A HISTORY OF THE BRITISH ARMY

A History of
The British Army

BY

THE HON. J. W. FORTESCUE

SECOND PART CONTINUED—FROM THE FALL OF THE BASTILLE
TO THE PEACE OF AMIENS

VOL. IV – PART I

1789–1801

The Naval & Military Press Ltd

Published by

The Naval & Military Press Ltd
Unit 5 Riverside, Brambleside
Bellbrook Industrial Estate
Uckfield, East Sussex
TN22 1QQ England

Tel: +44 (0)1825 749494

www.naval-military-press.com
www.nmarchive.com

Cover illustration shows **The Chelsea Pensioners reading the Waterloo Dispatch**, originally entitled **Chelsea Pensioners Receiving the London Gazette Extraordinary of Thursday, June 22, 1815, Announcing the Battle of Waterloo**. This painting, by David Wilkie, was commissioned by Arthur Wellesley, 1st Duke of Wellington in August 1816.
    It was exhibited at the Royal Academy summer exhibition in 1822, where it was so popular that a rail was installed to protect it from the thronging crowds. This was the first time that a rail was needed at the Royal Academy exhibition. The painting was retained by the Duke of Wellington and his descendants, and it is displayed at Apsley House.
    It shows old soldiers gathered around a wooden table outside the "Duke of York" public house, in Jew's Row off the King's Road in Chelsea. The Royal Hospital Chelsea is visible in the background to the left.
    One of the soldiers is reading the *Waterloo Gazette*, which published the Waterloo Dispatch sent by the Duke of Wellington immediately after the Battle of Waterloo on 18 June 1815. The dispatch, dated 19 June 1815, was reprinted in several editions of the *London Gazette* on 22 June 1815.
    The painting includes many portraits of characters identified in notes prepared by Wilkie, and include, from left to right:

- An artilleryman who has laid down his knapsack.
- A mounted orderly of the 7th Light Dragoons who has brought the Gazette, wearing a blue uniform with red pillbox hat.
- A soldier from the Life Guards, a sergeant from 42nd Foot (the Black Watch) who fought at the Battle of Barrosa in 1811, and one from the King's German Legion.
- A Chelsea pensioner who was at the Battle of Quebec with General Wolfe in 1759, standing and reading the Gazette.
- A soldier's wife, pregnant and ashen-faced, waiting for news of her husband's fate.
- A seated veteran eating an oyster (despite the consumption of oysters in June being prohibited by Act of Parliament).
- A black bandsman from the 1st Foot Guards (once a servant of General Moreau) who witnessed the execution of Louis XVI in 1793.
- An old soldier who fought under Wellington at the Battle of Assaye in 1803, and under the Marquis of Granby in the Seven Years' War in the 1750s and 1760s.
- A veteran with a wooden leg.
- An Irishman from the 11th Dragoons, talking to an elderly veteran, who served with General Eliott in the Great Siege of Gibraltar.
- A corporal from the Royal Horse Guards (the Blues) with his wife and son and the dog Old Duke which accompanied the regiment through Spain.
- A soldier from the Foot Guards leaning out from the window.

In the background, a Highlander is playing the bagpipes.

In reprinting in facsimile from the original, any imperfections are inevitably reproduced and the quality may fall short of modern type and cartographic standards.

PREFACE

IN offering to the public this new instalment of the *History of the British Army*, I feel constrained to accompany it with an apology. In my first volume I expressed the hope that I should tell the whole of my story down to the year 1870 in four volumes; and now the fourth volume proves to have carried the narrative no further than to the year 1803. I know not what plea to advance in my excuse, except the sheer ignorance avowed on a famous occasion by Dr. Johnson. I can only say that, until I had dug deep into the huge mass of military manuscripts at the Record Office, I had no conception either of the tasks that were set by Pitt to the British Army nor of the vast amount of work—thankless, indeed, and unprofitable—which it did, or strove to do, during the first ten years of the war of the French Revolution.

I am aware that in some quarters this excuse will avail me little. One critic, neither incompetent nor unkindly, has lamented that I have not ignored military operations altogether and confined myself strictly to an account of the Army's growth and administration. Gladly would I have done so, had it been practicable. But, in the first place, it is impossible to trace the reasons for changes and reforms without a detailed narrative of the Army's campaigns. I might go still further, and say that many changes and reforms are themselves undiscoverable except by minute examination of operations in the field. Secondly, it must be remembered that the most perfect administration and organisation in time of peace do not of themselves suffice, even with the addition of a competent commander in the field, to make an Army successful in war. An Army may be a very perfect instrument, but if improperly handled, or employed for unsuitable work, it may none the less fail. In England the handling of the Army lies with the Cabinet; and, since war is universally and rightly accepted as the only test of military efficiency, a History of the British Army must include a detailed study of all campaigns, so as to determine whether success or failure were due to the merits or demerits of the Army, which is the tool, or of the Cabinet, which is the workman, or of both. For throughout my work it has been my design (perhaps too ambitious) to endeavour to formulate our military experience of the past in all its branches, so as to give warning against repetition of old mistakes in the future. Lastly, I think the narrative of former wars worth the writing for the sake of the officers of the Army. Few British campaigns, except those of Wellington in the Peninsula, are familiar even to studious officers, and, in my humble judgment, it is a misfortune that the Peninsular War has always been treated by British writers as

PREFACE vii

an isolated incident, instead of as the climax of a long and deadly struggle,—as a solid success achieved at last after fifteen years of folly and failure.

As regards maps, the kindness of Messrs. Macmillan has enabled me to raise the standard greatly; and I hope that the result may prove satisfactory. No pains have been spared to perfect them, though the task has been one of inconceivable difficulty. The maps for the Helder campaign, for instance, are the result of the collation of a series ranging in date from early in the sixteenth century down to the corrected staff-map of 1900. Again, many of the places mentioned in the accounts of the West Indian campaigns have only been identified after much trouble and research, while some, particularly in St. Domingo, have defied all efforts at discovery. The brunt of this very arduous work has fallen upon Mr. H. W. Cribb of Mr. Emery Walker's firm, who has toiled at it not only with the zeal of a masterly workman, but with the enthusiasm of a collaborator. I cannot sufficiently express my obligations to his skill, his industry, his patience, and his great geographical knowledge. My own share in this part of the work has consisted chiefly in the collection of maps wherever I have been able to find them, and in visiting as many battlefields as my time and means permitted. The knowledge and experience of my brother, Colonel Charles Fortescue of the Rifle Brigade, who has been my companion on these expeditions, has assisted me greatly in turning my observations to good account.

For the rest, I must again tender my most grateful

thanks to Mr. Hubert Hall—that guardian angel of historical students at the Record Office—for invaluable help in the searching out of documents, and to Mr. G. K. Fortescue for the like good offices at the British Museum. My special gratitude is due also to Lord Londonderry, who has most generously thrown open to me, unasked, the treasures of the Castlereagh Papers; nor must the ties of kinship forbid me to record my thanks to my cousin, Mr. Bevill Fortescue, who has granted to me more than a kinsman's privileges in ransacking his noble collection of the Grenville Papers at Dropmore. Lastly, I would tender my respectful acknowledgments to those officers of the Army, known and unknown to me, who have been kind enough to notice my work with sympathy and appreciation; assuring them that their approbation is that which I seek chiefly to deserve and shall always value above all others.

J. W. F.

CONTENTS

BOOK XII

CHAPTER I

	PAGE
Political Affairs demand special Prominence in a History of the War of the French Revolution	3-7
The French Army before the Revolution	7
Choiseul's Reforms after 1763	8
Lewis the Sixteenth's Reforms after 1774	9
Effect of Service in America on the French Army	10
Proximate Causes of the Revolution	12
Mutiny of the French Guards	13
Formation of the National Guards	13
Helplessness of the Military Authorities	14
A paid Force of National Guards organised	15
Decay of Discipline in the Regular Forces	16
Military Reforms of the Constituent Assembly	17
Increased Demoralisation of the Regular Forces	18
The Mutiny at Nancy	19
Further Military Reforms of the Constituent Assembly	20
Civil Establishment of the Church; Brittany, La Vendée	21
The King's Unsuccessful Attempt to escape from Paris	22
The Constituent Assembly succeeded by the Legislative Assembly	22
Sweeping Reforms in the Regular Forces	23
Two-thirds of the Officers resign	24

CHAPTER II

	PAGE
The German Powers, Russia and Poland	26
Anxiety of the European Powers over the French Revolution	27
Efforts of the Emperor Leopold to bring about concerted Intervention of the Powers in France	28
Declaration of Pilnitz	29
Growth of an aggressive Spirit in France	30
The Girondists determine to pick a Quarrel with the Emperor	31
Death of the Emperor Leopold	32
The Empress Catherine tempts Prussia to abandon her Agreement with Austria and share in the Partition of Poland	33
The French declare War upon Austria	34
Miserable State of the French Army	35
Fatuous Military Measures of the Legislative Assembly	36
The French invade Belgium	37
Their ignominious Repulse	38
The Girondists resort to an insurrectionary Movement to avert a Reaction in Favour of the Monarchy	38
Thereby they place themselves in the Power of the Jacobins	39
Attack of 10th August on the Tuileries	40
The King dethroned; the Commune of Paris seizes the Government of France	41
Prussia summoned by Austria to join her in Resistance to French Aggression	41
Frederick William declines to do so without Indemnity	41
Distraction and Weakness of the Prussian Administration	42
Catherine sends a Russian Army into Poland	43
She bribes the Emperor Francis to abandon Leopold's Policy in Poland	44
Quarrel of the Emperor with the King of Prussia over the Question of Indemnities	45
Tardy Advance of the Austrian and Prussian Armies upon France	46
Abortive Measures of the French Government to increase the Army	47

CONTENTS

	PAGE
The September Massacres in Paris	47
Failure of the Prussian Army owing to internal Dissension; Action of Valmy	48
Retreat of the Prussians; bitter Feeling between them and the Austrians	49

CHAPTER III

The Revolutionary Crusade against Europe	50
French Invasion of Nice, Savoy, and the Ecclesiastical States of the Empire	50
French Designs against the kingdoms of Spain, Sardinia, and the Two Sicilies	51
Imbecility of the French Military Measures	52
Successful Invasion of Belgium by Dumouriez	53
The French Convention declares the Navigation of the Scheldt to be free	53
Attitude of the British Government towards the French Revolution	53
Pitt's Determination to maintain Neutrality	54
Talleyrand's Mission for a Treaty between France and England	54
Change of Attitude of France towards England after the Dethronement of Lewis the Sixteenth	55
Revolutionary Intrigues of Chauvelin in London	55
The United Provinces appeal to England for Protection in the event of French Aggression	56
The Convention's Manifesto forces Pitt to repressive Measures against revolutionary Movements in England	56
The Convention thereupon abstains from invading Holland	57
Repulses of the French in Nice and on the Rhine	57
Plunder of Belgium by the Commissioners of the French Convention	58
Pitt still strives to maintain Peace	58
The Polish Question; Catherine offers Prussia a Share in the Spoil	59

	PAGE
Prussian Troops enter Poland	60
Pitt's last Effort to save Poland	60
It is defeated by the Execution of the French King, and the consequent Certainty of War between France and England	60
Catherine guarantees to Prussia the Provinces occupied by Prussian Troops	60
France declares War against England; her Military Impotence	61
Dumouriez ordered to invade Holland	62
His Plan of Campaign	63
Plans of the Austrian and Prussian Commanders	63
Apathy of the Dutch regarding Defence of Holland	64
Lord Auckland begs for British Troops to hearten them	65
Dumouriez's dash into Holland	65

The Netherlands

A Brigade of British Guards hurried to Helvoetsluis	66
The Austrians attack Dumouriez's right flank with signal success	67
Dumouriez finally defeated at Neerwinden	68
He deserts to the Austrians; the French are driven out of the Netherlands	69

CHAPTER IV

The British Cabinet; William Pitt, Henry Dundas	70
Pitt commits the Direction of the War to Dundas	72
William Grenville, the Foreign Secretary	73
Pitt's Military Policy	74

The West Indies

Disturbances in the French West Indies	76
Flight of French Refugees to the English Islands	76
Large increase of English Garrisons in consequence	77
The British Forces at Home and Abroad	77

CONTENTS

	PAGE
French Emigrants beg the British Government to take over St. Domingo	78
Character of the French Emigrants	78
Dundas despatches Orders for the Occupation of the French Windward Islands	79

England

Augmentation of the Army	80
Further Regiments despatched to Holland	80
Their miserable quality	81
False system followed in the augmentation of the Army	81
Demands of the Fleet upon the Army	82
Consequent exhaustion of the Regiments of the Line	82
Forces raised for Home-Defence; the Fencibles	83
The Seventy-Eighth Highlanders raised	83

The Netherlands

Pitt decides to help Austria to gain Indemnities in French Territory	84
He sends a large Force of Cavalry to the Netherlands	85
He claims Dunkirk as England's Indemnity	85
The Emperor's Rapacity and its evil Effects	86
His Jealousy aroused by Prussia's gain of Polish Territory	86
He selects Baron Thugut as his chief Adviser	86
Thugut's tortuous Diplomacy	87
Conference of the Allied Powers at Antwerp	88
The Struggle for Indemnities	88
Hesitation of the British Government to commit itself to Operations on the Continent	88
Dunkirk reported too strong for Capture by the British Contingent	89
The Allies agree upon a Plan of Operations	90
Continued Hesitation and Evasion of the British Government	90
The Allied Armies; the Austrians and the Cordon-System	91
Prince Josias of Coburg-Saalfeld; Mack	92
General Defects of the Allied Armies	93

	PAGE
The Austrian Army	93
The Prussian and Hessian Troops	94
The Hanoverian and Dutch Troops	95
The British Troops	95
Frederick, Duke of York	96
Sir James Murray, Chief of the Staff	97
Helpless State of France; her Declaration of War against Spain	98
The Beginning of the Revolt of La Vendée	98
Madness of the Convention's Military Measures	99
Appointment of the Committee of Public Safety	100
Captain Lazare Carnot	100
His Journey to Dunkirk	101

CHAPTER V

The Netherlands

	PAGE
Dispositions of General Dampierre on the Northern Frontier of France	102, 103
Dispositions of the Allies opposed to him	103
Inactivity of Coburg	104
Dampierre attacks the Allies	105
The Coldstream Guards engaged at Vicoigne	105
Harsh Criticism of the Duke of York by his Officers	107
The new Tactics of the French	108
Dampierre's entrenched Camp at Famars	108
Coburg's Plan for the attack upon it	109
The Action of Famars	110
The Allies besiege Valenciennes	111
Carnot's unsuccessful Raid upon the British Base	112
Dundas's Superstition concerning Ostend	113
His Meddling with its Defence	113
Capture of Valenciennes	114
Internal Affairs of France; Fall of the Girondists	115
Fresh Subversion of Discipline in the French Army	115

CONTENTS

	PAGE
Revolt of Southern France and of Corsica against the Convention	116
Failure of the Allies to take advantage of it	117
Distracted Counsels of the Allies in Flanders	118
The Attack on Cæsar's Camp	119
Division of the Allied Forces for the Sieges of Dunkirk and Quesnoy	120
The Combat of Linselles	121
Dispositions of the covering Army for the Siege of Dunkirk	122
Dispositions of the besieging Army	123
Difficulties of the Siege from want of a co-operating Fleet	124
The Reasons why the Fleet did not appear	125
Reforms in the Military Administration of France	126
The "Workers" of the Committee of Public Safety	126
Carnot's Plans for the Relief of Dunkirk	127
Positions of the opposing Forces	128
Houchard's first Attack on the covering Army	129
His second and decisive Attack	131
The Duke of York raises the Siege of Dunkirk and retreats	132

CHAPTER VI

West Indies, Windward Sphere

British Expedition over Sea; Capture of Tobago, St. Pierre, and Miquelon	134
Failure of an Attack upon Martinique	135
Forebodings of a general Insurrection of Negroes in the West Indies	135

Toulon

The Revolt of Southern France; Lord Hood occupies Toulon	136
Events demand Alteration of Pitt's Military Policy	137
Spheres of Operations open to the British; Toulon	138
La Vendée	139

Windward Islands; St. Lucia and Martinique	139
Leeward Islands; St. Domingo	140
Confusion of Dundas's Ideas and Orders	140

The Netherlands

The Campaign in Flanders; Failure of Houchard to follow up his Success at Dunkirk	141
Houchard's Operations; critical Position of the Allies	142
Austrian Successes; complete Change of the Situation	142
Cavalry Combat of Avesnes-les-Sec	142
Reverses of the French in Alsace	143
Fury of the French Demagogues against the Generals; increased Demoralisation of the French Troops	143
Vacillation of the British Cabinet as to future Operations in Flanders	144
Coburg decides Matters by besieging Maubeuge	144
The Duke of York commands the covering Army	144
Confusion caused by Dundas's Interference	145
Jourdan advances to the Relief of Maubeuge	146
Coburg compelled to raise the Siege	147
Souham captures Furnes, and advances to Nieuport	147
Dundas sends a Force under General Grey to Ostend	148
Nieuport relieved, and the French driven back by the Duke of York	149
Continued Interference of Dundas with the Commanders	149
Close of the Campaign	150

CHAPTER VII

West Coast of France

The War in La Vendée	152
Dundas promises Help to the Vendeans	153
A Force collected under Lord Moira for the Purpose	154
The Expedition delayed by Confusion at Portsmouth	155
It arrives too late	156

CONTENTS

	PAGE
The Government still wedded to its West Indian Projects	156
Dundas's Precautions against Invasion	157

TOULON

The Operations at Toulon; the French Force before it strengthened by the Fall of Marseilles	157
Skirmish at Ollioule	158
Hood detaches a Squadron to Corsica	158
Lord Mulgrave arrives at Toulon; Rowland Hill and Thomas Graham on his Staff	159
The Force at his Disposal	159
Poor Quality of the Spanish Troops	159
Defences of Toulon described	160
The Fortification of Little Gibraltar	162
Napoleon Bonaparte arrives at Toulon	162
Victor surprises Mont Faron	163
Recapture of Mont Faron	163, 164
Plans of the French Commanders	165
Quarrels among the Allied Commanders	166
Dangerous Situation of the Allies	167
Increase of the French Force round Toulon	168
Ill-judged Manifesto of the British Cabinet	168
Disastrous Sortie of the Allies	169
The French capture Fort Mulgrave and Mont Faron	170, 171
Evacuation of Toulon by the Allies	171, 172
Hood's Share of the Responsibility for the Failure of the Allies	172
Extraordinary Behaviour of Henry Dundas	174-178

CHAPTER VIII

CORSICA

Corsica; Overtures of Paoli to Hood	179
Hood sails for Corsica	180
Destitute Condition of the Fleet and Army	181
Ill-feeling between Hood and David Dundas	181

HISTORY OF THE ARMY

	PAGE
Disembarkation near Mortella Point	182
Storming of the Convention Redoubt	183
San Fiorenzo occupied by the British	184
Reconnaissance towards Bastia	185
David Dundas decides that Bastia must be blockaded	186
Arrogant Behaviour of Hood thereupon	187
Dundas returns to England	187
Renewed Disputes between Hood and the new Commander	188
Hood's Operations against Bastia	189
Surrender of Bastia owing to Famine	190
Arrival of Charles Stuart as Commander-in-chief of the Mediterranean	191
Stuart sails to Calvi	192
Siege of Calvi	193
Surrender of Calvi	194
Dissension between Hood and Stuart	195
Causes of the Friction between Army and Navy	196
Evil results of basing Military Operations upon Naval Advice	198
The Crown of Corsica accepted by King George	199

CHAPTER IX

FRANCE

Affairs in France; the Rise of Hoche	200
Hoche drives the Austrians across the Rhine	201
Difficulties of Carnot and the "Workers"	201
Persecution of the French Generals by the Representatives of the People	202
Renewal of the System of Terror	202
La Vendée; Turreau's "Infernal Columns"	203
Gradual Improvement in the French Army	203, 204
Execution of Hébert and of Danton	205
Increased Power of the "Workers"; their Military Projects	205
Carnot's Resolution to concentrate the French Strength in Belgium	206

CONTENTS

England

	PAGE
Affairs in England; Coalition of Portland with Pitt	206
Ministerial Changes thereupon	207
New Secretariat for War established; Dundas appointed to hold it	208
The Opposition's Criticism of the War	208
Augmentation of the Army; Formation of the Seventy-ninth to the Ninety-second Foot	204-210
Devices of the Government to raise Recruits	211
The System of raising Men for Rank	212
Its appalling Evils	213, 214
Enlistment of foreign Troops	215
Neglect to train Light Infantry	215
Faulty training of the Light Cavalry	216
Irish Militia formed	217
Enrolment of Volunteers	217
Rise of the Yeomanry	218
False System pursued in regard to Volunteers	218
Affairs of the Coalition; Pitt's Endeavours to restore Amity	219

The Netherlands

Preparations for a new Campaign in Flanders	220
The Duke of York continued in Command of the British	221
Prussia threatens to withdraw her Troops from the Rhine	222
She is bribed into furnishing an Army by the Treaty of the Hague	223
Bad Condition of the Austrian Troops in Belgium	224
James Craig appointed Chief of the Duke of York's Staff	225
Bad Condition of the British Contingent in Belgium	225
Position of the Allied Forces on the Northern Frontier of France	226
False Distribution of the Duke of York's Corps	227
Carnot's Plan of Campaign in Belgium	228
Strength and Distribution of the French Forces on the Northern Frontier	229

	PAGE
The Emperor arrives at the Headquarters of the Allied Army	229
Decision to open the Campaign forthwith	230

CHAPTER X

THE NETHERLANDS

Campaign of 1794; the British Troops	231
Position of the French Army under Pichegru	232
Advance of the Allies; Action of 17th April	232, 233
Coburg besieges Landrecies	234
Description of the Country	235
Movements of the French to relieve Landrecies	235
Cavalry Action of Villers-en-Cauchies	236-239
Second Attempt by the French to relieve Landrecies	240
Cavalry Action of Beaumont	241-243
Movements of the French on the western Flank	244
Defeat of Clerfaye at Mouscron	245
The French capture Menin and Courtrai	246
The Duke of York marches to join Clerfaye in Western Flanders	248
He is attacked by the French on 10th May	248
Cavalry Action of Willems	249-251
March of Coburg with the main Army to the West	251
European Complications; Kosciusko's Rebellion in Poland	252
Its Influence in the Counsels of Prussia and Austria	252, 253
Junction of the Emperor and the main Army with the Duke of York at Tournai	253
Description of the Field of Operations	253
Dispositions of the French	254
Dispositions of the Allies	255
Mack's "Plan of Annihilation"	255
Battle of Turcoing; first Day, 17th May	256-259
Dangerous Disposition of the Allies at the Close of the first Day	260, 261
Battle of Turcoing; second Day, 18th May	262-269
Comments on the Conduct of the Austrians	269

CHAPTER XI

THE NETHERLANDS

	PAGE
Bitter Feeling of the British against the Austrians	271
Attack of the French upon the Allies at Tournai, 23rd May	272
Influence of Polish Affairs upon the Emperor's Counsels	273
Defeats of the French on the Rhine and Sambre	274
The Emperor decides to abandon the Austrian Netherlands	275
He announces his Departure for Vienna	275
Discouragement of the Austrian Troops	276
Pichegru advances in Western Flanders	277
He invests Ypres	277
Demoralisation at the Austrian Headquarters	278
Dangerous Situation of the Allies	279
Fall of Ypres; Coburg marches for the Sambre	281
Dundas sends a Force under Moira to Ostend	282
Defeat of Clerfaye at Deynse	283
Retreat of the Duke of York from Tournai	283
Defeat of Coburg at Fleurus; he retires on Brussels	283
Evacuation of Ostend by the British	284
Moira retires to Ghent	285
Continued Retreat of Coburg and the Duke of York	285
Fall of Nieuport; Massacre of the Emigrants of the Garrison	286
Continued Advance of the French	287
Coburg retires eastward	287
Weakening of the French Army by Robespierre's Orders	288
Continued Retreat of the Allies	289
The Duke of York evacuates Belgium	290
Final parting of the British and Austrians	290
Resignation of Coburg	291

CHAPTER XII

THE NETHERLANDS

The Prussians evade taking part in the Campaign in the Netherlands	292

HISTORY OF THE ARMY

	PAGE
Pitt sends an Embassy to Vienna to urge a Renewal of the Offensive in Belgium	293
Defeat of the Prussians at Kaiserslautern	294
Fall of Robespierre	294
His Responsibility for giving the Allies Breathing-Time in the Netherlands	294
Quality of the British Reinforcements sent to the Netherlands	295
Moira returns to England	295
Strength of the British Army	296
Disgraceful Indiscipline of the Officers	297
Defective Clothing of the British Troops	298
Shameful Condition of the Transport and Medical Service	299
The Military Problem set to the Duke of York	300
His Difficulties with the Dutch	300, 301
Dundas sends an independent Force under Lord Mulgrave to Flushing	302
Condition of Mulgrave's Troops	302, 303
The Emperor orders his Troops not to be employed in Defence of Belgium	304
Renewed Advance of Pichegru ; Retreat of the British	304
Action at Bokstel	305
The Duke of York retires to the Line of the Maas	306
Unwillingness of Clerfaye to work heartily with him	306, 307
Surrender of Fort Crevecoeur by the Dutch	308
The Duke retires to the Waal	309
Pitt guarantees a fresh Loan to Austria	309
Surrender of Bois-le-Duc by the Dutch	310
The French cross the Maas	311
They besiege Nimeguen	312
The Allies evacuate Nimeguen ; Misconduct of the Dutch	313
Sufferings of the Troops ; infamous Behaviour of the British Surgeons	314
The Duke of York summoned to London	315
The Command divided between Generals Harcourt and Walmoden	315
Faults of the Allies' Position	316

CONTENTS

	PAGE
Severe Frost sets in	316
The French cross the Waal in the Ice; Action of Geldermalsen	317
Second Action at Geldermalsen	318
Third Action at Geldermalsen	319
Walmoden retires behind the Leck	319
Disastrous Retreat of the British to the Yssel	320
Further Retreat upon the Ems	321
The French occupy the Dutch Netherlands	323
Order for the British Force to re-embark	323
Disgraceful End of Pitt's Expedition to the Low Countries	324

CHAPTER XIII

THE WEST INDIES; LEEWARD SPHERE

Dundas authorises British Protection of the Planters in St. Domingo	326
Agreement signed with the Planters of St. Domingo	327
Description of French St. Domingo or Haiti	327, 328
State of the Island in 1793	329
British Troops shipped from Jamaica to St. Domingo	330
Occupation of Jérémie and Mole St. Nicholas	331
Disadvantages of Mole St. Nicholas	332
Occupation of St. Marc	333
The Mulattos hostile to the British	333
Capture of Tiburon and L'Acul	335
Growing Distrust of the British by the People	336
Insurrection at Port-au-Prince	337
Rigaud's Attack upon Tiburon	337
Increasing Trouble in St. Domingo	338
Arrival of British Reinforcements, May 1794	339
Capture of Port-au-Prince	339
Mortality among the Troops	340
Disputes between Generals Whyte and Williamson	341
Rascality of the Commanders of Local Levies	341, 342

xxiv   HISTORY OF THE ARMY

	PAGE
Charmilli's Mission to England	343
He succeeds in deceiving Dundas	343
Captain Thomas Brisbane at St. Marc	344
Rigaud recovers Léogane	345
His fierce Attack on Fort Bizothon	346
His successful Attack on Tiburon	346, 347
Disastrous close of the Year 1794 in St. Domingo	347
Dundas's Failure to send Reinforcements	348

CHAPTER XIV

WEST INDIES; WINDWARD SPHERE

The Capture of the French Windward Islands was Pitt's First Object	350
General Grey and Sir John Jervis sail for Barbados	351
Grey's Difficulties at Barbados	352
He trains Light Infantry on the American Model	352

MARTINIQUE

His Plan for the Capture of Martinique	353
He sails for Martinique: his first Operations	354, 355
Operations of Generals Gordon and Thomas Dundas	356, 357
Dundas's March over Mont Pelée to St. Pierre	358, 359
Siege of Fort Bourbon	359
Action of the Heights of Sourier	360
Escalade of Fort Louis	361
Surrender of Fort Bourbon and final Capture of Martinique	361

ST. LUCIA

Grey sails to St. Lucia	362
Surrender of St. Lucia	363

GUADELOUPE

Grey sails to Guadeloupe	363
Storm of Fort Fleur d'Épée	364

CONTENTS

Capture of Guadeloupe	365
His Arrangements for holding the Islands	366
Death of Thomas Dundas	367
Negligence of the British Government in allowing French Reinforcements to sail to the West Indies	367
Recapture of Point-à-Pitre and Fleur d'Épée by the French	368, 369
Victor Hugues at Guadeloupe	370
Grey's Operations round Fleur d'Épée	371
His final Plan to recover it and Point-à-Pitre	372
Its disastrous Failure	373, 374
The Camp of Berville	374
Mortality among the Troops	375
Grey's Quarrel with Dundas as to Prize-Money	376-378
Continued Mortality among the Troops	379
Victor Hugues resumes the Offensive	379
Succession of Attacks on the Camp of Berville	380
Gallant Defence and final Surrender of the British	381
Prescott's Defence of Fort Matilda	382
The British driven from Guadeloupe	382
Ideal Harmony of Navy and Army in this Campaign	383
Appalling Loss of Life in both Services	384

CHAPTER XV

European Affairs; Poland

Suppression of the Polish Insurrection	386
Partition of Poland	387
Prussia makes Peace with France—Treaty of Bâle	388, 389
Wreck of the first Coalition	389

France

Improvement of internal Condition of France	388
Conciliatory Policy initiated in La Vendée	389
Reaction in favour of the Constitution of 1791	390
England's Prospects at the beginning of 1795	391
Alliance between the French and Dutch Republics	392

Attacks on the Dutch Colonies

	PAGE
The British Government resolves to take over the Dutch Colonies	392
Justification of this Action	393

The Cape of Good Hope

Sailing of the Advanced Expedition to the Cape of Good Hope	394
Correspondence of the Commanders with the Council of Regency at Cape Town	395
Condition of the Cape Colony in 1795	396
British Occupation of Simonstown	397
Craig's first March towards Cape Town	398
Difficulties of his Position	399
Arrival of Sir Alured Clarke and the main Expedition	400
The March upon Cape Town	400
Surrender of Cape Colony	401
The entire Army is left at Cape Colony, and the Bulk of the Fleet sails for Madras	402

Operations against the French and Dutch East Indies

Capture of Pondicherry	402
Capture of Trincomalee	403
Capture of Ceylon, Malacca, Amboyna, and Banda	404
These Operations did not affect the main Situation	405

Military Measures in England

The Duke of York appointed Commander-in-chief	406
Dearth of Troops in England	407
Shameful Measures of Government for recruiting in Ireland	407
Dearth of Seamen to man the Navy	408
The Duke of York's Plans of Reorganisation	408
Dundas's Scheme for enlisting foreign Recruits	409
Its Failure; the British Cavalry withdrawn from Germany	409, 410

CONTENTS

	PAGE
The Generals in the West Indies urge the Formation of Negro Regiments	411
Dundas refuses to sanction it	411

DESIGN FOR A DESCENT UPON BRITTANY

Hopes of the French Royalists	411
De Puisaye's Plan of a Descent approved by Pitt	412
The Expedition sails; naval Action off L'Orient	413
Capture of the Peninsula of Quiberon	414
Imbecility of the Royalist Agents	415
Annihilation of the Royalist Invaders by Hoche	415
A Force under Lord Moira ordered to Quiberon	416
British Negotiations with Charette	418
Subsidiary Force under Doyle ordered to the Islets of Quiberon	418
Moira resigns his Command; Doyle sails to Quiberon Bay	419
He occupies Isle d'Yeu	420
The Count of Artois refuses to land in France	421
The Scene with Charette	421
Perilous Position of Doyle	421
His Force withdrawn from Isle d'Yeu	422
Criminal Recklessness of Ministers in this Enterprise	422

CHAPTER XVI

WEST INDIES; WINDWARD SPHERE

Position of General Vaughan at the beginning of 1795	424
Exultation of the revolutionary Party at Guadeloupe	425
Arrival of French Reinforcements at Guadeloupe	425
Vaughan begins to raise Negro Levies	426

THE NEGRO REVOLT IN THE BRITISH WEST INDIES

GRENADA AND ST. VINCENT

The Rising in Grenada	426
Description of Grenada	427, 428

xxviii HISTORY OF THE ARMY

	PAGE
Lindsay's Operations—his Death	428
The Rising in St. Vincent; the Caribs	429
Arrival of British Reinforcements at Barbados	430
Their miserable Quality	431
Dundas again forbids Formation of Negro Regiments	431
He sends a Battalion to capture Demerara	431
Criminal Subservience of Ministers to the West India Committee	432
Measures of Vaughan in defiance of Dundas	433
General Design of his Operations in the British Islands	433

St. Lucia

Colonel James Stuart's Operations about Vieuxfort and Choiseul	434
His severe Repulse before Soufrière	435
Ravages of Yellow Fever among the Troops	436
The British driven from St. Lucia	436

Grenada

Colonel Campbell repulsed at Mount St. Catherine	437
Operations of Brigadier Nicolls	438
Ravages of Yellow Fever among the Troops	439
Discreditable Defeat of the British at Goyave	439
The French announce that the War shall be carried on with Humanity	440
The British driven from all Points except St. George's	441

St. Vincent

Successful Operations against the Caribs	441
The Sixtieth returns from Demerara to St. Vincent	442
Successful Operations to Windward	442
Adverse Effect of the Capture of St. Lucia upon St. Vincent	443
Operations to Leeward	443
Excessive Dispersal of the Troops to Windward	444
The Post of Owia surprised by the Enemy	444
The British withdrawn to the Hills round Kingston	445

CONTENTS xxix

	PAGE
Demoralisation of the Troops; their Misbehaviour at Vigie	445
Arrival of Reinforcements; Recapture of Vigie	446
Reoccupation of the Posts to Windward	447
Discreditable Defeat of the British at Mount William	448
The British again driven into Kingston	449

Dominica

Landing of Revolutionists at Pagoua Bay	449
Extraordinary March of the British to meet them	449
Annihilation of the invading Enemy	449

Martinique (the British Headquarters to Windward)

Vaughan's Difficulties owing to the Incapacity of Dundas	450
Dundas at last sanctions Formation of Negro Regiments	451
Death of Vaughan	451
Ravages of Yellow Fever among the Troops	451
Dundas's Approval of Negro Regiments comes too late	452
Insufficiency of the Reinforcements sent from England	452
The First and Second West India Regiments formed	453
Annihilation of a Party of French Invaders in Martinique	454
General Reflections upon the Windward Campaign	455

CHAPTER XVII

West Indies; Leeward Sphere

Situation in St. Domingo at the Opening of 1795	457
Deaths of Thomas Brisbane and Colonel Markham	458
Arrival of Reinforcements at St. Domingo	458
Williamson sails to St. Domingo to command in Person	458
Critical Situation at Port-au-Prince	459

The Maroon Revolt in Jamaica

Account of the Maroons	460
The Reasons for their Insurrection	461
Lord Balcarres detains the Reinforcements for St. Domingo at Jamaica	462

	PAGE
Futility of Balcarres's Operations against the Maroons	463
Colonel Walpole with the Seventeenth Light Dragoons subdues the Maroons	464
Walpole resigns his Commission owing to a Breach of his Treaty with the Maroons	465

St. Domingo

Arrival of Reinforcements at Mole St. Nicholas	466
Williamson's Operations checked by the Mortality among the Troops	467
Ministers resolve to send a large Force to St. Domingo	468
New Policy towards Mulattos and Negroes initiated	468
Improvement in the Outlook at St. Domingo	469
The Force for St. Domingo driven back to England by Tempest	470
Bad Effect of this Mishap upon the Negroes	470
Reinforcements from Europe reach both English and French	471
Bad Quality of the British Reinforcements	472
General Forbes begins Operations at Bombarde	472
His Army paralysed by Yellow Fever	473
Continued Improvement in British Prospects at St. Domingo	474
No Advantage can be taken of it from Dearth of Troops	475

CHAPTER XVIII

West Indies; Windward Sphere

Sir Ralph Abercromby selected to lead a large Force to the Windward Islands	477
Culpable Delay in the Despatch of this Force	478
Dundas desires to send it off imperfectly equipped	479
Abercromby refuses to sail till all is ready	480
Disastrous Dispersion of the Expedition by a Storm in the Channel	480
The Expedition sails again, and is again driven back	481
Alterations of Abercromby's Instructions	481
The Expedition again sails and reaches Barbados	482

CONTENTS

GRENADA

	PAGE
Abercromby at once despatches Troops to Grenada	483
Successful Operations of Nicolls in that Island	483
Enormous Difficulties of Abercromby	484
General Whyte is despatched to occupy Demerara	486

ST. LUCIA

Arrival of British Regiments; Abercromby sails for St. Lucia	486
His Disembarkation and Advance on Morne Fortuné	487
The Attack on Morne Chabot	488
The Disembarkation south of Castries	489
Miscarriage of the subsequent Operations	489
Death of Colonel Malcolm	489
Investment of Morne Fortuné	490
Repulse of the British Attack on Vigie	491
Capture of Morne Fortuné	492

ST. VINCENT

Abercromby sails to St. Vincent	493
Successful Operations there	493

GRENADA

Final Reduction of the Brigands in Grenada	494
Close of the Campaign	495
Appalling Mortality among the Troops	495
An Estimate of the Losses in the West Indies, 1794–1796	496

CHAPTER XIX

THE SITUATION IN EUROPE, 1795

Prussia accedes to the Treaty for Partition of Poland	497
Successes of the Austrians on the Rhine	497
Successes of the French in the Riviera	498

	PAGE
Triple Alliance of England, Austria, and Russia	499
Unwillingness of Austria to protect Germany	499
She is finally brought to consent to maintain her Army on the Rhine	500

France

The new Constitution under the Directory	500
Insurrection of 13th Vendémiaire crushed by Bonaparte	501
Defects of the new Constitution	501
Financial Difficulties of France	502
Pitt makes Overtures for Peace	502
They are insolently rejected	502
Catherine's Project for Conquest of Persia	503
Austrian Operations delayed by Thugut's Jealousy of Prussia	503

The Mediterranean

Bonaparte appointed to command the Army in Italy	503
His rapid Successes	505

The Dutch Colonies

The Directory prepares a Diversion against England at the Cape of Good Hope	506
The British Naval and Military Force at the Cape	507
Arrival of a Dutch Fleet in Saldanha Bay	507
Operations of General Craig and Commodore Elphinstone	508
Surrender of the Dutch Fleet	509

The Mediterranean

Bonaparte's successful Efforts to rouse Corsica against England	509
Nelson seizes Porto Ferrajo	510
Spain engages to declare War against England	510
Bonaparte's Victories at Lonato and Castiglione	510
Prussia signs a Treaty with France	511
The British Fleet ordered to evacuate the Mediterranean	511
Bonaparte's further Successes before Mantua	511

CONTENTS

Defeat of Moreau and Jourdan by the Archduke Charles at
  Würzburg 511
The French Design for Union of the Armies of Germany and
  Italy overthrown 511
Withdrawal of the British Fleet from the Mediterranean . 512

ENGLAND

Domestic Troubles in England 513
Danger of Pitt owing to his Misconduct of the War . . 514

IRELAND

Troubled State of Ireland; the United Irishmen . . . 515
Communication between the United Irishmen and the
  French Government 516
Lord Fitzwilliam's Viceroyalty 517
Bitter Feeling in Ireland upon his Recall 517
Rise of the Orange Society 517
Inefficiency of the Garrison in Ireland 518
Creation of the Yeomanry upon the Alarm of Invasion . . 519
Pitt again makes pacific Overtures to France . . . 519
Dundas's Project for seizing the Helder 520
Its ridiculous Failure 521
New Measures for obtaining Recruits 522
The Supplementary Militia and Provisional Cavalry formed . 523
Napoleon's Victories at Arcola 523
Thugut's Anger at Pitt's Overtures to France . . . 523
Death of the Empress Catherine 524
Insolent Dismissal of Lord Malmesbury from Paris . . 524
The French Fleet sails for Bantry Bay 524
Miscarriage of the Enterprise 525

THE MEDITERRANEAN

French Victory at Rivoli; Fall of Mantua 526
French Raid upon Fishguard 527
Dundas's Project for an Expedition to South America . . 528
It is fortunately abandoned 528

Victory of Sir John Jervis off Cape St. Vincent	529
Mutiny of the British Fleet at Spithead	529
Mutiny at the Nore	530
The Army's Pay suddenly increased	531
Pitt's Share of Responsibility for the Mutinies	531
Bonaparte advances into Carinthia	533
Preliminary Treaty of Leoben	533
The French occupy Venice and Corfu	534
Pitt again makes Overtures to France; Negotiations at Lille	535
The Revolution of the 18th Fructidor	535
Rupture of the Negotiations	536

CHAPTER XX

The West Indies; Windward Sphere

Abercromby sails with Orders to capture Trinidad and Porto Rico	537
Folly of the Government's Plans	538
Capture of Trinidad	540
Failure at Porto Rico	541
Increase of the West India Regiments	542
Opposition of the West Indian Planters to this Measure	542
Peace re-established in the Windward Islands	544

Leeward Sphere

New Policy of Ministers at St. Domingo	545
General Simcoe's Instructions	545
His Design to occupy Tortuga	546
Successful Attacks of the Negroes	547
Ill-faith of the white Proprietors at St. Domingo	547
Operations of Simcoe	548
Incapacity of his Subordinates	549
He reports the Policy of Ministers to be impracticable	550
The War of Posts begins again	551
Ministers resolve to evacuate all Posts except the Mole and Jérémie	552

CONTENTS

	PAGE
Combined offensive Movements of the Negro and Mulatto Leaders	553
Arrival of Colonel Maitland at St. Domingo	554
His peculiar Position	554
Skilful attack of Rigaud upon Jérémie	555
Evacuation of Port-au-Prince by the British	556
Maitland's Conciliation of Toussaint	556
Failure of his Attempt to capture Tiburon	557
Ministers again alter their Policy; Disgust of Maitland	558
The Military Situation in St. Domingo	559
Maitland decides to Evacuate St. Domingo by Convention with Rigaud and Toussaint	560
His Reasons for favouring Toussaint	561
Courage and Sagacity of Maitland's Decision	562
Fury of the Jamaica Planters	563
Toussaint's Rise to Supremacy in the Island	564
The Cost of the St. Domingo Campaigns to England	565

CHAPTER XXI

The Treaty of Campo Formio	567

IRELAND

Increasing trouble in Ireland	568
Preparation of a Dutch Expedition to invade Ireland	569
The Expedition abandoned	569
Demoralisation of the Troops in Ireland	570
Sir Ralph Abercromby goes Commander-in-chief to Dublin	571
His Difficulties in restoring Discipline	572
His famous General Order	573
His Situation considered	574
Intrigues of the Castle Officials against him	576
He resigns his Command	577
The King alone supports him	578
Difficulty in finding a Successor to him	579

The Mediterranean

	PAGE
Bonaparte's Return to Paris	579
His Schemes for Invasion of England	580
The Directory's Policy of general Aggression and Spoliation	580
French Proceedings in Holland, Italy, and Switzerland	581
Mystery of Bonaparte's secret Expedition	582
The Directory agrees to send it to Egypt	583
Extreme Hazard of this Enterprise	585
Bonaparte sails for Alexandria	585
The British Government decides to send a Fleet again to the Mediterranean	586

Diversion on the Coast of Holland

British Expedition to destroy the Bruges Canal at Ostend	587
Its disastrous Issue	588

Ireland

Outbreak of the Rebellion in Ireland	589
Worthlessness of the Irish Militia	590
Landing of Humbert in Killala Bay	591
The "Race of Castlebar"	592
Surrender of Humbert	594
Vindictive Suppression of the Rebellion in Connaught	594
Demoralisation of the British Troops in Ireland	595
Disbandment of the Fifth Dragoons	596
Insufficiency of the Government's Measures for Home Defence	597

CHAPTER XXII

The Mediterranean

Insufficiency of a Naval Force to fulfil the Government's Policy without an Army	599
Difficulties in obtaining Recruits	601
Charles Stuart's Force in Portugal	601
Insubordination of the French Part of it	602

CONTENTS

	PAGE
Impracticability of Stuart's Instructions from Dundas	603
The first Menace of Trouble in India	605
The Government's new Policy of Raids on Spanish Ports	605
Lord St. Vincent's Opinion of Charles Stuart	606
Nelson's Cruise in search of Bonaparte	607
The Battle of the Nile	607
Nelson returns from the Nile to Naples	608
Discontent with French Rule in Switzerland and Italy	609
Negotiations between Naples and Austria	610
Russia enters the Lists against France	611
Miserable internal Condition of France	611
Nelson, the Queen of Naples, and Lady Hamilton	612
Nelson's Eagerness to follow up the Victory of the Nile	614
Naples takes the Offensive	615
Collapse of the Neapolitans, and Flight of the Court to Palermo	615
Stuart's Preparations for Attack on Minorca	615
Course of the Expedition	616
Capture of Minorca	618
Audacity of Stuart's Campaign	619
Dundas's Ideas for future Operations	620
Stuart's Measures in Minorca	621
Nelson begs a Battalion from Stuart for Messina	623
Arrival of Stuart in Sicily	623
His masterly Designs for Use and Defence of the Island	624
Alliance of Russia, Turkey, and England	625
Prussia declines to be included in it	626
Austria after Hesitation joins the Alliance	627
Weak Points of the new Coalition	628
The Law of Conscription in France	628
Forces of the French and the Allies	629
Victory of the Archduke Charles at Stockach	629
Thugut's Jealousy of Prussia spoils the Archduke's Campaign	629
Successes of Suvorof in Italy	630
Successes of Nelson and Ruffo in the Neapolitan Dominions	631
Suvorof's Victory of the Trebbia	631

xxxviii HISTORY OF THE ARMY

	PAGE
Thugut's Folly thwarts Suvorof's Plans	632
Suvorof's Victory of Novi	632
Thugut again spoils his Projects	633
Nelson's Jealousy of the Russians in the Mediterranean	634
His extravagant Scheme for a Campaign in the Roman States	634
Defeat of Suvorof in Switzerland by Masséna	636
Bonaparte's Invasion of Syria	637
His Repulse before Acre	637
His Defeat of the Turks at Aboukir	638
His stealthy Flight from Egypt to France	638

CHAPTER XXIII

THE EXPEDITION TO NORTH HOLLAND

First Act for the Enlistment of Militiamen in the Line	639
Its Failure	640
Several Militia and Fencible Regiments volunteer for foreign Service	640
Treaty of England with Russia for Recovery of Holland	641
Second Act for Enlistment of Militiamen in the Line	641
Abercromby called in to advise as to the Operations	642
Difficulties of the projected Campaign	643
Abercromby declares against the Expedition	644
Dundas also adverse to it	645
The Question of Transport	646
First Instructions issued to Abercromby	647
Their absolute Futility	648
Second Set of Instructions issued to Abercromby	649
Vagueness and Indecision of the Ministry	650
Abercromby arrives off the Helder	651
Description of North Holland and the Coast	652
Dispositions of the French and Dutch to repel Abercromby	653
Action fought by Abercromby to effect his Disembarkation	654
The Enemy evacuate the Helder; Capture of the Dutch Fleet	657

CONTENTS

xxxix

	PAGE
The Rendezvous of the Militia at Barham Downs	658
The First Reinforcements sent to Abercromby	659
His Position on the Zype Canal	660
His Inability to move	661
Brune's Plan of Attack on the Zype Position	662
Brune's Attack on the Position	663
It is everywhere repulsed	664
Arrival of Reinforcements, British and Russian	665
The Duke of York subjected to a Council of War	666
Bad Equipment of his Troops	667
Early Failure of Supplies	667
The Duke's Difficulties with the Followers of the Prince of Orange	668

CHAPTER XXIV

THE EXPEDITION TO NORTH HOLLAND

Position of the French under General Brune	670
The Duke of York's Plan for Attack upon it	671
Abercromby's March upon Hoorn	672
The main Attack opened prematurely by the Russians	673
Rout of the Russians	676
The British Right compelled to fall back	677
Pulteney's Successes on the Left abandoned	679
Evil Consequences of the Failure to the Allied Forces	681
Arrival of more Russian Troops; a second Attack determined on	682
The Duke of York's Plans	683
Description of the Sand-Dunes of North Holland	684
The Action of Egmont-aan-Zee, 2nd October	687
The Duke of York gains a negative Victory	693
Dispositions of both Sides after the Battle	694
The Action of 6th October	695
Heavy Losses of the Allies	697
The Council of War advises a Retreat	698

xl   HISTORY OF THE ARMY

	PAGE
The Duke of York retires to the Zype	699
Extreme Danger of his Situation.	700
He agrees to evacuate North Holland under a Convention	701
Reflections on the Expedition; the Militia.	701
The Artillery	702
The Royal Waggon Train.	703
The Failure of Supplies	703
The Government's Excuses	707
Disingenuous Treatment of Abercromby by Dundas	708
Discussion of the Government's Object in the Expedition	709

CHAPTER XXV

The East Indies

	PAGE
Incompleteness of Cornwallis's Work after the Capture of Seringapatam in 1792.	711, 712
Madajee Scindia's Designs upon the Nizam.	712
Sir John Shore declines to protect the Nizam	713
Alienation of the Nizam by this Treatment	713
Rise of trained Troops under French Leaders	714
De Boigne and Perron with Scindia	714
Raymond with the Nizam.	715
Menace of these Troops to British Interests	715
Tippoo Sahib's Overtures to the French Government.	716
The Arrival of Ripaud at Mangalore.	716
Tippoo's Mission to Mauritius	717
Extraordinary Folly of M. Malartic	717
Dundas's Measures to reinforce India.	719
Arrival of Lord Mornington as Governor-general.	720
Dangerous Dispersion of the Forces of India	721
Mornington resolves to march upon Seringapatam	721
His successful Negotiations with the Nizam	721
His Transactions with the Mahrattas.	722
Difficulties of Transport for a Campaign in Mysore	722
The Military Commanders: Harris, Floyd, Wellesley.	723

CONTENTS

	PAGE
Mornington trusts Harris with full Powers	724
Composition of the Force: the Madras Army	725
The Nizam's Contingent and Bombay Army	726
Tippoo's March against the Bombay Army	727
His Repulse at Sedaseer	728
March of Harris	728
Enormous Multitude of his Transport Animals	729
His tortuous Movements to obtain Forage	730
The Action at Mallavelly	731
The March resumed	734
Arrival of the Army before Seringapatam	735
Wellesley's Mishap at Sultanpettah Tope	735
The Siege of Seringapatam	736
The Storm of Seringapatam	739
Burial of Tippoo Sahib	744
His military Blunders	745

CHAPTER XXVI

The East Indies

Arrival of a Convoy at Seringapatam	746
The Distribution of Prize-money and Partition of Mysore	747

The Pacification of Southern India

Disturbed State of India	748
Doondia Wao	749
His Force defeated and dispersed	750
Occupation of Soonda	751
Operations against Kistnapah Naik	752
Reappearance of Doondia Wao	753
Wellesley is ordered to hunt him down	753
Wellesley opens his Campaign	754
Failure drives him to new Methods	757
Final Defeat and Death of Doondia	758
Valuable Experience gained by Wellesley	759

xlii HISTORY OF THE ARMY

	PAGE
Operations against the Polygars	760
Severe Repulse of the British before Panjalamcoorchy	762
Final Storm of Panjalamcoorchy	763
Operations against the Murdoos	764
Failure of the Operations in the Sherewele Jungle	766
Final Capture of Caliarcoil	767
Operations against the Rajah of Bullam	767
Extraordinary Bravery of Lieutenant Parminter	768

CHAPTER XXVII

The Mediterranean

Bonaparte becomes First Consul of France	769
His amazing Energy in repairing the Directory's Blunders	770
Disruption of the Coalition of 1799	771
Quarrel between Russia and Austria	772
Quarrel between Russia and England	772
Thugut's Plans for the Campaign of 1800	773
Charles Stuart's Plan for Operations in the Mediterranean	774
The Convention of El Arish	774
Neglect of the British Army by Ministers	775
Dundas's Project for a Descent on Brest	775
His further Project of Operations near Belleisle	776
Charles Stuart quarrels with Ministers and resigns his Command	776
Maitland's Expedition to Belleisle	777
It is abandoned by Dundas's Order	779
Successes of the Austrians in the Riviera	780
Concentration of British Troops at Minorca	781
Abercromby appointed Commander-in-chief in the Mediterranean	782
His first Set of Instructions	782
His second Set of Instructions	783
Bonaparte's Advance over the Alps	783
Melas entreats for Troops from Minorca	784

CONTENTS

xliii

	PAGE
Battle of Marengo	785
Abercromby sails to Genoa to arrive too late	785
Melas again begs for British Troops	786
Abercromby decides not to co-operate with him	787
Successes of Moreau in Germany	787
Bonaparte's successful Negotiations with Russia and Spain	788
Third Set of Instructions sent to Abercromby by Dundas	789
The new Policy of Attacks upon Spanish Ports	789
Pulteney's abortive Attempt upon Ferrol	790
Indignation with Pulteney in England	791
Pulteney not to blame	792
Concentration of the Mediterranean Force at Gibraltar	793
Abortive Attempt upon Cadiz	793
Surrender of Malta; Close of the Campaign	794
Gross Misconduct of Military Affairs by the British Ministers	795
The true Reason for it	796
Nelson's Strictures upon the British Generals	797
Nelson's own Failures in Military Operations	798

CHAPTER XXVIII

The Mediterranean

French Treaty with Spain, and Attempt to revive the Armed Neutrality	799
Dundas's fourth Set of Instructions to Abercromby	799

The Expedition to Egypt

An Expedition to Egypt ordered	800
The Reasons of the Government for undertaking it	801
Change in the Situation owing to the gaining of the Tsar by Bonaparte	802
A Force from India to co-operate in Egypt	803
Abercromby's Difficulties	804

	PAGE
He concentrates his Force at Malta	805
Withdrawal of British Troops from Portugal	806
Increasing Hostility of Russia towards England	807
Battle of Hohenlinden ; Austria sues for Peace at any Price.	808
Abercromby arrives in Marmorice Bay	808
Apparent Hopelessness of the Task assigned to him	809
The Training of the Army for Disembarkation	810
Increase of Difficulties upon Abercromby	811
Bonaparte's Anxiety for Egypt	812
Abortive Cruise of Admiral Ganteaume	813
Quality of the French Army in Egypt.	814
Assassination of Kléber : Menou succeeds him	815
Menou's Blunders	816
Abercromby arrives off Alexandria	817
Dispositions of Menou	818
The Problem set to Abercromby	818
His Plan of Attack	819
The Disembarkation on the Peninsula of Aboukir	820
Storm of the Central Sand-hill by Moore	821
Landing of the Remainder of the Force	822
Losses of the Army and Navy in the Disembarkation	823
Position of the Army after the Action	824
Abercromby's Advance on the 11th of March	825
Attack of the French on the Ninetieth and Ninety-second	826
The Action becomes general	827
Close of the Action	829
Criticism of Abercromby's Proceedings	830
The British Position of the Roman Camp	831
Rapid Increase of Sickness	832
Menou's Plan of Attack on the British	833
The Action of the 21st of March	834
Comments upon the Action	839
The Losses of the British	840
The Losses of the French	842
The Death of Abercromby	843
Character of Abercromby	844

CONTENTS

CHAPTER XXIX

THE CAMPAIGN IN EGYPT

	PAGE
Bonaparte's diplomatic Successes	848
The Treaty of Lunéville and the Armed Neutrality	848
Resignation of Pitt	848
Hutchinson succeeds Abercromby	849
His Operations at Rosetta	849
His Advance up the Nile	850
Cabal of Officers against Hutchinson	851
He continues his Advance	852
The Turks successfully engage the French	853
Junction of the Turkish and British Armies	854
Surrender of Cairo by the French	855
Arrival of Reinforcements from England	856
The Indian Contingent	857
Its long Delay in reaching Cosseir	858
Baird's March across the Desert from Cosseir	859
The March of the Eighty-sixth across the Desert from Suez	860
Hutchinson's Operations against Alexandria	861
Capitulation of Menou	863
Comments on the Egyptian Campaign	863
Its incompetent Direction by Henry Dundas	865
The Armed Neutrality; Capture of the Danish and Swedish West Indies by the British	866
Nelson's Victory at Copenhagen	866
Bonaparte's Feints at Invasion of England	868
The Failure of his Diplomacy in Russia and in the Peninsula	868
Peace of Amiens signed	869

CHAPTER XXX

REVIEW OF THE PROGRESS OF THE ARMY FROM 1793 TO 1802

The Appointment of the Secretary of State for War	871
He becomes Secretary of State for War and Colonies	872

	PAGE
The Secretary at War; Yonge; Windham	872
Effect of a Coalition Ministry on the Military Administration	873
William Huskisson, the Under-Secretary of State for War	874
The Appointment of the Secretary of State for War an Administrative Failure	875
The Duke of York as Commander-in-chief	876
His Position in the Financial Aspect	877
He assumes absolute Control of the Military Side of the War Office	878
The Adjutant-general, Quartermaster-general, and Military Secretary	879
Limitations of the Duke's Power in Military Matters	879
The Master-general of the Ordnance, Lord Cornwallis	880
Unsatisfactory State of the Ordnance Office	881
Creation of the Staff Corps in consequence	881
The Treasury	881
Land Transport and Supply	882
Sea Transport	882
Dangers of Sea Transport in the Eighteenth Century	883
The Home Office	884
Its Friction with the War Office over the Militia	885
The Lords-Lieutenant and the Generals of Districts	885
The Union with Ireland and Disappearance of the Irish Establishment	886
The Regular Army: its Strength and Methods of Recruiting	887
The Militia: English, Scotch, and Irish	888
The Fencibles	889
Rise of the Ninety-third Highlanders	890
Fencibles for Foreign Garrisons	890
West India Regiments: Importance of their Establishment	891
The Provisional Cavalry	891
The Volunteers: Volunteer or Yeomanry Cavalry	892
Volunteer Infantry and Artillery	893
Voluntary Associations for Defence	893
Confusion in the Military Arrangements	894

CONTENTS

	PAGE
Foreign Troops: Difficulty and Obscurity of the Subject	895
The Enlistment of Foreign Levies in Principle a Blunder	896
The Pay of the Army	897
Change in the Status of Regimental Paymasters	898
Anomalies and Expense of the Change	899
The Clothing of the Army	899
Abortive Efforts to change the System	900
Reforms actually executed	902
The Housing of the Army	903
The Establishment of the Barrackmaster-general	903
Shameful Extravagance and Incapacity of the New Officer	904
The Housing of the Army in Barracks amounted to a Revolution in the Military System	906
The Branches of the Regular Army: the Cavalry	907
Report of the Board of General Officers upon the Mounted Troops	907
Disappearance of the old War-horse	908
Veterinary Surgeons	909
Defective Training of the Cavalry	910
General Money's Criticisms	911
The Artillery: Growth of the Horse Artillery	912
The Field Artillery: the First Corps of Drivers, 1794	913
The Second Corps of Drivers, 1801	914
The Artillery in the Field	914
The Engineers	915
The Royal Military Artificers	915
The Staff Corps	916
The Infantry: Battalions of Flank Companies	916
Long Delay in the Creation of true Light Infantry	917
The Making of the Rifle Brigade	918
Details of Dress and Drill in the Infantry	921
The Medical Service: its past History	922
The Reforms of 1798	923
The Chaplains' Department: Reforms	925
Military Education: the Staff College	926
The Royal Military College	927

xlviii   HISTORY OF THE ARMY

	PAGE
Signs of kinder Treatment of the Soldier	927
Good Service of the Duke of York	929

APPENDICES

A. Table of Regular Regiments raised, 1793–1802.	931
B. Pay of the Army	935
C. British and Irish Military Establishments, 1793–1802	938
D. Effective Strength of the Regular Army (exclusive of Artillery), 1793–1801, with the number of Recruits raised in each Year	940
E. List of Fencible Regiments for the Formation of which Letters of Service were issued, 1793–1802	941

INDEX 945

MAPS AND PLANS

(*In a separate volume.*)

CAMPAIGN OF THE NETHERLANDS, 1793–1795

1. Position of Famars.
2. Dunkirk.
3. Position of the opposing armies, April 1794.
4. Battle of Turcoing.
5. Avesnes-le-Sec, Villers en Cauchies, and Beaumont } on one sheet.
6. Willems

CAMPAIGN OF THE MEDITERRANEAN, 1793–1795

7. Toulon
8. Corsica } on one sheet.
9. Bastia
10. Calvi

CAMPAIGNS OF THE WEST INDIES,[1] 1793–1798

Leeward Sphere

11. Haiti, with inset of St. Domingo.
12. Jamaica.

Windward Sphere

13. Martinique } on one sheet, with inset of Point-à-Pitre and
14. Guadeloupe   the Camp of Berville.

---

[1] For general map of the West Indies see Volume III.

HISTORY OF THE ARMY

15. St. Lucia.
16. Castries.
17. St. Vincent ⎫
18. Grenada   ⎬ on one sheet.
19. Dominica   ⎭

CAMPAIGN OF NORTH HOLLAND, 1799

20. General Map of North Holland.
21. North Holland: Helder to Petten.
22.   „   „   Petten to Alkmaar.

23. Cape of Good Hope, with inset of Capetown and Simonstown.

GENERAL MAPS

24. THE NETHERLANDS, NORTH-EAST FRANCE, and the LOWER RHINE.
25. FRANCE, AND THE WESTERN MEDITERRANEAN, with five insets—(1) Malta, (2) Valetta, (3) Minorca, (4) Connaught, 1798, (5) Partitions of Poland.
26. EGYPT AND THE EASTERN MEDITERRANEAN, with three insets—(1) Peninsula of Alexandria, from Aboukir Bay to Alexandria, (2) The Battle of 21st March 1801, (3) The Valley of the Nile.
27. SOUTHERN INDIA, with two insets—(1) Seringapatam, (2) Ceylon.

ABBREVIATIONS USED IN REFERENCE TO THE ARCHIVES PRESERVED IN THE RECORD OFFICE

B.G.O. = Minutes of the Board of General Officers.
C.C.L.B. = Commander-in-chief's Letter Books.
H.O.M.E.B. = Home Office Military Entry Books.
S.C.L.B. = The Letter Books of the Secretary at War, known as the "Secretary's Common Letter Books."

BOOK XII

CHAPTER I

A VERY eminent military writer has recorded his opinion that the prodigious effects of the French Revolution in Europe were due less to new methods introduced by the French in the conduct of war, than to the changes which it wrought in state-craft and civil administration, in the character of governments, and in the condition of the people. The rulers of Europe attempted to combat novel forces of overwhelming strength by ordinary measures of antiquated design. Hence, he concludes, their blunder was a political one, and was not to be amended by any purely military expedient.[1]

To seek to evade the truth of this deep and searching criticism would be idle. War is at all times a political instrument. The military chief may indeed, so to speak, lay and fire the gun upon its mark; but the pattern of the gun itself, the nature of its ammunition, the time for bringing it into position, the choice of that position, and the selection of its target, are things which must be decided by the political commander. Therefore it is that war is never so formidable as when the powers both of soldier and statesman are united in a single man of genius. Let such a man arise, and let there be furnished ready to his hand the novel forces of overwhelming strength, to which Von Clausewitz alludes, and there follows the necessary consequence that he will be well-nigh irresistible. He can only be overcome by forces of like potency with.

[1] Von Clausewitz, *On War* (English translation), iii. 69.

his own, by the pride of the free peoples, the religious loyalty of the primitive, the vindictiveness of the conquered and despoiled, the rage and hatred of all. The war of the French Revolution may be described as the long struggle wherein the French nation rose up in arms to overthrow kings, and, having taken to herself a king, was herself overthrown by nations. No purely military narrative can relate aright the history of such a contest.

But the difficulties in the treatment of the subject do not begin nor end with the reaction of French political troubles upon Europe. At St. Petersburg the restless ambition of the Empress Catherine created as dangerous a centre of disturbance as did the fanaticism of the Revolutionary party at Paris. In France the lust of war and conquest was yet to be born; in Russia the combative instincts and military organisation of a half-civilised state were still in full vigour, terrible weapons in the hand of a very able, rapacious, and unscrupulous princess. Between these two lay the chaos which was known as the Holy Roman Empire, with a social and political organisation as rotten as that of France itself, and Poland in anarchy and confusion. The menace of danger simultaneously from East and West contributed more than any other cause to distract the energies of the two leading powers in Germany, and so to consolidate the strength both of Russia and France; with the ultimate result that within the space of two short years Austrian troops were seen marching with the French banners against Moscow, and with the Russian against Paris.

From the terrible embarrassments, which afflicted the German States, England was fortunately delivered by her insular position. Moreover, having freed herself from the trammels of the feudal system more than a century before France began to shake them off, she was little accessible to the temptations put forward by the French revolutionary propaganda. Hence, although she possessed a weak spot in Ireland, she was the great bulwark against the Revolution in the West of Europe.

In the East, Russia, through the backwardness of her civilisation, likewise opposed to it an impenetrable barrier, her people being too primitive to accept, even for misinterpretation, the wild ideas of the French fanatics. It is remarkable that, when all other armies were cowed, the soldiers of these two nations were never afraid to meet the French in the field; and to them accordingly it fell finally to play the chief part in breaking down the might of victorious France. If, as a very eminent French thinker has written, the French Revolution, though political, partook of the character of a great religious movement, then it may justly be said that England and Russia prevailed because of the faith that was in them, faith in their own political institutions.

It is therefore evident that at this stage of our narrative political affairs demand greater prominence than has hitherto been allotted to them; but this is only a feeble description of the true state of the case. It is not too much to say that many of the military operations of this period are absolutely unintelligible without a sufficient understanding of the political events that accompanied them. Again and again one army or another appears to be hopelessly beaten and the issue of the campaign to be decided, when suddenly, as if by magic, the whole situation is changed. Victorious commanders halt; great advantages are abandoned; sound dispositions give place to vicious; a tumultuous mob becomes an irresistible host, and once sturdy troops a disorganised rabble; and the secrets of these changes are to be found not in any masterly military manœuvre, but in some obscure intrigue of a Minister at Vienna, or in some stroke of violence by a faction at Paris. In such a tangle of complicated affairs the difficulties of the historian become very great. It is open to him, if he will, to assume perfect familiarity on the part of his readers with every detail in the story of the French Revolution; though in truth that event is summed up to many Englishmen in the single phrase, Reign of Terror. The Revolution, in fact, is placed on much the same footing with the earthquake at Lisbon, as a short though gigantic catastrophe; whereas, just as an earthquake consists not of a single huge upheaval but of innumerable shocks of less or greater violence, so is a Revolution made up of innumerable greater and less commotions. To follow the military operations of the British aright, necessity compels that occasionally certain of these commotions shall be dwelt upon in some detail; but, unless some account has been given of their forerunners in the general disturbance, these are raised to undue and disproportionate importance. On the other hand, a lengthy recital of the whole course of the French Revolution is, in such a work as this, out of the question; and it is therefore for the historian to extricate himself as best he can from an extremely embarrassing dilemma.

In this difficulty I have resorted to a middle course, which alone seemed to offer a satisfactory way of escape. The section of the French nation with which British military history is principally concerned is, of course, the French army, the army of the tricolour, whose fame will never be forgotten until wars have ceased from upon the earth. The story of its origin and of the early trials and vicissitudes through which it rose to a height of greatness hardly paralleled in human history, is not only full of interest in itself but replete with instruction for British officers and statesmen. Not until we understand how the French soldier was trained to beat the armies of the world can we realise how the British soldier was trained to beat the French. I therefore open the present volume with a brief account of the destruction of the old French army and of the first measures taken for the creation of the new, during the earlier years of the French Revolution. Some such preliminary sketch is absolutely necessary for the right understanding of that army's later growth and development, and of the differences in its quality when at various times it was confronted with our own forces in the field; and it will further be a means for recalling to readers the sequence of the principal events in the

Revolution itself. I am fully aware that the subject may be condemned as alien to a History of the British Army, and I feel constrained to apologise for dealing with it at length. But "novel forces of overwhelming strength" call for exceptional treatment. Victorious armies have ever learned from their enemies; and the British had much to learn from the French before they emerged victorious from the great war of the Revolution.

The French Army, as we have hitherto known it, was, like the English, recruited by voluntary enlistment, and was therefore composed of very similar elements, that is to say, of men who were of character too restless and turbulent for a peasant's life, or who had flown to the ranks to escape from troubles of one kind or another. About one-fourth of them, however, had been born and educated to better things; and these did not lightly bear the yoke of discipline. The term of service, unlike the English, was limited to eight years, after which a soldier could re-enlist for successive periods of two years, receiving a bounty for each such extension of his time. Finally, at the close of his military career there lay open to him a haven in the Hotel des Invalides, corresponding to our Chelsea Hospital. The service, however, was very far from attractive. The discipline was severe, the pay was bad —but fivepence a day—the food, clothing, and housing were no better than the pay, and there was no hope of advancement. A few, but only a very few, privates rose to be officers; for a commission was the special privilege of the nobility. Hence recruits could hardly be obtained but by the most cunning wiles of the crimp; and desertion rose to appalling proportions. Lastly, the Hotel des Invalides was too often closed to deserving veterans by the intrusion of civilians, whom the great nobles wished to reward, at the expense of the State, for some private service. In such an army it may readily be believed that there was abundant ground where the seeds of discontent could grow and ripen into a harvest of mutiny.[1]

The French officers, as a body, were little less discontented than the men. They were drawn, as has been said, almost exclusively from the nobility; but the nobility numbered twenty-five thousand families and was constantly increasing, inasmuch as certain official positions carried with them promotion to noble rank. The great majority of these families were miserably poor, yet all careers were closed to them except the military and the ecclesiastic; and, in both of these, high and lucrative station was the appanage of birth, not the reward of merit. Colonelcies frequently fell to children of sixteen and eighteen, belonging to the highest of the noble houses; and, except actually on parade, military rank was subordinate to social precedence. A commanding officer found himself, off duty, the inferior of captains of high lineage and historic name. Indeed, there was in every regiment an association of subalterns who undertook to maintain the tone which they conceived to be proper for their brother officers; nor did they stick at enforcing their decrees upon their superiors by horseplay, even in the public streets of a garrison town.[2] In brief, the discipline of the officers was deplorably bad.

Finally, the French army had been greatly demoralised by the disgrace that had fallen upon it during the Seven Years' War. Under incapable leaders and corrupt administration this great and famous force had been shamed by defeat after defeat into the belief that it was good for nothing. Upon the peace of 1763 Choiseul set himself with inconsiderate zeal to institute reforms which should save France from a repetition of such ignominy. Frederick the Great was the commander above all others who had humiliated the French; therefore, in Choiseul's view, all changes must be copied from the Prussian model. Veteran officers,

---

[1] Poisson, *L'Armée et la Garde Nationale*, i. 10-12; Dampmartin, ii. 368; Taine, *Ancien Régime*, ii. 301 (new edition).
[2] *Mémoires de Ségur*, i. 67, 200.

HISTORY OF THE ARMY

scarred with wounds but still fit and eager for service, were driven from the army; wild theories of training and tactics were propounded and frequently carried into practice; and the troops were made over to young and conceited generals, who worried the men and disgusted the officers by petty details of dress and drill, which they conceived to be the essence of the Prussian system. Worst of all, these reformers introduced the Prussian custom of striking men with the flat of the sword, forgetting that Frederick's soldiers were serfs, whereas the French peasant, for long before the Revolution, was generally the actual proprietor of his own plot of land.

At the accession of Lewis the Sixteenth in 1774 military reform proceeded upon more sensible lines. Colonelcies were no longer granted even to the greatest nobles until they had served for fourteen years; the system of purchase, which still survived in certain regiments, was gradually and skilfully abolished; and certain noble corps of the Household Troops were disbanded from motives of economy. But this last step in one respect made matters worse instead of better, for it signified a reduction of the number of appointments open to the nobility. The twenty-five thousand families were more than ever impoverished, and their bitter cry for commissions became intolerable to the Minister of War. In an evil hour, and against the advice of the Minister himself, it was decreed in 1781 that thenceforward every aspirant to a commission must produce a certificate from the King's Genealogist that he had four generations of noble ancestry to his credit. This was a cruel blow. Formerly no further certificate had been required than one signed by any two noblemen; and many a good officer of the middle class had obtained admission to the army by the payment of a small fee to two duly qualified though impecunious sponsors. Now, not only was this door closed, but thousands of young men, lately ennobled by the good service of their fathers or grandfathers to the State, were shut out from all employment except in the Church. This regulation, of itself sufficient to embitter the general discontent, was made doubly galling by being injudiciously enforced. The King, always weak and irresolute, sought refuge from the outcry of officers and the endless appeals of individuals for special favour, by placing the government of the army in the hands of a Council of War. Thus unity of command was destroyed; and this measure was thought by many to have given the finishing stroke to the discipline of the old French army.[1]

It must be remembered, further, that the experience of the French troops, who had served under Washington in America, had opened the eyes of at least some of them. Vast numbers of the men had indeed deserted rather than re-embark for France;[2] but those that returned were enthusiastically welcomed for their restoration of French glory at Yorktown. Little heed was paid to the many shameful failures which had attended the French operations at large. Lafayette, Rochambeau, and the brave men with them had vindicated the honour of the French arms; they had beaten the old enemy; they had established the free republic for which all classes in France, from the Queen downward, professed a sentimental affection. Many imagined that the Americans, with the aid of the French, had conquered for themselves the ideal state of society described by Jean Jacques Rousseau. They honoured, and most justly honoured, the name of Washington, but they had no conception of the qualities which really made him great. They talked of Cincinnatus and his brave legions; but they knew nothing of the cat-o'-nine-tails with which Cincinnatus compelled his legions to obedience. They admired the boldness with which a sheriff's officer had served a writ upon General Rochambeau himself in the midst of his staff; but they gave not a thought to the public spirit and the public opinion which lent to that writ its force. Full of the new gospel, that all men are not only perfectible but naturally good, the French ignored the substance of the American Revolution as a

[1] Dampmartin, i. 97-101, 133.   [2] Ségur, i. 404.

fit subject for practical study, but seized on its superficial forms as a theme for sentimental rhetoric. The officers of the army were naturally carried away by the prevailing current of feeling, and the more readily because the hero of the hour was one of themselves. Only a few of the old school recognised Lafayette for what he really was, one of the vainest and shallowest of men.

The army, therefore, was more than half disorganised before the Revolution actually broke out ; and, if it failed in time of need, there was practically no other force to preserve order in the kingdom. There existed indeed a militia, which was embodied annually for a month's training in time of peace, and in time of war was used to swell the ranks of the army to its full strength.[1] But the militia, which was recruited by ballot in the various parishes, was a most unpopular service, being so regulated as to constitute one of the most intolerable grievances of the poorest classes. The nobles, their servants, their dependents, and in fact all who could gain their protection, were exempted from service ; and the same privilege was further extended to several thousand officials of the middle class. Moreover, the purchase of substitutes was forbidden even to those who could afford it, lest the price of recruits for the regular army should thereby be raised. Besides the

---

[1] The French army at the beginning of 1789 numbered about 160,000 men, its nominal establishment being 178,000. Of this total the Household troops, viz. the Life Guards, Hundred Swiss, French Guards, and Swiss Guards (the two last each of 6 battalions), made up 8000. The infantry of the Line was composed of 79 French and 23 foreign regiments, each of 2 battalions (excepting the King's Regiment, which had 4) ; and the Light Infantry was made up of 12 battalions. The Artillery consisted of 7 regiments, each of 2 battalions, including sappers. The Cavalry consisted of 25 regiments of Cuirassiers, 18 of Dragoons, 6 of Hussars, and 2 of Mounted *Chasseurs*. The Militia consisted of 106 battalions, of which 79 were garrison-battalions, designed to feed the 79 regiments of the Line in time of war. This force, together with 421 companies for coast defence, raised the strength of the army in time of war to 287,000 men. See Poisson, i. 1-9 ; Rousset, *Les Volontaires*, pp. 1-3 ; Dampmartin, ii. 361.

army and the militia there existed for purposes of internal police the town-guards, maintained and controlled by the larger towns, and a mounted constabulary[1] under the immediate orders of the central government. This last, which seems to have been as effective for its duty and as summary in its procedure as the *Guardia Civil* of modern Spain, was a force of the very highest quality; but its numbers did not exceed eight thousand, whereas the population of France counted from twenty-four to twenty-five million souls.

It need only be added, on the one hand, that centuries of misgovernment and of maladministration, combined with oppressive game-laws and vexatious customs-duties, had raised up in France an enormous class of poachers, smugglers, and lawless and dangerous men, which the utmost severity was powerless to put down; and that, on the other hand, the government was centralised to an extreme degree, all power filtering downward from the sovereign through a hierarchy of thirty intendants to a vast number of subordinate officials. All functionaries, therefore, looked to Paris for direction, and hesitated to take any initiative without orders. The local authority and administration, both formal and informal, which is exercised in England by resident landowners, was unknown in France. The nobles claimed their privileges, giving no service in return; and only in the west and north-west, in La Vendée and Brittany, were to be found provincial magnates of the British type, who lived and moved among their own people. Hence any weakness or irresolution at headquarters paralysed executive action throughout the length and breadth of France; and if to such paralysis were added disaffection of the armed forces of the Crown, there remained little to save the country from anarchy.

1789. This is no place for examining the many complex and remote causes which conspired to bring about the Revolution; it must suffice to name only the proximate and immediate reasons for the final outbreak. The

---

[1] *Maréchaussée.*

first was the peril of national bankruptcy, which forced 1789. the King to summon, after an abeyance of nearly two centuries, an assembly of the three estates of the realm; the second was famine, due to the ruined harvest and the terrible and disastrous winter of the year 1788. The States-General met on the 4th of May 1789; but for weeks and months before there had been serious riots both in Paris and in the provinces, and as early as in February 1789 the Minister, Necker, had confessed, not without good warrant, that the troops were not to be trusted.[1] On the 27th of April several regiments were called out to quell a dangerous rising in Paris. On that day the troops did their duty; but on the 23rd of June 23. June, when the Commons-House of the States-General declared itself to be a National Assembly, the French Guards showed dangerous symptoms of mutiny. Thirty thousand regular soldiers had meanwhile been assembled in the environs of Paris; but the menace of their presence was more apparent than real. Mirabeau, the greatest July 8. of the Revolutionary leaders, did indeed declare that such a force was a threat to public tranquillity, and that the preservation of public order might well be committed to a militia of citizens; but the true danger lay rather in the inaction than the action of the troops. Bold and resolute handling might perhaps have restored the habit of discipline, but the King had set the seal on their disaffection by the well-meaning but fatal order that not a drop of blood should be shed.

Throughout the 12th and 13th of July Paris was a July 12-13. scene of the wildest disorder. The troops could not act even if they had been willing; and the city was only saved from general pillage by the hasty enrolment of twelve thousand citizens as a National Guard, under the orders of a committee which took upon itself the government of the capital. During these two days five out of six battalions of the French Guards mutinied and passed over to the side of the mob; and on the morning of the 14th they moved out with the populace July 14.

[1] *Mémoires de Malouet*, i. 289; *Mémoires de Bouillé*, p. 118.

1789. to the attack of the Bastille. No strong man was at hand with a disciplined force at his back to blast them off the face of the earth; they were left to work their will unmolested, and they received the keys of the fortress, intrinsically an insignificant conquest, by ignominious surrender. On the morrow every officer of the French Guards resigned; and this famous corps, after two centuries and a half of honourable life, passed disgracefully away, releasing, however, three men from its ranks to rise to the highest command, Lefebvre, Friant, and Lazare Hoche.

The consequences of this fatal day were incalculable. The King's authority was gone; no new sovereign power had risen to seize it; and the populace found the mastery in their own hands. "For every impartial man," wrote Malouet, one of the keenest of observers, "the terror dates from the 14th of July." On the
July 15. morrow the King, always weak and yielding, ordered the troops to retire from before Paris; and on the following day the generals who had commanded them, together with the Prince of Condé and the King's second brother, the Count of Artois, fled from the country. The reaction of these events upon the soldiery was immediate. In the week following the fall of the Bastille no fewer than six thousand men deserted from the troops outside Paris, to be welcomed and caressed by the mob within; and the influx was only checked by posting strong picquets of National Guards at the gates. In the provinces the example of Paris was followed with incredible rapidity. Everywhere bands of primitive militia sprang into existence, which seduced or overawed the troops, and seized all arms, magazines, and fortresses in the name of the nation. Everywhere likewise was seen indecision on the part of the military commanders, all waiting, as they had been taught, for
July 19-21. orders from the King. At Strasburg the rabble was left free to sack and pillage for three entire days under the eyes of eight thousand troops, which stood by with ordered arms waiting for the word of command

which never came. The commandant, Rochambeau, a 1789. gallant soldier whom we have seen before and shall see again, stood by in an agony of irresolution, but would say nothing except " Dear me, how dreadful ! "[1] There was no longer a government in France.

It is therefore small wonder that anarchy burst into flame all over the country. A furious revolt of peasants, partial indeed in the south and west, but elsewhere universal, swept the nobles from the land like hunted beasts. Their game was shot down, their forests destroyed, their houses burned by the hundred. Very few had the spirit to resist, and there was no one to defend them. The various bodies of provincial militia, all independent of each other, fought frequently among themselves for authority and still more for food ; and the regular troops, being viewed with suspicion by all, received no orders to act.[2] In Paris the zeal of the National Guards soon cooled, as was natural with men who had to attend to their own business ; and it was necessary to raise a paid force to take their place. The King authorised the enlistment of deserters from the regular army in this corps, thus practically encouraging the gravest of military crimes ; and, on Lafayette's recommendation, a force of sixty battalions was organised with a total strength of thirty thousand men, of whom seven thousand, made up chiefly of deserters and mutineers from the French Guards, were paid, and the remainder were civilians. A new uniform of a blue coat with red collar, and white waistcoat and breeches, was given to them—a dress which was soon to become famous,—and Lafayette himself, being placed at their head as commandant, found himself to all intent the most powerful man in France.

Well would it have been if Lafayette had proved, as he fondly imagined himself to be, a Washington ; but he differed as much from Washington as a paroquet from an eagle. This man, who had fought through the American War, and had seen the ability of the Anglo-

[1] Dampmartin, i. 103, *seq.*   [2] Poisson, i. 91-94, 101.

1789. Saxons for practical self-government, self-help, and self-organisation, could find no better counsel to lay before the National Assembly than three thin formulæ—that all men are free and equal, that all men have the right to resist oppression, and that all sovereignty is derived from the people. Moreover, in his blind conceit and malice against the only free people in Europe, he had already sent forth emissaries to propagate these precious doctrines for the undermining of Britain's influence at home and abroad, thus leading France to interference with others when she should have been minding her own business. The National Assembly was, unfortunately, but too well disposed to acclaim such folly. In vain men of sense, like Mirabeau, Malouet and Mounier, protested; the authority of the hero of America was too strong for them, and the Assembly gladly turned from the difficult task of reorganising France to the interminable recreation of defining the rights of man.

The mere phrase was sufficient to set the many turbulent brains in the army seething. On the 4th of August the nobility, by the general abdication of all feudal rights and privileges, enabled the Assembly to decree that commissions in the army were thenceforward open to all French citizens; and thereupon the non-commissioned officers and men of many regiments set themselves to draw up a military constitution to meet this new state of affairs. This led to discussion first of their own rights and the rights of their officers, and presently to the appointment of committees to correspond with other regiments and with the mutineers of the French Guards. Meanwhile the mob, under the guidance of the extreme party in the Revolution, continued to be the principal authority in the country; and Oct. 5. on the 5th of October the scum of Paris, male and female, was marched to Versailles to intimidate the King into certain constitutional concessions. Once again the old story was repeated. Lafayette allowed this ruffianly band to go on its way; some of the troops on guard at the palace were seduced to mutiny, the rest,

by the King's miserable weakness, were forbidden to fire. 1789.
The palace was invaded, and Lewis was brought away in
triumph to Paris. From that moment the hearts of the
best men in France misgave them that the rule of the
worst was no longer to be avoided. The National
Assembly, ever since the 14th of July, had worked
under the terrorism of hired rascals in the galleries ;
and after the 6th of October over one hundred members
seceded in disgust, while five times that number prepared to fly from the country. The three clearest and
ablest heads in Paris, Mirabeau, Mounier, and Mallet du
Pan, agreed independently of each other that civil war
would be preferable to a reign of brute violence, and
that the King ought to retire to the provinces and rally
all good citizens round him to avert the catastrophe by
force of arms.¹

The dealings of the National Assembly with the
question of military reorganisation were not calculated
to reassure anxious citizens. A committee had been
appointed at the beginning of October to report upon 1790.
the matter, and in March their recommendations were March.
carried into effect. It is enough to say of them that
voluntary enlistment was preferred to conscription, and
that the pay of the private soldiers was raised—measures
harmless enough in themselves but taken for no good
object. The increase of pay was designed as a bribe to
the men to transfer their allegiance from their officers to
the Assembly, while the choice of voluntary enlistment
was made an excuse for insinuating that all willing
recruits were necessarily drawn from the criminal class,
and for insulting the military profession at large.² All
provision for the restoration of discipline was omitted ;
and indeed the Assembly was so jealous and fearful of
the army that it spared no pains to undermine the
authority of the officers. The men were encouraged to
lay their complaints before it ; and the most flagrant
cases of insubordination received open sympathy from
the members. Matters grew still worse when the

¹ Taine, iii. 166, 167. ² Poisson, i. 190.

1790. administrative redistribution of France was accomplished. Thereby the country was divided into eighty-three departments, as the largest unit, and into forty-four thousand municipalities as the smallest; and among these tiny bodies over two million citizens were equipped with arms as National Guards, and called upon to exercise the sovereignty of the people. The regular troops were then placed under the orders of these municipalities, which were not slow to exercise their authority, interfering continually with that of the officers, and working hand in hand with agents from the Revolutionary clubs in Paris to ruin the discipline of the men. In such regiments as were already ill-governed, mutinous conduct became the rule during the spring of 1790, and early in June the Minister for War declared that the forces were falling into a state of utter anarchy.[1]

The finishing blow to the discipline of the army was given by a great festival held at Paris to celebrate the first anniversary of the fall of the Bastille. Since December 1789 it had become common, in the enthusiasm of the time, for large bodies of National Guards to meet at some centre, and there to swear fidelity to the King, the Assembly, and the Constitution. These federations, as they were called, were fruitful of demoralisation to the regular troops that took part in them, though they had their value in bringing the National Guards of the provinces and of the capital together, and of affiliating the one to the other. It was
July 14. resolved that, at the great federation of the 14th of July 1790, representatives of every department, of every regular regiment, and of all the National Guards should be present, to swear the usual oaths and to refresh the spirit of national concord. Never was device more perfectly successful. The detachments sent to Paris by the regular regiments were thoroughly corrupted during their stay, and returned to sow mutiny and insubordination broadcast among their comrades. Officers

[1] Taine, iv. 218-228.

CH. I HISTORY OF THE ARMY 19

coming back to duty from leave of absence were thunder- 1790.
struck, even in good regiments, at the change in their
men. So far, in many corps the officers had remedied
temporary disorder with little trouble ; but now matters
were completely altered. The men were sulky, discontented, and constantly seeking to provoke their
superiors, while they resented discipline as the token of
the accursed thing, aristocracy. The officers also were
divided among themselves according to their political
sympathies ; and the absence of many colonels, who
were anxious to avoid evil days, favoured indiscipline.
Mirabeau was now for disbanding the army altogether, before further mischief should ensue. The
Assembly also passed a sharp decree against insub- Aug. 6.
ordination ; but it was too late. At the end of August
three regiments, one of them Swiss, broke into open
mutiny at Nancy, seized the regimental money-chest,
and defied their officers. To their amazement they
found themselves put down with a strong hand. The
Marquis of Bouillé, a noble old soldier whose arm the
British had felt in the West Indies in 1778, marched
without hesitation against the mutineers, and crushed
them utterly after a pitched battle, which cost to victors Aug. 31.
and vanquished not fewer than three thousand men.

For the moment discipline seemed to have been
re-established. Bouillé received the thanks of the
Assembly and of the King, together with the offer of a
marshal's baton, which, however, he refused to accept
for service done against his own countrymen. The
mob of Paris, furious at the vindication of law and
order, assembled, fifty thousand strong, to intimidate the
Assembly into censure of the General, but recoiled
before the bayonets and cannon of the National Guard.
The revolted Swiss, being tried, according to their
privilege, by their compatriots of other corps in the
French service, were very severely dealt with, over
twenty being summarily hanged and fifty more sent to
the galleys. The Assembly also reiterated a former
decree forbidding soldiers to take part in political

1790. meetings or even to be admitted to them;[1] but here the movement in favour of discipline ended. Bouillé found himself powerless to punish the French mutineers of his own authority, though he committed them for trial; and the Assembly sent commissioners of its own to Nancy to inquire into the whole matter. Meanwhile the Assembly, in pursuance of its work of military reform, ordained that in future all military crimes should be tried by a jury, of which one-seventh should be non-commissioned officers and one-seventh privates, the proportion of jurors of the same rank as the prisoner being in all cases doubled.[2] Thus authority was still further withdrawn from the officers, and the enforcement even of legal penalties became doubtful if not
Nov. impossible. The party of violence in Paris recovered itself, and denounced the Minister of War so furiously that he resigned; while at the same time it waged, through its emissaries, relentless persecution against the troops that had been faithful to Bouillé. Finally, in December the commissioners returned from Nancy to recommend that the two mutinous French regiments should indeed be disbanded, but that the prosecution of the ringleaders should be dropped, all prisoners in confinement on account of the mutiny released, and intercession made with the Swiss Cantons on behalf of the soldiers condemned to the galleys.[3]

It seemed as though France had suddenly imbibed all the British prejudice against a standing army; but the evil was really more deeply seated. Mutiny was as active in the navy as in the army,[4] and indiscipline as rife in the civil as in the military departments. Mirabeau pleaded in vain for a strong Government with a Cabinet responsible to Parliament, after the English model; but even his genius and eloquence could not prevail, for the party of violence desired

---

[1] *Mémoires de Bouillé*, p. 243; Poisson, i. 289.
[2] Taine, iv. 15; *Mémoires de Bouillé*, p. 213.
[3] Poisson, i. 265-268.
[4] Mahan, *Sea Power in the French Revolution and Empire*, i. 41.

nothing so little as law and order. Meanwhile fiscal confusion had become worse confounded, for nothing is so expensive as anarchy. A gigantic effort had been made to restore financial equilibrium by confiscating the goods of the Church, and issuing paper money upon the credit of the funds thus appropriated; but this measure, by hasty and clumsy mismanagement, had only increased the general demoralisation. It paved the way, moreover, for an attack upon conscience, the last stronghold of moral authority, in a proposal for the civil constitution of the clergy. Hereby provision was made that all bishops and curates should thenceforth be elected, the one qualification for an elector being that, whatever his creed, he should have heard a mass. This blow against the rock of religious belief struck out instantly the sparks of civil war in Brittany and in the South; but the Assembly cared not the least. The Civil Constitution was decreed; and, since two-thirds of the clergy refused to recognise it, a further decree was made that all ecclesiastics must swear adherence to it on pain of destitution. Thus were sown the dragon's teeth which were to produce so terrible a harvest in La Vendée.

1790.

April.

May-June.
Nov. 27.

The patience of others besides priests also drew near to exhaustion at the close of 1790. The assault upon the Church was as grievous to the dull pious soul of the King as to any Breton peasant, and the durance wherein he was held at the Tuileries was intolerable to him. Slowly he came to the resolution to fly to some fortress on the northern frontier, where, under protection of Bouillé's loyal regiments and with the support of an Austrian force over the border, he could rally all loyal Frenchmen and good Catholics to restore order and authority in France. Long and weary was the correspondence upon the subject between old Bouillé, who knew his own mind, and the King, who did not. The project of an appeal to the provinces had long ago been urged by Mirabeau; but Mirabeau died before he could see it realised. The Jacobins (for so we may now

1791.
April 4.

1791. term the extreme party of violence), suspecting Bouillé, took from him his best regiments, and endeavoured to demoralise such as were left with him by practically revoking the prohibition of soldiers from attendance at political meetings. None the less the Marshal worked on quietly and strenuously; and at last the King, irritated by a fresh insult from the populace of Paris, accepted from him a very able plan to escape from the capital to Montmédy. There is no need to tell again the story of the flight to Varennes. Bouillé had arranged every detail on his side with military punctuality and precision. The King started twenty-four hours too late—his besetting sin in a life of irresolution
June 26. —and was brought back in ignominious procession to Paris.

The alarm at his escape and the terror of consequent invasion had been great; and the Jacobins did not fail to take advantage of it. Memorials poured into the Assembly crying out for the dethronement of the Sovereign who had betrayed his country; and finally a huge petition to the same effect was set out in the Champ de Mars for signature by the people at large. A turbulent crowd soon gathered round it, and the Municipal Council, taking the alarm, called out the
July 17. National Guard, which dispersed the populace by a single volley. So great was the terror inspired by this act of firmness that the fiercest of the revolutionary spirits quailed, and the most violent in speech hastened to hide themselves away. Had it been followed up by a resolute assertion of authority, the Revolution might have taken a very different course; but the flash of energy was but momentary, and the Assembly relapsed into weakness once more. In September, having fulfilled (as it supposed) the task of making the Constitution, and thus gained for itself the title of Constituent Assembly, this strange body was dissolved. In some respects it had done good work; but towards the reorganising of disorganised France it had done worse than nothing, chiefly because it persisted in reckoning

with men as with algebraic symbols instead of as incalculable forces of flesh and blood.

1791.

Meanwhile the last blow had been dealt to the army. For months the officers had endured with exemplary patience the insulting and vexatious domination of ignorant municipalities; obeying the orders of their unworthy masters, despite deliberate efforts to stir up insubordination among the men, with a loyalty which was beyond all praise. Not the most dutiful submission could avail them. Viewed as a body, there were no more industrious, able, and patriotic public servants in France; but they were nobles, and this was sufficient to identify them in the public mind with the worthless parasites of Versailles, who were a curse to every land which they entered. Moreover, to individual persecution there was added the shock, during the early months of 1791, of a succession of sweeping reforms in the military service. Some of these were doubtless good and sound; others wounded the sentimental susceptibilities of the army to the heart; others again were essentially vicious. Thus the whole of the famous Household troops, except the Swiss Guards, were abolished, and a new Constitutional Guard appointed for the Sovereign. The old historic titles of the regiments, whether suggesting royal favour, such as the King's, or territorial origin, such as Picardie and Champagne, were blotted out; and in infantry, cavalry, and artillery alike, numbers were substituted for them. The change was perhaps necessary, but any soldier can understand that it was unwelcome, and for a time may well have been even injurious. Far more noxious were the new regulations as to promotion. To place the highest commands within reach of deserving privates was doubtless in principle right; but to establish the elective system for the advancement of men and officers was, in view of recent experience in America, nothing short of imbecility. Yet this was the method deliberately chosen by the collective wisdom of France. For the appointment of a corporal all the corporals in a regiment

1791. suggested a name to their captains; the list thus formed was kept by the colonel; and on the occurrence of a vacancy the captain of the company chose three names from this list, of which the colonel selected one. The like procedure was observed in the case of every grade of non-commissioned officer. The degree of officer could be obtained either by rising through the ranks or by passing an examination; but one sub-lieutenancy in every four was reserved for non-commissioned officers, and was conferred alternatively by seniority and by selection, the latter term signifying at first election by the suffrages of all the officers.[1] One-third of the field-officers and one-half of the generals were likewise appointed by election; and the only gift left to the King to bestow was a marshal's baton. Here therefore were all powers of reward taken from the commanding officers, as well as all powers of punishment, which had already been made over to juries; and thus military discipline was reduced to an impossibility.[2]

The last straw which made the burden of military command insupportable was a new oath, tendered to all ranks after the flight to Varennes, from which the King's name was omitted. Though intellectually a superior body of men, taken as a whole, the French officers, owing to generations of hereditary service, regarded the person of the King with a sentimental devotion which was almost superstitious.[3] It was hard for them to see the Sovereign's function as the fountain of military honour abolished; it was insufferable even to think that he was no longer head of the army. Thousands resigned rather than take the oath; and by September 1791 two-thirds of the whole body of officers had been driven from the service to join in foreign lands the relatives whom a like persecution had hunted from their

[1] This procedure survived, curiously enough, till 1804; though subalterns had by that time learned to ascertain the colonel's pleasure before submitting to him a candidate for promotion from the ranks to a commission. *Mémoires de Fezensac*, p. 37.
[2] Poisson, i. 314 *sq.*; Taine, iv. 15, 16.
[3] *Mémoires de Marmont*, i. 25.

homes. The extreme party of the Revolution rejoiced. 1791.
France, they said, would be the sooner purged of aristocrats; under the new Constitution she had renounced the monarchical lust of conquest, and would need no army but for defence of her own territory; moreover, a people in arms, willingly obedient to officers of its own election, would be more than a match for the hired legions of any monarchical power. Such were the theories of the minority which had gained the upper hand in France. Already there were symptoms abroad of a war which might put them to the test.

CHAPTER II

1791. THE first outbreak of the Revolution in France found the rest of Europe so fully engrossed with other affairs as to attract comparatively little attention. A brief sketch has been given in a former chapter of the troubles that disturbed the Netherlands during the reign of the Emperor Joseph the Second, of that monarch's league with Russia against the Turks, and of the Triple Alliance whereby Pitt checkmated him. Mention has likewise been made of the dispute which arose between England and Spain in May 1789 over Nootka Sound, and of its happy termination, as also of Pitt's abortive efforts to stay the rapacious hand of the Empress Catherine in Turkey. But though the mere statement of these various incidents suffices to indicate the preoccupation of the different Courts, it does not touch the inwardness of the unrest which agitated the powers of Central and Eastern Europe. The Emperor Joseph died in February 1790, and made way for a wiser and more cautious prince in Leopold, the brother of Queen Marie Antoinette of France; but there remained always three disturbing elements—the mutual jealousy and suspicion of Austria and Prussia, the exhausted and anarchic condition of Poland, and the unscrupulous and insatiable ambition of the Empress Catherine of Russia.

Poland at this time was under the rule of Stanislaus, one of Catherine's discarded lovers, and therefore subject to Russian influence: a state of affairs which Prussia regarded with anger and dread. Prussia had never ceased to cherish the great Frederick's dream,

unrealized at the partition of 1772, of obtaining 1791.
Dantzig and Thorn from Poland; and Poland was
in consequence intensely bitter against her. Leopold,
meanwhile, deploring the division of German power in
presence of so formidable a rival as Catherine, was
inclined to reverse Joseph's policy of friendliness with
Russia and to seek closer relations with Prussia. He
made his overtures accordingly in February 1791 to
King Frederick William, who welcomed them as likely
to assure Austrian neutrality in case of a war with the
Empress. At the same time, however, Leopold took
advantage of Prussia's unpopularity to extend Austrian
influence in Poland, and to put forward the project of
making the Polish Crown hereditary in the Electoral
family of Saxony. Stanislaus accepted this proposal;
thereby at a stroke throwing off his dependence on May.
Russia, and establishing the preponderance of Austrian
influence within his realm. Frederick William was deeply
chagrined, for his advisers reckoned that, unless Poland
were an elective kingdom, there was no safety for
Prussia. Nevertheless he was inclined to resign himself to the situation if Austria would promise neutrality,
as before, in the event of a war between himself and
Catherine; and accordingly he asked Leopold to meet
him in conference at Pilnitz, on the outskirts of Dresden,
in order to settle the matter. After some hesitation the
Emperor on the 11th of June accepted the invitation,
in order to determine not only the details of the new
policy in Poland, but the attitude that was to be assumed
by the German powers towards France.

For by this time the Revolution had forced itself
rudely upon the attention of Europe in general and of
Leopold in particular. The invasion of the palace at
Versailles in October 1789 had shown it to be no
ordinary insurrection. It is true that the abolition of
feudal rights through France had early caused some
outcry among the German princes who still owned
property in Alsace; but this was a matter easily to be
adjusted. It is true also that the Elector of Trèves had

1791. allowed some of the emigrant nobles to form a rallying-point at Coblentz, while others had dispersed themselves broadcast over Europe, preaching vengeance against the Revolution. But the assembly at Coblentz though noisy was insignificant, and the emigrants, though they found much civility at foreign Courts, particularly at Berlin, found little else. The truth was that one and all of the crowned heads of Europe were in financial straits, and had little to give but fair words. King Gustavus of Sweden was indeed eager to take up the cause of the Royal Family of France in an enthusiastically chivalrous but unpractical fashion. But of the remaining powers Spain and Sardinia were ready only with plans for others to execute; Naples promised a few doles; and Frederick William of Prussia, while declaring himself quite ready to march an army into France, was careful to add the stipulation that Lewis the Sixteenth must pay for it. Leopold had formed the worst opinion of the emigrants; and his interest in French affairs was dictated wholly by sentiments of kinship, for policy led him to look to the East rather than the West. The project of the flight of King Lewis to Varennes forced him indeed to consent to the movement of his troops in Belgium [1] towards the French frontier, but the failure of the attempt wrought no change in his sentiments. It was his firm conviction that only the unanimous concert of all Europe could effectively oppose the Revolution; and in a circular of the 6th of July to the Powers he called upon them to come to an understanding to save King Lewis. But Leopold hoped to gain his point by menaces alone, without recourse to arms; and pressing forward his negotiations with Prussia in this spirit, he on the 25th of July concluded with her a preliminary treaty, whereby the two powers, among other matters, agreed to do their best to make the concert

---

[1] The use of the term Belgium as synonymous with the Austrian Netherlands is, of course, an anachronism, but it is so convenient that I shall continue to employ it, as also the expression Belgic Provinces, in that sense.

of Europe effective for the settlement of the troubles 1791. in France.

Shortly afterwards Catherine of Russia, released by Aug. 11. the preliminaries of Galatz from her war with the Turks, re-entered the political arena, and, furious at the ingratitude of Stanislaus, at once turned all her energies towards Poland. With the object of keeping that field to herself, she spared no efforts to entangle Austria in the difficulties of France, warmly supporting the negotiations for concerted intervention, joining Gustavus of Sweden in a treaty with the emigrant princes, and professing endless zeal for the cause of the French monarchy. But Leopold was watching European affairs as closely as Catherine herself. He gave orders forbidding large assemblies or enlistment of French royalists in his dominions ; and, on the eve of his departure for Pilnitz, he uncompromisingly rejected an offer from the Aug. 20. Count of Artois to cede Lorraine to Austria as the price of her armed interference. Having arrived at the place of meeting he found Frederick William in as sensible a frame of mind as himself. The two monarchs decided that there should be no intervention in the internal affairs of France without the concert of all the Powers, and, as the result of their labours, issued the famous Declaration of Pilnitz. Herein they set forth Aug. 27. that such concert was of the highest importance to enable the King of France to establish a monarchical government, which should assure the rights both of Sovereign and people ; that they themselves would act promptly to further that end ; and that meanwhile they would give orders to their troops to be ready. Since England had said positively that she would be no party to any such arrangement, the declaration was really no more than an empty form. No sooner, in fact, did Leopold hear that Lewis the Sixteenth had on the 14th of September accepted the Constitution prepared by the Constituent Assembly, than he informed the Powers that the desired object had been attained, and that the coalition was at an end.[1]

[1] Sybel, i. 258, 259, 279-314.

1791. In truth, it was not from Europe but from France that sprang the aggression which plunged the world into twenty years of war. Before the dissolution of the Constituent Assembly, elections had been held for a new one, wherein, partly by dexterity and partly by intimidation, the fanatical minority of violence had succeeded in gaining decided preponderance of representation. Moreover, by an act of incredible folly the members of the Constituent Assembly had debarred themselves from accepting seats in the new chamber. The result was that it contained not a man of experience, hardly a man of mark or of substance,—little indeed beyond empty heads and as empty purses. In such a hotbed of mediocrity it was natural that eloquence should overshadow less eminent weeds; and accordingly the most active and powerful party was that grouped round the deputies of the Gironde, who possessed the advantages of some personal distinction and much oratorical talent. Their opinions, however, were in many respects as radical as those of the mob of Paris itself. What France needed was patient and sustained labour in the building up of a new social and administrative order. What the Girondists desired was the reduction of the Sovereign to impotence, toward which the first step was the overthrow of the monarchical Constitution of 1791 by continual persecution of the nobles and the clergy, and if necessary by war. This object achieved, they trusted to the magic of sentiment and lofty speeches to accomplish the rest. Of their guiding spirits it must suffice to mention only the name of Brissot, who was in charge of the department of foreign affairs. He was no more than a shallow adventurer, who, having wandered through many lands without finding one which had need of him, was credited with wide knowledge of the world, and, being a journalist, could lay claim to omniscience. His dominant characteristic was extravagant self-conceit.

The Girondists lost no time in pushing forward the work of destruction. It was easy to carry motions

decreeing the banishment of non-juring priests, and 1791.
death to all emigrants who should fail to return before Nov. 7, 8.
the year was ended. It was still easier to speak insulting
words of every Sovereign in Europe; but it was not
so simple a matter to bring about war, for both the
moderate party, now represented by Lafayette, and the
extreme party, represented by Robespierre, were opposed
to it. Events, however, favoured them. The King,
while adjuring the emigrant princes to remain quiet, set
his veto on the wholesale condemnation of several
thousand Frenchmen to death; and the Girondists
seized this opportunity to denounce their Sovereign as
an intriguer with exiled nobles and foreign Powers.
At the same time, Lafayette, finding that his importance
was waning faster than was agreeable to his vanity,
conceived that his best chance of regaining his
ascendency was to obtain command of the army and
the direction of operations in the field. He therefore
threw in his lot with the Girondists, and joined them in
advocating war.

The next step, therefore, for the Girondists was to
pick a quarrel with Austria, and, if possible, to isolate
her from the rest of the European Powers. Emissaries
were accordingly sent to Berlin and to London, to gain,
if possible, both Prussia and England to the side of Nov. 29.
France; and on the 14th of December King Lewis,
pursuant to a vote of the Assembly, with great reluctance informed the Elector of Trèves that he should
treat him as an enemy unless the corps of emigrants in
his dominions were dissolved, and that he was moving
fifty thousand men to the frontier to enforce compliance.
This was a direct threat to violate the territory of the
Empire, and Leopold accordingly answered that he
should order his troops to prevent it; but at the same Dec. 21.
time he removed all ground of complaint by compelling
the emigrants to disperse forthwith. In alarm lest the
moderate party should yet gain the upper hand and
preserve constitutional monarchy, the Girondists resolved
to make war certain by provoking the Emperor still

1791. further.¹ "War," cried Brissot, "is a national benefit: the only calamity to be dreaded is that we should have no war." A vote of credit was carried on the 31st of December; and on the 11th of January 1792, the
1792. Assembly, with loud cries of "liberty or death," decreed that the Emperor should be called upon categorically to renounce his projects of an European congress, and to support France against the Powers on pain of war. A peremptory note of the 25th of January threatened hostilities definitely on the 1st of March unless these demands were conceded; but still Leopold returned a conciliatory though firm reply, emphasising his own desire for peace and exposing the motives of the Girondists in clamouring for war. None the less he grew nervous, and sought by a definite treaty of alliance with Prussia to make sure of her support, first in defence against a possible attack, and, secondly, in hastening the convocation of an European congress which, without attempting to stir up a counter-revolution in France, should curb the aggressive spirit of the
Feb. 7. dominant faction. This treaty he obtained, but at a heavy price. On the one hand, he failed to obtain from Prussia a guarantee of the new system which he had promoted in Poland; and on the other hand, he conceded in principle King Frederick William's fatal claim to indemnity for the cost of any military preparations, whether for the menace or the execution of war against France. Then suddenly, in the flower of his days, Leopold was stricken down by sickness, and in two
March 1. days he was dead.

The removal of his guiding hand was felt the more keenly owing to the precipitation of the crisis both in the East and the West. In Paris a sudden swerve of Lafayette towards the moderate party had given hopes of its triumph, but these, like all hopes founded upon that unstable man, had gone to wreck. The emigrant nobles, by adroit flattery, had persuaded the worthless King of Prussia that the time was come for him to act,

¹ Sybel, i. 338.

and to stir Austria to action in France, while Catherine's 1792.
troops were marching from the Turkish frontier upon
Poland. The new Emperor, Francis, who was but
twenty-four years of age, tried at first to pursue his
father's policy, and again pressed upon Frederick
William the acceptance of the Austrian system in
Poland ; but now the Empress Catherine came forward
with hints of a new partition of that kingdom, wherein
Prussia might have a share. Frederick William had
guaranteed the integrity of Poland in 1790, but the
temptation held out by the Empress was too strong for
him. War between France and Austria was inevitable,
and in that war he was not only bound but eager to take
part. Since therefore the German rulers could offer no
resistance to Russia in the East, it was plainly Prussia's
interest to take as high a price as possible for permitting
that which she had no power to prevent. Easy triumph
over the Jacobins, the re-establishment of King Lewis,
and a large share of Poland ; military glory, extension of
territory, patronage of a brother monarch in distress—
nothing could appeal more strongly to a Hohenzollern.
Principle counted for nothing. Frederick rejected the
overtures of Austria and threw in his lot with Russia.

Events in other quarters likewise conspired to
encourage the Girondists in their bellicose intentions.
King Gustavus of Sweden had lately been assassinated ;
a new Ministry, unfavourable to Austria, had gained
authority in Spain ; Pitt had given further testimony of
his persistent adherence to neutrality ; all of which
things, added to the death of Leopold and the new attitude
of Prussia, seemed to promise the complete isolation of
the Empire. Brissot and Lafayette now thought of little
but the advantages to be gained from the war. It was
nothing to them that civil strife was already raging with
savage ferocity in the south of France, that their foolish
decrees had kindled a furious contest between blacks
and whites in St. Domingo, that financial disorder was
rapidly growing to chaos. They had seized the oppor- Feb. 9.
tunity to sequestrate all the property of the emigrants,

1792. so that for the moment they were in no lack of money; and for the completion of their triumph they needed only to expel the present ministers of King Lewis, and to put men of their own choice in the vacated posts. This
March 23. last they duly accomplished on the 23rd of March, and assigned the portfolio of foreign affairs to Lieutenant-general Dumouriez. That officer was now in the fifty-fourth year of a stormy and chequered life; but, whether for military or diplomatic projects, he retained both in body and brain the restless activity of youth; and he plunged at once into wild schemes for the isolation of Prussia from Austria and for a coming campaign. He was the inventor of the term "natural frontiers," a phrase fraught with infinite mischief to France, whereby he signified, roughly speaking, the Rhine as France's boundary to north and east, and the Alps as her limit on the south, or in other words the annexation of Belgium and Savoy. Belgium, therefore, was the point at which he designed to attack Austria, counting much, as likewise did Brissot, upon a rising of the inhabitants in favour of France. Anxious to take the initiative before the Austrian forces on the frontier could be reinforced, he plied the Court of Vienna with a succession of insolent demands: but, failing even so to provoke her to aggression, he was ultimately obliged to ask the Assembly to declare war upon no particular pretext. At the last moment his heart misgave him, for he was a good soldier and doubted the quality of his troops; but he
April 20. could not draw back; and on the 20th April, to the infinite distress of King Lewis, the Assembly decreed war against Austria. Hardly yet has France ceased to pay the penalty for that act of thoughtless and wanton mischief.

Dumouriez's misgivings were well justified, for the
1791. French army had gone from bad to worse. On the alarm caused by the flight of the King to Varennes, the
July 3-17. Constituent Assembly had directed by successive decrees the embodiment of one hundred thousand volunteers into one hundred and sixty-nine battalions of National

Guards. These men received a higher rate of pay than that enjoyed by the regular army, and elected their own officers; captains and subalterns being chosen by each company, and field-officers by each entire battalion. A few of the new corps selected their officers and non-commissioned officers from the old militia, which had been lately disbanded; and these proved superior to the rest. But the vast majority followed the usual rule in such cases with the usual results. Sixty of the new battalions were formed rapidly, but then the movement flagged. Of the remainder a few were very slowly collected, but a great many never existed except on paper. Nor was this the only failing. The battalions when reviewed were found to contain a large proportion of boys and of undersized men, unfit to bear arms; and in some instances the recruits were no sooner brought together than three-fourths of them desired leave of absence, and did not hesitate to take it, whether granted or not. However, on the despatch of the menacing note to Austria of the 14th of December, the Minister of War announced the formation of an Army of Flanders under General Rochambeau, an Army of the Rhine under General Luckner, and an Army of the Centre, on the Meuse, under Lafayette; the hero of America having obtained his expected reward for his alliance with the Girondists. A circular was then sent round, requiring each department to provide the quota of volunteers assigned to it; and a fortnight later the Assembly decreed that all volunteers should be entitled to their discharge at the close of each campaign, on giving two months' notice to their captains, and that each campaign should be reckoned to have ended on the 1st of December in each year. The collective wisdom even of our own nation has rarely devised so fatuous an arrangement as this.

The Government then turned its thoughts to the regular army, and made the disquieting discovery that, apart from other defects, it was more than fifty thousand men short of its peace-establishment, and that the boasted volunteers, far from increasing the strength of

1792. the armed forces, had simply diverted from the army the ordinary supply of recruits. The obvious remedy was to incorporate the volunteers into the battalions of the Line, which step was recommended alike by the generals Jan. 16. and the Minister of War; but this was by no means to the taste of the Legislative Assembly. To subject willing patriots to regular military discipline, urged the orators, would impair the spirit of liberty and substitute for it a blind submission to the command of their chiefs; it would be far better to turn the Line into National Guards than National Guards into the Line. Here we see plainly the two stools between which the French Republic fell to the ground. Undisciplined men could not keep the foreign enemy at bay; disciplined men could enable their chiefs to seize supreme power. But the fall was not yet. The recommendations of soldiers and sensible men were rudely set aside; and the Assembly decreed boldly that in no case whatever should the Line be recruited from the embodied National Guards. Having thus exalted the volunteers in sight of the whole nation to the abasement of the Jan. 19-24. army, the Assembly sought to raise recruits for the Line by the offer of bounties, an expedient which is always vicious, and in such circumstances was foredoomed to be futile. In fact, the Girondists left no stone unturned to ruin the regular troops. Despite all their heavy trials, from which they had suffered incalculably, the old regiments still remained the only trustworthy force for the maintenance of order; and the fact stands to the eternal honour of the French officer. In every direction distracted municipalities called aloud for their services; but they were retained inactive at centres where the rule of the mob was dominant; and one noble Swiss regiment at Feb. 28. Marseilles at length laid down its arms and prepared to march home to its native canton rather than submit longer to insult.[1] Incessant criticism and constant changing of the Ministers of War also weakened authority at headquarters; and the grant of a free pardon to all deserters

---

[1] Poisson, i. 375 *sq.*

of the past two years, with the liberation of the Swiss mutineers of Nancy, set an additional premium upon insubordination.¹ Discipline and military spirit steadily deteriorated. At Béthune and Lille, for instance, the garrisons sent delegates to the Assembly to protest against the new regulations of 1791 and to denounce the Minister who had formulated a code of discipline, "which breathed slavery and tyranny." The deputies called the delegates to the Chamber, and bitterly attacked both Minister and generals in their presence. Finally, this same Assembly not only allowed the released mutineers of Nancy to be caressed in Paris as martyrs, but admitted them likewise to the honours of the sitting.²

1792.
Feb. 8.

With forces thus raised and trained the Girondists launched France into war. The armies, such as they were, were already massed on the frontier; and on the 29th of April the invasion of Belgium began. Rochambeau pushed forward a vanguard of some three to four thousand men under General Dillon from Lille upon Tournai, and General de Biron, on Dillon's right, marched from Quiévrain for Mons and Brussels, while Lafayette hastened the concentration of thirty thousand men at Givet for an advance on Namur. The results of this forward movement were beyond expression ludicrous. Dillon's men, on their first skirmish with a small party of Austrians, abandoned their guns and baggage and fled in wild disorder to Lille, where they

April 29.

¹ The following list of Ministers of War is instructive :—

1789, Latour du Pin.
16th November 1790, Duportail.
6th December 1791, Narbonne.
10th March 1792, de Grave.
8th May 1792, Servan.
3rd October 1792, Pache.
4th February 1793, Beurnonville.
6th April 1793, Bouchotte.

² The woollen night-cap, misnamed the cap of liberty, became the fashion after the apotheosis of these ruffians, who wore it as part of a convict's garb.

1792. massacred their commander and two more generals. Biron thereupon promptly fell back before a force of one-third of his strength; but an attack of Austrian hussars on his rearguard sufficed to set his troops flying in mad panic to Valenciennes, leaving three guns and a few prisoners behind them. Lafayette, whose army alone outnumbered the entire force of the Austrians in Belgium, therefore remained stationary at Givet; and the operations came to an abrupt end. The Assembly was furious with rage, and on the motion of the Minister of War passed, despite the opposition of Robespierre and the extreme party, stringent decrees for the punishment of offenders and for the prevention of such incidents in future. But the misfortune was not so easily to be remedied. The French levies, raw though they were, felt the shame of their disgrace when they came to themselves; but the few remaining officers of pre-revolutionary days were unable to endure such dishonour to the once proud army of France. Great numbers of them passed the frontier to join the emigrants, rather than be associated with such a rabble; and, in the case of three old German regiments of the French service, they were followed by a part or the whole of their men.

The dominant faction in Paris felt the danger of the situation, which was now enhanced by the commercial depression that inevitably accompanies war. To hearten themselves and the country, they carried a decree for the
May 5. raising of one hundred and seventy thousand additional volunteers; and, visiting the military failure on the
May 8. Minister of War, they replaced him by an old officer, Servan. But what the Girondists dreaded above all was a strong reaction in favour of the King and the Constitution of 1791; and to avert this they resolved to resort, as usual, to an insurrectionary movement. For this purpose they required a corps which would obey themselves only, since they were as jealous of the armed ruffians of Jacobinism as of the regular battalions; and Servan therefore carried through the Assembly a decree for the summoning of twenty thousand armed

men as delegates from every canton in France, to take 1792. part in the annual celebration of the 14th of July. Thereupon Lafayette again came round to the side June 4. of the moderate party; and Dumouriez, having first persuaded the King to dismiss his colleagues, resigned June 13. his office on the 17th June, and went to take command June 17. of the Army of the North. A new Ministry of Lafayette's followers was then formed; but the dismissal of the Girondists gave a welcome opportunity to the extreme Jacobins. A new leader, Jacques Danton, appeared at their head, who so far had played a comparatively obscure part, but none the less, as the moving spirit of the most violent of the political clubs, held the mob of Paris in leash against the day of insurrection. The King's veto on Servan's decree made a pretext, and on the 20th of June Danton, himself unseen, let June 20. slip the populace, which invaded and overran the Tuileries, and would probably have taken the King's life, had he not shown extraordinary coolness and courage. The rising, therefore, was a failure; and the new Minister, Monciel, was for taking strong measures and putting down the Jacobins once for all. His project would probably have succeeded, but for the irresolution of Lafayette and the weakness of the King, who as usual decided to give way, in the vain hope of conciliating the Assembly. Thereupon the Ministry resigned, and on the following day the Girondists per- July 10, 11. suaded the Assembly to declare the country in danger. They then flattered themselves that Lewis would recall them to power, and, piqued by his refusal to do so, resolved to depose him. Their hope was that they could use Servan's bands for their own purposes, and dismiss them from Paris as soon as their objects were attained; but having bound themselves hand and foot to the Jacobins, they were no longer free. As the various contingents reached Paris from the provinces, the best of them were passed on by the Jacobin leaders to a camp which was forming at Soissons, and only those that would serve for an insurrection were

1792. retained. On the 29th of July arrived some five hundred men from Marseilles, who possessed the fire, which was lacking in the mob of Paris, to lead others to an attack. Throughout the first days of August the Jacobins pursued a tumultuous agitation for the deposition of the King; on the 9th the municipality of Paris, by the mandate of the populace, was reconstituted for the avowed purpose of insurrection; and on the
Aug. 10. 10th the scum of Paris, with the men of Marseilles at their head, was poured forth to the storm of the Tuileries. There is no need to tell again the story which has been so pathetically commemorated by the chisel of Thorwaldsen. King Lewis allowed a savage conflict between his Swiss Guards and the mob to begin, but at the critical moment gave the troops the order to cease firing. The Guards, being soldiers, obeyed, and of course fell victims to the fury of the populace, which was under no command and subject to no control. Thus shamefully was the cause of order betrayed; and among the spectators of the conflict was one who witnessed the betrayal with unfeigned disgust, a young subaltern of artillery named Napoleon Bonaparte.

The conquerors hastened to gather the fruits of victory. Before the last dropping shots of the conflict had ceased, Vergniaud, the chief orator of the Girondists, had moved that the King should be suspended from his sovereignty, and that a National Convention should be summoned. At the same time commissioners galloped off to the armies on the frontier to secure the adhesion of the soldiery, telling them that a return to slavery was the only alternative. Lafayette might yet have saved all by marching his army to Paris, but as usual
Aug. 14. he hesitated, and within four days found his command taken from him, and himself obliged to fly into Belgium. There he was captured by the Austrians and for long kept in close confinement at Olmütz, where he need trouble us no more. The allegiance of the troops was thus gained with small difficulty, and meanwhile the Commune of Paris, after a feeble resistance from the

Assembly, established its omnipotence. The Royal Family was imprisoned at the Temple; a committee of vigilance was set up with power to arrest all suspected persons; and finally a revolutionary tribunal was erected to try them. An armed force was obtained by re-modelling the National Guard, with such recruits and such a system as best suited the Jacobin purpose. Pecuniary supplies were secured by the confiscation of the contents of the Royal palaces, of the treasures of the churches and the entire property of the emigrants, the aggregate value of which is reckoned to have exceeded two hundred millions sterling. As the Girondists made some feeble attempts to stem the flood of the Revolutionary tide, the Commune resolved so to manipulate the elections for the coming Convention that the power of the Jacobins should be absolute. Intimidation offered the simplest and shortest means of attaining this object, and accordingly it was arranged that on the first day of the elections there should be a great massacre of political opponents.[1] The pretext, which by chance was happily supported by news from the frontier, was the necessity for ridding the country of internal enemies while menaced by a foreign invasion.

1792.
Aug. 13.
Aug. 17.

Sept. 2.

It will naturally be asked how it was that France, which had opened an unprovoked campaign with signal disaster in April, was left practically undisturbed by foreign reprisals from May till the end of August. On the first declaration of war the Emperor had at once turned to his ally Frederick William of Prussia, and submitted to the Court of Berlin four different principles whereon to conduct the war. The first was to set all selfish projects absolutely aside; the second, to be content with King Lewis's promise to repay the expenses if restored to the throne; the third, to take pledges for such repayment by actual occupation of certain French fortresses; the fourth, that Prussia and Austria should each indemnify themselves by taking an equal extent of territory. The Prussian negotiator at once declared

[1] Sybel, i. 499.

1792. uncompromisingly for the fourth principle, saying that his country would not take part in the war without assurance of proper compensation; nor would all the warnings and deprecations of Austria move him from his decision. King Frederick William, however, still under the sway of the emigrants, declared himself ready to combat the Revolution first and think of indemnity later, and was not to be deterred from his purpose even by the protests of his reigning mistress. But the Prussia of that day was suffering little less than France from the decay of discipline. Frederick the Great had so organised the administration that everything turned on the personal directions of the Sovereign; and Frederick William was too idle, too weak, and too sensitive to the suggestions and impressions of the moment, for so great a position. The consequence was that public affairs were distracted between the intrigues of unstable men and improper women; every department interfered with the work of every other; diplomats meddled with military matters and generals with politics. Every soldier, therefore, took sides upon the question of the Austrian Alliance, and the great majority of the senior officers was bitterly opposed to it. Prominent among these was the Duke of Brunswick, under whom, as Hereditary Prince, the British had so often fought in the Seven Years' War. By reputation he was the first general in Europe; but advancing years and increasing responsibilities had confirmed in him a habit, very fatal to a soldier, of exaggerating the difficulties and questioning the equity of any enterprise entrusted to him. He had a morbid dread of meddling with the French Revolution, which alone sufficed to make him loathe the idea of a French war; but, above all, he detested the emigrant nobles and the Austrians with whom Prussia was to be allied. With a very bad grace, therefore, he furnished a plan of campaign; and with a still worse grace he learned that he was expected to march to Paris with an army of little more than one hundred and ten thousand men,

which, moreover, would not all be ready till the end of 1792.
July. "I am bored to death with all this," he wrote ;
"no good can come of it." However, the troops were
set in motion for the Rhine, and it was agreed that the
Emperor and King Frederick William should meet
at Mainz, in July, to settle the difficult question of
indemnities.

But many things were to happen before that meeting
could take place, for the Eastern centre of disturbance
in Europe was now in full activity. Though, as has
been seen, Frederick William had decided to part company with Austria and to attach himself to Russia upon
the Polish question, he still retained a vague desire to
combine with Austria so as to keep Russia in check ;
and he therefore began his negotiations with Catherine
by submitting to her his defensive alliance of February
1792 with Austria, to which both powers presently
asked her adhesion. Catherine, however, had no intention of permitting harmony between the two leading
potentates of Germany. Her interest lay in sowing
discord between them ; and she knew that, with Prussia
gained to her side and a French war fairly set on foot,
she could afford to laugh at Austria. She therefore
utterly rejected the treaty of February, declaring her
preference for a separate agreement with Prussia, and
meanwhile she ordered her troops to march directly April 8.
upon the southern frontier of Poland. On the 18th
of May thirty-two thousand Russian soldiers passed the
Polish border, and a week later Catherine definitely
proposed to Frederick William a separate alliance for a
war, upon disinterested principles, against the Revolution.
Frederick William, still bent upon a good understanding
with Austria, communicated this proposal to the Emperor
Francis, adding, however, the significant hint that, though
willing to abjure all indemnity from France, he should
look for compensation in Poland. This revelation
opened the eyes of the court of Vienna. So far Francis
had followed the policy of Leopold in seeking to
strengthen Poland against Russian aggression ; but those

1792. who knew him best felt sure that he would revert to more dangerous principles, and they were not disappointed. Francis was a man of despotic instincts, selfish, ignorant, indolent, and disingenuous. To gain as much as possible for himself, and to yield as little as possible to others—these were the false and shifting beacons by which, in a voyage of unexampled difficulty and peril, he attempted to steer the course of an empire.

Instantly, therefore, on hearing of Prussia's intentions concerning Poland, he felt that the acquisition of a Polish province would be as agreeable to himself as to his neighbours; and, accordingly, he agreed with Frederick William that Austria and Prussia in concert should claim a share in the protection of that country. Catherine, who desired nothing less, thereupon distracted the attention of Francis by suggesting to him to exchange the Austrian Netherlands for Bavaria, as a counterpoise to Russia's acquisitions in Poland. This exchange had been a favourite project with the Emperor Joseph, for not only had Belgium always proved in itself a troublesome possession to the House of Austria, but it carried with it the further danger of contiguity with France; whereas Joseph held that the true interest of the Hapsburgs was to consolidate their power and influence in the East. Francis, without hesitation, rushed at the bait; and on the 13th of July he signed a treaty with Catherine, whereby he bound himself to restore in concert with her the old order, or, in other words, anarchy, in Poland, overthrowing the new constitution which Leopold had established and promised to uphold. Meanwhile Catherine continued negotiations with Frederick William, who had fully approved the Bavarian exchange, in the happy expectation of a Polish province for himself. Ultimately the Empress concluded with him also a separate treaty of alliance, wherein, while obtaining valuable concessions for herself, she was careful to omit all mention of Prussia's expected indemnity, which, she said, must await the meeting of the King and Emperor at Mainz. Meanwhile her troops overran

Poland ; and the unhappy Stanislaus, on appealing to   1792.
Austria for help, found that Francis had deserted him.
Yielding, therefore, to the inevitable, he consented to
throw the country back into its previous confusion ; July 24.
and Catherine, secure in the military occupation of her
prize, resolved in secret that she would share it with no
man.[1]

On the 19th of July Francis and Frederick William July 19-21.
met at Mainz, amid a brilliant concourse of the German
princes ; and, while the principals busied themselves with
festivity upon festivity, their Ministers approached the
delicate business of indemnities. Fatal differences at
once made their appearance. The Prussians named
the modern province of Posen, or little short of it, for
their share of Poland. The Austrians retorted that the
exchange of Bavaria for Belgium was no equivalent for
such an extent of territory, and demanded the cession
of Anspach-Baireuth, which had been lately made over
to Prussia by the reigning Prince. Frederick William
rejected the proposal with anger, and therewith the
negotiations ended. Thus the two powers, leaving the
whole question of indemnities unsettled, entered upon
the war with mutual jealousy and suspicion. This alone
would have sufficed to wreck the coalition, but other
causes were not wanting. On the 23rd Frederick July 23.
William dropped down the Rhine to Coblentz, where he
was met by a horde of emigrant nobles loudly vaunting
the monarchic sympathies of the French peasants,
the weakness of the frontier fortresses, and, generally,
the simplicity of a direct march on Paris. This did
not soften the loathing which Brunswick felt for the
emigrants ; and their ridiculous pretensions, their
marked indiscipline, their petty jealousies and, above
all, their rapacity soon brought them into disrepute
in higher quarters. None the less, one of them was
suffered by the King and the Emperor to draw up the
manifesto to the French nation with which Brunswick
heralded his coming, a vain message of threatenings and

[1] Sybel, i. 462-476 ; ii. 143-152, 157-159.

1792. slaughter, which was priceless as a weapon to the Jacobin leaders, and injurious beyond calculation to the cause of monarchy.

But far more serious was the fact that so far the Austrians had brought to the scene of action but seventy-one thousand men instead of one hundred and six thousand, as they had promised, and that in consequence the army of invasion would fall very far short of the numbers originally assigned for the campaign. Brunswick's hatred towards the war increased, and he made up his mind to advance as slowly as possible. Twenty days were consumed in reaching the French frontier from Coblentz, while the Austrian generals, in thorough sympathy with him, crept as slowly to the rendezvous. Then, however, came the news of the insurrection of the 10th of August, which kindled in Frederick William a burning haste to reach Paris; and the movements became more rapid. Thus on the 20th the army arrived before Longwy, which capitulated
Aug. 23. after a short bombardment on the 23rd; and the first barrier on the road of the invaders was broken down.

On the news of the fall of Longwy the leaders in Paris woke to a sense of their danger, for so far, as we have seen, the factions had been intent on crushing their political opponents rather than the foreign enemy. It will be remembered that on the 5th of May a very large additional levy of volunteers had been decreed; but the ardour for this service had greatly cooled, and the attempt to form these new levies had been anything but successful. In fact, in the middle of June the War Department in Paris had only a very vague idea of the number of volunteers at its disposal, while it knew for certain that the regular troops were still twenty-seven thousand men short of their establishment. It was partly to meet this difficulty that, under a proclamation
July 11. of "fatherland in danger," all able-bodied citizens were called out for service, with orders to select from among themselves recruits sufficient to raise the armed force to four hundred and fifty thousand men. Of these, fifty

1792. intimidation the Party of Terror assured to itself an overwhelming majority in the elections at Paris, and the Commune arrogated to itself the government of France.

Aug. 31. Meanwhile Servan had ordered Dumouriez to station his army on the rugged heights of the Argonne, a strong but by no means impregnable position, as the best chance of checking the invasion of the Allies. But there was
Sept. 1. in reality little to be feared. On the very next day Brunswick, then arrived before Verdun, declared his intention not to pass the Meuse. Even the immediate
Sept. 2. and unexpected surrender of Verdun availed nothing to change his resolution; for, though King Frederick William insisted upon prosecuting the advance, Brunswick by calculated inactivity was still determined to have his own way. There is no need to enter into details of the campaign, which was remarkable chiefly for the glaring blunders committed by both sides; for the beginning and end of the story is that the Prussian army was paralysed by the discord between its General and its
Sept. 20. King. The climax came at the action of Valmy, when, after a trifling cannonade which cost neither side above two hundred men, the Prussian troops returned to camp, complaining bitterly that they were not allowed to fight, while the French boasted loudly that they had beaten the veterans of Frederick the Great.

As a matter of fact, Dumouriez, though he carried a bold face before his army, felt his situation to be so
Sept. 21. perilous that on the day following Valmy he opened negotiations with the Prussians, in the hope of gaining time. Brunswick joyfully welcomed these overtures; while Frederick William himself, growing nervous over Catherine's ominous silence as to Poland, began to wish that the war were over. Dumouriez saw his opportunity and pressed it; Danton, who had the charge of foreign affairs at Paris, perceived with unerring good sense the advantage of detaching Prussia from Austria, and despatched emissaries to pursue the negotiations. Thus a week was gained, and that week was decisive. In the expectation of a rapid march to Paris, no sufficient pro-

thousand was designed to complete the regiments of the 1792. Line, and the remainder to be incorporated into a multitude of volunteer-battalions, either already existing or shortly to be created. At the same time, the age for service was lowered to sixteen, all veterans were invited to rejoin the ranks, and bounties and pensions were offered to deserters from foreign armies. Practically this decree, by resorting to compulsion, admitted the failure of the voluntary system; but the omission to insist upon personal service completely destroyed the value of the levies. Regular enrolment of recruits gave way to a wide traffic in substitutes; and there resulted the inevitable army of naughty boys, decrepit old men, cripples, criminals and ragamuffins, a scourge to their country and a terror to their officers.[1] Nor was it only the men that failed; money, arms, ammunition, equipment, all alike were lacking, for the whole of the administrative service had been overset. Want of pay, food and clothing, together with uncertainty of command, will demoralise the best of troops under the best of officers; much more was it bound to break up the raw armies on the northern frontier of France. The deserters from these corps during July and August were counted by thousands, and to fill their places with the new recruits was to pour water into a sieve. Against this doubtful gain there followed, after the 10th of August, the passing of the whole of the Swiss troops, ten noble regiments, from the armies of France.

Moreover, though the Minister of War, Servan, might take alarm at the advance of the enemy, the Commune of Paris subordinated all military movements and forces to its own operations in the capital. On the 1st of September came the news that Brunswick had arrived before Verdun; and on the morrow some twelve Sept. 2. hundred select ruffians of Paris, well provided with arms and with liquor, were let loose for five days to the massacre of several hundreds of harmless men and women in the prisons of the city. By this measure of

[1] Rousset, pp. 73, 78.

CH. II   HISTORY OF THE ARMY   49

vision had been made by the Prussians for transport and 1792.
supply ; and a halt in an exhausted country signified to
it nothing less than starvation. Continual torrents of
rain aggravated the distress of famine, and dysentery
raged among the invaders with fearful violence. Meanwhile large reinforcements reached Dumouriez ; and
when Frederick William, on the 28th, suddenly wished Sept. 28.
to resume the advance, he found that the condition of
his army forbade it, and that far from advancing he
must retire. The negotiations, begun by chance, were
therefore continued of necessity ; and on the 30th the Sept. 30.
retreat began.

So long as their army was entangled in the defiles of
the Argonne, the Prussians seemed to favour a separate
peace ; but, no sooner was it safe in the plain, than they
refused to discuss even a suspension of arms wherein
Austria was not included. But already the Austrians
had formed the most dangerous suspicions of their
Allies, and on the 8th of October they withdrew from Oct. 8.
among them, resolving thenceforth to act with the
Prussians no more. Weakened by their defection,
Brunswick evacuated Longwy and Verdun ; and by the
22nd of October his army, frightfully reduced by Oct. 22.
sickness and railing furiously against the Austrians, had
repassed the frontiers of France.

CHAPTER III

1792. THE date of the first check of the Allies at Valmy may be said to mark definitely the launching of the revolu-
Sept. 21. tionary crusade upon Europe. On the day that followed it the Convention met, and, though the Jacobins had not the majority which they expected over the Girondists, yet both parties were agreed upon the main principle of their policy, namely, the overthrow of all kings and the affiliation to France of the republics that were to supplant them—in brief, the conquest and emancipation of the world. Dumouriez's agents had transmitted from all parts of Italy most encouraging reports of the spread of revolutionary ideas in that quarter; and events appeared fully to justify them. In fulfilment, therefore, of Dumouriez's aspirations after a natural frontier, General Montesquiou invaded Savoy on the night of the 21st of September with nineteen thousand men, and within a week was in possession of the country, practically unresisted. At the same time General Anselme entered the county of Nice with ten thousand men, and was received with warm welcome by the inhabitants. Lastly, General Custine, who had been appointed to command the army of the Rhine, had marked the growth of revolutionary sentiments among the people of the Ecclesiastical States, and obtained permission to enter them with eighteen thousand men. A noble by birth, Custine had embraced the revolutionary cause with the exaggerated ardour of a renegade, and with the thirst after new sensations of the jaded man of pleasure. "War to the tyrant's palace; peace to the poor man's

cottage," was the motto under which he advanced; and 1792. so rotten was the administration of the Bishoprics that the whole edifice crumbled down ignobly before his handful of men. Starting on the 28th of September, he in a few days mastered Speyer and Worms without difficulty; and the capture of these trifling towns sufficed to scare all the authorities from Kehl to Cologne into disgraceful panic and the most abject offers of surrender. On the 20th of October he entered Mainz, and for a moment Brunswick's army was alarmed lest he should throw himself across its line of retreat at Coblentz; but Custine, pursuant to the general scheme of widening the breach between the allied powers, spared the Prussians, and occupied only the imperial town of Frankfurt. From thence he spread his detachments north and south to carry the new gospel with them from the Lahn to the Neckar.

These successes, together with the humiliating retreat of the Allies, conspired to raise the hopes of the fanatics at Paris to an extravagant height. War promised not only to fulfil the wild dreams of idealists, but to relieve the increasing misery and destitution brought about by anarchy and financial disorder. France, in a word, having wasted her own substance, was to live by the plunder of her neighbours. In the hope, therefore, of obtaining the wealth of the South American mines, it was resolved to attack Spain, though that power was willing not only to withdraw her own army from the frontier, but to indemnify France for the expense of bringing her troops to confront them. Preparations were also made to assail in succession Sardinia and Naples, and finally to stir up the Turks against Austria and Russia.[1] Dumouriez again was anxious to make another attempt upon the Austrian Netherlands; but, at the same time, in order to promote the alienation of Prussia from Austria, he wished to evacuate Frankfurt, and to recall the army of the Rhine to the left bank of the river, lest the Prussians cantoned about Coblentz should resume

[1] Sybel, ii. 23.

1792. the offensive. Custine, however, who was full of wild projects for the total overthrow of the Empire, opposed him vehemently, and carried his point for the more ambitious policy. Dumouriez was therefore bidden to be content with the invasion of the Netherlands only, and in every way his operations were subordinated to Custine's.

To put such a slight upon a successful general was not the wisest way of opening a campaign, but it was of a piece with the entire military policy of the Republic. Wasteful and inefficient as had been the measures for the creation of an armed force from the beginning of the Revolution, they were innocent compared to those which followed the 10th of August. Several citizens having offered to levy troops, it was decided that every man might raise a corps who would, receiving about thirty pounds sterling for every horseman mounted and armed, and about six pounds for every foot soldier.[1] Needless to say, companies, squadrons, and battalions sprang into life, upon paper, with incredible rapidity; indeed, it was impossible to conceive a measure better calculated to corrupt a whole nation. Vast numbers of these corps never consisted of more than a few officers; those that did in fact possess men drew them from the volunteers; while the volunteer regiments in their turn tempted thousands of men to desert to them from the Line, in hope of promotion. To complete the mischief,

Oct. 3. the Convention elected a Jacobin Minister of War in the person of one Pache, an obscure clerk, who presided over this chaos of fraud with the benignant complacency of swindler-in-chief. As to discipline, it is sufficient to say that Dumouriez, who had by tact and firmness brought some order into his new battalions, was actually taken to task for oppression by so contemptible a creature as Marat.

However, after vexatious delays caused by the incompetence of Pache, Dumouriez, on the 28th of October, invaded Belgium; and from this point the

[1] Poisson, i. 494.

reader must be warned to follow military events in the 1792.
Low Countries with attention. Proclaiming that the
French were come only to liberate the inhabitants, and
that they would pay honestly for all supplies, he made
his advance in three columns; the left column of eighteen
thousand men moving from Lille upon Antwerp, the
right of sixteen thousand from Givet upon Namur, the
centre of forty thousand, under himself, from Quiévrain
upon Mons. On the 5th of November Dumouriez Nov. 5.
found the Austrians, about twenty thousand strong,
under General Clerfaye, drawn up on the heights of
Jemappe before Mons; and on the 6th he attacked Nov. 6.
them with a success that decided the issue of the campaign. Clerfaye was able to make good his retreat, but
town after town threw open its gates to the French; and
within a fortnight the invaders were practically masters
of the country. On the 16th of November the Conven- Nov. 16.
tion proclaimed the navigation of the Scheldt to be free,
in defiance of all previous treaties, and sent a flotilla up
to Antwerp; and Dumouriez eagerly sought permission
to proceed to the invasion and emancipation of Holland.
But at this point the Convention paused, for it knew
that the violation of Dutch territory could hardly fail to
embroil France with England.

The attitude of the British Government towards the
Revolution so far had been that of strict and even
benevolent neutrality. Pitt was essentially a minister
of peace. He had taken office at the close of a disastrous
and exhausting war; he had already restored credit and
stimulated trade by sagacious financial administration
and by other measures, of which a commercial treaty
with France was not the least conspicuous; and he
desired only the leisure to match his powers of statesmanship against still higher problems of social and
administrative reform. Burke, as is well known, had
taken alarm from the very first at the course pursued
by the Revolution, and not the less because sundry clubs
had sprung up in England, which not only openly
favoured the propagation of French principles, but

1792. carried on a correspondence with the Jacobin Club in Paris. Few prominent men, however, were to be found in the clubs that were actually affiliated to the Jacobins, though there were some of high station and influence, such as Lord Lansdowne, who held and expressed decidedly advanced opinions. As mischievous an utterance as any that was current in England was a speech of Fox in the House of Commons on the 5th of February 1790, wherein he took occasion to applaud the mutiny of the troops in France. In spite, however, of a disgraceful riot at Birmingham on the first anniversary of the fall of the Bastille, Ministers seem to have apprehended little danger from these societies until May 1792, when the notable increase of seditious publications at length called forth a proclamation warning all good citizens against their teaching. These occurrences, however, left Pitt unshaken in his determination to eschew all interference with the internal affairs of France; and Grenville, his foreign secretary, after the failure of Brunswick's invasion, indulged in pardonable self-gratulation that England had not been entangled in so discreditable an enterprise. The British Ambassador was indeed withdrawn from Paris after the 10th of August, for his own safety; but Pitt was still resolute and sanguine in the hope of keeping England out of the struggle. France also was at the outset not without inclination toward a good understanding with England, though the name of Pitt became early a bugbear to the Revolutionists; and, for some time before the two nations went to war, everything that might discredit the Revolution, whether in the way of reaction or of excess, was ascribed to the gold of Pitt. Nevertheless, when the Girondists made up their mind to war with Austria, they sent Talleyrand to London to propose a treaty, whereby England and France should mutually guarantee to each other their possessions within and without Europe, charging him at the same time to endeavour to raise a loan by offering as security the island of Tobago.[1] His instructions,

[1] *Dropmore Papers*, ii. 259, 260.

however, bade him negotiate with the Opposition, with 1792. the object of ousting Pitt if he should reject these overtures; and the envoy's frequent conferences with Fox and Sheridan ensured him a cool reception from the Prime Minister and Grenville. Talleyrand therefore gained nothing except genuine and reiterated assurances of England's wish for peace; and at the end of April he was replaced by Monsieur de Chauvelin, who had so far acted as his colleague.

Chauvelin at first displayed sanity of judgment and moderation of conduct; but after the 10th of August the ruling powers in Paris conceived distrust of England's peaceful professions, and despatched a number of agents to propagate revolutionary opinions in the kingdom. After the fall of the French monarchy, the republican societies in England had become noisier and bolder; and, after the retreat of Brunswick, circumstances conspired to turn Chauvelin gradually into the centre of a republican faction in Britain. His head at the best of times was none of the coolest; and the triumph of the Revolution drove him, even as other French nobles who had deserted their own order, to extravagant presumption and self-importance. Unaware that Grenville had long taken the measure of his ignorance and absurdity, he became more and more insolent in his tone, only to be answered with the coldest and haughtiest contempt. In fact, the apparent indifference of Ministers to the growth of disaffection and sedition in the kingdom alarmed many of their supporters; yet they were waiting only for the right moment to move with effect. It seems certain that Lebrun, the French Foreign Minister, counted upon a general rising in the British Isles in November, and looked forward to a grand alliance of the republics of France, Great Britain, and Ireland; and it is beyond question that some kind of a plot had actually been contrived for seizing the Tower of London and arming the populace. But still the Ministers reserved their force. "If the country is to be saved," wrote Grenville on the 14th of November, "the work

1792. must not be left to the hands of the Government, but every man must put his shoulder to it, according to his rank and situation in life, or it will not be done." "The conquest of Flanders," he added, " has, I believe, brought the business to a much nearer issue than any reasonable man could have believed a month ago."[1]

The movements of the French in Flanders could not indeed be overlooked, for England in 1788 and 1790 had guaranteed to Austria the possession of Belgium, and to Holland the exclusive navigation of the Scheldt and the maintenance of the House of Orange. On the 13th of November the Dutch Ambassador appealed to the British Court for protection for Holland in case of need. Pitt, as in duty bound, pledged himself to give it; but he still looked to a general peace as the surest means of attaining this object, and offered his mediation

Nov. 16. to Austria and Prussia for the purpose. As shall presently be seen, these two powers were absorbed by very different matters; but meanwhile there came a startling indication of the real intentions of France. On the 19th of November officials from an obscure German Duchy implored the Convention's assistance against the tyrants that oppressed them; whereupon the Convention solemnly decreed that France would grant succour and fraternity to all nations that desired liberty, and that orders would be given to her generals accordingly. The decree was then translated into several languages and scattered broadcast upon Europe, evoking sympathetic replies from various quarters, and notably from certain of the Societies in London. At length, at the end of November, Pitt saw that the time was come to move. Throughout his administration he had allowed the discipline and efficiency of the armed forces to go to naught; and he now discovered unpleasant symptoms of disaffection both in the army and the Militia. Two officers, Lord Sempill of the Third Guards and Lord Edward Fitzgerald of the Fifty-fourth, openly used

---

[1] *Dropmore Papers*, ii. 281. Marsh, *Politics of Great Britain and France. Courts and Cabinets of George III.*, pp. 226-228.

treasonable language and subscribed money to the French 1792. cause; and there was reason to fear that their example had been followed. Moreover, the offensive tone adopted by the French on the question of the Scheldt left no room for doubt that they meant to drive the British to extremities. Sempill, Fitzgerald and another officer were dismissed the service; and on the 1st of Dec. 1. December two-thirds of the Militia were called out for purposes of internal police, while Parliament was summoned to meet within a fortnight. The country welcomed these measures with a readiness which showed that it awaited only a signal to show its antipathy to the Revolution; and the French, realising that their projects for kindling insurrection had failed, directed Dumouriez to abstain from the invasion of Holland.[1]

This was the first rebuff encountered by the Revolution in its efforts to carry its gospel into other lands, and it was quickly followed by others. Anxious to secure a separate peace with Prussia, the French Government offered to conclude an offensive alliance with that power, holding out promises to remodel the map of Eastern Europe for her advantage, and even to guarantee the integrity of Holland—the very country which she had marked out for plunder. These overtures failed; the Prussians appeared before Frankfurt, Dec. 2. and within a fortnight compelled Custine to abandon the east bank of the Rhine. This was the first of a series of repulses. A foolish expedition despatched against Trèves in the middle of December was driven back with considerable loss; and the excesses of Anselme's troops had already made the French odious in Nice. In Belgium, matters were still worse. Dumouriez on his invasion had honestly resolved to keep faith with the people; but Pache, who was in alliance with the violent spirits in Paris, was as firmly determined to destroy the general's authority in the army and to sweep the wealth of the country into

[1] Sybel, ii. 52, 99. *Dropmore Papers*, ii. 334, 339, 340, 342, 344, 345, 349.

1792. Paris. He therefore undid the whole of Dumouriez's conciliatory work, ignored his promises, cancelled his contracts, and employed creatures favoured by himself to supply the army's wants. In the hands of these scoundrels the troops, abandoned to nakedness and starvation, were driven first to rapine and then to desertion by hundreds and even by thousands. The term of the first batch of volunteers was just expiring, and they marched away in whole companies. Moreover, since Dumouriez declined to despoil the country, Pache sent emissaries of his own to pillage and steal, a business which they thoroughly understood. Discontent grew apace among all classes in Belgium, and the more rapidly since the agents of the French Government sought to overawe the people into voting the incorporation of their country with France. Finally the Convention, impatient for the funds which it so urgently needed, decreed that, wherever the French troops might go, Commissioners should accompany them to reorganise the government, or in other words to confiscate the property of the well-to-do, and to force worthless French paper-money upon the poor. It was now plain that until the financial deficit on the books of the Revolution could be wiped out, there was no hope of rest for Europe.

Even so, however, Pitt did not abandon his efforts for peace. Though overtures made to the Opposition for concerted action had failed, he had triumphed in Parliament over Fox, who by a very foolish and mischievous speech had succeeded in reducing his followers to an insignificant minority. At the same time, in the country at large the change of feeling for the better had been so rapid as to seem to Ministers almost miraculous. Moreover, to their credit, neither Fox nor Sheridan opposed the moderate increase of seamen which Pitt asked for the Navy, nor a very small augmentation which he desired for the Army. But though thus strong at home, he could find little support abroad. Spain, having lately passed under the sway of the Queen's favourite, Godoy, rejected his overtures 1792. for an alliance; while Austria, when approached, talked about the exchange of Belgium for Bavaria, and the partition of Poland.[1]

The Emperor had in fact been haggling with Prussia all through November and December as to the price of her alliance for another campaign against France, and had reluctantly consented to an agreement that Prussia should take a Polish province, while Austria, after first reconquering Belgium from France, should content herself with exchanging it for Bavaria. The reconquest seemed fairly certain, since the States of Brabant had offered the Emperor a subsidy and forty thousand men if he would deliver them from the yoke of the Jacobins; but, in case it should fail, the Emperor hinted in the course of negotiations that he would look for compensation in Poland, or indemnify himself at the expense of France. Neither the Emperor nor the King seem to have considered the fatal consequences which were bound to follow upon such a policy as this last, though Leopold in his lifetime had repeatedly pointed them out; but when great potentates bring to high political transactions the morals and sagacity of the lowest class of horse-dealer, such results must be expected. Catherine, meanwhile, was in military occupation of the whole of Poland, and had no intention of giving an inch of it either to Austria or Prussia, if she could help it; but events forced her hand. The ripening of an insurrection in Poland and of conspiracies in Russia itself, with the fear that England might support Austria in opposing her designs, decided her to gain the friendship of Prussia without delay, by offering that country a share of the spoil. Frederick William, who had with reason grown very anxious over Catherine's proceedings, grasped eagerly at the prize. On the 6th of January 1793 he published a manifesto that the machinations of the Jacobins compelled him to occupy

[1] *Dropmore Papers,* ii. 345, 359.

1792. the Polish provinces adjoining his own territory, and on the 14th of January 1793 Prussian troops marched into those provinces in force.[1]

The event came as a shock to Europe. Pitt, foreseeing from it fatal results, protested vigorously, and even offered to waive his objections to the Bavarian exchange if Austria would make peace with France and join England in preserving the integrity of Poland. This bold stroke staggered even Catherine for a moment, but she was saved by the course taken by the Revolutionary Government. Some of the Girondists, who dreaded war with England and were now frightened at the speed at which France was hurrying into chaos, had returned to pacific views and seemed likely to head a reaction. During the last days of December and the first days of January, Girondists and Jacobins turned the impeachment of King Lewis into a trial of strength, and the issue was for some time doubtful. Finally, however, on the 15th of January 1793, the Jacobins carried the day for his condemnation and execution; and this triumph of the party of violence destroyed the last hope of peace between France and England, and therewith the last hope of averting the partition of Poland. Secure in the certainty that England's interference was no longer a thing to be apprehended, Catherine pursued her design;

1793. and on the 22nd of January 1793 she signed a treaty with King Frederick William, whereby she ensured to Prussia the Polish provinces occupied by her troops, but bound Prussia also not to make a separate peace with France until the Revolution should be annihilated. The Empress further stipulated that the whole transaction should be carefully concealed from the Austrians until it should be actually accomplished.

At about the same time the final crisis in England was brought about, as Catherine had foreseen, by events in Paris. Since Christmas 1792 Grenville had interchanged a succession of notes with Chauvelin, Maret, and other French officials, who, while often varying their

[1] Sybel, i. 560-565; ii. 160-165.

tone, failed always to meet Grenville's main points, namely, that England could not allow Belgium to be incorporated with France, nor tolerate an invasion of Holland. At last came the news of the execution of King Lewis on the 21st of January. England was thrilled with horror; and Pitt seized the moment to order Chauvelin to withdraw from the kingdom. His arrival in Paris brought matters to a head, and on the 7th of February Pitt received the expected news that on the 1st the Convention had declared war against England and Holland.

1793.

Feb. 7.

Probably there never was a moment in the whole history of France when her military impotence was so abject as on this declaration of war. The world's annals of military maladministration are rich and varied, but it is doubtful whether they afford any parallel to the unspeakable wickedness which characterised the three months of Pache's reign at the French War Office. It is sufficient to say that by the end of 1792 the French forces on the frontier had lost sixty thousand men by desertion alone, without counting those who had perished of cold, starvation, and sickness. The nominal establishment of the forces was eight hundred thousand men; and officers and staff for that number were actually on the pay-list. Official accounts further proclaimed that France had ten armies on foot; but, of these, two had never existed except in name, while the remaining eight did not comprise above one hundred and fifty thousand effective men, including regulars and volunteers; and they were not only lacking in arms and ammunition, but absolutely destitute in respect of pay, clothing, and equipment. It is hardly necessary to add that the troops, having been forced to live by brigandage during great part of the winter, had lost such discipline as their officers had contrived to instil into them; while the soldiers of the Line, who still wore the white coats of the Monarchy, were by no means friendly to the volunteers. The situation was so alarming that it was found

1793. necessary to displace Pache, though not with dishonour, and to make Beurnonville, an accomplished soldier, Feb. 4. Minister in his stead. Further, on receiving the report as to the lack of recruits, the Convention passed a series of decrees for a levy of six hundred thousand men; each commune being called upon to furnish its contingent, and, if the number of voluntary recruits were insufficient, to make up the number as it thought Feb. 14-21. best. Lastly, it was ordained that the Line and the volunteers should both alike enjoy the higher rate of pay and the privilege of electing officers, and should both wear the blue national uniform; a change which placed them upon an equal footing in every respect, except that the regulars were enlisted till the end of the war, and the volunteers for one year only.[1]

Further reforms were deferred till the close of the campaign; and it is easy to see that those above given could have little effect beyond putting an end to the volunteers by destroying their privileges. The levy itself necessarily required several weeks to collect, and, since personal service was not enforced, was not likely to be of any great value. Further, the execution of the King had alienated most of the older officers who remained, and among them Dumouriez himself. That General indeed had many causes of complaint against the ruling faction. His plan of campaign had been subordinated to Custine's; his cherished design of invading Holland had been checked; the operations of the entire army had been suspended; the whole of his honest and politic work in Belgium had been undone; the people had been driven into hostility by oppression, and the discipline of the army destroyed by starvation and want. On the 27th of January he secretly sent an agent to open negotiations with Lord Auckland at the Hague, and to arrange a conference with him; but, before the two could meet, war was declared, and Dumouriez was ordered to invade Holland forthwith. The Convention, thirsting for the wealth of the Bank

[1] Poisson, ii. 136, 163 *sq.* Rousset, pp. 161 *sq.*

of Amsterdam, was anxious to make sure of it before 1793. the Allies could put their strength into the field. Two months earlier, when his troops were heartened by the victory of Jemappe, no order could have been more welcome to Dumouriez than this; and even now, though he had few men upon whom he could depend, he resolved if possible to make good the defects of his army by swift and sudden action. The French troops on the northern frontier were very widely scattered, their cantonments extending north and south on the lower Meuse from Roermond to Maastricht, and east and west from the upper Rhine through Aachen to Liège and Namur. His original plan had been to turn all the waterways and fortresses that bar the entrance into Holland from the south, and to invade it by way of Nimeguen; but time was so precious that he resolved to collect a small force of but seventeen thousand men at Antwerp, and to march from thence with all secrecy direct upon Amsterdam. At the same time he directed thirty thousand men from the east under General Miranda to take the Dutch fortresses of Maastricht and Venloo, and then to make for Nimeguen. Speed, in his view, was everything, for the Austrians had already forty thousand men cantoned to the east of the Rhine, and were shortly to be reinforced.

Meanwhile the Allies were still making up their plans for the next campaign. Brunswick and Prince Frederick Josias of Coburg-Saalfeld, who had been appointed Commander-in-Chief of the Austrian army, met at Frankfurt, and, after many conferences between the 6th and the 14th of February, decided upon a scheme of operations, which by their own showing required forty thousand more men than they had any expectation of collecting. They saved themselves, however, by laying it down as a cardinal principle that, until Mainz was recovered from the French, the Allied forces must not attempt to pass from the east to the west bank of the Meuse. Belgium (so argued the Austrians) had been eaten up, and so long as the

1793. navigation of the Rhine was blocked at Mainz, the subsistence of the Imperial troops on the west of the Meuse must be difficult. Moreover, if the French should retire before an Austrian advance, and mass all their forces on the Rhine, then they might beat Brunswick, who, unless his retreat were assured by the possession of Mainz, would be in danger of utter destruction. The reader should take note of this decision, for not only is it the key to much that appears puzzling in the coming campaign, but it is an excellent example of the principle on which Coburg and Brunswick conducted war, namely, to look at risks first and at objects afterwards. The immediate problem of the defence of the Dutch provinces was left without so much as an attempt at solution. Both Grenville in England and Auckland at the Hague had long foreseen the certainty of a French attack upon them, and had strained every nerve to stir the authorities to action. But the Stadtholder was a man of almost inhuman dulness, apathy and stupidity; and all popular energy was paralysed by the spirit of faction, which, never inactive in Holland, had under the influence of French agents become almost a spirit of revolution. The Dutch army was so defective in training, equipment and discipline that it had ceased to exist as an efficient force; and its few foreign corps, which alone deserved the name of regiments, had been driven to mutiny by a reduction of their pay below the rate fixed by their contract. Even in January and February, Auckland wrote that the Stadtholder looked for British ships and British troops to save him,[1] and that the French party was derisively insinuating that England, nominally the faithful ally of the Dutch Republic, was content to desert her in the hour of danger. Finally, on the 15th of February he begged that the

---

[1] *Dropmore Papers*, Auckland to Grenville, 21st and 25th January; 14th and 15th February. *F.O. Holland*, 16th February 1793. And see *Auckland Correspondence* and *Dropmore Papers* generally, November 1792 to February 1793.

Duke of York might be sent over with a few officers of 1793. experience, even if without troops, to take command of the Dutch. " Men, commanders, ships and money," he wrote, " we could not ask for more if this country were a part of Yorkshire, but I incline to think that it should be considered so for the present; and if it is brought to a question whether we are to conquer it and keep it, or whether Dumouriez is to do it, I have no doubt as to the decision."

Still the British Government hesitated, for, thanks to its neglect of the Army, it possessed but a handful of troops, and was unwilling to move them to the Continent. Then suddenly, on the 16th of February, Feb. 16. Dumouriez dashed out from Antwerp with his tiny force in four columns. One small body instantly pushed northward towards Moerdyk, to collect boats for the passage of the arm of the sea called the Hollandsdiep; another marched upon Klundert and Willemstadt, a third north-eastward to attack Breda, and a fourth to the north-west to blockade Bergen-op-Zoom and Steenbergen. Everywhere his coming was welcomed by the Dutch. Breda, with large stores of munitions of war, was disgracefully surrendered on the 26th of Feb. 26. February; Klundert and Gertruydenberg fell in quick succession; Willemstadt was then besieged with the captured cannon, and by the 9th of March Dumouriez March 9. was prepared to essay the passage of the Hollandsdiep. But here his course was stayed, for his activity had stirred his enemies on every side.

On the 20th of February the seven battalions of Feb. 20. British Guards were suddenly paraded before the Horse Guards; and the Duke of York, announcing that the first battalions of the three regiments were ordered to proceed on active service, called for volunteers from the others to bring them up to strength. The whole brigade thereupon stepped forward as one man; and five days later the three battalions, numbering under two thousand men of all ranks and denominations, marched to Greenwich amid the cheers, and something

1793. more than the cheers, of an enormous and enthusiastic crowd.¹ By nightfall the whole were embarked upon vessels too small to carry more than two-thirds of their number in safety, without medicines or medical appliances, without the slightest reserve of ammunition, and of course without transport of any description. Their commander was Colonel Gerard Lake of the First Guards, and his orders were on no account to move his men above twenty-four hours' distance from Helvoetsluis, so as to be able to return on the shortest
March 1. notice. By the mercy of Heaven these troops safely reached that port, narrowly escaping a gale which would probably have condemned them either to drowning or asphyxiation; and four days later they proceeded to
March 5. Dort to oppose Dumouriez's passage of the Hollandsdiep. About the same time a flotilla of Dutch gunboats arrived in the Meuse, many of them manned by British sailors and flying British colours. Auckland, by threatening to take command in Holland himself, had at last compelled the miserable Stadtholder to issue orders for the defence of his country.²

But the obstacles which were multiplying in Dumouriez's front were as nothing to the storm that
Feb. 20. suddenly broke upon his flank. Miranda had duly moved up to the siege of Maastricht with a force inadequate to the task and, moreover, dangerously dispersed; but the Austrians, declaring themselves too weak to move, still remained torpid in their cantonments, perhaps the more stubbornly because the Prussian Agent at the Austrian headquarters was perpetually urging them to action. At last, however, Coburg
Feb. 26. on the 26th began to concentrate his forty thousand men and to pass them in five columns across the river;

¹ The head of the column was able to keep sober; the rear, under the endearments of the populace, subsided dead drunk on the road and was brought on in carts. *Narrative of an Officer of the Guards.*

² Lake to Dundas, 2nd March 1793. Lake's Instructions, 23rd February. Grenville to Auckland, 20th February 1793. *F.O. Holland*, Auckland to Grenville, 4th March 1793.

and on the 1st of March, to the great surprise of the French, he burst upon their cantonments on the Meuse, and for four days drove them in utter rout before him. Coburg himself and the left wing halted before Liège, but on the right the Archduke Charles, with the impetuosity of twenty-one years and the instinct of a born soldier, followed up the disorderly rabble from Maastricht southward upon Tongres, boldly attacking wherever he met the enemy. Such of the French as had been in action fled in all directions, abandoning everything; ten thousand deserters hurried across the frontier into France; and a small remnant took refuge behind the canal at Louvain, where it was joined by such French divisions as had not been engaged. Had Coburg pursued his advantage and advanced instantly with all his forces, he could have ended the campaign at once, for the people, furious at the exactions of the Jacobins, and, above all, at the theft of the plate from their churches, had turned savagely upon the retreating French. Instead of this he halted on the 5th, and wasted ten whole days in cantonments between Maastricht and Tongres. The Convention now ordered Dumouriez at once to proceed to Louvain and assume command, which he did with a very bad grace, leaving General Flers to take his place in Holland. His presence did much to restore confidence in the French army, and he was not a little helped by Coburg's inaction. Nevertheless the news that reached him was singularly disquieting. Fresh regiments were embarking from England for Helvoetsluis; two reinforcing columns of Austrians were advancing from the Rhine upon Namur; and eight thousand Prussians, under the Duke of Brunswick-Oels, had arrived at Bois-le-Duc on the 11th, and were moving with five thousand British and Dutch upon Breda, to cut off the troops on the Hollandsdiep from France and Dumouriez's own soldiers from Antwerp. In so desperate a situation there was no choice but to take the offensive.

On the 15th Coburg at last resumed his advance with March 15.

1793. March 1.

March 5.

March 9.

March 11.

1793. forty-two thousand men; and on the 16th Dumouriez marched with forty-eight thousand to meet him. On
March 18. the 18th the decisive action was fought at Neerwinden, when the French were totally defeated, with a loss of five thousand men and three guns. The volunteers and the National Guards were the troops that failed in the battle; and after it the men broke up and fled by whole battalions. Ten thousand deserted in the ten days following the action, and Dumouriez was fain to form a rearguard out of his artillery and his few battalions of the Line, and to fall back on Louvain. Coburg, who had lost about three thousand men, made little attempt at pursuit, keeping his main body halted at Tirlemont until the 22nd, but exhorting the Duke of Brunswick-Oels to hasten from Bois-le-Duc to Malines to cut off Dumouriez's retreat to Antwerp. The Duke, who had already permitted Flers to withdraw with impunity the bulk of his forces to Antwerp, was evidently not disposed to second Austrian operations with Prussian troops, for he refused to move. However, the advance of the Austrians compelled
Mar. 23-24. Dumouriez to evacuate first Louvain and then Brussels;
March 25. and on the 25th, finding himself obliged to abandon Namur also, he opened negotiations with Coburg. He had quarrelled with the Convention beyond hope of reconciliation over the iniquity of its rule in Belgium; and he now proposed that the French should retreat from the whole country, and that he should march to Paris to re-establish the monarchy, the Allies meanwhile halting on the frontier and receiving the fortress of Condé as a guarantee. An agreement to this effect was duly made with the Chief of the
March 27. Austrian Staff on the 27th, and a circular was issued from the Austrian headquarters, suggesting a conference of the representatives of the powers to decide as to the measures to be next taken.

There is no need to tell at length the story of Dumouriez's adventures during the following days. It must suffice that he was driven from the midst of his army, and on the 5th of April was fain to take refuge with the Austrians. Fragments of several corps and one complete regiment of Hussars followed him, unwilling to part with their beloved General; but several thousand French troops in Belgium and Holland, which might have been cut off to a man, were allowed to retire in peace to the frontier. None the less the fact remained that even a dilatory commander at the head of a force of discordant Allies had sufficed to drive the armies of the Revolution in shameful disorder from the Austrian Netherlands.

1793.
April 5.

CHAPTER IV

So far England's attitude towards the Revolution has been treated with little more fulness than that of the other nations of Europe: it is now time to examine more thoroughly her position and her circumstances. Her government at this period lay in the hands of three principal men, William Pitt, Henry Dundas, and William Grenville. Few Englishmen need information as to the great talents of Pitt, his capacity in administration, his skill in finance, his eloquence in debate, his integrity, his courage, and his patriotism; but there were two important matters of which Pitt had no knowledge, namely, of war and of the world. The man whom he chose, or rather who thrust himself upon Pitt, to supplement these defects was Henry Dundas. The son of a Lord Advocate of Scotland, Dundas was born seventeen years before Pitt, and had been called to the Scottish Bar while Pitt was still in the nursery. Sprung from a well-known legal family, and possessing not only ability of his own but a half-brother who was President of the Court of Session, he soon obtained a large practice, was made Solicitor-General for Scotland at twenty-four, and in 1774 was elected member of Parliament for Midlothian. Having some talent for speaking he soon made his mark in Parliament as one of the bitterest opponents of America, and, being made Lord Advocate in 1775, was one of Lord North's strongest supporters until that statesman's influence began to wane. By great adroitness he kept his place under the Rockingham Ministry of 1781, and in 1782 received from Lord Shelburne the Keepership of the Scottish Signet for life, with the patronage of all places in his own country, where for thirty years he reigned practically with autocratic power, returning such peers and such commoners to Parliament as he chose to nominate. In the year 1792 he was chairman of the Secret Committee appointed to report on the government of India, and gained much insight into the affairs of that country. It is characteristic of the man that he was foremost to accuse Warren Hastings in 1782, that he defended him at first in 1786 against Burke, and finally for no reason turned against him once more. His principles in fact were plastic; and he had a singularly keen eye for the form in which it would be most profitable to mould them. Having early perceived the promise of Pitt, he attached himself to that Minister, and became Treasurer of the Navy in Pitt's first administration. Finally, in 1791 Dundas received the seals of the Home Office, which gave him charge of the Colonies, and also, as shall be seen, of the conduct of the war.

By that time Dundas had become Pitt's closest friend and most trusted colleague. "Mr. Pitt, among the multitude of things which press upon him is at all times ready to accommodate himself to my call," wrote Dundas. "You know the difficulty [of the War Department] with other Departments," wrote Pitt in 1794, "even with the advantages of Dundas's turn for facilitating business and of every act being as much mine as his."[1] The alliance between two such men was strange. Pitt, though the wittiest and most delightful of persons when he consented to unbend, was naturally shy, haughty, reserved, and fastidious. Dundas was not only highly convivial over the bottle, as was the rule in those days, but genial to every one, never forgetting, to his credit, those who had known him before he rose to high office; yet his mind was coarse and his ideals not of the highest. Pitt was an upright man, and in public affairs at large a patriotic

[1] *Dropmore Papers*, ii. 396, 595.

and far-seeing statesman. Dundas was honest in so far as he never sought to enrich himself with the public money; he could on occasion shew fine qualities of courage and public spirit; but in political matters he was too often little more than an unscrupulous though very successful intriguer. Votes were the end and aim of all his actions, and the horizon of his policy was bounded by the next general election. Such a man may be a faithful servant to a successful master; but he can never be a loyal master to an unsuccessful servant. Nor, despite his undoubted industry and "turn for facilitating business," can I find that the man had really any great talent for administration. His State-papers are intolerably diffuse, verbose, and evasive of the point, while his orders, as shall be seen, are open to still harsher criticism. Probably, like Pitt, he was at his best in the House of Commons, where his speeches are said to have been eloquent, and were certainly disingenuous, but where his cheerful address and broad Scottish accent doubtless reconciled many to the chilling superiority of his young leader. Such was the man who from his knowledge of the world had gained Pitt's utmost confidence, and, as I believe, far greater ascendency over him than is generally supposed. To him, accordingly, was committed the direction of the war, with a sanguine trustfulness to which he responded with as sanguine self-confidence. Yet so profoundly ignorant was Dundas of war that he was not even conscious of his ignorance.

A man of very different character was William Grenville, who after holding the seals of the Home Office for two years had made them over to Dundas in 1791, and taken over those of the Foreign Office in their stead. A younger son of the George Grenville who had passed the Stamp Act, he possessed a mind of the like academic cast with his father's. Indefatigable industry joined to great natural gifts had made him one of the best informed men in England. As a classical scholar he was deeper and sounder than Pitt or Fox;

he was as familiar with Italian literature as with Greek ; he spoke French with a purity of accent which had deceived even Frenchmen as to his nationality, and he wrote it with a facility and correctness that were the envy of the diplomatic service. Withal he was deeply versed in history, and followed political, social, and religious movements all over Europe so closely, that few pamphlets of note or notoriety in any country failed to find their way to his library. He had, moreover, devoted as close attention to Indian and Colonial history as to European ; and, unlike most of his contemporaries he made a particular study of geography, sparing no pains to obtain the best maps, and amassing a collection of them which would not have been despised by any General Staff in Europe. And if Grenville's ideal of an English statesman's intellectual equipment was high, his conception of his duty to his country as a patriot and to himself as a gentleman was no whit lower. Intense pride and austerity of conduct forbade him even to recognise that there was more than one path for an upright and honourable man. Yet with all his great qualities he was diffident of his own powers, and painfully conscious that the gift of governing men had been denied to him. He could win their confidence and respect, but he could not command their sympathy ; and, too honest to charge others with a failing which he knew to be his own, he confessed it with genuine self-abasement and humbleness of heart. Through his willingness to efface himself his name has been little remembered in history; yet he brought to the councilboard not only knowledge, insight and sagacity, but a resolute will, dauntless courage, and inflexible constancy of purpose.

Pitt, as we have seen, had done his utmost to avoid war ; but, since war had been forced upon him, it behoved him, or Dundas for him, to frame a military policy. On the continent of Europe there were two principal objects which seemed vital to England, namely, the integrity of the Dutch Netherlands, and the maintenance of an effective barrier between them and France. Holland, as Lord Auckland said,[1] was practically a great military magazine and military chest; and Antwerp was a base for naval operations which, in the hands of France, would be a standing menace to England's safety. The Belgic barrier and the exclusive right of the Dutch to the navigation of the Scheldt were, in fact, not only matters of traditional foreign policy but an essential part of England's scheme of national defence; and Pitt imagined that he had secured both by the active diplomacy of Harris in 1787. Moreover, from the beginning of the Revolution he had watched the growing financial distress of France with the keen eye of a Chancellor of the Exchequer, and had made up his mind, not altogether unreasonably, that no country in such a state of disorganisation and bankruptcy as France could long support a war. He thought that he could fix a term at which her hand must drop the sword from sheer powerlessness, and he entered upon the contest in the assurance that the struggle could not be a long one. To hasten the process of financial exhaustion by destroying French trade over sea would, as he thought, be the surest and cheapest way of bringing the war to a close, as well as the means best suited to England's military resources; for, though she had practically no army, she possessed at any rate a navy and superiority at sea.

1789.
Aug. 20.
This policy once fixed, it was not difficult to decide where the naval force should be employed. Ever since the declaration of the Rights of Man by the National Assembly there had been unrest in the French West Indies generally, and especially in St. Domingo, the most important of them. The white planters everywhere took alarm at the doctrine that the blacks were free and equal to themselves; while the mulattos or coloured people, who were subject to degrading hardships and disabilities, claimed their privileges under this declaration, and were moreover encouraged by a philanthropic society, known as the Negro's Friends, in Paris.

[1] Auckland to Grenville, 14th February 1793.

The grant of a constitutional government to the island 1790. naturally kindled between the two parties dissensions, which were artfully inflamed by the partisans of royalty and of the old order. The quarrel was carried to Paris, where the violent language of Brissot and others of the Negro's Friends encouraged the hot-headed mulattos to organise an insurrection. It was put 1791. down without great difficulty, and the ringleaders March. were broken on the wheel; but this severity gave the Negro's Friends an opportunity to pass a decree asserting, at whatever cost, the equality of the coloured man with the white. "Perish the Colonies rather than one tittle of our principles," cried one of them; and therewith the full rights of citizenship were conceded May 15. to the coloured people at one stroke. The whites retorted by trampling the National Tricolour under foot, and even threatened to hoist British colours; but before they could organise themselves for defence the negro slaves in two districts, stirred by incendiary addresses from Paris, rose up in general insurrection Aug. against them, devastating and slaughtering with hideous barbarity. Alarmed at the ruin of the once rich and thriving French colonies, the Constituent Assembly in Paris rescinded its mischievous decree; but it was too Sept. 24. late. The mulattos joined the blacks; and the whites, aided by the garrison of regular troops, turned upon both with the fury of despair. The combatants outdid each other in a savage emulation of cruelty. Civil commissioners arrived from Paris and endeavoured to Christmas. restore peace, but in vain; a war of colour, once kindled, is not easily quenched; and they returned to France after three months, having accomplished nothing. The Legislative Assembly then put the finishing touch to 1792. the mischief by decreeing equality of rights with white April 4. men to all free mulattos and negroes, and by sending out violent Jacobins as commissioners to execute the decree in all the French islands. Those appointed to St. Domingo, by name Santhonax and Polverel, arrived there in September, and at once allied themselves with the Sept.

1792. blacks, in order to grow rich upon the plunder of the whites. Having deposed two governors who presumed to dispute their authority, they, at the beginning of 1793, became practically masters of the island.

As early as in September 1791 emissaries from the Governor and Assembly of St. Domingo had arrived at Jamaica to beg for troops, arms and ammunition, for defence against the negroes; whereupon the Governor, Lord Effingham, though, of course, unable to send the troops, had given a liberal supply of arms, receiving subsequently Grenville's approval for so doing. Later in the same year some of the principal planters appealed to the Ministers in England to send an armed force, which should take possession of St. Domingo in King George's name, and receive the allegiance of the inhabitants; and the request, though necessarily rejected at the time, seems not to have been forgotten. Meanwhile, as the disorder in St. Domingo increased, refugees began to swarm into Jamaica, where the planters became so nervous over the insurrection of half a million negroes within twenty-four hours' sail of their own shores, that they begged for a reinforcement of British troops. After much haggling the Assembly agreed to pay for the Twentieth Light Dragoons, and for two additional battalions of infantry; and thus by the beginning of 1793 the garrison of Jamaica, then a most unhealthy island, had been raised to double of its normal strength.[1] Like causes had produced like effects to windward also. In Martinique, Guadeloupe, and St. Lucia, as in St. Domingo, the proceedings of the National Assembly had embittered the feeling between the whites and the blacks; and fugitives from these colonies kept pouring into the English islands, particularly into Dominica, in such numbers as to cause serious alarm. It was necessary,

---

[1] Effingham to Grenville, 7th and 17th September 1791; Grenville to Effingham, 11th November 1791; Governor Sir A. Williamson to Dundas, 30th November 1791, 6th May 1792; Dundas to Williamson, 7th January 1792. B. Edwards, *History of St. Domingo*, p. 140.

therefore, to reinforce the British Colonies to windward 1792. also; and thus it came about that, before war had been declared, no fewer than nineteen battalions were actually in or on the way to the West Indies, for purposes not of aggression but of simple security against a general rising of the coloured population.[1]

Adding to these nineteen battalions nine more, which were stationed in India, we find that of eighty-one battalions of the British Line, more than one-third were quartered in climates so deadly that a Minister could safely reckon on the necessity of renewing the whole of each battalion every second year. These reinforcements for the West Indies were drawn from Gibraltar, a very important but, at that time, unhealthy naval station; from Ireland, which was in a state of veiled rebellion; and from Nova Scotia and Canada, where relations with the United States were anything but easy. The garrisons for these four places demanded some twenty-five battalions, leaving twenty-eight, besides the Guards and the Cavalry, to defend and keep order in Great Britain and the Channel Islands, to man the fleet, and to meet the multitudinous calls of an empire on the verge of war. The whole of these regiments at home were far below their strength, not exceeding in all fifteen thousand effective men; and no great effort had been made to increase them. It is true that early in December 1792 an order had been issued to enlarge the establishment of certain corps to the extent of six or seven thousand men; but it was idle to speak of an augmentation when there was hardly a regiment which could muster more than half of its unaugmented establishment. The standard of stature was lowered, the bounty was raised to five pounds, and commanding officers were ordered to rouse the activity of their recruiting parties, but to no purpose. Recruits at the end of 1792 still came in but slowly. The folly of ten years was not to be made good by the belated wisdom of a day.[2]

[1] Dundas to Maj.-gen. Cuyler (Barbados), 2nd January 1793.
[2] S.C.L.B. 8th and 27th December 1792.

1792. Such a situation would have made any thoughtful man pause before undertaking any aggressive action at a distance, but Dundas was not a thoughtful man. At the end of 1792 refugees from the French West Indies, with emigrant nobles at their back, again beset the British Ministry, and three planters from St. Domingo boldly offered the King the sovereignty of that island. To plead their cause they employed Monsieur Malouet, a gentleman lately driven to England by the violence of the Jacobins in Paris, who, being at once a friend of Grenville and acquainted both as a civil servant and a proprietor with St. Domingo, was thought by them to be an instrument of peculiar fitness. Malouet waited upon Grenville accordingly, and told him honestly that, though British protection would be as profitable to the English as to the French Colonies, yet the transfer of sovereignty was beyond the power of any number of French planters. With this the matter for the moment ended, as conducted between two honourable gentlemen; but unfortunately a great many of the refugees were of a very different stamp from Malouet or from the old Marquis of Bouillé, who worked with him. The retreat of the Duke of Brunswick had driven a fresh swarm of emigrant nobles to join the thousands of French exiles already in England; and a great many of them were extremely undesirable acquisitions. Some beyond question were high-minded gentlemen; but those who were most assiduous in besieging the British Ministry were simply selfish, avaricious adventurers. They were, however, extremely clever and accomplished men of the world, with plenty of tact, attractive address, persuasive tongues, and that peculiar air of high breeding which can transmute brazen impudence into the semblance of golden condescension. With Grenville, who was as high-bred as he was high-principled and as courteous as he was austere, their arts were powerless; and they therefore turned to Dundas, whose hatred of the Revolution was extravagant, and whose vanity, it must be feared, was less proof against the subtleties of

French flattery. With him they concluded an agree- 1792.
ment that, in return for British protection, St. Domingo
should be sequestrated to the British Crown until the
conclusion of peace—an agreement which they had
no authority to make, and which it was a political
blunder in Dundas to accept. But Dundas was essentially a sanguine man, and the ideas of the sanguine
Frenchmen were exactly consonant with his own. In
his view the hoisting of the British flag over the French
West Indies would revive memories of Chatham when
reported in the Gazette, would please and flatter the
public, would bring fresh trade to England, and above
all would gain the hearts of the West Indian merchants,
who possessed wealth and influence, votes and pocket-
boroughs. He never called to mind the disasters which
had resulted from trusting the American loyalists who
only twenty years before had, with far better warrant,
made like promises with the French loyalists. He had
no understanding, even if he had cognisance, of Clinton's
words to Sackville, "An inroad is no countenance, and
fortified places require garrisons." On the 12th of
January 1793 he sent three planters of St. Domingo 1793.
with a letter of recommendation to the Governor of
Jamaica, forbidding any action so long as peace endured,
but adding that in the event of war, which was highly
probable, it would certainly be part of the British
operations " to extend the protection of His Majesty's
arms to the French West Indies, and secure to them
the advantage of being subject to the Crown of Britain."
Moreover, directly after the declaration of war he sent Feb. 10.
orders to Barbados for the capture of Tobago ; and on
the 28th of February he despatched yet further instruc- Feb. 28.
tions for taking over, by concert with certain French
planters, the islands of Martinique, Guadeloupe, St.
Lucia and Mariegalante. Thus, though his troops
were insufficient to guard British territory alone, he
deliberately committed himself to the protection of four
foreign islands, one of them of very considerable extent
and all of them unhealthy ; and this not only against

1793. the armed force of France, but against a coloured population of nearly a million souls, some of them already insurgent, and all ripe for insurrection.[1]

Meanwhile as the month of January advanced and the prospect of war grew more certain, further orders were issued for augmenting the forces; and on the 25th Lord Amherst was appointed General on the Staff, as during the American War, with the duties though not with the title of Commander-in-Chief at the Horse Guards. Finally on the 11th of February a vote was submitted to Parliament for the increase of the army by twenty-five thousand men, a great number of which were raised by forming one hundred independent companies of one hundred men apiece, and drafting them into existing battalions. Just at this time, as we have seen, the apathy of the Stadtholder towards the entreaties of Lord Auckland compelled the Ministry to hasten three battalions of Guards, in a dangerous state of unreadiness, to Holland, but with express and repeated orders that they should be used for the protection of that country only.[2] It is perfectly plain that the Government had at first no intention of keeping these troops on the Continent; but their arrival, and still more that of the Duke of York, did so much to hearten the Dutch to activity, that on the 5th of March it was resolved to send the Fourteenth, Thirty-seventh, and Fifty-third Foot, completed by drafts from the new independent companies, to join the Duke as a brigade under Major-general Ralph Abercromby. These regiments, however, were subject to the same instructions as the Guards, namely, to remain within immediate reach of their transports in case their services should be required elsewhere. Their quality was such that the Adjutant-general felt constrained to apologise for them both to Abercromby and to the Duke of York. "I

Jan. 25.

Feb. 11.

March 5.

---

[1] *Mém. de Malouet*, ii. 193-197, 209-213. Dundas to Williamson, 12th January; to Maj.-gen. Cuyler, 10th February; to Maj.-Gen. Bruce, 28th February 1793.

[2] Dundas to York, 19th March 1793.

am afraid," he wrote to the Duke, "that you will not reap the advantage that you might have expected from the brigade of the Line just sent over to you, as so considerable a part of it is composed of nothing but undisciplined and raw recruits; and how they are to be disposed of until they can be taught their business I am at a loss to imagine. . . . I was not consulted upon the subject until it was too late to remedy the evil, but I hope that my remonstrances will be of some use in the modelling of troops for the Continent in future." It need hardly be added that, on their arrival in Holland, two out of the three battalions were found utterly unfit for service, the new recruits being old men and weakly boys, worse than the worst that had been accepted even at the period of greatest exhaustion during the American War. To send them on active service was, therefore, simply waste of money.[1]

But this was only one of the evils which ensued because an extremely ignorant civilian was too vain to consult his military advisers before giving military orders. Any soldier at the War Office could have told him that the method of raising independent companies to recruit existing regiments had been found wasteful and unsatisfactory in the past; and, indeed, at this very time the Chief Secretary Cooke wrote to him from Ireland a strong protest against the whole system. It was expensive, because it meant the provision of half-pay for their officers as soon as the men had been drafted out; it was unfair to old subalterns, because they were passed over by boys who by good fortune had raised recruits cheaply. It produced a bad class of recruit, because these young officers were poor judges of men; and finally it encouraged desertion, for the crimps, so long as they poured a certain number of recruits into the depots by a certain time, cared not

[1] *Dropmore Papers*, Auckland to Grenville, 5th and 13th March, 1793. S.C.L.B. 5th March; Abercromby's instructions, 9th March; Dundas to York, 15th March 1793; C.C.L.B. 2nd March; Adj.-gen. to York, 27th March, 12th April 1793. Calvert, pp. 53, 67.

1793. the least whether they deserted afterwards. Nor was Cooke content only to criticise, for he produced an alternative plan for allowing each of the fourteen battalions in Ireland to raise two additional companies of one hundred men apiece, and for granting to the commanding officers the privilege of recommending officers for them. The scheme was approved and was found to be most successful; but it was not introduced into England, where, on the contrary, the number of independent companies was still further increased.[1]

Again, the Adjutant-general, if consulted, could have warned Dundas to be chary of his battalions, since some of them would certainly be required for the Fleet. The King's Navy was labouring under the grievances which in four years were to drive the seamen to mutiny; and as a natural consequence men were hardly to be obtained Feb. 7. by any means. On the very day when the declaration of war was received, the Fleet swallowed up two battalions; and by the end of March it had absorbed so many men that only three regiments of the Line were to be found south of the Tweed. In fact the Horse Guards did not know where to turn for another battalion. This, however, did not prevent Dundas from presently sending another emissary to Jamaica, to commit England still more deeply to operations in the most leeward sphere of the West Indies. Yet he had no reserve of any description to rely upon, except fourteen thousand Hanoverians and eight thousand Hessians, which, pursuant to the time-honoured practice, were taken into British pay; and of these the latter only, being mercenaries pure and simple, could be counted upon for service beyond sea.[2]

Since the kingdom was thus stripped of regular troops, it was necessary to raise other forces for its

[1] *S.P. Ireland*, Cooke to Hobart, 23rd April; Westmoreland to Hobart, 27th April; Dundas to Westmoreland, 16th May, 31st July 1793; *S.C.L.B.* 18th May 1793.
[2] *S.C.L.B.* 7th February. *C.C.L.B.* Adj.-gen. to Duke of York, 2nd and 12th April 1793. Dundas to Williamson, 4th April 1793.

security; but this also was done as foolishly as possible. Early in February it was rightly and wisely decided to call out nineteen thousand additional Militia; but in the execution precisely the same mistake was made as in France. Personal service was not insisted upon; there arose a great demand for substitutes; and the Militia, instead of gaining a substantial increase, simply cut off from the Army the sources of its supply of recruits. In Scotland, which as yet had no Militia, recourse was made to the raising of Fencible regiments, that is to say, of regular troops enlisted for home-service and for the duration of the war only. This system had so far been applied only on a small scale, the regiments of Fencibles during the Seven Years' War and the American War of Independence having been but few;[1] but it now received great and sudden expansion. On the 2nd of March authority was issued for the raising of seven regiments of Fencible Infantry in Scotland at a stroke; besides one already authorised for the Isle of Man, and another, added in April, for the Orkney Islands.[2] With the leading magnates of Scotland at their head, these new corps were speedily completed; but there was one Scottish nobleman who went further than his peers, and raised a regiment in the Highlands for general service. This was Thomas Humberstone Mackenzie, afterwards the last Earl of Seaforth; and his regiment remains with us, still known by his name, but yet more famous under its number of the Seventy-eighth. The reader should take note of the Fencible regiments, for in the years before us we shall see them increased and multiplied in all three kingdoms. Meanwhile, he should remark that within a month of the declaration of war there were

1793.

Feb. 20.

[1] Duke of Argyll's and Earl of Sutherland's, 1759; Lord Fred. Campbell's, 1778; Earl of Sutherland's, Fauconberg's (Yorkshire), North's (Cinque Ports), 1779.
[2] Athol's or the Manx, Sir J. Grant's, Gower's (or Wemyss's), Eglinton's (or Montgomery's), Breadalbane's, Argyll's, Duke of Gordon's, Hopetoun's, Balfour's (Orkney). Their strength was 650 of all ranks, except the Manx, which were 323 strong.

1793. already three distinct forces, the Army, the Fencibles, and the Militia, all bidding against each other for the recruits which only the Regular Army could turn to efficient account.

It is not difficult to perceive the lurking possibilities of disaster in Dundas's military policy; but until April it showed at any rate a certain consistency. The despatch of troops to the Continent was treated as a temporary measure, designed for the protection of Holland only; and, though the Prince of Coburg had called upon the Duke of York to co-operate in his great sweeping movement from north-east to south-west, the Duke had complied only so far as his instructions and, it may be added, his lack of transport permitted.[1] But much, besides the expulsion of the French from Holland and Belgium, had occurred in March, all tending to embarrass England in the principal object of her Continental policy, the securing of a strong barrier between France and Holland. The fatal question of indemnity, first brought forward by the King of Prussia, had aroused the cupidity of his brother potentate in Austria, who valued the recovery of Belgium chiefly in order that he might exchange it for Bavaria. Pitt had for a moment been willing, as we have seen, to consent to the Bavarian exchange, for the sake of peace; but upon the outbreak of war he reverted to absolute rejection of it; and, in an evil hour,

March 2. the British Ambassador at Vienna, Sir Morton Eden, put forward a suggestion that Austria should be bribed to retain Belgium by the promise of an extension of her frontiers on the side of France. Realising that Austria

April 3. refused to act disinterestedly, Grenville reluctantly accepted the proposal; and at the same time the British Government seems to have taken it for granted that it must give the Emperor some assistance towards the conquest of the new barrier.[2]

Accordingly, since no more infantry was to be

[1] Murray to Dundas, 26th March 1793.
[2] Sybel, ii. 230; Grenville to Auckland, 3rd April 1793.

spared from England, eleven regiments of cavalry were 1793. ordered to prepare for service on the Continent, though March 21- their numbers were so weak that they could not between April 2. them muster more than twenty-three squadrons, or about two thousand five hundred of all ranks, fit for service. But, at the same time, the British Ministers shrank from supplying British troops for the advantage of other nations without gaining some equivalent to satisfy the electors of England ; wherefore they decided, apparently at the instance of Grenville's elder brother, Lord Buckingham, to claim Dunkirk as Great Britain's indemnity for the war. The choice, viewed from the standpoint of the party-politician, was a good one. Dunkirk, having been taken by Cromwell, sold by Charles the Second, and dismantled under the conditions imposed by the sword of Marlborough, possessed sentimental attractions to the public at large and to the Whigs in particular ; while, as a nest of privateers, its extirpation could not but be welcome not only to every merchant in England, but especially to the Chancellor of the Exchequer. No scheme of operations had yet been concerted with Austria, for, indeed, Coburg had advanced from the Roer before nearly all his forces had been collected ; but Pitt seems to have thought that, while the Austrian reinforcements were on their way to the front, the mixed force of British, Hanoverians, Hessians and Dutch might very well master Dunkirk in the course of April, afterwards leaving the Austrians in sufficient strength to pursue their operations in Flanders alone, while the British struck at some other part of France. Thus Pitt was not true even to his own plan of ruining his enemy by the destruction of her colonial trade. Moreover, it is difficult to define what he meant by some other part of France. The old Marquis of Bouillé, knowing that the heart of the Revolution could be pierced at Paris, had suggested a descent upon Havre with thirty thousand men ; and, as shall be seen, there was by this time another vulnerable point in the west of France. But why it should have been necessary

1793. to seek out a new point of attack, when troops were already massed or massing on the French frontier within twelve days' march of the capital, and with only a demoralised enemy before them, was a question which seems never to have occurred either to Pitt or to Dundas. There can be no doubt that they fell into a common pitfall of the British politician. They gave so much thought to the treaty which they should lay before Parliament at the close of the war, that they omitted to consider the means of bringing the war itself to a close.[1]

Meanwhile the omnivorous rapacity of the Emperor Francis was already reducing the coalition against France to hopeless weakness. The first trouble arose out of the project of the Bavarian exchange, which was so bitterly resented by the Wittelsbachs, the reigning house of Bavaria, that they not only raised difficulties about the passage of the Imperial troops through their territory to the Rhine, but refused to make over Mannheim to them as a place of farms. Much incensed, the Emperor detained his reserves from the front with the idea of seizing Bavaria by force, to which the Bavarians replied by detaining their troops likewise to watch them; and thus both were lost for service in active operations. This was a bad beginning; but still more fatal in its March 23. results was the communication to Vienna of the treaty between Russia and Prussia for the partition of Poland. The Emperor, furious at having been outdone by Frederick William in the gain of territory, dismissed his Ministers and took to himself a new adviser in Baron Thugut, an absolutely unprincipled politician, who cared for nothing but power and believed in nothing but success. To humour the greed of his master, he March 27. sent an emissary to England to press once again not only for her consent to the Bavarian exchange, but for

---

[1] *S.C.L.B.* 21st March, 2nd April; *C.C.L.B.* 25th March 1793. *Dropmore Papers*, ii. 360, 387-89. Buckingham to Grenville, 20th January; the King of Grenville, 29th March; Pitt to Grenville, 1st April 1793. Auckland to Grenville, 31st May 1793.

CH. IV HISTORY OF THE ARMY 87

the acquisition by Austria of certain places in Alsace also ; 1793.
agreeing in return that the Emperor should do his best
to increase the territory of Belgium by the conquest of
French fortresses, but adding that, unless England consented to the exchange of the Belgic Provinces thus
augmented, Austria would be obliged to take a portion
of Poland. Simultaneously he informed Russia and April 4.
Prussia, who had agreed to guarantee the Bavarian
exchange to Austria if she would subscribe to the treaty
of partition, that the Emperor renounced the exchange
and looked for indemnity both in France and Poland.
Finally, after hearing of the recapture of Belgium, he
again approached Sir Morton Eden and offered, if
England would conclude a close alliance with Austria,
to abandon the Bavarian exchange. Thugut appears to
have considered it a cardinal principle of statesmanship
to involve himself in a tangle of lies ; but this purpose-
less duplicity of course produced no good effect. Eden
announced that England was immovable upon the
Bavarian question, but would agree to concede indemnities of French territory. Frederick William simply
replied that, if Austria thwarted his designs on Poland,
he would withdraw all his troops from France except the
twenty thousand men that formed his contingent, as a
member of the Empire, to the Imperial army. This
placed the Emperor in a dilemma. He would gladly
have broken with Prussia, and drawn closer to England,
but Prussia could provide him with the troops that he
needed, while England could not. It then remained
for him to choose whether he would make peace with
France and give all his attention to Poland, or renounce
Poland and turn all his strength against France ; but in
his insane greed of territory he insisted upon trying to
gain everything. The result of this double-dealing
speedily told upon the military operations. Brunswick,
pursuant to agreement, had moved upon the 25th of
March against Custine before Mainz ; and in the
course of ten days he drove the French in utter confusion south of the Lauter. But beyond that point he

1793. did not press them; and Frederick William, though he blockaded Mainz, resolved to make any further offensive movements conditional upon Austria's good behaviour.

It was in such inauspicious circumstances that the representatives of the various powers met in conference at Antwerp. Coburg, who loathed the war and had hoped to end it by an agreement with Dumouriez, April 5. had issued a proclamation declaring himself to be the ally of all friends of order, and abjuring all projects of conquest in the Emperor's name. Instantly Austrians, Prussians, and English with one voice required him to withdraw it, and to publish a new declaration that he would prosecute the war vigorously. He did so, but with great reluctance; indeed, so bitter was his opposition to the new policy that he tried to open further negotiations with the Convention, and even furnished it with information which he ought to have kept to himself.[1] Meanwhile Lord Auckland announced that England, as well as the other powers, would expect an indemnity for her share in the war; whereupon the Dutch representative announced that, as every one else was taking compensation, he hoped that Holland's claims would not be forgotten.[2] The sharing of the lion's skin having thus been determined, the next thing was to decide upon a plan of operations for slaying the lion. A vague project was drawn out for the attack of the frontier-fortresses, in which Coburg reckoned upon the co-operation of over twenty thousand men, that is to say, of thirteen thousand Hanoverians and seven thousand five hundred British, in British pay, besides fifteen thousand Dutch. Dundas was staggered; for he had not yet the slightest idea what were the ultimate designs of either of the German powers, who, as he justly complained, were very backward to give an

---

[1] Sybel, ii. 142.

[2] The insisting upon an indemnity must have been the work of Pitt, probably under the influence of Dundas. Grenville trembled at the word indemnity. *Dropmore Papers*, ii. 392.

explicit account of their views either as to the conduct of 1793. the war or the termination of it. "We cannot advise the King," he wrote, "to give a blind co-operation to measures not distinctly explained." But he hinted that if the Austrians would spare a detachment to help the British to capture Dunkirk at once, England might make fewer difficulties about lending her troops for subsequent operations. The English, he explained, were prejudiced against Continental enterprises; wherefore it was important to convince the nation early that its troops in Holland were employed for an object intimately connected with the interests of Great Britain and the security of her commerce. "The early capture of Dunkirk by a Prince of the blood," he added, "would give much éclat to the commencement of the war." In other words, Dundas was ready to employ British troops in the Low Countries only for a political campaign, and not for the military purposes of the war—to use them, in fact, primarily to win votes rather than battles. The attitude is but too characteristic of British Ministers for War.[1]

Meanwhile the Allies on the frontiers of France remained inactive; the Austrians, indeed, blockading Condé, where the French kept them engaged with incessant affairs of outposts, but the British contingent still awaiting the orders which Dundas hesitated to give. In the third week of April the chief of the British staff reported that a considerable force of French was entrenched about Dunkirk, too strong to be attacked by the Duke of York's troops, and that there was no operation on which the latter could be employed except in support of the Austrians.[2] We shall presently recognise the unseen hand which had been working at Dunkirk. Ten days more of uncertainty passed away, and at last, on the 1st of May, Coburg produced a plan of operations. By the middle of May he hoped to have

May 1.

[1] Protocol of conference of 7th April. Dundas to Auckland and to Murray, 16th April; Auckland to Grenville, 19th April 1793.
[2] Murray to Dundas, 22nd April 1793.

1793. about ninety-two thousand men,[1] to which by the beginning of June would be added thirteen thousand more. He proposed, therefore, to hasten the fall of Condé by a bombardment, and then to advance with fifty-two thousand men to the siege of Valenciennes, leaving a cordon of some forty thousand to cover every imaginable point along a front of some fifty miles from Maubeuge on the Sambre to Ostend on the sea. Valenciennes might be expected to fall at the end of July, and then ten thousand men could be left to mask Lille, while fifty thousand marched to the siege of Dunkirk. If this plan were accepted, Coburg pledged himself to the Duke of York to lend his best good-will to the attack on Dunkirk. On this assurance the Duke recommended the plan to which at last Dundas gave his consent, on the understanding that the other powers in general and Austria in particular should give an immediate explanation of their ulterior views. England, he repeated, could not allow so large a force in her pay to be employed on operations whose object was undefined; and he emphasised the statement by an inquiry as to the security of Ostend, which so far had been the British port of disembarkation, evidently as a hint that England reserved her right to withdraw her troops at any moment.

This is a good instance of the manner in which British Ministers evade their responsibility. The British General had, nearly three weeks before, laid before Dundas the following issue. "There is no use for British troops in the Netherlands except to act in support of the Austrians. Their commander has submitted a plan based on the active co-operation of all our troops, present

---

[1] Prussians, 8000, of which 1800 cavalry; Austrians, 55,000, of which 10,000 cavalry; Dutch, 15,000, of which 2500 cavalry; Hanoverians, 12,000, of which 3000 cavalry; Hessians, 8000, of which 1500 cavalry; British, 7200, of which 3000 cavalry. Total, 105,200, of which 27,200 in the pay of England. About 5000 of the Austrians and the 8000 Hessians were not expected till June. Witzleben, ii. 117, 181-186. Coburg to York, 1st and 3rd May; Murray to Dundas, 5th May; Dundas to Murray, 10th May 1793.

and expected. We think the plan a good one. Are we 1793. to act with him, or are we not?" Upon this it was for the Ministry to say at once to Austria, "Our Generals favour your plan of campaign, but until we know your ultimate intentions we cannot take part in it. Unless you come to a definite understanding with us by a certain day, we shall order our troops on the spot to re-embark, and meanwhile we have suspended the march of our reinforcements." Instead of this they said in effect, "We approve the plan of campaign, and thereby commit our troops to it; but we reserve to ourselves the right to withdraw them, or, in other words, to wreck the operations, whenever we think proper." If, therefore, the enemy should in the meantime take the offensive and press the Austrians hard, which, as shall be seen, was what actually happened, the responsibility for granting or withholding British assistance was thrown entirely upon the General.

It remains to say a word of the plan itself, and of the troops and commanders who were appointed to carry it out. The enormous front along which Coburg proposed to disperse his force is an example of the system known as the cordon-system, which was in particular favour with the Austrians at this time. It consisted in covering every possible access to a theatre of war with some small body of troops, and had been formulated by Marshal Lacy upon the experience of the war of the Bavarian Succession in 1778, when he had held a front of fifty miles in the labyrinthine country of the Upper Elbe, and reduced the campaign to a mere scuffle of foraging parties. Well calculated to exclude the plague or contraband goods from a country, it was, of course, ridiculous against the invasion of an enemy; for it meant weakness at all points and strength at none, and in fact simply invited the destruction of the army in detail by a force of inferior strength. Nevertheless it was in high favour with all armies of Europe, excepting the British, at that time; and it was a matter of rule that, wherever the enemy stationed a battalion or a com-

1793. pany, a countervailing battalion or company must be posted over against it. The Austrians had suffered much from this system in their recent war with the Turks; but their commanders, of whom Coburg had been one, had learned little from the experience. Apart from his adherence to this new and utterly false fashion, which precluded the concentration of troops for a vigorous offensive, Coburg was a sound, slow, cautious commander of the old Austrian type, more intent upon preserving his own army than destroying the enemy's, and, perhaps, happiest when firmly set down to conduct a siege in form according to the most scientific principles. Withal he was a sensible and honourable gentleman, and extremely popular with his troops. The chief of his staff, and, by common report, the virtual Commander-in-Chief, was the unfortunate Mack, then a colonel forty years of age, who enjoyed the reputation of being the most scientific officer in Europe. The theory of war, as then understood in many quarters, assigned as the first object not the annihilation of the enemy's force in the field, but the possession of certain geographical points, which were called Strategic Objects. At this game of maps and coloured labels Mack excelled; and, when called upon to fight an action, he so elaborated his plans for the overwhelming of his enemies by the simultaneous onslaught of a number of converging columns that, if everything went right and every column reached exactly the appointed place at exactly the appointed time, he assured to himself not only victory but conquest. But, since he made no allowance for the possible failure of any one of his combinations through unforeseen contingencies or accidents of any description, Mack's actions were rarely successful and always unduly hazardous. He seems to have been an honest man, of real though misdirected ability; while his character gained for him a confidence and respect which the British in the field accorded to no other foreign officer. But though, as shall be seen, his methods by no means commended themselves to all

British commanders, they nevertheless made a fatally 1793.
favourable impression upon the British Ministry.

To judge with the wisdom that comes after the event, it may be said that the Allied Army was tactically deficient in two principal respects, namely, in the numerical weakness of its light infantry and in the faulty organisation of its artillery. Light infantry and light cavalry at this time were still treated mainly as accessories, useful for the "little war" (to use the French expression) of outposts and reconnaissance, but as something apart from the "great war," which was reserved for the more solid squadrons and battalions that enjoyed the dignity of a place in the formal Order of Battle. In fact, the work of outposts was supposed to fall wholly upon the light corps, while the regular troops husbanded their strength in security behind them. Hostilities with any nation which is driven back on primitive methods of self-defence, and which neither knows nor respects the contemporary usage of civilised warfare, invariably upset any such arrangement; and the British, after the experience of America, should have been awake to this truth. Indeed, in justice to the officers, many of them were alive to it; but Pitt, since 1783, had been more solicitous for the reduction than the training of the Army. In the matter of artillery the practice of all the nations was the same. Each battalion possessed its two guns, three-pounders or six-pounders, and the remainder of the ordnance was massed into a park, with or without an inner distribution into brigades or batteries. The handling of the artillery by the Count of Bückeburg at Minden had not yet found sufficient appreciation to be made the foundation of a system.[1]

The Austrian troops, in spite of the exhaustion of the long Turkish war, were for the most part worthy of their high reputation, and aroused at first the greatest admiration among British officers. They included, however, a certain number of irregular corps, both

[1] The authorities for this and the next paragraph are Ditfurth, i. 29, 35, 36; Witzleben, ii. 59; Calvert, p. 83; Sybel, ii. 154.

1793. horse and foot, chiefly Slavs, which were simply savage banditti of the most dangerous type. They would murder or plunder any one, friend or foe, even to the vedettes of their own army; and no Austrian general would trust himself among them without an escort. The quality of the higher officers was, however, unworthy that of the men, many of them being old, supine, and narrow-minded; and the corps of officers at large was sharply divided between two factions, which espoused the two opposite schools of Loudon and Lacy. The organisation also was imperfect, for, though the army was indeed distributed into brigades and divisions, these were not kept together, but all detachments were formed of squadrons and battalions arbitrarily collected and entrusted to a general as arbitrarily chosen, who knew no more of the men than they knew of him. In the matter of tactics the Austrians had made no progress since the Seven Years' War. Cavalry and infantry alike were still formed in three ranks, and the art of handling large bodies of cavalry had been nearly, though not wholly, forgotten.

The Prussians still enjoyed the fame which they had won under Frederick the Great, but they had not been improved by the false training observed by Cornwallis at their manœuvres; while their commander, von Knobelsdorf, though full of zeal, was also full of years, having passed his seventieth birthday. Superior to them were the Hessians, the majority of whom had served in America, where they had learned to manœuvre rapidly and to fight in dispersed order, though the lesson had never been practised since their return to their own land.[1] The Hessian Jäger were particularly good light troops, and were armed with rifles. The whole corps, moreover, was the more effective since it was equipped with regimental transport upon a lavish scale, and was therefore mobile and self-dependent.[2] On

---

[1] Ditfurth, i. 48.
[2] 231 horses, draught and pack, and 116 drivers, etc., per battalion of 1100 men, of which 82 horses and 34 men were for the

the whole, the Hessians seem to have been the most 1793.
valuable fighting men in the army, though they were
not exempt from the love of plunder, a failing which
mercenary veterans are apt to judge more leniently, at
certain times, than other troops. The Hanoverians
were then, as always, fine soldiers, but without the
advantage of the Hessians in experience and training.
The Dutch, being hastily raised, were ill organised,
disciplined, trained, and equipped.

The British, with the exception of the Guards, were,
in the opinion of foreign critics, very deficient in training and discipline, for precisely the same reason as the
Dutch, namely, persistent neglect. The cavalry was of
better material than the infantry, and was very well
mounted ; but both officers and men were so ignorant
of their work that, at first, they could not even throw
out vedettes and outposts without instruction from
foreigners. The field-guns were inferior to those of
the rest of the Allies ; the ammunition-waggons were
heavy and unwieldy ; and the horses were harnessed one
before the other instead of abreast, which made them
difficult to drive, and took up much room on the
road. The models of both harness and waggons were,
in fact, of Marlborough's time ; while the medical
arrangements, or what passed for such, were those of
a still remoter age. Discipline for the most part was
bad, especially among the officers, for reasons which
have been explained in a former chapter ; and, though
there were still among their infantry good men who
had learned their business in America, far too many
were absolutely ignorant as well as neglectful of their
duty. Hard drinking in all ranks accounted for much
both of the indiscipline and the neglect. To the men,
of course, drunkenness brought a flogging at the
halberts, but to the officers, unfortunately, it did not
necessarily mean punishment ; nor was it possible that
it should, when respectful consideration was shown to

officers. Each company had one four-horse waggon, and each battalion one pair-horse hospital-waggon.

1793. both Prime Minister and Secretary of State for War if they appeared incapably drunk at the House of Commons, because the leaders of the Opposition drank even harder than they. This vice of drunkenness was the most formidable with which good officers had to contend throughout the twenty years of the war, simply because it was a fashion set in high places.[1]

It was no easy task to command such a force as the British, Hanoverians and Hessians, under the orders of such a man as Dundas, and the immediate direction of such generals as Coburg and Mack. Frederick, Duke of York, second son of King George the Third, was in 1793 thirty years old. At the age of sixteen he had been sent to Berlin to study the profession of arms under the eye of Frederick the Great himself, and had returned with a practical knowledge which made him later an admirable Commander-in-Chief at the Horse Guards, but also with an undue preference for the weaker points of the stiff and formal Prussian system. In 1791 he had become Colonel of the Coldstream Guards, in which post he had at first shown himself enough of a martinet to excite discontent;[2] and, though he had wisely changed his ways after a year's experience, he was not at this time popular with his men, while his officers, who had been taught to look for preferment from politicians, resented his authority whether for good or ill. In this respect he was hampered by the same disadvantages as had beset Lord Stair in 1743; and, unfortunately, he did not possess the qualifications to gain the confidence of his troops in the field. He had the cool personal bravery which belongs to his race, but not the higher moral courage which gives constancy and patience in difficulty or misfortune; and hence he was at once sanguine and easily discouraged. He had learned his work, so far as it could be acquired by the industry of

---

[1] Ditfurth, i. 33; Witzleben, ii. 66. York to Dundas, 25th January 1794. Vol. iii. of this *History*, pp. 524, 525.
[2] *Dropmore Papers*, ii. 349.

a mediocre intellect, but he was slow of apprehension, 1793. without sagacity, penetration or width of view, and with so little imagination or resource that an unforeseen emergency confounded him. On the other hand, his dutiful loyalty and submission, in most trying circumstances, towards Coburg on the one hand, and the Cabinet on the other, were beyond all praise. The Ministry had some just doubts as to his fitness to command, but the King had set his heart upon the appointment; and indeed, where so many Serene Highnesses were gathered together, the superior rank of the Duke was a decided advantage. It was hoped, therefore, to make good his deficiencies by joining to him Sir James Murray, better known by the name which he afterwards assumed as Sir James Pulteney, nominally as Adjutant-general, but really as Chief of the Staff and something more; for it was to his correspondence that the Government looked for information and advice.

Murray was a singular character. He had served in the Seven Years' War; he had distinguished himself in the West Indies during the American War of Independence; and he had trained an intellect, which was of no common order, not only by shrewd observation of the world but by solid and extensive study. His knowledge was great, his grasp and outlook wide, his judgment cool and accurate, his indifference to danger and hardship absolute; but he was shy, awkward and diffident, with a dreamy indolence which led him too readily to surrender his own correct opinion, and to amuse himself with speculation upon the incorrect opinions of others.[1] When roused he could sum up a situation with an insight, terseness and vigour which showed how close was his hold upon facts; but he was not the helpmate who could make good the defects of the Duke of York. The situation, indeed, demanded a Marlborough, with the insight to see the one thing that was needed, and the tact and ascendency to bring cautious commanders, intriguing Ministers, narrow-

[1] Bunbury, *Great War with France*, p. 46.

1793. minded potentates and irresolute Cabinets into line, for the one true object,—an immediate march on Paris. Such a march could undoubtedly not have been made without risk, owing to the dearth of food in France; yet the opportunity was favourable, and the hazard was slight compared with the certain danger of delay. Already in
Feb. 19. February the Republic had wantonly made a fresh enemy by declaring war upon Spain; and the campaign in Belgium had produced results for which the most sanguine of her enemies could hardly have hoped. On the first
March 8. news of the Austrian successes, the Convention instantly formed a special tribunal for the trial of traitors and conspirators against France, and summoned two of the defeated generals to appear before it. This done, it proceeded to take measures for hastening the levy of the three hundred thousand men, decreed a fortnight before. The scenes of ridiculous enthusiasm, which had become usual in Paris, followed as a matter of course; but the multitude of men who, for various reasons, claimed exemption, was astonishing, and the rascality of many who were enrolled was flagrant. A great many of these rogues made a trade of fraudulent enlistment, receiving a bounty from several corps and selling the arms and clothing received from each of them; while the number of women, who claimed allowances for the removal of their husbands to the army, sufficed to warrant the belief that every recruit was a polygamist. In the provinces, both north and south, there was violent resistance to the levy; and on
March 10. the 10th of March, at Saint Florent le Vieil on the Loire, the peasants turned upon the troops which had been brought up to enforce the ballot, and, though armed only with cudgels, dispersed them and drove them from the town. That evening the alarm-bell rang in every church of the surrounding parishes; and five days later bands of peasants drove the National Guards from Chollet, some twenty miles south of Saint Florent, and took that town also. This was the first manifestation of a great counter-revolutionary

movement, famous in history as the revolt of La Vendée.

1793.

The Convention, however, did not at first realise the importance of this outbreak, in the critical state of things in the north. An attempt to reinforce Dumouriez at Louvain, by calling out ten thousand of the National Guards of the northern provinces, provided only a few worn-out men and boys,[1] whom the General contemptuously dismissed to their homes. Then came the defection of Dumouriez himself, which was well-nigh fatal to all military improvement. The General had disparaged the election of officers by their men; he had urged that the volunteers should be incorporated in the Line; he had tried to enforce discipline upon all; and, finally, he had turned traitor and taken some of his regular troops with him. It was therefore plain that discipline was an abomination, that all his recommendations were vicious, that the regular troops were not to be trusted, and that volunteers only were to be accounted faithful. Never was the regular army of France so near to total dissolution at the hands of its countrymen as at this moment of supreme military peril. Beurnonville, having tried to abolish abuses, was driven from the War Office; a good Jacobin, Bouchotte, with a still better Jacobin, Vincent, at his elbow, was installed in Beurnonville's place, and the whole of Pache's vile following returned with them to office.[2] A camp was ordered to be formed at Peronne, and in it were assembled, not with disgrace but with honour, all the soldiers who had been imprisoned by Dumouriez for misconduct, all the deserters, the cowards and the skulkers, who had fled from the army of Belgium. Further, it was resolved that representatives of the people, with absolute powers, should be sent to rally and reorganise the northern forces, and to set the fortresses in order. If ever a nation seemed bent upon compassing its own destruction by piling madness upon madness, it was the French at this moment.

April 6.

[1] Poisson, ii. 239, 240.   [2] Rousset, p. 183.

1793. Yet, amid all the confusion, there appeared the first sign of the powers which by terrible means were to reduce France and, through France, the whole Continent of Europe to discipline and order. On the 6th of April the Convention chose nine of its members, renewable by monthly election, to wield the Dictatorship of France, with the title of the Committee of Public Safety. On April 10. the 10th of April a rough Alsatian officer, Kellerman by name, whose gallantry had raised him from the ranks to a commission during the Seven Years' War, came forward with a scheme which preserved the famous regiments of the French Line. Finally, among the six representatives despatched to save the wreck of Dumouriez's army was Captain Lazare Carnot of the Engineers; by birth a younger son in a respectable family of Burgundy, by repute well known in Europe as an original thinker upon military matters in general, and upon the defence of fortresses in particular. Though now forty years of age and of twenty years' standing in the army, he was still a captain, for his military opinions had given offence in high quarters under the Monarchy; and it was as a simple captain that he was to appoint generals, and to organise victory under the Republic. Deeply read in theology and history, a passionate devotee of mathematics and of science, he had framed for himself high ideals, which, as he thought, the Revolution was appointed to fulfil; and he upheld its principles through good report and evil report, not with the Gallic effervescence that is bred of self-consciousness, but with the austere fanaticism of a Scot who takes his stand upon the Covenant. He believed; and in his faith he had buried all thought of self. Rank, wealth, fame alike were indifferent to this spare, stern, ascetic soldier. To give all that lay in him for the cause, to render faithful account of every trust reposed in him for the cause, to forward all that would further it, to combat all that could impede it—such were the principles that governed his conduct. With these motives to inspire him, with great natural gifts, and with every faculty of mind and body trained to the highest point, it is not surprising that his intellectual grasp was wide, his insight clear, his energy infectious, his industry indefatigable. Such was the man who in the early days of April hurried to the north, his brain teeming with thoughts, long since conceived, as to the training best suited to the French soldier, with his natural aptitude for attack. Five years before, while advocating a scheme of short service, he had written that it is war and not a lifetime in the barrack-yard that makes the old soldier.[1] To General Dampierre, who had been appointed on his recommendation to succeed Dumouriez, Carnot left it to apply this precept, while he himself, with ominous directness, hastened northward to repair the half-ruined fortress of Dunkirk.

[1] *Vie de Carnot*, i. 138.

CHAPTER V

1793. The effect of Carnot's arrival at Dunkirk in overthrowing Pitt's original plan has already been told. There can be no doubt that the French had full information of the Minister's designs, for it became a proverb that the most secret projects of the British War Office were always well known to the enemy and to everybody in England.[1] Nevertheless, if the British Cabinet had thereupon frankly abandoned any attempt upon Dunkirk, Carnot's labours might have been turned to naught. The French army was only slowly assembled during April, and even at the end of the month was of inferior force and scattered over a wide front; for the French were not free from the vices of the cordon-system, nor were likely to be, so long as civilians interfered with their military dispositions. Apart from the garrisons of Quesnoy, Valenciennes, Condé, Lille and Dunkirk, Dampierre kept ten thousand men on April. his right, under General Harville, between Maubeuge and Philippeville: ten thousand more, under General

---

[1] "The squadron of men of war and transports was collected, the commodore's flag hoisted, and the expedition sailed with *most secret* orders, which as usual were as well known to the enemy and everybody in England as to those by whom they were given" (Marryat, *The King's Own*, ch. vii. *ad init.*). Marryat attributes this failing to the multitude of counsellors that compose a Cabinet. He may be right, but those who are acquainted with the scandalous carelessness with which Ministers treat confidential military documents, find no difficulty in accounting for it otherwise. This evil still continues, and will continue until Cabinet Ministers are subjected to the same penalties for abuse of trust as other servants of the King.

Lamarlière, lay on his left, in an entrenched camp thrown 1793. up by Carnot at Cassel and at other points between Lille and Dunkirk; and five thousand at Nomain, Orchies, and Hasnon, covered the interval between Lille and the main army. This last, consisting of thirty thousand men under Dampierre's immediate command, lay in an entrenched camp at Famars, a little to the south of Valenciennes, with a detachment in another fortified position at Anzin, to the north-west of that town. In all, therefore, he had about fifty thousand men at hand for service in the field.

Meanwhile the Allies, who were still below their full April 23. strength, occupied the following positions. On their right, that is to say, to westward, six thousand Dutch and about three thousand Imperial troops, under the Hereditary Prince of Orange, lay at Furnes, Ypres and Menin; next to them two thousand five hundred British and about the same number of Austrians and Prussians, under the Duke of York, occupied Tournai; next to the Duke of York, Knobelsdorf, with about eight thousand Prussians, held the line of Maulde, Lecelles and Saint Amand on the Scarpe; next to Knobelsdorf, Clerfaye, with about twelve thousand men at Vicoigne and Raismes, and at Bruay and Fresnes, on the Scheldt, encompassed Condé on the south, while the Prince of Würtemberg with about five thousand men blockaded it on the north. At Onnaing, due south of Condé, lay the principal army, about fifteen thousand strong, with the advance guard at Saint Saulve; and to the east of the main army General Latour with about six thousand men occupied Bettignies, in observation of Maubeuge, with a detachment at Bavai to preserve communication between Bettignies and Onnaing. The total force of the Allies may thus be taken, roughly, at over sixty thousand men, not including thirty thousand Imperial troops under the Prince of Hohenlohe-Kirschberg, which were uselessly detained at Namur, Trèves and Luxemburg. The English cavalry, the Hanoverians and the Hessians, had not yet arrived, though the first detachments of the two former were drawing near to the front; but none the less the Allies were actually superior to the French in numbers, and very far superior in quality. The whole of their multitudinous posts were strongly entrenched; but it will be observed that, besides the essential defect of the enormous extension of their front, their line was cut in two by the river Scheldt, which gave the greater opportunity for a successful attack upon one or other of their wings. The general distribution of the Allies corresponded in the main with their lines of retreat, that of the British lying west to the sea, that of the Dutch north-east upon Antwerp, that of the Austrians east upon Namur; so that a successful attack upon the British would probably lay bare the Austrian right, and a decided defeat of the Austrians must certainly uncover the British left. With their usual jealousy for supreme control, the Austrians mixed a contingent of their own troops with the Allies in every section of the army, an arrangement which gave rise to infinite confusion, since it made even small detachments dependent on two or three different sources of supply. For each nation made provision for its own troops in its own way, and, owing to diversities of system and of differences in calibre of muskets and cannon, it was impossible to make any effort towards uniformity.

Still, the inactivity of Coburg during April was marvellous. It never occurred to him to overwhelm any one of Dampierre's isolated divisions of untrained men by concentrating a superior force upon it. He never reflected that, even if both sides adhered to the cordon-system, the French could bring up the whole manhood of their country to make their cordon stronger than his own at every point. He allowed Dampierre to school his troops with impunity by perpetual affairs of outposts, without remembering that the French could more easily replace two men than he could replace one. Finally (but this may be pardoned to him) he did not guess that, while he was wasting a campaign over formal sieges, the French would evolve from the 1793. experience of many skirmishes a new system of tactics —that they would abandon the old formal training, and, turning to account the indiscipline which springs from the principle of equality, would grant independence of action to the born fighting men, and trust to the national impetuosity to carry the rest forward in dense masses to the attack.

It is a shameful reproach to the Allies that, overmatched though he was in every respect, the French General took the initiative and made the first move of the campaign. On the 1st of May he assailed the whole line May 1. of the Allies from Saint Saulve to St. Amand ; but, the attacks being unintelligent and incoherent, he was beaten back at every point with a loss of two thousand men and several guns. Urged by the Convention to save Condé, he on the 8th essayed a second attempt, and on this May 8. occasion confined himself to demonstrations only upon the flanks of the Allies, concentrating a larger proportion of his force against Clerfaye's position in the centre. These sounder principles brought him within an ace of success. He himself directed a frontal attack from Anzin against Raismes and Vicoigne, and after four successive repulses carried the position of Raismes, excepting the village. Lamarlière meanwhile with little difficulty made his way towards St. Amand, while one of his divisions, crossing the Scarpe, pressed on unseen through the forest of Vicoigne, nearly to the road which leads from St. Amand to Valenciennes. There this division began to throw up a redoubt and batteries to cannonade Clerfaye's defences of Vicoigne, so as to cut off communication between him and Knobelsdorf, and to ensure a junction with the garrison of Valenciennes. The situation was critical, for, if the French succeeded in holding possession of the road, the post at Vicoigne was lost, and the whole line of the Allies was broken. Fortunately the Duke of York had moved three battalions of Guards to Nivelle, a little to the north of St. Amand, having promised Knobelsdorf help

1793.
May 8. in case of need; and at five o'clock in the evening the brigade came upon the scene, just as the French were gaining the upper hand of the Prussians. The country to north and west of Valenciennes is a level plain, broken only by the three forests, which bear the names of Marchiennes, Vicoigne, and Raismes, so that the Duke could see little or nothing of what was going forward until his troops were actually on the scene of action. The Coldstream, being first for duty, by Knobelsdorf's order entered the wood, and quickly driving the French back, followed them up to their entrenchments. There, however, they were met by musketry in front and a fierce fire of grape from a masked battery in flank; when, finding themselves unsupported by the Prussians, they fell back in good order with a loss of over seventy killed and wounded. Seeing, however, by the appearance of the red coats, that Knobelsdorf had been reinforced, Lamarlière's division made no further effort to advance; and Dampierre, while leading a last desperate assault upon Vicoigne from the front, was mortally wounded by a cannon-shot. This decided the fate of the day: his successor stopped the attack, and on the following morning

May 9. retreated. On the next day Clerfaye and Knobelsdorf stormed the enemy's newly-built batteries and captured their garrison of six hundred men, but failed to take the guns, which, according to the French custom of the time, had been withdrawn and kept limbered up for the night, in readiness for escape.[1] The loss of Clerfaye's and Knobelsdorf's corps in the two days was little short of eight hundred officers and men; that of the French was far heavier, and was aggravated by the death of Dampierre. It speaks highly for the man that with troops so raw he should have made so fine a fight against some of the best soldiers in Europe.

The losses suffered by the Coldstream Guards on the 8th were made the subject of much complaint both against Knobelsdorf and the Duke of York, and did not promote good feeling among the Allies in

[1] Calvert, p. 72.

the field. The battalion was, in fact, lucky to escape annihilation. Murray blamed Lieutenant-colonel Pennington, who was in command; but it seems that Knobelsdorf simply told him to enter the wood, which was full of dense undergrowth, without saying a word of the batteries or entrenchments hidden within it, though both an Austrian and a Prussian battalion had already suffered severely in an attempt to carry them. The Duke of York, who had never contemplated so foolhardy an attack, wisely thought it best to make no complaint. The battalion itself, to judge by a letter from one of the officers to Lord Buckingham, was very indignant with the Duke; and there is every probability that its complaints reached the ear of Pitt. I mention this because, though the matter is in itself a small one, it gives conclusive evidence of the incessant friction which arose from the indiscipline of the British officers and from the mistrust which the Allies felt for each other. It is safe to conjecture that this uninformed criticism of generals by their subordinate officers continued throughout the campaign; and the preservation of the letter above mentioned among Lord Grenville's papers is proof that such criticism was not disregarded by their powerful patrons at home. Unfortunately there is too much reason to fear that this evil even now is not unknown in our Army.[1]

During the following days the Allies were considerably strengthened by the arrival of successive detachments of Hanoverians and of one brigade of British cavalry under General Ralph Dundas;[2] but already Murray, with his American experience, had awoke to his weakness in light troops, and was recommending the acceptance of two offers to raise corps of foreign

[1] *Dropmore MSS.* Lieut.-colonel Freemantle to Buckingham, 13th May 1793. Calvert, p. 79. *Narrative by an Officer of the Guards,* i. 29-31. Murray to Dundas, 10th May (private) 1793. There are some significant omissions from his public letter of the same date as published in the Gazette. *Auckland Correspondence,* iii. 58.
[2] 7th, 11th, 15th, 16th Light Dragoons.

1793. riflemen and Polish Uhlans.¹ The primitive tactics of the French were beginning to tell. The raw levies understood war to signify the killing of the enemy—even of one man rather than none at all—and the saving of themselves. When therefore a mass of them was set in motion, the bravest men advanced, taking advantage of every shelter afforded by the ground, and did their utmost to shoot their opponents down; while the rest ran away or remained at a safe distance, to return in a fierce tumultuous swarm if the enemy showed signs of wavering, but not otherwise. However, on the 21st, Coburg, much rejoiced by the reinforcement of British and Hanoverians, judged himself strong enough to pursue his plan of campaign, and decided to drive the French from their camp at Famars preliminarily to the investment of Valenciennes. Meanwhile, to the general regret, Mack resigned his post on Coburg's staff, owing partly to ill-health, partly to his sense of Thugut's antagonism to him;² and the Prince of Hohenlohe, a veteran of seventy-one, was called from Luxemburg to take his place. It was, however, enough at that time that the attack should be designed by an Austrian General to ensure that it should be repugnant to all good sense.

May 21.

The entrenched camp of Famars embraced two broad parallel plateaux, divided by the little river Rhonelle, which lie immediately to the south of Valenciennes. The western plateau, that of Famars, has a length of about four miles, and abuts on the village of Artres; the eastern, which is broader and less clearly defined than the other, has a length of about three and a half miles, and terminates at the village of Préseau. Both are practically flat upon the summit, unenclosed, and covered with crops. The ascent to them is steepest from the west and south, and the valley dug between them by the Rhonelle, though not deep, plunges down so abruptly as to present sides of sharp though short declivity. The ridge of Famars was protected by a

¹ Murray to Dundas, 15th and 17th May 1793.
² Witzleben, ii. 194.

series of detached flêches and redoubts placed on every commanding point on the northern, western, and southern sides. The passages over the Rhonelle at Artres, and at Maresches, a mile and a half above it, were defended by strong entrenchments and batteries, and all the fords on this narrow but deep and sluggish stream had been destroyed. The eastern ridge was fortified by a continuous entrenchment with three redoubts, which was carried for nearly a mile along the length of the summit. The force at hand for its defence was about twenty-five thousand men, besides which five thousand men held the fortified position of Anzin; while a small detachment due west of it at Aubry maintained communication with the post of Hasnon, still further to north and west.

1793.

The attack of the main position was assigned to two principal columns, of which the left or southern was placed under command of the Duke of York, with orders to assemble his force on the heights between Préseau and Maresches, and to assail the right flank of the position. This column was made up of sixteen battalions, eighteen squadrons, and thirty-eight reserve-guns,[1] of which the brigade of Guards[2] and the eight squadrons of Dundas's brigade were British. The second principal column consisted of twelve battalions, of which three were the English of Abercromby's brigade,[3] twelve squadrons and twenty-three reserve-guns, with five pontoons, under the Austrian General Ferraris. His orders were to assemble between Saultain and Curgies, a little to the north-east of Préseau, to drive the enemy from their positions east of the Rhonelle, and to cross the river

[1] That is to say, guns not allotted to the infantry as battalion-guns.
[2] The brigade was reckoned at four battalions, the flank companies being massed into a fourth battalion.
[3] The Fourteenth and Fifty-third, with the flank companies of these two regiments and of the Thirty-seventh, massed into a third battalion. Witzleben (ii. 199) gives a larger number of British troops, calling all squadrons and battalions in British pay by the name English.

1793. itself, or at least feint to do so. Besides these, a third column under Count Colloredo was to observe Valenciennes from between Estreux and Onnaing, and to protect Ferraris's right flank; a fourth, further to the right, under Clerfaye, was to attack the entrenched camp of Anzin; a fifth still further to the right under Knobelsdorf was to march from St. Amand against Hasnon; and a sixth and seventh under the Crown Prince and Prince Frederick of Orange were to move respectively from Tournai upon Orchies, and from Menin upon Turcoing. Finally, on the extreme left or western flank, there were an eighth column, under General Otto, to protect the Duke of York's left by an advance by Villerspol upon Quesnoy, and a ninth to disquiet the French on the Sambre from Bavai. The scheme was typically Austrian; that is to say, too full of science to leave room for sense.

May 23. The morning broke in dense fog, so that the main attack did not begin until near seven o'clock, when the Duke of York's column, after marching most of the night, made its way with little resistance to Artres. There failing to force the passage of the river, which was defended by five batteries, the Duke left his heavy guns with about a third of his force to engage the French artillery, and proceeded with the rest higher up the stream to Maresches, where a ford was found, and the passage was with some trouble and delay accomplished. Meanwhile Ferraris attacked the long entrenchment on the eastern ridge, opening fire from three batteries, while Abercromby on the right and four Austrian battalions on the left advanced to the assault, and carried the works with little difficulty, capturing seven guns and over one hundred prisoners. Two French regiments of cavalry, which tried to turn the scale against the assaulting columns, were most gallantly charged by the Austrian Hussars and the Hanoverian Life Guards, and actually defeated, notwithstanding that the victorious troops had all the disadvantage of a steep ascent against them. Coburg then halted Ferraris's column, until further news should come of the Duke of York's advance. But the Duke, after making a wide turning movement by Querenaing and driving the French from their outlying defences, found himself at sunset at the foot of the most formidable ascent in the whole position, crowned at different points by four redoubts which flanked each other. Thereupon, since his men had been on foot for eighteen hours, he decided to defer the attack till next morning. Elsewhere, the success of the various columns was indifferent. Knobelsdorf could win no more than the outworks of Hasnon; Clerfaye failed to take the camp of Anzin; and, though the Prince of Orange drove the French from Orchies, his brother, Prince Frederick of Orange, was foiled before Turcoing. Coburg gave orders for renewal of the attack on the entrenchments of Famars and Anzin at daybreak of the 24th; but it was found that the French, after reinforcing the garrison of Valenciennes, had evacuated all their positions and retired to Bouchain. The trophies of the Allies were seventeen guns, captured at various points, and three hundred prisoners; and the further loss of the French was set down, doubtless with exaggeration, at three thousand killed and wounded. Even so the results of the day were unsatisfactory. The Austrians, of course, blamed the Duke of York; and Murray, without specifying who was in fault, wrote privately that a great deal more might have been done.[1] But, in truth, no one except an Austrian of that period could have looked for great results from so feeble and faulty a plan of attack.

1793. May 23.

May 24.

However, the ground was now clear for the siege of Valenciennes; and Coburg, as a compliment to the Duke of York, offered him the command of the besieging force, including fourteen thousand Austrians. There was much division in the British Cabinet over this piece of politeness, for Ministers were still in the dark as to Austria's general intentions; and some of

[1] Murray to Dundas, 24th May 1793.

1793. them feared that the troops under the Duke of York might be so much crippled by the siege of Valenciennes as to be unfit for the subsequent siege of Dunkirk. However, notwithstanding their suspicions of some sinister design on Austria's part, the Duke received permission to accept the command; though Coburg was careful to attach General Ferraris to his staff with secret orders to take the entire direction of the operations upon himself.[1] The chief of the English Engineers, Colonel Moncrieff, was urgent for storming the town without further ado, and was confident that, if his plans were followed, the place could be taken within twelve days; but though Murray was wholly of Moncrieff's opinion, Ferraris would not hear of it. A fortnight was therefore spent in collecting heavy artillery, after which

June 13. ground was duly broken on the 13th of June, before a greater and a lesser horn-work on the east side of the town. About twenty-five thousand men were actually employed on the siege, while the remainder, about thirty thousand men, formed the covering army; and, practically speaking, active operations upon both sides ceased except round the walls of the beleaguered fortress.

Yet, far away to westward, there had been a movement disquieting to the British. On the 29th of May forty transports, conveying the second brigade of British cavalry,[2] came into Ostend; whereupon Captain Carnot, knowing the slackness of the Dutch garrisons at Furnes and Nieuport, which covered that place, determined to surprise them from Dunkirk, and then by a swift march forward to seize and burn the British shipping. Moving

May 30. out accordingly on the night of the 30th, he reached Furnes at daybreak, drove the Dutch headlong from the town, and was hoping to follow them up to Nieuport,

[1] Witzleben, ii. 210-211. This author states that the Duke of York asked for the command of the siege, which I believe to be absolutely incorrect, and indeed incredible. See Murray to Dundas, 26th and 29th May; Dundas to Murray, 30th and 31st May 1793.
[2] Blues, Royals, Greys, Inniskillings.

1793. tions, with its inevitable consequence of strained relations between him and the General in the field.¹

Meanwhile the siege of Valenciennes went forward slowly and methodically, much more so, indeed, than seemed necessary either to Murray or to Moncrieff, though bad weather was accountable in some measure
July 10. for the delay. At length, on the 10th of July, Condé surrendered after a severe bombardment, and was occupied in the name of the Emperor Francis. Twelve
July 22. days later Mainz opened its gates to the Prussians, though the garrison was twenty thousand strong, and had still bread and wine to last for some days. Finally,
July 26. on the 26th, an assault was delivered in three columns upon the two horn-works of Valenciennes, one column being led by a storming party of the Guards, and supported by part of Abercromby's brigade. The attacks of all three succeeded with little loss, and Murray, after a strong altercation with the Austrian engineer, insisted, in defiance of Ferraris's orders, upon making a lodgment in the greater horn-work.² Thereupon,
July 28. on the 28th of July, the French General, Ferrand, capitulated. The place was taken over, like Condé, in the Emperor's name, amid the loud applause not only of the citizens but of the garrison, who trampled the tricolour under foot and hailed the Duke of York as King of France. All three of the captured garrisons were permitted to return to their own place, on condition that they should not fight against the Allies during the remainder of the war.

The French Government, however, found important employment for these troops at home; for during the months of May, June, and July matters in France had gone from bad to worse. The arbitrary interference
May 5. of the Jacobin Commune of Paris with property and commerce had irritated the better class of citizens all over the country; and Marseilles, Lyons, and all Brittany

¹ Dundas to Murray, 29th May, 14th June, 12th July; Murray to Dundas, 18th June and 16th July 1793.
² Murray to Dundas, 25th July.

when the whole of his troops with one accord fell to the 1793. plunder of the town, heedless of their officers, and in a short time were reeling or lying in all directions, hopelessly drunk. Far from seizing Ostend, he was thankful that the Dutch did not return and cut his helpless battalions to pieces.[1]

Nevertheless, the movement fulfilled the useful purpose of frightening the British Cabinet. Dundas was possessed by a kind of superstition respecting Ostend, having apparently some idea that it might be held as the gate of the Austrian Netherlands from the sea, even if the rest of the country were evacuated. Though the place itself was part of the Austrian dominions, the guardianship of the whole of the coast, and indeed of the right flank of the Allied army, was entrusted to the Dutch; and in spite of all protests the Dutch declined to do anything for its defence. Ostend was in fact indefensible, being divided by an unbridged estuary which cut it in two at every flood tide, and was safe from a French attack only for so long as Menin, Ypres, and Nieuport were held by the Allies. The Duke of York and Murray therefore regarded it as of no military value, though of some temporary convenience, looking upon Antwerp and the Scheldt as their true base and channel of communication with England. Nothing, however, would convince Dundas of Ostend's insignificance. He took the place under his own control, sent heavy ordnance to be mounted for its defence, appointed a special officer, General Ainslie, to take command of it, and plagued Murray so incessantly to fortify it that the Duke of York, for the sake of peace, consented to raise a few entrenchments on a small scale. The Duke had hardly done so, however, before he received a rebuke from Dundas for spending too much money; whereupon he, of course, suspended the work, being, as Murray said, at a loss to know how to proceed. This was the beginning of a more minute and persistent interference of Dundas with the conduct of the opera-

[1] *Vie de Carnot*, i. 321, *sq.*

burst into revolt. The news of the reverse at Famars, 1793. and of a disaster which had occurred two days later in La Vendée, only made the Commune more desperate. The Committee of Public Safety, supported by the Girondists, sought to conciliate both revolted towns and foreign enemies; but the Jacobins, by stirring the mob of Paris into insurrection, overawed the Convention into the total overthrow of the Girondists. The supremacy of June 2. the party of violence meant as usual the destruction of all obedience among the troops. At the end of April and during May, the Committee of Public Safety had passed sundry decrees[1] for reinforcing the army and for the improvement of its discipline, by the establishment of a military code and military courts, and by driving away the swarms of women who, whether as wives, mistresses, or actual soldiers, attached themselves to all ranks, from the General to the private. The base and contemptible Minister of War, Bouchotte, took good care that these salutary orders should not be executed. Custine, on succeeding to the command of the army in Flanders after the death of Dampierre, May 25. had by exhortation and a few terrible examples restored subordination in some measure, and gained the respect and confidence of his men. Bouchotte, insanely jealous of him, not only gave him no support but rather flooded his camp with low ruffians and with foul literature, for the deliberate encouragement of indiscipline.[2] The same influences were employed in La Vendée, where the volunteers deserted in whole battalions, and the basest pretexts were put forward for the evasion of service.[3] Nothing indeed but failure upon failure in the field could result from the policy of the Jacobins. Kellerman complained that his army of the Alps was hopelessly

[1] Poisson, ii. 335-344.
[2] *Ibid.* 344; Rousset, 218-231.
[3] Poisson, ii. 363 *sq.* The Vendéens let their prisoners go on parole, shaving their heads for greater certainty of identification. Thereupon great numbers of the French soldiers voluntarily shaved their heads in order to evade further service, pleading that their parole could not be violated.

1793. overmatched; and on the 12th of June the army of
June 12. Italy was utterly routed at Saorgio. Even the forces of corrupt and demoralised Spain successfully invaded Roussillon, captured Bellegarde, and threatened Ollioure and Perpignan. Yet Robespierre still held his shield over Bouchotte; and the Jacobins sought to escape from the consequences of their own folly by the execution of Custine, Biron, and other generals, and by the imprisonment, often followed by decapitation, of all officers who had met with defeat in the field. Thus did the countrymen of Voltaire emulate and outdo the countrymen of Admiral Byng. Further decrees, ordaining the death of all grown men and the destruction of all
July 26. property in Vendée, and stigmatising Pitt as the enemy of the human race, showed sufficiently that the ruling faction in Paris was animated by the fearful desperation which springs from the consciousness of guilt.

At the beginning of August, therefore, the position of France seemed to be, and in the presence of active and intelligent enemies would actually have been, hopeless. Not only in the north and east was danger threatening; it was still more urgent in the south, where Lyons, Marseilles, and above all Toulon, the great naval arsenal of the Mediterranean, were in arms against the Convention. Great Britain had concluded alliances
April 25. with Sardinia, with Spain, and with the Court of
May 25. Naples, in order to unite all the forces of the Medi-
July 12. terranean against France; and Lord Hood's fleet of fifteen ships, though disgracefully belated, and indeed only manned by the help of three British regiments, had anchored at Gibraltar on the 19th of June.[1] Moreover, Corsica also had risen against the Convention, under the leadership of the old patriot Paoli, the hero of many a London drawing-room during the days of his exile in England. Such a series of events could not but attract Dundas's eye more strongly to the

[1] The regiments were the 11th, 30th, and 69th. Hood hoisted his flag at Spithead on the 6th of May, and sailed the 24th of May.

Mediterranean; and in July he sent Colonel, Lord 1793. Mulgrave, a very capable officer, to Turin, to stir up both Sardinia and the Austrians in Italy to an advance upon Lyons. Meanwhile the Convention summoned Kellerman with the army of the Alps to overawe that rebellious city, which, however, girded herself for a siege rather than yield; and before Kellerman could take Aug. 8. measures to coerce her, he was recalled to his former station by a successful movement of the Piedmontese against his advanced posts. Mulgrave, however, sent no Aug. 19. very encouraging report from Turin. The King of Sardinia was eager for action in co-operation with the British fleet, but jealous of Austria. The Austrian General De Vins was also ready to march upon Lyons or Marseilles in command of an united force of Austrian, British, Sardinians, and Neapolitans, but only on condition that the various contingents were raised to a sufficient strength, and the arrangements for subsistence placed absolutely under his control. Altogether Dundas came to the conclusion that nothing could be done in the Mediterranean during 1793, though Mulgrave gave a promising account of Corsica's readiness to place herself under British protection. The Minister therefore contented himself with sketching an elaborate and characteristic plan for a future campaign in that sea during 1794, reckoning that by that time the troops in Flanders, as well as those under orders for the West Indies, would have finished their work and would be wholly at his disposal. None the less he continually warned the Duke of York that he should shortly withdraw eight thousand Hessians from the force on the frontier of France; although, in the distracted state of that country, the one thing needful was to prosecute the campaign in that quarter with energy.[1]

[1] Dundas to Mulgrave, 8th July; Mulgrave to Dundas, 19th August; Memorandum dated Wimbledon, 27th August 1793. This last document is unsigned, and not in Dundas's handwriting, nor in his style. Possibly it was prepared by Pitt when staying with Dundas at Wimbledon; but I take the mention of Dundas's residence to be plain evidence that it represents his opinion.

1793. Unfortunately, after the fall of Valenciennes the Allies in Flanders, far from pressing their advantage, fell to debating what they should do next. It had been already agreed that the Austrians should give up ten thousand men to the Duke of York for the siege of Dunkirk; but Coburg, seeing the danger of the plan, made a last effort to avert it by submitting a new scheme for taking the offensive in concert with Prussia; he himself to move south-east upon Maubeuge from Valenciennes, while the Prussians should advance south-west from Mainz upon Sarrelouis. King Frederick William gladly assented, but the Duke of York protested, as under his instructions he was bound to do; and he was upheld by a messenger who arrived from Vienna at Coburg's headquarters on the 6th of August. Thugut had been at work on one of his usual subtilties. He had soothed Pitt by renouncing the exchange of Belgium for Bavaria, but had begged that Prussia might not be informed of the renunciation; for he was still secretly bent on obtaining Bavaria by some means, and had resolved to purchase it by the cession of Alsace. Hence it was his wish that the King of Prussia, and particularly the Austrian troops under General Wurmser who were serving with him, should move south into Alsace, and that Coburg should pursue the plan, already agreed upon, of besieging Quesnoy, while the Duke of York invested Dunkirk. Coburg thereupon gave way, though with no very good grace; and it was resolved that, before his army was separated from the Duke's, a general action should be fought, as an essential preliminary to the subsequent operations.[1]

The position of the French under General Kilmain was known as that of Caesar's Camp, which lies on the left bank of the Scheldt about two miles above Bouchain; but in reality it formed an irregular quadrilateral, of which a part of Villars's famous lines of La Bassée formed the northern side. Facing due east,

[1] Sybel, ii. 370-373.

Kilmain's front was covered by the Scheldt from Bouchain to Cambrai, his rear by the river Agache, which runs into the Sensée a little to the south of Arleux, his right by the Sensée, and his left by the wood and heights of Bourlon from Cambrai to Marquion. All passages over the Scheldt were closed by entrenchments, and the valley itself was flooded; all passages over the Sensée were equally defended, while the right from Cambrai to Agache was strengthened by fieldworks and abatis. Such a position, held by sixty thousand men, was formidable, and Coburg accordingly resolved to turn it by the south. The turning column, consisting of fourteen thousand men under the Duke of York, was to assemble about Villers-en-Cauchies and Saint Aubert, and to cross the Scheldt at Masnières and Crevecoeur, about five miles south of Cambrai. A second column of about nine thousand men under the Austrian General Colleredo, and a third of about twelve thousand under General Clerfaye, were to force the passage of the Scheldt in the front of the position. The remainder of the army, little less than half of it, was uselessly frittered away in posts of observation.

Murray, foreseeing that the French would retire as soon as they perceived the turning movement, begged persistently that more cavalry should be given to the Duke of York, in order to inflict some punishment on them. His request was refused, and the result was exactly that which he had expected. The Duke, after a march of eleven hours on a day of extraordinary heat, found his troops too much exhausted to pass the river at Masnières; and Kilmain, withdrawing quietly in the night, made good his retreat upon Arras with little loss, though the British cavalry made a few prisoners. The Austrians, of course, blamed the Duke of York, though Coburg had sent Hohenlohe with him for the express purpose of superintending his operations; but the arrangements of the day opened Murray's eyes to the essential vices of the Austrian tactics. "We were not in force to attack the enemy," he wrote;

1793.

Aug. 7.

1793.
Aug. 7.
"the Duke's column was a long way from support, and between ourselves we were not sorry to see them go off." It was only after long schooling by disaster that the Austrians at last abandoned a system of which the rottenness was clear to the much despised Briton.[1]

After the engagement, Coburg pressed the Duke of York to remain with him for yet another fortnight, in order to renew the attack on the French army or to take Cambrai, the last fortress that blocked the way into France. But the Duke could only obey his instructions as to Dunkirk, which had lately been reiterated by Dundas;[2] and the two armies accordingly parted. Coburg, weakened by the withdrawal of nine thousand Prussian troops, and not yet compensated by the restoration of fourteen thousand Austrians from the Rhine, resolved to besiege Quesnoy, and meanwhile spread his force in several detachments from Denain to Bettignies. The Duke assembled his whole force of about thirty-seven thousand men[3] at Marchiennes

Aug. 13. on the Scarpe on the 13th of August, and on the 15th marched in two columns north-west by Baisieux and Turcoing upon Menin. From Baisieux the route lay across the front of the great fortress of Lille, and of the French fortified posts extending from that city

Aug. 18. to Dunkirk; and on the morning of the 18th, soon after the advanced guard of the southern column had moved from Turcoing, heavy firing was heard in the direction of Linselles, about two miles to the west of that place. The Prince of Orange, for reasons best known to himself, had seized the opportunity to sally out from Menin, and surprise the French posts of Blaton and Linselles, which being accomplished, he left two weak battalions to hold them, and retired.

[1] Ditfurth, i. 69. Witzleben, ii. 263-64. Murray to Dundas (private), 9th August 1793.
[2] Witzleben, ii. 264, 370. Dundas to Murray, 1st August 1793.
[3] Ditfurth, i. 73. $47\frac{1}{2}$ battalions, 58 squadrons. British, 5200 infantry, 1300 cavalry; Austrians, 10,000 infantry, 1000 cavalry; Hanoverians, 9000 infantry, 1600 cavalry; Hessians, 5500 infantry, 1500 cavalry. Total, 29,700 infantry, 5400 cavalry, 1900 artillery.

About mid-day the French returned with five thousand men and drove out the Dutch; and an hour or two later an aide-de-camp came galloping into Menin to ask for help. The Duke of York at once ordered out the brigade of Guards, which had just arrived at Menin after a severe march, with a few guns, under General Lake. The three battalions, without their flank companies, and therefore little over eleven hundred strong, at once turned out, and traversed the six miles to Linselles in little more than an hour, but, on reaching it, found not a Dutchman there. They were, however, saluted by a heavy fire of grape from batteries which they had supposed to be in possession of the Dutch; and thereupon Lake determined to attack at once.

1793.
Aug. 18.

The hill, on which the village of Linselles stands, is fairly steep on its northern face, and was further strengthened by two redoubts before the village itself and by a barrier of palisades on the road, while its flanks were secured by woods and ditches. Lake at once deployed into line under a heavy fire of grape, and, after firing three or four volleys, charged with the bayonet and drove the French from the redoubts and village. He then halted and re-formed on the southern side of the hill, not without apprehensions lest the enemy should rally and make a counter attack while he was still unsupported. Fortunately, however, the French were not equal to the attempt, being still of the inferior quality which was inevitable under the foolish administration of the Jacobins, and so puny in stature that the Guards cuffed and jostled them like a London mob, without condescending to kill them.[1] Lake was therefore left unmolested on his ground, until at nightfall six battalions of Hessians arrived, in reply to his urgent messages for reinforcement, to relieve him. His trophies were twelve guns, seventy prisoners, and a colour, but his losses amounted to one hundred and eighty-seven officers and men killed and wounded; and no real object whatever was gained. The action was un-

[1] Hamilton, *History of the Grenadier Guards*, ii. 285.

1793.
Aug. 18.
doubtedly most brilliant, and the conduct of the men beyond all praise; while Lake's swift decision to escape from a most dangerous situation by an immediate attack stamps him as a ready commander. But it is a grave reflection upon the Duke of York that he should so thoughtlessly have exposed some of his best troops to needless danger, leaving them isolated and unsupported for several hours. It is still less to his credit that, when he finally relieved them by a detachment of Hessians, he actually left these also isolated and unsupported within striking distance of a superior enemy during the whole night, for no better purpose than to rase some paltry French earthworks which a few hours would suffice to throw up again. Because the Prince of Orange was guilty of one act of signal foolishness, there was no occasion to outdo him by another.

At Menin the army was parted into two divisions. The first, consisting of the Hanoverians, ten British squadrons and foreign troops, or about fourteen thousand five hundred men, under the Hanoverian Marshal Freytag, was to form the covering army; the other, of nearly twenty-two thousand men, including the rest of the British troops, under the Duke in person, was
Aug. 19. appointed to besiege Dunkirk. On the 19th, Freytag marched from Menin by Ypres upon Poperinghe, which
Aug. 20. he occupied with his main body on the 20th, at the same time pushing his advanced guard further north-west to Rousbrugge on the Yser. On the following
Aug. 21. day a detachment of Hessians, with great skill and at small cost to themselves, drove the French from Oost Capel and Rexpoede into the fortress of Bergues, with the loss of eleven guns and some four hundred men; and Freytag then took up his line of posts to cover the besieging army. His left was stationed at Poperinghe, covered by the fortress of Ypres; and from thence the chain ran north-west to Proven on the Yser, and westward up that stream by Bambecque to Wylder, where it turned north, and passing midway between

Bergues and Rexpoede rested its right on a point called the White House, hard by the canal that runs from Bergues to Furnes. On the 23rd and 24th Freytag drove the French from Wormhoudt and Esquelbecque with the loss of nineteen guns, and surrounded Bergues by detachments at Warhem to east, Coudekerque to north, Sainte Quaedypre to south, and Steene to west. From this last an outer chain of posts was extended southward to Esquelbecque, and thence east by Wormhoudt and Herzeele to the Upper Yser at Houtkerque. The whole circuit thus embraced measured about twenty-one miles; from which it will be concluded that Freytag was a believer in the cordon-system.

1793.

Aug. 23, 24.

Meanwhile the Duke of York marched on the 20th to Furnes; and on the 22nd, moving thence parallel with the strand, he drove in the enemy's advanced posts upon the entrenched camp of Ghyvelde, which the French abandoned in the night. On the 24th, after several hours of sharp fighting, which cost the Allies nearly four hundred men,[1] the French were forced back from the suburb of Rosendahl into the town; whereupon the Duke entrenched himself in his chosen position, with his right resting on the sea and his left at Tetteghem, facing full upon the eastern side of the town and about two miles distant from the walls.

Aug. 20.
Aug. 22.

Aug. 24.

The field of operations for the Duke's army may be described roughly as a quadrilateral, of which the sea forms the northern side, the canal from Dunkirk to Bergues the west, the canal from Bergues to Furnes the south, and a line drawn from Furnes to the sea the east. From east to west the ground thus enclosed was divided roughly into two parallel strips; the northern half consisting of the sandhills known as the Dunes, together with a narrow plain of level sandy ground within them; and the southern half of a huge morass called the Great Moor, which consisted partly of stand-

[1] The British engaged were the flank companies of the Guards and Line, and Royal Artillery. Casualties, seventy-eight killed and wounded.

1793. ing water, partly of swamp, but was all open to inundation by admitting the tidal water from the sluices of Dunkirk. Tetteghem, which formed the left of the Duke's position, rested upon this swamp, and commanded the only road that led across it to the White House, and so to Freytag's army. The position itself was in many respects disadvantageous. It was much broken up by innumerable little ditches, hedges, and patches of brushwood, all of which the troops had to clear away with their side-arms for want of better tools; it was wholly destitute of drinking water, that in the canals being brackish, and that found in the wells unpalatable; and, finally, it lay open to the minutest inspection from the tower of Dunkirk Cathedral. But this was not the worst. The Duke had looked for a fleet to cover his right flank, which had suffered from the enemy's gunboats during the march upon Ghyvelde, and for transports bringing heavy artillery and other materials for the siege; and so far there was not a sign of them. "The principal object is to have what is wanted and to have it in time," Murray had written to Dundas in July; and Dundas had replied that he was preparing artillery for Dunkirk, but was in great

Aug. 27. want of gunners.[1] At last, on the 27th, the transports came with gunners, but without guns; on the
Aug. 29. 29th a frigate, the *Brilliant*, and a few armed cutters
Aug. 30. appeared off the coast; and on the 30th Admiral Macbride arrived to concert operations, but without his fleet.

By an arrangement, which was repeated at least once more during the war, Macbride's squadron, being intended to act with the Army, had been removed from the control of the Admiralty and placed under the orders of Dundas, so that he alone was responsible for this miscarriage.[2] "Why did you not earlier suggest to

---

[1] Murray to Dundas, 16th July; Dundas to Murray, 19th July 1793.
[2] *Dropmore Papers*, ii. 444. Dundas to Grenville, 12th October 1793.

me naval co-operation at Dunkirk ? " he wrote angrily 1793. to Murray on the 29th. "I had always a conceit in my own mind as to its usefulness, but I had no authority to quote for it." This is an instructive example of Dundas's methods as a War Minister. The project of besieging Dunkirk emanated from himself and his colleagues in the Cabinet, and from them alone. No military man approved it, though the Duke of York, out of loyalty to his masters, dutifully upheld it; and Dundas never quoted any authority but his own for undertaking it, nor for his constant interference with the conduct of the operations that preceded it. He had indeed a good many conceits in his own mind, the most fatal of which was that he understood how to conduct a campaign; and he had privately made vague inquiries of Murray, as to the need for naval co-operation, so far back as in April.[1] But the point was not one to be decided off-hand by a General, for the question was not whether a fleet would be useful, but whether it would be able to act in all weathers; and this purely naval matter appears never to have been considered at all. On the 15th of August, when the army was not yet committed to the siege, General Ainslie, the commandant at Ostend, warned Dundas that he had not realised the difficulties which might be raised by adverse weather at Dunkirk; and, as a matter of fact, the *Brilliant* and her little flotilla had not been on the coast three days before they were blown away from their station. It was doubtless owing to the uncertainty of naval assistance that Murray gave the apparently astounding opinion, that he regarded a squadron as useful though not very material to the siege. But, apart from this, Dundas had so often pressed the Duke of York to spare his eight thousand Hessians, which formed almost one-third of the force under his command, for another service, that it was impossible for the Duke to divine whether Ministers really intended to pursue their design against Dunkirk or not. If they did, he had

[1] Dundas to Murray, 16th April 1793.

1793. a right to look to them for a siege-train and for the necessary naval assistance, neither of which were forthcoming, partly because Dundas did not know his own mind, partly because he had committed himself to a multiplicity of operations beyond the power, after ten years of steady neglect,[1] of either Army or Navy to execute. However, as a substitute for the much-needed ships and guns, he sent to Murray a plan for the siege of Dunkirk, drawn up by no less skilled a hand than that of Lord Chancellor Loughborough, possibly with some hope that the deficiencies of Downing Street might be made good by the wisdom of the woolsack. There are times when the conceit of British politicians becomes touchingly ridiculous.

Very different was the change that had come over military administration in France during the same month of August. Upon the re-election of the Committee of Public Safety, which took place on the 10th, Barrère, who was a member, approached Prieur of the Côte d'Or with the words, "We none of us understand military matters. You are an officer of Engineers; will you join us?" "There is only one man in the Convention for the place," answered Prieur, "and that is Carnot; and I will be his second." Accordingly, on the 14th of August two new members were added to the Committee, namely, Carnot, who assumed control of the formation, training, and movements of the armies, and Prieur, who took charge of arms, ammunition, and hospitals. These, together with Robert Lindet, formed the most remarkable group in one of the most remarkable administrative bodies which has ever existed. Three of the members, Barrère, Billaud Varennes, and Collot d'Herbois, were known as the Revolutionaries, their business being to guide and inspire political emotions; three more, Robespierre, Couthon, and Saint Just, were concerned with legislative proposals, police, and the revolutionary tribunal, and bore the ominous name of the High Hands; but the last three, Carnot, Prieur, and Lindet,

Aug. 10.

Aug. 14.

---

[1] Calvert, vi. 118; Murray to Dundas, 3rd September.

1793. were to crush the cordon-system out of existence, hung like an angry cloud to the south of Dunkirk; but the Generals of the Allies took no heed. Murray, indeed, had heard with anxiety of the increase of the French force in his front, and had begged Coburg for reinforcements, which, however, could not be spared.[1] On the east Coburg was busy besieging Quesnoy, with corps of observation thrown out to east and west. He had called up eight thousand men under General Beaulieu from Namur to strengthen his weak cordon about Bouvines and Orchies; but to west of Beaulieu the space from Lannoy to Menin was guarded by some thirteen thousand Dutch—spiritless, disaffected troops, whose leader, the Prince of Orange, was half inclined to give up the contest because he could obtain no assurance as to his indemnity. West of the Dutch was the gossamer line of Freytag, and behind it lay the Duke of York, conscious, first, that Souham had opened the sluices, and that the steady rise of the inundation would shortly sever his communication with Freytag; secondly, that his right flank was under perpetual menace from the French gunboats; and thirdly, that his rear was insecure, since there was nothing to hinder the French from moving troops by sea. In this situation he was trying to take a fortress, which he was not strong enough to invest and which the enemy could consequently reinforce at any moment, by attacking it upon one side only without heavy artillery. He endeavoured to protect his flanks by throwing up entrenchments in the Dunes, but found that they filled with water at the depth of two feet; and he was fain to disarm a frigate at Nieuport and bring up her heavy guns to the front, in order to arm batteries, not only against the town, but towards the sea, to drive away the French gunboats. Thus at the beginning of September he was able to open fire; but meanwhile Houchard had not been idle, for on the

Aug. 27. 27th he fell in force upon the posts of Beaulieu and the Prince of Orange at Cysoing and Turcoing. He was

[1] Murray to Dundas, 28th and 31st August 1793.

were known simply as the Workers, a title which no 1793. men have ever more worthily earned.

Carnot's advent showed itself in prompt and energetic action. On the 16th of August a decree was passed for Aug. 16. a levy *en masse*, which, it was estimated, would add four hundred and fifty thousand men to the army; and, since all exemptions and substitutes were disallowed, the cream of the nation began for the first time to flow into the ranks. Moreover, on the 29th of August, the old Aug. 29. white coats of the Monarchy were abolished and the blue coat of the National Guard made uniform for the entire host, a significant hint that henceforth there were to be no further distinctions between regular troops and volunteers, but a single National Army. Prieur, on his side, set up manufactories of arms and gunpowder in Paris, and stimulated the search for saltpetre in all directions. The result of these measures lay hid in the future; but immediate and important movements were made on the northern frontier. Carnot, with true insight, had divined that England was in reality the most dangerous member of the Coalition, and that to foil her before Dunkirk would, from its political results, be the most telling of all military operations.[1] Withdrawing therefore several thousand troops from Coburg's front and from the army of the Moselle, he massed them to westward, until, on the 24th of August, there were, apart Aug. 24. from the eight thousand men in Dunkirk itself, some twenty-three thousand in the entrenched camp at Cassel, four thousand about Lille, and twelve to fifteen thousand more from the Moselle within a few days' march. Kilmain had been recalled after the retreat from Cæsar's camp, and replaced by General Houchard in supreme command. Among Houchard's subordinate generals was Jourdan. Dunkirk itself had for commandant General Souham, an energetic officer whose fame was soon to spread wide; and one of Souham's battalions was commanded by Lazare Hoche.

Thus new men and a new principle of war, which

[1] *Vie de Carnot,* i. 394.

beaten back by Beaulieu with the loss of four guns; 1793. but the Dutch abandoned Turcoing with suspicious alacrity, and would have retired to Tournai and Courtrai had not Murray sent a detachment to support them. "There is ill-will and disinclination to favour our present operations," wrote Murray; and indeed the fact is hardly surprising.[1] The marvel is that he and the Duke of York should have remained in so dangerous a position, when a successful attack by the enemy upon the Dutch and a bold push forward would have carried the French to Furnes, and cut off the whole of the army about Dunkirk beyond rescue. Indeed, though they knew it not, this operation had actually been projected at the French headquarters.[2]

With the arrival of his last reinforcements from the Moselle, Houchard resolved to attack the scattered posts of Freytag, the nearest of which lay little more than five miles from Cassel. Assembling thirty thousand men, he led them forward early in the morning of the 6th of September in five columns, under Generals Van- Sept. 6. damme, Hédouville, Colland, Jourdan, and himself, the three first against Poperinghe, Proven, and Rousbrugge, the two last against Wormhoudt, Herzeele, and Houtkerke. Though outnumbered by ten to one, the Hanoverians and Hessians fought most obstinately, and the troops opposed to Houchard and Jourdan would have held their own behind the Yser at Bambecque, had not the French already penetrated to Rexpoede in their rear. The fighting lasted all day, the garrison of Dunkirk at the same time keeping the besieging army employed by a sortie; and at night Freytag retired upon Hondschoote, ordering General Walmoden, who commanded the posts about Bergues, to withdraw all his troops to the same place. Taking the road by Rexpoede, in ignorance that it was actually occupied by the French, Freytag blundered into the midst of a French picquet, and was, with the young Prince Adol-

[1] Murray to Dundas, 31st August 1793.
[2] Sybel, ii. 417.

1793.   phus (afterwards Duke of Cambridge), wounded and
Sept. 6. taken. The Prince was rescued, but the Field-Marshal was secured, and would have remained a prisoner, had not General Walmoden, guessing that his chief might have fallen into a trap, marched at once upon Rexpoede, stormed it then and there, and delivered him. Walmoden then assumed command, and, resuming the retreat, took up a convex position before Hondschoote, with his right leaning on the Bergues canal, his centre just in advance of Hondschoote itself, and his left resting on the village of Leysele. The whole of his front was covered by a maze of small ditches and hedges, through which the only access was a single dyke leading into Hondschoote; but this broken ground, however valuable for defence, deprived the Allies of the use of their cavalry, which was the arm in which above all they overmatched the French. From thence Walmoden sent urgent messages to the Duke of York for reinforcements; and it is significant that, owing to the inundation, no troops could reach him except by way of Bergues. There was therefore no reason why Freytag's corps should not have been concentrated about Hondschoote, where it would have covered the besiegers quite as efficiently and with infinitely less risk. The British Commander-in-Chief cannot be acquitted of neglect herein, though Freytag must bear part of the blame for extreme dispersion of his force.

Houchard tried to follow up his success on the
Sept. 7. following day by a renewed attack, but his soldiers would not follow him; and Walmoden, though he took the precaution to send his heavy baggage to
Sept. 8. Furnes, repulsed him without difficulty. On the 8th, however, Houchard advanced with fresh troops to the assault, himself leading twenty battalions, covered by several guns, to the principal attack by the dyke; while a second column on his left, under General Leclerc, tried to force its way along the canal, and a third, under Colland and Hédouville, moved up from Rousbrugge against Leysele. The plan of attack was faulty,

for by holding Walmoden in front and pushing the main force round his left flank, which stood in the air at Leysele, Houchard must have compelled him to retire or to be driven into the swamp of the Great Moor. The new French tactics, however, made good the General's shortcomings. Taking cover cunningly behind every hedge, ditch, or bush, the French sharpshooters poured a deadly fire into the Hanoverians and Hessians, who stood exposed in their array of three ranks deep, discharging their volleys by platoons with perfect discipline, and pressing forward with the bayonet when the French ventured too near to them. But the volleys did little injury to dispersed and hidden skirmishers, and the charge with the bayonet was hardly more effective over such intricate ground; for the French did not await it, but ran back to the nearest hedge and resumed their fire from behind it. For four hours Walmoden's brave men held their own with the greatest gallantry in spite of heavy losses, until at noon their last reserves of ammunition were exhausted, when, their left flank being seriously threatened by Hédouville, the General gave the order to retire in two columns upon Furnes. A battalion of Hessians covered the retreat with splendid tenacity; and the wreck of the force took up a position between the two canals just to the south of Furnes. The infantry had lost at least a third of its numbers, perhaps even more; and the Hanoverians, by the confession of their own officers, were no longer to be depended upon.[1] It was no reproach to them that this should have been so, for no troops in the world can endure heavy punishment during consecutive days of unsuccessful fighting, and remain unshaken. Their losses had been very great, and their behaviour, by the admission both of friend and foe, most admirable.

1793.
Sept. 8.

On this same day the garrison of Dunkirk made a sally against the besiegers in the village of Rosendahl, but was repulsed, though not without loss to the

[1] Murray to Dundas (private), 9th September 1793.

1793. Allies; and in the afternoon came the news of Wal-
Sept. 8. moden's defeat. At four o'clock orders were given for
the heavy baggage to be sent back to Furnes, and at
eight a Council of War was held. The Duke of York
hoped to carry off his siege-guns, but the French,
having control of the sluices, had shut off the water
from the canal, so that it was no longer of use for
transport; and it was represented that delay might
mean the overpowering of Walmoden's army and the
cutting off of the Duke's retreat by Furnes. At
midnight therefore the besieging army retired in two
columns, with a confusion which shows the inefficiency
of the Duke's staff. Transport being scarce, the
waggons were so much overloaded that the animals
could hardly drag them, and the troops were constantly checked by fallen horses and overturned vehicles.
Further, no orders for the retreat were sent to the two
battalions in Tetteghem, and the whole of one column
was delayed until they could join it. It was thus ten
Sept. 9. o'clock on the morning of the 9th before the entire
force reached the camp at Furnes, fortunately without
the least molestation from the enemy.[1] There the Duke
effected his junction with Walmoden, but took the
precaution to send his heavy baggage to Ostend. He
had been fortunate in escaping from a most dangerous
position with no greater loss than that of his thirty-two
heavy guns; but incessant fighting, a swampy encamp-
ment, bad drinking-water and fever had grievously
thinned the ranks of his army. It was reported at the
time that the siege of Dunkirk had cost the Allies from
one cause and another nearly ten thousand men;[2] and
I am disposed to think that this estimate is not exaggerated. "Our whole enterprise is defeated and our
situation embarrassing in the extreme," wrote Murray.
"It is uncertain whether we can maintain ourselves
behind Furnes; at all events I think we shall hold good
behind the canal at Nieuport." This letter reached

[1] *Narrative of an Officer*, pp. 91-92; Ditfurth, i. 127-128.
[2] *Ibid.* pp. 91-93, and see Ditfurth, i. 126.

Downing Street on the 11th; and on that same day Macbride's fleet appeared before Nieuport, three weeks too late.

1793.
Sept. 11.

But the troops found some consolation for their failure in the momentous news that on the 26th of August Lord Hood, by the invitation of the inhabitants, had occupied Toulon.

CHAPTER VI

1793. DURING August and the first week of September the results of the Government's incoherent enterprises began to crowd one upon another with rapidity enough to bewilder a clearer head than that of Dundas. The forces that he had set in motion in the Colonies seemed at first to promise great results at small cost. On the
April 12. 12th of April General Cuyler, obedient to his instructions, embarked a force of about five hundred men[1] at Barbados, and sailed under convoy of Vice-admiral Sir John Laforey's squadron to Tobago. The enemy was prepared for his coming, for, as was usual with Dundas's secret expeditions, the whole island of Barbados was apprised of the project as early as the General;[2] but
April 14. none the less Cuyler landed on the 14th at Courland Bay, stormed on the same night the French fort that crowns the hill above Scarborough, and captured the island with trifling loss. The news of this success reached London on the 1st of June, and was followed a month later by that of the bloodless capture of St.
May 14. Pierre and Miquelon by a small force sent from Halifax; but the next intelligence from the west was less satisfactory. Though by no means overtrustful of the representations of the refugees from Martinique, whom Dundas had recommended to him, and who assured him that eight hundred men would suffice to take the island, General Bruce embarked about eleven hundred troops

[1] Flank companies 9th, nine companies 4/60th, 50 artillery.
[2] Cuyler to Dundas, 22nd March 1793.

at Barbados on the 10th of June,[1] and sailed for the island with Admiral Gardner's squadron. After concerting operations with the French Royalists, he landed his troops on the 16th at Case Navire, for an attack on St. Pierre ; but a panic, which set in among the Royalist levies on the morning fixed for the action, convinced him that it would be hopeless to trust them, and he accordingly re-embarked on the 21st for Barbados, carrying his pusillanimous allies away with him. Here, therefore, was an initial failure on the part of the monarchical party, which had promised such easy possession of the French West Indies ; and Bruce did not hesitate to add that, since the Republicans had admitted all black men to rights of government in Martinique, any further attack would be hopeless unless undertaken by a considerable force.

1793. June 10. June 16. June 21.

The news of this abortive expedition reached London on the 13th of August ; and shortly afterwards came a letter from a gentleman in Tobago, warning the Government that French emissaries were busy all over the West Indies, and that there was great danger of a general rising of the negroes for the expulsion of the white proprietors from all the islands.[2] Here was information important enough to make Pitt think twice before he pursued his policy of cutting off the financial resources of the Revolution by ruining French West Indian trade, to say nothing of the fact that the said trade was already practically ruined by civil war in the French islands. There were other weak points in the French armour besides the West Indies, so many indeed that Ministers might be excused for finding it difficult to determine which of them they should assail. The only method of overcoming that difficulty was that they should clearly define to themselves their object in making war.

Aug. 13. Aug. 29.

[1] Battalion companies of the 21st ; flank companies (apparently) of the 9th, 15th, 21st, 45th, 48th, 3/60th, 4/60th, 67th. Bruce speaks of eighteen flank companies, perhaps including details of the 25th and 29th, which were serving on the fleet as marines.
[2] Mr. Balfour to Dundas, 20th July 1793.

1793. First then, there was the counter-revolution in the south of France; where Lyons still defied the forces of the Convention, and where it was hoped that Sardinia, in return for the two hundred thousand pounds given her by the recent treaty, would intervene effectively, with Austria at her side. Next,[1] from this same quarter there came the very important but unexpected news that commissioners from Toulon, after some parley with Lord Hood, had agreed to declare for the Monarchy and the Constitution of 1791, and to give up to him the shipping, forts and arsenal, to be held in trust for King Lewis the Seventeenth until the end of the war. In return for this, however, they made the natural but very significant request that troops should be landed for their protection. Here, therefore, was the Government committed, though by no act of its own, to serious operations by land on the side of the Mediterranean. The responsibility assumed by Hood was very grave; and for a time he hesitated to incur it. "At present," he wrote, two days after issuing his public reply to the offers of the commissioners, "I have not troops sufficient to defend the works. Had I five or six thousand good troops I should soon end the war."[2] He therefore anchored at Hyères and, mindful of the British alliances with the Mediterranean powers, wrote to the British Ambassador at Naples for such forces as could be spared, at the same time asking help of the Spanish Admiral, Don Juan de Langara, who was lying with his squadron off the coast of Roussillon. Before, however, these reinforcements could arrive, he was so far satisfied by the assurances of the French that he

Aug. 28. sailed into Toulon harbour and, landing fifteen hundred marines and soldiers who were acting as such, occupied the principal forts that defended the outer harbour. While thus engaged he was joined by Langara with the

[1] The official despatch reached the Government on 13th September, but the fact was known to Pitt on the 7th. *Dropmore Papers*, i. 422.
[2] Hood to Dundas, 25th August 1793.

greater part of his squadron, who announced that he had one thousand troops ready to disembark at once, and had left four ships behind to bring three thousand more from the army in Roussillon. Full of gratitude, Hood gave Langara effusive thanks, and appointed Admiral Gravina, the Spanish officer next senior to Langara, to be commandant of Toulon.

All this was known to the Government by the 15th of September, by which time, as shall presently be told, more reassuring news had arrived from Flanders, to the effect that the French had been checked, and that Coburg's army had been liberated for action by the surrender of Quesnoy. It therefore behoved Ministers seriously to reconsider their military policy, and to make up their minds definitely whether their object in the war was to be, as they professed, resistance to unprovoked aggression and the overthrow of the Convention, or simple annexation of French possessions. In Flanders their great enterprise, undertaken with no military knowledge and for no military purpose, had failed; they were as much as ever in the dark as to the ultimate designs of Austria, and they could not but be sensible that remarkably little had been accomplished by the Allies on the Rhine. As a matter of fact Frederick William, having discovered a glaring instance of Thugut's duplicity in the matter of the Bavarian exchange, had at the end of August practically decided to withdraw from the Coalition. This was as yet unknown to the British Ministers, for their ambassador at Vienna, Sir Morton Eden, was completely duped by Thugut; but they were conscious of an increasing coolness on the part of Prussia towards the war against the Revolution. In such circumstances, although the northern frontier of France was, from its proximity, the most convenient sphere of operations for a British army, they might well consider the advisability of removing all their forces from that quarter in order to concentrate them at Toulon, which Lord Hood's negotiations had already engaged them to protect.

1793. French successes in the north could be only temporary and unprofitable if the Allies, by assisting the counter-revolution in the south, should deprive the Convention of the richest provinces of France. A French force at Antwerp itself would signify little, if the Allies could rally the party of order from Bordeaux to Marseilles to put down the tyranny at Paris.

On the other hand, it was no light task to hold Toulon against all the host that the Convention might turn upon it. Sir Charles Grey, when consulted by Pitt as to the force that would be required, declared that fifty thousand good soldiers would be no more than adequate; upon which Pitt dismissed him with the remark that he hoped that a smaller body would suffice.[1] Probably he rested his opinion on Lord Hood's phrase about ending the war with six thousand men, which was of course nonsense, and nonsense of a kind which naval officers at that period were far too ready to talk and Ministers to hear. Mallet du Pan, the clearest head in Europe, was urgent for making the counter-revolution in the south the centre of attack upon the Convention; but American experience had shown that the support of a disloyal faction is the most unstable of all foundations upon which to build the conduct of a war. Men of the same nation will fight each other like devils, but, when foreigners are called into the contest, all parties tend to combine against them. Moreover, the southern provinces were by no means unfavourable to the Revolution at large. On the contrary, they had enthusiastically acclaimed and supported it, until threatened with the massacre and pillage which had disgraced Paris in September 1792. It was therefore essential that the Allies should enter France in such strength as to be independent of all help from French forces in the field. It was certain that the worthless brothers of King Lewis the Sixteenth and their parasites would claim to place themselves at the head of any

---

[1] Brenton's *Naval History*, i. 101.

counter-revolution; and their presence alone might 1793. suffice first to paralyse and then to subvert it.

Again, it was doubtful whether any efficient force of the Allies, other than British, could be collected in the south. Sardinia was perfectly ready to advance at once to the rescue of Lyons if Austria would join her; and the Austrian General De Vins, being of the school of Loudoun, was anxious to show his superiority to his rivals Coburg and Clerfaye of the school of Lacy. But here again the mischievous rapacity of Thugut neutralised all action, for he would allow no Austrian troops to move from Italy unless Sardinia consented to concede the Novarese to Austria, indemnifying herself at the expense of France. The British Ministers were aware of this dispute about the Novarese, for Mulgrave had reported it,[1] and they had sufficient experience of the Imperial Court to divine that it would not quickly be settled. Apart from Austria and Sardinia, troops could be obtained from Naples and from Spain; but the assistance of two courts so effete and so corrupt was not likely to be efficient. In any case, it was certain that, if any real advantage was to be gained from the possession of Toulon, every British soldier must be withdrawn from other operations, and that the whole of England's military force must be assembled at that point. If this were impossible, it were best to instruct Hood to make sure of the French fleet, destroy the arsenal, and carry away the inhabitants who had yielded the place into his hands.

Then, besides Flanders and Toulon, there was La Vendée, where the contemptible ruffians whom the Jacobins had appointed to be generals were suffering defeat upon defeat. If by the help of the insurgents Nantes could be seized as a base, it was no very long march from Angers or Tours or Orléans to Paris; but here again it was not a small force that was required, but every British battalion that could be spared.

Lastly, if the Ministers wanted to secure indemnities

[1] Mulgrave to Dundas, 1st September 1793.

1793. only, the West Indies lay open to them. No doubt it would be of advantage to possess the famous harbour of St. Lucia, to deliver Dominica from the menace of Martinique, her neighbour to windward, and to master Guadeloupe, with the nest of privateers which preyed upon all British commerce in those seas. Above all, the capture of Haiti would ensure at once the security of Jamaica, the possession of a country whose wealth, though more than half destroyed, was still appreciable, and the transfer to a British garrison of St. Nicholas Mole, which, being the gate of the Windward Passage and the Gibraltar of the West Indies, would give safe transit for the trade of the archipelago to England. Such an enterprise, however, would equally demand the entire land-force of the British Isles. It would be necessary not only to take the islands but to hold them, and to hold them not only, as heretofore, against the climate and against the fleet and armies of France, but against the entire negro population, which the Revolution had summoned to its aid. There was, as there still is, abundance of records of former attacks upon all those islands, showing that at the best of times each British battalion in the West Indies required to be renewed in its entirety every two years, and at the worst of times might be completely extinguished by a single hot season. Of all plans, therefore, this would be the most difficult, the most perilous, the most costly in execution and maintenance, and the least damaging to France; not to mention the fact that the overthrow of the Convention, which had authorised the equality of the black man with the white, was really essential to its permanent success. Thus it should at least have been obvious to the Government that out of the four spheres of operations it could hope to act with effect in one alone; and then only by throwing into the chosen sphere every trained soldier that it could muster.

Blind to all such considerations, Ministers decided not to select one, or at most two, of these spheres, but to fritter away their handful of forces between all four.

Indeed, Dundas's orders between the 11th and 18th 1793. of September form a notable specimen of his ideas of carrying on war. The news of the failure at Dunkirk Sept. 11. had at first completely unnerved him; but, on realising how critical was the position of affairs in that quarter, he directed eight battalions[1] to embark for Ostend, as a temporary measure. Then he warned the Duke of York that five thousand of his Hessians must be held ready to sail to Toulon as soon as this reinforcement reached him, and that the eight battalions themselves would be required elsewhere at the beginning of October. On the same day he wrote to Lord Hood that everything must give way to the importance of holding Toulon; that he had appealed to Austria for troops; and that he would send Hood the five thousand Hessians aforesaid, as well as two battalions out of the five stationed at Gibraltar. Four days later he warned General Bruce to be ready to receive at Barbados fifteen battalions, which were under orders for active service in the West Indies. Lastly, at the same time or very little later, he framed a design for a descent upon St. Malo and for the occupation of the Isle D'Yeu, off the coast of La Vendée.[2] It is now time to return to Flanders, and to follow in detail the reaction of Dundas's genius upon the operations in that quarter.

In the first peril of the retreat from Dunkirk the British commanders seem to have entertained serious thoughts of re-embarkation;[3] but were reassured when Houchard did not follow up his stroke upon the force of Walmoden. For this the French general has been much blamed; and indeed his failure to destroy the Duke of York's army was made the excuse for bringing him shortly afterwards to the guillotine. But in truth Houchard had lost his true oppor-

[1] 3rd, 19th, 27th, 28th, 42nd, 54th, 57th, 59th.
[2] Dundas to Murray, 11th, 14th September; to Hood, 14th September; to Bruce, 18th September 1793; Pitt to Grenville, *Dropmore Papers*, ii. 43 (the conjectural date of September attached to this last is wrong, and should be changed to October).
[3] *Narrative of an Officer*, i. 92.

1793. tunity through the unskilfulness of his attack upon Walmoden, wherein his troops, already half starved and less than half disciplined, had been seriously shaken by their losses. He therefore reinforced the garrisons of Bergues and Dunkirk, and, in the hope of relieving Quesnoy, fell with thirty thousand men upon the flank of the Dutch cordon from Poperinghe and upon its front from Lille. His success was at first encouraging, for
Sept. 12, 13. he defeated his opponents completely with the loss of forty guns and three thousand men, and captured Menin. General Beaulieu, who had been dispatched with over four thousand Austrians to the assistance of the Dutch, for some reason refused to act with them, but checked the advance of the French beyond Menin, and occupied Courtrai. The Dutch fled in disorder to Bruges and Ghent; and for the moment it seemed as though communication between the Duke of York and Coburg was
Sept. 12. hopelessly severed. The Duke, after leaving a detachment under Abercromby at Furnes, had withdrawn to the rear of the canal between Nieuport and Dixmuyde, in order to secure his retreat to Ostend; but he now
Sept. 14. ordered Abercromby back to Nieuport, and marched with the bulk of his force eastward to Thorout, where he was joined by two battalions[1] from England. From
Sept. 15. thence on the 15th he moved southward to Roulers; and on that day the situation underwent a total change. Beaulieu, being attacked by Houchard before Courtrai, waited only for a reinforcement which the Duke had hurried forward to him, when, taking the offensive, he utterly routed the French, who fled in the wildest confusion, and, pursuing them to Menin, recaptured the
Sept. 16. town. The Duke entered Menin on the following day, where he received letters from Coburg who was already at Cysoing, not more than eighteen miles to the south, reporting that since the fall of Quesnoy he had gained
Sept. 12. a brilliant victory over one of Houchard's divisions at Avesnes-le-Sec. This action, which, though almost unknown to Englishmen, still remains one of the greatest

[1] 19th, 57th, three companies of the 42nd.

achievements in the history of cavalry, was not only 1793. most glorious to the Austrians in itself, but was important as showing that the new tactics of the undisciplined French army were inapplicable to any but a strongly enclosed country. Nine Austrian squadrons, counting some two thousand men, without a single gun, had utterly dispersed seven thousand French, chiefly infantry, cut down two thousand of them, captured two thousand more, and taken twenty guns, all with a loss to themselves of sixty-nine men. These successes effectually checked the advance of the French. Houchard, after the defeat at Menin, had already given the order to retreat; and the French retired to their former positions before Cassel, Lille, and Maubeuge.

Then arose the question what should be done next. The season was advancing, but events had marched rapidly in Paris since the revolt of Toulon. Following hard upon the news of Houchard's reverse came tidings that the Duke of Brunswick had defeated the French with a loss of four thousand men at Pirmasens, on the northern frontier of Alsace; and this succession of disasters stirred the Jacobins to the ferocity of panic. On the 17th two savage laws were passed, which practically Sept. 17. placed all lives and all property at the arbitrary disposal of the reigning faction; and then the demagogues turned with fury upon the generals. Loudest among them was Robespierre, who, profoundly jealous of any man who could do what he could not, was suspicious above all of soldiers. Thanks to his denunciations, Houchard and his staff were recalled under accusation of treason; Sept. 21. and thereby another blow was added to the many already struck at the army. The troops were greatly demoralised by the continual change of commanders,[1] whom the Commissioners of the Convention promoted or deposed at their arbitrary pleasure; and the commanders themselves were not less demoralised by the certain prospect of death if they failed to achieve the impossible with troops that were neither fed, nor clothed,

[1] Poisson, ii. 525-526.

1793. nor paid, nor disciplined. The Allies, therefore, could still reasonably look for success from a concentration of their whole army and a vigorous offensive.

Dundas, since the failure at Dunkirk, had become suddenly an advocate for keeping the whole of the forces together, and for making an attack upon the enemy before undertaking any further enterprise;[1] but with what precise object a general action was to be fought he did not say, for the very sufficient reason that he did not know. The British Ministers, so far as they favoured any operations at all in Flanders, would have preferred a second attempt upon Dunkirk; but they gave, or professed to give, a free hand to the commanders, flattering themselves that, if the attempt were abandoned, the British troops would be the sooner released for service at Toulon and, above all, in the West Indies. Coburg, on the other hand, had already put forward what was at any rate a definite plan, though upon the old lines. He wished to besiege Maubeuge, which was certainly an important point, since it formed the chief link in the communications between the French armies of the north about Lille, and of the Ardennes about Givet and Philippeville, while its entrenched camp made it a point for a formidable concentration of the French forces at large. Moreover, it obstructed the passage of the Austrian troops from east to west, compelling all reinforcements from Luxemburg to fetch a compass by Namur and Charleroi before they could join the army of Flanders. The Dutch agreed to come forward again to further the operations; and before the British Government, upon Murray's representation, could finally make up its mind to co-operate with the Austrians, Coburg had crossed the Sambre with forty thousand men and invested Maubeuge.[2]

Thereupon there followed the usual distribution of troops into a cordon. The besieging force numbered

[1] Dundas to Murray, 13th September 1793.
[2] Dundas to Murray, 13th, 14th, and 28th September; 14th October. Murray to Dundas, 14th and 15th October 1793.

fourteen thousand, the covering army, including twelve 1793. thousand Dutch, twenty-six thousand men ; and to the Duke of York was entrusted the task of protecting Flanders along a front of some forty-five miles, from Cysoing to Nieuport. For this purpose Coburg gave him about sixteen thousand Austrian troops in addition to those in the pay of Britain ; but, owing to the vagaries of the British Minister for War, the corps was exposed to the most dangerous risk. Hardly had the eight reinforcing battalions from England joined the army in Flanders, before Dundas ordered four of them to return at once, and the remainder as soon as possible. Further, not content even with this, he gave Murray to understand that the embarkation of the Hessian corps from Flanders was only deferred, and hinted that a part of his artillerymen might also be spared for Toulon. Now Dundas knew perfectly well that the troops had passed through a very severe campaign, had fought several actions and had suffered heavy losses ; he knew perfectly well that no adequate steps had been taken for filling up the gaps in the ranks ; he could hardly have been ignorant that winter was approaching ; and Murray had twice warned him that the French were rapidly increasing their forces between Lille and the sea. Yet the Minister, though he had given the generals nominally a free hand, calmly withdrew battalion after battalion, until at last Murray told him plainly of the danger of the situation. The state of the army was most distressing : the force in British pay was reduced to twelve thousand fighting men, or less than half of its original numbers ; the sick and wounded of the whole army under the Duke's command numbered at least nine thousand, or more than one-fourth ; the troops were dangerously dispersed along a very wide front ; and, though Murray did not mention this, the Austrian Government had deprecated all field-fortification, on account of the damage that might ensue to meadows and the banks of canals.[1] Finally, he gave warning

[1] Ditfurth, i. 147.

1793. that, if the enemy made an attack, the Duke would be obliged to abandon Ostend. Dundas's reply to this was very characteristic. Without a word to Murray he ordered the Commandant at Ostend to retain the second batch of four battalions which, by his own order, had been sent there for re-embarkation to England; and he wrote an angry letter to Abercromby, a subordinate officer, first expressing horror at the idea of abandoning Ostend, and then regretting that attempts had been made to keep those same four battalions in Flanders. "It would be impossible," he wrote, "to restrain the just indignation of the country, if, for the sake of feeding an army under a Prince of the blood, so substantial an interest to this country as that of the French West Indies had been sacrificed."[1]

Apart from the fact that such language, especially when addressed to a subordinate concerning his chief, was utterly unbecoming a Minister and a gentleman, it was not obvious why an army should be starved, whether in the matter of empty ranks or of empty stomachs, simply because it happened to be commanded by a Prince of the blood. If its presence in Flanders were an embarrassment to the Government, the simple remedy was to withdraw it altogether, rather than leave it so weak as to be in peril of destruction; for there was no lack of employment for the troops elsewhere. This amazing outburst is no solitary instance of Dundas's bad taste, much less an unique example of his incapacity.

Meanwhile Murray's apprehensions increased; and events soon came to justify them. Jourdan, on Carnot's recommendation, had succeeded Houchard in command of the army of the north; and, with Carnot himself at his back, he now concentrated forty-five thousand men Oct. 7. at Guise for the relief of Maubeuge, leaving the remainder of his troops, some sixty thousand men, extended in a long line to the sea. Coburg sent pressing entreaties for reinforcements to the Duke of York, who at once

[1] Murray to Dundas, 6th October. Dundas to Ainslie, 12th October; to Abercromby, 13th October 1793.

moved about nine thousand men to Cysoing, and leav- 1793.
ing half of them there, proceeded with the rest—chiefly Oct. 10.
the wreck of the British troops—to join hands with the
Austrian advanced corps a little to the south of Quesnoy
at Englefontaine. It was, however, to no purpose, for
Jourdan, having increased his force to sixty thousand
men, attacked Coburg furiously on the 15th and 16th at Oct. 15, 16.
Wattignies, and, despite very heavy loss to himself both
in men and in guns, compelled him to raise the siege of
Maubeuge. The Dutch, who had not behaved well in
the action, retired to Mons; but Coburg moved his headquarters to no greater distance than Bavai. He was
there meditating further attacks upon the French, when
the Committee of Public Safety, intoxicated with the
success at Wattignies, ordered Jourdan peremptorily to Oct. 18.
take the offensive and to drive the hordes of the tyrant
into the Sambre, which river, it may be observed, at that
moment flowed between the opposing armies. A second
and still more ludicrous order bade him keep his force Oct. 22.
together, menace several remote points simultaneously,
operate in two divisions against Mons and Tournai,
and withal act with prudence. Jourdan, however, not
daring to attempt the passage of the Sambre, sent on the
20th one division to assail Marchiennes, and another
under Souham against all the Allied posts from Cysoing
to Werwicq, which last was held by six thousand men
under Count Erbach. Both attacks were successful,
though Marchiennes was retaken on the 24th; and on
the 22nd Erbach was forced to fall back to Tournai and Oct. 22.
Courtrai, abandoning even Menin. On the 22nd likewise
a division from Cassel attacked Ypres, while another
from Dunkirk under Vandamme captured Furnes, and,
pressing northward with twelve thousand men, opened on
the 24th the bombardment of Nieuport. The town had Oct. 24.
been but hastily fortified, and the garrison consisted of
only two weak Hessian battalions, a few dragoons, and the
British Fifty-third Regiment, in all fewer than thirteen
hundred men. For the moment it seemed certain that
the British would be cut off from their base.

1793. Murray, foreseeing this, had ordered all stores, beyond what was necessary for the moment, to be removed from Ostend. The Commandant disembarked some of the four battalions which, pursuant to Dundas's order, were about to sail to England; and Dundas, on hearing of the situation, at once sent Major-general Grey, the appointed Commander of the West Indian expedition, with four more battalions[1] to take charge of the troops at Ostend, giving him full liberty to defend it or to bring away the whole of the eight battalions, as he might think best, without reference to the Duke of York. Meanwhile he clamoured for reports as to the intentions of Coburg, and for explanation of the reasons for the possible abandonment of Ostend; for it had not yet occurred to him that the French, by attacking in overwhelming force, might compel the Commander of the Allies to conform to their plan of operations instead of pursuing his own.[2]

However, matters soon righted themselves. The

Oct. 24. French were driven back with heavy loss from Cysoing and Orchies. The garrison of Nieuport held its own gallantly, being reinforced on the 27th by another battalion of Hessians and by a few gunners from Ostend; and meanwhile the Duke of York was hastening back from Englefontaine and Tournai, while Coburg followed him westward with half of his army as far as Solesmes, midway between Cambrai and Landrecies. On the evening of

Oct. 28. the 28th Grey arrived at Ostend, and at once sent the Forty-second and four companies of Light Infantry to the help of Nieuport. On the same evening the Duke of York having reached Camphin, a few miles east of Cysoing, detached Abercromby with four battalions and two squadrons[3] northward against the French post

---

[1] 3rd, 28th, 54th, 59th. They had already made one voyage to Ostend and back.

[2] Murray to Dundas, 18th October; Ainslie to Dundas, 23rd October; Dundas to Grey, 26th October; to Murray, 27th October 1793.

[3] Two Austrian battalions, 3rd Guards, flank battalion of Guards, one squadron 7th L.D., and one squadron 15th L.D.

at Lannoy. The place was captured with little loss, and 1793. the British Light Dragoons did terrible execution in the pursuit of the flying enemy. On the following night Oct. 29. another division, under the Austrian General Kray, made a brilliant attack upon the post of Marchiennes, driving out the French with a loss of nearly two thousand men and twelve guns, at a cost to itself of fewer than one hundred casualties. Meanwhile the French, on hearing of the Duke of York's advance upon their flank, had retired from Menin and Ypres; and early on the next morning Vandamme, fearing to be cut Oct. 30. off, retreated from before Nieuport, leaving four guns and a quantity of ammunition behind him. So easy was it to change the whole face of affairs by concentrating a compact force against one point and rolling up a cordon from end to end. It is almost comical to observe how at first both sides used the cordon-system; how the French, after abandoning it with success, relapsed into it once more; and finally how the Allies, also abandoning it under British direction, in their turn gained the upper hand.

Throughout this anxious period the interference of Dundas with the operations had been incessant, and his tone by no means the most courteous. The incoherence and folly of his orders may best be judged from a summary of the reply which Murray at length found time to write on the 20th of October. "Let me point out to you," he wrote, in effect, "that the same messenger brought to me from you, first, advice to besiege St. Quentin; secondly, orders to keep a body of troops at Ostend; and, thirdly, strong exhortations against division or detachment of our force. As to Ostend, if Nieuport holds out, it is safe for the winter; and I see no reason why Nieuport should not hold out. As to St. Quentin, this means taking a train of artillery there in the month of November. It means also that twenty thousand out of Coburg's twenty-five thousand men must be detached, while the remaining five thousand remain quietly between three fortified towns and a forest, from which

1793. fifty thousand men may attack them from all sides at any time. Further, the detached force must draw its subsistence from a distance of forty miles across the whole French army without any other protection than that of those five thousand men." "I beg pardon," he continued, "for taking up your time with this kind of argument, which it was not your intention to enter into, but I think it is right to show that, perhaps, people in England are not more infallible in their judgments than those upon the Continent." Irony so keen sped home even through the dense armour of Dundas's conceit. "You have not sufficiently weighed the feeling of this country," he answered, taking refuge in bluster, "if you think that any successes could have counter-balanced the loss of Ostend." Murray hastened to soothe him by pointing out that the Duke of York, though against his own military judgment, had strictly obeyed the Cabinet's instructions as to the protection of Ostend, and that it was not Grey who had saved it but the Duke himself, who, before he knew of Grey's arrival, had forced Vandamme to retire by threatening his communications.[1]

This sharp passage of arms silenced Dundas for the time, though, as will be seen, it taught him little wisdom for the future. Meanwhile, after a few small affairs of outposts, the campaign came to an end. The Emperor of Austria sent orders to Coburg to fight a general action, for no particular object; and the Committee of Public Safety gave the like instructions to Jourdan, in the hope that he might be able to advance to Namur and so to threaten the Austrian line of communication. But neither was in a position to obey. The campaign had been most arduous, as a war of posts must always be, not only from the innumerable minor actions, but from the strain imposed on the troops by constant vigilance and by endless marching to and fro to reinforce the threatened points of the cordon. The

[1] Murray to Dundas, 30th October and 12th November; Dundas to Murray, 8th November 1793.

losses on the side of the Allies had been great : those of 1793.
the French had been enormous, not only in men but
in material, for the Allies had taken from them over two
hundred guns. In brief, both armies were thoroughly
exhausted ; and yet the Allies had accomplished comparatively little, owing partly to the false plan imposed
by England, partly to the false tactics of the Austrian
commanders, still more to the misunderstandings and
jealousy that make coherent action so difficult in an army
composed of many nations. On the Rhine likewise
little had been effected. Soon after the victory of
Pirmasens the King of Prussia left his army for Posen ;
and, though the Austrian General Wurmser drove the Oct. 13.
French in utter confusion from the lines of Weissen-
burg, yet, in consequence of faulty dispositions and of
the half-hearted co-operation of the Prussian troops,
an advantage which might have been decisive was turned
to little account. Prussia, in truth, was not anxious to
aid Austria in gaining Alsace; while the Polish question,
as always, kept the two powers in an attitude of mutual
suspicion and mistrust. There was nothing, therefore,
left to the Allies but to take up cantonments for the
winter, which they accordingly did, while Grey and
the whole of the eight battalions with him returned
to England. The Allies had missed their chance in
Flanders ; it is now necessary to see what other
opportunities the British had lost elsewhere.

CHAPTER VII

1793. THE revolt of La Vendée had begun, as has been told, on the 10th of March 1793; and from that day until the 29th of June, when the insurgents were defeated in their attempt to capture Nantes, their career had been one of unbroken success. The district comprehended under the name of La Vendée was about seventy miles square, being bounded on the west by the ocean, on the north by the Loire, on the east by the road from Saumur on the Loire to Niort, and on the south by the course of the river Sèvre from Niort to the sea. Within these limits lies a blind, broken and difficult country of rolling hills, small enclosures, strong fences and innumerable by-roads and lanes, offering every advantage to those who are well acquainted with it, but puzzling beyond measure to the stranger. Here the gentry lived on their estates and were the natural leaders of the people; and by the end of April three gentlemen had formed very rude but efficient armies each of about ten thousand men. Few of these were regularly trained, but all were ready to assemble and fight when summoned, and after the action to return quietly to their work. Their tactics were simple enough. The boldest men and the best marksmen, knowing the country intimately, crept unseen round the flanks and rear of their enemy, harassing and alarming them into disorder; and at the right moment the remainder rushed in a tumultuous mass upon the front, and as a rule carried all before them. The principal leaders were the Marquis of Bonchamp, an accomplished soldier of real genius; D'Elbée, who

CH. VII HISTORY OF THE ARMY 153

had served in the cavalry, and Charette, a lieutenant 1793. in the Navy; but over these Cathelineau, who was not of the gentry, had held supreme command until his death in action before Nantes, when Stofflet, formerly a gamekeeper, after an interval succeeded him. After their failure at Nantes the insurgents still continued to fight with varying success, till on the 17th of July they inflicted on the Republican troops at Coron a defeat so crushing as to raise their ascendency higher than ever. Not long afterwards Monsieur Tinteniac came over to London as an emissary from the Vendeans to ask for arms, ammunition and artillerymen; but meanwhile the French regular troops, which had been released by the capitulation of Mainz, were sent to combat the insurgents; and, after many reverses, due to the incompetence of the Jacobin commanders, General Kléber won a great victory for the Republic at Oct. 17. Chollet. Bonchamp and D'Elbée fell in this action; but Larochejacquelin took command, led the wreck of Oct. 18. the Vendeans—thirty thousand fighting men and half as many useless mouths—over the Loire, and marching northward defeated his pursuers at Laval. This victory Oct. 25. not only retrieved the defeat of Chollet, but practically left it open to the insurgents to march, if they would, even to Paris.

A few days later, however, two emissaries arrived from England, bringing assurances that the British Government was well disposed to help the Vendeans, and had an expedition ready to join them at Granville or at any other point that they might select. How Dundas could have been so shameless as to hold out hopes of this kind to them, it is difficult to explain, for he was well aware that he could not send them a man;[1] and, indeed, it is said that an emigrant officer at Jersey warned them not to repose too much confidence in his promises. So far nothing had been done except to appoint Lord Moira, better known to us as the Lord Rawdon who had so

[1] *Dropmore Papers*, i. 431. This letter is conjecturally dated September. It should be 24th or 25th October.

1793.   greatly distinguished himself in America, to command
the expedition. However, the poor Frenchmen trusted
the British Minister, made their way northward slowly
Nov. 12. and irresolutely to Granville, attempted on the 12th
of November to surprise it, and were completely
defeated. On that very day, and not earlier, appeared
the first sign of preparation in England. Then Lord
Moira submitted a memorandum asking for twelve
thousand men, of which two hundred were to be
artillerymen with twenty guns, for a descent upon
France; his plan being either to capture the island of
Noirmoutier, a little southward of the mouth of the
Loire, and thence in concert with the insurgents to attack
Nantes, or, if the insurgents could master St. Malo, to
land there and push south upon Rennes. Dundas had
not a man to give to Moira at the moment; but
another division of four thousand Hessians had recently
joined the Duke of York, and as many more mercenaries
from Baden and Hesse-Darmstadt were expected in
Flanders by the end of the month. He, therefore,
ordered the four thousand Hessians to be embarked at
Ostend as soon as possible, and, taking from Grey the
eight battalions which had spent so much time wander-
ing backwards and forwards across the German Ocean,
made them over to Moira. Artillerymen, however,
were so scarce that not more than one hundred, of
which one-third were recruits, could be collected for
Nov. 17. him; and Moira on the 17th wrote that, if he was to
be confronted with deficiencies like these, he thought
the Ministers had better arrange the expedition without
consulting him, for he could not be responsible for any
shortcomings. Dundas therefore addressed Murray,
begging that the Duke of York would spare a company
of gunners; but the Duke himself was so short of
artillerymen that he had been obliged to lay up two
of his field-howitzers in order to provide crews for
the cannon at Nieuport; and Dundas dared not weaken
Nieuport lest he should endanger his darling post of
Ostend. The artillery had been neglected and allowed

to deteriorate between 1784 and 1792;[1] no attempt had been made to augment it until 1793; and this was the not unnatural result.[2]

1793.

By some means Moira was persuaded to be content with something over one hundred gunners; and then arose a difficulty about guns, which were to have been supplied to him at Portsmouth but which were not forthcoming. Dundas wrote airily to Murray that the expedition to Brittany would sail on the 22nd of November; but both he himself and the Master-General of the Ordnance did their best, with considerable success, to ensure that it should not. Portsmouth had been selected as the place from which the West Indian expedition should start, and, since it was leaving England just at the time when it ought to have arrived at its destination, Grey was hastening his preparations with feverish energy, while Sir John Jervis, the Commodore who was to escort him, had even gone the length of seizing every lighter and boat in the harbour. "The confusion here is incredible," wrote Moira from Portsmouth on the 26th of November. "If Admiral Macbride and I had not slaved like dray-horses, things would not have been so forward. Between ourselves, I fear desperately that we shall find the Royalists beaten." Moira's fears were realised. He sailed on the 1st of December with less than half the force which he had requested, for the Hessians had not yet joined him; but on arriving before Cherbourg and coasting on to La Hogue next day, he found his signals on the coast unanswered, and not a sign of a Royalist. The insurgents had indeed won a victory at Antrain, some thirty miles south of Granville, on the 21st of November, and had for a moment decided to march to that town once more. But other counsels prevailed. They turned back to the

Nov. 26.

Dec. 1.

---

[1] It seems that this was the worst period through which the corps ever passed. Duncan, *History of the Royal Artillery*, ii. 13. Like the rest of the army, it suffered from insufficiency of pay.

[2] Moira to Nepean, 17th November; Dundas to Murray, 15th November; Murray to Dundas, 25th November 1793.

1793. Loire, and after an unsuccessful attack upon Angers recrossed the river, to be finally overthrown at Savenay on the 23rd of December. This ended the "great war" of La Vendée, though the guerilla warfare was still long to continue. Moira meanwhile returned to Guernsey with his whole force. Had he sailed on the 22nd he might conceivably have reached the coast in time to be of service. On the 2nd of December he was, by no fault of his own, too late.[1]

Dec. 23.

Here, therefore, was the project upon La Vendée come to naught, with the further result of depriving General Grey of one half of the force intended for the West Indian expedition. It was, therefore, a question for the Ministers whether Grey should be allowed to proceed at all; but nothing was further from their thoughts than to abandon their enterprise against the French Antilles. Pitt was firmly wedded to the scheme at the cost of all other objects, as also were Dundas and Grenville; and though Lord Auckland urged upon Grenville that the great object of Europe was to destroy the Convention, and that the fate not only of the war but of "the whole existing race of mankind" might be risked by the pursuit of conquests, yet no heed was paid to him.[2] Intelligence had been received of the landing, to be presently narrated, of British troops from Jamaica in St. Domingo, which had called forth the warm approval of Dundas;[3] and Grey had accord-

---

[1] Duncan, ii. 58. Moira to Nepean, 23rd, 25th, 26th November; to Dundas, 2nd December 1793. Edmund Burke took an interest in this expedition, and submitted a memorandum of 19th November, suggesting the employment of gunboats.

[2] *Dropmore Papers*, ii. 415, 443, 454. Pitt to Dundas, 11th October; Auckland to Grenville, 7th November 1793. Dundas received not a little encouragement in this folly from Lord Westmoreland, the Lord-Lieutenant of Ireland. "I fear our army in Flanders is ruined. I hope, however, that will not interfere with your West Indian schemes. Money will answer there [in Flanders]; and I am sure a thousand men in the West Indies will tell more than five thousand in Flanders." Westmoreland to Dundas, 28th and 30th September 1793. *S.P. Ireland.*

[3] Dundas to Williamson, 9th November 1793.

ingly been permitted to sail for Barbados on the 26th of 1793.
November. It was still possible to send Moira's troops
to join him, for Grey had started with only a part of his
storeships, and Jervis had left men-of-war to escort the
rest. There were, however, vague rumours of an intended descent by the French upon England ; the Brest
squadron was still at liberty ; and Lord Howe, with
the Channel fleet, preferred to lie in wait at Torbay
against the time when the enemy should put to sea,
rather than attempt to blockade them in Brest.
Dundas, having still command of Macbride's squadron, therefore took upon himself the task of ascertaining
how far the menace of invasion was real ; and in effect
Macbride's ships and Moira's battalions were kept in
hand to deal with a possible invasion of the French
or, if needed, to make a counter-descent upon France.[1]
The troops, therefore, stayed on board ship about
Southampton and the Isle of Wight for long after the
news of Savenay had arrived ; and the men, being overcrowded in the transports, fell sick and died by scores
of typhus-fever.[2] But never for a moment, during these
months from October to December, does it seem to have
occurred to Dundas that these unfortunate eight battalions, which had made so many useless voyages to Ostend
and elsewhere, were urgently required at Toulon.

Hood, it will be remembered, had occupied Toulon
on the 28th of August, and had on the same day been Aug. 28.
joined by the Spanish squadron under Langara. At the
moment when he entered upon negotiations with the
Royalists in the town, the forces of the Revolution, being
fully employed with the reduction of Marseilles and
Lyons, were none of them at hand ; but Marseilles fell
almost immediately, and the army of General Carteaux

---

[1] *Dropmore Papers*, Dundas to Grenville, 12th October 1793.
[2] Moira to Nepean, 8th December 1793. Monthly return of
eight battalions, 1st January 1794—4500 men, 800 sick, 32 deaths.
Return of nine battalions, 1st February 1794—5000 men, 900 sick,
25 deaths. Return of 1st March 1794—870 sick, 47 deaths. Dr.
Hayes to Cathcart, 1st February 1794.

1793. was thereby released to march upon Toulon. Hood reckoned Carteaux's force to be ten thousand strong, and was aware that it was to be joined by another army of uncertain strength; but he looked upon their coming with little alarm; and indeed his first brush with them seemed
Aug. 31. to justify his contempt. On the 31st of August a first detachment of about seven hundred and fifty French appeared at Ollioule, a village some three miles to the north-west of Toulon; whereupon on the same afternoon Captain Elphinstone of the Royal Navy marched out with six hundred troops, half British and half Spanish, to dislodge them. Though without artillery, Elphinstone promptly stormed the village, which was a post of remarkable strength, drove the enemy from it and captured four guns, all with a loss to himself of no more than twenty killed and wounded. There was, however, unavoidable danger in the town itself from five thousand turbulent seamen, who had been turned ashore from the disorganised French fleet; and Hood was not easy until he had disarmed four of the captured
Sept. 14. French vessels that were in worst repair, and shipped the seamen off in them to Rochefort, Brest, and L'Orient. Meanwhile the French force outside Toulon increased daily; but the Admiral seemed to be so little alive to the true nature of the situation that, on the 8th of September, he detached some of his ships under Commodore Linzee to Corsica, with instructions to blockade Bastia, San Fiorenzo, and Calvi, to offer to transport the French garrisons there to France, and, if possible, to reduce the forts. How he proposed to hold the forts, if reduced, he did not explain; and, indeed, it will presently appear but too evident that Hood, though an admirable seaman, was as ignorant as a Cabinet Minister of the conduct of operations ashore.[1]

Fortunately on the 6th of September Lord Mulgrave arrived at Toulon, having hastened thither from Turin upon the first intelligence of the occupation, and by

[1] Hood to Dundas, 13th and 14th September; to Linzee, 8th September 1793.

Hood's appointment assumed command of the British 1793.
troops. He brought with him as his aide-de-camp
Captain Rowland Hill, a young officer of but two years'
service, who had lately gained his rank by raising an
independent company. At Toulon, moreover, Mulgrave
took to himself an extraordinary aide-de-camp in Mr.
Thomas Graham of Balgowan, a gentleman forty-five
years of age, who, having lost his beautiful wife in 1792,
had joined Lord Hood's fleet as a volunteer in the hope
of distraction from his sorrow. Mulgrave took by no
means so sanguine a view of affairs as did the Admiral.
The force at his disposal was about twelve hundred men
of the Eleventh, Twenty-fifth, Thirtieth, and Sixty-
ninth Foot, all of them really part of the fleet's complement, with rather over three thousand Spaniards.
The latter, however, as he soon discovered, were, with
two solitary exceptions, utterly worthless, both officers
and men ; being the refuse of the Spanish regular army
and militia, with a strong infusion of convicts collected
on the coast of Barbary. In fact they were so wretched
a rabble that the Spanish General Ricardos had refused
to take them under his command in Roussillon. Again,
rightly or wrongly, Mulgrave distrusted the so-called
Royalists in the town; and, more important than all, the
French had naturally made little provision for the defence
of Toulon from the side of the land.

When first disembarked, the company-officers of the
British troops had been turned ashore to take up and to
fortify such positions as they thought best, there being
no general officer nor engineer to form a complete
scheme of defence ; for though there were officers of the
French Engineers in the town, who professed to give
assistance, these were judged to be not above suspicion.
On his first visit to the lines of defence Mulgrave noticed
one post, held by Spaniards, which was dangerously
exposed, and begged that it might be evacuated; but
before this could be done the French attacked and
drove out the garrison, with a loss of seventy killed,
wounded, and prisoners. The Spaniards made hardly a

1793. show of resistance, the French Royalists offered as little; and it was left to the British to cover the retreat.[1] The only hopeful feature was that the Spanish Admiral Gravina, who was by birth a Sicilian, was a very gallant officer, and most cordial in co-operation with his British colleague.

The defence of Toulon, on the land side, was in truth a very formidable undertaking. The harbour consists of a deep inlet, running, roughly speaking, from east to west, and branching out at the western or inner end into the shape of a cross. On the southern side the shaft of the cross is shut off by a peninsula about two miles long, which is connected by a very narrow isthmus with the mainland. The peninsula bears the name of Cepet, and the isthmus that of Les Sablettes. The southern arm of the cross is formed by another peninsula, known as the heights of La Grasse, which terminates to seaward in two small promontories, of which the southern bears the name of Balaguier, and the northern that of Eguillette. Over against Eguillette on the northern shore is another isthmus, with a building known as the Great Tower at the extremity; and these two points, Eguillette and Great Tower, formed the gate of the inner harbour. Within this inner harbour, at the head of the northern arm of the cross, stands Toulon itself, with its docks to seaward and its bastioned defences to landward. But the ramparts of the city alone were of little profit for its protection, being commanded on each hand by clusters of steep hills, and dominated by the lofty ridge of Mont Faron immediately in rear. Even in those days the town was within range of bombardment from several points on the land side, and accordingly a ring of outworks had been traced, and in some cases begun, upon all the surrounding hills. These were the posts now taken up by the Allies.

Beginning on the south-east of the town, Fort La Malgue stood on an eminence on the northern shore for the defence of the outer harbour; next, to north of

[1] Mulgrave to Dundas, 8th September 1793.

this, was Fort St. Catherine on an isolated hill; then 1793. Fort Artigues on a low spur of Mont Faron; then Fort Faron on one of the lower peaks; and finally Fort Croix de Faron on the highest peak of all, at the eastern extremity. The ridge of Mont Faron itself is about two and a half miles long, steep and rugged on the southern face, and along the northern front so precipitous that it was thought inaccessible. Indeed the only approach from the north was a zig-zag path, too narrow to admit two men abreast, called the Pas de la Masque, which reached the summit about half-way along the length of the ridge. It was therefore thought sufficient protection for the northern face to place a strong piquet at the head of this path, though Graham, who was something of a mountaineer, showed by practical example that an active man could ascend the cliff at more than one point to west of it. To the north-west of Mont Faron stood another work, Fort des Pomets, ill-placed because commanded by a higher ridge to west of it. A smaller work to south of this served to connect it with the lower and upper forts of St. Antoine on the western slopes of Mont Faron; and from thence minor posts, over against the western front of the town, carried the line southward down to the Fort of Malbousquet, which commanded both the town and the harbour. The whole circuit of these defences extended for some eight miles. They were not well designed, for they made little provision for mutual support; but the key of the whole was the Fort Croix de Faron, from which the remaining posts on the eastern side could be rendered in succession untenable. Incomplete though the works were, the fatigue imposed upon the troops by the routine of duty over this great perimeter was very severe. The men, having no tents, were much exposed to the weather; and Mulgrave dared not throw great labour upon them to improve the defences, lest he should wear them out. The strain bore hardest of all upon the British, who, since the Spaniards could not be trusted, were divided among all the posts. Altogether Mulgrave, though

1793. fairly confident, felt so uncertain for his safety that one of his first cares was to take such measures as he could for securing his retreat, and for burning the arsenal and dockyard.[1]

Before he had been in Toulon a fortnight, trouble began. Carteaux on the west and General Lapoype on the east received reinforcements and heavy guns; and Sept. 18, 19. on the 18th and 19th Carteaux opened fire from three batteries upon the heights at the head of the inner harbour, which were not silenced by the British men-of-war until several sailors had been killed and wounded, Sept. 20. and a gunboat sunk. On the following day Hood declared, quite correctly, that if the enemy obtained possession of Balaguier and Eguillette, the fleet would be driven from the harbour; and accordingly on the Sept. 21. 21st Mulgrave scraped together five hundred men, and, landing between Balaguier and Eguillette, selected a hill at the western end of the peninsula for the site of a redoubt, which should completely cover the outer roadstead. The French, attempting to disturb them, were quickly driven off; and the work proceeded with such rapidity that the guns were mounted within three days. The fort was named Fort Mulgrave, and the post together with its outworks received, from its strength, the title of Little Gibraltar. At the same time a detachment was established within range of Little Gibraltar on the isthmus of Les Sablettes, in order to prevent the enemy from giving annoyance from thence. Thus the perimeter of the defences was extended from eight to at least ten miles; and the British, who, even including seamen, were under fifteen hundred strong, were divided among eleven different posts.[2]

Such a distribution could not but be hazardous in the extreme; the more so since there had arrived a Sept. 16. few days before in Carteaux's camp a young Lieutenant-colonel, by name Napoleon Bonaparte, who had been appointed by Carnot to take the command of his

[1] Mulgrave to Dundas, 15th September 1793.
[2] Ibid. 24, 26th, 27th September 1793.

artillery. Fortunately, on the 27th, Hood was rein- 1793.
forced by a battalion of nearly eight hundred Sardinians, Sept. 27.
six Sardinian ships of war, and by two thousand Neapolitan
soldiers, with a promise of four thousand more
to follow. The former were excellent troops, the latter
not to be trusted ; but, to Mulgrave's disappointment,
the Austrians still showed disinclination to furnish
troops for Toulon. Meanwhile the enemy became
active, Lapoype being an accomplished officer and
having under him an able subordinate, the future
Marshal Victor. To Victor's leadership Lapoype confided
eight hundred men, who, at two o'clock on the
morning of the 1st of October, advanced from the
village of Revest, north and a little west of Toulon, Oct. 1.
against the northern face of Mont Faron. Two hundred
of them, contriving with great difficulty to ascend the
cliffs to west of the Pas de la Masque, took the British
piquet at the head of it in rear, while the rest attacked
it in front. The piquet, only sixty men strong, at once
fell back, and the French, pressing on to the redoubt
at the summit, found the work deserted by its Spanish
garrison. Thereupon they at once occupied it, and
having received a reinforcement of one thousand men,
saw themselves in comfortable possession of the whole
length of Mont Faron and of the key of Toulon.

By seven o'clock the state of affairs was known in
the town ; and the commanders of the various nations,
meeting in council, decided that the mountain must be
recaptured at once. At eight o'clock two columns sallied
forth, one of two hundred and fifty British and three
hundred Piedmontese to assail Mont Faron from the
north-west, the other of about nine hundred Neapolitans,
Piedmontese, and Spaniards to ascend it from the southwest.
The day was intensely hot, and the climb up the
rugged and almost perpendicular acclivity was extremely
fatiguing to the troops ; but the French offered no opposition
to either column beyond a single harmless
volley from a small party at long range. The two
columns then united at the western end of the mountain,

1793.
Oct. 1.
and prepared to advance over a succession of transverse ridges to the highest point, where the French were drawn up before the redoubt. The direct approach to their front from the westward was straitened by a deep ravine to a width of not more than twenty yards of level ground; their right was protected by the cliff on the northern face, and their left was thrown back *en potence* along the southern crest of the ravine. These troops on their left, however, were, as Mulgrave perceived, unskilfully disposed, being drawn up upon the very summit instead of somewhat below the brow, and therefore unable to command the ascent. He therefore advanced himself with great display from the west against the front of the French, while Gravina, availing himself of every fold in the ground, worked round unperceived to their left, and Captain Elphinstone led four hundred men from a redoubt, in which he had been stationed, on the southern slope. Just as Elphinstone's and Gravina's men suddenly appeared over the crest on the French flank, Mulgrave and his men rushed straight upon their front; and the enemy broke and fled in panic and confusion. About one hundred were killed on the spot, as many more leaped over the precipice, another two or three hundred were wounded, and sixty were taken; while the casualties of the Allies little exceeded seventy hurt or slain. Of the injured men nearly one half were British, but the success would have been cheaply gained, had not Admiral Gravina, the one capable officer among the Spaniards, been unfortunately among the wounded.

On its own small scale this was a very brilliant little action, for the French had the advantage in numbers, unity, and position, and the troops of the Allies, owing to want of equipment, were obliged to undergo a very fatiguing day's work without a drop of water. The two men who actually led the way in these two columns are worthy of remark. He of Gravina's column was a Spanish sergeant of Marines named Moreno, who, by Mulgrave's account, was the one brave man besides Gravina in the Spanish contingent. The leading man of Mulgrave's column was Thomas Graham, who here 1793. came under fire for the first time, was wounded in the hand, and distinguished himself so greatly, not only by courage but by his astonishing military instinct and eye for ground, that on Mulgrave's persuasion he resolved, in spite of his years, to seek a new career as a soldier. It was at this time that Graham formed a friendship with Captain Rowland Hill, which did not end until December 1842, when General Lord Hill died, and his comrade General Lord Lynedoch, grieved to the heart, followed him within a year.[1]

Thus the key of Toulon was recovered, and Mulgrave resolved to secure it with five hundred men in future; but the Neapolitans showed such dismay when appointed to hold it, that it was necessary to replace them by British and Piedmontese.[2] Nevertheless, with a man such as Bonaparte in command of the French artillery, the respite was not likely to be long. He and his superiors were perfectly clear as to the right plan of action, namely to master the peninsulas of Cepet and Eguillette and drive the English fleet from the harbour. Within a week after the recapture of Faron, three French batteries had been erected against the heights of La Grasse, one on the west, and two to the southward. To redress this, on the night of the 8th, Captain Brereton Oct. 8. with a small party of British and Piedmontese sallied forth against the two last, bayonetted or took one hundred of their garrisons, and destroyed the heavy pieces of artillery mounted in the batteries. The loss of the British did not exceed ten killed and wounded, but even this was serious when the number of trustworthy troops was so small; the more so since, on the 9th of Oct. 9. October, Lyons, after a desperate resistance, at last fell, and released a large body of French troops to serve before Toulon. Some three thousand more Spaniards

[1] Cottin, *Toulon et les Anglais*, pp. 218-220; Mulgrave to Dundas (official and private), 30th October 1793. Delavoye, *Life of Lord Lynedoch*, pp. 66-79.
[2] Mulgrave to Dundas, 3rd and 10th October; Brereton to Mulgrave, 9th October.

1793. and Neapolitans had meanwhile arrived, but it was only with great difficulty that two hundred additional British soldiers were collected from various ships; and the preponderance of Spanish troops gave Gravina's incapable successors the better right to claim a leading share in the direction of operations. Most unfortunately too the naval chiefs, in anxiety for their ships, resolved, against the opinion of the military, to occupy Cap Le Brun, about a mile to the south of Fort La Malgue on
Oct. 15. the northern shore of the harbour. On the 15th the French attacked and carried this post, in spite of a vigorous resistance from a handful of British soldiers and French emigrants. The place was soon recaptured; but, when Mulgrave with great readiness made his dispositions for turning the mishap to instant and telling advantage, the Spaniards insisted on taking the lead, and from sheer ignorance and incompetence ruined the whole plan. Thus not only were valuable British and Piedmontese lives sacrificed, but the enormous perimeter of defence was still further extended.[1]

Oct. 20. A new difficulty then arose. The Spanish Court took upon itself, without a word to its Allies, to appoint Gravina Commander-in-Chief of the combined forces, a step which was the more distressing to the British since they held the man himself in high honour, and were there-
Oct. 26. fore unwilling to oppose him. The British Admiral's anxieties were next increased by an order from Dundas to embark the men of the Thirtieth Regiment, and to send them with four ships to Gibraltar for service in some other part of the world. With the greatest reluctance Hood withdrew part of his seamen from the shore and sent away the four ships; but, supported by Mulgrave, he declined to part with a single soldier until reinforcements should arrive. On the 27th, at last, seven hundred and fifty men of the Royals,[2] Eighteenth, and Royal Artillery arrived from Gib-

---

[1] Mulgrave to Dundas, 3rd and 10th October; Brereton to Mulgrave, 9th October.
[2] The second battalion (2/1st).

raltar, together with General O'Hara, who had been 1793. appointed Commander-in-Chief, and Major-general David Dundas, his second in command. Both were struck by the extreme weakness of the position, owing to its vast extent, the want of mutual support between the various posts, the worthlessness of all but the British and Piedmontese troops, and the difficulties caused by divided command and by the variety of languages spoken in the force. O'Hara was an excellent linguist, but even this could not secure unanimity; and it was useless to give orders even in the best of Spanish or in the Neapolitan dialect, when the officers of those nationalities had not the slightest idea how to execute them. For two months, moreover, although the British Ministers had known of the occupation of Toulon, they had despatched neither supplies nor stores to the troops. The season was far advanced, yet neither tents, camp-equipage, nor field-guns had been provided for the men disembarked by Hood. And meanwhile the energetic Bonaparte was not only collecting and organising a siege-train, but had already mounted guns, which ranged over much of the inner harbour, and had matured his plan of attack. Eguillette was the point upon which his eye was continually fixed; and O'Hara had already noted with dismay that communication with this peninsula and that of Cepet was possible only by water, and was liable to be interrupted by bad weather. So ill did both he and David Dundas think of the situation that he warned Hood to be prepared for mishaps; and both Hood and O'Hara gave Henry Dundas to understand that Toulon was practically invested, that the only chance of holding it was to take the offensive, which was impossible with such a force as was at their disposal, and that their tenure of the place was precarious in the extreme.[1]

These letters appear not to have reached London

[1] Mulgrave to Dundas (public and private), 18th October 1793. O'Hara to Dundas, 13th November, enclosing letter to Hood of 11th November; David Dundas to Henry Dundas, 12th November 1793.

1793. for some time; but Mulgrave, who had left the army on the coming of O'Hara and David Dundas, arrived there about the 23rd of November, and gave an account of affairs which so frightened both Pitt and Henry Dundas as to draw from the latter an order to Hood to destroy, in any case, the French fleet and arsenal.[1] Meanwhile all circumstances conspired to aid the enemy. On the 10th of October new power had been given to their Executive by a decree declaring the Government to be Revolutionary, and vesting the supreme administration in the Committee of Public Safety. This measure greatly strengthened Carnot's hands. Already he had succeeded in recalling the incompetent Carteaux, who was by profession a painter; and though Jacobin influence was still strong enough to procure the appointment of a doctor, Doppel, to succeed him, yet the reign of the medical man was short. On the evening
Nov. 15. of the 15th of November the French attacked Fort Mulgrave, but were beaten off by the First Royals with very heavy loss; and shortly afterwards Doppel was replaced by a competent soldier, Dugommier. At the same time successes in Savoy, and the driving of the Sardinians over the Alps, liberated several thousand more Frenchmen for the siege of Toulon, while a successful action in Roussillon relieved the Republic of much anxiety in that quarter. Lastly, on the 20th
Nov. 20. of November, Hood, O'Hara, and Sir Gilbert Elliot, a civilian who had been joined with them as Commissioner for the government of Toulon, issued a declaration prepared by the Cabinet in the name of King George, which wrought untold mischief to the cause of the Allies. It ran to the effect that, when monarchy should be re-established in France, and a treaty concluded for the restoration of all conquests taken by her from the Allies, for just indemnity on account of their expenses and for proper security for the future, then Toulon should be given back according to Lord Hood's original agree-

[1] *Dropmore Papers*, ii. 471. Dundas to Hood, 23rd November 1793.

ment. But inasmuch as Hood's original declaration 1793. specified only that he held Toulon in trust for King Louis the Seventeenth until peace should be made, this new manifesto amounted to a breach of faith, which the besiegers outside the town and the disaffected within it did not fail to charge against England.

Meanwhile no more troops came from Gibraltar; not an Austrian soldier appeared from Italy, whither Hood had sent ships for them; the pretensions of Langara, whether just or unjust, became more exacting, and Hood therefore more impatient; and, worst of all, sickness was so rife that over three thousand men were in hospital. The returns of the Spanish and Neapolitan officers showed a strength of six thousand troops for each nation; but there was no account of the number of effective men, and no voucher for the truth of the musters. In any case the only trustworthy troops were the British and Sardinians, numbering some three thousand five hundred men, for a task which needed twenty-five thousand.[1]

At length came a real disaster. On the 29th of Nov. 29. November a sortie of twenty-three hundred of all nations was led by David Dundas against a French battery, which had been recently erected at Aresnes, due north of Malbousquet, and had greatly annoyed the garrison of that work. The country being strongly enclosed, the troops advanced in four columns, of which four hundred British formed the left, and succeeded in surprising and taking the battery; but, instead of re-forming on the captured height, the men rushed onward in pursuit with increasing disorder, and, finally encountering far superior numbers, were driven back with very heavy loss. The British alone[2] left behind them just over two hundred killed, wounded, and prisoners; which loss was the more serious since the casualties included twelve officers, and officers were

[1] O'Hara to Henry Dundas, 22nd November and 12th December. David Dundas to same, 22nd November. Hood to same, 26th November 1793. [2] 2/1st, 11th, 18th, 25th, 30th, 69th.

1793. already none too plentiful. Among the twelve was O'Hara himself, who had ridden up to the captured batteries, in the hope (according to one account) of meeting his death, and was there wounded and taken. The reverse, as David Dundas wrote, was due entirely to the nature and bad discipline of the troops, and was not redeemed by the spiking of six guns and the acknowledged loss of over two hundred killed and wounded by the French. Its gravest consequence was that the British were too much weakened to take their former share in the defence of the outposts. "The fabric totters," wrote David Dundas, "but we will prop it if we can."[1]

It was not long before the fabric fell. The numbers of the enemy were further increased by the arrival of six or eight seasoned battalions from the Var, so that the French troops amounted to between thirty and forty thousand men,[2] whereas the Allies had already four thousand sick and wounded in hospital, and David Dundas had learned that no greater reinforcements were to be expected from England than three hundred Light Dragoons. "If we are not speedily relieved," wrote both Hood and David Dundas, "we shall soon have more men fit for hospital than for service." On the 18th the end came. For some days, pursuant to Bonaparte's plan, heavy fire had been kept up against all the posts of the Allies, and in particular upon the extremities of the line at Cap Brun and

Dec. 16. Eguillette. At two o'clock in the morning of the 16th five batteries opened a heavy bombardment on Fort Mulgrave, doing much damage and inflicting heavy

Dec. 17. loss; and at the same hour on the morning of the 17th the French attacked the post in great strength. For about half an hour the resistance was stout; and then the Spaniards, who held the northern defences of the work, deserted the battery and fled. Captain Connolly of the

---

[1] Napoleon's *Correspondence*, i. 23. David Dundas to Henry Dundas, 30th November, 1st and 2nd December 1793. Cottin, p. 277.

[2] Napoleon himself gives the number on the 7th of December as thirty thousand men. *Correspondence*, i. 23.

Eighteenth, who commanded the British at Fort Mul- 1793.
grave, detached an officer and thirty-six men, who retook Dec. 17.
the battery and defended it for a time with success; but
the enemy advanced in increasing numbers, the Spaniards
utterly refused to come forward again, and by four
o'clock the remnant of the Eighteenth were borne down
and driven out. Hardly had the firing ceased on the
peninsula when it began on the height of Faron. For the
second time the French made their way up the cliff by
the face that was thought inaccessible; the Spaniards and
Neapolitans fled from all their posts at the first fire, and
the small parties of British scattered among them were
left alone. One little group of the Eleventh fought on
until but five men were left, but against four thousand
Frenchmen further resistance was impossible; and the
officers, collecting such few men as they could, retired
to the posts on the southern side of Mont Faron.

Thus the circle of the Allies' defences was broken
at its two most vital points, and was no longer tenable
on land or water. Early on the morning of the 18th Dec. 18.
Langara came to Hood, clamouring for a Council
of War, at which it was quickly decided that the
captured posts could not be retaken by the fifteen
hundred men in reserve in Toulon. All arrangements
were then made for a methodical retreat. The troops
were withdrawn from the isthmus of Eguillette, and
from the posts immediately imperilled by the loss of
Faron; and in the night the fleet took up a new
station in the outer roadstead. But here all order
ended. Without saying a word to the other commanders, the Neapolitans on that night stole out of the
town, evacuated Cepet, Sablettes, Malbousquet, and Cap
Brun, and, after ordering the Piedmontese also to quit
the post last named, embarked and sailed away. The
Spaniards at Malbousquet, seeing the Neapolitans retire,
retired also; and thus the enemy was enabled to occupy
this work and other of the deserted defences, and to
cannonade the town. At ten that night the ships and
the arsenal were kindled for destruction, the French in

1793. Malbousquet pouring a continual fire on the British
Dec. 18. seamen engaged in the work. The Spaniards had been
charged with the duty of firing the ships in the basin
before the town ; but, finding themselves driven back by
musketry from one of them, they abandoned the attempt,
and avenged themselves by kindling, instead of sinking,
two powder-ships, the explosion of which shook two
British gunboats to pieces, killed and wounded not a
few of the sailors, and might well have made an end of
all of them. In all this behaviour of the Spanish there
was much to justify suspicion of treachery, more than
enough to prove the certainty of ill-will. The whole
garrison was then drawn into Fort La Malgue, from
Dec. 19. whence it embarked on the morning of the 19th ;
Major Koehler, the Engineer who had so much distinguished himself in Gibraltar, being the last man to
leave the shore, after spiking every gun in the fort.
But none the less it was found impossible to embark
the heavy baggage. Three of the British field-guns also
were accidentally left behind, and the rest were stowed
away so hastily that their carriages and other fittings
were distributed on many different ships. Fortunately
the weather was favourable, or fleet, army, and a swarm
of fugitives which had flown to the ships, must all
inevitably have perished.[1] The nations then separated,
each to its own place ; and Hood, encumbered by
several hundred refugees, and with his troops worn out,
naked, and destitute, cast anchor in Hyères Bay.

So ended this ill-fated enterprise, hastily undertaken,
inefficiently directed, inadequately supported. So far
as blame can be attached to any of the British commanders on the spot, the chief burden must fall upon
Hood. What his own opinion about Toulon may have
been it is difficult to say, for he had the gift, born of
great moral courage, of never betraying the slightest
misgiving in the most perilous crisis ;[2] but it is certain

---

[1] *Life of Lord Minto*, ii. 201.
[2] See *Journal of Sir John Moore*, i. 52 ; Delavoye's *Life of Lord Lynedoch*, p. 75.

that when Mulgrave went home, Hood shared his alarm 1793. as to the insecurity of the place, and made no secret of it to Henry Dundas. The Admiral was, however, an overbearing and difficult man, particularly in his relations with the Army, as he had already shown at St. Kitts in 1782.[1] Mulgrave, who only commanded the troops by Hood's own appointment, seems to have handled him with much tact; but O'Hara and David Dundas, who were of higher and more independent rank, found him less practicable. It is true that the Admiral for the second time confessed his misgivings on hearing O'Hara's opinion as to the danger of the situation; but it seems that he and David Dundas, who succeeded to the command after the capture of O'Hara, were on bad terms from the first. Hood's usually contemptuous attitude towards military officers may possibly have been stiffened by the distance which separated him socially from the poor, awkward but haughty Scot who had risen from small beginnings to high professional rank; and, if Hood was obstinate, undoubtedly Dundas on his side was tenacious of his own opinion, and with justice, for in ability and knowledge of his own business he was no whit the Admiral's inferior.

It is beyond question that David Dundas urged Hood very early in the day to evacuate Toulon, to destroy the arsenal, and to ruin or carry off the French fleet, and that O'Hara was strongly of the same opinion as his subordinate. Both pointed out that the only real method of defending the place was to take the offensive, an operation of extreme difficulty, not only because the troops were utterly destitute of transport, but because the whole country round was mountainous, wooded, and broken by ravines, was traversed by few roads, and was withal so barren as to afford no subsistence to an army. It was therefore obvious that any advance must depend entirely on the accumulation of supplies and transport from the British Isles; and Hood knew better than any man the length

[1] *Journal of Sir John Moore,* i. 256.

of communication with them by sea. Finally the counter-revolution at Lyons, which alone had justified the original occupation, had been crushed; Mulgrave's observations had made it clear that no help was to be expected from Austria, and indeed Hood himself had acknowledged, on the 24th of November, that he had abandoned all hope of it. Nevertheless the Admiral refused to hear of evacuation;[1] and the result was that he was driven after heavy loss to a hasty retreat, that the destruction of the French fleet and arsenal was consequently very imperfect, and that fifteen ships of war were left undamaged, to become the nucleus of a French Mediterranean squadron. Moreover the crews of his own vessels, already dependent on the army for the best of their men, were very dangerously weakened—a fact which, as shall be seen, brought him into further collision with the military authorities, and was the true cause of the failure of all his operations. It is therefore evident that a heavy responsibility lies upon him, and upon him alone, whether he erred ignorantly or with knowledge. The truth seems to be that his seventy years had intensified his natural defects of temper, and developed in him an unpleasant form of cunning, which led him to run great risks whenever he could claim all credit in case of success, and shift the blame on others in case of failure.

But more extraordinary by far than Hood's was the behaviour of Henry Dundas. On the 14th of September he had declared that everything must give way to the importance of Toulon; on the 26th he had written to O'Hara and Hood that he would send as soon as possible one thousand cavalry and two thousand infantry from Ireland, besides five thousand Hessians, who were to follow as soon as they were ready, and two battalions already ordered from Gibraltar. As the reader has seen, none of these troops, except two weak

---

[1] "Lord Hood is perhaps over confident, and will never admit the slightest doubt of our keeping the place." Sir G. Elliot to Lady Elliot, 24th November 1793. *Life of Lord Minto*, i. 191.

battalions and a few gunners, or about eight hundred men in all, from Gibraltar ever arrived at Toulon. One weak regiment of cavalry was indeed embarked, though too late to be of use; but the infantry from Ireland was given to Grey for the West Indies, and the five thousand Hessians were assigned to Moira for Brittany. Yet not one word of these changes was announced to the naval or military commanders at Toulon; and Hood on the 16th of December, three weeks after Grey had sailed for Barbados, was beside himself with joy at the thought that the West Indian expedition was to be abandoned and the troops sent to him. Even when writing to O'Hara on the 18th of December, Henry Dundas merely announced that three battalions were on the eve of embarkation to join him, without a hint that the remainder of the reinforcements had been diverted to another service. On the other hand, he calmly assumed that the General had at least seventeen thousand men under his command, when as a matter of fact he had never more than twelve thousand bayonets. Yet the Minister had long known, from Mulgrave's information, that two-thirds even of the twelve thousand were worthless, and the rest almost worn out with excessive duty, fatigue, and exposure. Finally, though he had himself confessed his own uneasiness to Hood upon O'Hara's report, he wrote in reply to the confirmatory warning of David Dundas a letter so extraordinary that, with slight abridgment of its intolerable verbosity, it must for once be quoted at length:—

"Your letter and General O'Hara's are not calculated to inspire us with good spirits or confidence in the exertions to be made at Toulon. You mention all your difficulties but none of your resources. Toulon came into our hands when we were unprepared for any such event, and was held by a handful of British troops and seamen, and those Spaniards whom it is now the tone to consider as good for nothing. No sooner do we send reinforcements, after the most vigorous exertions, I

1793. believe, ever made in the same period of time, than we are accosted with despatches which are little short of announcing the abandonment of the place, and give us hardly a ray of hope. No doubt General O'Hara will do his best, but there is no occasion to enhance his merit by an exaggerated statement of difficulties, without mentioning the relative position of the enemy which diminishes the force of his apprehensions. We require no stimulus to induce us to give every additional force to Toulon, but let us at least have the satisfaction of thinking that our exertions at home will be answered by your exertions abroad. Again, you and O'Hara lead me to suppose that defence would be easy, but that the fleet and harbour also require defence. But you do not state that the harbour could be abandoned without giving up the communications by sea, nor do you appear to have considered the subject with Lord Hood, so as to report whether, if the fleet were withdrawn, your task of defence would be proportionately lessened. Lord Hood says nothing of it, and it never occurs to you that you only state a difficulty and say nothing of the means of removing it." . . . "Nobody" (to give the concluding sentence in Dundas's exact words),—"nobody carries to a higher pitch than I do the propriety and indeed the duty of Ministers to support the character and reputations of the officers they employ. I think that we are even in honour bound to uphold their errors and defend their mistakes; but while I have the honour to serve His Majesty, I will set my face against the invidious practice of every officer, when he goes upon service, sitting down to make a catalogue of difficulties and grievances, which never has, nor never can have a good effect upon any service, and must always expose the person doing so to the suspicion of beginning his service with preparatory apology for his failure. I am no soldier and therefore not entitled to form a judgment, but I can say that such a train of thinking and acting would augur ill for vigorous exertions in civil life."[1]

[1] Henry Dundas to David Dundas, 20th December 1793.

Such was the reward of an honest soldier who had 1793. the courage to give his true opinion, however unpalatable, rather than prophesy smooth things to please the Government. The best commentary on the letter is the fact that the Allies had been driven from Toulon two days before it was written; but setting aside the bluster about the "vigorous exertions," which had not succeeded in embarking more than about three hundred men in three months from England to the Mediterranean, it is singular to note how utterly this Minister of War failed to grasp plain facts. In the first place it is incomprehensible how the harbour could have been abandoned without giving up the communication by sea. The British troops (excepting the few which came from Gibraltar), as well as the seamen, formed part of the complement of Hood's fleet, which was already undermanned and could not have gone away without them; and hence the withdrawal of the ships necessarily meant the withdrawal of the garrison also. If therefore the fleet had retired to Hyères, the French could speedily have captured the batteries at Eguillette, Cepet, and Cap Brun, which would have prevented it from entering Toulon again. Thus supplies and stores would have been cut off; there was already dearth in the neighbourhood; and the disaffected section of the population in the town would have done their utmost to hasten a surrender. As to Henry Dundas's loyalty to his commanders, the reader will later have many opportunities of judging for himself. Meanwhile it is sufficient to note that this man, who, being no soldier, was by his own confession not entitled to form a judgment on military matters, nevertheless arrogated to himself the right to call in question the verdict passed by three Generals upon some of the troops serving under them, and to answer one of them, who had done no more than confirm the opinion of the other two upon a purely military matter, not only with rebuke but with insulting imputation of base motives. The consequence of this outrageous behaviour will soon be apparent; and indeed

1793. the reader has already seen enough of Dundas to judge that war under the guidance of such a man must inevitably end in disaster.

> AUTHORITIES.—The original despatches as to Toulon are in *S.P. Admiralty, Admiral's despatches*, Mediterranean, 391, and *H.O. Admiralty*, 212-213. The records are abominably confused, according to the practice of our public offices at the time. Cottin's *Toulon et les Anglais* gives the French account of the matter. *Nelson's Despatches*; *Correspondence de Napoléon*; Barrow's *Life of Lord Hood*; Lady Minto's *Life of Lord Minto*; *Mémoires de Marmont*; and the *Diary of Sir John Moore* afford useful auxiliary material.

CHAPTER VIII

Hood with his fleet and transports arrived on the 20th and 21st of December in Hyères Bay, where they lay inactive for the next five weeks, the Admiral awaiting his victualling ships, and David Dundas looking for reinforcements of men and material. Hood, however, had by the 23rd made up his mind to go to Corsica as soon as he could, in order to assist the national party, led by Paoli, to throw off the yoke of the French. The posts held by French garrisons in the island were but three, namely, the defences of the Bay of San Fiorenzo,[1] Bastia, and Calvi; the two first being situated to west and east of the long promontory which forms the northern extremity of Corsica, while Calvi lies at the northern angle of the west coast. It will be remembered that Hood had detached five sloops of his squadron under Commodore Linzee in September to blockade these three places and to endeavour to reduce the forts, with the co-operation of the Corsicans ashore. But at the moment of trial the Corsicans failed; and Linzee withdrew with two ships very seriously damaged, the usual result of pitting wooden walls against masonry. Hood, who was already suspicious of Paoli, was none too well pleased at this mishap;[2] but when the Corsican leader, on the 4th of January 1794, wrote to him offering to place the island without reserve under British protection, the Admiral, though without instructions from

1793.
Dec. 21.

[1] Now called St. Florent; but I have preserved the Italian form as having been used in all contemporary British documents.
[2] Hood to Admiralty (with enclosures from Linzee), 6th October 1793.

1793. home, accepted the proposal, on condition that the representatives of Corsica should enter into a convention
Dec. 31. on the subject. On the 31st of December the Fiftieth and Fifty-first Regiments, jointly seven hundred strong, had arrived from Gibraltar, the latter under the command of Lieutenant-colonel John Moore, the very able man who as an ensign had distinguished himself at Penobscot in 1779. An English officer, Lieutenant-colonel Cooke, had already given some account of the defences of the French posts and of the numbers of the Corsican levies; and it was resolved to send Moore and Major Koehler to report more fully as to the
1794. practicability of an attack, and to concert operations
Jan. 12. with Paoli. They sailed accordingly on the 12th of January, and with them Sir Gilbert Elliot, who was now charged with the negotiation of an agreement with the Corsican patriots.[1]

Jan. 24. On the 24th Hood weighed anchor for Corsica, but, being driven off by a gale, put into Porto Ferrajo in the island of Elba. There Moore joined him and submitted his report, to the effect that, with the help of the inhabitants, upon which he saw fair reason to count, there was good hope of a successful attack even with the small number of troops at disposal. As a matter of fact, Moore's estimate of the French numbers, which he reckoned from the best of his intelligence to be under two thousand men,[2] was too low by one half; while the British forces, including those detailed for service as marines on board the fleet, little exceeded the supposed numbers of the French.[3] The fleet itself was so

[1] Hood to Dundas, 7th January 1794, enclosing correspondence with Paoli and Cooke's report.
[2] *Journal of Sir John Moore*, i. 51.
[3] A return of 7th January 1794 gives the strength at 102 officers, 2341 N.C.O. and men, of which 239 sick and wounded. The troops consisted of R.A. 2/1st, 11th, 18th, 25th, 30th, 69th. This is evidently incorrect, and is probably founded on some return made previous to the 17th of December. The numbers, as I reckon, are too great by one-third, and therefore the addition of the 50th and 51st would bring the total up to something over 2000 men.

short of its complement of seamen, from sickness and 1794. other causes, that Hood was obliged to apply to the Grand Master of Malta for the loan of one hundred sailors, and, failing to obtain even half as many, to seek out others at Naples.[1] Thus it was impossible to spare the whole of the troops for service ashore; and the want of supplies and stores was as great as that of men. The confusion of the retreat from Toulon had left to the British no artillery except four light howitzers and two mortars, which had been sent from Gibraltar; and not one item of ordnance-stores had been received from England. Camp-equipment the soldiers had never had, and great part of their baggage had been lost, so that, as David Dundas said, they began the world naked and destitute. Yet again, the fleet was in want of provisions; for, though the Admiralty had promised to send victualling ships in November 1793, none had arrived in January; and indeed they were still lacking even in May 1794. Worst of all, there was no good feeling between the chiefs of the army and of the fleet. David Dundas was still chafing under the disastrous results which had followed upon Hood's obstinate neglect of his advice at Toulon; and the Admiral had since shown him great discourtesy by ordering Moore and Koehler to visit Paoli without, in the first instance, consulting their military superior, and by causing Moore to address his report to himself as Commander-in-chief of both fleet and army. Dundas let the matter pass, lest the King's service should suffer; but with Sir Gilbert Elliot paying assiduous court to Hood, and with Henry Dundas's disgraceful letter of the 20th of December in his pocket, it was only natural that the General should have longed for deliverance from so thankless a situation.

After some days of preparation at Porto Ferrajo Feb. 6. the fleet sailed on the 6th and 7th of February for the Gulf of San Fiorenzo, in order to secure a safe anchorage as a base of future operations. Moore had provided

[1] Hood to Dundas, 10th March 1794.

1794. a clear and concise report as to its defences, and the method of overcoming them. The Gulf of San Fiorenzo is an inlet about three miles long, with a width of about three miles at its entrance on the north, narrowing gradually to about nine hundred yards at its head, on the south. On the western shore the ingress is marked by the promontory of Mortella Point, a little to the south of which stood a tower which, under the perverted name of the Martello tower, has become famous in history. This structure was of solid masonry with walls fifteen feet thick, and mounted two eighteen-pounders and one six-pounder. A like tower stood at Fornali, about two miles higher up the harbour upon the same shore, covering two powerful batteries to seaward; while on a detached hill, in rear of it and about two hundred and fifty feet above the sea, the French had thrown up a formidable work which was known as the Convention Redoubt. This last, with its twenty-one heavy guns, was to become the key of San Fiorenzo.

Feb. 7. On the 7th Commodore Linzee anchored the transports in a bay immediately to westward of Mortella Point, and on the same day Dundas, after some hesitation, disembarked about fourteen hundred troops,[1] one hundred and twenty seamen, and two light guns. On Feb. 8. the following day a line-of-battle ship and a frigate cannonaded the Mortella tower, but were driven off with serious damage and a loss of over sixty killed and wounded, leaving the tower itself and its garrison of thirty-eight men wholly unhurt. Meanwhile Moore, with about seven hundred of the Royals, Fifty-first, and seamen, and two light guns, advanced for seven or eight miles over an extremely rugged country to the rear of the Convention Redoubt, which he found to have been so much strengthened since his former reconnaissance that attack was hopeless with the small force at his disposal. Dundas therefore raised a battery of four guns on the shore, one hundred and fifty yards Feb. 10. from the Mortella tower, and after two days' firing

[1] Detachments of 2/1st, 11th, 25th, 30th, 50th, 51st, 69th.

succeeded in forcing it to surrender. The capture of 1794. the tower permitted heavy guns to be landed on the western shore of the bay, thus saving much heavy carriage by land; but Dundas despaired of dragging them over the rocky country to the heights which commanded the Convention Redoubt. Moore and Koehler were, however, urgent that the attempt should be made, and Dundas wisely yielded to their representations.[1]

The troops were therefore encamped on Monte Revinco, some twelve hundred feet above the sea and in rear of the Redoubt; and the naval officers and seamen by extraordinary skill and industry contrived to hoist six heavy guns to two positions selected by Koehler, the one on a hill with a summit of almost perpendicular rock seven hundred feet above the sea, the other on a height of less difficult access. This was accomplished between the 12th and the 16th, on which latter day the batteries Feb. 16. opened a plunging fire upon the Redoubt at a range of from eight hundred to one thousand yards; and on the 17th Dundas gave his orders for the assault to be Feb. 17. delivered soon after moonrise. Moore, with the Royals and Fifty-first, was to move upon an advanced angle of the Redoubt; and the Fiftieth and Twenty-fifth were to march along the shore and then turn, the one upon the centre and the other upon the seaward face, while a party of Corsican levies lay in wait between the Redoubt and the tower to cut off the enemy's retreat. At half-past eight the three columns advanced in perfect silence. Moore's, having the advantage of easier ground, was the first to enter the works; but the French held firm, and French and English stood for a moment with crossed bayonets until the other British columns came in and decided the matter. For a short time the French in the tower and in the other defences of

[1] "We never should have had any footing in Corsica but for the perseverance of myself and Moore. This Lord Hood declared to me on the public parade at San Fiorenzo."—Koehler to Lord Grenville, *Dropmore MSS.*

1794.
Feb. 17. Fornali poured a heavy fire of grape into the captured redoubt; but presently they abandoned the whole position and fled to the eastern shore. The British loss was no more than fifty-two killed and wounded; that of the French was about one hundred killed and wounded, and seventy prisoners, out of a garrison of five hundred and fifty. The Corsicans, who should have cut off the fugitives, were too active in pillaging the dead and injured to attend to other matters; and thus over three hundred good French troops escaped to San Fiorenzo. This misfortune was not without serious consequence to the subsequent operations.[1]

Feb. 18. On the 18th the fleet anchored safely in the bay, and, the French having withdrawn the garrison of San Fiorenzo to Bastia, the British occupied the former
Feb. 19. town on the following day. The next object therefore for the British commanders was the capture of Bastia, which is not above eight miles distant from San Fiorenzo as the crow flies, but is divided from it by a range of mountains, rising in places to a height of three thousand feet above the sea. There was even then a good road connecting the two towns, which crossed the range at the Col de Teghimé,[2] seventeen hundred feet above the sea; but its windings round the lower hills and spurs fully doubled the direct distance between them. A narrow gorge on the western slope of the mountains made the task of severing communications between San Fiorenzo and Bastia an easy one; wherefore Dundas,
Feb. 21. on the 21st, ordered Moore to camp with the Fiftieth, Fifty-first, and Sixty-ninth at this spot, and pushed forward his Corsicans to drive away some parties of French which occupied the summit of the mountain.

[1] David Dundas to Henry Dundas, 21st February 1794. James's *Naval History*, i. 189. *Diary of Sir John Moore*, i. 48-61. I must add that from errors in transcription, or some other cause, much of this part of Moore's diary is almost unintelligible as printed. The fact appears to have escaped the notice of the editor.

[2] This name is misprinted Titime in the *Diary of Sir John Moore*.

On the 23rd he himself ascended Teghimé in company 1794. with Moore to reconnoitre Bastia, when the situation Feb. 23. became plain. From the highest ridge of the mountain the ground slopes down for some distance to the east, and then rises again to a second and lower crest marked by the village of Cardo, from which it finally descends more steeply to the sea. From this lower crest of Cardo the final slope, though much broken by ravines, divides itself into two principal ridges, upon the commanding points of which stood the defences of Bastia on the side of the land—Fort Straforello to the northwest, Fort San Gaetano about seven hundred yards to the south and west of it, Fort de la Croix about five hundred yards to east of San Gaetano, and Fort Montserato about six hundred yards south-west of La Croix. All of these were built of masonry and advantageously situated, but all of them equally were commanded within easy range from the crest above them. Dundas therefore ordered his Corsicans to occupy this crest, and moved the Sixty-ninth forward to a position on Feb. 24. the slopes of Teghimé within twelve hundred yards of the forts, where, after further reconnaissance, he ordered the Fifty-first to join it, placing both regiments under command of Moore. Before Moore could reach his post, however, the French sallied out from Bastia, Feb. 25. drove the Corsicans from their positions, burned the village of Cardo, which was one of their principal defences, and began to entrench themselves with feverish activity upon the crest where Dundas had hoped to build his batteries. Moore spent one night in dense fog and Feb. 26. bitter cold on the heights of Teghimé, listening to the clink of the French picks and shovels; and on the 27th Feb. 27. Dundas ordered the troops to retire to their old position at the gorge, within three miles of San Fiorenzo, having made up his mind that an attack on Bastia was too hazardous, and that the place must be blockaded until starvation should compel its surrender.

It seems possible that, if Dundas had pushed his regular troops, as well as the Corsicans, directly to the

1794. ridge of Cardo, he might have held that ground and captured the forts of Bastia with little further difficulty, for the French had been shaken by their defeat at Fornali. Moore, with the spirit and enterprise of youth, had been for this course, and so also was Hood, though from his ignorance of military operations his opinion was of little value. Yet the movement would have been hazardous, and Dundas was not without warrant for his hesitation. By intercepted letters he had ascertained that the French in Bastia had fourteen hundred troops of the Line, the crews of two frigates, and a number of Corsicans, making in all a force superior to his own. It was impossible for his army to act with the fleet on the east coast, owing to the uncertainty of the weather and the strength of the seaward batteries of Bastia. The country was absolutely barren. The distance to the ridge of Cardo from San Fiorenzo was from ten to twelve miles, and, though the road was good, he had not nor could obtain a single wheeled vehicle to bring up supplies and stores. He could and did provide mules, but these were few and of small size. He would also have been obliged to keep troops on Teghimé, a bleak and exposed situation, to cover the retreat of those on the ridge of Cardo, and his force was miserably deficient in clothing, camp-equipment, and medical stores. Nevertheless, it is certain that, had the Corsicans held the ridge of Cardo, Dundas would have persisted in the attempt in spite of all difficulties; but, that ridge once lost to him and fortified by the French, the enterprise, by the admission of all soldiers, became impossible with the force at his command. He therefore decided, pending the arrival of reinforcements which Henry Dundas had long ago promised him, to blockade Bastia from the shore, while Hood did the like from the sea, in order to reduce it by famine.

On hearing of Dundas's resolution not to attack, Hood peremptorily required of him the troops that had been embarked as marines, and gave him to understand that he considered the operations abandoned by the General to be perfectly feasible. This opinion was the more insolent, inasmuch as the Admiral had never looked at the ground at all, whereas Dundas, who knew his profession well, had carefully reconnoitred it on three successive days. Hood then in a most arrogant fashion asserted his claim to supreme control of all the forces naval and military, declaring that Dundas's command of the troops had come to an end after the evacuation of Toulon, and that it was only by his own courtesy that the General had been permitted to direct the operations against Fornali and Mortella. To this Dundas answered very civilly and sarcastically that, if the Admiral really possessed the powers that he claimed, he had better have asserted them earlier, so that he might have ministered to the many wants and distresses of the troops, and relieved the General of all embarrassment and anxiety on their account. Dundas added that, having permission from the Secretary of State to go home on sick-leave, he proposed to return as soon as the Admiral would grant him a sloop to sail to Leghorn; but that if Hood would produce his authority and the Royal instructions for taking command of the troops, he would lay them before the military officers, who would cheerfully follow his Lordship's orders. It is significant that Hood when forwarding his correspondence with Dundas to England carefully omitted to include this letter, for, as a matter of fact, he could have shown no such authority as Dundas required. However, without a word to the General, he sent three of his captains privately to Moore and to another of the field-officers, to ascertain their views as to the feasibility of an attack; and he was somewhat taken aback when Moore answered that it was not for a subordinate to speak when the opinions of his superior had been openly declared. A few days later David Dundas embarked for his voyage home. His departure was a great misfortune, but it is difficult to see what else he could have done, looking to the behaviour of

1794.

March 11.

1794. Hood and the shameful treatment meted out to him by Henry Dundas.[1]

After his departure the command developed upon Colonel D'Aubant of the Engineers, a feeble and incompetent officer, upon whom Hood promptly turned with the same peremptory tone that he had used towards Dundas, quoting the opinions of his flag-officers, and even joining Sir Gilbert Elliot with himself in a remonstrance which demanded immediate action. Of what weight the views of a civilian could be in such a matter, it is not easy to see; but in those days, as in more recent times, all civilians,[2] whether Ministers, Ambassadors, or Governors, thought themselves qualified to direct military operations; and it was only the opinion of soldiers that counted for nothing. However, on Hood's suggestion, D'Aubant agreed that the flag-officers of the fleet should meet the field-officers of the army in a Council of War; and on the following
March 16. day Moore and Koehler, as competent men as could have been found in Europe, again reconnoitred the French position. They reported that the only point from which Bastia could be successfully assailed was from the west, and that the French defences on that side were now by nature and art too strong to be attacked with the small British force. Thereupon
March 18, Hood, who was not blind to Moore's capacity, wrote
19. to Henry Dundas the substance of his opinions, and confessed that Bastia must be starved into submission.

Nevertheless, when the Council of War again met
March 20. two days later, the flag-officers, not one of whom had seen the ground, unanimously declared in favour of an attack, while the field-officers, who were all of them familiar with the position, as unanimously pronounced against it. It so happened, however, that Sub-

[1] *Diary of Sir John Moore*, i. 65-69. David Dundas to Henry Dundas, 10th and 14th March. Hood to Dundas, 18th March 1794 (with enclosures).

[2] Occasionally the civilians quarrelled with each other over this interference, as, for instance, Pitt and Lord Elgin.—*Dropmore Papers*, ii. 476.

lieutenant Duncan of the Artillery had opined that the 1794. enemy could be effectively annoyed if batteries were erected on a ridge to the north of Bastia; and, on the strength of this very young officer's judgment, Hood demanded from D'Aubant not only the six hundred men who had been given to the fleet as marines, but also gunners, officers, guns and stores, some of which were granted and some, after unedifying squabbles, refused by the irresolute Colonel. This done, the Admiral sailed away to the east coast to play April 2. the soldier, still urging D'Aubant to attack vigorously from the western side, or in other words to attempt with one thousand men an operation already declared to be impracticable for sixteen hundred.[1] Arrived before Bastia, Hood, on the 4th of April, landed twelve April 4. hundred soldiers and seamen, and on the next day wrote to Henry Dundas that his batteries would open fire within forty-eight hours, and that he expected to be in possession of Bastia within ten days after.[2]

Foul weather, however, delayed the landing of the stores; and the 11th of April had come before the Admiral had finished the erection of his batteries to the north of Bastia, on a high ridge parallel to that on which the outworks stood.[3] On that day he opened fire on the April 11. town, the citadel, and the nearest of the French fortifications from thirteen pieces ashore and from a floating

[1] D'Aubant to Dundas, 2nd April; Hood to Dundas, 5th April 1794, with their enclosures. Nelson took credit for having persuaded Hood to attempt this attack, concealing from him the fact that the garrison of Bastia was nearly 4000 strong (*Despatches*, ii. 6). He even took the trouble to write to Sir W. Hamilton (27th March 1794) that the garrison was 800 strong, apparently for the sake of disparaging the military commanders (*Dropmore MSS.*). We shall see that this was not the only occasion on which Nelson showed utter ignorance of the nature of operations ashore.

[2] This throws some doubt on General Maurice's conjecture (*Diary of Sir John Moore*, i. 24) that Hood was playing "a game of bluff" and "playing to the gallery at home" in making this attack. He seems to have persuaded himself, in spite of previous misgivings, that it would be successful.

[3] Moore calls the ridge by the name of Capanelli or Campanalli, but the name does not appear on modern French maps.

1794.
April 11.

battery at sea; but the floating battery was speedily destroyed by red-hot shot, and the fire from the shore batteries was ineffective, because, as Moore and Koehler had noted, the range was too great. A fortnight passed, but still Bastia held out; and then Hood began to blame D'Aubant for not encamping his troops on the heights of Teghimé, declaring that a mere demonstration would suffice to bring about the fall of the town. This of course was nonsense, and not the less certainly nonsense because Elliot joined Hood in urging it upon D'Aubant; but for once D'Aubant was resolute in his refusal. At length, on the 15th of May, drafts for the Fiftieth and Fifty-first arrived at San Fiorenzo, together with the remnant of the Eighteenth, which had remained on the fleet; and D'Aubant, after eagerly offering his assistance to Hood, by whom the message was received with little grace, solemnly marched his men up to the heights of Teghimé. But this proved mere parade, for, before he could make up his mind to any movement, the garrison of Bastia, three thousand five hundred strong, surrendered, having exhausted the whole of its provisions. Hood of course claimed credit for the success, and wrote to Dundas in bitter terms of the apathy of the military officers; nor can it be doubted that D'Aubant was an useless encumbrance to both army and navy. The fact remains, however, that Bastia was reduced by starvation only, and that Hood's operations ashore, undertaken directly against the advice of Moore and Koehler, were futile and absurd, wasting much valuable ammunition, which was none too plentiful, and not hastening the fall of the place by one day. Moore, indeed, after inspection of the ground, declared that by an enemy of the slightest enterprise the Admiral's force might have been destroyed.[1] Yet Hood had

May 15.

---

[1] Koehler was of the same opinion. "I have documents to prove that the difference of opinion which took place with respect to Bastia was not only the salvation of the troops, but the real cause of the taking of the place; for, had the troops been employed

undertaken this operation on the vague opinion of a 1794. subaltern of artillery; and he equally supported his arguments in favour of an attack from Teghimé by the opinion of a junior field-officer, which was scouted by his more capable fellows as absurd. The Admiral, in fact, was so overbearing that he considered no member of the army to be capable who did not at once subscribe to his views and truckle to his authority as well in military as in naval affairs.[1]

No sooner, therefore, had Bastia been occupied by the British than Hood demanded two regiments from D'Aubant, and prepared to hurry to Calvi in order to play the soldier before that place also. Fortunately, however, on the 25th of May, there arrived a new May 25. Commander-in-chief, with a commission as Lieutenant-general of Corsica and of the whole of the Mediterranean except Gibraltar, which exempted him from the busy interference of the Admiral. This was Charles Stuart, a younger son of the house of Bute, and a man of talent so rare both as a commander and an administrator, that the imbecility of Henry Dundas alone prevented him from winning a name in history even before his premature death. D'Aubant, on his arrival, was very rightly recalled; and Stuart set himself forthwith to ease the friction between army and navy, and to cultivate good relations with the Admiral. A week later the General embarked for Calvi to reconnoitre the June 1. fortress; and during his absence the Twelfth Light June 3. Dragoons, which had been originally intended for service in Toulon, arrived, after a long and troublesome voyage, at San Fiorenzo, in a country where mounted troops were absolutely useless. Stuart had hardly June 5.

in the manner proposed by his Lordship [Hood], their defeat must have ensued. . . . These are not ideas of my own only, but facts at this time generally agreed to by those troops that were employed on that service."—Koehler to Lord Grenville, 9th July 1774. *Dropmore MSS.*

[1] Hood to Dundas, 5th, 14th, 25th, 29th April, 14th May, with their enclosures; D'Aubant to Dundas, 13th May 1794. *Diary of Sir John Moore*, i. 80-99.

1794. returned before news came that the French fleet had sailed from Toulon, escorting a force for the reinforcement of Calvi; whereupon Hood promptly put to sea,
June 10. but, being baffled in an attempt to get between the enemy and the French shore, left Admiral Hotham to blockade them and himself repaired to Genoa. First, however,
June 9. he detached Captain Nelson in the *Agamemnon* to superintend the embarkation of the troops at Bastia;
June 13. and on the 13th Stuart sailed with a force of fifteen hundred of all ranks, calling at Mortella Bay for ammunition and for drafts, numbering about eight
June 16. hundred men, which had arrived from Gibraltar. On the night of the 17th the ships found a precarious anchorage[1] to the west of Cape Revellata, a promontory
June 18. about two miles west of Calvi. On the morrow a landing-place was selected at Port Agro, an inlet about two and a half miles south of the anchorage and the
June 19. same distance south-west of Calvi; and on the 19th the troops landed and encamped on the heights above the town.

Calvi stands at the end of a peninsula formed by a ridge of rocky hills, which, opposite Port Agro, has a height of over nine hundred feet, and from thence slopes down with a general trend from south-west to north-east for some two miles to the sea. The town itself was strongly fortified, and was further protected by important outworks. These were, Fort Mozzello, a pentagon built of stone with a heavy gun on each face, situated on rising ground about eight hundred yards west of the town, with a battery, called the Fountain Battery, of six guns on its northern side; the San Francesco Battery of three guns, standing on a rocky hill washed by the sea; and Fort Monteciesco, with one heavy gun and five or six field-guns, built on a steep rock over two thousand yards south-west of Calvi, so as to command, in concert with two frigates in the bay, the communications between the town and

[1] The *Agamemnon* anchored in 63 fathoms on a rocky bottom.—Nelson's *Journal of the Siege of Calvi.*

the country to southward. One and all of these works, 1794. however, were dominated by the heights above; and Stuart formed the project of erecting four separate batteries on the same night. Of these one was to silence Monteciesco, and another to cover the construction of the most important battery of all, which was to be thrown up within seven hundred and fifty yards of Mozzello without the digging of a single trench. Bad weather delayed the landing of the troops and stores for two days; and the labour of making roads and hauling heavy guns to the appointed spot, nine hundred feet above the sea, was enormous. The work, however, went forward rapidly and with perfect unanimity, until Hood, who on the 19th of June had returned to Mortella Bay, June 19. again caused unpleasantness by demanding of General Trigge at Bastia, without a word to Stuart, forty soldiers to act as marines. Stuart, who was as resolute a man as Hood himself, despatched a strong protest; and when the Admiral, a few days later, wrote to Stuart enclosing a summons to the garrison of Calvi, the General declined to send it in, and begged to be allowed to carry on the operations by himself. This peremptory answer silenced the Admiral and brought his interference effectually to an end.

In the first days of July the battery against Monteciesco was completed, and on the 4th it opened July 4. fire, inflicting much damage on the fort. Stuart used the opportunity on the night of the 6th to make a July 6. feint attack upon Monteciesco, and, favoured by this diversion, duly established a battery of six heavy guns within seven hundred yards of Mozzello, in addition to the covering battery higher up the hill. For the next ten days the guns in the advanced works exchanged a savage and destructive cannonade with Mozzello and the Fountain Battery. On the 12th Nelson received July 12. the wound that cost him the sight of his right eye; and on the 14th Stuart, who up to that day had slept in the battery every night, was obliged to withdraw from it by exhaustion and ill-health. "No man in the

1794.
July 18.

expedition," wrote Nelson, "has undergone the fatigue of the General." But at last, on the 18th, the breach in Mozzello was seen to be practicable; and the assault was appointed to take place one hour before daybreak on the following day. The Fiftieth undertook the task of constructing during the night a new battery, as a

July 19.

feint, three hundred yards to south-west of Mozzello, and took post there, with the Fifty-first in reserve; while at the appointed hour the Eighteenth, under Lieutenant-colonel Wemyss, and the flank-companies of the whole force under Moore, fell, the one upon the Fountain Battery and the other upon Fort Mozzello itself. Both works were carried at the first rush with little loss, Moore receiving a wound in the head, which, however, did not keep him for an hour from his duty. The town still refusing to capitulate, the soldiers and seamen, though already overworked, with the greatest cheerfulness raised new batteries and dragged into position more heavy guns, which opened fire on the

July 31.

31st. The garrison replied by a general salvo, which soon died away into a few dropping shots and ceased, though not before a ball had slain Lieutenant William Byron of the Eighteenth, and thereby assured the peerage of Byron to a very handsome and unruly little boy of six, who was before long to become famous. Stuart then again summoned the town; and, after some negotiations, it was agreed that the garrison should surrender on the 10th of August, unless relieved before that day by an expedition from France.

Aug. 10.

The 10th of August came without bringing succour to the garrison, which accordingly surrendered. The loss of the British troops during the siege did not exceed ninety, nor that of the sailors a dozen, killed and wounded; but the amount of sickness for the three weeks before the fall of the town was terrible. More than two-thirds of the besiegers were in hospital, and the remaining third, utterly exhausted by the severity of their labours[1]

---

[1] "Perhaps there was never so much work done by so few men in the same space of time." *Diary of Sir John Moore*, i. 114.

and by the heat and unhealthiness of the climate during 1794. the dog-days, kept dropping down daily. Stuart himself had a month earlier asked for sick leave as soon as Calvi should be taken; and it was evidently a relief to all when the place surrendered, for another week would have prostrated the entire force. Hood, however, who had not gone near Calvi until the 27th of July, was bitterly chagrined because his name was not included in the capitulation; and he so far forgot himself in his vexation that he wrote to Dundas's Under Secretary of State, accusing Stuart of sacrificing his men from a spirit of tenderness towards the beleaguered garrison. Calvi, as he averred, would have been reduced to surrender a fortnight earlier by two days' bombardment, owing to the want of shelter and of ammunition in the town; and, in support of this allegation, he forwarded a vague statement by an irresponsible French officer, which Stuart's own vision and the list of stores captured at the fall of the town alike proved to be false. It is true that Hood at this time was so ill that he was obliged to ask for leave of absence; but it is not surprising that Moore, on learning of this example of the Admiral's spite against Stuart, should have characterised it as alike stupid and infamous.[1]

A new cause of dissension between General and Admiral arose soon after. Hood, desiring to relieve the squadron which was blockading the French fleet, and being as usual short of men, demanded of Stuart four complete regiments. To this Stuart, having fewer than eight hundred men fit for duty in the whole island, replied that he could spare only as many soldiers as had originally come from England in the fleet. This number accordingly he sent on board, but retained the best men, who had served him so well at Calvi, for service ashore, as they deserved. The result was a chorus of complaint from the captains of the fleet. " The troops sent to the ships are all of them

[1] Hood to Admiralty, 9th and 27th August; to Nepean, 17th August 1794. *Diary of Sir John Moore*, i. 153.

1794. raw boy recruits, without beds and with no covering but a regimental blanket . . . some have no clothing but what is on their backs . . . our decks are so leaky that few of the men can sleep dry in their hammocks . . . much less the ninety soldiers who have no beds." Such was the burden of their cry, nor was it unreasonable; but it seems never to have occurred to them that it was far harder on the General than on themselves that the only recruits furnished to him should have been children; that their clothing, which he had no means of supplying, should be deficient; and that, with over a thousand men in hospital, he could find no beds to give them. It appears from the comments of one of the captains that the soldiers originally brought from England were strong and active men, "better qualified for the duty of the afterguard than the majority of the seamen"; but it was asking a great deal of a General, who was responsible for the safety of several fortresses, to give up all his best soldiers to furl the mainsails of the fleet.[1]

The truth is that the persistent neglect of the Navy and Army by Ministers during the past ten years of peace had practically reduced the two services to the strength of one. A great part of the Navy was constantly ashore in those years, doing the work of soldiers, and a great part of the Army was on the fleet doing the work of sailors. Such a condition of things rarely fails to bring about friction, since it means the constant placing of seamen under the command of Generals and of soldiers under the command of Admirals. There is this further injustice about the system also, that whereas naval officers can easily distinguish themselves ashore—as indeed they rarely fail to do—it is extremely difficult, if not impossible, for military officers to distinguish themselves afloat. There are many Englishmen who could name several actions in which the Navy has distinguished itself on land; but probably there is not one in ten thousand who is aware of the part played by

[1] Hood to Admiralty, 20th September 1794, with enclosures.

the regiments of the Line in many of our great fights 1794. at sea. These very sieges of Bastia and Calvi are remembered—if, indeed, they be remembered at all among us—by the fact that Nelson took part in them; and such success as attended them is commonly ascribed to the blue-jackets. Yet this view of the operations is absolutely erroneous. The skill, energy and bravery of the seamen were extraordinary, as no men more willingly testified than David Dundas and Stuart; but it was Moore and Koehler who chose the positions for the attack on Fornali, and insisted that heavy guns could be brought up to them. At Calvi, again, Nelson's zeal and industry were indefatigable; but the extremely able dispositions whereby Stuart mastered the town emanated from the General alone, and Nelson did no more than carry out his instructions. The only military operation which Hood and Nelson designed and executed entirely by themselves, was the attack on Bastia from the northward; and this, as all the military officers had predicted and as events inexorably proved, was absolutely futile and ridiculous.

The point is worth insisting upon, because the popular sentiment respecting the expedition to Corsica is traditional, having been encouraged, partly through ignorance, partly through prejudice, by the Ministers. They, in common with most of the nation, observed that the Navy during the first years of this war was uniformly successful and the Army uniformly unsuccessful; and, consequently, they made up their minds that naval commanders must always be right and military commanders wrong. How entirely they ignored their own share in the military failures is a matter which will frequently engage our attention in the years before us; but, apart from this, they took no account of the fact that the enemy opposed to the fleet was far less formidable than that opposed to the Army. The French navy never to the very end of the war recovered from the demoralisation which it suffered at the Revolution; it was never more efficient as

1794. compared with the British, than the half-trained levies which the Duke of York defeated again and again in 1793 and 1794. The French army, on the other hand, emerged from the Revolution as the most terrible weapon ever known in the history of war, humiliating the most redoubtable hosts of Europe. The British nation at large very excusably shared this error with the Ministry; and, since both Cabinets and nations are far more generous in granting indiscriminate praise to success than conscientious in allotting the blame for failure, both conspired to exalt the Navy as incomparable and the Army as useless. As a mere matter of sentiment this opinion would have been harmless; but, unfortunately, it was the cause of real mischief, which, as it seems to me, may be traced in great measure to the arrogant and contemptuous attitude which Hood assumed, and taught his officers to assume, towards the Army. It is, indeed, true that Hood, after returning home in November 1794, was never again employed; but he, and possibly others of the old school, had set the tone, and it was encouraged by the long succession of naval victories and military reverses. Thus it was that naval officers, following his example, laid down the law about military matters of which they knew absolutely nothing, and put forward military projects which Ministers, in their ignorance and thirst for showy successes, accepted without sufficient inquiry or consideration. Yet at the time when Hood exhibited these airs of superiority, the Navy, through the fault of the Government, was in a thoroughly bad state; and already there were symptoms in his fleet of the mutiny which finally came to a head in 1797. It was not till the school of Hood had passed away that the true glories of the Navy began; and the head of the new school, John Jervis, had learned from Saunders and Wolfe at Quebec to make himself the most perfect of colleagues to a General.[1]

---

[1] I trust that I shall not be accused of endeavouring to revive old jealousies between the Army and Navy. In these days, when

HISTORY OF THE ARMY

Meanwhile, as the result of the operations, the French had been driven from Corsica ; whereupon the Corsicans solemnly offered to King George the Crown of the island, which was accepted on his behalf by the Commissioners, Lord Hood and Sir Gilbert Elliot. Thus the British gained a valuable naval station in the Mediterranean, to have and to hold for so long as might suit the caprice of one of the most ungovernable communities in Europe.

1794.

June 19.

AUTHORITIES.—The original papers respecting the operations in Corsica are in *H.O. Admiralty*, 213-217, and *W.O. Orig. Corresp.* 168. The papers are much confused and incomplete. Next to the original papers, Nelson's *Despatches* and the *Diary of Sir John Moore* are the most valuable authorities. Very reluctantly I am obliged to call attention to the very careless and inadequate treatment of the *Diary of Sir John Moore* by the editor in all campaigns preceding the war in the Peninsula. The work has been scamped ; the maps are worthless ; and the result is that the *Diary* demands nothing less than a new edition revised by a competent editor.

---

the two services are drawn closer together than ever before,—when naval officers attend the Staff College and military officers the Naval College at Greenwich,—it may, I hope, be permitted to me to write the truth without fear or favour. My admiration for the Navy is unbounded ; and, in past days, I have received such kindness and hospitality from naval officers as I shall always remember with pleasure and gratitude. But I still think it is time for us to look a little less to the successes, and a little more to the shortcomings of the Navy during the Great War ; for only those who have looked behind the scenes can realise how serious these shortcomings were.

CHAPTER IX

1793. It is now necessary to revert to the relative conditions of France and the Allies at the close of 1793. The British enterprises against the French at Dunkirk, in La Vendée, and at Toulon had one and all failed; but the tale of disaster was even then not fully told. Upon arrogating to itself the appointment of Generals in the field, the Committee of Public Safety Oct.-Nov. had appointed Pichegru and Hoche to command respectively the armies of the Rhine and Moselle. Pichegru had been a non-commissioned officer of artillery before the Revolution, had since obtained command of a battalion of volunteers, and, by assiduous courting of the Jacobin leaders, had become a Lieutenant-general without seeing a shot fired. Hoche, as we have seen, had risen from the ranks of the French Guards, had distinguished himself in high command at Dunkirk, and, above all, had attracted Carnot's attention by a memorandum condemning the dispersion of troops after the Austrian manner, and advocating everywhere concentration and a vigorous offensive. "This young fellow will go far," said Carnot, as he handed the document to Robespierre. "A very dangerous man!" objected the other, who dreaded the success of any man except himself. The task prescribed to Hoche was to relieve Landau, then blockaded by the Prussians; but he found his army in such ill condition that he hesitated to attempt anything until strengthened by Pichegru, when he made a general attack upon the Prussians under the Duke of

Brunswick at Kaiserslautern, and was beaten back with 1793. heavy loss. Thanks to Carnot's influence, however, Nov. 28-30. his failure was forgiven to him; and his new project, that he should reinforce Pichegru with two-thirds of his troops and fall upon the Austrians under General Wurmser at Hagenau, was approved. Wurmser perceived the gathering storm, and appealed to Brunswick for help; but King Frederick William had expressly forbidden the Duke to engage himself in any important operations, and the Prussians did not move until too late. On the 23rd of December Hoche Dec. 23. opened his attack with great skill and success, and would have annihilated Wurmser, had not Brunswick interfered at the last moment to check the pursuit of Dec. 26. the French. The Austrian commander, furious because Brunswick had not supported him from the first, then returned to the eastern bank of the Rhine, thus uncovering the Prussian left, and obliging them likewise to abandon the greater part of the Palatinate, and to content themselves with protecting the neighbourhood of Mainz. Landau, therefore, was recaptured by the French; the eastern frontier of France was purged of the enemy; and, above all, the ill-feeling between Austria and Prussia was more than ever embittered. Broadly speaking, the French by the close of the year had contended successfully alike with the Coalition and with internal foes, having lost ground only in the Eastern Pyrenees to Spain, the enemy from which it could be most easily recovered.

Nevertheless the authority of the Committee of Public Safety was by no means yet fully assured. The Commune of Paris, representing the most infamous of the population, had been jealous of it from the first; and the useful service of the little band of Workers had been accomplished only with great difficulty and by constant concessions to the party of violence. Representatives of the people vested with arbitrary powers still accompanied the armies, interfering with the operations, punishing by summary

1793. execution the slightest fault or failure, whether realised or merely suspected, levying barbarous and oppressive requisitions, and thus driving officers, men, and civil population alike to despair. In no army was this policy of terror more ruthlessly pursued than in that of the Rhine, where unlimited powers were exercised by the representatives Lebas and St. Just, of whom the latter, a young man of twenty-six, gave himself the airs of omnipotent Jove, with a guillotine for thunderbolt. A campaign, however, cannot be won solely by decapitation of one's own troops; and in the winter of 1793-1794 this fact began to impress itself, in respect not only of the army but of France at large, upon some of the ruling men in Paris. But it was no easy matter to convince the unspeakable rogues of the Commune of Paris that terror, which had brought to them personally enormous profit, was, as a national policy, a failure. Early in December 1793 the Committee of Public Safety took several measures to abridge the powers of the Commune; and some of the men who had in earlier days been most violent favoured the reaction towards a milder rule; but none the less Collot d'Herbois, who had been the author of most atrocious cruelties at Lyons since the recapture of the city, continued to obtain official approval of his conduct. Dread of summary restoration of order by some victorious General continually haunted the minds of many of the leaders, and notably of Robespierre; and, since the only idea of this last was to support whichever party was at the moment the stronger, he upheld

Dec. 25. Collot, and sought popularity by proposing the execution of another batch of Generals. Thus the opening of the new year witnessed a complete revival of the system of terror.

Immediate mischief was the inevitable result. Carnot had wished after the victory of Savenay to institute a policy of conciliation in La Vendée; but, on the contrary, a ruffianly soldier named Turreau was let loose upon the district with his "infernal

columns," as if to exterminate a herd of wild beasts. 1793.
The country was laid waste, the villages were burned,
and such victims as could not escape the soldiery were
swept into Nantes, to be murdered after such manner
as might please the still greater ruffian, Carrier. Thereupon the people at once took up arms again. A
smuggler bearing the nickname of Chouan [1] organised
a band of his fellows for revenge, and was soon
imitated by others. Charette and Stofflet again came
forward as leaders; and there began a desultory guerilla
war, fraught with constant disaster to the Republican
troops, which gnawed deeply into the heart of France.
At the same time, as if to increase the difficulties of
its capable commanders in the field, the Convention
lent a ready ear to all complaints against them. The
Representatives attached to the armies, with the true
instinct of politicians of all times and nations, were
careful to take to themselves the credit for every victory,
and to impute to the military the blame for every reverse; 1794.
and a savage decree was passed that any General con- Jan. 1.
demned to death should be executed in front of his
own troops. Successful commanders ran as great a
risk as unsuccessful. Kléber, Marceau, Lapoype, and
Bonaparte were one and all denounced in the spring of
1794 by the civilians who had aspired to direct them
in the field; and it was only by much labour and
cunning that Carnot was able to save their lives.

Nevertheless, despite all drawbacks, there was progress towards improvement in the French army.
True, there was still shameful rascality on the part of
contractors,[2] which was countenanced by Bouchotte
under the protection of Robespierre, and which
caused much suffering and desertion. The levy *en
masse* again had proved a failure; but, on the other
hand, compulsion to personal service, without exemption
of any kind, had forced a better class of recruit into 1793.
the ranks; and it was wisely determined to incorporate Nov. 22.
these new levies with the battalions at the front, which

[1] *Chat huant.* [2] Poisson, iii. 139 *seq.*

1793. possessed officers and non-commissioned officers of experience to train them. Finally, the reorganisation of the army into demi-brigades, consisting each of two battalions of volunteers and one battalion of
1794. regulars, was, after long delay, decreed and gradu-
Jan. 8. ally brought about. Innumerable useless corps were swept away; the establishments of existing corps were increased; and the law as to election of officers was practically, though tacitly, ignored.¹ At the same time a succession of decrees forbade the attendance of deputations from regiments upon the Convention, strove to check abuses and waste in the matter of
Feb. 12. requisitions, and made a new regulation that no soldier should rise to any grade of command—from corporal
Feb. 15. to general—who could not read and write. All this wrought for discipline and efficiency, for many of the Colonels and Generals appointed by the Jacobins, being unable to read a map or even a letter, had brought about great confusion at the War Office and frequent disaster in the field.² At the same time, strenuous efforts were made to improve the cavalry, which had hitherto been absolutely useless; and its establishment was fixed at twenty-nine regiments of heavy and fifty-four of light cavalry, or ninety-six thousand men in all. The horse-artillery also, after but a single year of existence, was augmented to eight thousand men, and the field-artillery, including detachments for battalion guns, to twenty-six thousand men. The whole force of France at the beginning of 1794 reached six hundred thousand effective men, or about half of the figure which, from motives of policy or conceit, was invariably assigned to it by the orators of Paris.

Moreover, to turn military improvements to the best advantage, events conspired to throw power more and more into the hands of the Committee of Public Safety. By a clever decree, the Committee contrived to disarm the hired ruffians who supported the Com-

¹ Poisson, 239-248; Rousset, pp. 293, 299.
² Ibid. 123-124, 236, 249; also generally, pp. 78-148.

mune, and to make over their weapons to the army; 1793. and this blow was followed three months later by the Dec. 22. accusation and execution of the leaders of the Commune itself, including Hébert, the supreme ruffian, and Ronsin and Vincent, two of the greatest scoundrels 1794. in the War Office. The next attack was directed March 29. against Danton and others, who had recognised the failure of the policy of terror, and wished to end it; and accordingly he and his followers went to the guillotine on the 5th of April. This was the work of April 5. Robespierre, who at one time had been the firm ally of both of these factions, but was now seeking supreme power in order to carry out certain ideas of his own for the social regeneration of France. Being an absolutely mediocre man, of the type which small provincial journals delight to honour with the title of "our talented townsman," he was wholly lacking in the ability and experience required for the business of administration; and he seems to have agreed, without knowing what he did, to the abolition of Ministers for departments and the substitution of boards, responsible to the Committee of Public Safety, in their place. Hereby the little knot of Workers, who had real capacity as well as boundless industry, gained an affluence of power, and the military service an increase of efficiency; for their labours were too high for the control of a petty lawyer who possessed no gift but that of composing bad essays, and knew no resource but that of cutting off heads. Nor was the activity of the Workers confined to France alone. Revolutionary agents had been busy all over Europe with persuasive tongues and still more persuasive purses. They had bribed high officials to second Carnot's military projects by conspiracies at Turin, Naples, Florence, and Genoa; they had met with much encouragement in Holland, and counted on further success in Switzerland; they had made some impression upon Denmark, had half gained Sweden, and had spared no expense to rouse the Turk against Austria. The cost of these

1794. negotiations was enormous, but the Government of France was playing for high stakes, knowing well that without victory in all quarters in the coming campaign, bankruptcy and starvation must inevitably bring down the Revolution with a crash.

On the military side Carnot had decided to strike at important points only, and elsewhere to stand on the defensive. In the south he designed to invade Italy, hoping that treachery at Turin would make the work easy; but the principal struggle, as he knew, must be fought out in Belgium. He did not, however, confine his schemes of aggression to that quarter only. He recognised with true insight that Britain was France's most formidable enemy; and he had actually projected and prepared for an invasion of England, with the help of the Brest fleet, and for a march upon London. The plan was bold, indeed wild in its extravagance, being founded on a false idea that disaffection in England was as deeply seated and as widely spread in action as it was noisy and inflated in speech. None the less the bare menace of invasion served a useful purpose—to scare and disconcert the British Government.[1]

Jan. 21. In truth it must have been with no very pleasant feelings that Ministers met Parliament in January 1794, having no better news to lay before the Houses than a tale of failure in all quarters. Pitt had, at least, the consolation that a section of the Whigs, headed by the Duke of Portland, in the same month announced to him their intention of separating themselves from Fox, and of giving the Ministry an independent support. It was, however, felt that such an arrangement could neither be satisfactory nor of long continuance, since, as Sir Gilbert Elliot put it, Portland's party would be no more than "a detached auxiliary force, to act on one occasion, to retire on another, and to be a perpetual object of anxiety to those whom they meant

[1] Sybel, iii. 26-27; *Vie de Carnot*, i. 470; *Dropmore Papers*, ii. 501.

to serve, of hope to the enemy and of speculation to the rest of the world.[1] Moreover, there were members of it, most notably William Windham, who were extremely dissatisfied with the military policy, or want of policy, initiated by Dundas.[2] Negotiations were, therefore, set on foot for the inclusion of Portland and some of his friends in the Cabinet ; and, after six full months spent in bargaining, it was finally arranged, on the 11th of July 1794, that Portland should become Second Secretary of State, Lord Fitzwilliam Lord President, and Lord Spencer Lord Privy Seal, while Windham displaced the incompetent and corrupt Sir George Yonge as Secretary at War. It may be well to add at once that in December Lord Spencer exchanged the Privy Seal for the Admiralty with the capable but indolent Lord Chatham, while Lord Mansfield took over the Presidency of the Council, and Lord Fitzwilliam accepted the Lord Lieutenancy of Ireland.

But these changes were accompanied by a reform of the greatest importance in the history of our military administration. Pitt was resolute in refusing to permit the War Department to lie in the Duke of Portland's hands ; wherein he was probably right, for the Duke, though he carried with him votes in the House of Commons, brought nothing to the Council Board beyond a certain ponderous irresolution. Pitt thereupon arranged, though with some difficulty, that Portland should administer the Home Department, including the Colonies, but should have no authority over naval and military business, for control of which he created a third and new

[1] *Life of Lord Minto*, ii. 383.
[2] "I think, if you see Dundas, it may not be amiss to urge the danger of running after distant objects while the great object lies still—of hunting the sheep till you have killed the dog. The most fatal error will be, I apprehend, the seeking to preserve the popularity of the war by feeding the avarice of the nation with conquests."—Windham to Mr. Elliot, December 1793. *Life of Lord Minto*, ii. 196.

Secretariat of State for War. In itself this measure was valuable and sound, but it was absolutely vitiated by the selection of Henry Dundas to fill the new post. In the face of the shameful blunders of the past eighteen months this appointment was almost criminal; but Pitt's ignorance of war was unfortunately surpassed only by his infatuated trust in his friend. Thus Henry Dundas became the First Secretary of State for War, the very worst man that could possibly have been chosen to found the traditions of such an office. His methods have found faithful imitation by all too many of his successors.[1]

So much may be said by anticipation of events which, though not actually accomplished, were practically assured at the opening of the session of 1794. But the secession of Portland's following by no means left the Opposition without keen critics of the conduct of military affairs. Tarleton the guerilla-leader of the American war, though a vain and shallow man, knew enough to hit the many weak points of Henry Dundas's enterprises, and he was backed by one abler and more solid than himself, Major Thomas Maitland, of the Sixty-second Foot, a brother of the extreme radical, Lord Lauderdale. We shall see more of Maitland, who is still remembered at Malta as "King Tom," in the years before us. Fox also, though as usual guilty of opposition which was purely factious, rightly pressed home upon the Government the duty of defining to themselves what was their true object. If, he argued, the purpose of the war was to substitute some form of government for the present tyranny in France, then Toulon was worth more than the West Indies; if on the other hand it was to obtain permanent possessions, then the West Indies were worth more than Toulon. To this the Government answered by the mouth of Jenkinson, that their end was to destroy the existing government in France; but both he and Pitt added

---

[1] Pitt to Grenville, 5th and 7th July 1794. *Dropmore Papers*, ii. 595, 597.

that Toulon was not to be considered of such importance as to justify a sacrifice of the opportunity for acquiring the French West Indies. Plainer evidence could not have been given of the utter unfitness of both to direct a formidable war.[1]

1794.

But the Government's measures for the augmentation of the regular Army, though not yet criticised in Parliament, were still more questionable than its military policy. In the first place, from blind assurance of an easy triumph, no sufficient provision had been made in time for raising additional men; and the result was that in October 1793 it was a matter of the greatest difficulty to furnish a draft of one hundred men to stop the gaps in Abercromby's brigade in Flanders.[2] In August, however, Alan Cameron of Erracht after much importunity had received permission to raise a regiment of Highlanders without levy-money, and with a special stipulation that the men should not be drafted; and thus was created the Seventy-ninth or Cameron Highlanders. In September 1793, new regiments began to follow each other more rapidly. First came a battalion formed by Lord Paget, whom we shall know better as a leader of cavalry under the successive titles of Lord Uxbridge and Marquis of Anglesey. The commission which he received to command it was the first that he ever held in the Army; and the regiment took, and still keeps, the number of the Eightieth. Then came in succession Colonel John Doyle's regiment, now the Eighty-seventh; Colonel Albermarle Bertie's, now the Eighty-first; Colonel Thomas De Burgh's, recruited chiefly in Connaught and still known as the Eighty-eighth Connaught Rangers; Major-general Leigh's, now the Eighty-second; and finally three Scottish battalions raised by Colonels Ferrier, Halkett, and Cunninghame, who had

[1] *Parliamentary History*, vol. xxxi.; Debates of 21st January, 3rd February, 10th April, 1794.
[2] Adj.-gen. to the Duke of York, *C.C.L.B.*, 31st October 1793.

1794. left the Scots Brigade of Holland during the American War and now tried to make a new brigade for their own land. Thus after a separation of over a century the old comrades of the Buffs rejoined them in Great Britain. In November other regiments were added, namely, General Bernard's, now the Eighty-fourth; General Cuyler's, now the Eighty-sixth; Colonel Nugent's, recruited by Lord Buckingham among his tenants at Stowe, now the Eighty-fifth; Colonel Fitch's, formed chiefly of recruits from Dublin, now the Eighty-third; and Colonel Crosbie's, now the Eighty-ninth.[1] From January to October 1794, there was a deluge of new battalions, of which it must suffice to mention here a second battalion of the Seventy-eighth, and three which began life in February, namely, that raised by Mr. Thomas Graham, the volunteer of Toulon, which was and still is the Ninetieth, and two Highland corps formed by Colonel Duncan Campbell and Lord Huntly, which though originally distinguished by other numbers[2] are known to us as the Ninety-first and Ninety-second Highlanders. Five regiments of Light Dragoons raised in February and March must also be mentioned, since we shall meet with them not unfrequently, namely, Beaumont's, Fielding's, Fullarton's, Loftus's, and Gwyn's, which were raised without expense to the Government, and bore the numbers

March 7. Twenty-one to Twenty-five. Lastly, attention must be called to a notable new departure in the formation of a Corps of Waggoners in five companies, with a total strength of six hundred non-commissioned officers and men, one-tenth of them artificers. This was the first attempt at a military organisation of the transport-service.

It was reckoned that, in one way and another, at least thirty thousand men were enlisted for the regular Army

---

[1] These regiments are arranged according to the dates of their letters of service. See Appendix A at the end of the volume, giving a list of all the corps raised from 1798 to 1803.

[2] Campbell's was originally numbered 98th; Huntly's 100th.

between November 1793 and March 1794,[1] and the 1794. number was the more astonishing since Fencibles and substitutes for the Militia had absorbed a large number of recruits. It would, however, be a fallacy to suppose that Ministers had yet thought out any regular plan for continual filling of the ranks; on the contrary, they had resorted to a variety of hasty expedients founded upon no fixed principle, and therefore unfitted to meet more than a temporary emergency. Such procedure is invariably wasteful and extravagant in the highest degree; but Yonge and Dundas honestly believed themselves to have found true economy in a clever and specious scheme put forward by one of the Generals in Ireland, for defraying the cost of new levies by the sale of commissions.[2] The experiment was tried on a grand

---

[1] Adj.-gen. to Prince Edward, *C.C.L.B.*, 17th March 1794.

[2] *C.C.L.B.*, Adj.-gen. to Lieut.-gen. Cunninghame, 8th October 1793.

Here is an example of the scheme as used for raising a regiment of 10 companies each of 60 men.

Proceeds of sale of 1 Lieut.-colonelcy, 1 Majority,
1 Company, 1 Lieutenancy, 1 Ensigncy,
amount to £9250
Cost of 600 men at £15 9000
                                        Balance . . £250

Another scheme for augmenting battalions of infantry. As soon as 450 approved recruits have been raised, there shall be added to it a Lieutenant-colonel, and a Major.

The Major will pay for his Lieut.-colonelcy . £600
The senior Captain will pay for his senior Majority   700
Another Captain   ,,   ,,   junior Majority   550
Two Companies thus vacated will sell for . .   2800
Levy-money of £5 granted by Government for
450 men   2250
                                        Total . . £6900
Cost of 450 men at £15 (£10 bounty and £5
levy-money) would be   6750
                                        Balance . . £150

Thus the country is saved all expense but £5 a man levy-money.

S.C.L.B., 15th April, 1st and 12th November 1793; 20th January 1794.

1794. scale and with high hopes, not unmingled with misgiving, on the part of officers; and indeed the prospect of raising a large number of men without charge to the country was sufficiently alluring. None the less the scheme failed completely,[1] as is the common fate of all projects which aspire to obtain a costly article at a trifling outlay.

Beyond this experiment the Government could think of no better plan for augmenting the Army than to encourage young men of means to raise men for rank, or in other words to offer them rank in the Army in proportion to the number of recruits that they could produce. This was an old system which hitherto had been confined chiefly to the raising of independent companies, and had therefore led to no higher rank than that of Captain. Even then it had been vicious and had been repeatedly condemned; and it was no good sign that in 1793 a Lieutenant had advertised in the London papers, offering two thousand guineas to any one who could raise him one hundred recruits in six weeks, and get them passed at Chatham.[2] But it was now extended to the raising of a multitude of battalions which, for the most part, were no sooner formed than they were disbanded, and drafted into other corps. Thereby of course the men were easily absorbed, but not so the officers, to whom the Government had pledged itself to give half-pay; and thus it was possible for a young man to obtain a pension for life from his country on investing a sufficient sum to raise a few score of recruits.[3] But this was the least of the evils of the system. There was instantly a rush to obtain letters of service; and commissions became a drug in the market. It was said that over one hundred commissions were signed in a single day,[4] while the

---

[1] *S.C.L.B.*, 9th July 1794.   [2] *Star*, 13th April 1793.

[3] One Lieutenant drew half-pay for 80 years after the drafting of the 104th (Royal Manchester Volunteers), which was one of these ephemeral corps. *Records and Badges of the British Army*, p. 833.

[4] *St. James's Chronicle*, 26th April 1794.

Gazette could not keep pace with the incessant promotions. 1794. The Army-brokers, who in the days of purchase negotiated for officers the sale of commissions, exchanges, and the like, carried on openly a most scandalous traffic. "In a few weeks," to use the indignant language of an officer of the Guards, "they would dance any beardless youth, who would come up to their price, from one newly raised corps to another, and for a greater douceur, by an exchange into an old regiment, would procure him a permanent situation in the standing Army." The evils that flowed from this system were incredible. Officers who had been driven to sell out of the Army by their debts or their misconduct, were able after a lucky turn at play to purchase reinstatement for themselves with the rank of Lieutenant-colonel. Undesirable characters, such as keepers of gambling-houses, contrived to buy for their sons the command of regiments; and mere children were exalted in the course of a few weeks to the dignity of field-officers. One proud parent, indeed, requested leave of absence for one of these infant Lieutenant-colonels, on the ground that he was not yet fit to be taken from school. It must be noted, too, that, thanks to the Army-brokers, these evils were not confined to the new regiments, but were spread, by means of exchange, all over the Army; and, since the great majority of the regiments were abroad on active service, the old officers, who were daily facing danger and death, suddenly found themselves inferior in rank to men undistinguished by birth or intellect, and without the smallest pretension to military ability.

Little less dangerous was the enormous encouragement given to crimping by the sudden demand from all quarters for recruits. The Navy, as has been seen, was unable to find its complement of men for the fleet, despite the fact that the Common Council of London in January 1793 had offered an additional bounty of two pounds to seamen;[1] and now there was thrown

[1] *Public Advertiser*, 2nd February 1793.

1794. into competition with the press-gang a race of greedy, unscrupulous scoundrels, some of them holding and disgracing the King's commission, who made profit out of every boy or man that they could lay hold of by fair means or foul. Thus the ranks were filled, as Tarleton phrased it, with infancy and dotage; recruiting became a mere matter of gambling; and the price of men rose to thirty pounds a head.[1] So large a sum set a premium on every description of rascality in the trepanning of recruits by violence or by guile; and the ordinary Englishman does not lightly bear with oppression of this kind. At length, on one day in August, an unfortunate lunatic, who had been enlisted by a sergeant and locked up in a brothel—the synonym for a recruiting-house—in London, hurled himself out of a window in the third story, into the street. Instantly a mob assembled, which delivered a succession of riotous attacks upon all houses of this description, and was only suppressed, after several days of disorder, by the calling out of the Guards and six regiments of cavalry.[2] Pitt defended the system on the ground that the Navy as well as the Army would be manned, by the turning over of soldiers to reinforce the marines; but this is only another instance of Pitt's callous ignorance and self-deception. The truth is that while doing nothing, and probably worse than nothing, for the Navy, it destroyed the efficiency of the Army for a time, and but for the timely interposition of a capable soldier would have destroyed it permanently. Who was responsible for the introduction of the system it is not easy to say, for there were so many disgraceful circumstances attending it that the whole subject was hushed up, and is now extremely obscure; but assuredly it was not Lord Amherst, nor is it credible that it can have been any soldier. It is safe to assert that it was the work of civilians; and if we seek among the civilians at the War Office for the two men of tried conceit,

[1] *St. James's Chronicle*, 19th July 1794.
[2] *Ibid.* 19th August 1794.

unwisdom, and incapacity, we can find them at once in 1794. Sir George Yonge and Henry Dundas.[1]

Meanwhile new levies, even when raised under these false conditions, were not to be produced in a moment; and thirty thousand recruits were not to be reckoned, even by the most sanguine of Ministers, as equivalent to the same number of old soldiers. The Government, therefore, renewed its contract for the hire of Hanoverians and Hessians on a greater scale, raising the total number of them to close upon thirty-four thousand men. To these were added five foreign corps, which were intended to supplement the dearth of light troops from which the British contingent had suffered so much during the campaign of 1793. As early as in May of that year, one Captain George Ramsay had offered to raise a small body of foreign riflemen, and had after some delay been permitted to enlist also a corps of Uhlans. Thus originated three corps which, in honour of the Commander-in-Chief in Flanders, were called by the name of York Chasseurs, York Rangers, and York Hussars. The formation of the remaining two, the Prince of Salm's Hussars and Hompesch's Hussars, was only authorised in February 1794, and consequently they were not ready for service at the opening of the campaign. No effort had been made to provide British soldiers for the work of light infantry, except by raising eight additional light companies for the

[1] *Narrative by an Officer of the Guards*, ii. 76-79; Bunbury, *Great War with France*, Introd. p. xx.; *St. James's Chronicle*, 27th January 1795 (debate on Army Estimates of 21st January); *Journal of Sir Henry Calvert*, pp. 360, 384-85. The letters of Lady Sarah Lennox (the mother of the Napiers) throw a curious light on the scramble for promotion through the enlistment of recruits at this period. "Think of my bad luck about recruits. If I had seen an officer one fortnight sooner who is here, he would have sold me 20 at 11 guineas per man. Is not that unfortunate; but they are now gone. My Dublin stock too, which was 40, has been reduced to 26," ii. 109, *and see also* ii. 101. "Is there any chance of recruiting men of five feet four inches for 10 guineas, and as much under as possible, in your neighbourhood." Evidently the wives of poor officers plunged into speculation to help their husbands with recruits.

1794. Brigade of Guards, the men of which were distinguished by round hats with large green feathers, trousers instead of breeches and gaiters, and fusils instead of muskets. But with these details of dress their qualifications as light troops were exhausted; for they received no sufficient instruction in their peculiar duty.[1]

The Light Dragoons likewise continued to belie their name, being trained in reality simply as cavalry of the line of battle; but for this, probably, the civil rather than the military authorities of the Army were responsible, for at this period it was literally impossible to obtain officers for the mounted troops. It will be remembered that before the outbreak of the war the Adjutant-general had constantly, but in vain, endeavoured to obtain an increase of the wholly inadequate pittance of pay meted out to subalterns of dragoons. Even in peace the burdens laid upon them were too heavy to be borne, and to these were now added inadequate compensation for losses in the field, only eighteen pounds being granted to replace a charger which had cost thirty-five. The consequences became immediately apparent. The Duke of York was obliged to beg that the cornetcies of regiments serving in the Low Countries might be given away, since purchasers for them could not be found.[2] Thus the Light Dragoons were untaught, because there were no officers to teach them; patrols and advanced detachments lacked the daring and adventurous leading of youth; and one of the highest schools for the training of subalterns was wholly neglected. It is hardly possible to estimate the evil consequences of Pitt's misdirected parsimony, in devoting to the hire of mercenaries the money which should have been spent in the improvement of the British Army.

So much must be said of the regular forces; but the year 1794 was not less remarkable for an enormous increase in the number of the Fencible regiments,

[1] S.C.L.B. 15th April 1793. *Daily Chronicle*, 16th April 1793.
[2] York to Dundas, January 1794.

Militia and Volunteers, all due to Carnot's menace of 1794. invasion. The estimate for the Fencible Cavalry provided in March 1794 for forty troops; by May this figure had already risen to ninety-two troops, and was still rising. Next, the number of the embodied Militia for England was augmented to thirty-six thousand; while by an Act of the Irish Parliament, passed in 1793, sixteen thousand additional Militia were levied in Ireland. This latter was an entirely new departure; and it need hardly be said that the first ballots drawn on the west of St. George's Channel led to serious rioting.[1] Provision was also made in the estimates, and a Bill was introduced for the raising of six thousand Militia in Scotland; but this measure was for the moment deferred, in order that familiarity might ultimately facilitate its passing. The formation of the Scottish Militia, however, appears to have been begun in anticipation,[2] and men were enlisted who, later in the year, were formed into over twenty battalions of Fencible infantry. The extension of the ballot throughout the three kingdoms, though not actually completed until the passing of the Scottish Militia Act in 1797, must be regarded as the most important military step taken since the passing of the Militia Act of 1757 by the elder Pitt; and due credit should be allowed to the Government for it.

Oct. 15- Nov. 20.

Meanwhile, to augment the English Militia to the prescribed figure, an Act was passed, after the model of that of 1778, empowering the Lord-Lieutenants to enrol volunteers, to be added to the Militia, and to be entitled to the same bounty, subsistence, and clothing. Finally, in April, was passed an Act, limited to the duration of the war, authorising the formation of district corps or companies of Volunteers, to be entitled to pay and subject to military discipline if called out for invasion or in aid of the civil power. This was the first attempt to summon the

[1] *Chronicle*, June 1793.
[2] *St. James's Chronicle*, 24th and 26th July 1793.

1794. manhood of the kingdom to arms; for, though Shelburne in the peril of 1782 had sent a circular to all the Mayors and Lord-Lieutenants in England with the object of forming a levy *en masse*, yet the hastening of the peace, by Rodney's victory of the Saints and by the relief of Gibraltar, had rendered any elaboration of the plan unnecessary. Now, however, there sprang up an infinity of Volunteer corps, infantry, artillery, and light horse or Yeomanry Cavalry, first in single companies and troops, but very soon in battalions and regiments. The first of the Volunteer corps appears to have been the five Associated Companies of St. George's, Hanover Square, which was formed in anticipation of the Act;[1] the first of the Yeomanry was Lord Winchelsea's three troops of "Gentlemen and Yeomanry," raised by the County of Rutland.[2] The rapidity with which these Volunteers were raised would be flattering to the national vanity were it not susceptible of a commonplace explanation. By a certain clause in the Act Volunteers were exempted from service in the Militia, upon producing a certificate that they had attended exercise punctually during six weeks previously to the hearing of appeals against the Militia list. This dissociation of the Volunteers from the Militia was a great and disastrous blunder, which has never yet been thoroughly repaired. It is, however, sufficient to note for the present that the Government had deliberately set up three different descriptions of auxiliary forces, Militia, Fencibles, and Volunteers, all competing with each other and with the regular Army. The number of regular troops provided for in the estimates of 1794 (reckoning the Irish establishment at fourteen thousand) was one hundred and seventy-five thousand men, besides thirty-four thousand foreign troops, four thousand Fencibles, and fifty-two thousand Militia; or, say, two hundred and sixty-five thousand men in all.

Simultaneously with these efforts at home, Pitt worked strenuously to restore unity and vigour to the

[1] *S.C.L.B.* 26th March 1794. [2] *Ibid.* 29th April 1794.

Coalition. The relations of the coalesced powers at 1794. the close of 1793 were in the highest degree unsatisfactory. The Empress Catherine, still insatiable, despite the deterioration of her forces and the exhaustion of her treasury, had resumed her old designs upon Turkey, and had set a large force in motion towards Constantinople. The Emperor Francis, still under the guidance of Thugut and full of vague plans for increasing his territory, was drawing closer to the Empress in the hope of obtaining her countenance to the annexation of Venice by Austria, if indemnity in France should fail, and of sharing with her the ultimate partition of Turkey. Both were bitterly incensed against Prussia: Catherine because King Frederick William had diverted his troops from the invasion of France to the strengthening of his position in Poland; Francis from jealousy that his rival should have enlarged his boundaries, when he himself had not. Frederick William, as has been seen, had practically withdrawn his forces from active operations on the Rhine; and accordingly in December 1793 Pitt had sent Lord Malmesbury to Berlin to ascertain (if, indeed, anything could be ascertained in such a centre of intrigue and falsehood) what might be Prussia's motive for retiring from the struggle. In reply to Malmesbury, Frederick William, having obtained his desire in Poland, declared himself eager to continue the contest against the Jacobins, but absolutely prevented by lack of money. Thereupon Pitt proposed to give Prussia a subsidy of two millions Feb. 5. sterling, of which England should pay three-fifths, and Holland and Austria each one-fifth. This was a liberal offer; and, since it was certain that Holland would raise no objection, it lay practically with Austria to give effect to it. It was well known that Austria was in financial straits, that Hungary was full of unrest and the Belgic Provinces much cooled in their loyalty, and that, apart from these troubles at home, the Emperor had contrived to quarrel with Sardinia abroad. Hence it was beyond question that Austria could not carry on the

1794. war without Prussia's assistance ; and, forasmuch as Francis had already despatched emissaries to Berlin to discuss the operations to be undertaken in the spring, the natural presumption was that he would gladly close with Pitt's proposal.

The British Government thereupon bestirred itself to frame its projects for the coming campaign. The Duke of York left Belgium for London on the 6th of
Feb. 12. February ; and a few days later Mack, now advanced to the rank of Major-general, arrived there likewise to concert plans with the Ministers. The Austrian genius had shortly before submitted[1] a scheme calculated for a force of three hundred and forty thousand men, which had been received with great satisfaction by the British Cabinet and the Duke of York ; but, since there was no earthly possibility that the Coalition could put that number of men into the field, the whole of this elaborate creation was valueless. Both Mack and Coburg, however, pressed for a concentration of forces and a march on Paris, though neither of them could conceive the feasibility of taking the offensive without leaving one hundred and twenty thousand men behind them to guard the frontier from the Meuse to the sea. The prime question, therefore, was one of men, and Pitt on his side promised his utmost endeavour to increase the British contingent to a figure which should ensure a genuine total of forty thousand fighting soldiers. As to the means whereby this force should be produced, Pitt was remarkably vague, being clear only that he could not spare the few thousand men under Lord Moira's command, since he wished to hold them ready to sail to any part of the British coast which might be threatened by a French invasion. Moira, therefore, though one of the ablest officers in the Army and adored by the men, was kept inactive, while his troops sickened and died of gaol-fever in overcrowded transports at Jersey.[2] However, Pitt

[1] York to Dundas, 2nd February 1794 (with enclosures).
[2] Dr. Hayes to Lord Cathcart, 1st February 1794 ; Monthly returns, 1st February to 1st May ; Ditfurth, ii. 32.

made up his forty thousand men to his own satisfaction 1794. by naming various reinforcements, which he hoped to pour into Flanders during the summer and autumn; for it was one of the delusions of this gifted man, as also of his friend Dundas, that an army of twenty thousand men, supplemented by monthly driblets of two thousand men during ten months, is the same thing as an army of forty thousand men ready for the field at the opening of the campaign.

The next requisite was that the Austrian, Prussian, and British contingents should each of them possess a siege-train, since, according to Mack, it was essential for the Allies to master every fortress on the French frontier from the Meuse to the sea. Pitt promised this also, on behalf of the British; and then arose the question of commanders. Though well aware that the King's assent would be wrung from him only by extreme pressure, the Ministers were for recalling the Duke of York and appointing Lord Cornwallis, who had just returned from India, in his place. Herein they were undoubtedly right, for, after all allowance made for the extreme difficulty of his position, the Duke did not shine in the field. The Ministers, however, blamed him especially for the failure before Dunkirk, wherein they themselves were chiefly in fault; and Mack, prompted apparently by the King, found little difficulty in making excuses for the Duke, who from the first had condemned the idea of attacking Dunkirk at all. It was finally arranged that he should retain command of the British contingent, but that he should be kept always in the neighbourhood of the principal army, with a few thousand Austrians attached to his own corps, so as to subordinate him the more completely to the Austrian Commander-in-Chief. This compromise bears so clearly the mark of the British politician that its origin cannot be doubtful. It is of a kind that may serve for the construction of a Cabinet, but it is not suitable for war, and was particularly ill-fitted to the projected campaign. For the rest, Pitt declared himself satisfied

1794. that the command should remain with Coburg, who was deservedly most popular among the Austrian troops; and Mack rejoiced the heart of the British Cabinet by announcing that the Emperor would direct the operations as Generalissimo in person. Altogether the results of the conference were considered to be so satisfactory that the King presented Mack with a jewelled sword as a reward for his good service.¹

The British Government's satisfaction was soon proved to be premature. The discussion of future operations with the Court of Berlin was, in fact, only a trick of Thugut to keep as many Prussian troops as possible on the French frontier; and the whole intent of the Emperor's taking personal command was that Coburg and other honest men in his army, who profoundly distrusted his chief adviser, should be kept under proper restraint. Thugut now declared, in answer to Pitt's proposals, that Austria would not advance a penny towards the subsidies for the Prussian army, being well able to dispense with every part of it beyond the twenty thousand men which formed its contribution towards the forces of the Empire. In fact, he was so madly jealous and fearful of Prussia at this time that he secretly proposed to Russia a scheme for a joint March 11. attack upon her. On learning the Emperor's decision, King Frederick William ordered Marshal Möllendorf to begin the withdrawal of his troops from the Rhine. Coburg was in consternation, for he knew that, without Prussian help, the execution of the approved plan of campaign would be impossible. He therefore asked the Duke of York to join him in requesting Möllendorf to delay his retirement, and despatched letter after letter to Vienna, adjuring the Emperor in terms of touching devotion and patriotism to send every man that he could raise to Flanders, and to work loyally with Prussia to crush the terrible power of the Revolution while there was yet time. Möllendorf courteously acceded to his desire; but the Prince's

¹ Witzleben, iii. 64 *seq.*

protests fell on deaf ears in the Imperial capital. 1794.
There were over sixty thousand men ready for service
at Vienna, but from his insane dread of Prussian
aggression, Thugut would not part with one of them ;
and Coburg's only reward for his faithful and disinterested counsel was rude and ungracious rebuke.
Just at the critical moment, however, Lord Malmesbury checked the further withdrawal of the Prussian
troops, by threatening to break off all negotiation for a
subsidy unless they remained on the Rhine until he
could receive further instructions from London. This
brought the impecunious King to reason, for without
English money he was lost. Shortly afterwards the parley
was, with Pitt's sanction, resumed ; and there was much
haggling over the sphere wherein the Prussian troops
should be employed, Frederick William declaring that
for operations on the Rhine he would furnish eighty
thousand men, but for Belgium not more than fifty
thousand. Finally, Malmesbury succeeded in com-
promising matters ; and a treaty was signed at the
Hague on the 19th of April, whereby Prussia, in con- April 19.
sideration of a lump sum of £300,000 and a subsidy
of £50,000 a month, engaged herself to provide sixty-
two thousand men, to be employed wherever Great
Britain and Holland, their paymasters, should think fit.
Ten days later Fox in the House of Commons predicted April 30.
that this would be a useless waste of money ; and it
will be seen that he was a true prophet.[1]

Meanwhile Coburg was doing his utmost to prepare
his army for the heavy work that lay before it ; but
the Austrian forces had not improved since the previous year. Heavy losses had brought many young
soldiers into the ranks ; and, owing to the extreme
extension of his line of cantonments, the troops had
gained little rest during the winter. The French
delivered as many as forty-five petty attacks between
the 6th of January and the 26th of March, each one

[1] Sybel, iii. 49-65 ; York to Dundas, 22nd March, 3rd April
1794 ; Witzleben, iii. 70-84.

of which meant the setting of many detachments in motion for long and harassing matches. Moreover, owing to the decay of the Emperor's popularity in Belgium, the people would do little or nothing for the troops; and, Coburg being unwilling to take from the inhabitants what they refused to give, the men suffered greatly from want of food, fuel, and shelter. Money would, of course, have overcome all difficulties, but, though the Prince begged piteously for it, he could obtain none from Vienna; and the consequences were most cruel. "Some regiments," he wrote in February, "have been without bread for several days, and two contractors have been driven to suicide." On the other hand, taking a true measure of his enemy, Coburg had issued instructions that the French must be attacked at all times and in all circumstances, and that, even in the defence of a position, at least a third of the men should be kept ready for a counter-attack. But there was one clause in his orders which seems to give the key to many an Austrian defeat. "Men defending entrenchments will sit in the banquette, arms in hand, until the enemy comes within three hundred paces, or even somewhat nearer, and then open a heavy fire." British troops were accustomed to hold their fire until the enemy was within thirty paces; and hence it was that the French Army of Italy, when they met them in Egypt, found the red coats tougher adversaries than the white.[1]

Among the rest of the Allies matters were little better than with the Austrians. The Hessians in Flanders were far below their proper strength, sickness and constant skirmishes having swallowed up the additional recruits furnished during the winter; while the brigade which had been attached to Moira's force left one hundred dead and two hundred and fifty invalided in the Isle of Wight, over and above five hundred sick men whom they carried with them to Ostend.[2] As to the British, everything was, as usual, behindhand, though

---

[1] Witzleben, iii. 91, 62, 29; Ditfurth, ii. 10 *sqq.*, 28.
[2] Ditfurth, ii. 30, 31.

the Duke of York had now a more energetic Chief of Staff than Murray in Colonel James Craig, whom we saw last at Wilmington in 1781. Recognising from his American experience how serious was the Duke's deficiency in light troops, Craig tried to hire some from Prussia, but without success. There was a difficulty about the British siege-train, for it was discovered, some weeks after the Duke had made requisition for it, that the application had been mislaid at the Office of Ordnance. Though Dundas made profuse promises of British drafts and reinforcements, to the number of five thousand men, not one thousand of these had arrived by the middle of March, and Abercromby's brigade was quite unfit to take the field. The remount-horses were discovered to be very bad. Artillery-drivers, moreover, the dearth of which had been represented by the Duke for quite six months, were found to be so scarce in England that the Master-General was fain to seek them, though without success, in Hanover. A fresh disappointment arose in the matter of foreign troops, for it proved impossible to obtain three thousand Brunswickers, whom Dundas had counted upon taking over from the Dutch into the British service. Rapidly the forty thousand soldiers promised by Pitt dwindled away; and Craig resigned himself to the inevitable fact that the deficiency would amount to at least ten thousand men. But this was not, to his thinking, the most formidable danger. With a boldness which must have shocked Pitt and Dundas, he wrote to the War Office a very strong and damaging criticism of the cordon-system, and predicted that nothing but misfortune could attend Generals who upon principle preferred dispersion to concentration.[1]

1794.

So the month of March passed away, the unhappy Coburg waiting in anxious suspense to know first,

[1] Craig to Nepean, 7th, 22nd, 31st March, 11th April; to York, 7th, 15th, 16th March; York to Dundas, 9th, 22nd, 26th March, 1794.

1794. when the troops that composed his heterogeneous army would be ready ; secondly, what their numbers might be when they were ready ; and thirdly, what the Emperor would expect him to do with them when it should please him to honour headquarters with his presence. Meanwhile Coburg had even in February given orders for the contraction of his cantonments; and at the beginning of April, after much shifting, his force occupied the following positions.

The Right or western Wing of the Allied Army, covering maritime Flanders, was entrusted to Clerfaye with a force of Austrians, Hessians, and Hanoverians, who thus occupied the ground formerly entrusted to the British and Dutch. His headquarters were at Tournai, where an entrenched camp had been thrown up. In his front also Orchies and Marchiennes had been strengthened by field-works ; and on his right efforts had been made to restore the defences of Menin, Ypres, and Nieuport, though, except in the case of Ypres, with little result. The effective strength of Clerfaye's army in the field, after deduction of garrisons for the strong places, was about twenty-four thousand men.

On Clerfaye's left, and connected with it by a detachment of five thousand men under General Wurmb at Denain on the Scheldt, stood the Centre or principal army, consisting of about twenty-two thousand men under the Duke of York, about forty-three thousand men under Coburg himself, and of about nineteen thousand Dutch under the Prince of Orange. The Duke occupied the right with headquarters at St. Amand, Coburg the centre with headquarters at Valenciennes, and the Prince of Orange the left with headquarters at Bavai. It was reckoned that, after providing for garrisons, Coburg could spare sixty-five thousand men for active operations.

The Left Wing consisted of twenty-seven thousand Dutch and Austrians under Count Kaunitz, which were stretched over the space from Bettignies, a little to the north of Maubeuge, to Dinant on the Meuse.

To these must be added fifteen thousand more 1794. Austrians under General Beaulieu, cantoned between Namur and Tréves, bringing the grand total of the Allied force to something over one hundred and sixty thousand men, of which at the very most one hundred and twenty thousand were free for work in the field.[1]

It will be noticed that the corps of Clerfaye and of the Duke of York had exchanged the places which they had occupied during the previous year, pursuant to the design of the British Ministers that the Duke of York should be kept under the immediate eye of Coburg. The first result of this interference was to spoil Clerfaye's temper for the whole campaign; for he judged his force too weak for its task of defending the maritime provinces; and indeed it was only by the positive orders of Coburg that he consented to hold the command.[2] The whole arrangement, in fact, was calculated to cause confusion. It was bad enough that the lines of retreat for the British and Austrians should be in exactly opposite directions; and the obvious course, upon the change of the Duke of York's station, would have been to have shifted his base to Antwerp. But far from this, not only was his base continued at Ostend, but, to make matters worse, a brigade of British was placed under Clerfaye's command, and a respectable number of Austrians under the Duke of York's; so that in case of mishap, not only must the lines of retreat for the right and right centre intersect each other, but neither corps could retire upon its base without leading several of its regiments in the wrong direction.

Meanwhile on the French side Carnot had girded himself for a supreme effort. "We must finish matters this year," he wrote to Pichegru on the 11th of February; "unless we make rapid progress and anni-

[1] Ditfurth (ii. 43) reckons the field force at from 120,000 to 130,000, but he includes British troops which were not on the spot, and reckons the strength of those present at too high a rate.
[2] Witzleben, iii. 94.

1794. hilate the enemy to the last man within three months, all is lost. To begin again next year would mean for us to perish of hunger and exhaustion." He therefore decided to combine the armies of the North, of the Ardennes and of the Moselle, and to mass two hundred and fifty thousand men along the line from Dunkirk to the Meuse. Of these about one hundred thousand were to move upon Ypres, march thence upon Ghent, master maritime Flanders, and then wheel eastward upon Brussels; while at the same time another hundred thousand were to advance upon Namur and Liège, and sever communication with Luxemburg. In other words, he designed to turn and envelop both flanks of the Allied Army, leaving about fifty thousand men to stand on the defensive in the intermediate space between Bouchain and Maubeuge.

Of the many eminent critics who have passed judgment upon this plan, there is not one who has failed to point out and condemn its defects; and indeed it is obvious that if the Allies, neglecting small detachments, should fall with their full strength upon either wing of the enemy, they might annihilate it. An advance of the French in overwhelming strength upon the communications of the Allies about Namur would have been equally effective and far less hazardous. Yet Carnot prescribed the invasion of the maritime provinces as the first object, partly no doubt with a view to the ultimate invasion of England, but chiefly, as I conceive, with the political object of threatening the retreat of the British and thus overawing the most formidable power in the Coalition. It is worth while to recall that in 1815 Wellington looked for Napoleon to turn the western flank of the Allies and cut the British off from the sea, and that he dreaded such a movement so much that he made his dispositions at Waterloo with a view to prevent it. Wellington's action has been as sharply criticised as Carnot's; and yet, when two such men agree upon such a point, their opinion is at least worth serious consideration. In any case, the threatening of the lines of communication both east and west was 1794. quite sufficient to distract the councils of the Allies, to set them quarrelling as to which among themselves should be sacrificed to the others, and so perhaps to bring about political discord and the rupture of the Coalition.

At the end of March Pichegru gave the strength of the army of the North at two hundred and six thousand, and of the army of the Ardennes at thirty-seven thousand men, making a total of two hundred and forty-three thousand present under arms, of which one hundred and eighty-three thousand were free for service in the field. The army of the North at the beginning of April was thus distributed. The Left Wing, seventy-one thousand men, extended from Dunkirk by Cassel and Lille to Pont-à-Marque; the Centre, forty-seven thousand men, from Arleux (near Douai) by Cambrai, Bouchain, and Bohain to Etreux, a little to the north of Guise; the Right Wing, thirty-six thousand men, from Avesnes by Cerfontaine, St. Rémy, and St. Waast to Maubeuge. This made a total of one hundred and fifty-four thousand men ready for the field; one half of them, under such leaders as Moreau and Souham, standing on the frontier of maritime Flanders. As early as on the 11th of March Carnot ordered Pichegru to begin the advance on Ypres; but the General, though willing to train his troops by countless skirmishes, made no movement until the 29th of March, when he attacked the Austrian advanced posts at Le Cateau with thirty thousand men, and was beaten back with the loss of twelve hundred killed and wounded and four guns. "It is dangerous," he reported, "to match our young troops against the enemy so soon"; and therewith his operations incontinently ceased.

Meanwhile Coburg, still awaiting his orders, made no attempt to overwhelm any one of the scattered French divisions. At last on the 2nd of April the April 2. Emperor quitted Vienna, reached Brussels in company with his brothers, the Archdukes Charles and Joseph on

1794.
April 14.
the 9th, and on the 14th joined Coburg at Valenciennes. The Prince then laid before him the danger of the Allied position, with both wings too weak to take the offensive against an enemy which was reported to be three hundred thousand strong; and followed this up by recommending the advance of the centre to the siege of Landrecies, for which Mack had prepared one of his usual elaborate schemes. Thus the Austrians reverted once more to a war of petty sieges, which could produce no decisive result. Indeed the only thing to be said for operations in the selected quarter was that the country was open and well suited to cavalry, in which arm the Allies were far superior both in quantity and quality to the French. The Emperor approved the plan; and the troops were set in motion forthwith, nominally for a great review to be held in the Emperor's honour near Le Cateau. Thus, despite all Carnot's efforts to take the initiative, it fell to the Allies to open the new campaign.

CHAPTER X

ON the 16th of April, as had been arranged, the whole 1794. of the main army was inspected by the Emperor on the April 16. heights of Cateau. The British infantry was represented, as in the last campaign, by three battalions of Guards, with a fourth battalion formed out of their flank-companies, and Abercromby's brigade of the Fourteenth, Thirty-seventh, and Fifty-third. These last had at length received their first instalment of recruits to make good their losses during 1793, in the shape of a draft which was described as "much resembling Falstaff's men, and as lightly clad as any Carmagnole battalion"[1] of the French Army. The cavalry numbered twenty-eight squadrons, drawn from fourteen regiments[2] and organised into four brigades,

---

[1] Calvert, p. 187.
[2] Three squadrons of the 1st Dragoon Guards, two squadrons each of the Blues, 2nd, 3rd, 5th, 6th Dragoon Guards, 1st Royals, 2nd Greys, 6th Inniskilling Dragoons, 7th, 11th, 15th, 16th Light Dragoons. The 8th and 14th Light Dragoons were embarked or embarking to join the army. It has been a matter of much difficulty to discover how these regiments were brigaded.

Harcourt's Brigade. (?) 1st, 5th, 6th D.G. = 7 squadrons.
Mansel's Brigade. (?) Blues, 3rd D.G., Royals = 6 squadrons.
Laurie's Brigade. (certainly), Bays, Greys, Inniskillings = 6 squadrons.
Ralph Dundas's Brigade. 7th, 11th, 15th, 16th Light Dragoons, 1st squadron of the Carbineers = 9 squadrons.

After the death of Mansel on the 26th of April, Dundas took over his brigade, and Colonel Vyse took Dundas's. But the regiments seem to have been much shifted from one brigade to another.

Calvert, pp. 197, 204. *Cannon's Records*, Royal Horse Guards, p. 102.

1794. three of heavy and one of light dragoons, the last being supplemented by a picked squadron of the Carbineers under the command of Captain Stapleton Cotton, a lad of twenty, who in later years was to earn the title of Viscount Combermere. The review over, the Emperor took up his quarters in Le Cateau, whither the commanders forthwith repaired to him for orders.

April 17. The French troops under Pichegru in the immediate front of the Emperor consisted of three divisions, with an average strength of twelve thousand men each, extended along an entrenched position some eighteen miles long, on the wooded heights of Bohain and Nouvion. Of these Fromentin's division held Catillon on the Sambre, a village rather over four miles east and south of Le Cateau; westward of Fromentin, Ballaud's division lay astride the road from Le Cateau to Guise, at Arbre de Guise and Ribeauville; and, still farther to west and south, Goguet's division held the ground about Vaux, Prémont, and Bohain. The nearest French troops beyond these to westward were fifteen thousand men under Chappuis about Cambrai; while to eastward three divisions of the French right wing, numbering some thirty thousand men, lined the Sambre from St. Waast to Maubeuge.

There was therefore an opportunity of overwhelming one or other of these isolated bodies; but the Austrians clung religiously to their old methods. The force was divided into eight columns, three of which were directed to move north-westward toward Cambrai, so as to check any movement from that side. These need trouble us no more. Of the remaining five, two on the left were ordered to drive the enemy out of Catillon, cross the Sambre, and after clearing the forest of Nouvion to push forward their light troops. One column in the centre, under Coburg's personal command, was designed to move by Ribeauville upon Wassigny to master the heights farther to southward; while two more on the right, under the Duke of York and Sir William Erskine, were to advance, the former upon Vaux, the latter upon Prémont, to drive the enemy from their entrenched positions there and at Bohain, and to press their light 1794. troops forward upon Le Catelet. All commanders April 17. were expressly ordered to halt the main portion of their troops on the captured ground, so that there was no intention of pursuing the enemy in the event of success.

It would be tedious to describe so feeble an operation. The scene of the engagement is a country much broken by ravines and hollow roads, so that the heavy artillery of some of the columns was with difficulty brought forward; but the French, being in a manner surprised, were manœuvred out of their positions with little trouble or loss. The Duke of York's and Erskine's columns alone encountered resistance worth mentioning, but they found little difficulty in turning the French entrenchments, while the Austrian Hussars and a squadron of the Sixteenth Light Dragoons succeeded in cutting down great numbers of the retreating enemy. Altogether the Allies lost fewer than seven hundred killed and wounded, while the action was reckoned to have cost the French over two thousand men, besides from twenty to thirty guns, of which eleven were captured by the British columns. Beyond this the French were little molested in their retreat to Guise, and the trifling success of the day was marred by disgraceful plundering and burning on the part of the Allied troops after the engagement. The British had already shown tendencies in this direction, but had been checked by the Duke of York, who had hanged two offenders, caught red-handed, on the spot, without even the form of a drum-head court-martial. Now, however, the Austrians led the way in misconduct, either led astray by some of their savage auxiliaries, or in aimless revenge for their starvation during the winter; and the British were only too ready to follow the example.[1]

On the following day the army halted between April 18. Nouvion and Prémont, pushing its outposts farther to southward, while detachments of Austrians were

[1] Ditfurth, ii. 54. Craig to Nepean, 18th April 1794.

1794. posted also at Prisches, a few miles north of Nouvion, and at La Capelle, Fontenelle, and Garmouset to eastward, so as to cover the left flank and rear of the army. Thereupon the Prince of Orange, whose troops had been advanced towards Cambrai on the 17th, countermarched to Le Cateau, and assembling his force at Forest, about three miles to the north of it, on the
April 20. 20th fell upon the enemy's posts over against Landrecies on the left bank of the Sambre. After a hard struggle, which cost him one thousand men and the French twice as many, he carried the French position, and at once opened the trenches before the town.
April 21. On the following day Pichegru delivered feeble and incoherent assaults upon the positions of Prisches and Nouvion, and upon the heights to the south of Wassigny, all of which were beaten off with the loss to him of many men and four guns. Further desultory fighting
April 22. at the advanced posts on the next day was equally unfavourable to Pichegru, as indeed he deserved for his folly in not concentrating the thirty thousand men, who lay ready to his hand at Maubeuge, for an overwhelming attack.

Coburg then judged it safe to proceed with the siege in earnest, and, withdrawing the covering army to the north, formed it in a huge semicircle around the besieging force. His left wing curved round from the heights that lie to eastward of Landrecies, and between it and the village of Maroilles, southward to Prisches, thence south-east across the Rivierette to Le Sart, and thence by Fesmy to the Sambre, the whole line being strongly entrenched, with several bridges thrown over the Rivierette. The force allotted for the defence of this tract was thirty-two battalions, fifty squadrons, and twenty-six light companies, the left under General Alvintzy, the right under General Kinsky. On the western bank of the Sambre the right wing completed the semicircle, with a total of twenty-six battalions and seventy-six squadrons. The first section of the defences on this side ran westward of Catillon to the Selle, from which stream the Duke 1794. of York's army carried the line north-westward to the road from Le Cateau to Cambrai. This, a broad paved way, runs straight as an arrow over the long waves of rolling ground that lie between the two towns, the undulations rising to their highest at the village of Inchy, upon which the Duke rested his right. The position thus occupied by the Allies was over twenty miles in extent, following a chain of hills of easy slope but seamed to east of Catillon by deep water-courses and hollows, and broken by small copses and enclosures in the neighbourhood of the villages. Westward from Catillon, however, towards Cambrai the hills subside into a broad plain, not unlike Salisbury Plain, except that the undulations are far longer and the acclivities therefore less severe. Covered with crops but unenclosed, its gentle slopes and unseen folds present an ideal field for the action and manœuvres of cavalry.

On the 23rd intelligence reached the Allies that April 23. fifteen thousand of the enemy had moved out from Cambrai in three columns towards the north-east, were driving in the outposts along the lower Selle, and had even crossed that river, apparently with the object of intercepting the Emperor Francis, who was returning from a visit to Brussels, to rejoin the headquarters of the army. The Austrian General Otto, receiving information of these movements from Major-general Sentheresky at St. Hilaire, between four and five miles north-west of Inchy, at once joined him there; and reconnoitring farther north he found the enemy, apparently about ten thousand strong, near the village of Villers-en-Cauchies. Having with him only two squadrons of the Fifteenth Light Dragoons and as many of the Austrian Leopold Hussars, making together little more than three hundred sabres, Otto fell back to St. Hilaire, and sent a message to the Duke of York for reinforcements. Late at night he was joined by the Eleventh Light Dragoons, two squadrons of the

1794.
April 24.

Austrian Zeschwitz Cuirassiers, and Mansel's brigade of the Blues, Royals, and Third Dragoon Guards, the whole numbering ten squadrons.

Early on the following morning he again moved northward down the valley of the Selle, keeping the Fifteenth and Leopold Hussars in advance and the remainder in support; and at about seven o'clock the four advanced squadrons came upon a force of French light cavalry of twice or thrice their strength in a long belt of dwarf coppice, near the village of Montrecourt, and about two miles east of Villers-en-Cauchies. Being attacked on their left flank the French horsemen at once retreated with precipitation for a quarter of a mile, when they rallied, and then retired steadily westward, covered by a cloud of skirmishers. Finally they re-formed between Villers-en-Cauchies and Avesnes-le-Sec, fronting to eastward, and masking a force of unknown strength in their rear. Otto appears to have followed up this cavalry with great speed, for, on looking round for his supports, he could nowhere discover them. He halted the advanced squadrons, but, perceiving that he had already committed them too deeply, he assembled the officers and told them briefly that there was nothing for it but to attack. The English and Austrian officers then crossed swords in pledge that they would charge home; and it was agreed that the British should attack in front, and the Austrians on the enemy's left flank towards Avesnes-le-Sec, which was already a name of good omen in the annals of the Austrian cavalry.

The Fifteenth led by Captain Aylett now advanced at a rapid trot, breaking into a gallop at one hundred and fifty yards from the French cavalry. These did not await the shock but wheeled outwards, right and left, and retired at speed, unmasking a line of French skirmishers and guns, which opened fire before their front was clear and killed several of their own soldiers. In rear of the artillery six French battalions, or about three thousand men, were massed together in quadrate formation of oblong shape,¹ with the front rank kneeling. A volley from the eastern face of this square, together with a discharge of grape from the guns, checked the attack for a moment; but, cheered on by their officers, the Fifteenth swept through the battery and dashed straight upon the bayonets. The French infantry seems to have stood till the last moment, for Aylett fell with a deep thrust through the body, and four other officers had their horses wounded under them; but the onset of the Dragoons was irresistible. One half of the square was dispersed instantly; and the other half, after firing a volley, broke up likewise before the charge of the Fifteenth, and fled in wild disorder. In rear of the square were more French squadrons, upon which those that retired from the front had been re-formed; but these had given way before the impetuous attack of the Austrian Hussars, and for half a mile the sabres of both Austrians and British dealt terrible havoc among the flying Frenchmen.²

1794. April 24.

Leaving, however, the Austrians to pursue the infantry towards Cambrai, the Fifteenth, now commanded by Captain Pocklington, passed on to the road from Villers-en-Cauchies to Bouchain, dispersed a long line of fifty guns and ammunition-waggons, which were retiring to the north-west, and continued the chase until the guns of Bouchain itself opened fire upon them, and a relieving force came out to save the convoy. Meanwhile not a sign appeared of the supporting

¹ So say the records of the 15th Hussars. I suspect that there were two squares with the guns between them, as at Avesnes-le-Sec on 12th September 1793. Two squares side by side would give an appearance of oblong shape to the formation.

² The records of the 15th Hussars for some reason seek to excuse the slaughter of the fugitives, by mentioning that the National Convention had decreed that no quarter should be given to the English; and this mistake has been copied by Sir Evelyn Wood in his excellent account of the action in *Achievements of Cavalry*. As a matter of fact the decree was not made until the 26th of May; and three hundred men need no excuse for taking no prisoners when attacking five thousand.

1794.
April 24.
squadrons which might have ensured the capture of the artillery; and Pocklington, observing other forces of the enemy closing in upon him from every side, rallied his men and retired at a trot. The blue uniform of the Light Dragoons, however, caused the French to mistake them for friends; and it was not until they were close to Villers-en-Cauchies that Pocklington perceived that he was cut off. The enemy was, in fact, established in his front, blocking the road with infantry and artillery at a point where a causeway carried it across a valley, though to the south of the village there were visible the scarlet coats of Mansel's brigade. Wheeling about, therefore, for a short time, Pocklington checked the pursuers that were following him from Bouchain, and then, wheeling once more to his proper front, he galloped through the French amid a heavy fire of grape and musketry with little loss, and safely rejoined his comrades.

Things, however, had not gone well with Mansel and his brigade. Whether it was by Otto's fault or by his own that he had gone astray, and whether he attempted and failed in an attack upon the French who were obstructing Pocklington's retreat, is a mystery. We know only that Craig reported, with great regret, that the brigade had behaved ill; that he attributed the fault mainly to Mansel, whom after the action of the 17th he had already reported as an incompetent officer; but that the troops also were to blame, though the Royals had immediately recovered themselves and protected the retreat of the other two regiments. More curious still, the list of casualties shows that the Third Dragoon Guards suffered the very heavy loss of thirty-eight men and forty-six horses killed, besides nine more men wounded and missing, though the casualties of the Royals and the Blues were trifling.[1] From this I infer that Mansel led his brigade to the sound of the guns, and,

[1] In *Cannon's Records* of the 3rd Dragoon Guards these casualties are ascribed to the action of the 26th of April. Whether the mistake be due to accident or to design, it is to be regretted.

being ordered to attack the fresh division of the enemy that had come upon the ground, contrived by irresolution and mismanagement to bring the Third Dragoon Guards under enfilading fire of the French cannon, and to throw the whole of the six squadrons into confusion. In any case it is certain that the brilliant attack of the Fifteenth was insufficiently supported, and that Mansel and his brigade, justly or unjustly, lay under reproach, until two days later they redeemed their good name beyond all chance of cavil. The casualties of the French in this action were eight hundred men killed and four hundred wounded, besides three guns taken; while the Fifteenth escaped with a loss of thirty-one men and thirty-seven horses killed and wounded, and the Leopold Hussars with a loss of ten men and eleven horses killed and wounded and the same number missing. The Emperor of Austria conferred on the officers of the Fifteenth a gold medal and the much-coveted order of Maria Theresa; and the regiment still bears on its appointments the name of Villers-en-Cauchies. With a little more luck, or, it may be, a little better management, Otto would have achieved one of the greatest successes ever recorded of cavalry against infantry, and annihilated the whole of the force that had moved out from Cambrai.

1794.
April 24.

As matters stood, however, the reverse to the French produced little effect on Pichegru. Successive reinforcements had more than made good his losses; and on the 24th of April the combined strength of the armies of the North and of the Ardennes, not counting fifty thousand men employed as garrisons, was little short of two hundred thousand men free for service in the field, or nearly two to one of Coburg's force. Relying upon this numerical superiority the French General started for Lille, in order from thence to direct operations against Clerfaye. At the same time, however, he set his troops in motion to raise the siege of Landrecies, directing General Charbonnier with thirty

1794. thousand men of the army of the Ardennes to attack Kaunitz on the extreme left wing of the Allies, while at the same time General Ferrand with forty-five thousand from Guise should fall on the covering army on the east and south, and General Chappuis with thirty thousand men from Cambrai should assail the Duke of York on the west.

April 26. Accordingly, early in the morning of the 26th the French engaged the covering army simultaneously at all points. On the east General Fromentin with twenty-two thousand men assailed Maroilles and Prisches, and after a long and severe struggle captured the latter position, severing for the time communications between Alvintzy and Kinsky. Alvintzy himself was disabled by two wounds, and the situation was for a time most critical until the Archduke Charles, who had succeeded to the command of Alvintzy's troops, by a final and skilful effort recovered the lost ground and drove the French over the Little Helpe. This enabled him to reinforce the centre under General Bellegarde, who with some difficulty was defending the line from Oisy to Nouvion against twenty-three thousand men. Thereupon Bellegarde instantly took the offensive, completely defeated the French, and captured from them nine guns.

But far more brilliant was the success of the Allies on the west, where Chappuis led one column along the high-road from Cambrai to Le Cateau, while a second column of four thousand men advanced upon the same point by a parallel course through the villages of Ligny and Bertry, a little farther to the south. Favoured by a dense fog the two columns succeeded in driving the advanced posts of the Allies from the villages of Inchy and Beaumont on the high-road, and of Troisvilles, Bertry, and Maurois immediately to south of them; which done, they proceeded to form behind the ridge on which these villages stand, for the main attack. Before the formation was complete the fog cleared; and the Duke, observing that Chappuis's left flank was in the air, made a great demonstration with his artillery against the French front, sent a few light troops to engage their right, and calling all his cavalry to his own right, formed them unseen in a fold in the ground between Inchy and Bethencourt, a village a little to westward of it.[1] The squadrons were drawn up in three lines, the six squadrons of the Austrian Cuirassiers of Zeschwitz forming the first line under Colonel Prince Schwarzenberg, Mansel's brigade the second line, and the First and Fifth Dragoon Guards and Sixteenth Light Dragoons the third, the whole of the nineteen squadrons being under command of General Otto.[2]

1794.
April 26.

In this order they moved off, Otto advancing with great caution, and skilfully taking advantage of every dip and hollow to conceal his movements. A body of French Cavalry was first encountered and immediately overthrown, General Chappuis, who was with them, being taken prisoner. Then the last ridge was passed and the squadrons saw their prey before them— over twenty thousand French infantry drawn up with their guns in order of battle, serenely facing eastward without thought of the storm that was bursting on them from the north. There was no hesitation, for Schwarzenberg was an impetuous leader, and the Cuirassiers had been disappointed of distinction at Villers-en-Cauchies; the Blues, Royals, and Third Dragoon

[1] Going over the ground, my companion and myself fixed upon a hollow about half a mile to west of Inchy, and on the north side of the road, as the spot where Otto concentrated his squadrons out of sight of the French. The left flank of the French infantry, upon which the attack was opened, we reckoned to have stood in a hollow about half a mile south-east of Inchy. After very careful study of the ground, I put forward these conjectures with some confidence.

[2] The establishment of an Austrian Cuirassier Regiment was six squadrons; the British regiments, as originally organised in 1793, should have made thirteen squadrons; but I imagine that losses had reduced one or other of them to a single squadron, for both Witzleben (iii. 132) and Ditfurth (ii. 57) give the number as six Austrian and twelve British squadrons.

1794.
April 26.
Guards had a stain to wipe away; the King's and Fifth Dragoon Guards were eager for opportunity to show their mettle; and the Sixteenth Light Dragoons, being the only Light Dragoons present, were anxious to prove that they could do as well as the Fifteenth. The trumpets rang out, and with wild cheering white coats, red coats, and blue coats whirled down upon the left flank and rear of the French. The French guns, hastily wheeled round, opened a furious fire of grape, while the infantry began as furious a fire of musketry; but the charging squadrons took no heed. Mansel, stung by the imputation of cowardice, which had been thrown out to account for his mishap on the 24th, had vowed that he would not come back alive, and dashing far ahead of his men into the thick of the enemy went down at once; but Colonel Vyse, of the King's Dragoon Guards, taking command of both brigades, led them as straight as Mansel. In a very few minutes the whole mass of the French was broken up and flying southward in wild disorder, with the sabres hewing mercilessly among them.

The misfortunes of the enemy did not end here, for one of their detachments, which had been pushed forward to Troisvilles, was driven back by a couple of British guns under Colonel Congreve, and joined the rest in flight. Meanwhile Chappuis's second column had advanced a little beyond Maurois with its guns, when the appearance of the fugitives warned them to retire; but in this quarter, too, there was a vigilant Austrian officer, Major Stepheicz, with two squadrons of the Archduke Ferdinand's Hussars and four of the Seventh and Eleventh British Light Dragoons. Following up the French column he drove its rearguard in upon the main body a little to westward of Maretz, and a few miles further on fell upon the main body also, dispersed it utterly, and captured ten guns. Twelve hundred Frenchmen were killed in this part of the field alone, so terrible was the Austrian hussar in pursuit; two thousand more had fallen under the sabres of Otto's division, which likewise captured twenty-two guns and three hundred and fifty prisoners. The shattered fragments of the French infantry fled by a wide detour to Cambrai; and Pichegru's attack on this side was not merely beaten off, but his troops were literally hunted from the field.

1794.
April 26.

So ended the greatest day in the annals of the British horse, perhaps the greater since the glory of it was shared with the most renowned cavalry in Europe. The loss of the Austrians was nine officers, two hundred and twenty-eight men, and two hundred and eight horses; that of the British, six officers, one hundred and fifty-six men, and two hundred and eighty-nine horses, killed, wounded, and missing. The British regiments that suffered most heavily were the Blues and the Third Dragoon Guards, each of which had sixteen men and twenty-five horses killed outright; and the determination of the Third to prove that the harsh criticism of their comrades on the 24th was unjust, is shown by the fact that five out of the six officers injured in the charge belonged to them. Mansel, the Brigadier, who was also their Colonel, died as has been told. Of the Captains one, his own son, was overpowered and taken in a desperate effort to extricate his father, and another was wounded. Of the Lieutenants one was killed and another, if not two more, wounded. The Major in command, however, had the good fortune not only to escape unhurt but to receive the sword of General Chappuis. The total loss of the covering army was just under fifteen hundred men; that of the French was reckoned, probably with less exaggeration than usual, at seven thousand, while the guns taken from them numbered forty-one.

On the following day the Emperor ordered his army to devote itself to singing a *Te Deum* and to solemn thanksgiving, which was very right and proper, but might well have been deferred for forty-eight hours until the full fruits of the victory had been gathered. For although there were four fortresses, Avesnes, Guise,

April 27.

1794. Cambrai, and Maubeuge, within easy distance as a refuge for fugitives, another day's pursuit would assuredly have swept up many hundred stragglers, while the mere sight of the Allied troops would probably have sufficed to set the French levies running once more. There was however better excuse than usual for inaction, for among General Chappuis's papers had been found evidence that a most formidable stroke was about to fall, if it had not already fallen, upon Flanders. It is now necessary to narrate the course of events in that quarter, namely, on the right or western wing of the Allies.

April 23. On the 23rd of April a force from Cambrai, acting in concert with that which was beaten on the 24th at Villers-en-Cauchies, had moved northward against Wurmb's corps of communication at Denain, and, but for the arrival of Clerfaye with some eight thousand men from Tournai, would have driven it across the Scheldt. On the 24th, 26th, and 27th the harassing of the advanced posts of the Allies about Denain continued, and meanwhile the true attack was developed, pursuant to Carnot's plans, on the extreme left of the

April 24. French line. On the 24th Michaud's division of twelve thousand men marched from Dunkirk, part of it towards Nieuport on the north, the rest upon Ypres to south-east, sweeping back the feeble posts between the two places. Simultaneously Moreau's division of twenty-one thousand men moved eastward from Cassel upon Ypres, and drove all the outlying detachments on that side to take shelter under the ramparts. Then, leaving some of Michaud's division at Messines to watch

April 25-27. the fortress from the south, Moreau pursued his way eastward against Menin, and surrounded that fortress upon all sides. At the same time Souham's division of thirty thousand men, under the personal direction of Pichegru, advanced from Lille north-eastward upon Mouscron, drove back upon Dottignies the weak detachment that defended it, and captured Courtrai, which was

April 26. practically without a garrison. General Oynhausen, however, restored matters somewhat by collecting troops from Tournai at Dottignies and retaking the position of Mouscron, where reinforcements arrived in the nick of time to strengthen him.

1794.
April 28.

The papers found upon Chappuis gave Coburg the key to all these movements; and on the evening of the 26th he sent twelve battalions and ten squadrons under General Erskine from his own army to St. Amand, bidding Clerfaye to recall at once to their proper stations the reinforcements which he had imprudently hurried to Denain. Clerfaye accordingly hastened by forced marches through Tournai to Mouscron, which he reached on the 28th, raising the garrison of that place to ten thousand men, exclusive of about two thousand more in the detached posts of Coyghem and Dottignies. The relief of Menin was his first and most urgent object, and he had fully resolved to attempt it on the 30th; but Pichegru was too quick for him. On the 29th the two columns under Generals Souham and Bertin fell, the one upon Clerfaye's front, the other upon his left flank and rear, with a superiority of three to one, and after a hard struggle forced him from his position. The Austrian General seems to have begun his retreat in good order, but the movement speedily degenerated into a flight; and when he rallied his beaten troops at Dottignies he was the weaker by two thousand men killed and wounded and twenty-three guns. Happily six of the battalions sent from the army before Landrecies had by that time reached Dottignies, and, with these to hearten his demoralised force, he retired eastward to Espierres, on the western bank of the Scheldt.

April 29.

This defeat decided the fate of Menin. The garrison consisted of rather more than two thousand men, chiefly Hanoverians, but in part French Emigrants, which latter if captured could expect nothing but the guillotine. The commandant, Count Hammerstein, therefore decided to cut his way out through the besiegers, and with the fortune that favours the brave,

1794.
April 30. succeeded during the night of the 30th in forcing his passage northward to Thourout and thence to Bruges. Thus Menin and Courtrai, the two gates of the Lys, were lost, and a gap was broken in the long cordon of the Allies. Along the whole of the right wing there was something like a panic, and the roads were choked with long trains of supplies and stores flying northward to Brussels and Ghent. At Ostend there had lately arrived the Eighth Light Dragoons and the Thirty-eighth and Fifty-fifth Foot, sadly belated, since the infantry, with Dundas's usual wisdom, had been embarked at Bristol; but General Stewart, the commandant at Ostend, did not think it prudent after Clerfaye's defeat to send them down country.[1] Happily Pichegru did not pursue his advantage as he ought.

May 3. He did indeed push a detachment northward from Menin upon Roulers, which was attacked and defeated with a loss of two hundred men and three guns by three squadrons of the Allied Cavalry;[2] but there his activity ceased; and he solemnly sat himself down about Moorseele on the left bank of the Lys, with one flank resting on Menin and the other on Courtrai, as if to allow time for Coburg's army to come up in his front.[3]

April 28. Coburg meanwhile had passed through no enviable days. On the 28th news reached him that Kaunitz on his left wing had been forced back by overwhelming numbers to the Sambre, while on his right wing Pichegru had made his way to Courtrai; but, however serious the outlook, he was still tied for the present to the miserable and useless fortress of Landrecies. By a strange irony Mack on that very day submitted a plan of future operations, whereby Bouchain, Cambrai,

[1] Stewart to Dundas, 30th April; Craig to Nepean, 25th April; Adjutant-general to Duke of York, 22nd April, 1794. These two unfortunate battalions spent three weeks on the passage.

[2] York to Dundas, 6th May 1794.

[3] It is curious to note that Jomini's account makes the French force front to the south, whereas Craig conceived of it as facing to the north; so that evidently it was prepared to face either way.

Avesnes, and Maubeuge were in succession to be 1794. besieged;[1] but circumstances on the occasion were too strong for pedantry. Landrecies fortunately fell on the 30th, and Coburg on the same day ordered the April 30. Duke of York to lead the rest of his force with all speed to Clerfaye's assistance, and to drive the French from Flanders.

Heavy rain, however, delayed the Duke's progress; and it was not until the 3rd of May that he May 3. reached Tournai, where he reunited Erskine's force with his own and pushed forward a strong detachment three miles westward to Marquain and Lamain, releasing five thousand men, which had hitherto held those points, to join Clerfaye. The front thus occupied by the Allies, from Tournai in the south to Espierres in the north, was from seven to eight miles long and faced due west, their objective being the right flank and communications of the French left wing. The British brigade at Ostend, namely the Twelfth, Thirty-eighth, and Fifty-fifth under Major-general Whyte, and the Eighth Light Dragoons, were by this time on their way to Clerfaye's army; and the united force of Clerfaye and the Duke of York was now reckoned at about forty thousand men.[2] Pichegru, on the other hand, had from forty to fifty thousand between Menin and Courtrai, and twenty thousand more under General Bonnaud (who had succeeded Chappuis) at Sainghin, about five miles south-east of Lille, to act as a reserve. At Clerfaye's proposal it was agreed that on the 5th of May he himself should cross the Lys a little below Courtrai and fall upon that place from the north, while simultaneously the Duke of York should move

[1] Witzleben, ii. 167. Memorandum of the 28th of April in *W. O. Corres.*

[2] Clerfaye (including the reinforcements from Ostend), nineteen thousand; Walmoden at Warcoing, six thousand; Duke of York at Tournai, eighteen thousand (Craig to Dundas, 6th May 1794). Witzleben, however, reckons the united force at thirty thousand men only (iii. 143), and Ditfurth gives but four thousand men to Walmoden.

1794. eastward to cut it off from Lille. After all, however, Clerfaye, whether from diffidence or mere frowardness, would not venture on the attempt. Appeal was made to the Emperor Francis to give him positive orders to attack, but meanwhile Bonnaud concentrated over
May 8-9. twenty-five thousand men between Bouvines and Anstaing, a little to the west of Marquain, as if to threaten the Duke's left. When the Emperor's orders at last reached Clerfaye, he first wasted four days in reconnoitring, and at last made but a feeble attack on the 10th, contenting himself with the capture of the outermost fringe of Courtrai.

Pichegru seems to have had good information of Clerfaye's movements and possibly even of his intentions, for he left Moreau's division alone to deal with him; and, having moved Souham's division to the east
May 10. bank of the Lys, himself on the same day attacked the line of the Allies in force. Souham advanced against the Hanoverians on the Allied right, but, though he forced the posts of Dottignies and Coyghem, was repulsed from Espierres. On the left of the Allies thirty thousand French moved out in two columns against the Duke of York's entrenched position between Lamain and Hertain; the stronger column of the two, which included five thousand cavalry, following the main road from Lille to Tournai, the other turning south-east from Bouvines by Cysoing upon Bachy, as if to turn the Duke's left flank. This latter column was checked by a couple of battalions and three squadrons under command of an Austrian officer at Bachy, and was unable to penetrate further. The other and more formidable body carried the advanced posts of Baisieux, upon the main road, and of Camphin about a mile to south of it, and forming on the plain between these two villages opened a furious cannonade from howitzers and heavy guns. Thereupon the Duke, perceiving a gap in the enemy's line, whereby the right of their main body was uncovered, ordered sixteen squadrons of British Dragoons and two of Austrian hussars to advance

into the plain of Cysoing by the low ground that lies south of the heights of Lamain, and from thence to attack.

1794.
May 10.

The cavalry obeyed with alacrity; but the ground on the plain, though perfectly level and unenclosed, was much broken by patches of cole-seed, grown in trenches after the manner of celery, which checked the progress of the heavy dragoons. Moreover the French infantry, for the first time since the Revolution, threw themselves into squares and faced the galloping horsemen with admirable firmness. Nine regiments of cavalry in succession charged up to the bayonets, but with insufficient speed, and fell back baffled.[1] Nevertheless they followed the French up the plain from south to north, until, a little to westward of Camphin, their left came under the fire of some French heavy batteries, established on the gently rising ground before the village of Gruson. The Duke then ordered a brigade of British infantry to move forward between that village and Baisieux, at the same time sending down four battalions along the track which the cavalry had taken, to support their attack. The French infantry thereupon retreated from Camphin in a northerly direction towards the village of Willems, their cavalry covering the movement; while the British cavalry, now reinforced by six more squadrons, hovered about them watching for their opportunity to attack. At length they fell upon the French horsemen on both flanks, and utterly overthrew them, after which they renewed their attempt upon the infantry, but again without success. At last, however, a little to the south of Willems, the battalion-guns of the British infantry came up and opened fire, when the French, after receiving a few shots, began to waver. The squadrons again charged, and an officer of the Greys, galloping straight at the largest of the squares, knocked down three men as he rode into it, wheeled his horse round and overthrew six more, and thus made a gap for the

[1] *Life of Lord Combermere*, i. 38.

1794.
May 10.
entry of his men. The sight of one square broken and dispersed demoralised the remainder of the French. Two more squares were ridden down, and for the third time the British sabres had free play among the French infantry. Over four hundred prisoners were taken, thirteen guns were captured, and it was reckoned that from one to two thousand men were cut down. The loss of the British was thirty men killed, six officers and seventy-seven men wounded, ninety horses killed and one hundred and forty wounded and missing, the Sixth Dragoon Guards being the regiment that suffered most heavily. It is hardly necessary to call attention to the arm which was lacking on this day, or to point out that a single battery of horse-artillery would have enabled the cavalry to break the squares at the first onset, would greatly have increased the enemy's losses, and would have made the day's operations more decisive. Not for eighteen years was the British cavalry destined again to ride over French battalions as they rode on this day; and then Stapleton Cotton was fated once more to be present, leading not a squadron of Carbineers, but a whole division of horse to the charge at Salamanca. But the 10th of May 1794 is chiefly memorable as marking the date on which the new French infantry showed itself not unworthy of the old.[1]

May 11.
May 12.
After the action the French main body retired once more across the Lys to its old camp between Menin and Courtrai; but on the 11th Souham attacked Clerfaye in his position at Lendelede, about four miles north of Courtrai, and after an obstinate engagement forced him to retire still further northward to Thielt,

[1] The regiments engaged were the Blues, Second, Third, Sixth Dragoon Guards; First, Second, Sixth Dragoons; Seventh, Eleventh, Fifteenth, Sixteenth Light Dragoons. Which were engaged throughout and which came up as reinforcements, I have been unable to discover. The account of the action is drawn chiefly from Calvert, *Journal*, pp. 203-205. *Narrative of an Officer*, ii. 41. Ditfurth, ii. 75. *Life of Lord Combermere*, i. 38-39. The first is the most important.

with the loss of fifteen hundred men and two guns. 1794.
Meanwhile the Duke of York, in spite of his success
on the 10th, became anxious as to his position in
presence of numbers so overwhelmingly superior, and
pressed Coburg to send him reinforcements. At the
Emperor's headquarters, however, there was some
hesitation whether the principal army should move
eastward to the assistance of Kaunitz on the Sambre,
or westward for the salvation of Flanders. The first
idea was to make a demonstration towards Cambrai
with a part of the force; the next to make a rapid
march and invest Avesnes, also with only a part of
the force, in order to take pressure off Kaunitz. The
idea of moving with the whole army to any given
point seems to have occurred to none of the Austrian
Generals. Then came the Duke of York's application May 11.
for help, whereupon General Kinsky was ordered with
some six thousand horse and foot to Denain, to enable
Wurmb's detachment at that place to join the Duke
of York at Tournai. One day later arrived news May 12.
from Kaunitz that he had been compelled to fall back
still further northward from the Sambre, and was
attacked on all sides; the fact being that Carnot on
the 30th of April had directed fifteen thousand men
from the army of the Rhine to join the army of the
Ardennes, so as to ensure decisive superiority on the
Sambre. Upon this, Coburg determined that the
subdivision of the army into fragments must cease,
and called upon the Emperor to choose between the
Sambre and Flanders, as the sphere of action for the
entire force. Intelligence of a successful engagement
fought by Kaunitz and of Clerfaye's retreat to Thielt
inclined the Emperor to Flanders; and though, even
then, Austrian pedantry insisted that some eight thousand
men under the Prince of Orange must remain in the
vicinity of Landrecies, yet the bulk of the army on the
14th commenced its march westward. May 14.

This movement, however, was by no means to
the taste of some of the Emperor's advisers; and it

1794. becomes necessary at this point to turn for a moment from the western to the eastern centre of European disturbance, and to glance at the influence which events in Poland had exerted upon the Imperial Cabinet. It has already been said that Thugut's only object in persuading the Emperor to take personal command in the field, was that the operations might subserve his own policy. With this view the Minister prepared to remove to Valenciennes, which was to be the political headquarters of the Empire during the Emperor's stay in the Netherlands; but before he could leave Vienna he was startled by the news of a general rising in Poland. This insurrection under the leadership of
March 25. Kosciusko broke out on the 25th of March, and spread with a rapidity and success which left the Russians absolutely helpless. Catherine, greedy for the partition of Turkey, had already moved the best of her troops southwards; and the only force of any kind upon the spot was that of Prussia, which fact in itself was
April 20. enough to kindle Thugut's jealousy. On the 20th of April Kosciusko, after two days' fighting, captured
April 25. Warsaw; and five days later Catherine, while asking the Emperor for the troops due to her by treaty, mentioned also how greatly she needed the help of the Prussians, from whom likewise she had claimed assistance. Meanwhile King Frederick William, growing nervous lest the rebellion should infect also his own Polish provinces, after some hesitation decided to throw the Treaty of the Hague to the winds; wherefore, withdrawing twenty thousand of his troops from the Rhine, he left Berlin on the 14th of May to take personal command of his army in Poland.

All this was gall and wormwood to Thugut, and the more so because Kosciusko had expressed a wish to place Austrian troops in occupation of Poland rather than yield it to the Prussians. He became more and more anxious to have done with France, if possible by a separate peace with the Republic, and to devote all Austria's energies to the thwarting of Prussia in the

East. The embitterment of his hostility towards 1794. Prussia brought him more than ever in conflict with Coburg and Mack, who desired above all things a good understanding with the second great power of Germany; but, unfortunately, he found two officers of like sentiments with himself in the Prince of Waldeck, who held a high position on the Staff, and General Rollin, who of all men possessed greatest influence with the Emperor. It was therefore with profound dissatisfaction that Thugut's ignoble clique saw the mass of the Austrian troops drawn nearer to France and further from Poland; and though outwardly they swallowed their ill-humour, yet they had every intention of compassing their own ends, even by means the most infamous.[1]

On the 15th of May the Emperor joined the Duke of York at Tournai, and the Archduke Charles brought the Austrian Army from Landrecies to St. Amand, eleven miles to south of it. The field, on which the decisive action was to be fought, was one that had drunk deep of human blood. It may be described as the parallelogram enclosed by a line drawn south-eastward from Courtrai to Tournai, thence south-westward to Pont-à-Marque, thence north-westward through Lille to Wervicq, and thence north-eastward back to Courtrai. To east it is bounded by the Scheldt, to north by the Lys; and through the midst of it, flowing first from south to north past Pont-à-Marque and Cysoing to Lannoy, and thence westward into the Deule and so to the Lys, runs the Marque, a stream impassable except by bridges, owing to soft bottom and swampy banks. The principal bridges were those of Pont-à-Marque on the great road to Paris, and Pont-à-Tressin on the road from Tournai to Lille; but there were others on by-roads at Louvil, Bouvines, Gruson, Tressin, L'Hempenpont, Pont-à-Breug and Marque, most of them fortified and strongly held by the French. Two

May 15.

[1] Sybel, iii. 118-120. Witzleben, iii. 157-167.

smaller streams of the same character as the Marque, but running from west to east, form also important obstacles within this arena, namely, the Espierres-brook, which has its source close to Roubaix and flows into the Scheldt at Espierres, and the Baisieux-brook, which rising near Hertain joins the Scheldt at Pont-à-Chin. The ground is mostly level, with the exception of the undulating heights that rise from the Lys, the low ridge upon which stood the villages of Roubaix and Lannoy, and the group of hills about Tournai itself; but it was thickly studded with villages, linked together by chains of innumerable cottages and farm-houses, which were all of them enclosed by hedges. The fields were cut up by swampy brooks and by a ramification of wide drains, which, with other enclosures, practically forbade the movements of troops except by road. The roads, however, even then were many; and the principal highways were nearly broad enough to permit an advance in column of half-companies;[1] but all of them, as well as the waterways, were lined with trees, making it extremely difficult to see the movements of troops from a distance. Thus it was and is a country unfit for cavalry, and far better adapted in that day to the tactics of the French than of the Allied infantry.[2]

Within the parallelogram the French were somewhat widely scattered. Osten's division of ten thousand men lay at Pont-à-Marque. To the left or northward of it the bulk of Bonnaud's division of twenty thousand men was encamped at Sainghin, with detachments occupying also Pont-à-Tressin and Lannoy, further north upon the Marque. Souham's division of twenty-eight thousand, and Moreau's of twenty-two thousand men lay on the south bank of the Lys between Courtrai and Aelbeke, a village nearly four miles

[1] Ditfurth, ii. 90. He says actually that there was nearly room for the full width of a company, of course in triple rank.
[2] Great part of the battle-field is now built over. Lille alone covers a vast extent of it, and Roubaix and Lannoy are to all intent part and parcel of Lille. But the general character of the ground, and in particular its blindness, remains unchanged.

south of it, with Thierry's brigade at Mouscron, and 1794. Compère's brigade at Turcoing to preserve communication with Bonnaud. In all, the French army numbered eighty-two thousand men.

Against this force Coburg could pit sixty-two thousand, twelve thousand of them cavalry. Of the Allied army, fourteen thousand under the Archduke Charles were at St. Amand; seventeen thousand under the Duke of York at Tournai; nine thousand under Kinsky at Marquain; four thousand Hanoverians under General von dem Bussche at Warcoing, on the Scheldt; and, lastly, sixteen thousand men under Clerfaye were at Oyghem, about five miles north and east of Courtrai on the north bank of the Lys. The whole of these troops, excepting Clerfaye's corps, could easily be concentrated within twelve hours at Tournai, from which a swift and resolute attack upon the southern flank of Souham and Moreau, by Roubaix, Mouveaux and Bondues, might have cut them off from Lille, driven them into the arms of Clerfaye and overwhelmed them. The Austrians, however, were not to be weaned from their own methods, and accordingly on the 16th Mack prepared an elaborate plan, which he designed, and even declared, to be a plan of annihilation.

The army was as usual to be divided. The first May 16. column, of four thousand Hanoverians under Bussche, was to march by Dottignies upon Mouscron, detaching a third of its strength northward on the high road from Tournai to Courtrai, and, having captured Mouscron, was to open communication with the second column. The second column, of twelve battalions and ten squadrons, or about ten thousand men, under Field-Marshal Otto, was to advance by Leers and Wattrelos upon Turcoing. The third column, of twelve battalions and ten squadrons under the Duke of York, was to move by Lannoy against Mouveaux, sixteen British squadrons being held in reserve at Hertain under General Erskine. The fourth column, of ten battalions and sixteen squadrons under Count

1794. Kinsky, was to be employed partly in covering the Duke's left flank; but the bulk of it was to advance on Bouvines and there force the passage of the Marque. The fifth column, of seventeen battalions and thirty-two squadrons under the Archduke Charles, was to march to Pont-à-Marque, sending a small detachment northward by Templeuve to preserve communication with the fourth column. Having gained the passage of the Marque the Archduke was to attack the enemy on the western side of the river, and, after leaving detachments to guard the bridges, to wheel northward, unite forces with Kinsky and move up with him to join the Duke of York at Mouveaux. Finally the sixth column under Clerfaye was to march from Oyghem on the left bank of the Lys, force the passage of the river above Menin on the morning of the 17th, and manœuvre in rear of the enemy about Mouscron and Turcoing. Thus the design was to attack the enemy's front with half the army, turn both their flanks with the remainder, and destroy the French irremediably; but whether the surest way of attaining this object was to disperse the troops in isolated columns over a front of twenty miles in a blind and strongly enclosed country—this was a question over which Craig, at any rate, shook his head.

May 17. Miscarriages of the great plan began early. Clerfaye did not receive his orders for the movement towards Menin until late on the morning of the 16th, and did not march until the evening. His progress was much delayed by the heavy sandy roads, and, consequently, it was the afternoon of the 17th before his corps reached Wervicq, and attempted to cross the Lys by the bridge. The French, however, had covered it by entrenchments which blocked his passage; and, when the pontoons were asked for, it was found that by some mistake they had been left behind. Several hours were wasted while they were coming up, and the pontoon-bridge was consequently not laid until late at night, when a few battalions only crossed the river, the remainder of the force bivouacking on the left bank.

The general result was that Clerfaye's corps, one-fourth 1794. of the whole army, counted for nothing in the first May 17. day's operations.¹

The march of the remaining columns was begun in a thick fog which rendered concerted movements difficult, and the Austrian Staff seems to have made no allowance for the varying distances to be covered by the columns; Kinsky having little more than seven miles to traverse from Froidmont to Bouvines, whereas the Archduke Charles had fully fifteen miles from St. Amand to Pont-à-Marque. Bussche concentrated at St. Leger, a little to west of Warcoing in the night, advanced upon Mouscron, and captured it, but was driven out again with very heavy loss, and forced back to Dottignies. For this misfortune Mack was chiefly responsible, by directing the detachment of so large a proportion of this column on a perfectly aimless errand towards Courtrai. Otto, on Bussche's left, fared better, driving Compère's troops from Leers, Wattrelos, and Turcoing; but, unfortunately, with no further result than to join them to Thierry's brigade behind Mouscron, to the greater discomfiture of the unfortunate Hanoverians.

To the left and south of Otto the Duke of York with about ten thousand men ² advanced by Templeuve upon Lannoy which, after a sharp cannonade, he attacked with the brigade of Guards in front while the Light Dragoons turned it by the left; but the enemy beat so hasty a retreat that they escaped with little loss. Leaving two Hessian battalions in Lannoy, the Duke pushed on to Roubaix, where the enemy stood, with greater force both of infantry and artillery, in an entrenched position; but, in spite of a very obstinate resistance, the Guards carried this post also with the bayonet. Having no intelligence of the

¹ Witzleben (iii. 197-198) considers the slowness both of Clerfaye and the Archduke Charles on this day to have been inexcusable.

² Brigade of Guards (4 battalions); 14th, 37th, 53rd Foot; 2 Hessian and 5 Austrian battalions; 7th, 15th, 16th Light Dragoons (6 squadrons); 4 squadrons of Austrian Hussars.

1794.
May 17. columns on his right and left, the Duke rightly decided to leave his advanced guard at Roubaix, and to fall back with his main body to Lannoy; when to his dismay he received a positive command from the Emperor himself, who with the Headquarter-Staff had accompanied the rear of his column, to push on to the attack of Mouveaux. This order was sheer folly, unless indeed it were dictated by wanton and deliberate wickedness;[1] but it was reiterated in spite of all protests, and though the evening was falling and the troops were weary with a long and harassing day's work under a burning sun, the Duke reluctantly obeyed. The French position at Mouveaux was enclosed by palisades and entrenchments and flanked by redoubts; but for the third time the brigade of Guards drove the enemy out brilliantly with the bayonet. The Seventh and Fifteenth Light Dragoons under Abercromby's personal direction at once pressed forward in pursuit, and galloping round the village, which had been kindled by the flying French, overtook the fugitives, and cut down three hundred of them. Three guns were captured; and one small party of the Fifteenth actually rode into the French camp at Bondues,[2] nearly two miles to west of Mouveaux, and set the troops there running in every direction. The main body of the Duke's column then bivouacked astride of the road between Mouveaux and Roubaix.

[1] Hamilton (*History of the Grenadier Guards*, ii. 304) says, I know not on what authority, that the pretext for this order was that Clerfaye required assistance. It is certain that the Austrian Headquarters had heard nothing and knew nothing of Clerfaye's situation at this time, so that, if General Hamilton's story be more than mere gossip, the order was probably urged by Waldeck or some other of Mack's enemies, with the object of bringing his elaborate combinations into contempt. The fact that the British would be the chief sufferers in case of mishap, would rather have encouraged this faction in the Austrian Staff to the measure.

[2] The *Gazette* prints this place as Bouderes; and the mistake has been copied into many regimental histories. It is only one among innumerable instances of the slovenliness of the clerks of the War Office at that time.

With the two columns south of the Duke, however, 1794. affairs had gone but indifferently. Kinsky's advance May 17. from Froidmont was delayed by a message from the Archduke Charles, to the effect that his force could not possibly reach the Marque at the appointed hour of six in the morning; but in due time Kinsky moved forward to Bouvines, and drove the French from their entrenchments. The enemy, however, broke down the bridge over the Marque as they retired, and, until the advance of the Archduke began to make itself felt, Kinsky was unable to repair it, since the passage was commanded by a battery of heavy guns. The Archduke's column had meanwhile left St. Amand at ten o'clock on the evening of the 16th, and after driving back the French advanced posts at Templeuve[1] and Cappelle, a little to east of Pont-à-Marque, finally succeeded in forcing the passage of the river at that point. But it was not till two o'clock in the afternoon, instead of six in the morning of the 17th, that his army had passed to the west bank of the Marque; and his soldiers were too much exhausted to move further than Lesquin, a little east of the road between Pont-à-Marque and Lille. There he bivouacked on the heights between Lesquin and Peronne, a village about three miles to south-east of it; his men having been on foot for twenty-two hours, marched more than twenty miles over bad roads, and fought a sharp action for the passage of the river. His advance, however, had forced the enemy to evacuate Sainghin, and thus enabled Kinsky to repair the bridge at Bouvines; but none the less Kinsky, with excess of caution, would not cross the river, and encamped for the night on the right bank, which was for him the wrong bank, of the Marque.

At the beginning of this day the French commanders had no information of any movements of the Allies beyond the march of Clerfaye; and, accordingly, the divisions of Souham and Moreau, together with Van-

[1] Not to be confounded with the village of the same name further north, on the road from Tournai to Lannoy.

1794.
May 17. damme's brigade, had crossed to the left bank of the Lys. The advance of the Allies from the east and the combats about Turcoing, however, soon undeceived them. Pichegru being, as Soult said, fortunately absent, Generals Souham, Moreau, Macdonald, and Reynier met in council at Menin; and on the evening of the 17th they decided to make new dispositions and to set their troops at once in motion. Vandamme's brigade alone was left on the north bank of the Lys to watch Clerfaye, and the remainder of the troops on that site crossed the river to take up their appointed stations. Malbrancq's brigade was posted between Roncq and Blancfour, villages lying from three to four miles due south from Menin on the road to Lille; to the left of Malbrancq, Macdonald's brigade crowned the heights of Mount Halluin; the rest of Souham's division, under Generals Daendels and Jardon, lay some three miles away to the east of Macdonald, occupying a line between Aelbeke and Belleghem, a village lying a little to the south of Courtrai; and the gap between Macdonald and these troops was filled by the brigades of Compère and Thierry about Mouscron. Thus the formation of the French left wing was that of a double echelon; the three divisions being arranged at the three angles of an isosceles triangle, with the van at the apex, Mouscron, and the rear before Menin and Courtrai. The right wing, consisting of Bonnaud's and Osten's divisions, some thirty thousand strong, was assembled about Flers, two miles and a half to the east of Lille; where orders arrived on the evening of the 17th from Souham that a general attack was designed for the morrow, in which the duty of Bonnaud's division would be to march upon Lannoy and Roubaix.

It was not without anxiety that the reports from the various columns of the Allies were awaited on the evening of the 17th at the Austrian headquarters at Templeuve. The failures of Bussche to capture Mouscron, and of the Archduke Charles to reach the point assigned to him, had sufficed to mar Mack's plans; and of Clerfaye

there was no news whatever. Orders were therefore 1794.
sent at three o'clock next morning to the Archduke May 17-18.
Charles to march at once with his own and Kinsky's
corps upon Lannoy; while the Duke of York and Otto
were directed to attack Mouscron at noon, in the hope
that before that time something would have been heard
of Clerfaye. But it seems to have occurred to none
of the Austrian Staff that the disposition of the Allied
Army, as prescribed by Mack, positively invited the
French to take the offensive. On this night Bussche
lay at Dottignies and Coyghem with his weakened corps
of Hanoverians. On his left the main body of Otto's
column, seven and a half battalions and three squadrons,
was at Turcoing, with detachments of two battalions at
Wattrelos, and of three battalions and three squadrons
at Leers, on the line of his retreat. Thus his force was
distributed in isolated patches along a length of five
miles, with its right flank not only unprotected, but
actually threatened by a superior force of the enemy,
lying within three miles both of Turcoing and Wattrelos.

On Otto's left the Duke of York's column was as
dangerously dispersed. The Guards, with the Seventh
and Fifteenth Light Dragoons, under Abercromby, were
at Mouveaux; four Austrian battalions and the Sixteenth
Light Dragoons were at Roubaix; the Fourteenth,
Thirty-seventh, and Fifty-third were on the road
between Roubaix and Lille, in order to repel any attack
from the garrison of the latter place; two Hessian
battalions lay at Lannoy, and four squadrons of Austrian
hussars were engaged in patrolling. The Duke's right
was indeed covered, but his left was exposed to attack
not only by the garrison of Lille but by Bonnaud's
superior force about Flers; and thus both his column
and Otto's practically passed the night pent in on three
sides by forces of thrice their strength. To the left, or
southward, there was a gap of four miles between the
Duke's troops and the nearest of Kinsky's detachments,
which lay at Pont-à-Tressin and Chereng, with the main
body still further south at Bouvines; while the Arch-

1794.
May 17-18. duke Charles, with nearly one-fourth of the whole army, lay over against him at Sainghin on the other side of the Marque, with advanced detachments pushed far to the south-west at Seclin. Finally, Clerfaye, with rather more than a fourth of the entire Allied force, was still on the western side of the Lys at Wervicq. Certainly the dispositions lent themselves to a plan of annihilation.

May 18. At three o'clock on the morning of the 18th, while Coburg was signing the orders for his troops, the French army began its march to the attack. On the south Osten's division was left about Flers and Lezennes, to watch the Archduke Charles and Kinsky; while Bonnaud, dividing his eighteen thousand men into two columns, directed them northward, the one by L'Hempenpont upon Lannoy, the other by Pont-à-Breug upon Roubaix. Simultaneously Malbrancq's brigade marched south from Roncq upon Mouveaux; Macdonald's from Mount Halluin upon the western front of Turcoing; Compère's from Mouscron upon the northern front; Thierry's, also from Mouscron, together with Daendels's from Aelbeke, upon Wattrelos; while Jardon's brigade moved from Belleghem towards Dottignies to hold the Hanoverians in check. Excluding this last brigade, sixty thousand men in all were thus turned upon the six posts in which the eighteen thousand men under Otto and the Duke of York were dispersed.

Otto's force, being nearer to the enemy, was the first to feel the weight of the attack. General Montfrault, who commanded at Turcoing, perceiving the overwhelming strength of the enemy, begged reinforcements from the Duke of York, who sent him two Austrian battalions from Roubaix, but with strict orders that they should return in the event of their arriving too late to save the town. As a matter of fact they did arrive too late, for the garrison had already been driven from Turcoing; but none the less they attached themselves, as was perhaps natural, to Montfrault, who stood fast on the eastern skirts of the town and held back the enemy for a time, until a French battery unlimbering on ground to the north of him, forced him to retire. Seeing himself threatened by large bodies of cavalry, Montfrault formed his troops into a large square, with four battalions and light artillery in front, one battalion on each flank, and the cavalry in the rear. In this order he fell back, his heavy artillery and waggons being enclosed in the centre of the square, and his light troops skirmishing on all four sides. It was about half-past eight when he began his retrograde movement; but already Wattrelos, the first post on his rear, was in possession of the enemy. The garrison, two Hessian battalions, had manfully resisted an attack of six times their number until eight o'clock, when, finding themselves in danger of being surrounded, they retired, and, with the help of two companies sent forward by General Otto, withdrew successfully to Leers. Montfrault thereupon found himself compelled to leave the main road for a by-way, which ran between Wattrelos and Roubaix, in order to continue his retreat.

1794. May 18.

Between six and seven o'clock, rather later than the opening of the attack on Turcoing and Wattrelos, Bonnaud's two columns came up from the south upon Lannoy and Roubaix; and shortly afterwards Malbrancq's brigade from the north fell upon Mouveaux, while a part of the French force that had captured Turcoing appeared also on the north of Roubaix. The Duke of York despatched urgent messages to recall the two Austrian battalions which he had sent to Otto, but of course in vain; and meanwhile he made such head as he could with his handful of troops against overwhelming odds. The troops at Mouveaux were disposed in two sides of a square, the left showing a front towards the east at Mouveaux, the guns stationed in the angle at the northern end of the village, and the right thrown back to the hamlet of Le Fresnoy. To the south, the British brigade of the Line under Major-general Fox, near Croix, sought to bar the way against part of Bonnaud's division from Lille; but to defend the rest of the ground there

1794.
May 18.

were but three Austrian battalions. Of these half a battalion was stationed in Roubaix itself, and the remainder echeloned to the right rear of Fox's brigade behind the sources of the Espierres brook, which ran along the southern skirts of the village. These Austrian battalions seem to have been the first to give way, and one of them, by Craig's account, did not behave as it ought; but they were pressed hard both in front and on their right flank, which, owing to the absence of the two battalions sent to Otto, was wholly uncovered. One brigade of Bonnaud's division therefore succeeded in forcing its way between Mouveaux and Roubaix to Le Fresnoy; and the Duke thus saw Abercromby and the brigade of Guards absolutely cut off from him. Moreover, though he knew it not, the victorious French of Thierry's and Daendels's brigades were coming down from Wattrelos upon his rear. Seldom has a General found himself, through no fault of his own, in a more extraordinary position. He had been assured that the Archduke Charles would join him from the south, and he had therefore ordered Abercromby to defend Mouveaux to the last extremity; but not a sign of an Austrian was to be seen whether to south or north. His first instinct was to ride to the Guards at Mouveaux; but this was seen to be out of the question. He then tried to make his way to Fox's brigade, but found that the French were in possession of the suburbs of Roubaix, and that he was cut off from this brigade also. Realising then that, his Austrian battalions being dispersed, he had not a man left to him except two squadrons of the Sixteenth Light Dragoons, he took a small escort from them and rode to Wattrelos, hoping to obtain from Otto the means for extricating the Guards. Meanwhile he sent orders to Abercromby to retire to the heights on the east side of Roubaix.

Montfrault, however, had fared ill in his attempt to withdraw. Until he reached the ground between Wattrelos and Roubaix, his square preserved good order; but being attacked at that point by overpowering numbers from the south as well as from north and west, it was broken up, and fled in disorder towards Leers. Meanwhile General Fox, finding himself absolutely isolated, at length gave the order for his brigade, which so far had held its own, to retire. The retreat began in perfect order, and the brigade, having successfully fought its way to the road at Lannoy, followed it for some distance, under incessant fire from all sides, until checked by a battery covered by an abatis, which the French had thrown up on the road. The first shots from this battery struck down several men, and Fox for the moment feared that surrender would be inevitable; but fortunately in the ranks of the Fourteenth was a French emigrant who knew the district well, and undertook to lead the brigade across country. It pursued its retreat therefore under constant fire of artillery and musketry in front and on both flanks, and with cavalry constantly threatening its rear; but it kept its assailants at bay, and at one moment made so sharp a counter-attack as to take temporary possession of some French guns. Thus partly by good luck, partly by good conduct, partly by the misconduct and mismanagement of the enemy, the three battalions contrived to reach Leers, with the loss of all their battalion-guns excepting one, and of nine officers and five hundred and twenty-five men out of eleven hundred and twenty. The greatest credit was given to General Fox for the coolness, skill, and patience with which he extricated his brigade.

1794.
May 18.

Abercromby appears to have begun his retreat from Mouveaux at about nine o'clock, but of necessity very slowly, having with him a considerable number of guns. The retirement was conducted in perfect order as far as Roubaix, the Seventh and Fifteenth Light Dragoons covering the rear with great gallantry. At Roubaix the French, though in occupation of the suburbs, were not in possession of the little walled town, which was still held by a dismounted squadron of the Sixteenth Light Dragoons. The place consisted of a single long street, the direct continuation of which led to Wattrelos, while, just outside the eastern gate, the road to Lannoy turned sharply to the right, being bordered on one side by a deep ditch and on the other by the Espierres brook. To defile through the town took necessarily much time, but the guns emerged safely and the Guards also. Next to the Guards were the Austrian Hussars, still in the street; then in rear of them a party of the Fifteenth; next to this party were the Sixteenth, who were formed up in the market-place; and in rear of all were the remainder of the Fifteenth, holding the pursuing French in check. All was still in order when a French gun posted on the Wattrelos branch of the street suddenly opened fire from the edge of the town, sending shot after shot among the Austrian Hussars. The ordeal would have been a severe one for any troops, and presently the Hussars dismounted and tried to find a way out among the houses, but in vain. The trial became unendurable as the French pressed on and opened fire on all sides upon the horsemen thus pent in for slaughter; and at last the whole body remounted, galloped wildly down the road, swung round the corner, where the French infantry thrust vainly at them with their bayonets, and raced onward for three or four hundred yards, when the foremost troopers suddenly found the way blocked by horseless guns. The French had brought a second gun to enfilade the road to Lannoy, and the drivers of the British cannon had fled. The shock of this mass of galloping horsemen suddenly checked was appalling. In an instant the ground was strewn with men and horses, kicking and struggling in frantic confusion, while a number of bât-horses dashed into the ranks of the Guards, plunging and lashing out, with their loads hanging under their bellies. For a short time the disorder appears to have been beyond remedy, for a belt of wood surrounding the town gave excellent shelter to the French sharpshooters, who had a very easy target in the mass of struggling men and animals. Very soon, however, the Guards recovered themselves, and cleared a way for the cavalry to pass

on beyond the wood to open ground. There the Light 1794.
Dragoons rallied, the rear-guard was re-formed, and the May 18.
retreat, always under heavy fire, was resumed towards
Lannoy.

That village, which was enclosed by a low earthen
rampart and a shallow ditch, had likewise been attacked
early by one of Bonnaud's brigades from Lille, but had
been defended with the greatest gallantry by two
battalions of Hessians, who were apparently still in
possession when the British troops approached it,
though surrounded on the west side, and indeed nearly
on all sides, by the French.[1] The British officers,
however, could see no sign of a friendly garrison, and
Colonel Congreve was actually wheeling his cannon
round to open fire on the place, when there galloped up
to them some blue-coated horsemen, who, being mistaken for Hessians, were allowed to approach without
molestation, and succeeded in cutting the traces of

[1] The evidence upon this point is very conflicting. All the
English accounts state that, when the British reached Lannoy on
their retreat, the place was in possession of the French. Ditfurth,
on the other hand (ii. 133, 137 *seq.*), is very positive that it was
held by the Hessians until 1 p.m., which, in his opinion, was long
after the British would have reached it; and the evidence which
he adduces is very strong. Against this, it is certain that the
British would have been only too thankful to rally at Lannoy if
they could, and that they were greatly disappointed to find themselves cut off from it. It is also to be noted that Ditfurth rakes up
everything that he can to the discredit of the English, but was not
at the pains to read a single English account of the action, except
the Duke of York's letter as published in the *Gazette*, and that his
account of their movements is consequently full of errors. I incline
to the opinion that the Hessians were still in Lannoy, but that the
French around them were so numerous as to cut the British off
from it—in fact, that the French practically held it invested, with
a covering force powerful enough to keep the British at a distance.
The same was the case at Roubaix, which the Sixteenth Light
Dragoons contrived to hold till Abercromby retreated, though the
Austrians, the Duke of York, and Abercromby himself all believed
it to be in the hands of the French. It still remains to be explained
why the Hessians made no sign of their presence when Abercromby's
column approached, for the British artillerymen actually began to
lay their guns upon it in the assurance that it was in the enemy's
hands.

1794.
May 18.
some of the guns before they were discovered. The Guards then perceiving their retreat to be cut off, faced about against their pursuers, and, leaving the high road, made their way across country as best they could southeastward to Marquain. The Hessians in Lannoy, either before or shortly after this, were forced to evacuate the village, and, finding the road to Leers blocked by the enemy, were likewise obliged to make their way across country in disorder, losing out of nine hundred officers and men some three hundred and thirty, of whom two hundred were cut off and captured in Lannoy itself.

Meanwhile the Duke of York, conspicuous by the star on his breast, had been hunted all over the country by the enemy's dragoons, and had escaped, as he frankly owned, only by the speed of his horse. On reaching Wattrelos he found it in the hands of the French, but passing beyond it under constant fire he came upon a gallant little party of Hessians still holding the bridge of the Espierres brook. These by a final attack with the bayonet gained a little respite for him, but were presently swept away from the bridge, and escaped only by fording the brook neck-deep. The Duke, thinking apparently that the bridge was lost, or not knowing of its existence, spurred his horse into the brook; but the animal rearing up and refusing to enter the water, he dismounted, scrambled over on foot, and taking a horse from one of his aide-de-camps, at last succeeded in finding Otto. About Leers and Nechin the fragments of Otto's force, together with some of the Duke of York's men, rallied upon the few battalions that held these places. The French did not press their advantage, and at half-past four the action came to an end. The loss of the Allies was about three thousand men killed, wounded, and missing, which was relatively slight, for, with proper management and conduct on the part of the French, not a man of the Duke's and Otto's columns would have escaped alive. The Brigade of Guards lost one hundred and ninety-six officers and men killed, wounded, and missing, the flank-companies being the heaviest sufferers ; while the Seventh, Fifteenth, and Sixteenth Light Dragoons, who by general admission behaved admirably, lost fifty-two men and ninety-two horses. The total loss of the British of all ranks was nine hundred and thirty, besides which nineteen out of their twenty-eight guns were captured.

1794.
May 18.

It may be asked what the rest of the army was doing on this day, while these two columns, together less than one-third of the whole, were in process of annihilation. The answer is that, for some reason, it observed a conspiracy of inaction. Bussche sat still at Dottignies exchanging occasional shots with Jardon's brigade. Clerfaye crossed the Lys near Wervicq at seven o'clock in the morning, and turning eastward advanced between Bousbecque and Linselles, where he was met by Vandamme's brigade, which numbered eight thousand men against his sixteen thousand. He engaged the French, overthrew their right wing, took eight guns, and then remained stationary ; until, being informed of the approach of more French troops about Bondues, he withdrew to the Lys, which he recrossed on the next day, and thence retreated northward. The behaviour of Kinsky and of the Archduke Charles was still more extraordinary. Kinsky, on being asked by one of his officers for orders at six o'clock in the morning, replied that he was sick and no longer in command. The Archduke Charles received at five in the morning the order to move at once upon Lannoy, a distance of six miles, so that his troops might well have come upon the scene of action between eight and nine. He did not march till noon, though within sound of the guns, nor did he strike the road from Tournai to Lille until three, when he received orders to return to Tournai. The military renown justly earned later by the Archduke forbids us to believe that this delay was due to ignorance ; and the fact that, though the Duke of York had early informed the Emperor of his danger, not a word was sent to

1794. hasten the Archduke or Kinsky, shows clearly that their torpidity was not unexpected nor disapproved at headquarters. Jealousy of the Duke of York and of Mack are among the reasons assigned to account for the general paralysis of the Austrian commanders; but possibly the true reason was that Thugut was sick of the war in Belgium, and wished the English to sicken of it also. Why he should have chosen the slaughter of several hundred British and Austrians as the best means of forwarding his purpose, and how he persuaded Austrian officers to second him therein, are matters which only an Austrian can determine. For us it must suffice that the decisive battle of the campaign was lost by the deliberate design of the Imperial Generals. Before long they were to learn that those who court defeat for dishonest ends may, when they least desire it, find defeat thrust upon them.[1]

[1] There are few actions which I have found so difficult to describe as this of the 18th of May. I have drawn my account from Witzleben, iii. 201-230; Ditfurth, ii. 130-157; Jomini; *Narrative of an Officer*, ii. 47-51; Cannon's *Records of the Seventh and Fifteenth Hussars and Sixteenth Lancers*; Calvert's *Journal*; and Craig's letters to Nepean of 19th May 1794 (Record Office).

CHAPTER XI

THE entire army of the Allies, with the exception of 1794.
Clerfaye's corps, was gathered into camp about Tournai
in the course of the 19th, the Emperor being received May 19.
in silence when he rode into the town, while the Duke
of York was loudly cheered by the inhabitants.[1] The
condition of the army was very far from satisfactory.
The troops themselves, or at any rate the British, were
not seriously shaken by the rout of the previous day;
but the Emperor and the Austrian commanders were
much discouraged, and the animosity of the various
nations towards each other was dangerously embittered.
The British, above all, were furious against the Austrians
for leaving them to be overwhelmed without so much
as an attempt to assist them. "It is impossible," wrote
Craig to the War Office, "to bring the Austrians to
act except in small corps. I lament that we should be
destined as victims of their folly and ignorance. Do
not be surprised at the word ignorance: I am every day
more and more convinced that they have not an officer
among them." These were hard words, but they were
true and just, though the Archduke Charles in later
days redeemed himself from this reproach. However,
for the moment the commanders laid aside their May 20.
differences and agreed that the attack should be
renewed, this time with united forces, upon Mouscron;
and meanwhile Coburg dispersed the whole army in a
semicircle around Tournai; the advanced posts running
from Camphin on the south by Baisieux, Willems,

[1] Calvert, p. 269.

1794. Nechin, Leers, Estaimpuis, and St. Legers to Espierres, while the inner circle of entrenchments ran from the Scheldt on the north by Froyennes, Marquain, and Lamain to the suburb of St. Martin and the citadel of Tournai itself.

The French Generals, as already narrated, made no effort to follow up their victory of the 18th, but awaited the return of Pichegru, who, on the news of the victory, hastened from the Sambre to turn it to account. On the 22nd, after a consultation with his officers, Pichegru decided to make a general attack upon Coburg's position, and directed that Souham with four brigades,[1] numbering from thirty to forty thousand men, should assail it on the right or northern half of its front from Espierres to Leers, while Bonnaud's division should fall upon its left about Templeuve, and Osten's division should make a demonstration still further to the south about Baisieux.

May 23. On the following day between six and seven o'clock in the morning the action began; and after long and hard fighting the Allies were finally driven from three important points, namely, Blandain and the hill of La Croisette immediately adjacent to it, a little to the west of Tournai, and Pont-à-Chin upon the Scheldt, a little below the city. To abandon to the enemy these posts, particularly Pont-à-Chin, which lay on the direct road from Courtrai to Tournai and commanded the navigation of the Scheldt, was impossible; and Coburg decided that they must be recovered at any cost. Throughout this long day's fighting the troops that had borne the brunt of the work on the 18th had been held in reserve; but at about six o'clock in the evening Fox's brigade of the British Line was called out to recover Pont-à-Chin, which had already been taken and retaken three or four times. The brigade went into this action with fewer than six hundred men, having lost half of its numbers just four days before; but the three gallant regiments, though

[1] The French brigades at this period were of the strength of divisions.

unsupported, carried the village unhesitatingly with the 1794. bayonet, pressed on to the low heights to south of May 22. it, swept everything before them, so far as their front extended, and captured seven cannon. The day ended, after a severe struggle of fifteen hours, in the retreat of the French, with the loss of some six thousand men and seven guns; the fire, both of musketry and artillery, having been the heaviest ever remembered by the oldest soldiers present. Both sides, however, fought for the most part in dispersed formation, and inflicted, comparatively speaking, little damage upon each other. The one exception was Fox's brigade. "Had their order of attack," wrote Calvert, "been adopted by the Allies in general, the day would probably have ended in the ruin of the French." But the losses of the brigade amounted to one hundred and twenty killed, wounded, and missing; and there are few troops that can be trusted, after losing half their numbers on Sunday, to storm a position held by a superior force and lose one-fifth of their remnant on Thursday. Some indeed claim that but for this handful of British soldiers the day would have been lost to the Allies;[1] but whether this be true or not, the 22nd of May should be a great anniversary for the Fourteenth, Thirty-Seventh, and Fifty-Third.

It was directly after this action that the course of events in Poland began to tell upon the councils of the Imperial Headquarters at Tournai. On the 23rd, Mack, May 23. disgusted by the failure of his elaborate plans, resigned his post as Chief of the Staff, and, having first expressed his opinion that the reconquest of Belgium was hopeless, retired for the time into private life. His successor, Waldeck, being a fellow-conspirator with Thugut, was still more eager for the evacuation of the Netherlands; and the Emperor was easily tempted to share their views. On the 24th a Council of War was held for May 24. form's sake, wherein the Emperor set forth the situation in such a light as to gain a ready vote from his

[1] Jones, *Campaign of 1794*. The author was a captain in the Fourteenth.

1794. Generals that further efforts in the Netherlands were
May 24. useless. The Duke of York alone pleaded earnestly
for a renewal of the attack upon Flanders; and, as fate
ordained it, his representations were seconded by unexpected successes of the Allies on the Sambre and in
the Palatinate. On the 24th Marshal Möllendorf and
the Prussians surprised the French about Kaiserslautern
and drove them back with a loss of three thousand
men and twenty guns; and on the same day Count
Kaunitz gained a still more important victory on the
Sambre. The fact was that serious differences had
arisen at Paris between Carnot on the one side and
Robespierre and St. Just on the other, because Carnot
insisted on keeping the direction of the military operations in his own hands. Robespierre, to whom the
art of war was as incomprehensible as a Chinese manuscript, was furious with jealousy and rage. "At the
first reverse, Carnot's head shall fall," cried the despicable creature, galled by the cold contempt with which
his inflexible colleague rebuffed his attempts at interference; and to re-establish civil influence at the seat
of war, St. Just, Lebas, and five more Commissioners
set out on the 2nd of May for the army of the Sambre.
There they introduced the rule of terror in its worst
form, and with it, of course, confusion unspeakable.
They fought with the Generals, they fought among
themselves; and in the midst of this chaos St. Just
took upon himself the supreme direction of the opera-
May 18, 20, tions whereby the Austrians were to be crushed. Four
22, 24. several times he ordered the army to pass the Sambre,
wasting the lives of his troops with obstinate imbe-
May 24. cility. Finally he gave Kaunitz the opportunity for a
counter-attack, in which, with inconsiderable loss to
themselves, the Austrians routed the French completely,
killing and wounding two thousand men, and capturing
three thousand more, besides fifty pieces of cannon.

This heavy blow to the French right wing offered
a fair occasion for the Allies to renew the offensive
in Western Flanders; and the Duke of York urged this

step upon his colleagues with all his might. The British 1794.
Government too, reckoning that the troops, promised
by Prussia in return for a British subsidy, must be nearly
ready, decided to send out Lord Cornwallis to concert
operations with Möllendorf, and directed him also to consult the Emperor and the Duke of York on his way to the
Prussian Headquarters. But, as has already been told,
King Frederick William was occupied rather with Poland
than France at the moment; and he had also been much
irritated by certain dispositions which had been proposed for his army by Mack in the middle of May.
"I am astonished at the fashion in which Mack thinks
to make use of my troops," wrote the King. "Does
Mack imagine that we can live on air?" echoed
Möllendorf;[1] both of them being secretly delighted
with so good an excuse for remaining inactive. Then
suddenly, on the 29th of May, the Allied Camp at May 29.
Tournai was thrown into consternation by the announcement that the Emperor was about to return
to Vienna. Aided by the defeat of the 18th, Thugut
had succeeded in persuading his imperial master to
abandon the Austrian Netherlands; and even Mack,
the unpopular Quartermaster-general, had supported
him by recommending not only the evacuation of the
country but the conclusion of peace with France.

The truth was that jealousy of Prussia had prevailed
over all other considerations, and that the Emperor had
decided to offer help to the Empress Catherine in quelling the Polish insurrection. He hoped, however, at the
same time to delude Prussia into keeping thirty thousand
men upon the Rhine, and England into furnishing a
subsidy for the ostensible prosecution of the war with
France; and it was therefore imperative upon him to
conceal his intentions. He accordingly gave out that
the object of his departure was to hasten the recruiting
of his forces; and in his final letter to Coburg, who
very unwillingly retained the command, he gave him
only vague instructions to adapt his action to the

[1] Witzleben, iii. 168-169.

exigencies of the campaign and to save his troops as much as possible. But this duplicity deceived no one, and the less because Waldeck, before he had succeeded Mack as Chief of the Staff, had openly declared that the war in Belgium must be ended. The Austrian troops were profoundly discouraged, and two-thirds of the officers asked permission to retire. They can hardly be blamed, for the succession of murderous actions fought by the Allies against the French on the northern frontier of France, between the 17th of April and the 22nd of May 1794, has few parallels in the history of war. For a month Austrians, British, and Germans had contended almost unceasingly against superior numbers, slaying or taking, not without heavy loss to themselves, French soldiers by the ten thousand, and capturing French cannon by the score. Yet all had been to no purpose, partly because the leaders had deliberately chosen a foolish plan of operations, partly because they had steadily refused to follow up their successes, partly because on the 18th of May they had held two-thirds of the army inactive within sound of the guns which were overwhelming their comrades. The bravest men will not fight upon such terms. They will not be butchered to serve the intrigues of politicians whose dishonesty would disgrace a sergeant, and of potentates whose incapacity would disqualify a corporal. In days to come Austria was to pay dearly in Italy for the 29th of May 1794.[1]

Immediately before the Emperor's departure came news from Kaunitz that the French had again crossed the Sambre in force ; which compelled Coburg to send him large reinforcements, and thus to weaken the right and centre of the Allies in order to strengthen their left. At the same time, for the sake of keeping the Dutch in good humour, Coburg was obliged to give the supreme command in that quarter to the Crown Prince of Orange, to the natural disgust of Kaunitz, who had shown much ability and achieved great successes. The great safe-

[1] Sybel, iii. 120-125. York to Dundas, 26th May 1794 (with enclosures).

guard, however, to eastward was that St. Just insisted 1794. upon controlling the French operations ; and it need not be said that against such an adversary even the Prince of Orange was victorious. But far more serious were the movements of the French on the western flank. Apprised of Coburg's detachment of troops to the Sambre, hoping still to further Carnot's projects for invasion of England, and above all conscious of the advantage offered to French tactics by the enclosed country of Western Flanders, Pichegru determined to prosecute his operations on that side. Accordingly, leaving between thirty and forty thousand men in positions about Mouscron and Menin to hold Coburg in check, he marched with about the same number on Ypres. On the 1st of June about fifteen thousand June 1. men surrounded the fortress on the west and south, and opened their first parallel ; while some twenty thousand more under Souham took post about Passchendaele, about six miles to the north-east, to cover the siege from Clerfaye, who was lying at Thielt. On that same day, by a curious irony, Lord Howe defeated the Brest fleet, taking eight French ships and sinking two more. This action, in which the regiments on the fleet, and particularly the Sixty-Ninth,[1] played no inconspicuous part, closed for the present all Carnot's projects of an invasion.

The event, however, in no way disturbed the plans of Pichegru. On the 4th of June Clerfaye contrived June 4. to pass two battalions into Ypres to strengthen the garrison ; but he declared himself unable, with the fifteen thousand men that remained to him, to relieve the place unless he were reinforced. By express command of the Emperor, who had lingered at Brussels on his homeward journey, Coburg sent him some ten thousand men in two detachments, reckoning that, after the recent victory on the Sambre, he could safely draw a few troops from that quarter. Clerfaye, however, continued to display the sluggishness which had characterised his

[1] Captain William Parker to the Admiralty, 3rd June 1794.

1794.
June 6. conduct from the beginning of the campaign. On the 6th, before his reinforcements had reached him, he made a feeble advance against Souham in four columns,
June 10. and was of course unsuccessful; and on the 10th, when his force had been raised to over twenty thousand men, he was assailed and defeated with loss by Souham before he could make up his mind to act. On that same day Coburg had designed to make a diversion in Clerfaye's favour, by an attack on Mouscron, upon a plan calculated so exactly to expose the Duke of York's column to destruction, as on the 18th of May, that the Duke refused to accept it until it was altered. This, however, was of small importance, for the French, having perfect information of the intended movements, appeared in every direction in such force that the enterprise was abandoned. The state of things at the Austrian headquarters was indeed almost beyond belief. Insensible to all ideas of duty and discipline, the young staff-officers, described by Craig as "in general the most contemptible of puppies," had talked openly of the projected movement in the coffee-houses at noon, though the Duke of York received no information of it until ten hours later, nor any orders until four o'clock on the next morning. "Mack used to keep these gentry in order," wrote Craig, "and, had he been here, the prison would have been full of them next day; but indeed it would never have happened." Meanwhile Clerfaye remained so incurably supine that the
June 12. Duke of York more than once entreated Coburg to entrust the relief of Ypres to himself, but in vain.
June 13. Roused by repeated orders to attack, Clerfaye at last moved against Souham in five columns, gained some advantage at first, captured ten guns, and then as usual sat still until Souham had gathered troops sufficient for a counter attack, when he immediately retired to his old position at Thielt.

This sealed the fate of Ypres, the key of maritime Flanders, the chief support of the right flank of the Allies, the bulwark which protected the British communications with Ostend. The Duke of York pleaded hard for a last 1794. effort to save it, by a march of the whole army to join Clerfaye ; but without success. " The truth is," wrote Craig, " that the Austrian army is incapable of further action. The men are disheartened and the officers disgusted and disunited." It was finally decided that, to cover Ostend and the Dutch frontier, Clerfaye should take up a position between the Lys and the Scheldt about Deynse, some ten miles to the south-west of Ghent ; keeping half of his force between Bruges and Ostend, and sending the Eighth Light Dragoons, Thirty-eighth and Fifty-fifth, which had formed part of his force, to Ostend. " We are too weak by ten thousand men to hold this defensive position," wrote Craig ; " if the French see their chance and push Clerfaye, they will force us to abandon this position about Tournai and will pass the Scheldt in spite of us ; and then ten to one we shall find ourselves separated from him and beaten in detail. . . . Sooner than hold the defensive position I would concentrate the whole army, eighty thousand men, march to the Sambre, attack them at any risk and march back again. . . . You may expect to hear from us soon in Holland." Clearly there was one among the despised British officers who could have taught the Austrians a lesson.[1]

The situation was indeed a desperate one. The Austrians, having taken no pains to restore the fortifications of Tournai, had thrown up an entrenched camp for its protection on the western side. These lines extended from the city southward along the Scheldt to Maulde, and required so many men for their defence that few could be spared for active operations. Some seven thousand Frenchmen at Mons-en-Pévèle kept the left of the Allies in continual alarm for the safety of Orchies, which was the key of Maulde and of the passage of the Scheldt at Mortagne ; for if that passage were forced, the communication between Coburg and

[1] Duke of York to Dundas, 10th, 13th, 14th June 1794. Craig to Nepean, 10th, 13th, 14th June 1794. Calvert, pp. 238-253.

1794. the army of the Sambre would be endangered. A little to the north of Mons-en-Pévèle was the entire garrison of Lille, and still further to the north, between Lille and Menin, stood from twenty to thirty thousand more French troops. Behind this screen to westward, from fifty thousand to sixty thousand of the enemy were engaged as the besieging and covering armies at Ypres; and far beyond them to the north lay the right wing of the Allies under Clerfaye, stretched in a weak attenuated line from Ostend to the Lys, and only maintaining communication with Tournai by the circuitous route of the Scheldt. On the eastern flank the French had now some seventy-five thousand men on the Sambre, with a capable leader in Jourdan, albeit one still hampered by the interference of St. Just; and this was the only quarter in which recent events had gone favourably for the Allies. Such a situation could not last long, and the strain upon Coburg must have been
June 16. cruelly severe. On the 16th, however, there came a gleam of hope. The French on that day again passed the Sambre, but for the fifth time were driven back with heavy loss; and Coburg, having summoned four
June 18. battalions from that quarter, determined on the 18th to march and join with Clerfaye in a final attempt to relieve Ypres. The troops were already in motion, when in the evening the news came that the French had crossed the Sambre for the sixth time, and successfully invested Charleroi. Thereupon the enterprise was
June 19. abandoned. On the following day Ypres surrendered, and thus Carnot's original plan of turning both flanks of the Allies began, after two months of murderous fighting, to accomplish itself.

Enabled by the fall of Ypres to turn the whole of his attention to eastward, Coburg at once proposed that he should march with all the Austrian troops to Charleroi, and leave the Duke of York to guard the line of the Scheldt from Tournai to Condé. The Duke answered that his instructions were to keep the whole of the troops in British pay together, but that, if

ordered, he would gladly lead the whole of them with 1794.
Coburg to the Sambre. Since, however, his force was
absolutely inadequate to guard the line of the Scheldt,
he insisted that, if it were left behind, an Austrian
garrison should remain at Tournai, and that he himself
should take up a position on the eastern bank of the
Scheldt between that city and Oudenarde, so as to
ensure his retreat in case of mishap.

The offer to march to the Sambre was fair, and it is difficult to understand why Coburg did not embrace it; for, if the battle on the Sambre were lost, it would obviously be impossible for the Duke's troops to remain isolated in Flanders. Coburg did, however, reject it, though he consented to station about five thousand Austrians under General Kray between Denain and Orchies, promising that, if he succeeded in forcing back the enemy on the Sambre, he would return without delay, but that, in the event of his failure, he should not expect the Duke of York to maintain his position on the Scheldt. He also took the significant step of transferring the Austrian hospitals and stores at Valenciennes, as well as the magazines about Tournai, to Brussels and Antwerp; the removal of the stores at Brussels having begun some time before.[1] Finally, on the 21st, he marched away; and June 21. the Duke, since the corps in British pay had now shrunk to seven thousand men, contracted his quarters, and took up a new position closer to Tournai.

But meanwhile the news that Ostend was in danger had, as usual, stirred Dundas to unwonted exertion in England. He still made a fetish of the place, and his original intention seems to have been to defend it, without any particular reference to the Duke of York's operations. On the 17th of June, therefore, he ordered Lord Moira's force in the Isle of Wight and the Channel Islands to sail for Ostend at once, together with drafts of recruits and three fresh regiments from Ireland, making in all a reinforcement of about ten thousand

[1] Duke of York to Dundas, 28th June 1794. Ditfurth, ii. 171-172.

1794.
June 21.
men. On the 20th Moira's troops embarked, and on the 21st the Eighth, the Forty-Fourth, and the recruits arrived at Ostend. The drafts, it must be remarked, arrived without arms or military appointments of any kind; and it was only a fog at sea that prevented a whole regiment, the Ninetieth, from being also landed there without either arms or clothing, Dundas having ordered it to embark without enquiry as to these details.[1] But Pichegru meanwhile did not remain idle, and leaving Ypres on the 20th marched upon Clerfaye's position at Deynse. The Austrian General, after a short defence of his entrenchments, retired, with the

June 23. loss of not a few men and three guns, first to Ghent, and then beyond it, finally taking up a position on the north side of the canal that runs from Ghent to Sluys,

June 24. where he was presently joined by his detachments from

June 25. Bruges. On the 25th of June there arrived at Ostend, after a voyage of nineteen days from Cork, one squadron of the Fourteenth Light Dragoons and the Thirty-third regiment, the latter under the command of an officer whose name it still bears, but who was then an impecunious younger son of five-and-twenty, possessed indeed of some skill in playing the violin, but still distinguished by no higher title than that of Colonel

June 26. Arthur Wellesley. On the morrow Moira with the last of the reinforcements[2] also reached Ostend, where he found an advanced guard of the French within four miles of the town, a large force of several thousand men close behind it, and the Commandant very wisely embarking his garrison with a view to retreat. The whole district was in a state of panic; but Moira promptly landed the whole of his men, and having observed the difficulties of defending Ostend, and the military worthlessness of the place, quietly selected his fighting ground outside it. "I am not at all satisfied with my position," he wrote calmly to Dundas, "but since you appear to attach im-

[1] Calvert, 277. *Life of Lord Lynedoch*, 91.
[2] 3rd, 19th, 27th, 28th, 40th, 42nd, 54th, 57th, 59th, 63rd, 87th, 89th.

portance to the town I will do my best to maintain it." 1794.
"The defences are so detestable," he added cheerfully to Nepean, "that I shall go into the open field if we must come to blows. If you are to lose everything it does not signify if you are beaten into the bargain."[1] It is dangerous for a General, be he even so able as Moira, to address an English Minister of War in this strain; for, in the event of mishap, the words may be brought up as evidence against him in Parliament to prove that he was reckless, careless, neglectful, or despondent.

During these days the Duke of York remained in painful suspense at Tournai, until the news of Clerfaye's defeat on the 23rd warned him to move northward without delay. As Craig had perceived, the French by crossing the Scheldt at Oudenarde could prevent the Duke of York from joining Clerfaye, crush both armies in detail, and then, passing eastward, could annihilate Coburg. The Duke therefore called in Kray's Austrians June 24. for the defence of Tournai, and marched north-eastward on the right bank of the Scheldt to Renaix, where he learned that on the same day a French corps had June 25. summoned Oudenarde. On the morrow Pichegru crossed the Lys at Deynse with the main body of his army, and striking south from thence encamped on the 27th at Huysse, between four and five miles north of June 27. Oudenarde. On that same night came a message from Coburg to the Duke of York that on the previous day June 26. he had made his attack on the French about Charleroi and had failed. This was the battle of Fleurus, which had been suddenly broken off by the Austrian commander before decisive advantage had been gained by either side; and it is still a question whether Coburg's action was dictated by the requirements of Thugut's policy or by his own military judgment. However that may be, he retreated in good order upon Brussels, halting on the 27th in a position running from Soignies June 27. on the west through Braine L'Alleud to Gembloux on

[1] Moira to Dundas and to Nepean, 26th June 1794.

1794. the east. This movement uncovered the Duke of York's left rear, and placed him in a most dangerous position. He had with him barely ten thousand men, nearly half of them cavalry, which in so close a country were of little service; and from the church-tower at Oudenarde he could see thirty thousand of the enemy in his front. The French, by passing the Scheldt, could at any time cut off his retreat to the north, in which case his only line of safety lay eastward towards Grammont; and this in its turn would be closed if Coburg should continue his retrograde movement towards Namur, which was his first stage on the road to Vienna.

June 28. On the morning of the 28th the enemy appeared in force before Oudenarde, showing every sign of making the dreaded movement across the river; and the Duke despatched orders to Moira to join Clerfaye immediately. For two days Pichegru continued his menaces on the Scheldt, and then suddenly on the evening of the
June 30. 30th he retired, having received orders from Paris to occupy Nieuport, Ostend, and the island of Walcheren in force, with a view to the invasion of England. Ostend, which, together with Nieuport, Henry Dundas had kept under his own orders, was evacuated in good time, while directions to that purport were still on their way from England. Moira's instructions extended no further than to the defence of Ostend, but, in the critical circumstances of the case, he proposed to join his force to Clerfaye, and to act with him against the French left. Clerfaye at first welcomed the offer, but, on hearing of the misfortune of Fleurus, declared that he could make no engagement with the British whatever. This was unpleasant for Moira, who had counted on the help of the Austrians in protecting the transport of his camp-equipage on the canal from Bruges to Ghent. The situation was dangerous, for the French were in force at three different places within two hours' march of the canal, bent upon preventing his junction with Clerfaye. Without a moment's hesitation Moira sent his baggage northward

to Sluys, and by a rapid march made his way to Ghent, 1794. just in time to anticipate a movement made by the French to intercept him. Thus a valuable reinforcement was secured to the Allies; and three more perilous days were passed without mishap, thanks rather to the Committee of Safety at Paris than to the Austrian commanders in the field.[1]

On the evening of the 30th the Duke of York rode June 30. over from Renaix to Braine L'Alleud to consult Coburg; and it was then agreed that Clerfaye's force should change places with the Duke's, so as to bring the Austrian corps nearer to its own main army, and the British contingent nearer to the sea. At the actual conference both Coburg and the Archduke Charles declared that, having no orders from the Emperor to evacuate the Austrian Netherlands, they felt bound in honour to defend them. Waldeck indeed opposed even a withdrawal from the line of the Scheldt. All this, however, was mere trifling, for two days later Coburg wrote July 2. that his right wing had been driven back from Soignies, and that the Duke would do well to retire to a position appointed him between Brussels and Antwerp. The fall of Mons on the 1st of July having also laid bare the Duke's left flank and rear, he took the hint, and while protesting against the desertion of the country, gave his orders for retreat in the morning by way of Grammont and thence upon Alost. Tournai, through the courtesy of the French, was peaceably evacuated by the Austrians, though Condé, Valenciennes, Landrecies, and Quesnoy were held. The line of the Scheldt was abandoned, and the Duke of York's troops were withdrawn from every garrison except Nieuport. As to this last the Duke, as in duty bound, asked for Dundas's July 2. orders, saying that, if the Government wished to reconquer Flanders, the place should be kept; otherwise the garrison, which included five hundred French emi-

[1] Duke of York to Dundas, 28th June, 2nd July; Craig to Nepean, 27th June; Moira to Dundas, 28th and 29th June, 1st July 1794.

1794. grants, should not for pity's sake be exposed to the risk of capture.

Then followed a miserable tragedy. Dundas, apparently before the receipt of this letter, wrote on the 3rd of July to General Diepenbrock, the Commandant at Nieuport, promising to send transports for the embarkation of the garrison, if necessary, but adding that the Government attached great importance to the retention of the place. Within two days the French had broken ground before the miserable little port, where the water was so shallow that ships could not come near the shore; July 16. and less than a fortnight later the unfortunate garrison, which included a few British troops, was compelled to surrender. Forthwith the French massed the emigrants in the ditch of the fort and played upon them with grape-shot until the whole of them were destroyed. It was well known that this would inevitably be the fate of those unhappy men if they fell into the hands of the Republicans; and German authors have not hesitated to censure the Duke of York because, according to the current, though unjust, opinion, he neglected to order the evacuation of Nieuport while there was yet time. It were, indeed, devoutly to be wished that the Duke had respected Dundas less, and had withdrawn the garrison without consulting him, though it is manifest that he would thereby have drawn upon himself the censure of the Government. The blame, therefore, for this shameful business must remain with Dundas; and it was a very great misfortune for England that he was not called to account for it.[1]

Meanwhile the Duke continued his retreat northward down the river Dendre, reaching Lombeek Ste. Catherine, about eight miles west of Brussels, on the July 5. 4th of July. On the morrow the leaders of the coalesced armies again met in conference at Waterloo, when it was decided that Clerfaye's force should pass

[1] York to Dundas, 2nd and 3rd July; Dundas to Diepenbrock, 3rd and 7th July; Diepenbrock to Dundas, 5th July 1794.

eastwards towards Brussels, and that the army of the 1794. Allies should ultimately occupy a line from Antwerp, by Louvain, Wavre, and Gembloux, to Namur, but that until the 7th, at any rate, the line in advance of Brussels, extending from Alost by Braine-le-Comte and Nivelles to Sombref, should be maintained. Ghent had already been evacuated; and accordingly on the next day Clerfaye's force began its march to join Coburg, while Moira moved to Alost and brought his troops for the first time under the Duke's personal command. But Jourdan meanwhile was not inactive. On the 6th July 6. he attacked the whole line of the Austrians from Braine-le-Comte to Gembloux; and, though beaten back after hard fighting on the east, where a concentrated attack might have given him possession of the Austrian line of communications, he succeeded in pushing Coburg's right wing back from Braine-le-Comte and Nivelles to Waterloo. Thereupon Coburg warned the Duke of York that he must retire eastward and cancel the agreement made on the 5th. The Duke answered with cold sarcasm that it was a new thing for the Austrians to retire before thirty thousand Frenchmen, and appealed to the Archduke Charles to keep Coburg to his engagements; but received from him only a sad reply that orders must be obeyed. On the 7th and 8th Jourdan renewed his attacks, directing the best of his strength against the Austrian left, which he forced back to the battlefield of Ramillies. He then immediately invested Namur; upon which Coburg, fearing to be cut off from the Meuse, ordered the whole of his army to retire July 7. upon Tirlemont.

The Duke meanwhile, since his left was uncovered by the retreat of the Austrians, withdrew, at Coburg's request, very slowly northward to Assche, and thence struck north-eastward to the Dyle, which he crossed at Malines, fixing his headquarters at Contich, some eight miles north of that city. A new line of defence was then taken up, which sufficiently showed the divided councils of the Allies. On the right the

1794.
July.
British contingent, now numbering some thirty thousand men, was posted on the Dyle from Antwerp to Malines. On its left the Prince of Orange with the Dutch troops and from two to three thousand Austrians covered the line from Malines to Louvain; and from Louvain the rest of the Austrian army, between forty-five and fifty thousand men, was extended in a south-easterly direction by Tirlemont, Landen, and Waremme to the Meuse, with a detachment of four thousand more on the eastern bank of that river, and between it and the Ourthe. Thus the British and Dutch, who desired to defend Holland, could be deserted at any moment which the Emperor should select for the pursuit of his own particular object, namely, to carry his army away to share the plunder of Poland. Craig, for his part, felt no doubt whatever that the British and Dutch would very soon be left to their own resources.[1]

The reader may have felt surprised that, with a force of nearly one hundred and fifty thousand men, the French should not have pressed the Allies harder, and made an end of them long before. The fact was that the Committee of Public Safety had interfered with the Generals on the 4th of July, by an order that the recapture of Valenciennes, Condé, Landrecies, and Quesnoy should take precedence of any further operations; and accordingly the army in Belgium had been weakened to provide for this service. This was the work of Robespierre, who at the time was inclined towards peace; and indeed peace appears to have been a common topic of conversation between the French and Austrian outposts from the beginning of July.[2] Thirty thousand French soldiers were accordingly withdrawn to Valenciennes, as many more were wasted in occupying ports of embarkation for England, and the remainder were ordered to push the Allies completely

---

[1] Coburg to York, 7th and 8th July; York to Coburg, 7th July; to Dundas, 7th and 10th July; Craig to Nepean, 11th July 1794.

[2] Sybel, iii. 150-152, 171. Craig to Nepean, 4th July 1794.

out of Belgium, and then to occupy a cordon from 1794. Antwerp to Namur. Pichegru, therefore, took command in person of the left wing, and on the 12th July 12. moved with eighteen thousand men against Malines, while Jourdan on the right simultaneously advanced against Louvain, Jodoigne, and Huy on the Meuse. On the evening of the 12th Pichegru drove the Duke of York's advanced posts into Malines, where they were promptly reinforced; but the fortifications of the town were in ruins, and, on renewing the attack on the 15th, the French captured the place with little difficulty. July 15. The troops charged with the defence were Hessians and Dutch; and it appears certain that the conduct of one or the other of them was not irreproachable, though there are indications also that the Duke himself was partly responsible for the mishap.

The Duke then threw his left back along the line of the Nethe from Lierre to Duffel; but meanwhile Jourdan had on the same day mastered Louvain, and July 15. in the course of the two following days Jodoigne and Namur also. The Dutch troops about Louvain, upon the loss of that town, fell back northward across the Demer, while the Austrians retired eastward; and thus the line of the Allies was fairly broken owing to their own divergent plans. The Duke of York had already in these days concerted operations with the Prince of Orange for the recapture of Malines on the 18th,[1] when July 18. he received a letter from Coburg saying that, owing to the loss of that place and of Louvain, he had ordered the troops formerly stationed at the latter city to fall back to Diest, and was himself withdrawing from Tirlemont to Landen. The Duke begged him before doing so to essay a general forward movement, but received only a vague and unsatisfactory reply; and on the morning of the 20th a staff-officer, while inspecting the left of July 20. the Dutch position, discovered that the Austrians at Diest were already retreating south-eastward on Hasselt, Coburg having given them orders to this effect without

[1] York to Dundas, 15th, 19th, 20th, 23rd July 1794.

VOL. IV U

1794. saying a word of his intentions to the Duke of York.
July 22. With his left flank thus again laid bare, the Duke was
July 24. obliged to evacuate Antwerp and retire due north from it across the Dutch frontier to Rozendahl. Coburg likewise fell back to eastward, crossed the Meuse at Maastricht, and took up a position about seven miles south and east of that fortress at Fouron le Comte. Thus the British and Austrians were finally parted.

It cannot be said that either of them was sorry to take leave of the other. Even in 1793 their relations had not been too cordial, for the Austrians, in their jealousy, would never allow foreign troops to pass through their fortified towns, even during a forced march; and thus the British were frequently condemned to make long and fatiguing detours.[1] But the betrayal of the Duke of York's column on the 18th of May, and the subsequent operations, deliberately contrived to hasten the evacuation of the Netherlands, converted the dislike of the British for the Austrians into the bitterest hatred and contempt. At headquarters, again, the presence of a soldier such as Craig, with ideas far more enlightened than those of the Austrians, and with some means of insisting upon them through the medium of the Duke of York, can hardly have contributed to harmony. It may be added that the Austrian troops were as severe in their criticism of their chiefs, and particularly of Waldeck, as were any of the British, proclaiming loudly that the abandonment of Belgium was due to French gold.[2] In fact the Austrian army, between heavy losses and deep distrust of its leaders, was utterly demoralised; nor is it surprising that this should have been so. It is indeed more than probable that, if Coburg had wished to make a stand after the action of Fleurus, his men would not have supported him. Of course Coburg had to bear the responsibility for all this, and to digest as best he might some very bitter reproaches from the Duke of

[1] *Narrative of an Officer of the Guards*, ii. 35.
[2] Craig to Nepean, 11th July 1794.

York; yet it seems that in truth he was the person 1794. the least to blame. Though as a commander in the field he was slow, unenterprising, enamoured of vicious methods, and possessed of no military quality except that of looking carefully to the wants of his troops, yet he did not lack insight, sound sense, imperturbable calm, and the instinct of honesty and straightforwardness. His name is forgotten in England, though his portrait is still occasionally to be found in English print-shops, showing that at one time he had gained a certain fame, which was destined speedily to perish. It can only be said of him that he was beloved by his men, that he bore the sins of others without complaining, and that he was a loyal servant to an unfaithful master.

CHAPTER XII

1794. WHILE the Allies in the Netherlands were thus giving way on all sides during the months of June and July, the British Government naturally bethought itself of the sixty thousand men which it had agreed to hire from Prussia for operations in that quarter. The Ministers had reckoned that these troops would be ready by the end of May; and accordingly, as has been told, Lord Cornwallis was sent from England to arrange with Marshal Möllendorf as to the part to be taken by the Prussians in the campaign. Visiting the Duke of York on the way, Cornwallis agreed with him that the protection of West Flanders, and, if possible, the siege of Lille, were the matters of most urgent importance; and he formulated his request to Möllen-
June 20. dorf accordingly. He soon discovered that he had been sent upon a fool's errand. Möllendorf, instead of sixty thousand, had but forty thousand men, deficient in stores and supplies and absolutely wanting in transport, which he declared himself unable to furnish without ready money from England. The real difficulty was that the Allies were all at variance as to the use that should be made of the Prussian troops. England wanted them to aid in recovering West Flanders. Holland would at first have preferred them to remain upon the Rhine, but presently yielded to the demands of England. The Emperor of Austria not only raised strong objections to the march of Prussian troops to Belgium, but claimed thirty thousand of the sixty thousand men for the protection of the

Empire, declaring that their removal from the Rhine would expose all Germany to the ravages of the French. Between these conflicting claims Möllendorf found little difficulty in sitting still and doing nothing, which was precisely what the advisers of King Frederick William most desired. By the 18th of June Cornwallis had made up his mind that scanty help was to be expected from Prussia, at any rate during the present campaign; and neither he nor Lord Malmesbury was slow to express very decided opinions as to the ill-faith of the Prussian Court.[1]

This was the situation when the failure of the Austrian attack at Fleurus determined the Emperor to evacuate the Low Countries. That potentate thereupon reversed his language as to the Prussian contingent, and urged that Möllendorf should advance into Belgium; nor did he hesitate, on the 15th of July, to order Coburg still to defend the Austrian Netherlands, though he said nothing about sending reinforcements to enable him to do so. This despicable lying and trickery had, of course, but one object, that of drawing more money from England under false pretences. The English Government, however, though it had learned that no reliance was to be placed on Thugut's statements or promises, decided in the middle of July to send Lord Spencer and Thomas Grenville to Vienna, to urge once more the renewal of the offensive in Belgium. So far, therefore, the Emperor seemed likely to gain his point; and since the King of Prussia had shown remarkable weakness in dealing with the insurrection in Poland, Francis had every reason to hope that decisive action in that country would be delayed, until his own and the Russian armies could appear there in sufficient force to dictate the final settlement according to their own desires. The Prussian Ministers, on the other hand, when they learned of the

1794.

July 19.

[1] Cornwallis to Dundas, 8th and 18th June 1794, and see *Cornwallis Correspondence*, ii. 239-255; *Malmesbury Correspondence*; *Dropmore Papers*, ii. 564-566, 577, 592, 594.

1794. despatch of Spencer and Grenville to Vienna, became nervous lest England should transfer the promised subsidy from her to Austria; and they began to turn their thoughts to the negotiations of a separate peace with France.[1]

Meanwhile, through the energy of Carnot, reinforcements had been found for the French army of the Rhine, which, after a fortnight's hard fighting on the heights about Kaiserslautern, forced Möllendorf to retire under the guns of Mainz with a loss of two thousand men and sixteen guns. The Austrian troops on the Rhine thereupon withdrew from the left bank of the river; and the miscarriage of a plan, concerted a fortnight later for recovery of the lost ground, set the Generals of the two nations quarrelling more bitterly than ever. The end of July brought yet another stroke of good luck to France in the overthrow of Robespierre and the execution of himself, St. Just, and other of his principal colleagues. Robespierre's latest achievement as a military administrator had been to decree that no quarter should be shown to British or Hanoverians in the field, an order which was disobeyed by the French troops and laughed at by the British. The supreme imbecility, apart from all other faults, of his rule had brought France to the last stage of exhaustion; and, indeed, if the Allies had succeeded in keeping the French armies out of Belgium, the latter must have perished of starvation.[2] Robespierre's death marked the close of the Terror and the beginning of a return to common sense in the matter of administration. The man, however, had lived long enough to waste the energies of the armies of the North in the recovery of the four captured fortresses in the frontier, when they should have been scattering the Allies to the four winds; and thus it came about that the Duke of York enjoyed a few weeks' respite for the formation of new plans.

July 2-13.
July 28.

[1] Sybel, iii. 240-243.
[2] Poisson, iv. 262.

It was fortunate for him that it was so, for he now found himself in serious trouble with his army. This was the result of the insane system, allowed by Dundas, of raising men for rank. The regiments despatched to Holland contained only a very few old soldiers mixed with great numbers of recruits, who were utterly without training and discipline. "Many of them do not know one end of a fire-lock from the other," wrote Craig, "and will never know it." Six of the battalions had been deprived of their flank-companies, that is to say, of their best men, to make up General Grey's force in the West Indies; and no sooner did the new levies find themselves released from the crimping-house and the gaol for active service, than they fell to plundering in all directions. The Duke was obliged to issue a very severe order on the 27th of July[1] to call the army to its senses; but, with such officers as had been obtained under Dundas's scheme, it was impossible to expect the slightest obedience. In the first place the army was lamentably deficient in Brigadiers and Generals of division. Moira had only accepted the command of his force on the condition that he should not serve in Flanders; and though, in view of the perilous condition of the Allies when he landed, he had waived his objections for the time, yet there was another obstacle not so easily to be overcome. Albeit enjoying an independent command of eight thousand men, Moira was almost the junior Major-general of the army. Major-general Crosbie, who was with him, also held a more important command than his seniors, such as Ralph Abercromby and David Dundas, the latter of whom joined the Duke of York at the end of July. Both Moira and Crosbie, therefore, went home, from delicacy towards the feelings of their superiors; and the loss of Moira was bitterly regretted as that of a very able officer who was idolised by his men.

The British troops now consisted of four brigades

[1] Ditfurth, iii. 217.

1794.
July.
of cavalry and seven of infantry,[1] making altogether some twenty-five thousand men; but for all these there were, after the departure of Moira and Crosbie, only four Generals — David Dundas, Stewart, Abercromby, and Fox, the last of whom was fully employed as Quartermaster-general. This was the more serious because the commanders of the new battalions, who had been juggled into seniority by the Government and the army-brokers, were not fit to command a company, much less a brigade. Some of them were boys of twenty-one who knew nothing of

---

[1] CAVALRY—

David Dundas's Brigade—2nd, 6th D.G.; 2nd, 6th D.
Ralph Dundas's Brigade—Blues; 3rd, 5th D.G.; 1st D.
Laurie's Brigade—7th, 11th, 15th, 16th L.D.
Vyse's Brigade—1st D.G.; 8th, 14th L.D.

Foreign Troops—

Uhlans Brittaniques, Irving's Hussars, Choiseul's Hussars.

INFANTRY—

First Brigade—3rd, 88th, 63rd.
Second Brigade—8th,[1] 44th,[1] 33rd.[1]
Third Brigade—12th,[1] 55th,[1] 38th.
Fourth Brigade—14th, 53rd, 37th.
Fifth Brigade—19th, 54th, 42nd.
Sixth Brigade—27th, 89th, 28th.
Seventh Brigade—40th,[1] 59th, 57th, 87th.

Foreign Troops—

Loyal Emigrants, York Rangers, Rohan's Regiment.

British Cavalry,	165 officers,	4,350	N.C.O.s and men.
Hanoverians and Hessians	168 „	2,939	„
Total Cavalry	333 „	7,289	„
British Infantry,	583 „	21,170	„
Hanoverians and Hessians	322	„ 8,722	„
Total .	1,238 „	37,181	„

Total of all arms, including artillery, etc., say, 1300 officers, 40,000 N.C.O.s and men.

---

[1] The flank companies of these battalions were in the West Indies.

their simplest duties. Though they went cheerfully 1794. into action, they looked upon the whole campaign as an July. elaborate picnic, for which they did not fail to provide themselves with abundance of comforts ; and thus the baggage-columns were filled with private waggons under the charge of insubordinate drivers. The junior officers, who were so scarce that few regiments had as many subalterns as companies, appear in many cases to have been worse than the senior, as is always to be expected when commissions are to be obtained for the asking ; nor with bad examples before them were they likely to improve. Thrust into the Army to satisfy the claims of dependents, constituents, importunate creditors, and discarded concubines, many of these young men were at once a disgrace and an encumbrance to the force. Hard drinking, which was the fashion then in all classes from highest to lowest, was, of course, sedulously cultivated by these aspirants to the rank of gentleman ; and it was no uncommon thing for regiments to start on the march under charge of the Adjutant and Sergeant-major only, while the officers stayed behind, to come galloping up several hours later, full of wine, careless where they rode, careless of the confusion into which they threw the columns, careless of everything but the place appointed for the end of the march, if by chance they were sober enough to have remembered it. These evils, too, were extremely difficult to check, for in 1794, as in 1744, political interest rather than meritorious service was the road to promotion. While the shameful traffic of the army-brokers and the raising of endless new regiments continued, every officer who could command money or interest was sure of obtaining advancement at home without the knowledge of his chief in the field, and had, therefore, not only no encouragement to do his duty, but an actual reason for avoiding it. Thus the men were very imperfectly disciplined ; there were no efficient company-officers to look after them ; no efficient Colonels to look after the company-officers ; no

1794. Generals to look after the Colonels. Craig sought
July. a remedy in begging for more Generals. "We cannot get on," he wrote, on the 5th of August, "without a good supply and a supply of good. The evil to the discipline of the army increases every day, and is likely to become very serious."[1]

But the Duke's difficulties did not end with the defects of his officers and men. It had lately become the practice in time of peace to issue to each regiment the materials for its clothing, to be made up by the regiment itself, a system which had probably been designed to obtain for the Colonels the largest possible profit. Nor must the Colonels be blamed herein, for they were expected to make that profit, which in those days was practically the only emolument open to general officers. It was, of course, impossible for troops in the field to spend three or four months in making up their clothes; and the result was that the Duke's army was left almost naked. Moreover, in the hurry of raising innumerable new corps, the responsibility for such details as clothing, accounts, musters, and so forth had been overlooked; the new officers knew nothing of the extremely complex methods of military finance;[2] and the sudden vast increase of business thrown upon agents and officials was greater than they could immediately bear. Finally, quite apart from these failings in respect of the raiment of entire battalions, no effort whatever was made to clothe the recruits who were sent out to fill up the gaps in the various corps. These unfortunate men, on being drafted into the depôts in England, received what was called slop-clothing, which signified a linen jacket and trousers; and it is an actual fact that many of them were sent on

[1] Craig to Nepean, 5th August 1794; Ditfurth, ii. 213 *seq.*; Memorandum of the Duke of York, 23rd December 1794; Calvert, pp. 385-386; see vol. ii. of this *History*, p. 88.

[2] No officer could hope to master these mysteries without the help of two fat little duodecimo volumes called *The Regimental Companion*, and a third and slighter volume entitled *Military Finance*.

active service in this dress, without waistcoat, drawers, 1794. or stockings. The result was that the Duke of York's July. corps was in a worse state in respect of clothing than had been hitherto recorded of any British army.¹

Another great difficulty, of which Craig had complained again and again, was the want of drivers for the artillery. Lord Moira had brought with him guns but no drivers; and there were but two captains (not enough, as Craig said, to do a fortieth part of the work) at disposal for the superintendence of a huge mass of horses. Thus a new train of artillery, which had been sent out to replace the cannon lost at Turcoing, became a positive embarrassment. The Commissariat also, as used so often to happen with British armies, was in a very bad state. The men of the new corps of Royal Waggoners had been recruited in London, and were the worst refuse of the population. They were known, in fact, as the "Newgate Blues." "A greater set of scoundrels never disgraced an army," wrote Craig, in his usual pithy style. "I believe it to be true that half of them, if not taken from the hulks, have at times visited them. . . . They have committed every species of villainy, and treat their horses badly." But the very worst department of all was that of the hospitals, wherein the abuses were so terrible that men hardly liked to speak of them. In December 1793 the inhabitants of one of the English ports had been dumbfounded by the arrival of one hundred invalid soldiers from Ostend in indescribable distress. They had been on board ship for a week in the bitter wintry weather, without so much as straw to lie upon. Some of them were dead; others died on being carried ashore. No provision had been made for their comfort on landing, and but for the compassion of the gentry, who subscribed money for their relief, the poor fellows might well have perished.² Nothing was done to

¹ Craig to Nepean, 31st August; Craig's Memorandum of 23rd December 1794.
² *Sunday Reformer*, 29th December 1793.

1794. amend this state of things. Dundas's idea of putting
July. an army in the field was to land raw men on a foreign
shore, and to expect discipline, arms, ammunition,
clothing, victuals, medical stores, and medical treatment
to descend on them from Heaven. Some kind of a
medical staff was improvised out of drunken apothe-
caries, broken-down practitioners, and rogues of every
description, who were provided under some cheap
contract; the charges of respectable members of the
medical profession being deemed exorbitant. "The
dreadful mismanagement of the hospital is beyond
description," wrote Craig, "and the remedy beyond
my power. Every branch and every fibre of every
branch draws a contrary way. I really doubt if there
will be any way to get any good from this department
but by tying them all together and sending them to
you to be changed for a new set."[1]

Such was the composition of the force with which
the Duke of York now undertook, in concert with the
Dutch, to protect Holland, or, in other words, to conduct
that most delicate and trying of operations—manœuvring
with inferior numbers over a wide front to hold a
superior force in check. The first difficulty arose
with the Dutch, for the Prince of Orange, apparently
enamoured of the Austrian methods, was eager to scatter
the troops over a multitude of different points; but
this the Duke, with Craig at his back, steadily refused
to do. The Prince then urged that the Dutch fortresses
should be garrisoned by British troops; but the said
fortresses were all in bad condition, and were repairing
only with that incredible slowness which was peculiar
to the Dutch Government. The Duke, therefore,
refused this also; feeling tolerably sure that, if he
consented, his battalions would be sacrificed piecemeal
for the defence of Holland, while the Dutch looked on
without raising a man to help them. The two gates

[1] Craig to Nepean, 12th and 31st August, 5th and 8th
September 1794. The class of medical officer obtained by Government is described in *Autobiography of Sir J. M'Grigor*, pp. 93, 94.

of Holland on the south were Bergen-op-Zoom and Breda, and on the east Grave and Nimeguen, with the fortress of Bois-le-Duc midway between Breda and Nimeguen. The two eastern gates were safe so long as the Austrians retained Maastricht and their position on the Meuse; but the Austrians were not to be trusted. Accordingly, the Duke resolved to garrison Breda, Bergen-op-Zoom, and, if possible, Bois-le-Duc with Dutch troops; himself taking up a position on the north bank of the river Aa, with his right resting on Bois-le-Duc and his left on the great morass called the Peel. From this central point he judged that he could move to the help of any of the Dutch fortresses to southward, cover the province of Gelderland, and keep Grave and Nimeguen within reach in case of mishap on that side.

1794. July.

He was about to march thither from Rozendahl when the news came that Moreau, who was advancing northward along the coast after the capture of Nieuport, had driven back the Dutch posts and had besieged Sluys. The Prince of Orange thereupon besought the Duke to stand fast, producing a letter from Coburg which contained not only an assurance of his ability to hold the passage of the Meuse, but even a hint of possible offensive movements. After some hesitation the Duke consented to a compromise by moving to Osterhout, a little to the north-east of Breda, so as to give some countenance both to Breda and Bergen-op-Zoom. He marched, accordingly, on the 31st of July, unmolested by the enemy, who were in force around Antwerp; and the Prince of Orange then came to the wise but rather belated decision to evacuate all the Dutch fortresses to the south of the Scheldt. The Duke, therefore, lent him a strong detachment of his men to hold communications between Breda and Bergen-op-Zoom, so as to release Dutch troops to cover the retreat of these garrisons and to relieve Sluys.[1]

July 31.

Aug. 8.

[1] York to Dundas, 25th, 27th, 30th July, 1st and 6th August; Craig to Nepean, 25th July 1794.

1794. Just at this moment Henry Dundas, hearing of Moreau's advance, and having by chance a few troops unemployed, decided to send a naval armament to Flushing, together with five battalions under Lord Mulgrave, for the defence of the Dutch territories in that quarter. As was his rule in such cases, Dundas kept Mulgrave under his own immediate command, but withal instructed him not to go against any order of the Duke of York,—an arrangement admirably calculated to paralyse the force and to raise discord between the commanders. Mulgrave, who had started
Aug. 17. apart from his troops, reached Flushing on the 17th, and finding that none of them had arrived, occupied himself in examining the situation. He was soon satisfied that the French had no further designs for the campaign than to take Sluys and Flushing, as ports from which to ship the harvest of the Austrian Netherlands to France. Meanwhile, the Dutch no sooner heard of his coming than they suspended their operations for the relief of Sluys, in the hope that Mulgrave would do the work for them; and the French, having also full intelligence of everything, increased their force at Sluys to twenty-five thousand men, which made the relief practically impossible. Dundas, meanwhile, wrote with the greatest confidence of the success of that operation, which his own interference had condemned to failure; announcing also that Mulgrave's force, which had not yet even arrived at Flushing, would be required elsewhere in a month. At length
Aug. 26. the five battalions sailed into Flushing on the 26th, nominally thirty-two hundred strong, and actually with the following qualifications for immediate service in the field. The Thirty-first[1] was composed chiefly of recruits, of whom two hundred and forty were unarmed. The Seventy-ninth had but one officer to each company, and but eight rounds of ball-ammunition a man. The Eighty-fourth had twenty rounds a man,

[1] Its flank companies, and those of the 34th, were detained for the West Indies.

but, the regiment having never ceased marching from quarter to quarter ever since it had been raised, the men were wholly untrained. The Eighty-fifth had thirty rounds a man, but half of the soldiers had never had arms in their hands. The Thirty-fourth alone appears to have been fit and ready for work. Fortunately there was no work for them to do, for Sluys surrendered on the very day of their arrival; and Mulgrave, after landing them at Flushing to learn the elements of their business, suggested that at least two of the battalions had better remain there and be made into soldiers, instead of sailing to certain annihilation in the West Indies. To this Dundas agreed, for he purposed to take from the Duke of York ten of Moira's battalions, and was well content to leave him inferior troops in their place. Meanwhile, as a specimen of utter imbecility, this despatch of Mulgrave's detachment has few equals even in English military annals. The mere promise of help was sufficient to relax the exertions of the Dutch. The troops were embarked so late as to miss the object of the expedition, and, even if they had been embarked in time, they were of quality too poor to have accomplished it. In brief, the whole enterprise bears the unmistakable mark of Henry Dundas.[1]

Meanwhile Spencer and Grenville had throughout August pursued their negotiations at Vienna with very indifferent success. One point Thugut was ready to concede, namely, the recall of Coburg, who indeed resigned on the 9th of August, being worn down in body and mind, and thoroughly disgusted with his command. But Thugut absolutely refused to order troops from the Rhine to Belgium, and demanded the guarantee of a loan of three millions for the present campaign besides a new subsidy for the next. It was necessary to refer these pretensions to the Cabinet in London;

[1] Dundas to Mulgrave, 7th and 13th August; Mulgrave to Dundas, 17th, 19th, 26th, 30th August, 3rd September; Dundas to York, 22nd August 1794.

1794. and long before the reference had even been made, the
Aug. 12, 14. Austrian Council of War ordered Clerfaye, who was to succeed Coburg, to devote all his efforts to the defence not of Belgium but of Luxemburg, Mainz, and Mannheim. But though the Allies were idle, the French were not; and, thanks in part to a threat of the Committee of Public Safety to massacre the garrisons unless the fortresses were delivered, they had recovered both Quesnoy and Landrecies by the 15th of August. The fall of Sluys, and the recall of the troops detached to Walcheren also enabled Pichegru to begin a forward
Aug. 27. movement, and on the 27th he advanced from Antwerp north-eastward to Hoogstraeten, driving in all the Dutch posts, and seeming to threaten the turning of the Duke of York's left. The Duke, thereupon, on
Aug. 30. the advice of a Council of War, retired on the 30th to his chosen position between Bois-le-Duc and the Peel, while Pichegru sent a strong detachment eastward to occupy Einhoven in force.[1]

Meanwhile a message had reached the Duke of York from Clerfaye, suggesting a general forward movement to save the beleaguered cities of Valenciennes
Sept. 1. and Condé; and on the 1st of September a conference was held between the Allied commanders at Bois-le-Duc to consider the proposal. It was not yet known to them, apparently, that Valenciennes had already surrendered to the French on the 29th of August, and that Condé was at the last gasp; and there was some talk among them of an advance of the British to recapture Antwerp, while the Austrians on the Meuse protected their rear. The news that both fortresses had fallen, and that the French forces thus liberated for the field were hastening to the front, naturally deranged this plan; and though

[1] On the 29th of August the Duke reorganised his force as follows:

First Brigade—Maj.-gen. Stewart, 3rd, 40th, 55th, 59th, 89th.
Second Brigade— 8th, 27th, 28th, 57th.
Third Brigade— 12th, 33rd, 42nd, 44th.
Fourth Brigade—Maj.-gen. Fox, 14th, 37th, 38th, 63rd.
Fifth Brigade— 19th, 53rd, 54th, 88th.

the Duke was anxious still to make the attempt, Craig 1794. perceived little hope of success, chiefly because he could not trust the Austrians to give hearty co-operation. In truth, the Allies had let slip the favourable moment through their own dissensions, and the opportunity was not to recur again. On the 4th of September Sept. 4. Pichegru marched northward from Hoogstraeten to Meerle, as if to threaten Breda, but on the 10th turned eastward, after leaving a detachment before that place, and on the 12th reached Oosterwyk. On the following day he attacked the Duke's advanced posts at Bokstel, Sept. 13. and on the 14th captured them, making two battalions of Darmstadt-Hessians prisoners. This was an unpleasant mishap, for these troops had hitherto always behaved admirably; but, though they complained of the Duke for not supporting them, the Duke in his secret report declared them to have been panic-stricken. Alive, however, to the importance of regaining this post and the line of the Dommel, the Duke ordered Abercromby forward next day with ten battalions and as many Sept. 15. squadrons of British, to recover the lost ground. The movement was very nearly disastrous, for Abercromby only just missed falling into the midst of Pichegru's main army, which was on march to the eastward; but quickly apprehending the situation, he withdrew his troops in excellent order with the loss of about ninety men, two-thirds of them prisoners. This skirmish is notable both because it brought Colonel Arthur Wellesley of the Thirty-third under fire for the first time, and because it led to the trial of four officers, three of them belonging to a most distinguished regiment, for cowardice. This was a healthy sign, for it showed that the older officers were bent on ridding the Army at the earliest possible moment of the worthless comrades imposed on them by Dundas.[1]

On the same day the Duke received information that this demonstration against Bokstel was but a feint, the main force of the enemy, reported to be eighty thousand

[1] Craig to Dundas, 19th September 1794.

1794. strong, being in motion to turn his left. His intelligence seems to have been extremely vague and imperfect at this time; but being dissatisfied with his position, to which, owing to dry weather, neither the Peel nor the Aa afforded adequate protection, he decided that the retention of it was not worth the risk of being cut off from his retreat to the Maas. He therefore retired on

Sept. 16. the next day to that river, crossed it at Grave and took up a position on the north bank, with his headquarters at Wychen, a few miles to the north of Grave. It then remained for him to make his dispositions to defend the line of the river, the unprotected portion of which extended for some seventy-five miles from Fort Loevestein, at the western end of the Bommeler Waert[1] on to the west, to Venloo on the east. Any effective defence with the forces at his disposal was impossible, and the Duke therefore arranged that all troops in British pay should be sent to him from West Flanders, and that the Dutch, who were sitting inactive behind their fortresses, should send men to repair and to defend Crevecoeur and Bommel.

The Duke's next effort was to concert offensive operations with Clerfaye, who lay on his left; and he had the greater hopes of a favourable issue, since the new Secretary at War, William Windham, was already on his way to that officer on a mission from London. But the Austrian Commander also had been unfortunate.

Sept. 17-18. On the 17th and 18th General Latour's corps of seven thousand men, which guarded his left on the Ourthe, was driven back by a greatly superior force of Jourdan's right wing under General Schérer; whereupon Clerfaye, who had watched the whole process without moving one soldier of his forty thousand to save Latour, immediately retired behind the Roer, leaving eight thousand men as a garrison for Maastricht. The Austrian General

[1] The Bommeler Waert is the triangular tongue of land enclosed between the Waal and the Meuse immediately to the east of Gorkum. It is very nearly an island, the entrance to it from the east being very narrow and defended by a fort, then, as now, called Fort St. Andries.

therefore rejected all idea of the offensive as impossible, but consented to maintain communication with the Duke if he would extend his left to Venloo, which, like all the Dutch fortresses, was in miserable repair and without a sufficient garrison. The Duke agreed, and so the matter was arranged; Clerfaye, however, giving the Duke clearly to understand that if his right were turned he should cross the Rhine.[1]

1794.

The Duke thereupon made his plans for protecting a line of from seventy-five to ninety-five miles of river with a force of thirty thousand soldiers of all ranks, the sick list having by this time claimed close upon seven thousand men of his army. His right from the Bommeler Waert to Grave was held by about five thousand Hessians, their main body being stationed at Alfen, a little to the east of the island; Grave was held by two Dutch battalions; east of Grave four brigades of infantry and two of cavalry lay about Mook; Abercromby, with two more brigades of infantry and one of cavalry, stood higher up the river at Gennep; and six thousand Hanoverians under Walmoden prolonged the line from Gennep to Venloo, with their main body at Well. Craig, however, did not deceive himself as to the inevitable issue, being firmly convinced that there was an understanding between the Austrians and French; wherein he appears to have been correct.[2] "We shall have to fall back behind the Waal," he wrote; "depend on it, this will happen in a few days . . . and in a fortnight the Austrians will be behind the Rhine." Jourdan followed up the Austrians, leaving Kléber to invest Maastricht; whereupon Clerfaye, who had sixty thousand men behind

[1] York to Dundas, 19th, 21st, 22nd September (enclosing correspondence with Clerfaye); Craig to Dundas, 19th September 1794.
[2] Craig to Nepean, 20th September 1794. Sybel, iii. 432 *note*. From this it appears that all documentary evidence of the agreement has been carefully destroyed, but that there is a hint of secret negotiations actually proceeding on the 18th of September 1794.

1794. the Roer, forthwith called loudly on the Duke of York to relieve that fortress. Grenville at the Foreign Office, anticipating something of the kind, had already despatched urgent representations to Vienna requiring the concurrence of the Austrians in this operation, but of course to no purpose. The Duke, by advice of Abercromby and Walmoden, sent Craig to stir up Clerfaye, and, that the Austrians might have no pretext for complaint, moved sixteen thousand men at great risk towards Venloo. But all was perfectly useless, for Clerfaye declined to budge. An attack of the French Oct. 2. on his position on the 2nd of October gave him the excuse that he wanted ; and he immediately retreated across the Rhine.[1]

Sept. 22. Pichegru meanwhile, on the 22nd of September, had completely invested Bois-le-Duc, and sent two divisions forward to line the Maas over against the Duke of York's position. The French were now in the greatest distress from want of provisions, which had to be brought from Antwerp in waggons, and that by long detours in order to circumvent the Dutch fortresses. It was therefore imperative for Pichegru to possess Bois-le-Duc as an advanced base ; and the place was the more difficult for him to master since he had no siege-artillery. Unfortunately the cowardice of the Dutch delivered to him Sept. 24. all that he wanted. On the 24th he opened a feeble bombardment with his field-pieces upon Fort Crevecoeur, which guarded the passage into the Isle of Sept. 28. Bommel from the south ; and on the 28th, the place, though amply provisioned and in a good state of defence, was yielded up by the Dutch Commandant. Thereby Pichegru gained not only forty-two heavy guns, but the command of the sluices whereby the inundation of Bois-le-Duc could be let flow or drawn off. The loss of Crevecoeur did not improve the good feeling of the British towards the Dutch, who, from the

[1] York to Dundas, 25th and 29th September, 1st and 3rd October ; Craig to Nepean, 1st October ; Grenville to York, 25th September 1794.

first entry of the Duke of York into their country, 1794, had showed the bitterest animosity against his men. Intelligence now reached the Duke that a general Sept. 30. insurrection of the French party in the United Provinces was imminent ; and three days later the retreat of Oct. 3. Clerfaye compelled him to retire northward across the Waal, over which he had already thrown a bridge of boats. The movement was conducted with some confusion owing to the mismanagement of the Duke's Staff ; but Pichegru suffered the Allies to shuffle themselves without the slightest molestation into their appointed positions. The Hessians held the Bommeler Waert on the south bank of the Waal, and the line of the Linge over against it on the north bank. At the village of Geldermalsen on the Linge the right of the British joined the left of the Hessians, extending from thence eastward along the Waal to the road from Nimeguen to Arnheim ; where the Hanoverians carried the line to its end at the parting of the Waal and the Leck, maintaining communication with Clerfaye's Austrians at Emmerick. Nimeguen, though ill-fortified and provided for, was also held on the southern bank of the Waal.

By this time even the long-suffering Cabinet in England was growing weary of paying subsidies to Austria and Prussia for service which they never rendered. On the 4th of October Dundas advised Oct. 4. the Duke of York that the Government had resolved to give them no more money, and ordered him to cut off the allowance hitherto paid to Clerfaye unless he agreed to active concert of operations. Thugut, however, had in many respects gained his point. The British Government, thinking that a bad ally was better than none, had consented on the 14th of September to guarantee to Austria a loan of three millions in consideration of her services during the first campaign ; at the same time renouncing a project which had been put forward for placing Clerfaye's force, together with the Duke of York's, under the supreme command of

1794. Cornwallis. Thugut was jubilant; for everything was going as he wished. In Poland, Suvorof was rapidly putting down the insurrection, in stemming which the Prussian Generals had shown the greatest feebleness; Belgium was already abandoned, as he had desired; and the Cabinet of London had rewarded Austria for her treachery by financial assistance. In the circumstances he could not do less than give promises of effectual help in the defence of Holland, though of course without the slightest intention to fulfil them.

Meanwhile the behaviour of the Dutch grew more and more suspicious. Bois-le-Duc was disgracefully
Oct. 10. surrendered on the 10th of October by the Commandant; and a regiment of French emigrants, which formed part of the garrison, having been denied permission to cut its way through the besiegers, was massacred in cold blood. On the same day, by a curious coincidence, the British Government warned the Dutch that, unless they exerted themselves, the British army should be withdrawn; at the same time proposing to put the Duke of Brunswick in command of the British and Dutch forces in order to keep them together. Then a
Oct. 18. week later, as if to bribe the Stadtholder to compliance, Dundas authorised the payment of one hundred thousand pounds to the Dutch, which was simply so much money wasted; for the Prince of Orange would do nothing for the defence of the country, and wished to employ the British for the repression of his own rebellious subjects. How, in the face of the Duke of York's letters, the British Ministers in London hesitated to order the immediate withdrawal of the army is incomprehensible, except on the supposition that they still trusted to the proved ill faith of the Emperor Francis.[1]

The French, meanwhile, continued to follow up their advantages. Jourdan, on the east, after leaving detachments to besiege Venloo and Maastricht, had
Oct. 6. occupied Cologne on the 6th of October, and drawn

[1] Dundas to York, 10th, 12th, 16th, 18th October; York to Dundas, 16th, 18th, 23rd October 1794.

up his army in face of Clerfaye's main body, which was 1794. extended along the Rhine from Duisburg to Bonn and beyond. Moreau, who had taken over the command owing to Pichegru's illness, also pushed forward seven thousand men in front of Grave, posted thirty thousand between Ravestein (a little to west of Grave) and Bois-le-Duc, and ten thousand men opposite the Bommeler Waert. On the 18th he began to lay a bridge of boats Oct. 18. over the Meuse at Alfen, and, being allowed by scandalous carelessness on the part of the Allies to complete it, passed a considerable force over the river. On the 19th he attacked the posts at Apeltern and Oct. 19. Druten, to east and north-east of Alfen, carried them after a very obstinate resistance from the Thirty-seventh and Rohan's Emigrants, and succeeded in capturing the greater number of the Thirty-seventh,[1] who had mistaken a party of French Hussars for the Emigrant cavalry in the British service. At the same time intelligence came that a strong French detachment had passed the Meuse between Roermond and Venloo, and was heading for Cleve, thus threatening to turn the Duke's left. Accordingly, in his public despatch, the Duke announced that he was about to draw the whole army to the north of the Waal; but privately he reported that he could not do so, since the Dutch, in spite of many promises, had made no effort to put Nimeguen in a state of defence. On the 20th the Oct. 20. French threw a permanent bridge across the Meuse a little to the north-west of Ravestein at Batenburg, and two days later began a new series of attacks upon the advanced posts, at the same time making demonstrations about St. Andries on the Bommeler Waert. By the 27th the troops round Nimeguen had been driven Oct. 27. into the outskirts of the town, and the Duke, who had transferred his headquarters to Arnheim, called all of

[1] Craig explained that this was owing chiefly to the inexperience of a young Colonel. Thus the army-brokers had contrived to lift children to the command even of regiments that had been eighteen months on active service.

1794. them except fourteen battalions to the north bank of the Waal. The French main body then took up a position between Grave and Nimeguen, threatening to seize the two eastern keys of Holland.

Oct. 28. At this critical moment Clerfaye paid a visit to the Duke at Arnheim, and promised that by the 3rd of November a corps of some seven thousand Austrians under General Werneck should arrive to assist in an offensive movement from Nimeguen. At the same time some effort was made to persuade Möllendorf to move to the Rhine about Bonn, and to support Clerfaye's left. But the British Government had recently, though none too soon, cut off the subsidy to the Prussians; and Möllendorf's answer was that his orders were to send twenty thousand of his men to South Prussia and fifteen thousand men to Westphalia, so that evidently nothing was to be expected from that

Nov. 1. quarter. On the 1st of November the French broke ground before Nimeguen, and on the same day Werneck announced that his corps could not arrive before the 7th. Meanwhile the French erected batteries a little above Nimeguen at Ooi, which, though silenced for a time by the guns of the Allies on the opposite bank, so seriously damaged the bridge of boats that General Walmoden, who was in command, thought it prudent to withdraw the greater part of the garrison to

Nov. 4. the northern bank. On the 4th, however, he made a sortie with the troops that remained, including six British battalions, supported by seventeen squadrons of British and Hanoverian cavalry.[1] The British, advancing under a very heavy fire, swept the enemy out of their trenches without drawing a trigger, and the cavalry pursuing the fugitives inflicted on them heavy loss. The casualties of the Allies in this affair were over three hundred killed and wounded; but, though

[1] The troops engaged were the 15th Light Dragoons, 8th, 27th, 28th, 55th, 63rd, 78th. The last-named regiment, together with the 80th, had arrived at Flushing at the end of September, when Dundas intended to withdraw some of the older regiments for service in the West Indies.

the sortie checked the progress of the French for the time, yet by the 7th they had not only repaired the batteries destroyed by the Allies, but had erected another which brought a cross fire to bear on the bridge of boats. Moreover, a letter arrived from Werneck that his arrival at Nimeguen, which he had fixed for the 7th, would be impossible until the 16th— a message which the Duke rightly interpreted to signify that he would not come at all.

On the night of the 7th, therefore, the bridge was repaired sufficiently to enable the garrison to evacuate the place; and the troops filed across the river. Two Dutch battalions were the last to leave the place under the Dutch General Haak, who, most improperly, was the first man of his nation to set foot on the bridge. As he did so, a shot struck one of the pontoons with some effect, whereupon he immediately ran across the bridge crying out that all was lost, and reported with shameless mendacity that all his troops had passed over except the rearguard. Upon this the pontoon-bridge was immediately fired, since a flying bridge had already been prepared for the passage of the rear-guard. As luck would have it, however, a shot from the French batteries cut the hawser; the flying bridge began to swing round; and, to save it from running foul of the kindled boats, the sailors dropped the anchor and so brought it up. When the burning pontoons had floated away, some British seamen, who were employed on the bridge, were for cutting it adrift, but the Dutchmen would not allow them to do so, preferring certain capture to the risk of a few cannon-shot. Thus eleven hundred of them were taken, either through their own cowardice or through that of Haak — a lamentable occurrence in an army which in the past had approved itself to be of incomparable steadfastness and valour.[1]

The Duke, therefore, now held the line of the Waal including the Bommeler Waert, and might well hope to

[1] York to Dundas, 7th and 11th November; Craig to Nepean, 10th November 1794.

1794. hold it, if the Dutch did their duty, until the army went into winter quarters. He had already put most of his cavalry into cantonments across the Yssel, but the Dutch threw every possible obstacle in the way of providing for the comfort of the troops. The weather too grew wintry, and the men, miserably clothed and housed in open barns, began to fall down very fast from cold and typhus fever. None of them had greatcoats except some of the Guards, Fourteenth, Thirty-seventh, and Fifty-third, who had received those which had been provided by public subscription in 1793, and which were now worn out. Flannel waistcoats had been supplied to the rest by their officers, who had subscribed over a thousand pounds for the purpose; and it appears that, without exaggeration, they had little other clothing. Sheer nakedness, in fact, had been the cause of much, though not of all, of the plundering that had disgraced the army; and this evil had been aggravated by the bitter hostility of the inhabitants towards the British. Not content with resenting real outrages, which were far too abundant, they never ceased flying to the Duke with frivolous and groundless complaints; and so disobliging were the authorities that Lord St. Helens, Ambassador at the Hague, tried for two months in vain to find places where the British might be allowed to establish additional hospitals. On

Nov. 27. the 27th of November the infantry in British pay numbered twenty-one thousand and the sick nearly eleven thousand; and when a man was ordered to hospital his comrades would exclaim, "Ah, poor fellow, we shall see thee no more, for thou art under orders for the shambles." On one occasion five hundred invalids were embarked from Arnheim in barges under charge of a single surgeon's mate, without sufficient provisions, without even sufficient straw, and brought to Rhenen, where they were left on board for want of sufficient space to admit them to the hospital. A Dutch gentleman counted at one time the bodies of forty-two men who had thus perished of neglect in the barges and had been thrown out dead on to the bank. Meanwhile the rascals who bore the name of surgeon's mates charged forty thousand pounds for wine for the sick, and, not content with robbing the State by themselves drinking what was supplied, actually plundered the helpless patients committed to their care. Such was the economy of Dundas's military administration—to obtain recruits by the offer of lavish bounties, to break down their health by giving them insufficient clothing, and to contract with scoundrels so to maltreat them, medically, that they should not recover.[1]

Fortunately for himself the Duke of York was summoned home on the 27th of November to hold personal communication[2] with Ministers; and indeed it seemed as if the campaign were ended. Upon his departure he placed the British troops under Lieutenant-general Harcourt, and the foreign troops in British pay under Lieutenant-general Walmoden, apparently dividing the supreme command between the two. This arrangement was evidently due to the Duke's unwillingness to subject the British to the Hanoverian Walmoden, who was senior to Harcourt; but, even so, it seems to be absolutely indefensible. The French, being exhausted by the campaign, went into temporary cantonments, Moreau's division on the west bank of the Rhine over against the line from Wesel to Emmerick, Souham's in and about Nimeguen, Bonnaud's between the Meuse and the Waal, and the remainder about Bois-le-Duc and Grave. The Allies were distributed along the north bank of the Waal from Tiel eastward to the Pannarden Canal, which connects the Waal with the Leck (as the Rhine from Arnheim downward is called), the Dutch taking charge of the Bommeler

[1] *Narrative of an Officer of the Guards*, ii. 89-91; York to Dundas, 27th November 1794; Harcourt to York, 15th December 1794.
[2] Ditfurth, who never loses an opportunity of abusing the English, of course puts a discreditable construction upon the Duke's departure, not knowing that he was sent for by Ministers (ii. 313).

1794. Waert. Eastward from the Pannarden Canal to Wesel the Allied left was to be covered by thirty thousand Austrians under General Alvintzy, which Clerfaye, on the instance of Henry Dundas, agreed to furnish for a payment of one hundred thousand pounds a month.

The Allies' line of defence seems to have been wrongly chosen, for, owing to the Pannarden Canal, the mass of the waters of the Waal was returned into the Leck, from which cause the Leck was less liable to be frozen. Harcourt had endeavoured to establish a second bridge over the Rhine besides that of the Arnheim, but the Dutch, from malice or negligence, obstructed the forwarding of the materials, as indeed they obstructed everything that might help the British. Altogether the situation was not a happy one, for, though rain had fallen continuously from the beginning of November, there was no saying when a frost might set in and turn the rivers into stable ice. Moreover, Moreau, roused by orders from Paris, became active again. On Dec. 11. the 11th of December the French crossed the Waal in boats at several different points to the attack of the Allied posts, and, though beaten back, left behind them an unpleasant sense of insecurity.[1]

On the 16th Pichegru returned and resumed the Dec. 18. command, and on the 18th the weather changed from rain to a severe frost. In a very few days the Maas and Waal were full of floating ice, which began to pack together, threatening to cover the whole breadth of their streams; while on the Leck the rapidity of the current swept away the bridge of boats at Arnheim. Harcourt, foreseeing that before long the ice on the Waal would become passable by the enemy, prepared to retreat northward. Just at this most critical moment, moreover, there arrived orders from Dundas that seven British battalions of his army were required for service elsewhere; that of these seven the Fortieth, Forty-fourth, and Sixty-third must march to Helvoets-

[1] York to Dundas, 27th and 29th November; Harcourt to York, 11th and 15th December 1794. Ditfurth, ii. 310.

luys at once ; and that Alvintzy, who so far had thrown 1794. every possible difficulty in the way of co-operation with the Allies, must find troops to take their place. Further, it was now ascertained that the Dutch had gone far in negotiation with the French, and there were strong rumours that an armistice had been concluded between them. Meanwhile the cold increased ; sentries were frozen at their posts ; and the ice on the Waal, in front of the Allies, became strong enough to give passage to the French, while that on the Leck in their rear, though thick enough to prevent the passage of boats, was too thin to bear cavalry or artillery. Harcourt's anxiety was extreme ; and he begged Dundas urgently for some further instructions as to the duty expected of him, since the order to weaken the force by sending home seven battalions was not in itself of any great assistance.

Affairs were in this condition when, on the 27th, Dec. 27. the French crossed the Meuse on the ice to the Bommeler Waert, surprised the Dutch posts there, and pushed on by Bommel over the frozen Waal to Tuil. The Dutch at this place fled instantly without firing a shot, some of the fugitives running on even to Utrecht. At Meteren, a few miles north of Tuil, the French were checked by the Hessians ; but, with their right flank exposed by the flight of the Dutch, it was doubtful whether these could maintain their position. Their commander, however, General Dalwig, decided to stand fast, and ascertained by reconnaissance next day that the French did not exceed two thousand Dec. 28. men ; whereupon Walmoden ordered ten battalions and six squadrons of British and Emigrants under David Dundas to Geldermalsen, a short distance north of Meteren, in the hope of annihilating this foolhardy French detachment. Accordingly, at one o'clock on the morning of the 30th, the force moved Dec. 30. out from Meteren in three columns, two of them to move direct upon Tuil from the north and north-east, while the third, under Lord Cathcart, fetched a compass

1794. to close in upon the enemy from the west. Cathcart's column unfortunately found the roads impassable and never came into action; but Dundas nevertheless attacked without him, and drove the French, after a sharp fight, from their entrenchments and across the Waal, with the loss of four guns and many killed and wounded, while his own casualties did not exceed fifty. This checked the ardour of the enemy for the moment, and during a few days there was peace upon the Waal.[1]

Walmoden now reinforced his right about Tuil, for the news had reached him that the fortresses of Gertruydenburg and Heusden, on the extreme right of the Allied line, were in serious danger; and on the 3rd of January 1795 he shifted his quarters to Amerongen, due north of Tiel, and on the north bank of the Leck. Grave at this same time capitulated, and released a large number of French troops for the field. Moreau's division therefore took up cantonments over against Alvintzy's corps from Xanten down the Rhine to the Pannarden Canal. Souham's division, now transferred to Macdonald, occupied the space between the Meuse and Waal as far as the point opposite to Tiel; two more divisions were in the Bommeler Waert, and yet two more about Gertruydenburg and Breda. On the 3rd of January the weather again became intensely cold, and at noon on the 4th two French detachments from the Bommeler Waert marched over the ice, drove in the posts before Tuil and at Hesselt, a little to the east of it, after hard fighting, and thus gained a passage by which they could move westward on the north bank of the Waal. On the following day the French attacked Tuil itself, whereupon the Dutch gunners at once fled from their batteries on the river; but, advancing from thence against Geldermalsen, the enemy was repulsed with

1795.
Jan. 3.

Jan. 4.

Jan. 5.

[1] Dundas to Harcourt, 13th and 24th December; Harcourt to Dundas, 23rd December; to York, 25th and 29th December; Walmoden to York, 22nd, 25th, 29th December 1794, 1st January 1795. The regiments engaged in the action were the 19th, 33rd, 42nd, 78th, 80th.

some loss by the Thirty-third, Forty-second, and 1795. Seventy-eighth, under the direction of General David Dundas. It was, however, plain that these posts could not be held against a strong attack so long as frost practically neutralised their natural defences; and Walmoden recalled Dundas and all the troops in that quarter to the north side of the Leck, in order to take up a new line of cantonments extending from Arnheim on the east by Wageningen, Reenen, Amerongen, and Wyk-by-Duurstede to Honswyk.

A sudden thaw on the 6th offered hopes of re- Jan. 6. establishing the old position on the Waal, and orders were issued on the 7th for a reconnaissance in force of the whole line of the French posts on the following day; but on the morning of the 8th the frost Jan. 8. abruptly set in again, though not before the troops were already in motion beyond power of recall. On the right, Dundas succeeded in driving the enemy from their posts on the Linge to the Waal, and in recovering Buren and Tiel. The brunt of the work fell upon the Fourteenth, Twenty-seventh, and Twenty-eighth under Lord Cathcart; and these drove the enemy in succession from the villages of Buurmalsen and Geldermalsen and captured a gun, not, however, without a loss of one hundred and thirty men to themselves. On the left the orders seem to have miscarried, probably through the confusion due to divided command. Before the operation could be carried any further, Pichegru, finding that the ice on the Waal was stronger than ever, on the 10th fell upon the Allied line in Jan. 10. great force at three different points between the Pannarden Canal and Tiel. The attack was repulsed upon the right, but the Austrians were forced back on the left flank, and Walmoden ordered the whole force to withdraw once more behind the Leck. This was effected with little loss; Colonel Coote's brigade of the Fortieth, Fiftieth, and Seventy-ninth being the only British forces severely engaged. Walmoden had fully intended to continue the retreat eastward across the

1795. Yssel; but Lord St. Helens, at the Hague, unfortunately protested against this, and another thaw enabled Walmoden to acquiesce. On the night of the 12th frost again set in more severely than ever, and on the 14th the French attacked along the whole line from Arnheim to Reenen. They were beaten back with heavy loss; but Walmoden, feeling that he was unable
Jan. 15. to hold his ground, on the following morning gave the order for a further retreat.

The days that followed are amongst the most tragical in the history of the Army. During November and December the discipline of the troops in Holland had greatly improved, but with the coming of the frost and the hardships that attended the constant alarms and marches on the Waal, it had once more broken down completely. Certain regiments of French emigrants, which had joined the army late in the year, were the worst offenders; but it seems certain that some of the British were not far behind them. The country to the north of Arnheim is at the best of times an inhospitable waste, and there were few dwellings and few trees to give shelter or fuel after a dreary march through dense and chilling mist over snow twice thawed and refrozen. Marauders from the regiments of every nationality swarmed round the columns; the drivers of the waggons freed themselves from all control, and the line of march was disorderly beyond description. When the day was ended, the troops of different nations fought for such scanty comforts as were to be found; and once there was a pitched battle between the Guards and the Hessians, who had been on bad terms with each other from the beginning of the campaign. Day after day the cold steadily increased; and those of the army that woke on the morning of the 17th of January saw about them such a sight as they never forgot. Far as the eye could reach over the whitened plain were scattered gun-limbers, waggons full of baggage, of stores, or of sick men, sutlers' carts and private carriages. Beside them lay the horses, dead; around them scores and hundreds of soldiers, dead;

CH. XII HISTORY OF THE ARMY 321

here a straggler who had staggered on to the bivouac 1795. and dropped to sleep in the arms of the frost; there a group of British and Germans round an empty rum-cask; here forty English Guardsmen huddled together about a plundered waggon; there a pack-horse with a woman lying alongside it, and a baby, swathed in rags, peeping out of the pack, with its mother's milk turned to ice upon its lips,—one and all stark, frozen, dead. Had the retreat lasted but three or four days longer, not a man would have escaped; and the catastrophe would have found a place in history side by side with the destruction of the host of Sennacherib and with the still more terrible disaster of the retreat from Moscow.[1]

By the 19th the surviving fragments of the battalions Jan. 19. reached their destination on the Yssel, where they were cantoned on the west side of the river from Zutphen to the sea. But there was no hope of long repose for them there. Harcourt perceived clearly that the re-embarkation of his force was now the only resource left to him, and that the place of embarkation must be on the Weser, since the lack of supplies and the incapacity of his commissariat officers would inevitably forbid him to remain long on the Ems. Within a week, want of victuals and the hostility of the inhabitants compelled him to continue his retreat from the Yssel; and on the 27th the march eastward was resumed, the main body Jan. 27-29. of the British retiring towards Osnabrück, the Germans upon Münster. One detachment of British,[2] however, was sent northward under Lord Cathcart's command to fetch a compass through West Friesland and along the borders of Groningen, in order to ascertain whether the people of these provinces were as disaffected as their fellows towards the House of Orange. By whose orders this isolated force was despatched upon such an errand is uncertain; it is only known that the column was

[1] Jones, *Campaign of 1794*, pp. 171-175; Ditfurth, ii. 362 *sq.*; *Narrative of an Officer of the Guards*, ii. 100-104.
[2] 15th Light Dragoons; 27th, 28th, 80th, and 84th Foot.

1795. followed up and incessantly harassed by the enemy, and that it was not very successful in discovering friendly sentiments among the Dutch. Upon reaching the Ems, the army halted, and on the 5th February took up cantonments on the western bank of the river, Cathcart on the extreme north guarding the passes of the Bourtanger Moor from the Dollart southward, while Abercromby fixed his headquarters farther to south and west of the river at Bentheim, and the Hanoverians retired to Münster.

The state of the troops by this time was worse than ever, for thousands of sick had perforce been left behind on the Yssel. "Your army is destroyed," wrote Walmoden to the Duke of York; "the officers, their carriages, and a large train are safe, but the men are destroyed. The army has now no more than six thousand fighting men, but it has all the drawbacks of thirty-three battalions, and consumes a vast quantity of forage." A more terrible reproach was never yet levelled against any force; nevertheless it was rather the politicians than the military commanders who had made such a reproach possible, by flinging commissions broadcast to any man or even child who could afford to satisfy the crimps. Upon entering German territory the men met with kindlier treatment from the inhabitants; but the infamous conduct of the French Emigrant Corps threatened to turn the Germans also into enemies. It now became abundantly clear that most of these regiments were simply frauds, imposed upon the English Ministers by a band of unscrupulous adventurers. But the English army, of course, had to bear the burden of their sins; and the Hanoverians and Hessians, naturally espousing the cause of their countrymen, turned upon the British with a bitterness which destroyed all cohesion between the nations of the Allies.[1]

Meanwhile the French, after leaving their opponents

[1] Walmoden to York, 3rd February; Harcourt to York (three letters), 11th February 1795.

to retreat unmolested from the Leck, resumed their 1795. advance, and at the end of January occupied Kampen and Zwolle on the Yssel. They made, however, no attempt to hinder the further retirement of the Allies; and their movements for the next fortnight were of the most leisurely description. Then arrived rumours of a French understanding with Prussia, of the neutralisation of North Germany, and of a line of demarcation to be drawn according to the actual territory occupied by the opposing armies. The French at once woke to the importance of gaining immediate possession of Groningen and East Friesland, and General Macdonald's corps was detached to invade Groningen, while those of Moreau and Vandamme remained in observation on the Yssel. On the 19th of February Macdonald occupied the town of Groningen, and thence turning eastward he, on the 27th, attacked Cathcart's fortified Feb. 27. posts at Winschoten. He was repulsed; but two days later the attack was renewed with success by General March 1. Reynier, and Cathcart was forced to retreat, which he did with great dexterity, crossing the Ems upon the 3rd. The entire British force then fell back to the March 3. east bank of the Ems to hold the line from Emden to Rheine, headquarters being fixed at Osnabrück.

Five days later the British Cabinet at last decided to withdraw its troops from the Continent, and on the 11th Harcourt, to his infinite relief, received intimation March 11. that transports for twenty-three thousand men were on their way to him. The Hanoverians were in consternation over the danger to which Hanover was exposed by this measure, but there was no help for it. A few days later Prussian troops arrived to hold the line of March 16. the Ems, and on the 22nd the British began their march to Bremen for embarkation. The Prussians did their utmost by obstruction, discourtesy, and insolence to disoblige them on their passage through the country; but this was natural, for they had always professed contempt for the British as a nation of traders, and a tradesman is never so despicable to a

1795.
April 14.
dishonest customer as when he refuses to grant him further credit. Finally, on the 14th of April, the infantry and part of the artillery took ship for England, leaving the remainder of the artillery and the whole of the cavalry behind them under Lord Cathcart and David Dundas. The number embarked was nearly fifteen thousand, some proportion of the sick having been recovered; so that the losses after the retreat from the Leck must have amounted to about six thousand men, of which not a tithe were killed or wounded in action. Thus disgracefully ended the first expedition of Pitt and Dundas to the Low Countries.

AUTHORITIES.—The British despatches relating to the expeditions to Flanders will be found in *W.O. Orig. Corresp.* 46-48, and in Entry Book No. 11. The number of private letters included in this collection makes it of unusual value. For the campaigns at large the best accounts known to me are in Ditfurth's *Die Hessen in den Feldzügen, 1793, 1794, und 1795* (Kassel, 1839), and in Witzleben's *Prinz Friedrich Josias von Coburg-Saalfeld* (Berlin, 1859), which is not a little built upon Ditfurth, but contains much that is valuable of its own and a superb atlas of maps. On the French side the short memoir of David and the life of Pichegru are of little worth compared with the narrative of Jomini. Marshal Macdonald's *Mémoires* are disappointing at this period. Of English printed accounts the most important is Jones's *Historical Journal of the British Campaign in 1794.* The *Journal* of Corporal James Brown of the Coldstream Guards supplies a few interesting details. Sir H. Calvert's *Journal and Correspondence* is often of value; and there is a great deal of most useful information in the footnotes to the miserable doggerel called the *Narrative of an Officer of the Guards.* Unfortunately the author, like Brown and Calvert, was a Coldstreamer, for which reason all three confine themselves chiefly to the doings of the brigade of Guards. The regimental histories of the 14th Foot and 15th Hussars have occasionally interesting material, but, taken altogether, the regimental records are disappointing.

CHAPTER XIII

THE course of our history during the years 1793 and 1794 has led us so far through no very pleasant places. It is now, however, time to explore the darkest and most forbidding tract in the whole of it, and to bring to light, if possible, the true story of the West Indian expeditions, which were the most essential feature in Pitt's military policy. The task is not an easy one, for the Government early found good reason to hush up the details of many of the most important transactions. Moreover, for reasons which will appear as the narrative proceeds, but few of the principal actors or witnesses at that dismal theatre of war ever returned to tell the tale, and those few were glad to keep silence and, if possible, to forget all that they had heard or seen. None the less, a knowledge of these obscure enterprises is of the first importance towards a right understanding of our position in Europe from 1793 to 1798. The secret of England's impotence for the first six years of the war may be said to lie in the two fatal words, St. Domingo.

In a former chapter there have been briefly recorded the facts of the great insurrection of negroes which was kindled in that island by the extravagance of the fanatics in Paris, of the siding of the Commissioners sent from France in 1792 with the blacks against the whites, of the appeals of the white refugees to Henry Dundas for British protection, and of the despatch of certain of these by Dundas with credentials to the Governor of Jamaica at the beginning of 1793. Since that time matters

1793. had gone from bad to worse in St. Domingo. The governing powers at Paris, awaking to the mischief wrought by the Commissioners Santhonax and Polverel, sent out a new Governor from France to place the island in a state of defence. This gentleman arrived on the island in May 1793; but he was defied with armed force by the Civil Commissioners, who called the revolted slaves to their aid, promising them perfect freedom in future and the plunder of the city of Cap François. One band of about three thousand negroes took the Commissioners at their word, burned down half
June 21-23. of the town, and massacred indiscriminately the white inhabitants. This atrocity naturally heightened the desire of the planters to obtain British protection; and the little knot of them, who had been sent out by Dundas, became at once preternaturally active among their compatriots in the less disturbed districts of the island.

Foremost and busiest among these emissaries was a planter named Charmilli, an extremely specious, clever, and accomplished rogue, who many years afterwards appeared in Sir John Moore's camp in Spain at a very critical time. He had evidently completely deceived Dundas, and, furnished with that Minister's credentials, found little difficulty in imposing himself also upon General Sir Adam Williamson, who was Governor of Jamaica. In June Dundas authorised Williamson to sign a capitulation accepting the temporary surrender of St. Domingo to the British, and gave him discretion even to employ a part of his troops in taking possession of the island. Charmilli thereupon became anxious for a regiment to be sent over at once; but Williamson was not so trustful as to lend aid to these adventurers without a written agreement, nor so foolish as to neglect the fact that the naval force of the French in St. Domingo was superior to that of the British at Jamaica. Charmilli wisely did not press him, but urged his compatriots to hasten the drawing of a capitulation. Early in September the precious document arrived. It set forth, among other details, that certain individuals, calling themselves the proprietors of 1793. St. Domingo, implored the protection of King George, swore allegiance to him, and accepted the rule of his appointed Governor, aided by a council of six of themselves. The only doubtful point was whether these men, or indeed any others, possessed the slightest authority from the inhabitants thus to transfer the island from France to England; but Williamson either forbore to examine this detail, or accepted the assurances of Charmilli's glib tongue as satisfactory. The capitulation was duly signed, and England was committed to the protection of St. Domingo. This was the first of a long series of blunders.

It must be explained first that British officials, when they spoke of St. Domingo, usually only meant that portion of the island, now known as Haiti, which belonged to the French. This amounted to little more than one-third of the whole, namely, a solid block at the western end of what may be termed the main trunk of the island, and of two long peninsulas projecting from it far out to westward. Haiti, in fact, much resembles a human hand cut off at the wrist, and with the first and fourth fingers only extended; St. Domingo proper, or the Spanish portion of the island, representing the arm from the wrist to the elbow-joint. The solid block, or (to maintain the simile) the hand of Haiti, measures, roughly speaking, about one hundred and twenty-five miles north and south by seventy-five miles east and west. Of the two peninsulas or fingers, the northern projects for some fifty miles westward beyond the mainland, tapering gradually from east to west from a breadth of twenty-eight miles to thirteen miles. Its western extremity is marked by the historic port of Mole St. Nicholas, the Gibraltar of the West Indies and the key of the Windward Passage. The southern peninsula runs westward from the mainland for a distance of close upon one hundred and forty miles, with an average breadth from north to south of twenty miles. Its western extremity bears the name

1793. of Cape Tiburon. The great bay formed by the two peninsulas was commonly known to the English as the Bight of Léogane, which name it will be convenient to retain. The country is almost everywhere mountainous, though with occasional broad and rich plains, the general trend of the ridges being from east to west, and the altitude rising frequently to three thousand and sometimes to six thousand feet. The roads were not numerous and for the most part followed the line of the coast, the passes across the two peninsulas from north to south being very few; and indeed it was the remarkable facility for transport by water, due to the peculiar configuration of the coast, which gave to the colony much of its value.

The distribution of the country for administrative purposes shows how complete was the dependence upon the sea for communication. The Northern Province of Haiti consisted of the extreme north coast from the Spanish frontier on the east to Mole St. Nicholas on the west. It included, besides the Mole, the once thriving town of Port de Paix, and Cap François, the latter formerly a beautiful city, which had risen to greatness through the vicinity of a plain, measuring some six hundred square miles, of the richest land in the world. The Western Province simply comprised the entire coast-line of the Bight of Léogane from Mole St. Nicholas to Cape Tiburon, together with four principal towns, namely, St. Marc, in the very centre of the Bight of Léogane; Port-au-Prince, the capital, in a deep inlet to south of it; Léogane, a little to the west of it; and Jérémie, close to the western end of the southern peninsula. Port-au-Prince had been ruined by an earthquake in 1770, and was moreover low-lying and most unhealthy; but the source of its wealth was the adjoining plain of Cul-de-Sac, containing some three hundred square miles of most fertile land. The Southern Province comprehended the southern coast-line from Cape Tiburon on the west back to the Spanish frontier on the east, with two towns, Aux

Cayes and Jacmel, neither of which possessed a safe 1793. anchorage. For purposes of local administration and of defence the country was distributed, under the old order, into fifty-two parishes, each of which supported one or more companies of white militia, a company of mulattos and a company of free blacks. The population of Haiti in 1790 had been officially stated at thirty thousand whites, twenty-five thousand coloured, and close upon half a million negroes. Thus even in its peaceful days it was no small charge to make over and to accept by a stroke of the pen.

But in 1793 the condition of the island multiplied the burden of government a thousandfold. The country was in a hideous state of anarchy, torn asunder by the most furious passions of caste, colour, and political fanticism. Of the white proprietors, formerly the governing race, not a few had perished by massacre, and fully half had fled across the sea. Of those that remained, a few were patriotic citizens, who honestly desired the restoration of law and order ; but the great majority were men who had everything to gain and nothing to lose by lawlessness and confusion. The coloured people had already shown savage animosity against the whites by a rising, in which they had called the negroes to their aid, in the Western and Southern Provinces; and, being neither white nor black, they formed a most dangerous and irreconcilable element. As to the negroes themselves, those of the Northern Province, after ruining the town and plain of Cap François, had retired to the mountains, where, under the wise instruction of one of their leaders, Jean François, they were planting provisions so as to make themselves independent of the regular settlements. They were reckoned, probably with exaggeration, to number forty thousand armed men. Amid all this chaos the only semblance of power and authority was vested in the Commissioners, Santhonax and Polverel, who had under their orders some six thousand regular troops, about fourteen thousand white militia, and a band of desperate

1793. ruffians of all colours, making in all some twenty-five thousand more or less disciplined and organised men. These, however, were necessarily dispersed over a very wide area in various garrisons; and some of the regular troops were certainly disloyal to the Commissioners. On the first menace, therefore, of an English attack, Santhonax and Polverel published a proclamation abolishing slavery, and promising freedom to all slaves who would join their standard. Comparatively few of the servile population responded to the call, many preferring to remain and share the fortunes of their masters; but vast numbers betook themselves to the mountains to enjoy a freedom of their own choosing. Thus the most formidable of all the forces in Haiti was multiplied many-fold at the very moment of the British occupation. It was the force which later defied and defeated the best troops of Napoleon himself.

Yet, beguiled by the tongues of Charmilli and his colleagues, Dundas and Williamson boldly thrust the right hand of England into this hornet's nest, never doubting their word as to the amiable and pacific disposition of the hornets. Williamson's garrison at Jamaica, which included seven complete battalions, besides a regiment of light dragoons and three companies of artillery, numbered something less than three thousand of all ranks. Immediately upon signing the capitulation he ordered the Thirteenth, the flank companies of the Forty-ninth, and a small detachment of artillery with four guns—in all about seven hundred men—to embark on board the men-of-war in the

Sept. 9. harbour; and on the 9th of September the squadron of four frigates and smaller craft made sail to windward under Commodore Ford. Nor should mention of the military commander be forgotten, for he was Lieutenant-colonel John Whitelocke of the Thirteenth, a name which later events were to connect indissolubly with foolish expeditions.

Sept. 19. On the 19th the squadron arrived before its destination at Jérémie on the southern peninsula, which had long been the headquarters of Charmilli and his 1793. colleagues, and so far had not been touched either by Civil Commissioners or rebel negroes. There all went well. A deputation at once came off to welcome the ships, and within a few hours the troops were landed, and the British flag was hoisted on the two forts that guarded the harbour. Ford then sailed across the Bight to Mole St. Nicholas, taking a French officer on board with him; and there again, after some anxious Sept. 22. hours, he was welcomed by the garrison, which was dreading an attack of rebellious negroes. A hasty message was sent to Whitelocke at Jérémie for a company of the Forty-ninth; the French regiment of Dillon, a mere handful of men, passed into English pay; the rest of the garrison swore allegiance; and the Gibraltar of the West Indies, with large stores of war, likewise passed into British hands. Williamson made speed to reinforce it by the battalion-companies of the Forty-ninth. He was not afraid thus to weaken his garrison at Jamaica, because Dundas had promised him considerable reinforcements in the course of the winter; but he was nervous at the scattering of these isolated garrisons over distant posts, while he still felt uncertain as to the command of the sea.[1]

At the beginning of October an unpleasant incident gave the British for the first time an idea of the untrustworthiness of the planters of St. Domingo. The occupation of Jérémie involved also the occupation of a post called Irois, over thirty miles distant from it by road and quite close to Tiburon. The late commandant of the garrison at Tiburon came into Irois with a plan for the capture of the place; and it was arranged that Whitelocke should attack it by sea, while a certain M. Duval engaged himself to lead five hundred men against it by land. Whitelocke duly appeared with his force at the appointed place on the 3rd of October; but Oct. 3. Duval, having failed to raise his men, did not present

[1] Williamson to Dundas, 8th September and 17th October 1793.

1793. himself, and Whitelocke, after some slight loss, abandoned the attack. Still more disquieting was the report sent from Mole St. Nicholas by Colonel Dansey of the Forty-ninth. The Gibraltar of the West Indies, though impregnable from the sea, was commanded, like the city of Toulon, from the adjacent hills to landward; and its only security lay in the extreme difficulty of bringing even light cannon to the summit of these hills, and in the scarcity of water among them. The enemy had for ten days been threatening an attack from Jean Rabel, only eight miles to eastward, and the British garrison was insufficient for safety. The inhabitants of the nearest village, Bombarde, were friendly, had sold to the British fresh provisions, and had even formed a small body of three hundred militia, which, however, owing to impatience of discipline, was useless. On the other hand, some of the French soldiers taken into British pay had deserted; and there was only just sufficient infantry to supply the necessary guards in the circuit of two miles embraced by the defences of the Mole. As to artillerymen, there were in one post only twelve of them to guard and man twenty guns. Most ominous of all, though the season was the healthiest of the year, the men had already begun to fall down with sickness.[1]

Williamson would gladly have reinforced the Mole, but he had barely fifteen hundred troops left in Jamaica, and the Assembly was already beginning to complain of the undue weakening of the garrison. He hardened himself, however, to send the flank-companies of the Sixty-second to Jérémie early in December; and owing to this, or to some other unknown cause, the parishes of Haiti were seized with a sudden epidemic of surrender. St. Marc and Gonaives, in the Bight of Léogane, tendered their submission to the Commandant of the Mole; Verrettes and Petite Rivière, to north-east and south-east of St. Marc, together with Jean Rabel, followed their example. Simultaneously

[1] Williamson to Dundas, 19th October; Dansey to Williamson, 25th October 1793.

the south also began to submit, Léogane taking the 1793. lead, though the remote towns of Jacmel and Saltrou, to east, were but little after her. The garrison at the Mole had already dwindled to little over two hundred men, and that of Jérémie to fewer than four hundred ; yet it was necessary to weaken them still further by detachments for some of the new possessions. Tiny bodies of British troops were therefore measured out by scores, tens, and even smaller numbers, to occupy, in company with a handful of local levies, St. Marc and Léogane. At the latter place they were opposed, but, though they were able to brush their enemy aside, they had the mortification to see the whole of the fertile plain of Léogane destroyed by fire, for want of a few hundred soldiers to protect it. At St. Marc the Commandant, Captain Thomas Brisbane,[1] was obliged to decline the surrender of Mirebalais, from lack of men to send there. 1794. The complete submission of the island seemed so near Jan. 2. that Commodore Ford summoned Santhonax to yield up Port-au-Prince ; and Williamson, in full confidence that the capital would be soon in his hands, despatched Jan. 17. another of his attenuated battalions, the Twentieth, to Jérémie, to be at hand to take it into possession.[2]

All now seemed to be going well. Irregular corps of French colonists, white and coloured, were formed at the centres of Jérémie, the Mole, and St. Marc, and a valuable body of some three or four hundred negroes, under a black leader named Jean Kina, was further taken into service at Jérémie. Speaking generally, however, the mulattos hung aloof from the British. They were dissatisfied with a clause of the capitulation, which granted them only the privileges accorded to their class in the British colonies ; whereas they demanded the restitution of equal rights with white men, which had been given to them by a decree of King Lewis the

[1] Brisbane in contemporary documents is called by his local rank of major, and later lieutenant-colonel.
[2] Williamson to Dundas, 15th December 1793 and 19th January 1794.

1794. Fourteenth in 1685. Williamson did not hesitate to affirm that the concession of this claim would give the British peaceable possession of the whole of the Western and Southern Provinces, or, in other words, of four-fifths of the country; and his officers in command at the various stations reported strongly to the same effect. He felt himself bound, however, by the terms of the capitulation, which had been cunningly drafted by Charmilli and his peers for their own advantage. Affecting to speak in the name of the whole colony and accepted as its representatives by Dundas, they claimed and obtained from Williamson the principal posts in the civil administration, and had no idea of admitting others to share the plunder with them. Nevertheless they grew nervous over the attitude of the British officers on the question of the mulattos; and Charmilli wrote vehement letters to Dundas in condemnation of their views. The success of Williamson's slender force was, as he averred, due entirely to the influence of himself and his friends; and, when the expected reinforcements arrived, the whole colony would doubtless submit to the government of King George.[1]

Dundas, meanwhile, had written, on the 13th of December, approving of the agreement made with Charmilli and of the occupation of Jérémie and the Mole, and adding that two battalions would sail from England for Jamaica immediately. On the strength of this promised reinforcement, he ordered that five hundred more men should be transferred from Jamaica to St. Domingo immediately, thus showing that he was prepared to direct operations in the West Indies as well as in Flanders from his desk in Downing Street. Williamson had hardly five hundred men to send, but he embarked the first battalion of the First Royals, which was barely four hundred strong, for the safety of the Mole; thereby reducing the garrison of Jamaica to dangerous weakness. Meanwhile Whitelocke had

[1] Williamson to Dundas, 17th January; Charmilli to Dundas, 26th and 29th January 1794.

improved the position at Jérémie by a second and success- 1794. ful attack upon Tiburon. Embarking a small portion of his garrison on three frigates of the fleet, he arranged with his colonial auxiliaries at Irois that he should force a landing and attack Tiburon from the beach, while they should fetch a compass through the mountains and post themselves so as to cut off the enemy's retreat to the west. On the evening of the 2nd of February Feb. 2. the landing was most gallantly forced in the face of some eight hundred of the enemy by the flank companies of the Thirteenth, Twentieth, and Forty-ninth under Major Brent Spencer. These troops, without pausing to fire, attacked directly with the bayonet, and generated such panic that their opponents abandoned their posts in the night, leaving one hundred and fifty prisoners and twenty-five guns in the hands of the British. Nevertheless the bulk of the enemy escaped, Whitelocke's auxiliaries not daring to perform the part assigned to them. However, this success rendered the Windward Passage doubly secure, and gained for the British practically undisturbed possession of the whole of the southern peninsula west of Aux Cayes.

Encouraged by this success, and thinking possibly that a bold offensive policy was, in view of his extreme weakness, the safest, Whitelocke determined to reduce all outlying posts about Port-au-Prince which might impede an attack upon the capital. The first of these was l'Acul, about six miles west of Léogane,[1] a fortified post from which a savage band under a savage leader was perpetually making forays. It was stormed with Feb. 18. little difficulty and loss by the same flank-companies of the Thirteenth, Twentieth, and Forty-ninth, led by Whitelocke himself, under a heavy fire of grape and musketry; and the adjoining parish of Grande Goave thereupon at once surrendered and took the oath of allegiance. The garrison of Léogane was now increased at the expense of Jérémie, and a reconnaissance was

[1] Such is the distance given by Williamson in his despatch; but the only Acul to be found on the map is twenty miles west of Léogane.

1794. made with a view to the attack of Fort Bizothon, which commanded the approach to Port-au-Prince from the west; but the force was judged too weak to attempt an attack. The squadron thereupon maintained the blockade of Port-au-Prince, in the hope that dearth of provisions and intestine discord might deliver the city into the hands of the British. Nevertheless the eyes of Williamson were by this time opened; and he warned Dundas that, if St. Domingo were ceded to Britain, it would need a garrison of five or six thousand men for many years.

But the people of St. Domingo had now recovered from the first shock of the British invasion, and begun to look about them. They saw that the red-coats were but a handful of men, for the four battalions sent by Williamson had never numbered more than nine hundred effective soldiers, and that these were only with the greatest difficulty able to hold the posts which they occupied. The enemy opposed to the British was denominated by the generic name of brigands, which was probably the most accurate term that could be found; but though these bands were actuated by no common impulse but that of murder and rapine, they were nevertheless most formidable. Such of the inhabitants as were well affected to the British began to despair. They had capitulated upon condition that they should be protected, or, in other words, that the invaders should restore order; but this was impossible without more troops; and though the British officers never ceased to tell of large reinforcements coming from England, yet it was noticed that those reinforcements never came. The people began to suspect that they had been deceived; and there were not wanting insidious counsellors to encourage them in their distrust. Looking, indeed, to the scandalous recklessness and mismanagement of Dundas, it is impossible for an Englishman to deny that their suspicion was well founded.[1]

[1] Williamson to Dundas, 9th February, 2nd and 10th March, and 28th April 1794.

A sudden outbreak at Port-au-Prince, due to the 1794. pressure of the blockade by the fleet, threw the helplessness of the British into glaring relief. The blacks, rising up in insurrection, attacked one of the French regular regiments in their barracks, with loud threats of massacre; and in a few hours two thousand white March 22. refugees, including over one hundred soldiers, fled in terror over the sea, destitute almost of everything, and threw themselves upon the British commander at Léogane for protection. The British garrison there and at l'Acul numbered two hundred and twenty men, of whom eighty only were fit for duty; and the unhappy officer was at his wits' end. But this was not the worst. Williamson, in his crying need for troops, had formed two legions of black and coloured men, the one under M. de Montalembert, a white planter, for Jérémie and Léogane, the other under a faithful mulatto named La Pointe, for the district of St. Marc. These were in principle wise and prudent precautions; but the favour shown to the mulattos made the whites furious, without reconciling the coloured people at large. The general unrest soon found vent in action. Early in April some mulattos, who had sworn allegiance, rose and surprised one of Whitelocke's outlying posts, commanded by a French officer, at Jean Rabel. Before dawn of the 16th April 16. a mulatto named Rigaud, who had for long past led one of the most formidable and savage bands in the southern peninsula, fell suddenly with two thousand men and a single small field-gun upon the fortified post at Tiburon. At six o'clock, after three hours' fighting, the magazine of the fort was by some mischance exploded, disabling all the gunners and dismounting the guns; and it was only after two hours more of a desperate struggle that the garrison finally beat the assailants off. The troops in the fort expended forty thousand rounds of ball-cartridge in this affair—an extraordinary number in those days—and lost twenty-eight men killed and one hundred and nine seriously wounded. The brigands left one hundred and seventy dead on the field,

1794. proving that they were no despicable nor irresolute enemy.¹

Troubles now began to multiply upon the British. At St. Marc, Brisbane, an extremely able officer and administrator, had persuaded the Spaniards to send a garrison of two hundred men to Gonaives. On the April 30. 30th of April a small party of negroes summoned this post, whereupon the Spanish troops promptly evacuated the place and abandoned the French inhabitants to massacre ; the motive being jealousy lest the British should reap the profit of the rich plains in the vicinity. On the following day there was a misfortune in another quarter. A strong body of mulattos had established themselves in a fort by the once friendly village of Bombarde, as a standing menace to Mole St. Nicholas. Whitelocke therefore decided to fall upon them by surprise, and to that end despatched Major Brent Spencer with two hundred troops and a few militia, in all possible secrecy, on the night of the 30th of April. On approach-
May 1. ing the place at dawn, however, Spencer found the enemy in force and fully prepared; and though, by the advice of a French officer, he made an attack, he was beaten off with the loss of some forty killed, wounded, and prisoners. This was a serious matter in the dearth of British troops, for the Mole was none too strongly
May 3. held. Two days later an attack was made upon the post of l'Acul, hard by Léogane, with the same desperate valour as at Tiburon, but was fortunately repulsed at little cost to the tiny garrison. The situation was becoming very critical. The sickly season was approaching ; eight long months had passed away without the appearance of a single soldier from England, and, unless reinforcements arrived speedily, there was every reason to fear that they might arrive too late.

¹ Captain Hardyman to Whitelocke, 17th April 1794. The British engaged must have been some of the Thirteenth Foot, to which regiment Hardyman belonged. The casualty-list (not given by Hardyman) is taken from Bryan Edwards, *History of the West Indies* (8vo 1807), iii. 165. I assume it to include the losses of the auxiliary troops as well as of the regulars.

On the 19th of May, however, the long-expected succours sailed at last into the harbour of Mole St. Nicholas. They consisted of the battalion-companies of the Twenty-second, Twenty-third, and Forty-first regiments, in all some sixteen hundred men under Major-general Whyte, which had been detached by General Grey upon the close of his operations, shortly to be described, to windward. Finding the garrison much straitened by the revolt of the natives all round, Whyte constructed a new line of defence; and then, with the concurrence of Whitelocke and the Commodore, he sailed at once to Port-au-Prince. On the 31st he arrived in the bay, and, ordering the militia of Arcahais and Léogane to threaten the city from the west and north, detached three hundred British and some Colonial troops to land a mile to west of Fort Bizothon under the cannon of two sloops of war. After four hours' firing the guns of the fort were silenced; and the troops, having been disembarked in the evening, made their way by a circuitous route towards it. At about six o'clock a violent thunderstorm came on, of which Captain Daniel of the Forty-first took advantage two hours later to make a dash at the fort with the bayonet. He had with him only sixty men of the advanced guard, but the vigour and surprise of his attack sufficed to give him possession of the work with trifling loss. Whyte then landed other troops on the north side of the town, while the fleet stood in close to it, sweeping the beach and enfilading the trenches with its cannon; and on the 4th of June the enemy spiked the guns of the defences and evacuated the town. One hundred and one pieces of ordnance and twenty-two ships, with cargoes worth nearly half a million sterling, were the trophies of the captors; and the British flag, at the request of the inhabitants, was hoisted with ceremony. The losses of the besiegers were slight; and the operations generally appear to have been conducted with commendable skill.

1794.   Here therefore was the capital of French St. Domingo in British hands; and Williamson, though he flattered himself with no extravagant hopes as to the reaction of this victory upon the rest of the country, hoped at least that it might not be without effect. On the very heels of the success, however, there followed a ghastly warning. The flank-companies of the Twenty-second, Twenty-third, and Forty-first, which had been despatched by General Grey from windward to rejoin
June 8. their battalions, sailed into Port-au-Prince on the 8th of June, numbering a little over two hundred and fifty men. They had left Guadeloupe four hundred and twenty strong; twenty-seven had been thrown overboard between Guadeloupe and Jamaica, and over one hundred had been landed at Jamaica to die. The rest of the troops began also to fall down equally fast. On the 29th of June the seven battalions in St. Domingo numbered rather more than seventeen hundred men sick and two thousand sound; by the 17th of July thirty-four out of sixty-four officers, recently landed, were dead; and by the end of August seven hundred and twenty-nine men had perished likewise. All military operations were necessarily suspended by the end of July; and the whole attention of Williamson was directed to the raising of levies from among the inhabitants.

Here, however, a serious difficulty arose at once. General Whyte, who had been sent to St. Domingo by Grey as one of his very best officers, had conceived that, being the senior officer on the spot, he would be charged with the administration of the territory under the protection of the British; but to his disgust he discovered that Williamson at Jamaica had already disposed of all patronage, and that he himself could do nothing without that General's sanction. The cancelling of one of his proclamations by superior order did not mend matters, and in high dudgeon he asked for leave to return to England. Meanwhile Williamson insisted, very foolishly, that all business at St. Domingo must be transacted through 1794. Jamaica, which meant that it must be delayed for a term varying from a fortnight to three weeks. Whyte, like Williamson, was bent on the employment of black troops as far as possible, and had built high hopes upon a negotiation with a band of five thousand negroes, called the Legion Egalité, which had offered to join the British on condition of receiving freedom and protection. Whyte, confident that he had satisfied them upon both points, agreed to take them bodily into the British service; but three weeks expired before the transaction could receive final sanction from Jamaica, and in the interval the negroes, growing suspicious, retired to their fastnesses in the mountains. Whyte's discontent was not diminished by this incident, and the contention between the two Generals was growing hot, when Whyte's departure for England brought the dispute none too speedily to a close.[1]

The absence of the Commander-in-Chief from St. Domingo, however, was in many respects a great evil. Williamson soon succeeded in raising Colonial corps to the number of over three thousand men, white and black, but these troops required officers who could speak the peculiar dialect which is known as Creole French. Hence Williamson could not avoid appointing French colonists and proprietors to the new levies; and he appears to have chosen them with little circumspection and to have superintended their doings with little care. Many of the officers thus chosen were brave and skilful leaders, but there appear to have been very few who had the slightest idea of honesty or principle. The results were in every sense costly beyond estimation. Men of any character or of no character asked and obtained permission to raise a corps in the district to which they belonged. Such individuals received bounty, clothing, and rations for their soldiers, rank and

[1] Williamson to Dundas (enclosing correspondence with Whyte), 15th and 17th July, 1st August; Whyte to Dundas, 20th July 1794.

1794. large allowances for themselves. Very soon, pleading the necessity of patrols and the efficiency of cavalry in the plains, they added to their corps a troop of horse, and gave it the name of a legion. They then enrolled their own negroes as soldiers, set those soldiers to cultivate either their own estate or land sequestrated from others for their own profit, put the men's pay into their own pockets and gave or withheld rations according to their own convenience. Having, moreover, this armed force at their disposal, they could use it for such purposes of plunder, extortion, or revenge as best suited them. It may easily be understood, therefore, that such rascals were not very eager to see the war ended; and there were not a few of them. These evils did not attain, of course, to enormous proportions at once, but it is significant that M. de Montalembert, who, though a brave man, proved subsequently to be one of the worst offenders, was the first to raise a legion. A swarm of Emigrants, or, as Williamson more truly called them, adventurers, recently shaken from the skirts of the exiled Princes of France, poured into St. Domingo at this time, clamouring for commands and appointments with an eagerness that showed the keenness of their scent for plunder. "They think," wrote the old General, "that though they have no property, something may be got here. I put not one of them into any office whatever."

Williamson, however, spoke too confidently. Whitelocke had carried home the despatches announcing the capture of Port-au-Prince, and Whitelocke held the opinion, loathsome to the French proprietors, that the privileges claimed by the mulattos ought to be conceded to them. Immediately, therefore, the ubiquitous Charmilli hurried back to England with a letter of recommendation from Williamson, who, completely deceived by the man, had appointed him to be second in command of Montalembert's legion. He brought with him a petition from the proprietors at St. Domingo, urging, doubtless with perfect good sense and justice, the need for immediate reinforcements; and he was ready himself with a sheaf of suggestions. All the 1794. negro corps ought, he said, to be increased; five or six hundred French officers should be sent out to command them; one or two thousand men should be recruited from French peasants, deserters, and prisoners of war; he had a friend in Alsace who would supply four hundred men at five guineas a head; he himself would raise a *Légion Britannique* twelve hundred strong, at sixteen guineas a head; and he begged that it might be placed in the British Line, with British pay, and officers holding the King's Commission. He was careful to add that, of course, he would need an advance of funds for preliminary expenses; but he would keep careful accounts and the Colony would repay every shilling. And lastly, he urged that the British Government should advance three hundred thousand pounds a year to St. Domingo, to be defrayed by a tax on its produce, which was worth, according to his estimate, two millions annually. Mingled with these proposals, all of them designed for no honest purpose, were a few remarkably sound and sensible recommendations; for the man, though a rogue, was assuredly no fool. Pitt and Dundas hesitated for long, but Charmilli by steady persistence gained his letter of service to raise two corps, one of cavalry and one of infantry. "You are the protector of St. Domingo," he wrote to Dundas in exultation. For more than two years this adventurer and others like unto him preyed upon St. Domingo undetected, or at any rate unchecked, until the spirit of peculation and rascality had spread almost beyond remedy into every branch of the service. Then at last, but too late, there came, as shall be seen, a strong man who purged them away.[1]

Such was the fate that was preparing for this unhappy island; and in the autumn of 1794, when the

[1] Williamson to Dundas, 1st and 9th August, 13th September 1794; Simcoe to Dundas, 12th April; Maitland to Simcoe, 26th April; to Dundas, 8th May; to Huskisson, 6th June 1797. Whitelocke's report and Charmilli's letters will be found in *Colonial Office Transmissions*, 733 (Record Office).

1794. British soldiers were dying like rotten sheep, all hope seemed to centre in a single officer, Captain Thomas Brisbane of the Forty-ninth Foot. His station at St. Marc was a most important position, which at once commanded the communication between the north and south of the island, covered the northern flank of Port-au-Prince, and protected the rich plains of the Artibonite on one side and of Boucassin and Arcahais on the other against the incursion of the negroes in the mountains. The ascendency of this officer must have been remarkable. With no more than eighty British soldiers, a handful of French regulars, about three hundred reluctant Spaniards, the local militia, and a black legion of his own raising—in all about twelve hundred men—he was the terror alike of Republican troops and of negro brigands over an area of one August. thousand square miles. He brought the negro chief, Toussaint L'Ouverture, who was later to become the master of Haiti, to submission, with surrender of the territory which he had conquered; and he prevailed on ten thousand revolted slaves to return to work with their masters, enlisting four hundred of them in the British service for five years with promise of their freedom at the end. Brisbane was still following up his successes at a distant point on the Artibonite, leaving the town of St. Marc to the care of forty English con-
Sept. 6. valescents, when, on the 6th of September, the mulattos, seduced by the promises of the French Commissioners, broke into treacherous revolt, massacred all inhabitants that were obnoxious to them, and burned half of the town. The little band of invalids retired to a fort on the sea-shore and defended itself most gallantly for two days, until relieved by a frigate from Mole St. Nicholas; and meanwhile Brisbane returned. The negro bands of Toussaint had joined the mulattos in overwhelming force, and for eleven days not an hour passed without firing, either in the repulse of attacks or the breaking up of ambuscades. But the black men enlisted by the British remained faithful, fighting most gallantly for

their white leader; and on the 19th Brisbane received a 1794.
reinforcement which enabled him to take the offensive. Sept. 19.
Then he instantly attacked, and drove the brigands,
with the loss of many prisoners, across the Artibonite.
Thus by the extraordinary energy of a single man St.
Marc was preserved, and with it Port-au-Prince, and
probably the rest of the British possessions in St.
Domingo. "Too much cannot be said in his praise
nor done to reward him and his garrison," wrote
Williamson. That this eulogy was no more than just
may be gathered from the fact that, while pressing his
operations with all possible vigour, Brisbane was himself
for some days so much weakened by fever that he
could not write, but was obliged to make his reports
in French through a native amanuensis, having no
Englishman to share the burden with him. It is
pathetic to think that such service should ever have
been forgotten.[1]

Thus the deadly months of July, August, and
September came painfully to an end; but the British
force had practically come to an end also, and its
weakness was an invitation to fresh attack by any
discontented faction of the inhabitants. News of
the battle of Turcoing and of other French successes
in Europe had also reached St. Domingo, and were
not without their effect. The mulattos as usual
were the most active in mischief — the mulattos
whom the selfishness of Charmilli and his gang
had alienated, and whom Williamson had fully nine
months before asked for powers to conciliate. Rigaud
organised a revolt, similar to that of St. Marc, at
Léogane where there was no Brisbane to suppress it,
mastered the whole district, and massacred every French
planter that he could find. The loss of this place
endangered Port-au-Prince seriously from the west;
and Rigaud determined to complete his work by the
capture of Fort Bizothon, the principal bulwark of the

[1] Williamson to Dundas, 1st September; to Portland, 10th
October 1794 (both enclosing letters from Brisbane).

1794. town upon that side. With a silence and secrecy most creditable to himself and to his troops, he assembled two thousand men close under the works during the night of the 4th December, and early on the morning
Dec. 5. of the 5th, just as the moon set, launched them in three columns simultaneously upon the two posts which constituted the defences of Bizothon. The garrison consisted of but one hundred and twenty British soldiers, relics of flank-companies and also apparently of three battalions; but they were on the alert, and the attack was instantly checked. None the less the assault was sharp and the peril for a time great. All three of the officers in the place—Captain Grant of the Thirteenth, Lieutenant Hamilton of the Twenty-second, and Lieutenant Clunes of the First Royals—were severely wounded very early in the action; but all three tied up their wounds and stuck to their work, and after about an hour of hard fighting the enemy withdrew. The little garrison lost twenty-two of its number killed and wounded. The enemy carried away most of their dead for a little distance; but the bodies actually found numbered two hundred and fifty, no small testimony to the ferocious courage of the assailants.[1]

Baffled but not dismayed by this repulse, Rigaud now resolved to attempt another and more formidable enterprise. His headquarters were at Aux Cayes, a central position from which he could strike at any point upon the southern peninsula; and, having failed in the east, he now turned his attention to the west. Having completed his preparations, he sailed on the
Dec. 23. 23rd of December with one brig of sixteen guns, three armed schooners, and about three thousand men of all
Dec. 25. colours and descriptions, and at daybreak on Christmas Day opened his attack upon the post of Tiburon. A small armed vessel in the harbour offered a most gallant resistance to Rigaud's flotilla; but the astute mulatto, landing five field-pieces, battered her heavily from the

[1] Williamson to Dundas, 20th December 1794.

shore, and at last blew her up with a red-hot shot. 1794. He then turned his guns upon the garrison, which numbered four hundred and eighty men, chiefly of Jean Kina's black corps; bringing up also a mortar which threw a fifty-pound shell, and pouring in a constant fire of musketry. In a very short time the guns of the defenders were dismounted, the artillerymen killed, and a fourth of the force disabled, the enemy latterly dropping every shell into the fort. Nevertheless the blacks and whites held out bravely, until at last, on the 29th, a shell exploded in the ditch where Kina's men Dec. 29. were lying. The trial was too hard for these half-trained levies; they rose in panic, lowered the drawbridge by force, and fled in wild confusion to Jérémie. The commandant, Lieutenant Bradford of the Twenty-third, then formed an advanced and rear guard of his few remaining men, put his wounded in the midst, and, retreating in such order as he could, forced his way through an ambuscade of the enemy at Irois and brought the wreck of his force safely to Jérémie. Another officer, Lieutenant Baskerville, who, owing to wounds received in a former action, could not be moved from the fort, blew out his brains as Rigaud entered it. It was reckoned that three hundred of the garrison were killed or wounded, and it seems that most of the latter fell into the enemy's hands and were massacred. The war was rapidly becoming a savage contest in which quarter was neither given nor taken.

Thus disastrously ended the year 1794 in St. Domingo. Fifteen months had passed since the British had set foot in it, and in the whole of that time they had received in reinforcements from England fewer than nine hundred men. On the 1st of January 1795, when the disaster at Tiburon was still unknown, the seven battalions in the island, eked out by a few drafts despatched during the autumn months from Jamaica and by a few officers from England, numbered just under eleven hundred of all ranks fit for duty, and over seven hundred sick; and yet this was the healthy season. Nor was it only the army that had suffered. The squadron, never strong enough for its work, was practically disabled by the mortality among its crews; and this was a most serious matter. Not only were expeditions, such as that of Rigaud, left free to overwhelm such forts as they chose, but privateers from Jacmel and Aux Cayes were able to make havoc of British merchantmen in the south. Moreover ships from America, St. Thomas, and, as usual, from the British Leeward Islands, poured provisions, arms, and ammunition into Port-de-Paix to enable the Republicans to continue the struggle. The lack of an adequate naval force had long been represented by Williamson, Whitelocke, Charmilli, and many others; yet the want was never supplied.

If we turn to the records of the War Minister's department for explanations of this neglect, we find a maze of contradictory orders, which of themselves form a bitter comment upon his conduct of military affairs. Alarmed and, to do him justice, infinitely distressed by the mortality among the troops, Dundas undertook to provide reinforcements in abundance. At the end of August he promised "very speedily" the despatch of two battalions of seventeen hundred men, to be followed shortly by two Catholic regiments from Ireland, and by four or five hundred light cavalry, for which last Williamson had long been entreating. At the beginning of September he declared that the first reinforcement for St. Domingo would consist of three complete regiments, together well over two thousand strong. Three weeks later he announced that one of these regiments was unfit for service, that, in consequence, only two of the three would sail, and that, owing to the multitude of pressing calls for troops, he could not say when other reinforcements would be sent. Early in December he wrote that unforeseen delays had taken place in raising the Catholic corps, and that the two regiments embarked in September were still at Plymouth waiting for a favourable wind;

but he added that the establishment of St. Domingo had been fixed at six thousand men, and, computing the seven battalions already there at twenty-three hundred men, promised two thousand drafts to bring them up to that strength. A fortnight later he reported that yet another arrangement was to be made.[1] The two long-delayed regiments—the Eighty-first and Lieutenant-colonel Murray's[2]—had actually sailed on the 17th of December; and now the Fortieth, Forty-fourth, and Sixty-third were to be withdrawn from the Continent to St. Domingo, and the whole of these five battalions supplemented by three thousand drafts. The three regiments last named were, as will be remembered, those required of General Harcourt at one of the most critical periods of his retreat through Holland, and, needless to say, were not forthcoming; but it was characteristic of Dundas that, while hesitating to order the re-embarkation of the entire army in Flanders, he was ready to take battalions out of the fighting line, abandoning the rest to the risk of being overwhelmed. Nevertheless, as has already been seen, not one of all these regiments had reached St. Domingo by the end of 1794. Something more than adverse winds and misfortunes in the Low Countries was needed to account for this; and to explain the mystery it will now be necessary to turn to General Grey's operations to windward.

[1] Dundas to Williamson, 25th August, 4th and 28th September, 8th and 23rd December 1794.
[2] Then numbered 96th.

CHAPTER XIV

It will be remembered that though Dundas had early involved himself in negotiations with the planters of St. Domingo, that island was not the field which he had originally selected for the development of Pitt's military policy. He had cast his eye first to windward upon Martinique and Guadeloupe, where the excesses of the fanatical party in Paris had wrought little less confusion than in St. Domingo; and, pursuant to his orders, Tobago had already been captured, and an 1793. abortive attempt had been made upon Martinique. It
Aug. 2. was immediately upon the news of this failure that the first orders were given for General Grey's force to prepare for foreign service; and until November it was a settled arrangement that Grey should take with him fourteen complete regiments of infantry and the flank-companies of fourteen more, besides artillery. In addition to these Dundas, in September, advised General Bruce at Barbados that transports would be despatched from England to bring to that island the flank-companies of all the regiments in the Windward Islands, and that they ought all to be assembled there by the last week in November. The summer of 1793, however, was very sickly; and Bruce in August sent an ominous report that officers and men were dying so fast that before long they would be too few to perform the daily duties. In October, as will be remembered, Grey was sent with four battalions on a fool's errand to Ostend;
Nov. 11. but on his return he received his instructions, which bade him attack Martinique, Guadeloupe, and St. Lucia,

and empowered him to offer favourable terms to any 1793. French island which was prepared to surrender. The operations to windward being concluded, or, at his discretion, not concluded, he was to proceed to St. Domingo; and it is abundantly evident that Dundas hoped to accomplish the capture of all the French islands both to windward and leeward in a single campaign.[1]

Less than a week later, however, Dundas took away eight of Grey's battalions for Lord Moira's expedition by La Vendée; and, since Grey's force was thus reduced by one half, new instructions were drawn up, which left him free to select his own object of attack, but expressed a hope that at any rate he would be able to master St. Lucia and Guadeloupe and to send reinforcements to St. Domingo. This point settled, Grey joined Sir John Jervis at Portsmouth to hasten the preparations; and at last, losing all patience, they sailed away on the 26th of November, leaving a man-of-war to Nov. 26. convoy an ordnance-store ship, which, as was usual in those days, was not ready. In truth, in spite of warnings and entreaties reiterated for a full century by Governors, Generals, and Admirals in the West Indies, the expedition had started nearly two months too late.

Arriving at Barbados on the 6th of January, Grey 1794. found things in none too promising a condition. The bulk of the transports had sailed from Cork, and the General expected to find them arrived before him; but, on the contrary, the troops did not even begin to appear until the day after his coming. General Bruce had sailed to England sick almost unto death in November, and Colonel John Whyte, whom we have already seen in St. Domingo, was temporarily in command. Whyte had secured exact plans of the fortresses

[1] *C.C.L.B.*, 2nd August; Adjutant-general to General Cunynghame, 8th October; *C.O.*, Bruce to Dundas, 30th August; Dundas to Bruce, 18th September; to Grey, 11th and 12th November 1793.

1794. and excellent information from French officers, who had been driven from their posts by the Revolution; but he had received no orders for the concentration of other troops than the flank-companies, and had therefore sent away two battalions from Barbados to leeward. Even the flank-companies themselves were not fully assembled, as indeed was natural, for Dundas had overlooked the fact that it would take the transports weeks to beat up against the trade-wind to Barbados. Another difficulty was the procuring of negroes, of which, according to the usual practice, four men were to be attached to each company of white infantry for fatigue-duties; for the West Indian planter, thoroughly demoralised by the profits of slave-owning, smuggling, and piracy during more than a century of wars, refused to part with his negroes except at an exorbitant price. Then, as the transports gradually came in, the soldiers were found to be very unhealthy. The hospital-ship, which should have accompanied them, had not been ready in time, and the result was that twelve hundred men were on the sick list. Matters, however, quickly improved. President Bishop of Barbados set a patriotic example by offering several of his negroes for the service of the Army, and declining all compensation for them. Jervis, with whom Grey was on most affectionate terms, was indefatigable in giving assistance; and all ranks of both services worked heartily together. Nor should it be omitted that Grey ordered every officer of the Light Companies to repair for a course of instruction to one of his brigadiers, Thomas Dundas, in order to restore " the perfection of Light Infantry attained during the American war." Thus was begun at Barbados the work which Moore was ten years later to perfect at Shorncliffe.[1]

In the midst of these preparations there arrived an anxious letter from Henry Dundas, informing the General that, while leaving his discretion still unfettered,

[1] Whyte to Dundas, 20th December 1793; Prescott to Dundas, 1st January; Grey to Dundas, 7th and 15th January 1794.

the Government would not disapprove the postponement of operations in the Windward Islands until he had dealt with St. Domingo. He added that, being most anxious for all the West Indian objects to be attained in one campaign, he was sending two more battalions to Jamaica, in order to make Williamson wholly independent of Grey's force. To this Grey returned the unanswerable reply that, if he sent a detachment to St. Domingo, he would be too weak for any operations to windward, and that if he sailed to St. Domingo with his whole force he could never in the teeth of the trade-wind beat back to Martinique. But it was a special characteristic of Dundas's military plans that he never provided force enough to attain his object, and ignored such trifling circumstances as trade-winds. Nevertheless, though Grey on his outward journey had despaired, owing to his weakness in numbers, of the capture of Martinique, he had since taken the bold decision of striking his first blow at this, the most formidable of all the Windward Islands. He reckoned that he had at his disposal more than six thousand men; his information told that at least as many, of one description or another, were ready to resist him at Martinique under a brave and skilful officer, de Rochambeau. But at Martinique there had been adopted a false system of defence. Not only were there two powerful fortresses, Fort Bourbon and Fort Royal, to guard the capital, but the entire coast, to say nothing of the country inland, was studded with an incredible number of batteries, isolated and without unity for any scheme of general resistance. Such a system necessarily signified dispersion of force, and upon the weakness of this dispersion Grey founded his plan of attack.[1]

By the end of January the missing troops had been gathered in from the islands to leeward; and, the preparations being complete, the entire armament of nineteen ships of war, escorting a force of nearly seven

[1] Dundas to Grey, 18th December 1793; Grey to Dundas, 20th January 1794.

1794. thousand soldiers,[1] sailed on the 3rd of February from
Feb. 5. Barbados. On the 5th of February the fleet and transports approached the south-east coast of Martinique, and parted into three divisions. The first, under Commodore Thompson and General Thomas Dundas, made for the Bay of Galion on the east coast of the island; the second, under Captain Rogers of H.M.S. *Quebec* and Colonel Sir Charles Gordon, steered for Case de Navire, a little to the north of Fort Royal Bay, on the west coast; the third, under Jervis and Grey, stood in to the Bay of Marin, at the eastern angle of the south coast, and dropped anchor off Point de Borgnesse. Grey, having to deal with a dispersed force, had no idea of tempting it to unite. At about five o'clock in the evening part of Grey's division began to disembark into its flat boats, whereupon the battery on Point de Borgnesse opened fire, which was returned by the fleet; but on the landing of the troops the enemy fled from the battery in disorder. Having destroyed the works

[1] The force was brigaded as follows :—
First Brigade.—Sir C. Gordon. 15th, 39th, 43rd.
Second Brigade.—Thomas Dundas. 56th, 63rd, 64th.
Third Brigade.—John Whyte. 6th, 58th, 70th.

Grenadier Battalions.—Colonel Campbell.

1st Battalion.—Grenadier companies of 6th, 8th, 12th, 17th, 22nd, 23rd, 31st, 41st, and 56th.

2nd Battalion.—Grenadier companies of 9th, 33rd, 34th, 38th, 40th, 44th, 55th, and 66th.

3rd Battalion.—Granadier companies of 15th, 21st, 39th, 43rd, 56th, 60th, 64th, and 70th.

Light Infantry Battalions.—Colonel Myers.

1st Battalion.—Light companies of 6th, 8th, 12th, 17th, 22nd, 23rd, 31st, and 68th.

2nd Battalion.—Light companies of 15th, 31st, 34th, 35th, 38th, 40th, 41st, 44th, and 55th.

3rd Battalion.—Light companies of 21st, 39th, 43rd, 56th, 58th, 60th, 64th, and 65th.

The flank-companies that came from Ireland with Grey without their battalion-companies were those of the 8th, 12th, 17th, 22nd, 23rd, 31st, 33rd, 34th, 35th, 38th, 40th, 44th, and 55th. Fifty men of the 7th, 10th, 11th, 15th, and 16th Light Dragoons also sailed with the expedition.

and the guns the soldiers re-embarked, and the fleet, 1794. steering a little to north-westward, silenced another battery at the village of Sainte Luce. On the following morning the gunboats of the fleet made a feint attack Feb. 6. upon the town of Marin, while Grey landed his whole division, two thousand five hundred strong, at Trois Rivières, a little to the west of Sainte Luce. He himself then advanced with one column by a very difficult and mountainous road to Rivière Salée, at the Feb. 7. same time detaching a battalion of light infantry under Whyte to westward to take the seaward batteries on Cape Solomon and Point Bourgos in rear. By the following day Whyte had fulfilled his mission, cutting off the retreat of both garrisons and taking them prisoners. Meanwhile Rochambeau sent a force across the bay from Port Royal to cut off Whyte, in his turn, from the main body at Rivière Salée ; but Grey was on the watch, and this detachment, being attacked on the same night with the bayonet, according to his favourite method, was driven out headlong. The capture of the batteries at Point Bourgos and Cape Solomon enabled the shipping to move up to Grande Anse d'Arlet, from which with enormous difficulty the seamen contrived to carry supplies and stores through mountain and forest to Whyte, who now took up a position on a hill within four hundred yards of Ilet à Ramiers, or Pigeon Island.

This rocky islet, which is about one hundred feet high and three hundred yards in circuit at the summit, mounted twenty-two pieces of the heaviest ordnance, and, having vast stores of ammunition besides apparatus for heating shot, effectually barred the entrance of the fleet into the harbour. Within two days, however, Grey's engineers had brought up and placed in battery two six-inch howitzers, which, taking the defences in reverse, reduced the garrison to surrender after two hours' firing, Feb. 11. with a loss of forty killed and wounded out of two hundred men. The fleet then sailed into Fort Royal Feb. 12. Bay, hugging its southern shore, while the guns of Fort

1794. Louis on the northern shore strove in vain to throw shell into the ships. Thus Grey effectually established himself to the south of Fort Royal, with the fleet in close touch with him for transport and supply, having weakened the enemy's force by three or four hundred men at very slight cost to himself.

To the north of Fort Royal Gordon had done his
Feb. 8. work with equal success. Landing at Case de Navire, he found the enemy occupying the road to Fort Royal and the heights above it in force; and he was therefore obliged to strike into the mountains, and by wide and unseen turning movements, through dense forests and over the steepest of hills and ravines, to manœuvre the enemy out of all their positions in succession. By the
Feb. 12. 12th the work was done, with little loss though with great fatigue to the troops; the five batteries mounted between Case de Navire and Negro Point were in Gordon's hands, and his force was encamped within a league of Fort Royal.

On the east coast, likewise, Dundas had performed his part with the greatest skill and energy. Galion Bay is formed by a slender peninsula which juts out like a hook from the mainland, forming a roadstead on the southern side, and on the northern a snug little haven, called Trinité Harbour, which was defended by two
Feb. 5. small forts. A small battery on the point at the entrance to the bay was quickly silenced by the ships, and Dundas, after landing his men at the neck of the
Feb. 6. peninsula, halted them for the night, and next morning pushed northward over the isthmus upon Trinité itself. This place was under the charge of General Bellegarde, a mulatto, with a force of his own colour; and Dundas was much harassed during his advance by a brisk fire from sharpshooters concealed in the sugar-cane fields. These, however, were cleared away with the bayonet, and Dundas, marching straight upon a strong post on an eminence in rear of Trinité, drove the enemy from it after a brief resistance, and at once sent two detachments to attack the forts, which were hurriedly evacuated

by the mulattos without firing a shot. That night Belle- 1794.
garde set fire to the town of Trinité and fled to the
mountains; and on the following morning Dundas, Feb. 7.
having left a garrison to hold the place, turned inland
after him, making for a lofty peak among the mountains
called Gros Morne, which was strongly fortified and
said to be held by Bellegarde in force. On reaching it,
however, at midnight, Dundas found it abandoned by the
enemy, and hastened to occupy it himself, for this was
the prize that he sought. Gros Morne commanded
what was practically the only inland communication
between the north and south of Martinique; and
with Trinité held on the coast-road on one side, and
Case de Navire on the other, the island was fairly cut
in twain.

Leaving the Sixty-fourth to hold Gros Morne,
Dundas continued his movement southward, and at
noon of the 9th occupied Morne Bruneau, a command- Feb. 9.
ing height about three miles north of Fort Royal, from
which the British caught sight of the outposts of the
citadel of Fort Bourbon. From thence he despatched
three companies under Lieutenant-colonel Craddock to Feb. 10.
seize a good landing-place for his supplies on the Cohé
de Lamentin, and a larger force to two more commanding points, apparently to eastward. The whole of
these detachments were fiercely attacked on the nights
of the 10th and 11th by Bellegarde's forces, but held
their own successfully. On the 13th Grey sent forward Feb. 13.
part of his force under General Prescott to join Dundas
at Bruneau, and on the following day moved thither Feb. 14.
himself with the rest of the troops from Rivière Salée.
Thus the junction between the two forces which had
been landed on the north and south of Fort Royal
Harbour was successfully effected.

On the same evening Dundas, according to concerted
arrangement, returned with the second battalion of
Grenadiers, the light companies of the Thirty-third and
Fortieth, and the Sixty-fifth Regiment, to Trinité.
There he gave the two light companies and the Sixty-

1794. fifth to Colonel Campbell, with orders to make their way north-westward by a path through the forest, to climb to the summit of a huge spur of mountain which runs southward from Mont Pelée, and to look for his arrival on the same ridge, a mile or two farther north, on the morning of the 16th. Meanwhile he himself, with his small but superb body of Grenadiers, took the road along the coast from Trinité northward to the river Capot, his baggage following him by sea. Thence turning westward, he entered upon the long and weary ascent of the rugged steep which was to lead him to the pass of La Calebasse, hard by the crater of Mont Pelée, some four thousand feet above the sea. Looking to the extraordinary difficulty of the country, the march of these two columns along two narrow tracks through this maze of forest and ravine appears to me to be a very remarkable military feat. Dundas left Trinité at five on the evening of
Feb. 15. the 15th, and, allowing his troops only three hours' halt at the Capot, reached the heights of La Calebasse
Feb. 16. before daybreak of the 16th; having traversed at least twenty miles, half of the distance over the roughest and steepest of ground, within twelve hours. Such an exertion is a hard trial in the tropics; and when he reached the final ascent of La Calebasse, where the road was barred by a battery and a considerable force of the enemy, his men were so much exhausted that he was obliged to grant them a short rest. Being called upon to advance, however, they scaled the craggy slope with such alacrity that their opponents would not stand, but destroyed the guns and fled. Moving southward along the ridge, Dundas found Campbell's column, which had been arrested when within half a mile of its appointed destination by five or six hundred of the enemy in a strong position, and was now hotly engaged. Sending forward a small detachment of his wearied soldiers, Dundas cleared the French from the front of Campbell's column, only to find that Campbell had been killed earlier in the day, while leading a charge

with the bayonet. He was then recalled to his own column by another attack, which he repulsed with heavy loss ; and his worn-out troops were then left for a short time in peace upon Morne Rouge.

At two o'clock on the following morning three companies of Grenadiers, with the flints removed (according to Grey's rule) from their muskets, stole forward to the attack of a redoubt which still obstructed the British advance. The enemy, however, had been so roughly handled that they had abandoned the work, leaving two guns behind them ; and the two columns then marched down the long descent upon their appointed object, the town of St. Pierre. As they approached it from the rear, eight ships of the squadron were seen in the bay in its front ; and on entering the town Dundas found it already in the possession of a force which Grey had landed upon its northern flank, while yet another detachment, under Colonel Myers, stood before it on the south. Thus St. Pierre, the wealthy commercial capital of Martinique, passed almost without resistance into Grey's hands, thanks chiefly to the extraordinary march of Dundas and Campbell across the island from sea to sea.

Fort Bourbon and Fort Louis, the two permanent defences of Fort Royal, now alone remained to be dealt with. The latter was situated on a long low spit which juts out into the harbour ; but the former was a far more formidable work, constructed shortly before the Revolution under the superintendence of the Marquis of Bouillé, upon the heights immediately to north of the town. It was an irregular polygon adapted to the configuration of the ground, with a detached redoubt at the northern or landward extremity ; but, as was inevitable in so mountainous a country, it was commanded by adjacent hills, notably by the heights of Sourier, immediately to the north. On those heights Bellegarde had encamped with a considerable number of troops, and Grey had fixed one o'clock on the morning of the 19th as the time for

1794. driving the French out with one of his favourite attacks with the bayonet. To his great joy, however, at Feb. 18. noon on the 18th he saw the mulatto leader descend from his position with part of his force, evidently bent upon attacking the British left, and cutting it off from its communication with the harbour. Grey reinforced that part of his line to hold him in check, and meanwhile ordered a battalion of Grenadiers and two of Light Infantry to advance with all speed upon Bellegarde's camp at Sourier. Hurrying across the valley which divided the opposing armies, these troops came first upon the enemy in the forest below the position, drove them from thence, and, following them up an almost inaccessible slope, swept them out of the camp. In due time the remainder of Bellegarde's force, completely repulsed in its attack, returned to Sourier, to be saluted by a cannonade from its own captured guns and a heavy fire from the British Grenadiers. The unfortunate men fled in panic to Fort Bourbon, where Rochambeau shut the gates in their faces; and the British, pursuing too precipitately, suffered some loss Feb. 28. from the guns of the fortress. Ten days later Bellegarde and three hundred of his men surrendered, he and his second in command being sent to Boston, while the remainder were made prisoners of war. Thus the heights of Sourier, the capture of which should have cost the British dear, fell into their hands at a trifling sacrifice of men, thanks to the unerring swiftness of their General's eye, and the foolish temerity of their enemy.[1]

It now remained to besiege and capture Fort Louis and Fort Bourbon, which promised to be the heaviest part of the task. Grey at once called in every man that could be spared from outlying posts for the attempt; and the sailors of the fleet were set to work to cut roads, and to bring guns up to the heights of Sourier. The perfect understanding between the chiefs of the fleet and army

[1] Grey to Dundas, 16th March 1794. Willyams, *Campaign in the West Indies*, pp. 1-55.

caused the two services to work together with un- 1794.
exampled harmony, and Grey gained the hearts of the
blue-jackets for ever by promising that they should have
a battery of their own. Their difficulties, however, were
greatly increased by unusually persistent rain; and the
troops would have suffered much had not Grey taken
the precaution, before leaving England, to obtain flannel
shirts for them. By the 6th of March, nevertheless, all
was ready. Batteries had been erected at eight hundred
yards' distance on the neighbouring heights of Morne
Tortenson to west, of Sourier to north, and of Point
Carrière to east; and on the 7th a heavy fire was March 7.
opened upon the two forts from land and sea. Within
ten days the guns had been pushed up to within five
hundred yards of the fortress; a new battery was
erected on Point Carrière at a range of not more than
two hundred yards from Fort Louis; and the fire of
the British became overwhelming. Finally, on the
20th the *Asia* and *Zebra* led the way for a flotilla of March 20.
small boats to Fort Louis; Captain Faulkner of the
Zebra ran his ship aground under the very walls; and
the blue-jackets, swarming after him, carried the fort
by escalade. At the same time a battalion of Grenadiers
and another of Light Infantry forced the entrance to
the town of Fort Royal, and hoisting the British colours
changed the name to Fort Edward, in honour of the
Duke of Kent, who had joined the force a few days
before. Seeing the town with all its stores and supplies
to be lost, Rochambeau hung out the white flag. The
British fire had been so fierce that hardly an inch of the
fortress was untouched by shot; his garrison had been
reduced from twelve hundred to nine hundred men;
and altogether he had made a most gallant defence.
On the 23rd, therefore, the garrison marched out March 23.
with military honours and laid down their arms,
Grey engaging to ship them to France, on condition
that they should not serve again during the current
war. Thus Martinique passed under the sway of King
George.

1794. The casualties of the British troops in the whole of the operations did not exceed three hundred and fifty killed and wounded, which speaks not a little for Grey's skill. "The General means to carry the business through with as little loss as possible, and with the strictest attention to the preservation of the troops." Such were the words of a General Order published on the 22nd of January; and he adhered to them. Nevertheless the work had been very severe, and the hardship, which the officers shared in every respect with their men, had been very great. The troops—thanks to Grey's firmness in hanging a couple of marauders, who had been taken red-handed—had behaved quite admirably; and they were cheered by the prospect of prize-money through the capture of a vast quantity of produce at St. Pierre. Lastly, the store of artillery and munitions taken at Fort Royal was so enormous as to make Grey's mind easy as to a sufficiency for his own future operations. None the less he did not fail during the course of the siege to ask Dundas for speedy reinforcements, to enable him not only to take but to retain possession of the islands.[1]

Leaving the Fifteenth, Thirty-ninth, Fifty-sixth, Fifty-eighth, Sixty-fourth, and Seventieth under General Prescott at Martinique, Grey embarked the remainder of his troops on the 30th of March, and after some delay through windless weather reached April 1. St. Lucia on the 1st of April. There he pursued the same tactics as at Martinique. One division was landed at Anse du Cap, just to westward of the extreme northerly point of the island; a second at Anse du Choc, a few miles further south and immediately to north of Castries Harbour; a third at Anse Latoc, immediately to south of the same harbour; and a fourth at Marigot, a little to south of Anse Latoc. Their function was very simple, namely, to march along the coast, taking the seaward batteries in reverse, and to meet at the Morne Fortuné so as to invest that fortress

[1] Grey to Dundas, 16th and 25th March 1794.

completely. By the morning of the 2nd this was done. 1794.
The fleet anchored comfortably in Cul de Sac Bay, and April 2.
in the evening the forces had wound themselves so
closely around the Morne that Grey gave orders to
Colonel Coote to storm a redoubt and two batteries
adjoining the main fortress. The task seems to have
been accomplished with the bayonet and by surprise,
for Coote killed thirty of the enemy without losing a
man. This success had its due effect, for the Commandant, General Ricard, capitulated on the same
night, and was shortly afterwards shipped, together
with the one hundred and twenty men that formed his
regular garrison, to France. Prince Edward thereupon
changed the name of the fortress to Fort Charlotte,
which it bears to this day.

The Sixth and Ninth were left under command of
Sir Charles Gordon to hold St. Lucia; and Grey, re-embarking on the 4th of April, returned to Martinique, April 4.
whence, after shipping supplies and stores, he sailed
again on the 8th for Guadeloupe. A detachment of April 8.
the squadron and transports waited on the way to
capture the small islands called the Saints, while Grey
and Jervis, sailing on, anchored off the entrance to Point-à-Pitre on the 10th. At one o'clock on the morning of
the 11th Grey landed with about one thousand soldiers April 11.
and seamen at Grand Bay,[1] on the southern shore of
Grande Terre, under a heavy fire from Fort Fleur
d'Épée and its outworks, which defended the bay. The
landing was effected with little or no loss, thanks to the
gallantry of Captain Lord Garlies of the *Winchelsea*,
who laid his ship close under the batteries, and silenced
them with his broadside. In the course of the 11th
the rest of the transports arrived; by the evening the
six battalions of Grenadiers and Light Infantry, besides
five hundred seamen, had been disembarked; and Grey
then made his dispositions for a general attack.

[1] Grey calls this the Bay of Gozier, and speaks of the fire of Fort
Gozier; but study of the map convinces me that the description in
the text is correct.

1794. The most menacing of the defences was Fort Fleur d'Épée, where the enemy was assembled in force. It was situated on the summit of a hill, with a half-moon battery cut out of the slope below it, and to seaward was consequently very formidable; but it was commanded by a second fort on Morne Mascotte, a hill a musket-shot in rear of it, which if taken by an enemy necessarily rendered it untenable. Grey therefore placed one detachment of troops under Prince Edward to attack Morne Mascotte; a second under Thomas Dundas to assail Fleur d'Épée from the rear, and to cut off its communication with Point-à-Pitre and the other defences to westward; and a third under Colonel Symes, the chief of his staff and an excellent officer, to follow the road along the coast and co-operate with Dundas. The

April 12. time of attack was fixed for five o'clock in the morning, and strict orders were given that not a shot must be fired, but that the whole of the work must be done with the bayonet. The several divisions had marched separately, according to the distance which they had to traverse; and all were in their appointed places when exactly at five o'clock the signal was given by the firing of a gun from Jervis's flagship, the *Boyne*. The men instantly rushed on, swept the picquets before them, though not until the alarm had been given, and swarmed up the hill upon Fort Fleur d'Épée under a tremendous fire of grape and musketry. The bluejackets hoisted each other into the embrasures; the soldiers dashed at the gates, and after a sharp struggle burst them open; and, the enemy still resisting stoutly within the fort, there followed a murderous contest in the darkness, until the Frenchmen at last fled in all directions in boats or by land into Point-à-Pitre. The loss of the British in this assault on La Fleur d'Épée was fifteen killed and sixty wounded, thirteen of the wounded belonging to the Navy. Of the enemy sixty were killed, fifty-five wounded, and over one hundred taken prisoners. This success gave Grey possession of the inner defences of Point-à-Pitre and of the northern half of the island, which is called Grande Terre. 1794.

It was not long before the southern half, or Guadeloupe proper, went the way of Grande Terre. Leaving garrisons at Point-à-Pitre and other important posts, Grey on the 14th sailed over to the other side of the bay, effected a landing without resistance at Petit Bourg, and turning southward followed the road along the coast towards Basseterre. On the 17th Thomas Dundas with another division of troops landed seven miles northwest of that town, and also turned southward to meet Grey; and on the 21st the two forces effected their junction in rear of Basseterre. There is no need to give details of the operations, which had consisted simply of turning the enemy out of their seaward batteries by taking them in reverse, or, if stronger means were necessary, by attacking them at night with the bayonet. On the morning of the 21st General Collot, seeing the last defences of Basseterre fallen, capitulated; and Grey thus added Guadeloupe to his other conquests. It had cost him eleven men killed, wounded, and missing, raising his casualties in the capture of the entire island to eighty-six. Yet Guadeloupe had nearly six thousand men fit to bear arms, or at least twice as many as Grey could land against them; weapons had actually been issued to four thousand of them, and many of the posts captured by the British were of exceeding strength. The whole campaign is an extraordinary example of the power of a small and efficient army working in perfect harmony with a small and efficient squadron upon a fortified coast. Collot had nearly nine hundred men, including fifty regular troops, shut up in one of the defences of Basseterre. One-third of that number, mobile and free to harass the flanks and rear of Grey's columns, would have given the British more trouble than twenty batteries. April 14. April 17. April 21.

It was now, however, Grey's turn to bear the burden of defending the islands which he had taken. His force was insufficient to do more than retain them;

1794. indeed, but for the three battalions promised by Dundas, he would hardly have encumbered himself with further conquests after Martinique, for his men were beginning to break down fast from sickness after the exertions of two months' incessant work in the tropics. He and Jervis, therefore, proposed that both of them should come home, in order to concert the operations for the next campaign, and to recruit their health so as to enable them to undertake it. Meanwhile there was much to be done in organising the civil government, and in making arrangements for internal police, to which end Grey formed a corps of two hundred and fifty rangers, half mounted and half dismounted, for the three islands. Another source of much trouble was the produce taken as prize-of-war, Dundas having given Grey long instructions, based upon a precedent of 1695, as to the division and distribution of all booty, but withheld the commission to erect a prize-court.

May 6. This duty kept Grey busy until May, on the 6th of which month, after long delay through foul winds, the battalion-companies of the Twenty-second, Twenty-third, Thirty-fifth, and Forty-first from Ireland reached him at Martinique. Having warning from the British consul at Virginia that a French fleet was in Hampton Roads, and that the Americans seemed disposed to declare war against England, Grey detained the Thirty-fifth, but sent the rest forward at once to Jamaica, together with General Whyte. It has already been related how on the 19th of May three of these four battalions arrived with Whyte at St. Domingo, and were at once employed in that theatre of operations.

Grey then turned his thoughts for a moment towards an expedition to Cayenne, in order to root the French completely out of the West Indies; but hearing that the force in that colony was considerable, he abandoned the project, and despatched the flank companies of the Twenty-second, Twenty-third, Forty-first, and Thirty-fifth to St. Domingo to rejoin their battalion-companies. Meanwhile he paid visits of inspection to St. Lucia and Guadeloupe, and was entertained at dinner at the latter place by General Thomas Dundas on the 31st of May. In the middle of the meal their host complained suddenly of illness and left the table, whereupon Grey and Jervis, who were extending their tour of inspection to Antigua and St. Kitts, took leave of him without misgiving, and proceeded on their voyage. In three days Thomas Dundas, a most excellent officer, was dead. Yellow fever, the white man's most formidable enemy in the West Indies, had opened its campaign to windward; and the General at Guadaloupe was one of the first to fall before it.[1]

1794.
May 31.

Those days of peace in the last fortnight of May were the last that the West Indies were to know for many months; and by a strange irony they coincided with the first and only hours of triumph which Pitt was to enjoy from his fatuous military policy. On the 20th of May the thanks of both Houses of Parliament were voted to Grey, Jervis, and the men under their command; and on the following day Henry Dundas forwarded the votes with effusion to the West Indies. Some comfort, indeed, Ministers needed, for the news of the disaster of Turcoing had just reached them; and they found it, as they thought, in Grey's success. Dundas wrote to the General, granting him leave to come home, and asking him to report as to the garrisons that would be necessary to hold the conquered islands, upon the supposition, first that the French could, and secondly that they could not, send a force from Europe to recover them. But Dundas gave not a thought to a French squadron with a convoy of transports which had slipped out of Rochefort on the 23rd of April and was already far on its way to the West Indies; and he took no measures to despatch reinforcements before November. Far from that, indeed, he wrote only exhortations to Grey to send every man that he could spare to St. Domingo, from which the

[1] Grey to Dundas, 12th, 13th, 22nd, 29th April; 3rd and 6th May 1794.

1794. trade-wind forbade them to return to windward; and all this he did with the records of many former expeditions at hand to show that any force sent to the West Indies was invariably reduced to a shadow at the close of the sickly months which follow upon the campaigning season. Lastly, Dundas gave Grey no information as to the attitude of America. As a matter of fact the French vessels in Hampton Roads were the escort of a convoy of provision-ships, upon the safe arrival of which hung the issue, whether France should or should not perish of starvation. Not a ship was appointed to watch them, though Lord Howe was sent to sea to intercept them at the eastern shore of the Atlantic. The escorting fleet was that which he defeated on the 1st of June, but the escape of the convoy with its cargo to France was at the moment well worth the sacrifice of seven line-of-battle ships.

June 5. Thus it happened that, early on the morning of the 5th of June, Grey and Jervis received at St. Kitts intelligence that seven ships and fifteen hundred troops had arrived from France at Guadeloupe; which message was presently followed by a second reporting the death of Thomas Dundas. Without delay the General em-
June 7. barked, and on the 7th arrived at Guadeloupe, where to his astonishment he found Point-à-Pitre and the whole of its defences in the enemy's hands. It appeared that on the first arrival of the French troops, Lieutenant-colonel Drummond of the Forty-third had at once asked for reinforcements; his garrison at Fort Fleur d'Épée being so much weakened by sickness that he had fewer than one hundred and twenty men fit for duty. Thomas Dundas at the moment was dying or dead, and his successor seems to have been so much upset that he sent Drummond's letter to Grey at St. Kitts, and only on the 5th of June recovered himself enough to order more troops to Fleur d'Épée. Meanwhile, however, the merchants of Point-à-Pitre and the French royalists came into the fort, raising the strength of the garrison to three hundred men; and on the

evening of the 5th the royalists begged permission to make a sally upon the enemy, who so far had contented themselves with burning and plundering. Drummond consented, for according to his information the French reinforcements were not numerous, besides which he had good reason to suppose that they would be drunk; and he therefore placed nearly two hundred royalist volunteers under one of his own officers for the sortie. The party had not marched far from the fort when a couple of shots threw them into a panic; many threw away their arms and deserted; some ran back to the fort, and only thirty stood by their leader. At one o'clock on the morning of the 6th the French made a general attack upon the fort with some fifteen hundred men. Drummond, who was ready for them, repulsed their first assault with very heavy loss; but on the cessation of fire the royalists were again seized with panic, cried out that all was lost and made a rush for the gate. The men of the Forty-third tried hard to stop them, but half of them succeeded in opening the gate and flying to the town before they could be overpowered; and by the time that the gate was closed, the enemy had swarmed over the deserted ramparts and almost surrounded Drummond and his handful of soldiers. The British commander rallied his men, but they were overwhelmed by the numbers of the enemy and the rush of the panic-stricken civilians; and finally he withdrew with about one-third of his garrison, and, gathering in two small outlying detachments, crossed the water to Guadeloupe. Many assigned treachery as the explanation of the behaviour of the royalists; but Grey had noticed that they were a miserable crew, and had refused to employ them either at Guadeloupe or at Martinique. The life of the white planter in the tropics, what with the enervation of the damp tropical heat, the luxury afforded by innumerable slaves, and the terror of a servile rebellion, was not calculated to produce a courageous race.[1]

1794.
June 5.

June 6.

[1] Grey to Dundas, 11th, 12th, 13th, 14th June; to Nepean, 14th June 1794.

1794. A day or two later Grey learned what manner of men he had to deal with, through a proclamation signed by Victor Hugues and Pierre Chrétien, Commissioners of the Convention, whereby all good republicans were summoned to rally to them on pain of being considered rebels and traitors. Further proclamations published an Act of the Convention, abolishing slavery and admitting all black men to equal privileges with whites, and initiated the organisation of paid volunteers to throw off the yoke of the English.[1] It was evident that the Convention intended to rouse the entire black population against the British; and Victor Hugues was well fitted to be the leader of the movement. He was a mulatto who had been public prosecutor at Rochefort during the Reign of Terror, and ought by right to have shared the fate of Fouquier-Tinville; instead of which destiny spared him to execute, as he boasted, twelve hundred royalists in Guadeloupe, and to cause indirectly the loss of an incalculable number of lives. He possessed, nevertheless, audacity and vigour as well as brutality, and as a leader of an excitable race such as the negroes was most formidable. Grey upon arrival made Basseterre his headquarters and summoned reinforcements from the other islands, while the fleet blockaded the French ships in Point-à-Pitre. Colonel Francis Dundas, a very capable officer, commanded the British troops at Petit Bourg, opposite that town, with a formidable battery, besides frigates and gunboats, to protect his flanks; but the troops were greatly debilitated by the climate, and the mortality both of officers and men had been so great that Grey seriously doubted his ability to retake Grande Terre. Hugues, however, without waiting for him to move, boldly sent a force across the bay, which, after a little burning and plundering, took post at Pointe St. Jean, a headland which forms the inner harbour of Point-à-Pitre on the western side. The French had not been there forty-eight

[1] Enclosed in Grey to Dundas, 13th June; 9th September 1794.

hours, when, on the night of the 13th, Francis Dundas 1794. fell suddenly upon them with the bayonet, killed nearly June 13. two hundred on the spot, drove the rest into the harbour, where several were drowned, and captured their whole camp with a loss to himself of but nine men wounded.[1] It was a cheering little success, but Grey did not deceive himself by overvaluing it, nor cease to press on Henry Dundas the need for reinforcements.

In the following days British detachments, which had been called in from the various islands, arrived at Guadeloupe; and early in the morning of the 19th June 19. Grey effected a landing without loss or molestation upon the opposite shore of Grande Terre, occupied the village of Gozier, and began to throw up batteries against Fort Fleur d'Épée. On the 22nd a detachment of Grena- June 22. diers and seamen was sent to surprise a strong post of the enemy at St. Ann's, on the coast some seven miles to eastward, and performed its task most successfully, bayoneting four hundred of the enemy, destroying all their guns and returning to camp with the loss of but one man wounded. The next task was to clear the road from Gozier to Fort Fleur d'Épée, which was commanded by a strong position of the enemy; and accordingly on the night of the 25th six companies June 25. were detached under Colonel Fisher to fetch a wide compass by a most difficult path, and to take the enemy in rear. This also was satisfactorily accomplished, the enemy flying away in panic and leaving Fisher to establish himself in their position and on some adjacent heights. The French, however, still occupying a chain of high and wooded ground between this post and Morne Mascotte, Grey, unperceived by them, reinforced Fisher by troops drawn from Petit Bourg; and on the 27th Brigadier Symes attacked the position on all June 27. sides, drove the enemy in confusion to Morne Mascotte, and from thence into Fort Fleur d'Épée. The loss of

[1] So Grey's letter to Dundas of 14th June 1794; but Willyams, who is the authority for the enemy's losses, gives the British casualties at seven killed and twelve wounded.

1794.
June 27.
Morne Mascotte roused the French commanders to fury; and gathering together a mixed force of all colours they advanced that same afternoon to recapture it, covered by a tremendous fire from the guns of Fleur d'Épée. So fierce was the tempest of shot upon Morne Mascotte that the British Grenadiers lay flat on their faces until the enemy's columns were close upon them, when they sprang to their feet, and after a savage exchange of musketry at a few yards' range drove their foes headlong down the hill with the bayonet. Two

June 29. days later, however, the French leaders again collected fifteen hundred men, clothing mulattos and blacks alike in the national uniform, and, with the same reckless disregard of life as had characterised the operations in the Low Countries, launched them for the second time at Morne Mascotte, only to be hurled back with even greater slaughter by Grey's favourite Light Infantry and Grenadiers.

The incessant fighting, however, was beginning to tell heavily upon the sickly and debilitated British soldiers. Since they had left England not one scrap of stores had been sent to them; their clothes were in rags, and they had no shoes to their feet. The rainy season had set in with the usual gloomy, steaming heat, alternating with the fierce glare of a vertical sun. The hurricane season was almost come, when the fleet would no longer be safe at sea; and everything pointed to the need of finishing the campaign at a stroke, while the enemy was still discouraged by slaughter and defeat. Grey therefore decided to detach a part of his force under Brigadier Symes to attack the enemy at Point-à-Pitre, hoping either to surprise Morne de Gouvernment, a strongly fortified hill commanding the town, or at any rate to destroy the supplies deposited in the town itself, and so to compel the French to withdraw from it. He, meanwhile, remained in person with the rest of the troops at Morne Mascotte, ready at a given signal of Symes's success to advance and storm Fort Fleur d'Épée, which had been heavily bombarded by his batteries for some days past. Accordingly, on the night of the 1st of July, Symes set out with two battalions of Light Infantry, one of Grenadiers, and one of seamen, all of them so weak in numbers as to be battalions only in name. The night was intensely dark; the road lay through deep wooded ravines; and the guides by ignorance or mistake led the columns so directly upon the outposts of the enemy, as to destroy all hope of taking them by surprise. It seems that Symes thereupon abandoned the idea of an attack upon Morne de Gouvernment, and ordered the leading battalion of Light Infantry to change direction from the Morne to the town. Meanwhile, however, a part of the column, headed by the seamen, seems to have blundered, with no clear idea of its object, into the street, where it at once found itself under a tremendous fire of grape from Morne de Gouvernment, from the ships in the harbour and from batteries erected in tiers on the roads. Many officers were struck down; and the men, bewildered and too much exhausted to move, for the first time forgot the lesson which a score of successful night-attacks had taught them, loaded their muskets, and as invariably happens upon such occasions, fired upon each other. The confusion then became appalling. Symes was badly wounded; the troops that were firing could not be controlled; those that remained in hand were so worn down by their march that they could not advance. In some quarters a few men stormed the enemy's batteries at the bayonet's point with all their old impetuosity; in others they broke into the houses, from which a heavy fire was poured upon them, and killed every soul that they could find. To all intent their object, the destruction of the magazines, was within their grasp; but there was no possibility of directing them upon it. At last Colonel Fisher sounded the retreat, gathered together such fragments of the force as he could collect, formed a rear-guard of Grenadiers, which kept the enemy most gallantly at bay, and, with the help of reinforcements furnished by Grey,

1794. brought back his weary remnant in safety to Morne Mascotte.[1]

The losses in this disastrous repulse are not ascertainable, but must have been very great. The casualties from the renewal of the operations in Guadeloupe on the 10th of June to the 2nd of July amounted, including those of the seamen serving ashore, to one hundred and twenty, including thirteen officers, killed, three hundred and sixty, including thirteen officers, wounded, and seventy-two missing; and it may be reckoned that quite five-sixths of these fell in the attack of the 1st of July. Symes, despite Grey's assurances that he had done all that was humanly possible, took his failure so grievously to heart that he died of his wounds. Grey was bitterly disappointed (for he had been as confident of carrying Fleur d'Épée as of Symes's success), but blamed no one, unless it were himself, for asking too much of his troops. He would not believe, and with good reason, that the men who had before won such astonishing little victories against all disadvantages of position, numbers, and climate, could fail him unless they were physically incapable of doing their work. It was hard that fortune should turn against him just when he most sorely needed her help, but though greatly afflicted by the grievous loss of officers, he did not repine. On the very evening of the action he began to
July 4. embark his heavy artillery, and two days later he withdrew the whole of his force from Grande Terre without the further loss of a man or of a single article of stores.

He then sent back to their former stations seven companies, which he had withdrawn from the other Windward Islands, and fortified a strong quadrilateral post, known as the position of Berville, on the isthmus west of the Rivière Salée. His object herein was to cut off Guadeloupe proper completely from Grande Terre, and to ensure himself a base from which, as soon as reinforcements should arrive, he could renew

[1] Grey to Dundas (enclosing Symes's report), 8th July; to Nepean, 9th July 1794.

his attack with success. It may be questioned whether 1794. he would not have done more wisely to evacuate the island altogether, for this quadrilateral upon low ground adjoining a marsh was extremely unhealthy ; the troops were already perishing fast ; and the garrisons of the other islands were none too strong. On the other hand the Government had attached great importance to the conquest of the whole of the islands, and it was not unreasonable to suppose that, on hearing of the departure of the French reinforcements from Rochefort, Dundas would at once have sent British reinforcements to countervail them. It was not easy, in such circumstances, to come to a decision, for Grey knew nothing of what was passing in Europe and had not yet grasped the extreme incapacity of Dundas. He therefore left forty-eight companies,[1] numbering in all eighteen hundred men, together with local corps of emigrants and royalists, under Brigadier Graham, at Berville, and himself repaired to Martinique, where he took up his headquarters at St. Pierre.

Though he had received permission to return home, he and Jervis determined to remain at their posts until relieved, for the situation was now most critical. The success of Victor Hugues at Point-à-Pitre had encouraged many secret enemies in the French islands to throw off the mask, and the sight of the British troops dying daily before their eyes did not tend to repress them. In the ten islands to windward, which were in British possession at the beginning of July, there were nominally thirteen complete battalions and twenty-eight companies of infantry, besides four or five companies of artillery. The whole of the troops did not comprise more than forty-five hundred of all ranks fit for duty, with a sick list of twelve hundred ; and Grey was again obliged to press earnestly, not only for reinforcements,

[1] 1st battalion Grenadiers, 1st battalion Light Infantry, 35th, 39th, 43rd, 65th, in all forty-eight companies besides two of artillery. The garrison was shortly afterwards increased, and the troops somewhat changed.

1794. but for new clothing and necessaries for his men. "You seem to have totally forgotten us," he wrote to Nepean; and the reproach was only too just. To these anxieties were added domestic troubles. It was discovered that Sir Charles Gordon, who, after excellent service in the field, had been appointed to the chief command at St. Lucia, had been guilty of peculation, rather perhaps through error and weakness than vice; and it was necessary to try him by court-martial. General Prescott, again, an able but quarrelsome officer, had fallen at variance with the provincial government at Martinique; and Grey was obliged to transfer him to the command at Fort Matilda in Basseterre, Guadeloupe. Then, strangely enough, Benedict Arnold appeared on the scene. He had been captured by Victor Hugues while visiting Guadeloupe on some mercantile business, and by great good fortune had made his escape. With amazing assurance he asked for a command as senior Brigadier-general, and, on the strength of his service to the British in the American Revolution, fastened himself on to Grey with a tenacity which the General's undisguised disgust was powerless to shake. Finally, at the end of July, there arrived a letter from Dundas which drove both Grey and Jervis to resign their commands, and insist that their successors might be sent out immediately.[1]

The purport of this letter was to cancel all that had been done by Grey in the matter of prize-money, as being, in the Advocate-General's opinion, illegal, and to hold him convicted, on the bare statement of certain merchants in London, of rapacity, extortion, and oppression; firstly, because he and Jervis had sold the produce captured in the various ports for the benefit of the captors; secondly, because he had accepted a pecuniary composition for that which had been taken in the warehouses ashore. The real truth was that, in consequence of the threatened abolition of slavery, a

[1] Grey to Dundas, 18th July; to Nepean, 18th and 19th July 1794.

great many British West India merchants had either 1794.
invested their capital in the French and other foreign
islands, or were carrying on illicit trade with them, so
that the seizure of this produce endangered the repayment of the money due to these merchants from their
French clients. Their agents had at first tried to buy up
this prize-property at their own figure; but the captors
would not accept their price. They had then tried to
insinuate themselves as prize-agents; but the captors
would have none of them. Finally, they hurried to
England and laid before Pitt their charges of extortion
against the commanders.

Now it was an incontestable fact that Generals and
Admirals had, in the past, been guilty of such extortion;
and both Pitt and Dundas were perfectly right to make
the fullest inquiry into any such accusations of the like
misconduct against Grey and Jervis. But to accept
the charges as true without hearing one word from the
commanders in their defence, and to rebuke them upon
such accusations as convicted wrong-doers, was worthy
neither of a gentleman nor a statesman; and the fact
that Pitt actually did so stands as a very grave reflection
upon his character. Grey and Jervis were naturally
furious, and protested most strongly, not only against
the insult to themselves, but against the wrong done to
the troops, some of whom had been punished for plundering because they could count upon legitimate prize.
" If this army be deprived of its prize-money," wrote
Grey, " many of the officers must be ruined. Every
article they purchase is so dear that double their pay
cannot support them, and the hoped-for prize-money
was the only resource to extricate them." Pitt and
Dundas had not thought of this, being accustomed,
as Wellington said of a later Ministry, to regard officers
as stocks and stones. Moreover, Dundas had quite
forgotten, when delivering his homily upon rapacity
and oppression, that he had himself issued regulations
for the division of prize-money, and had sanctioned a
detailed scheme, drawn up by Grey at his own request,

1794. to meet all difficulties therein. Seizing upon this weak point, Grey plied him with the question, "If, according to the Advocate-General's opinion, none of our prize is lawful prize, why did you issue special rules for its distribution among us?" To this it need hardly be said that he received no satisfactory answer.

To anticipate the final close of the controversy, it may be added that Grey and Jervis determined to fight the matter out, and did so after their return with great success. The Government tried to evade the issue by shuffling and procrastination; whereupon Grey's eldest son, Charles, a most effective speaker, who is now remembered as Lord Grey of the Reform Bill, rose in the House of Commons to move for papers upon the subject. Then the Government decided to change its tone. The West India merchants very foolishly brought the matter before the House for their own purposes, whereupon both Ministry and Opposition united to crush them, and to repeat their sense of the good services of Grey and Jervis. Considering that Pitt had severely censured them both only twelve months before, and that Fox, in the precisely parallel affair of St. Eustatius in 1781, had found no abuse too violent for Rodney, the situation was inexpressibly ludicrous; but as long as politicians sacrifice justice to the winning of votes, so long must such situations continually recur. Finally, after endless obstruction, £378,000 was divided in 1806 between the captors, or rather between their representatives; and though the sum might seem large, it was not nearly large enough to provide sufficient pensions for all the women who were made widows in this campaign.[1]

This episode, coming at a time when Grey was hoping for reinforcements rather than rebukes, was not

[1] Dundas to Grey, 9th June; Grey to Dundas, 28th July, to Nepean, 29th July, to Portland, 15th September 1794; Grey to Nepean, 14th February, to Dundas, 2nd March; Jervis to Nepean, 9th and 11th February; statement of the case, 7th March; Grey to Dundas, 13th and 25th April, 1st May 1795; Hawkesbury to Dundas, 1st March 1796. In the *Grey MSS.*, most kindly thrown open to me by Lord Grey, there is a mass of papers on this subject.

cheering to him ; but such incidents were forgotten in 1794. his dismay over the frightful death-rate among the troops and the growing audacity of the bands of hostile negroes, which, in the Windward Islands as in St. Domingo, were known as the brigands. Constant patrolling by the black rangers alone repressed them in Martinique, where the white soldiers fit for duty on the 1st of September had shrunk to six hundred men ; and in St. Lucia it had been necessary to take the offensive against them. But the centre of greatest danger was of course Guadeloupe, where the ravages of yellow fever were appalling. The returns of the 1st of September show that of fifty-five companies of infantry and artillery in the camp of Berville three hundred and thirty men had died since the 1st of August, nearly fifteen hundred men were sick, and barely five hundred fit for duty. Grey sent a circular to the Governors of the various islands asking if between them they could raise for him fifteen hundred white men, but the deadly fever was not sparing the white man in any quarter ; and from every side came the answer that compliance with his request was impossible.

The French white troops must also without doubt have suffered extremely, for it was long before Hugues again took the offensive ; but at length, on the night of the 26th of September, a large body of troops, dis- Sept. 26. tributed among several small vessels, evaded the British ships in the darkness and disembarked in two bodies, one of them at Goyave, a little to the south of Petit Bourg, the other at Lamentin, on the north side of the isthmus which connects Grande Terre with Guadeloupe. Graham at once called every possible man to the camp at Berville, and strengthened his position to the utmost of his power ; but he had no more than two hundred and fifty regular troops and three hundred royalists fit to stand to arms, and even these were too much worn down by sickness to be called effective. He was therefore unable to check the enemy's advance. The French who had landed at Goyave at once marched

1794. north upon Petit Bourg, where lay the British hospital, with a weak guard of convalescents and royalists under Colonel Drummond. Unable to make any resistance, Drummond retired to Bacchus Point, the next headland to northward, while the men-of-war hastily sent out boats to remove the sick from the hospital; but the work was not completed before the French entered Petit Bourg and proceeded to massacre every sick man that they could find. Then, before Drummond and his party could be embarked, they surrounded Bacchus Point, where there was a small battery pointing to seaward, and compelled him and the little garrison, after spiking their guns, to surrender. The occupation of this point cut off communication between the camp of Berville and the British men-of-war; and the French, advancing from thence, effected their junction with their comrades at Lamentin, and took up positions which completely invested the camp on the side of the land.

The enemy at once began to construct batteries, one of which, situated on a slight eminence, partly commanded the camp; and at four o'clock on the morning of
Sept. 30. the 30th, under cover of a heavy cannonade, they delivered a furious and most determined assault. The British, of whom many were so weak that they could hardly crawl to their appointed places, fought with extraordinary spirit; some of the royalists who joined them in the lines behaved as worthily; and, after three hours' fighting, the enemy were beaten off with very heavy loss. The loss of the British was slight, but Graham was severely, and his second in command mortally, wounded. Moreover, on the same day the French gunboats forced the British shipping out of the bay of Petit Bourg; and Jervis, who had hurried to the scene of action from Martinique, found it impossible to reopen communication with the camp at Berville. What passed on the following day is extremely uncertain, for Graham, being wounded, was unable to see, and no one else appears to have survived to tell. There is reason, however, to believe that between the 29th of September and the 6th of October the

French assaulted the camp five several times, and that 1794. they acknowledged their force to have numbered three thousand, and their casualties to have been nine hundred. But after a week of such work the gallant little garrison could do no more. Two officers and twenty-five men had been killed, five officers and fifty-one men wounded ; and on the 6th of October, Graham, finding himself Oct. 6. hopelessly cut off from all help, his provisions reduced to two days' supply, and his men hardly able to stand, surrendered on condition that the British troops should march out with the honours of war and be shipped by first opportunity to Great Britain. Thereupon one hundred and twenty-five ghastly figures staggered out of the lines, "fitter for hospital than to be under arms,"—all that remained of what had once been three battalions and twenty-three companies of infantry and two companies of artillery.[1] For a whole year, despite the capitulation, they were detained as prisoners ; but they died so rapidly in the weeks that followed the surrender that probably few of them ever saw England again. Yet though the tale of their noble service must remain for ever but half told, the records of the British Army contain no grander example of heroism than this of the dying garrison of the Camp of Berville.[2]

Victor Hugues, as was natural, at once followed up his success. Having massacred the royalists, he moved southward with two thousand men along the coast of Guadeloupe upon Basseterre, devastating the estates and burning the houses of the planters as he went. At

[1] The troops represented in the surrender were the 1st battalions of Grenadiers and of Light Infantry, the 39th, 43rd, and 65th, each of ten companies, and three companies of the 56th.

[2] Grey to Dundas, 16th and 24th October 1794, the latter enclosing letters from Graham of 21st and 22nd October, with a plan on which are noted a few details of the defence. Willyams gives also an account at some length, but since it differs from that of Graham upon matters which occurred before Graham was wounded, and is inaccurate in one or two minor points, I hesitate to accept it. The three battalions mentioned in the text were the 39th, 43rd, and 65th.

1794. Basseterre lay Prescott with a weak and sickly force, which there was little means of strengthening; and, while sending to him every man that he could spare, Grey foresaw that, unless troops should arrive from England shortly, the whole island of Guadeloupe must be lost. In March he had first represented the need for speedy reinforcements; in July he had pressed urgently for at least six thousand men, adding that, if that number were impossible, at any rate twelve hundred should be sent out at once in men-of-war to save the delay of convoy. Yet not a man had arrived, and Dundas had only written late in September to say that three battalions were then sailing but had been delayed by weather.

October. News of the unrest among the negroes in all the British islands increased Grey's anxiety, and he warned Dundas that, unless he were immediately strengthened, there was no saying where the enemy's successes would end.[1] Prescott, meanwhile, upon hearing of Hugues's approach, destroyed all outlying batteries and posts, and drew all his men into the fort at the southern end of Basseterre town, called by the British Fort Matilda. Admiral Jervis also, on the 9th of October, anchored his flagship in Basseterre Road, promising to give him every assistance. But it would serve no purpose to give an account of the siege which followed. It must suffice to say that, though the fort was in the worst possible repair, Prescott with the help of the fleet contrived to hold it from the 14th

Dec. 10. of October till the 10th of December, when, most of his guns being dismounted and the defences practically in ruins, he managed by great skill to embark the whole of his garrison, about six hundred of all ranks, without loss, and to carry them safely to Martinique. Thus after a bare eight months of precarious tenure, Guadeloupe was lost.[2]

Nov. 27. A fortnight before the evacuation of Fort Matilda

---

[1] Grey to Dundas, 8th and 17th July, 19th and 24th October 1794.
[2] Grey to Portland, 6th November; Prescott to Vaughan and to Admiral Caldwell, 11th December 1794.

Grey and Jervis sailed home together in the *Boyne*, 1794. having been relieved by Sir John Vaughan and Admiral Caldwell. Both had long been quite worn out by hard work, anxiety, and distress over the mortality among their men ; Grey in particular having since October been so much weakened by dysentery that he could hardly drag himself out of bed. Devotedly attached to each other, they had worked together not only with good will but with enthusiasm ; and the result had been a perfection of harmony, and even of sympathy, between Army and Navy which is absolutely without a parallel in the annals of the two services. The astonishing success of the campaign, viewed as a whole, must be ascribed chiefly to the thoroughness of co-operation between General and Admiral ; for it extended from them through all ranks of their subordinates. General Prescott, for instance, a veteran of fifty years' service, though very capable and brave as a lion, was touchy and cantankerous to the last degree ; he was not well disposed towards the Navy, having had a dispute, and one not altogether unreasonable, with Hood at St. Kitts in 1781 ; and but for the firmness and tact of Grey he would have quarrelled even with him, having been very unwilling to take the command at Basseterre. Yet so loyally and unselfishly did Jervis and his officers throw themselves into the thankless and dangerous work of harassing the besiegers of Fort Matilda from the sea, that the old man fell to his task with joy, earned the respect of the whole squadron by the skill and gallantry of his defence, and after the evacuation of the place recorded his thanks to the Navy in terms of touching gratitude and admiration.

It is most noteworthy, also, that this good feeling between fleet and troops survived all the adversity which came at the close of the campaign. It would have been easy for either service to throw the blame of the failure at Point-à-Pitre upon the other ; but neither dreamed for a moment of doing so. Grey was far too popular among the seamen for them to rejoice in his

1794. failure, and too great an admirer of the Navy to permit the Army to say a disrespectful word of it. Dissimilar though Grey and Jervis were in many respects, both took the greatest care of their men, Grey extending to them a thoughtfulness which was perhaps foreign to the sterner nature of Jervis. Thus, after the storm of Fort Fleur d'Épée, an exhausted gunner threw himself upon the only table that had escaped destruction, and fell asleep; but, when Grey presently came to the table to write his despatches, he would not allow the man to be disturbed. On the other hand, it was Jervis who had the forethought to provide Teneriffe wine for his men, to save them from being poisoned with new rum, and Grey who caught eagerly at the idea and imitated him.[1] This care on the part of their commanders accounts for the sustained ardour of the men in toiling, as they did, for so long as they could stand upright, notwithstanding hardship, exhaustion, and the terrifying spectacle of comrades perishing by scores of yellow fever.

Altogether it was a very honourable campaign to Grey and Jervis, and, if it was brought to naught by the neglect and improvidence of the Ministry, the fault lay not with them. But the cost of life was appalling. Of the officers who sailed to Martinique with Grey, twenty-seven were killed or died of their wounds, and one hundred and seventy died of yellow fever and other diseases incident to the climate. Even the few that survived had almost all of them been stricken, and had gone home as invalids. Of the men it is impossible to give so accurate an account. All that can be said is that, when Vaughan took over the command, the British troops in the whole of the islands to windward, representing fourteen battalions and twenty-eight companies of infantry, five or six companies of artillery, and half a squadron of light dragoons, numbered in all just over two thousand rank and file fit for duty, and just over twelve hundred sick. It is to be gathered, therefore, that of Grey's original seven thousand men at least five

[1] Grey to Dundas, 17th December 1793.

thousand had perished. The losses of the Navy 1794. were also enormous, but it is impossible to reckon them even approximately. The transport-vessels suffered even more severely than the men-of-war, their casualties being reckoned at forty-six masters and eleven hundred men dead, chiefly of yellow fever. These poor fellows had borne no small share in the thankless duty of landing troops and stores and dragging artillery ashore, not unfrequently under heavy fire. If the losses of the Army, Navy, and transports be added together, it is probably beneath the mark to say that twelve thousand Englishmen were buried in the West Indies in 1794. And this was nothing new. Ever since Cromwell sent his expedition to Hispaniola in 1654, the rule had held good that to assemble any great number of white men together in the West Indies was the certain way to bring about an epidemic of yellow fever, which would not only annihilate them but destroy multitudes of the white settlers also. The records of these expeditions were as accessible to Ministers then as now; and they had full warning that on this occasion they would have to fight not only poor sickly Frenchmen, but the negro population of the West Indies. Yet they poured their troops into these pestilent islands, in the expectation that thereby they would destroy the power of France, only to discover, when it was too late, that they had practically destroyed the British Army.

CHAPTER XV

1794. So the fateful year 1794 passed away, leaving France exhausted indeed, but triumphant. Great though had been the sacrifices which she had made, yet it was not through them, but through the divisions among the Allies, that she had been saved; and the true cause of those divisions lay in Poland. The Prussian generals had dealt feebly and timidly with the insurrection, but in August a strong man from Russia, Suvorof, had come upon the scene; and after three months of fighting
Nov. 8. the fall of Warsaw crushed finally the hopes of the Polish patriots. This was the end of Poland, the helpless victim offered up for the safety of revolutionary France. Prussia and Austria at once came truckling to Russia's feet for a share of the spoil, each putting forth her claims in eager jealousy against the other; and the Empress Catherine, exulting in her position of arbiter between them, resolved not indeed to drive Prussia to desperation, but to favour Austria above her rival, since she needed Austrian help for the partition of Turkey. She therefore made her award of the despoiled territory in the proportion of two thousand square miles to Prussia, three thousand square miles, carved out of provinces which Prussia had claimed for her own, to Austria, and six thousand square miles to herself. King Frederick William in bitter disappointment refused to accept such
Dec. 1. a settlement, and despatched an emissary to Bâle to make peace with France, so that his hands might be free to vindicate his claims upon the two other powers by force of arms. Thugut likewise was at first dis-

satisfied with Austria's share in the plunder, but decided 1794. to yield if Russia would acquiesce in the exchange of Belgium for Bavaria, and the annexation of Venetia by the Emperor. Since Prussia sulkily held aloof, Russia and Austria arranged the partition of Poland without 1795. her; and on the 3rd of January 1795 the two parties Jan. 3. signed a secret agreement, mutually guaranteeing to defend each other in case of a Prussian attack. Further, in return for Russia's consent to the Bavarian exchange, to the acquisition of Venetia and to some profit from the dismemberment of Turkey, Austria renewed her alliance of 1782 with Russia in the event of a Turkish war.

Ignorant of these details, but full of resentment, King Frederick William, at the request of the French Government, pursued his negotiations at Paris. The Jan. 7. time was not wholly propitious, for the conquest of Holland had somewhat revived the old recklessness which had originally launched France into war. On the day after the Prussian negotiator's first interview with Jan. 8. the Committee of Public Safety, envoys arrived from the Prince of Orange to sue for peace, but were contemptuously dismissed for offering too little in exchange for it. The armies of Souham and Moreau, meantime, speedily placed the whole of Holland and the Dutch fleet at the disposal of France, and forced the Stadtholder to take refuge in England. The Committee of Public Safety thereupon took a high tone even with Prussia, insisting that the Rhine must become the eastern boundary of France; and Frederick William, dreading lest Austria should anticipate him in making a separate peace, was afraid to meet this demand by a rupture of the negotiations. The French, however, knowing in their hearts that the safety of the Republic depended on detaching Prussia from the Coalition, did not press him too hard; and by the end of January the two parties had reached a sufficiently good understanding to arrange that Möllendorf should not be molested on his retreat from the Rhine to Westphalia. Finally, on the 5th of April was signed the agreement April 5.

1795. known as the Treaty of Bâle. Hereby it was concluded that France should retain the Prussian provinces on the western bank of the Rhine, pending a final settlement at a general peace; and a secret article added that, if those provinces should pass definitely into the hands of France, Prussia should receive an indemnity. Some difficulty arose as to the line of demarcation to be laid down between the two states, France being unwilling to allow it to cover Hanover; but Prussia set this question at rest by engaging herself to enforce Hanover's neutrality by a military occupation of that kingdom with her own troops. Meanwhile Tuscany had already come to terms with France in February; and in March Spain also

Mar. 22. made overtures for a separate treaty, relinquishing them only under a threat from Grenville that peace with France would assuredly bring upon her war with England.

Thus the first Coalition, which had so formidably menaced the young Republic, was irretrievably wrecked; and, in spite of her exhaustion and extreme financial distress, the internal affairs of France had also mended somewhat since the fall of Robespierre and the end of

Aug. 15. the Terror. The Government was so reconstituted that the Convention itself became the centre of power; while the Committee of Public Safety, though still charged with the direction of foreign affairs and of war, sank to the level of one among many administrative sub-committees. There was a general reaction against Jacobinism and ruffianism; and an effort of the Jacobins

Sept. 6. to regain power in September accomplished little but to involve Carnot, Prieur and Lindet in the odium which was attached to all colleagues of Robespierre, and to

Nov. 9. drive them from office. At last, on the 9th of November, the Jacobin Club was attacked by the organised bands of the more respectable citizens, and was finally closed three days later. In the course of the next three weeks freedom of conscience was re-established, and the most absurd and pernicious of Robespierre's economic decrees repealed; and the country, relieved by the removal of these burdens, began slowly to recover.

Most important, perhaps, of all changes of feeling in 1795. France, was a general inclination to initiate a new policy towards La Vendée. The infernal columns of Turreau, while guilty of infamous cruelties, had suffered repeated defeats, and had been compelled to abandon Poitou 1794. and Anjou; whereupon Carnot, despite the opposition June. of Robespierre, had insisted on sending another General to carry on the war on more humane principles. The contest, however, continued, until in October General Oct. Canclaux declared in favour of Carnot's contention, that it was for the Government to make the first overtures to conciliate La Vendée. In Brittany the case was the same. There, though there was no general rising, bands had been organised by Count Joseph de Puisaye and Georges Cadoudal, which the French Government had found it impossible to put down; and Hoche, the ablest General in the French service, who had been appointed to subdue them, speedily came to the like conclusion with Canclaux. The matter was the more urgent, since both Vendeans and Bretons had entered into correspondence with England; and Puisaye, who, though devoid of military talent, was a very brave and adventurous enthusiast, had an address at once so weighty and so winning that it could hardly fail to make an impression on British Ministers. The Con- vention therefore in December proclaimed an amnesty Dec. for all who should lay down their arms within a month; and direct overtures were made to the Vendean leaders, Stofflet and Charette. The former declined to abandon 1795. the monarchy, but Charette in February 1795 signed an Feb. agreement whereby, in return for important concessions, he bound himself to recognise the Republic. Similar measures of conciliation in Brittany were equally success- ful; and all circumstances seemed to conspire to bring the lamentable struggle in the two provinces to an end.

These sensible reforms enraged the Jacobins beyond measure; and on the restoration of the banished Girond- ists to their seats in the Convention the extremists tried once again to recover their ascendancy by rousing

1795. the mob of Paris to insurrection. But they were firmly
April 2. repressed; and after this outbreak all traces of the Terror were effaced. Divine service in the churches, though forbidden by law, commenced again; emigrants began to return, and some of their confiscated property was restored. The Chouans in Brittany signed a treaty of peace,
May 2. and on the 2nd of May even Stofflet agreed to accept the same terms as Charette. Unfortunately, however, the Government had no efficient force with which to keep order. Savage reprisals were wreaked on the Terrorists in the south; while the Jacobins, taking advantage of the dearness of bread, kindled yet another rising against
May 20. the Convention in Paris, which was only suppressed after two days of riot and tumult. A new National Guard of respectable citizens was then organised, and extreme republicanism made way for a strong inclination towards the Constitution of 1791. This revulsion of feeling was foolishly construed by the Bourbons as a reaction in favour of the old order. They could have made no greater blunder. The Revolution did indeed change its character after the Terror. The reign of popular idols and of great impostors was over. The men who had played leading parts had all been massacred or exiled; and there was no emulation among those who came after them to share such a fate. No man therefore aspired to the dangerous station of a leader, and, in fact, to use the words of Sainte Beuve, the rule of leaders gave place to the rule of schemers. Still the Convention remained collectively a formidable body. Albeit composed of pigmies, yet, as Mallet du Pan said, "when it acted under a common impulse, it possessed the herculean strength of a man in delirium." The people too, though disillusioned and longing for rest and peace, still retained their passion for equality and their consuming hatred of tyranny; while the troops in the field, whatever their political differences at home, forgot everything in the presence of the enemy except their common jealousy for the honour of the Fatherland.

Such was the condition of France; and such, visible

in its broad outline though not yet clearly defined, the 1795. prospect which confronted the British Ministry at the beginning of 1795. The Coalition was dissolved in bitterness and disaster. In the Mediterranean the British had indeed gained Corsica, but they held it by a most precarious tenure. In the West Indies they had taken Guadeloupe, Martinique, and St. Lucia to windward; but they had already lost Guadeloupe, and in the two remaining islands they could hardly hold their own. They had also obtained a footing to leeward in St. Domingo; but the want of troops to hold the ports on the southern coast gave the French privateers the opportunity to inflict very considerable losses on British trade. Moreover, the waste of men had been enormous. Both from windward and leeward the British Generals were crying urgently for reinforcements; and General Vaughan had written from Martinique that if the Government relied upon white troops alone in the West Indies, the whole army of Great Britain would not suffice to defend them.[1] The whole army of Great Britain was a term of derision by the time when Vaughan's letter reached Dundas, for practically all the regular troops worthy of the name had been destroyed; and yet, after the disasters of the Allies in the Low Countries, even the distress of the Generals in the West Indies could not entitle them to the first claim for help. Holland was lost, the English party in the Netherlands extinguished, and the French party omnipotent; and England's old continental policy was brought to naught. Formerly England and the United Provinces had been ranked together as the Maritime Powers; now the term had no longer any meaning. The Dutch patriots abolished the form of Government which had been the triumph of Harris's diplomacy in 1787, published a proclamation as to the rights of man, and reconstituted the administration more or less upon the principles of the Revolution. There was no mistaking the tendency of these innova-

[1] Vaughan to Dundas, 25th December 1794.

1795.
May 15.
tions; and it can have been little surprise to the British Ministry when, on the 15th of May, France concluded with the Dutch Republic an alliance offensive and defensive, whereby she gained the use of the Dutch fleet, the maintenance, at Holland's expense, of twenty-five thousand men, nominally as garrisons for the Dutch fortresses, and a contribution of four and a half millions sterling.

But, even if Holland were lost, there might be hope of saving the Dutch colonies; and as early as on the 4th of January 1795 one of the house of Baring wrote to urge upon Dundas the importance of seizing the Cape of Good Hope, to say nothing of other Dutch possessions, before the French could lay hands upon them. Dundas's familiarity with Indian affairs and, to his credit it must be added, his peculiar appreciation of the value of our Indian Empire, made him alert to see the danger. Negotiations were at once opened with the exiled Stadtholder; and on the 7th of February the Prince of Orange on his behalf wrote directions to the Governor and to the officer commanding the Dutch fleet at the Cape, to admit the British troops and ships as allies, and, if the British naval officers were senior, to place the Dutch ships under their orders. A similar order was also given to the Dutch colonies in the Indian seas, the British Government, upon its side, agreeing to restore them upon a general peace. Captain Blankett, having greater knowledge of the Indian seas than any other officer, was selected to command the squadron bound to the Dutch settlements, and he was instructed to take with him as many soldiers of the Seventy-eighth[1] as he could embark upon his ships, and to sail at once, together with Major-general Craig, to the Cape. If the Dutch resisted him, he was authorised either to employ force at once, or to await a reinforcement of more ships and three more battalions, which would follow him as soon as possible; but the vital point was that any troops despatched by the French

[1] The second battalion.

party in Holland should be intercepted. If the enter- 1795. prise should fail, he was to proceed to San Salvador, better known to us now as Bahia, in Brazil, there to await the arrival of the main body of the expedition. At the same time orders were despatched to the Commander-in-Chief and Senior Naval Officer in the East Indies to secure in like manner, by the Stadtholder's authority, the Dutch territories in that quarter. Among these preference was to be given to Cochin, Ceylon, and the Moluccas; but supreme importance was wisely attached to the exclusion of the French from Trincomalee.[1]

Here, therefore, despite the hostages already given to fortune in the West Indies, and the desperate situation of the British troops there both to windward and leeward, Dundas added to all existing embarrassments yet another sphere of operations and further responsibility both for administration and defence. On the whole, however, it seems to me that some justification can be pleaded for his policy. In the first place, it was important to sever French communication with India; and in the second, there were to be considered not only the direct inconvenience and danger that would accrue from the occupation of the Cape itself by a hostile power, but the indirect bearing of such occupation upon the capability of Mauritius for mischief. At the moment Mauritius was innocuous from want of means to fit out cruisers; but with the Cape at hand to supply her she would become, as she had become once before, from 1695 to 1697, a nest of privateers, secure and unassailable except among their own rocks.[2] More-

[1] Francis Baring to Dundas, 4th and 12th February; Prince of Orange to Governor and Naval Commander at the Cape, 7th February; Dundas to Blankett and to Craig, 16th February; to Commander-in-Chief and Naval Officer commanding East Indies, 19th February 1795. The original letter of the Stadtholder to his Minister at St. James's ordering the delivery of the Dutch colonies to the British is among the *Dropmore MSS.*

[2] Blankett to Dundas, 25th January 1794. For the damage done to our Indian trade in William III.'s reign see *Cal. S. P. Col.* 1696-97, 1697-98.

1795. over the duty of finding garrisons for all the conquered places, excepting the Cape, was made over to the Commander-in-Chief in the East Indies, so that the drain of British troops was not likely to be great. None the less Dundas, who had been so reckless already in flinging his troops into the tropics, contrived that this expedition should involve, as shall be seen in due time, sacrifices which need never have been necessary.

By cutting down the numbers of his seamen to the lowest point, and refusing to embark the soldiers' wives, who, in the proportion of five to each company, then and long after accompanied every regiment on active service, Blankett contrived to pack rather over five hundred men of the Seventy-eighth on board the four ships that composed his squadron. Craig begged for two battalion-guns for them, but was answered that none were to be spared; and ultimately, after protracted delay owing to contrary winds, March. the squadron sailed in the beginning of March. The preparations for the despatch of the main expedition had gone forward before Blankett started, and Dundas, uneasy over the long detention of the advanced ships, decided that the principal squadron should also sail direct to the Cape, without waiting for the embarkation of the troops. Captain Elphinstone, the Commodore, was therefore ordered to make his way forthwith to the Cape, with discretion to take the colony by force if surrender should be refused; but the troops were not to follow until later, making Bahia their first port of call, where Elphinstone might leave a convoy to escort them onward if he thought fit. If the Colony surrendered, or if the previous arrival of the French made his enterprise impossible, he was to proceed at once to Madras in order to secure the Dutch colonies in the East Indies. With these instructions Elphinstone sailed not many days after Blankett. By the beginning of May the troops also were ready, namely, the Eighty-fourth, Ninety-first, and Edmeston's Foot,[1] numbering two thousand five hundred men, in addition to the five hundred sent forward with Craig. Major-general Alured Clarke was in command, and his instructions, like Elphinstone's, bade him keep in view the ulterior purposes of the expedition in the East Indies, as well as the immediate object at the Cape. But, though free and even copious in the matter of instructions, Dundas was less profuse in the matter of money, and the unfortunate General, despite his entreaties, was despatched to sea without any military chest whatever.[2]

1795.

As fate ordained it, Blankett's ships were condemned to a tedious passage, and on arriving off the Cape on the 10th of June, fell in by great good fortune with Elphinstone's squadron. On the 12th the entire fleet anchored in False Bay; and Craig and Elphinstone sent a joint letter, enclosing the orders of the Prince of Orange to the Council of Regency which wielded the government at Cape Town. The answer was singularly vague. The Council undertook to supply the fleet with provisions, but deprecated the landing of men, except in small parties and unarmed; they professed gratitude for British protection, and declared that they would invoke the fleet's assistance in case of attack; but at the same time they intimated that they were in a position to defend themselves, and requested the British commanders to oblige them with a statement of the strength of their army. Ascertaining that Dutch troops were encamped at a pass that guarded the road to Cape Town, Craig and Elphinstone quickly divined that force would be necessary to obtain possession of the Colony, and at once despatched a vessel not only to hasten the coming of Clarke's battalions, but to bring every man who could be spared from St. Helena.

June 12.

[1] The 91st was then numbered the 98th, and Edmeston's was numbered 95th. The battalions of the 78th and 84th were each of them the second of those regiments.
[2] Blankett to Dundas, 25th and 28th February; Dundas to Craig, 2nd March; to Elphinstone, 21st March; to Clarke, 4th May; Clarke to Huskisson, 7th and 12th May 1795.

1795. The Cape Colony indeed was at that time in a very curious condition. It had been founded in 1652 by the Dutch East India Company. Three years later certain Dutch soldiers and sailors obtained grants of land in the interior and became the first free burghers of the Cape. The Company was not a good master; and with an unlimited country behind them, the burghers acquired the evil habit of withdrawing themselves from its control, and "trekking" away from its authority as fast as it was extended to reach them. In 1793 matters had come to a climax. The Company, not content with levying exorbitant taxes and enforcing oppressive monopolies, had instituted a paper-currency, which it had employed so ingeniously for purposes of extortion and tyranny that it had driven the burghers almost into rebellion. There were, when the British anchored in False Bay, three different parties in Cape Colony: firstly, the few monopolists who represented the Company; secondly, the French party, which included the principal merchants and inhabitants of Cape Town; and thirdly, the back-settlers or Boers, who had determined to set up an independent republic. The people at large were, as Craig said, "infested with the rankest poison of Jacobinism," and, though the Company had been able to terrorise them in Cape Town, the country districts, and notably Graaf Reinet, were in open revolt. They longed indeed for the arrival of their allies from France; and, the British squadron having been mistaken for the French, the Boer militia had swarmed down into the town, to the terror of the servants of the detested Company. It was, however, certain that not one of the three parties was friendly to the British; wherefore, having no artillery to match against an excellent train possessed by the Dutch, the British

June 18. commanders decided to temporise. They waited on the Governor, but found that he received the Stadtholder's letter with studied neglect, and that the Stadtholder's name was the reverse of a recommendation to his good offices. They thereupon took note that the Company's paper-money, nominally worth a quarter 1795. of a million sterling, was depreciated fifty per cent; they insinuated that, whereas the French could only give paper for paper, the English might liquidate the whole in cash. They could have used no subtler nor more telling diplomacy.

On the 28th of June there arrived at the Cape two June 28. vessels under American colours, with orders from the French Convention for all Dutch ships to assemble in French ports, and for the proclamation of the doctrines of the Revolution in the Colony. These documents were promptly seized and impounded by Elphinstone. But meanwhile the Governor on the 27th refused to supply June 27. more fresh provisions to the British, and drove in all the cattle from the country between the Cape of Good Hope and Cape Town, so as to ensure that the invaders should take no fresh meat for themselves. This was annoying because there was much scurvy on board the fleet; and Craig, having no money, could not buy from persons who were inclined to be friendly. However, since the Dutch could place eight hundred regular troops and two thousand militia in the field, and Craig could bring but sixteen hundred soldiers and seamen to meet them, there was nothing for him but to possess his soul in patience. Moreover the attitude of the Governor became daily more hostile. He had already ordered June 30. the inhabitants to withdraw from Simonstown, and he now threatened to burn it, whereupon Craig on the 14th of July occupied it with three hundred and fifty July 14. of the Seventy-eighth and four hundred and fifty marines. A few days later shots were fired at his patrols by the Boer militia and Hottentots on the surrounding hills; and Craig and Elphinstone, who worked most cordially together, decided to open the road to Cape Town without further delay. Two battalions of seamen were disembarked, making the land-force up to sixteen hundred men; and, after many days delay through foul winds, the smaller vessels of the squadron at noon on the 7th of August stood in Aug. 7.

1795.
Aug. 7.
towards the western shore of False Bay, preceded by a gunboat and the launches of the fleet, armed with carronades. At the same time Craig began his march northward along the coast from Simonstown, taking care to keep the flotilla always a hundred yards in advance of his column.

In truth the operation thus initiated would not have been an easy one against a well-trained enemy. For six miles the road from Simonstown to Cape Town runs along the shore, closely pent in between high hills and the sea. At the point where it turns inland from the beach, the only outlet lies through a defile formed by the flat-topped mountain called the Muizenberg, which rises to a height of sixteen hundred feet on the western side, and by a broad lagoon on the eastern side. The Dutch were encamped in a strong position for the defence of this defile, and having plenty of artillery had erected batteries to bear upon the ships as well as to command the approaches by land. Craig, on the other hand, had, despite his remonstrances, been sent from England without a single gun of any description. The fire of the flotilla, however, told quickly upon the nerves of the defenders. After a few shots the enemy abandoned in quick succession a seaward battery of two heavy guns and a seaward advanced post containing two howitzers and a field-gun; and when the ships turned their cannon upon the main camp from as close range as the shallowness of the water would permit, the Dutch hastily retreated, carrying off the rest of their artillery before Craig was within reach to prevent them. They rallied, however, on the ridge of steep and rocky heights a little beyond their camp, but were driven on, notwithstanding the protection afforded by a battery on the other side of the lagoon, by the light company of the Seventy-eighth. The skirmishing ended only with sunset, and at the close of the day Craig found himself stronger than he had been at the beginning by the possession of five pieces of ordnance.

Aug. 8. On the following morning the enemy, having drawn

out all their forces from Cape Town, advanced with 1795. eight guns to attack Craig, but finding him strongly posted and being received with fire from their own captured cannon, they prudently withdrew. On the morrow arrived a ship from St. Helena with four Aug. 9. hundred men and nine field-pieces for the British, but with little ammunition; and the following days were given up to the landing and transporting of supplies and stores,—a work of extreme difficulty since there were neither vehicles nor animals, and consequently everything had to be carried by the men. The question of transport was indeed that which made the capture of Cape Town an almost insoluble problem. The enemy was evidently disposed to offer a stubborn resistance, and Craig had insufficient soldiers even to meet him on the battlefield. If, therefore, by happy chance he succeeded in penetrating to Cape Town, he could still spare no troops to guard the twelve miles of road that separated him from his base at Simon's Bay, so as to ensure the regular transmission of supplies; while the season forbade the ships to enter Table Bay and open a shorter line of communication. He tried to surprise the militia on the 27th of August, in the hope of kindling a panic Aug. 27. among the burghers, but the venture failed owing to the ignorance and timidity of the guides; and the only result was to stimulate the enemy to such vigilance as to destroy all hope of a second, more successful, attempt.

Meanwhile burghers and Hottentots continued daily to fire at long range upon the camp from the surrounding hills, and on the 1st of September inflicted some Sept. 1. loss upon a picquet which had been more careful to take shelter from their bullets than to observe their movements. Supplies were now beginning to fail, and Craig had made up his mind to a desperate attack at all hazards within six days, when on the 3rd the enemy, Sept. 3. encouraged by their little success on the 1st, advanced against his position with every possible man and eighteen field-guns. Craig had made all preparations to receive them, when at the critical moment the signal of a fleet

1795. in the offing caused the Dutch to hesitate; and the appearance of fourteen ships decided them to abandon their project and to retire. The fleet proved to be the transports bringing Clarke's battalions from Bahia, where Elphinstone's despatch-vessel had found them on the 22nd of July. The men were soon landed; and then once again the entire force, both soldiers and seamen, was employed in the work of beasts of burden, dragging up through deep sand stores sufficient to form a depot at Muizenberg for the final advance. The labour was most trying, and the situation was the more anxious for the commanders, since no provision of bread and spirits had been brought by Clarke's force, and consequently the entire army was thrown upon the fleet for its supplies. This was no fault of Clarke, who had pressed upon the Government his need of a commissary and funds; rather, it was only another among many examples of the improvidence with which the Government sent expeditions to sea.

However, the commanders were fain to make the best of things as they found them, and to put both fleet and army upon short allowance. The magazine was with great difficulty formed, and on the 14th a sufficient guard was left to protect it, while the main body advanced upon Cape Town without a draught-animal of any description whatever. The men carried four days' supplies; the guns were dragged by volunteers from the crews of the transports; and all supplies, stores, and ammunition were transported by the labour of the seamen and soldiers of the expedition. The Boers hovered around the column, mounted with rifles of large bore and long range; and, the ground being favourable for their tactics, Clarke dreaded lest his column should be greatly harassed on the march. But the light company of the Seventy-eighth knew the work of true light infantry; a light company of seamen formed by Craig, under the command of Lieutenant Campbell of H.M.S. *Echo*, proved itself quite as efficient as the Seventy-eighth; and the precautions taken by the

Sept. 14.

General were so sound, that the march of six miles 1795. to Wynberg cost but one man killed and seventeen wounded. At Wynberg the enemy were assembled in force with nine guns in a strong position; but, being threatened in front and on both flanks, and alarmed by the sailing of three ships into Table Bay, they retired before the British could reach the top of the hill to close with them. Clarke pursued them for two miles, when, his overburdened troops being unable to go further, he halted and bivouacked for the night where he stood. On the following morning the Governor asked for Sept. 15. forty-eight hours to arrange a capitulation; but within twenty-four the Colony and town were surrendered, the British undertaking to maintain the paper-money at its existing value. The casualties of all ranks of the British did not exceed four killed and sixty wounded. The regular troops of the enemy, which were made prisoners, numbered six hundred infantry and four hundred artillery; and, had there been unity and good feeling among the inhabitants of the Colony, the British force could never have achieved this success. Meanwhile the story of the expedition is particularly worthy the study of civilians as exemplifying the difficulty of carrying on operations, even when the line of communications is but twelve miles long, without transport. The lesson, as shall be seen, was entirely thrown away upon Dundas the unteachable.[1]

Nevertheless, the situation was not by any means cleared up by the surrender. With the exception of a few merchants, the entire Colony was hostile to the British; and Craig reported that, should a French force arrive, every Dutchman would give it assistance if he dared. The Dutch gunners were to a man infected with Jacobinism; and several of the Boers went away in arms, accompanied by a French sedition-monger, declaring that they would not submit to the capitula-

[1] Elphinstone to Dundas, 15th August, 12th and 23rd September; Craig to same, 21st September; Clarke to same, 22nd September 1795.

1795. tion. These burghers were the despair of Craig. "It is hardly possible," he wrote, "to convey an idea of the ignorance, the credulity, and the stupid pride of the people, and particularly of the Boers. The most absurd ideas as to their strength and importance are prevalent among them, nor indeed is there any opinion on any subject too ridiculous or too grossly unjust not to be adopted by them, if recommended by a few of the popular leaders." Dundas in his instructions, which were founded on most erroneous information, had signified to Elphinstone and Clarke that half of their force would suffice amply to hold the place; but both Clarke and Craig agreed that it would be unsafe to reduce the garrison below three thousand men, and that consequently no troops could be spared for India. It was decided, therefore, that not a soldier should be withdrawn, though three ships under Blankett's command would furnish a sufficient naval force for the station. Accordingly, upon the 15th of November Elphinstone and Clarke sailed with the rest of the fleet for Madras.[1]

Nov. 15.

But the initiative against the Dutch colonies had been taken in India long before their arrival. The outbreak of war with France had led to the usual attack upon Pondicherry, which had surrendered, after a siege of twelve days, on the 22nd August 1793.[2] At the end of April 1794 an expedition to Mauritius was projected, but abandoned; and then all operations were suspended until the conquest of Holland by France. The first step after this event was taken from England by a Mr. Hugh Cleghorn, who at his own request started for Switzerland to secure the detachment of a Swiss regiment, the property of M. de Meuron, from the

[1] Craig to Dundas, 23rd September, 9th October, 23rd December; Clarke to Dundas, 24th September and 11th October; Elphinstone to Dundas, 10th October 1795.

[2] The force engaged numbered over ten thousand men, of whom over four thousand were Europeans of the 19th L.D., Royal Artillery, 36th, 52nd, 72nd, 73rd, 102nd, and the whole or part of two more battalions of Madras Europeans.

service of the Dutch East India Company. Taking 1795. de Meuron with him, Cleghorn flew to India with all possible speed, arrived too late to save the two companies at Cochin, but secured five companies at Colombo in the nick of time. By October 1795 de Meuron's regiment, numbering nearly one thousand good soldiers, had passed into the British service.[1]

The news of the conquest of Holland did not reach Calcutta until June, but was no sooner received than preparations were begun to despatch forces against Ceylon and the Dutch possessions in Malacca. The force for Ceylon consisted of the Seventy-second, and the flank-companies of the Seventy-first and Seventy-third, making about eleven hundred Europeans, inclusive of artillery, besides two battalions of Native Infantry; the whole being under the command of Colonel James Stuart of the Seventy-second. Sailing from Madras on the 30th of July and convoyed by the East Indian Squadron under Commodore Rainier, the armament anchored in a bay to the north of the fort of Trincomalee on the 1st of August. As at Cape Aug. 1. Town, the Commodore refused to surrender the place; and accordingly the troops disembarked and dragged up their supplies and stores over three miles of sandy beach without the slightest molestation. The fort being too strong to be carried by assault, ground was broken on the evening of the 18th; the batteries opened fire on the 23rd; and on the 26th the garrison, Aug. 26. numbering over thirteen hundred of all ranks, capitulated. Fort Oostenburg, the other principal defence of the place, with a garrison of two hundred and fifty men, thereupon surrendered also; and Trincomalee passed into the hands of the British at cost of about seventy men, native and European, killed and wounded.

The force was then broken up for the time in order to capture various outlying settlements on the coast. The fort at Batticaloa surrendered to a detachment of

[1] *R.O. Col. Corres. Ceylon,* 1.

1795. the Seventy-second on the 18th of September; Jaffna-
Sept. 18. patam, close to the northern extremity of the island,
Sept. 24. fell on the 24th to Stuart himself with the flank-companies of the Seventy-first and Seventy-third and a few companies of Native Infantry; Moeletivoe, a little to the east of the northern extremity, capitulated
Oct. 1. to a detachment of the Fifty-second on the 1st of October; the fort and island of Manaar on the west coast, about forty miles south of Jaffnapatam, was captured by detachments of the Seventy-first and
Oct. 5. Seventy-third on the 5th of October; and Calpentyn, about fifty miles south of Manaar, was surrendered to a
Nov. 13. small body of native troops on the 13th of November. After some delay owing to the north-east monsoon, the troops were again assembled at Negombo, about twenty miles north of Colombo, at the beginning of February 1796, and reinforced by fresh regiments from Madras and Bombay; those from the latter place having captured Cochin on their way. Finally, with
1796. a total strength of about two thousand Europeans[1]
Feb. 7. and four thousand native troops, Stuart on the 7th began his march upon Colombo. The enemy had erected batteries to bar his passage of the river Malwan, but evacuated them without resistance; nor was it until the British were within a day's march of the
Feb. 12. town that the Dutch attacked a post held by the flank-companies of the Seventy-third, and were driven off with loss. On the 12th likewise the British fleet
Feb. 15. anchored in the harbour; and on the 15th Colombo, though defended by a garrison of nearly three thousand fighting men, capitulated without resistance. Thus Ceylon was mastered with little difficulty; and the expedition to Malacca, which had sailed for its destination on the same day, was fully as successful. The fort at Malacca fell on the 18th of August 1795; and detachments from thence took possession of Amboyna on the 17th of February, and of Banda in the beginning of March 1796. With this, to antici-

[1] 52nd, 72nd, 73rd, 77th. The 72nd did not march to Colombo.

pate matters somewhat, the conquest of the Dutch East 1796.
Indian possessions was practically complete.

The whole of these operations were, however, desul- 1795.
tory and, in a manner, negative. They prevented France
indeed from reaping the full advantages arising from the
conquest of Holland, but they could do her no actual
damage. They could not react in the slightest degree,
so far as France was concerned, upon the state of affairs
in the West Indies, nor could they simplify—rather
indeed they complicated—the military problems which
in England clamoured loud for solution. It was all very
well to send little expeditions to the Dutch possessions,
and to gain a little cheap credit by the publication of
such successes in the *Gazette*; but the fact remained
that Ministers had deliberately selected the West Indies
as the principal sphere of active operations. They
had already so far neglected this sphere as to allow a
French expedition to reach Guadeloupe from Rochefort,
without sending a single man to General Grey to
enable him to combat it; and the result had been, as
they knew, that Guadeloupe had been converted into
a hot-bed for the propagation of revolutionary doctrines,
and into the headquarters of a general rising of the
blacks against the whites. The mere escape of this
expedition from Rochefort was something of a reproach
upon the naval administration; yet another reinforcement of sixteen ships and six thousand men, bound
for Point-à-Pitre, sailed from Brest on the 17th of
November 1794; and once more there was not a British
ship at hand to molest it. The simple truth was that
the state of the Navy at this time was as bad as that of
the Army, and from precisely the same causes, namely,
under-payment of the men and persistent neglect of
the service by the Government.

At the beginning of 1795 it became obvious that the
war could be carried on in no satisfactory way by the
system of temporary expedients and makeshifts which
had hitherto been the only resource of Ministers. A
step was therefore taken towards the re-establishment

1795. of the Army's discipline and efficiency by the appointment of the Duke of York to be Field Marshal Commanding-in-Chief, in the room of Lord Amherst, who
Feb. 13. had hitherto acted as the head of the Army with the title of General on the Staff. To whom this appointment was due is uncertain. The Duke was not popular nor held in any very high esteem in the country, for it was the fashion to ascribe all the misfortunes in the Low Countries to him; and Pitt, when moving the King for his recall, hinted that unless the Duke relinquished his command, his conduct would inevitably be severely censured in Parliament "to the disadvantage of the Government and the obstruction of the vigorous conduct of the war." It seems probable, therefore, that the King himself was primarily responsible for the selection of the Duke; and, if this be so, the act was one of the most useful of his reign. At the same time Lord Cornwallis was appointed Master-General of the Ordnance in place of the Duke of Richmond, receiving therewith a seat in the Cabinet, which gave him, as he acknowledged, almost the entire military responsibility in Council. He sneered at the appointment of the Duke of York, as was perhaps natural; but the sequel will show which was really the more valuable servant, Cornwallis as the military adviser of the Government, or the Duke of York as the military administrator of the Army.[1]

The next question was that of men, a question affecting the Duke of York more closely than Cornwallis. When the Duke took over the command, an invasion of England was looked upon as certain; in fact Cornwallis "could not see what else the French could do";[2] yet at the end of February, the entire force in England, Regulars, Militia, and Fencibles, numbered but ten

---

[1] Pitt to the King, 23rd November 1794. I am indebted to Mr. Hubert Hall for the opportunity of taking a copy of this letter, which for long was undiscoverable. *Cornwallis Correspondence*, ii. 283-287.

[2] *Cornwallis Correspondence*, ii. 285.

thousand cavalry and fifty thousand infantry, whereas the Commanders of the various districts, apart from London, then reported their requirements to be seventy-six thousand infantry and eleven thousand cavalry It was true that the return of thirty battalions from the Continent was shortly expected, but these could not be reckoned at more than twelve thousand men, whereas twenty-six thousand were wanted. In Scotland again, there were but four thousand infantry and fifteen hundred cavalry, whereas there were needed ten thousand infantry and two thousand cavalry. Nor was this the worst. The creation of innumerable new corps of infantry had completely prevented the recruiting of the old regiments ; and these new corps, though nearly complete, were not only composed of the worst material, but were undisciplined to the point even of open mutiny, owing to the ignorance and inexperience of their officers. The Duke quickly decided to end this state of affairs by disbanding the new corps and drafting their men into the old regiments; but this could not be done at a stroke, and even when accomplished did not make raw recruits immediately into soldiers.

Moreover, there arose the question how more men were to be found when these were exhausted. On the 20th of October 1794 the Government had suddenly sanctioned the raising of fifteen battalions of Fencible infantry on a single day, and had added to them twelve more battalions before the end of the year. Being then apparently at its wits' end to obtain recruits for the regulars, it had made in December a contract with an individual, bearing the rank of Captain, to supply four thousand recruits from Ireland at twenty guineas a head. This last measure was a climax of wickedness and folly, leading to deeds of atrocity and crime of which old officers even sixty years later could not speak without shame and indignation.[1] It was found too that fraudulent recruiting agents were abroad, and

[1] *S.C.L.B.*, 20th October, 15th November, 8th December 1794 ; Bunbury, *Great War with France,* p. xxi.

1795. it was consequently necessary in March to cancel all beating-orders for the time. Then in May 1795 all recruiting for the Army was practically suspended, owing to the demand for seamen. No fewer than four Acts were passed in the spring of that year to facilitate the manning of the Navy—one to raise men in the ports of England, another to levy them in the counties of Scotland, a third to sweep in all rogues and vagabonds, and a fourth to draw seafaring men from the Militia. But the Fencibles, as well as the Militia, had encroached upon the Navy's supply of recruits; and an order was necessary to make the Commanding Officers disgorge them. Finally, it appears that in June there were no fewer than fifteen regiments serving in the fleet. It is hardly surprising that, though the Admiralty had been transferred in December 1794 from the indolent rule of Lord Chatham to the more efficient and energetic Lord Spencer, the operations of the Navy during the first six months of 1795 should have been of the feeblest description.[1]

It will easily be understood that amid such confusion as this there was little hope of reducing matters speedily to order. The Duke of York knew exactly what he wanted, namely, to reduce the number of regiments, which had risen to one hundred and thirty-five of infantry, to the figure of at most one hundred; to make up the whole of the battalions to an uniform strength; to give them two depot-companies in order to facilitate the work of recruiting, and to make any new battalions into second battalions for existing regiments. But the recruiting market had been so completely demoralised that it was difficult to formulate any definite scheme; and there was no addition to the Army worthy of notice in the first six months of 1795, beyond that of four regiments of Light Dragoons. These, formed by drafts both from the old regiments of

---

[1] Duke of York to Dundas, 24th February and 29th July; Sir A. Gordon to Duke of York, 13th March; *C.C.L.B.*, 11th April; *S.C.L.B.*, 24th June 1795.

cavalry and from the new ephemeral corps of infantry, 1795, raised the corps of Light Dragoons to twenty-nine in all.[1]

The increase of this arm was due in part, probably, to the projected despatch of a number of Light Dragoons to the West Indies,—in part to the fact that the whole of the cavalry of the army of Flanders was still, for no possible advantage, detained in Germany. The Treaty of Bâle had broken up the entire defence of North Germany by withdrawing Prussia from the contest; and there was practically no shelter for Hanover except behind the line of demarcation which had been accepted for his own selfish ends by King Frederick William. To obtain this shelter it was necessary for Hanover to adopt neutrality under Prussian protection, which could not but offend Austria and discourage all combatants against France; but on the other hand the country was too weak to contend single-handed with France, and it was absurd to think that three thousand British cavalry could be of the slightest assistance. Yet this tiny body of British troops was kept in Germany until the end of 1795, when, owing to the acceptance of neutrality by the Hanoverian Regency, they were at last brought back to England. Dundas, however, had high hopes of making use of them, while abroad, as a recruiting agency, and counted upon raising a number of foreign regiments for service in the West Indies. He was disappointed. The crimps of all nations were upon the spot; and both the King of Prussia and the Hanoverian Regency threw every obstacle in the way of the British, both in the matter of recruiting and embarking the levies. Dundas had hoped to gather up a great many Dutch soldiers who were still loyal to the House of Orange; but here again Prussia and the Hanoverian Regency interposed, and though officers were procurable, it was impossible to secure many men. In all, however, it seems that nineteen corps of cavalry and infantry, French and

[1] S.C.L.B., 30th March 1795.

1795. German, were embarked for England from the Elbe before the end of the year.[1] The Dutch, of whom some eight hundred officers and three thousand men were receiving British pay, were left behind, though with promises that a Dutch corps would yet be formed in the Isle of Wight, and that employment would be found for some of them in that refuge of the destitute foreigner, the Sixtieth Regiment.

But, once again, all these shifts at home and abroad were of no profit to the West Indies, from which quarter, as shall presently be told, the accounts became worse and worse. The officers on the spot had repeatedly pointed out the remedy, namely, to form regiments of negroes; and Grey had set the example by actually organising his corps of black rangers in Martinique. Nor does it seem that the Government itself was adverse to this policy on principle, for Grenville, upon the menace of war with Spain in the matter of Nootka Sound, had suggested the formation of black corps in Jamaica even in 1790.[2] But the British slave-owners in the West Indies lived in mortal terror of their negroes, and dreaded above all any measure which could in the slightest degree improve their social standing or increase their self-respect. They could use the vast wealth of West Indian trade to work upon the financial susceptibilities of Pitt; they could employ their command of rotten boroughs to play upon the tenderest feelings of Dundas; and they had the powerful West Indian Committee in London to turn these powers to the best account. British Ministers, for some mysterious reason, have never yet had the courage to stand up against the West Indian merchants; and Dundas, as has been seen from his ready acceptance of the accusations against Grey and Jervis, was no excep-

[1] Harcourt to Henry Dundas, 18th April; David Dundas to Henry Dundas, 6th, 11th, 14th, 31st July, 13th August, 12th November; Henry Dundas to David Dundas, 21st, 31st July and 20th September 1795.

[2] Grenville to Effingham, 6th and 23rd October; 6th November 1790.

tion. He wrote, therefore, in February to Vaughan at 1795. Martinique forbidding further levies of black troops; stating vaguely that there was much objection to the employment of them in large numbers, and that in his own opinion it would be a dangerous measure to match them, at so critical a moment, against men of their own race.[1] Considering that three Generals upon the spot, Grey, Williamson, and Vaughan, besides several of their subordinates, had agreed that the only chance of saving the West Indies lay in the raising of black regiments, this calm assertion of the superior wisdom of Downing Street was certainly a marvellous example of assurance. But it was much more than this. It was a deliberate renunciation of the only resource whereby Ministers could hope to pursue their chosen military policy.

Yet, notwithstanding the rapid growth of danger in the West Indies, and the gigantic obligations so recklessly incurred in that quarter; notwithstanding the additional responsibility undertaken by the annexation of the Cape; notwithstanding the fact that there was hardly a battalion in England really fit to take the field,—Ministers were still not content without taking in hand yet another expedition. As has already been narrated, the French royalists had built high hopes on the general reaction of opinion in France since the end of the Terror; the exiled princes deluding themselves with the idea that the people's thoughts were fixed upon them, whereas really they were turned to the little Dauphin, the son of Lewis the Sixteenth and Marie Antoinette. The story of the slow torture of this unfortunate child for eighteen long months is perhaps the darkest page in the bloody record of the Revolution, but his death in June destroyed all hope of reversion to the Constitution of 1791. However, the royalists were too blind to perceive this, perhaps the more naturally since their agents had for some time been active in La Vendée and Brittany. The bitterness

[1] Dundas to Vaughan, 19th February 1795.

1795. of the past struggle was too fresh in those provinces to make it easy even for Charette or Stofflet to constrain their former followers to live at peace with the republicans. Quarrels constantly arose between the two May. parties, and finally in May a royalist agent gave the order, in the name of the King of France, to several Vendean Chiefs to recommence hostilities.

Meanwhile Puisaye had for eight months been in England, plying his suasive tongue upon the British Ministers, to gain them over to his own plan for a descent upon the coast of Brittany. His idea was that the expedition should be essentially a French one, that the British should promise indeed money, arms, and a fleet, but that no troops should be disembarked except corps of French Emigrants; and he pledged himself that, at the mere sight of the British fleet, the Bretons would again rise in arms. Pitt approved the design, mainly upon the representations of Windham, who to the last took upon himself the sole responsibility for the expedition; and the fact is remarkable, because Windham was the one civilian of the period whose views upon military subjects are entitled to some small respect. Accordingly, stores of clothing, arms and ammunition were collected; and Puisaye invited all the emigrants in Europe to throng to the British ports for the great adventure. They came in swarms. Count d'Hervilly collected fifteen hundred at Cowes; as many or more were enrolled by an English agent among the waifs and strays that hung about the British cavalry on the Weser; and to these in an evil hour the British Ministers determined to add over sixteen hundred French prisoners of war from among the thousands detained in England. D'Hervilly, an old soldier and a rigid royalist, was against the inclusion of such doubtful elements in his force; but he was overruled, though at whose instigation it is impossible to say. We know only that Windham had very reasonably wished the whole expedition to have been conducted in far greater force than was actually attempted; but whether he was answerable for this

particular blunder is unrecorded; nor, curiously enough, 1795.
can I find a sign of Cornwallis's share, if indeed he had
any share, in the whole transaction.

Meanwhile the old hostility between royalists and
republicans revived rapidly both in Brittany and La
Vendée; and at the end of May, Hoche, without
awaiting orders, seized several of the royalist leaders,
and set two and thirty columns in motion to traverse
the entire country. Thereupon civil war kindled itself
with all its old intensity from end to end of Brittany,
and Puisaye saw that the moment had come to act.
Accordingly, on the 17th of June Sir John Warren's June 17.
squadron of eight ships sailed from Cowes, carrying
thirty-five hundred men under d'Hervilly's command,
with uniforms, muskets, and ammunition for twenty
or thirty thousand more. Lord Bridport with fifteen
ships of the line covered their passage, while two small
squadrons under Sir Sidney Smith and Sir Richard
Strahan made feint attacks on the coast of Normandy
and Brittany. On the 22nd the French fleet of twelve
sail of the line under Admiral Villaret-Joyeuse was
sighted, and on the 23rd Bridport engaged it off June 23.
L'Orient, took three ships after a desultory action of
three hours, and then, calling his own fleet off, allowed
the rest of the French to escape. However, the action
cleared the sea for the expedition, and on the 25th June 25.
Warren dropped anchor off Carnac, between Morbihan
Bay and the peninsula of Quiberon.

The Chouans of this district were all of them afoot, but
d'Hervilly from excess of caution would not disembark
till the 27th. Meanwhile the Chouans thrust back the June 27.
nearest posts of the republicans about Auray, took
possession of that town, and pushed their advanced guard
eastward to Vannes, at the head of Morbihan Bay. This
success raised their hopes to the highest point; and
indeed a bold advance of the royalists in force could
hardly have failed to destroy the dispersed forces of
Hoche. That General saw the danger, and collecting
such men as he could—a bare two thousand—fell boldly

1795. upon the Chouans at Vannes and drove them back towards Auray. Puisaye entreated d'Hervilly to advance and crush this redoubtable adversary while he could, but d'Hervilly would not stir an inch until he was sure of his retreat; and since there had been some jealousy, owing to the vagueness of Windham's instructions, as to whether he or Puisaye was superior in command, he was the more obstinate in clinging to his own resolution. At length, however, on the 29th of June he attacked, in combination with British gunboats, the peninsula of Quiberon, a barren and waterless tongue of land some nine miles long and twelve furlongs wide, joined to the mainland by a narrow isthmus, whereon stood a fort still known as Fort Penthièvre. The garrison of this place, seven hundred strong, laid down its arms after a feeble resistance on the 3rd of July, and many of the soldiers passed into the ranks of the royalists. The news flew quickly to England, and Pitt in great elation despatched a ship of war to fetch the Count of Artois from the Elbe that he might place himself at the head of the invasion.

June 29.

July 3.

But meanwhile Hoche, having collected five thousand men, had on the same day driven back the Chouans at Auray; and these last, furious at finding themselves unsupported by d'Hervilly, complained loudly to Puisaye that they had been betrayed. Moreover, at that precise moment a foolish meddling priest, who had been a royalist agent at Paris, wrote to inform d'Hervilly that Puisaye was a traitor, and to order both him and the chiefs of the Chouans, in the French King's name, to suspend operations. Simultaneously this same miserable busybody instructed Charette, who was prepared to come to the assistance of Brittany, that the landing at Quiberon was but a feint, and that he must keep quiet until the true landing was effected in La Vendée. Other royalist agents were equally busy making mischief between Charette and Stofflet; and in fact these ill-chosen instruments and their two despicable masters, Lewis the Eighteenth and the Count of Artois, seem to have left no stone unturned to alienate their adherents, and to justify the wisdom of France in driving so contemptible a royal family from its midst. Much embarrassed, d'Hervilly withdrew to the peninsula of Quiberon, declining to move until further instructions should arrive from England. Of the Chouans many dispersed in dudgeon, and the remainder huddled themselves miserably into the narrow space chosen by d'Hervilly, while their chiefs consumed three priceless days in the work of reconciling d'Hervilly with Puisaye.

1795.

By this time Hoche had assembled a large force; and, as if to give him the time to make it larger, d'Hervilly projected an extravagant plan for an attack, after the Austrian model, in a multitude of columns upon the 16th of July. The natural result was that d'Hervilly's column alone appeared at the rendezvous at the appointed time, and was hunted back by overwhelming numbers into the peninsula with heavy loss. D'Hervilly himself was mortally wounded, and, but for the fire of the British gunboats, the republicans would have carried Fort Penthièvre there and then. During the action the second division of fifteen hundred Emigrants arrived from England and was pent up with the rest within the peninsula. The rest of the story is soon told. The French prisoners, who had been forced into the ranks of the Emigrants by the British Government, deserted by scores to Hoche; one of them undertook to guide Hoche's troops safely into Fort Penthièvre with the connivance of some comrades in the garrison; and on the night of the 19th the fort was gained without difficulty. The unhappy royalists fled to the end of the peninsula; but there was some delay, owing to a misunderstanding, before the boats arrived from the fleet to take them off; and, when these arrived, they were almost swamped by the rush of panic-stricken creatures that struggled to enter them. A few brave men stood and exchanged fire steadily with the republicans, but all discipline had disappeared; and,

July 16.

July 19.

1795. after eighteen hundred men, women and children had
escaped to the fleet, the survivors, some six thousand
July 27. men, laid down their arms. On the 27th of July, at
the instance of Tallien, the Convention resolved to
celebrate the occasion by a great massacre; and after
some weeks delay M. de Sombreuil, the leader of the
second division of Emigrants, and six hundred of his
companions were shot. Thereupon Charette immediately put to death an equal number of republican
prisoners; and thus once again the hideous sore of
La Vendée was reopened to its lowest depths.

The failure of the expedition struck dismay into the
French royal family and the British Cabinet. Pitt, on
hearing of the eligibility of Quiberon as a station for
shipping, had resolved without any delay to send
three thousand troops to occupy it, and to add to
these, as soon as possible, eleven thousand more
infantry and three thousand cavalry. Lord Moira
accepted the command of the whole, and on the 14th
and 15th of July received his instructions to proceed
to Quiberon and to act as auxiliary to the Count of
Artois's army, with power to raise and take into British
pay a force not exceeding fifteen thousand French. At
the same time General Graham was ordered to embark
immediately at Southampton with the advanced force
of three thousand men. He did so accordingly, but
the transports were detained by foul winds; and indeed
it was fortunate that this was so, for otherwise they
would have started but half armed. "I hope the
delay will enable Graham to complete his regiments
with firelocks, which were seriously deficient," wrote
Moira from Southampton. "The Forty-second,
Seventy-eighth, Nineteenth and Fourth Dragoon
Guards are here. The foot want arms; the cavalry
saddles. I hear that the Fortieth are a serviceable body
of men, but they have never fired powder yet." The
ruthless irony with which Moira stated bald facts was
more scathing than any vociferous complaint.

A few days later came the news of the disaster

at Quiberon, but this did not decide the British 1795. Ministers to abandon their expedition. At about the same time arrived the intelligence that Spain, intimidated by a victorious advance of the French to the Ebro, had on the 22nd of July signed a treaty of peace with France, July 22. under which she agreed to make over to that country the Spanish portion of St. Domingo. This incident naturally turned the British Government's thoughts again to the West Indies, but still Ministers hankered after some action on the French coast. In November 1794, when urging upon the King the recall of the Duke of York, Pitt had written that the only chance of decisive success for the British arms lay in directing their principal exertions towards a junction with the royalists in the maritime provinces of France. This, undeniably, was in itself a sound and sensible opinion. Though the Government may be excused for having failed immediately to realise the fact, Brittany and La Vendée were, as it seems to me, the quarter in which the entire armed force of Britain might from the first have been most profitably employed; even if, for the sake of harmony with the Allies, the hired troops of Hanover and Hesse had been made over to Coburg for the operations in the Low Countries. But it was ridiculous for Pitt to speak of devoting the "principal exertions" of the British arms to that field in 1795, when he had already committed them irrevocably to the West Indies. It was Pitt's hopeless incapacity to realise what he had done, what he was doing, and what he wanted to do with his armed forces, that made him so deplorable as a Minister of War. He tried to juggle with men as dexterous treasurers juggle with balance-sheets, transferring sums from the accounts of one fund to the accounts of another, and taking credit for the same sum under both accounts on the plea that the transfer is only temporary. The method is unsound even in finance : in war it means disaster.

However, early in July an emissary was despatched to Charette with autograph letters from Windham and

1795. Grenville, promising assistance and asking information as to the form in which that assistance could most profitably be bestowed. This gentleman found Charette sore and disappointed. "The British Ministers!" he said, "Why they have abandoned me during two whole years at a time when, with a little help, I could have finished the war by re-establishing monarchy." However, after venting his indignation against Puisaye and his jealousy of his subordinates, Stofflet and Sapineau, Charette softened, and declared that he had south of the Loire eighty thousand men, of whom fifty thousand had been in action a hundred times and would follow him anywhere. He wanted, he said, only powder, arms, and a prince of the blood to take his place at the head of the royal army.[1] Even before the return of this emissary, a letter from Charette to the Count of Artois had inspired that prince with an ardent desire to land on the coast of La Vendée, even alone; and, since Windham also pressed continually for some definite determination as to the help to be given to the royalists, the Government finally decided to escort Artois to the coast.

Aug. 11. Accordingly, on the 11th of August Moira was instructed to embark the Twelfth, Seventy-eighth, Eightieth, and Ninetieth Regiments,[2] together with a few of the Fourteenth Light Dragoons and a sufficiency of artillery and stores, and to send them under command of Major-general John Doyle to the islets of Hedic and Houat, which lie off the coast of France a little to the south of Quiberon. From thence Doyle was, if possible, to capture the island of Noirmoutier, a little to the south of the mouth of the Loire, and to give out that he held it in trust for the royal and catholic army of France, as a depot for the supply of arms to the royalists. If Noirmoutier proved to be unsuitable for the purpose, he might take Isle

[1] See this emissary's very interesting report in *Dropmore Papers*, iii. 105.
[2] The first battalions only of the 78th and 90th.

CH. XV HISTORY OF THE ARMY 419

d'Yeu, a little farther to the south, in its stead, or even 1795. in addition to it. Lastly, as if to call attention to his own weakness, he was to publish a proclamation expressing regret that the British Government, owing to the disaster at Quiberon and the peace recently concluded by Spain, was unable to do more. But to make up for such paltry deficiencies as this, the Count of Artois in person accompanied the expedition.[1]

There followed immediately the incidents which usually attended an embarkation at this period. Drafts were brought down to make the four battalions up to a strength of one thousand men apiece; but these recruits were so execrable and displayed so mutinous a spirit that the Colonels refused to take them on board. The result was that the force numbered only thirty-three hundred instead of four thousand. No sooner, too, had the destination of the expedition been communicated most secretly to Moira, than it was openly proclaimed and discussed at length in the newspapers. Moira lost all patience, and, after pleading in vain for another battalion for Doyle, begged Huskisson for Heaven's sake to procure him relief from his command. Finally on the 26th arrived three regiments Aug. 26. of foreign cavalry, which made the force complete; and, with a final request for forage and fresh meat to be sent after him, Doyle sailed away under escort of Rear-admiral Harvey's squadron. "What we are to accomplish with so small a force I am at a loss to guess," wrote Colonel Thomas Graham of the Ninetieth; and indeed there must have been many who were as much puzzled as he. However, on the 12th Sept. 12. of September the transports anchored in Quiberon Bay, and Doyle entered into communication with Charette. But it soon appeared that the attempt upon Noirmoutier was impracticable. The sands which connect the island, or rather the peninsula, with the mainland, were seldom covered to a greater depth than two or

[1] Dundas to Moira, 11th, 12th, 13th August 1795; *Dropmore Papers*, iii. pp. 95-96, 98-102.

1795. three feet of water, so that there was really no adequate protection for the stores, intended for the royalists, against the overwhelming force which the republicans could employ to capture them. Hoche had already collected a very formidable body of troops; and Charette naturally declared himself unable to hold a large extent of beach against a superior force, while the stores were landed and carried into the interior of the country.

Knowing himself to be too weak to undertake any offensive operation Doyle thereupon sailed to Isle d'Yeu, which was at once surrendered by its small garrison on Sept. 29. the 29th. The island is six miles long by four broad, and contained at that time eighteen hundred inhabitants, who, being royalists, received the British well. There were in it, however, neither forage, nor pasture, nor sufficient corn to feed the inhabitants, nor more than about forty oxen and a few miserable sheep. In this place, which contained but one dangerous roadstead, Doyle found himself set down at the approach of the autumnal equinox, with seven days' provisions and three weeks' fuel at short allowance. He had two thousand hungry horses and not a scrap of food for them, and could find no shelter for his men except by dispersing them dangerously among several straggling villages. His force was insufficient to defend the island against a regular attack, and his transports had been taken from him, so that he could not re-embark to retreat.

However, the news that the Count of Artois was at hand had roused the greatest enthusiasm among the Vendeans. The leaders laid aside all their jealousies, Oct. 5. and, when on the 5th of October an emissary announced to Charette the prince's orders to advance to the coast, the whole body moved off with eager delight, overthrowing the republican posts that lay on their way. But Oct. 10. five days later, when the Vendean army was within two miles of the shore, there came a second messenger to say that the prince had deferred his landing to a more propitious season, but had sent a sword of honour as 1795. a compliment to the General. Pale with rage Charette took the bauble in his hand, and for a time remained silent. Then at last he spoke. "Tell the prince," he said vehemently, "that he has sent me my death-warrant. To-day I have fifteen thousand men behind me; to-morrow I shall not have three hundred. There is nothing left for me but to choose between flight and death, and I choose death." He kept his word, though he struggled yet for six months against the inevitable; and meanwhile the Count of Artois remained irresolute at Isle d'Yeu.

But the prince's anxieties were as nothing to those of the unfortunate Doyle. Foul weather prevented his provision-ships at Quiberon from coming near him; the men were sickening fast from exposure; five hundred horses (though he had prudently sent his cavalry back to England) were dying of hunger; there was not a candle among the whole of the force, and it seemed likely that not only the troops but every one of the inhabitants might perish of starvation. Thanks to the noble devotion and incomparable seamanship of the officers of the Royal Navy, sufficient supplies were landed from time to time, though at considerable risk, to keep the men alive; but it was not until the 7th of November, nearly Nov. 7. six weeks after the original disembarkation, that three months' provisions were at last accumulated from the ships at Quiberon. A week later Doyle received from Dundas a letter, dated on the 19th of October, which seems to have contained an order for the embarkation of the troops on Admiral Harvey's squadron; but the shipping both of men and stores was a difficult matter owing to the danger of the roadstead. Moreover, the supplies on the squadron had run so low that the Admiral would not take the risk of taking the men on board and being driven to sea with more mouths than he could feed; nor could he embark the stores on shore before the men, lest once again he should be driven to sea, and the men on the island should

1795.
Dec.
starve before he could return to them. Harvey therefore sent to England for transports; but ultimately it seems that the troops were after all by good fortune embarked upon the squadron at the beginning of December, and reached England at the end of the same month very thankful for their deliverance.

After close study of a great number of English expeditions I incline to the opinion that this to Isle d'Yeu was the most disgraceful, in point of negligence and recklessness, that was ever thrust by a British Minister upon a British General. It is perfectly plain that no pains whatever were taken to obtain accurate information either as to Noirmoutier or Isle d'Yeu before the force was despatched to sea, and moreover that Ministers had really not the vaguest notion of what they meant it to accomplish. If they intended it to land and act with the Vendeans, it was too weak to be of the slightest value. If they designed it, as they professed, to seize and guard some island on the French coast, as a depot from which to furnish the Vendeans with supplies and stores, then it should have been fully equipped with victuals for several months and with the means of erecting shelter ; and the cavalry, with its two thousand horses, should have been left at home. But to consign three thousand infantry and two thousand cavalry, without any reserves of food or forage, in the month of September to a barren rock in the Atlantic, where there was no safe landing-place and consequently no assured communication with the outer world—this was something more than a blunder : it was a crime. It was no fault of Dundas that Doyle's troops, together with the whole of the inhabitants of Isle d'Yeu, were not starved to death. So great were the risks of the voyage that, though the garrison would have given almost any price for soap and candles, no adventurer would hazard the shipment of a cargo to the island. As it was, over one hundred horses perished of starvation on the island, while the cavalry which were sent back to England had not forage enough even for the

CHAPTER XVI

1794. LET us now return to the West Indies, and see how matters were faring there, while the Government was playing at invasions of France in Europe. To windward we left General Vaughan in his headquarters at Martinique with a force of about two thousand men fit for duty, to defend eleven different islands. Of the conquests made by Grey, Guadeloupe had been lost, but Martinique and St. Lucia remained, the two latter absorbing between them fully half of the troops that survived; and Grey had written in July that the security of the windward group of islands, from St. Kitt's to Tobago, demanded a garrison of eleven thousand men. In reply to this Dundas had announced in September the despatch of six battalions, and in December of seven more, together with three thousand five hundred drafts. The first division of these was detained by repeated foul winds, a misfortune for which it would be unjust to hold any human authority responsible, did we not know from the accounts of General Grey's preparations in 1793 that expeditions were never ready to sail when the wind was fair. Whatever one's suspicions, however, it would be unkind to assume, in the absence of direct evidence, that any cause but the weather was answerable for the fact that, up to the end of 1794, no reinforcements reached the Windward Islands from England except one hundred men of the Seventeenth Regiment, on a transport which apparently had been blown out to sea. Nor was it until the 21st of December that the Forty-sixth, Sixty-

return voyage, and threw more than two hundred horses 1795. overboard before they were half way home. Probably, therefore, the total loss in horses was from four to five hundred. As to the men, the returns show that over two hundred re-embarked sick from Isle d'Yeu, and that forty-five died outright among the infantry alone, from dysentery consequent upon exposure. A more wanton and wicked waste of lives, resources and money was never perpetrated; and though the loss was trifling compared to what it might have been, and the affair consequently attracted little notice, yet the fact by no means palliates the criminal carelessness of Henry Dundas, nor lightens the responsibility of Pitt for allowing, after repeated demonstrations of his incapacity, this deplorable impostor to continue in office as the supreme director of the war.

first, and Sixty-eighth Regiments arrived at Martinique 1794. from Gibraltar.

Meanwhile the successes of Victor Hugues at Guadeloupe had raised the revolutionary party to the highest pitch of elation. Upon the recapture of Guadeloupe he had issued an insolent proclamation, disguised in rather singular English, to announce that the bones of Thomas Dundas should be "deterred" and thrown to the four winds, as a protest against the crimes of the English against humanity, and that a monument should be erected to commemorate the fact. Thereupon Mariegalante promptly hoisted the national flag; and in St. Lucia discontent and disaffection ripened into what was practically open revolt. The troops could not follow the insurgent negroes into the labyrinth of wooded mountains which was their base of operations; nor could all the vigilance of the fleet prevent constant communication between them and Point-à-Pitre. Before the end of December Vaughan with remarkable keenness of insight comprehended the true significance of the situation, and gave the opinion, already recorded in these pages, that the whole army of Great Britain would not suffice to defend the Windward Islands. He therefore urged that it was high time to arm and train a regiment of negroes, obtaining the men either from the various islands, if the local governments would grant them, or, if that were impracticable, to import them direct from Africa.[1]

1795. Jan. 6.
A few days later five French ships of war and ten armed transports, with six thousand troops on board, arrived off Guadeloupe, and, though chased by a British frigate, made their way safely into Point-à-Pitre with the loss of but one vessel, containing four hundred soldiers. It was somewhat remarkable that the French reinforcements should not have suffered from the foul winds which so long retarded the English, but it is evident that they did not. The whole of the British

[1] Dundas to Grey, 17th July, 28th September, 19th December; Vaughan to Dundas, 21st and 25th December 1794.

1795. islands, as usual, shrieked to Vaughan for protection; but, meanwhile, the depredations of the insurgent negroes in St. Lucia became so serious that he was obliged to send a detachment to that island immediately; after which he wisely set about raising black levies without waiting for the approval of Government. January passed away, and February. Two French frigates from America joined Victor Hugues at Guadeloupe, but not a man reached Vaughan from England; and he was not deluded by Dundas's fair words about reinforcements, which, though always starting, seemed never to arrive. "In numbers," he wrote, "your letters of December promise a considerable addition to our force, but the effective strength of soldiers lies in their age and discipline"; and he sought comfort in the report of one of his officers in St. Lucia that a small body of negroes, lately recruited, had shown remarkable bravery in action. Meanwhile he had noticed with uneasiness that mischief was brewing at Point-à-Pitre. The bay was blockaded by the British frigates, which succeeded in capturing a second transport with two hundred troops on board; but they could not control the innumerable small craft which crept under cover of night from their haven beneath Fort Fleur d'Épée, and hugging the shore closely, made their way from island to island of the Archipelago, landing arms and men and sowing broadcast the seed of insurrection. Since the expulsion of the British from Guadeloupe the air had daily become more electric, and in the first week of March the storm broke.[1]

March 2. The evening of the 2nd of March closed in at Grenada in perfect peace, and with so little suspicion of mischief, that the Governor, Mr. Home, was actually absent from his capital, St. George's, on a journey to the leeward coast. Before dawn, came the news that the negroes had risen in the night, captured him and forty other whites at Goyave and massacred every

[1] Vaughan to Dundas, 11th January, 19th February, 2nd March 1795.

white man at Grenville, on the windward coast. The intelligence of this disaster reached Vaughan on the 5th and was followed on the 10th by a message from St. Vincent, saying that the Caribs in the north of that island also had broken into insurrection at the instigation of the French, and were devastating the whole colony. At the same time the officer in command at St. Lucia reported that despite of all his efforts the brigands were gaining ground, while from Guadeloupe came proclamations threatening the guillotine to any Frenchmen who joined the British, reprisals for all republicans executed by them, and menaces of attack upon Antigua and upon all the British islands. There is no denying to Victor Hugues, ruffian though he was, the merit of great skill and energy in the organisation of these simultaneous outbreaks. The fortunate chance which threw Governor Home into the hands of the brigands was instantly turned to account. Julien Fédon, a mulatto, who headed the rising in Grenada, and Besson, a Commissioner despatched thither by Hugues, at once issued a manifesto, declaring that the heads of the captured Governor and of his fellow-prisoners should answer for the good behaviour of the inhabitants of that island. Thereupon the negroes flocked to Fédon's banner by hundreds and even thousands; and not black men only but Frenchmen of all classes and colours, whether through terror or inclination, threw in their lot with the insurgents and fought by their side. The warning given to Dundas and unheeded by him in 1793 was being terribly justified; for the greater part of the negroes in the West Indies were now in open revolt.

1795. March 5.

Fully realising the seriousness of the situation, Vaughan judged the salvation of Grenada to be the most important object; wherefore, denuding St. Lucia at great risk of about one hundred and fifty men, he sent them under Lieutenant-colonel Lindsay of the Forty-sixth to St. George's. The island of Grenada is of oval shape, with an extreme length of abouty twenty

1795. miles from north to south and an average breadth of ten from east to west. Like its sister islands it is a confused mass of volcanic mountains, varying from fifteen hundred to three thousand feet in height, steep, rugged, and clad in dense forest. St. George's, the capital, stands on a beautiful inlet a little above the southern extremity of the western coast, its defences being Fort St. George, situated on a headland which commands the entrance to the harbour from the north, and three more forts, which were then still incomplete, upon a ridge to the east of the town called Richmond Hill. Grenville lies in a bay about half way up the eastern or windward coast; Goyave stands nearly opposite to it on the leeward coast, at the foot of the highest range of hills in the island; and there is a fourth little town at Sauteurs close to the extreme northern point.

March 12. On arriving at St. George's, Lindsay discovered that the senior member of Council, Mr. Mackenzie, had already begun operations by sending one hundred and fifty men, or more than three-fourths of the garrison, by sea to attack the position of the brigands about Goyave from the south, while the local militia were intended to fall upon it from the north. However, since the whole of the militia had taken refuge in the shipping, this com-

March 9. bination came to naught; and the troops after a slight skirmish returned to St. George's. Meanwhile, there arrived three British men-of-war, from which some marines were landed for the defence of the capital, and also three armed vessels with about forty men, which the Spanish Governor of Trinidad, being entreated for aid, had generously spared from his own tiny garrison. Accordingly, a few days after his land-

March 17. ing Lindsay marched upon one of the insurgents' posts and carried it with the loss of fifteen men killed and wounded, but was prevented by heavy rain from

March 22. doing more. Then, grievous to relate, this excellent officer was seized with fever, and in a fit of delirium destroyed himself. From that moment, the enemy being nearly five thousand strong, active operations were suspended; the troops were withdrawn to the hills about St. George's; and the island was perforce abandoned to the desolation of the brigands. Only at sea the frigates and armed schooners cruised round Grenada, endeavouring, not always unsuccessfully, to intercept the arms and stores which Hugues kept pouring in from Guadeloupe.[1]

1795.

In St. Vincent the outlook was equally gloomy. This island is of much the same size, shape, and description as Grenada; the capital, Kingston, lying at the head of an open roadstead at the southern corner of the leeward coast. About a mile to eastward of Kingston rises the commanding height of Dorsetshire Hill, and here the Carib King, incited to revolt by the emissaries of Hugues, had pitched his camp, directly threatening the town. He had not been there many days before he was attacked and utterly defeated by a force of seamen and soldiers under Captain Skinner of H.M.S. *Zebra* and Captain Campbell of the Forty-sixth. King Chateaugai himself with twenty of his followers was killed, and seventy-five more were wounded or taken. Two guns, of course supplied to him by the French, were captured; and in his camp was found a proclamation calling upon all Frenchmen to unite with Chateaugai in the cause of liberty, and threatening to burn their estates and murder their wives and children if they hung back. Brissot had been guillotined nine months before, but not soon enough to prevent this poor savage from being enticed, with the whole of his race, to destruction. The only reassuring incident in St. Vincent was that the negroes showed as hearty detestation of the Caribs as did the whites; and Governor Seaton begged earnestly for permission to raise a black regiment. But until this could be accomplished, he was powerless. The whole of the windward half of the island had been relinquished to the brigands, who were now proceeding to devastate the leeward side also. The local militia was untrust-

March.

[1] Vaughan to Dundas, 15th, 26th, 27th March 1795.

1795. worthy unless supported by regular troops, and the only regular troops were a handful of sickly men of the Sixtieth,[1] and a weak company of the Forty-sixth, which had been sent by Vaughan from Martinique immediately upon the first outbreak of the insurrection. In St. Vincent, therefore, as in Grenada, the British held little beyond Fort Charlotte, which guards the entrance to the roadstead of Kingston itself. In St. Lucia likewise the revolted negroes, headed by leaders from Guadeloupe, had increased so greatly both in numbers and arms that the British held no more than Morne Fortuné and the town of Castries, both of which were seriously threatened by large bodies of the enemy.[2]

The reinforcements promised by Dundas, however, were now due to arrive at Barbados; and Vaughan sent a staff-officer thither to meet the transports, with orders to detach three battalions without delay to Grenada. The name of this officer is worth recording, for he was Major Thomas Picton of the Fifty-eighth Foot. The convoy duly reached Barbados on the 30th of March, and was found to contain no more than five battalions, numbering together twenty-seven hundred men, instead of the eleven battalions and a large body of drafts which had been promised by Dundas in his last letters. Nor was the quality of the reinforcements superior to the quantity. At ordinary times the Second, Twenty-fifth, Twenty-ninth, Thirty-fourth, and Forty-fifth, were regiments that would have dissatisfied no General. But the three first had only recently been delivered from service on the fleet; the Thirty-fourth had parted with its best men by giving over its flank-companies to General Grey at the end of 1793; and the Forty-fifth, having been reduced to extreme weakness by previous service in the West Indies, had been drafted out at the beginning of 1794 and was practically

March 30.

[1] 4th battalion.
[2] Vaughan to Dundas, 18th and 25th March 1795 (with enclosures).

a new battalion. The whole of these troops were raw 1795. and young; and the Forty-fifth in particular, having been completed by a number of recruits upon the eve of embarkation, was, as Vaughan said, totally unfit for service in any climate. The boys that filled its ranks were not strong enough to carry their arms; their clothing was wholly unsuited to the tropics; and it was therefore not surprising that over two hundred of them were on the sick list before they had been a fortnight in the West Indies. It was in fact simply murder to send them out, and every soldier at the Horse Guards knew it; but the Ministers in their insufferable conceit thought it unnecessary either to seek or to accept their advice.

Moreover, Dundas appeared to imagine that it really did not signify very much whether the reinforcements consisted of three thousand boys or ten thousand men. His despatches to Vaughan by this convoy urged him first to take the Dutch possessions in the West Indies, though on second thoughts he feared that this might be impossible. Five of the battalions destined for the West Indies had, he explained, been detained for so long on board ship that sickness, or in plain words, typhus fever, had broken out among them, for which reason it had been found necessary to disembark them; but none the less he positively forbade the formation of black regiments. Finally, he announced that, on the representation of the British merchants trading to Demerara, he proposed to send the Third Battalion of the Sixtieth direct to that place, and ordered Vaughan to tell the Dutch Governor to be ready to receive it. According to previous instructions, force was to be employed if the Dutch offered resistance, so that practically Dundas committed Vaughan, who could hardly hold his own in the Windward Islands, to offensive operations five hundred miles away from his base, in the most pestiferous spot on the coast of the Caribbean Sea. And this enterprise was to be executed by a battalion which had been

1795. annihilated by yellow fever in 1793, and hastily recomposed of a heterogeneous collection of French, Dutch, and Germans, chiefly skulkers and deserters, whom the hope of British pay had attracted to Guernsey. Moreover, the expedition to Demerara was to be undertaken, almost avowedly, not for the furtherance of any object in the war, but to secure the profits of a clique of merchants who had ventured their capital, from motives the reverse of patriotic, in the Dutch Colonies. It was nothing that a British General, worn down with anxiety and overwork, was striving with a handful of sickly exhausted troops to stem the overwhelming flood of negro insurrection; nothing, that six hundred men in British pay should be shipped off together with their British officers at huge expense to their death; nothing, that other merchants and planters in the British West Indies should have their property exposed to devastation and themselves and their families to unspeakable outrage and massacre. Such considerations were not to be weighed against the sacred property of the "West India interest," which could rally to its banner over fourscore votes in the House of Commons, and scrupled not to use them for its own selfish objects.[1]

Vaughan, however, was blessed with a certain obstinacy and, perhaps fortunately in the circumstances, with an extremely uncertain temper. After a just protest against the iniquity of sending to him troops of such quality as the last reinforcements, he attacked Dundas upon the question of raising black regiments with commendable directness of speech. "I cannot but reflect with great regret that a set of self-interested merchants, who will not give a small part to save the whole, should be attended to in conducting operations in these countries instead of the Commander-in-Chief, who can have no motive but his own credit and the success of His Majesty's arms.

[1] Vaughan to Dundas, 16th April; Dundas to Vaughan (four letters), 19th February 1795.

I hope that the Ministry will yet weigh this important point. . . . I do not hesitate to say that unless my advice be taken, these Colonies will very soon be wrested from us. The French blacks will invade us and gain ours by the promise of freedom." However, being a sensible man, he did not wait for Ministers to change their minds, but gave Dundas to understand that he would take the matter into his own hands. The legislatures of the islands which had so far escaped injury, though composed of planters, decided to arm their negroes for defence and were readily supplied by the General with weapons. Vaughan also augmented the two corps of black rangers, whereby alone he had retained control of St. Lucia and Martinique, to eight hundred men; but beyond this, in the face of Dundas's instructions, he did not venture to go; and, if the consequences proved to be disastrous, it is not he but Dundas who must be held responsible for them.[1] Meanwhile he quickly made up his mind as to the disposal of the five battalions just arrived at Barbados. Picton, on his own responsibility, sent the Twenty-fifth and Twenty-ninth to Grenada, and the three remaining battalions to Martinique, where Vaughan kept the Second and Forty-fifth, but despatched the Thirty-fourth and Sixty-first to St. Lucia, and the Forty-sixth to St. Vincent, the two regiments last named being far superior to the rest. The entire force in the Windward Islands was returned on the 18th of April at rather under five thousand men; and it will now be convenient to follow separately the operations in the various islands during the year.

In all of them, it must be explained, the general object was the same, namely, to drive the brigands from the various little ports by which they received their arms and stores from Guadeloupe, and, having occupied these places, to follow the various bands inland, capture their posts and depots, and break them up until the prospect of starvation in the jungle should drive them to surrender.

[1] Vaughan to Dundas, 16th and 18th April 1795.

1795. In St. Lucia, Lieutenant-colonel James Stewart of the Sixty-eighth, an excellent officer, held command, and no sooner received his reinforcements than he sailed for Vieuxfort, at the southern extremity of the island. His troops consisted of the Sixty-first, the flank-companies of the Ninth and Sixty-eighth, and a black corps raised by Captain Malcolm, which had frequently done excellent service; the whole numbering, perhaps, six hundred whites and four hundred negroes. Disembarking in a
April 16. neighbouring bay he advanced on the 16th of April upon Vieuxfort, which was abandoned, after a slight skirmish, by the brigands, together with a considerable quantity of stores and ammunition. Leaving a garrison
April 18. in the town, Stewart followed up the enemy on the 18th; though so much hampered by want of transport that he could take but four pieces of artillery with him. These guns were dragged by soldiers and seamen from H.M.S. *Blanche*, while the remainder of his stores followed him by sea. His course lay westward along the coast to Laborie, which he found evacuated by the enemy, and thence to Choiseul, which he reached, after
April 19. a very severe march, on the evening of the 19th. From thence his path turned northward over a tangle of steep and wooded hills upon Soufrière, the enemy's most important post on the west coast of the island. Con-
April 20. tinuing his march on the 20th he found the whole force of his opponents in motion to attack him; but the Ninth and Malcolm's Rangers, falling into an ambuscade, made such slaughter of their opponents while extricating themselves, that the main body of the brigands retired before Stewart could reach them. On the following
April 21. day, after the guns had with enormous labour been brought forward, he again came up with the enemy in a strong position. But it was too late in the afternoon to attack; and the exhausted troops bivouacked for the night under continual showers of tropical rain.
April 22. Advancing again on the morrow the British at about eleven o'clock in the morning came in sight of the enemy's main position, strongly entrenched on com-

manding ground astride of the road to Soufrière. The brigands' right was covered by a lofty mountain, their left by a hill with a breastwork thrown up on its brow and an impassable morass at its foot ; and the road was barred by a thick parapet of earth and stones. Evidently the ground had been chosen and fortified by some military man who knew his profession. Stewart thereupon halted his guns on the road under protection of two companies, sent the black rangers to try to ascend the mountain so as to turn the enemy's right, detached eight companies to attempt a still wider turning movement upon the same side, and ordered the remaining troops to march round the morass, and then to climb the hill and assail the enemy's left flank. While these manœuvres were going forward, Stewart moved a company of the Sixty-first a little in advance of the guns on the road, whereupon the enemy at once opened upon it a very heavy fire. Excited by the sound the black rangers on the mountain's side opened fire likewise, and presently the whole of the British soldiers followed the example, expending an alarming proportion of their ammunition to no purpose, before they could be checked. The brigands then advanced in dense columns along the road upon Stewart's guns, with a coolness and intrepidity which was quite new in them ; nor were they finally driven back by the light companies of the Sixty-first and Sixty-eighth until they had made two attacks and suffered very heavily. The two companies pursued them to the parapet, from whence they were in turn repulsed with considerable loss. The action was prolonged from noon till seven in the evening without any decisive result, when, the British having spent all their ammunition and thrown away, under the stress of the tropical sun, the provisions supplied to them for the march, Stewart was compelled to fall back to his nearest depot of supplies and stores at Choiseul. He retreated accordingly at eight o'clock in the evening, and reached Choiseul in safety, though the men were so much exhausted that they could hardly drag the guns. The

1795. April 22.

1795.
April 22.
enemy fortunately had been punished too severely to venture to pursue them, or Stewart could hardly have escaped a great disaster.

Nevertheless the mishap was sufficiently serious. The casualties in the action amounted to over one hundred of the British killed and wounded, while the total loss of the entire force between the 15th and 22nd was nine officers and more than one hundred and sixty men. The steadiness of the enemy's troops and the skill with which they had been handled were not less disconcerting than the unfortunate excitability of the black rangers, which had led the white soldiers astray. Not daring to divide his force by leaving detachments at Choiseul and Laborie, Stewart withdrew to Vieuxfort, threw into it a garrison of about two hundred men, chiefly negroes, and brought the rest back to Morne Fortuné. He omitted not, however, to warn General Vaughan that, unless further protected by cruisers at sea, the post of Vieuxfort would be in the greatest possible danger.

May.
Then the month of May came in, and with it returned the yellow fever. The brigands allowed the plague to work its will among the troops in St. Lucia for five weeks,
June 6. and then on the 6th of June they attacked and took the British post at Gros Islet, apparently without any difficulty whatever. The men, completely worn down by death, sickness and fatigue, had lost all heart; and there were even a few who in desperation deserted to the
June 17. enemy. On the night of the 17th the brigands delivered a second attack upon the Vigie with the same fatal success; and Stewart, seeing that the harbour would very soon be unsafe for British shipping, embarked his
June 18. garrison quietly on the night of the 18th and carried it to Martinique. The total number of white troops that evacuated St. Lucia was just over fourteen hundred, of whom over six hundred were sick. A comparison of the morning-state of the 18th of June and the embarkation-state at eight o'clock of the same evening shows that one officer and seven men died in the course

of the day.¹ So ended for the present the British 1795. occupation of St. Lucia.

In Grenada, which had received its reinforcements direct from Barbados, the operations were begun earlier than in St. Lucia. On the 2nd of April Lieutenant-April 2. colonel Archibald Campbell of the Twenty-ninth landed his own regiment and the Twenty-fifth at Goyave, but to his dismay found himself under the orders of the President of the Council. This gentleman, Mr. Mackenzie, proceeded to divide his force into three parts for simultaneous advance from Goyave, St. George's and Grenville upon the enemy's main position at Mount St. Catherine, the highest and steepest mountain in the island. The plan was too thoroughly in conformity with Austrian methods to come to other than an absurd conclusion, the more certainly because Grenville was at the time in the enemy's hands; but poor Mackenzie regarded himself seriously as a commander, and urged an immediate attack upon the insurgents' principal stronghold, using taunts which unfortunately stung Campbell into making the attempt. The position of the brigands was in fact of extraordinary natural strength. Their camp covered a considerable extent of cleared ground, above which the mountain rose in three successive tiers. First came a steep but accessible slope, at the head of which were mounted two ninepounder guns; then came a rocky precipice, on the summit of which, commanding the lower ground and the only path of access, was another field-gun, besides swivels and wall-pieces; from this a steep acclivity led to a farther bluff, armed with another gun; and from this last the rock rose abruptly to the topmost peak of the mountain. Such was the natural citadel, held by six or seven hundred desperate men, which Campbell attempted to carry with about three hundred raw recruits, stiffened by about half that number of seamen. The troops, young though they were, behaved very April 8.

¹ Stewart to Vaughan, 25th April, 13th, 18th, 19th June (enclosed in Vaughan to Dundas, 9th May and 2nd June 1795).

1795.
April 8. well, and in spite of all obstacles nearly reached the gun at the summit of the first precipice, but were driven back by a heavy fire of musketry and by stones rolled down by the brigands. Heavy rain had made the mountain's side so slippery that they were quite exhausted by this effort, and Campbell was forced to retreat with a loss of three officers killed and eighty rank and file killed and wounded. This was the natural result of the direction of operations by a civilian; and, difficult though his position was, Campbell was greatly to blame for having listened to Mackenzie's representations for a moment. Vaughan, upon hearing of the mishap, at once sent Lieutenant-colonel Nicolls to take command in Grenada with the rank of Brigadier, so as to settle the question of command once for all.[1]

The consequences of this defeat were felt immediately. Fédon cut the throats of Governor Home and his forty fellow-prisoners, and the negroes ran off in flocks to join the brigands, who rapidly increased to a strength of nearly ten thousand men. Nicolls, however, upon his arrival saw the futility of Mackenzie's dispositions in scattering troops in detachments all over the interior, and determined to try the effect of a concentrated attack. Removing, therefore, Campbell's men from their position on the heights above Goyave,
April 26. he succeeded on the 26th of April in driving the enemy from Grenville, but failed in an attempt to cut them
April 29. off from the interior, though he forced them to abandon five guns. Realising that to follow the brigands into the forest would be simply to destroy his force to no purpose, he occupied strong posts at Sauteurs, Goyave and Grenville in order to cut off supplies from Guadeloupe, and organised a corps of two hundred and fifty negroes to destroy the provision-grounds of the insurgents. In several skirmishes he caused them serious loss, and was making fair progress, when the month of

[1] Vaughan to Dundas, 16th April 1795, enclosing Campbell to Vaughan, 10th April.

May as usual brought with it the scourge of yellow 1795. fever.

Then the young soldiers of the Twenty-fifth and Twenty-ninth began at once to fall down terribly fast. Twenty died in the first week of the month, and on the 10th six expired on a single day. So long as he could, Nicolls continued to harass the insurgents with considerable success; but by the middle of June June. so many of the white soldiers had perished that he was obliged to recall some of his black levies for the protection of St. George's. After the evacuation of St. Lucia, Vaughan had reinforced him by a part of the Sixty-eighth Regiment; but as the summer advanced the mortality increased. More than two hundred and fifty out of fourteen hundred and fifty men died in Grenada alone between the 7th and 23rd of July, while July. the number of the effective was reduced within the same period from twelve hundred and eighty to eight hundred and eighty. The inevitable results followed. Early in August two schooners from Guadeloupe had August. contrived to land arms, ammunition and provision for the insurgents, just when they had been reduced almost to destitution; and the whole of the good work accomplished by Nicolls was undone. A small reinforcement of the Sixty-eighth was sent to Grenada from Martinique after this misfortune, and the sickly season gradually wore itself to its close; but yellow fever had demoralised the men whom it had not killed, and the history of St. Lucia was repeated. On the night of the 15th of Oct. 15. October, during heavy rain, the brigands attacked the British post on the heights above Goyave, and carried it almost immediately. The position was very strong; the garrison consisted of about one hundred and fifty white troops and as many blacks; and it appears that the picquets stood and fought bravely, but that they were not supported by the main body. The casualties were few. The prisoners taken by the enemy did not exceed forty, all of whom were invalids too weak to retire with the rest of the force to St. George's;

1795. but the whole incident was felt to be anything but creditable.¹

Nov. In November the war abruptly assumed a new and unexpected complexion. The decay of the system of terror in France suddenly reacted upon the West Indies; and a Commissioner from Guadeloupe was sent to arrest Fédon, that he might be tried and punished for his barbarities, and to inform Nicolls that the war should be carried on thenceforward with humanity, and only for the great object of effecting the abolition of slavery. Though not in itself unpleasing, this announcement caused the greatest anxiety to the British Commanders, for they could not tell what its effect might be on their loyal negroes. The arrival at Martinique of four battalions² from England at the end of September had enabled a few soldiers to be spared for Grenada; but these were not enough to make head against the increasing strength of the brigands, for Fédon, defying the authorities at Guadeloupe, persisted

Dec. in retaining his command. At the end of December two large schooners full of men from Guadeloupe contrived to sail unmolested into St. Andrew's Bay, immediately to south of Grenville; and these reinforcements made a show of investing Pilot Hill, the position from which the British commanded Grenville Bay. Gradu-

1796. ally gathering men together, they, on the night of the
Feb. 17. 17th of February 1796, carried off a British sloop laden with ammunition, and seriously threatened the post itself and the entrance to Grenville Harbour. Twelve

Feb. 29. days later the British perforce evacuated Pilot Hill without the loss of a soldier, but abandoning five guns. Want of men was the only cause of this misfortune. Nicolls, in spite of such petty reinforcements as had reached him from Martinique, had fewer than seven hundred troops fit for duty in the island, and was

¹ Nicolls to Vaughan, 3rd and 12th May, 22nd June; to General Irving, 19th August; to General Leigh, 18th October. Returns enclosed in Vaughan to Dundas, 8th July 1795.
² 40th, 54th, 59th, 79th.

therefore unable to afford more than fifty white and two hundred and fifty black soldiers for the defence of Pilot Hill against five times that number of negroes, led by white officers and amply supplied with artillery. Thus, after a year of incessant petty combats and the loss of many hundred men from sickness, the British in Grenada found themselves at the beginning of 1796 in much the same condition as at the beginning of 1795 —just able to hold the town of St. George's, and not without misgiving lest they should be driven from the island altogether.[1]

In St. Vincent the struggle was even more varied and bitter than in the other islands. On the arrival of the reinforcements from England at the beginning of April, Vaughan at once sent the Forty-sixth, a regiment of men and not of boys, to Kingston; and through their help the enemy was driven forthwith from the lower ground into the mountains. The British then established themselves firmly at three posts outside Kingston, namely, Calliaqua, a little port from two to three miles east of the town ; Chateau Belair, another little haven on the western coast ; and Sion Hill, upon the eastern flank of Kingston town. This arrangement, though necessary in order to exclude any help sent to the insurgents from Guadeloupe, signified very heavy work for the men ; for the French had set up a new King of the Caribs in place of Chateaugai, and an attack upon Calliaqua on the 19th of April showed that these savages were still active. The British, however, with the help of some black rangers, were strong enough to take the offensive ; and at the end of April a party of the rangers, with a few bluejackets and thirty men of the Forty-sixth, attacked and took a Carib camp with extraordinary gallantry. The only access to this camp was by a zig-zag path cut on the face of the precipice, with every angle defended by a swivel-gun ; yet the stronghold was stormed with a loss of little more than twenty killed and wounded. Nevertheless a week later

1796.

1795.

April 10.

April 19.

April 26.

the May 7.

[1] Nicolls to Leigh, 21st, 23rd, 29th February 1796.

1795. enemy, after a hard fight, drove back a British post on Dorsetshire Hill, and would not yield it, when attacked on the following day, until twenty-three of their white leaders, besides numbers of blacks, had been killed.

Governor Seton then begged for reinforcements; but Vaughan could spare him none until the beginning of June, when the Third battalion of the Sixtieth arrived at Barbados from Demerara, where the Dutch Governor had refused to allow it to land. If Dundas had done his duty to his country instead of truckling to a parcel of greedy merchants, this battalion might have arrived in time to save St. Lucia, instead of spending weeks sailing the sea on a fool's errand. Since, however, it had come too late for St. Lucia, Vaughan sent it to St. Vincent; whereupon Lieutenant-colonel Leighton of the Forty-sixth at once started with about eight hundred men of his own regiment, of the Sixtieth, of black troops and artillery, to drive the enemy from the windward side of the island. On the 12th he stormed a very strong position called Vigie, which lay upon the left flank of his line of advance up the eastern coast, destroying over two hundred of the insurgents and capturing their white commandant, though not without the loss of four officers and nearly sixty white soldiers killed and wounded. He then pushed on as rapidly as the heat, an extremely strong and dangerous country, and his difficulties of transport would allow him, to Mount Young, the easternmost peak on the chain of hills now called Black Ridge, which completely commands the road along the eastern coast. Short though the distance was, he did not reach it until the 16th; and even so eight men died from exhaustion on the third day's march. Arrived there, he fortified Mount Young and the peak immediately to west of it, and pushed out his parties northward to destroy the canoes of the Caribs and to lay waste all the country upon which they could live, so as to drive them to starvation in the mountains.[1]

[1] Governor Seton to Vaughan, 16th and 29th April; Leighton

So far all had gone well in St. Vincent; and though 1795. a war of posts in the tropics could not but tell heavily upon the troops, yet yellow fever at least had spared them. But St. Lucia had been recovered by the French, and this was a very serious matter for St. Vincent, which lies not more than forty miles from it and, if anything, slightly to leeward. At the beginning of July, July. moreover, the French, reinforced by regular troops from St. Lucia, established themselves in greatly superior numbers on a hill near the British post at Chateau Belair; whereupon Governor Seton very foolishly directed Colonel Prevost of the Sixtieth to attack them with thirty British soldiers and seventy coloured militia. The attack was of course repulsed; and the leeward side of the island, which had for the most part escaped devastation and still abounded in supplies, was laid at the enemy's mercy. Seton wrote to beg reinforcements from Martinique; but none could be spared, for two-thirds of the garrison were in hospital, and the men were dying at the rate of seventy-five a week. He was therefore obliged to weaken Leighton's force by transferring a part of it from the windward to the leeward coast; and on the 5th of August, after marching from midnight till eight Aug. 5. in the morning through deep woods and ravines, a little column of two hundred of the Forty-sixth and Sixtieth stormed the French position above Chateau Belair, drove the enemy to the woods with heavy loss both in killed and prisoners, and captured two guns. The casualties of the British in this affair were sixty killed and wounded, including three officers; of which number one officer and no fewer than forty-four men belonged to the Forty-sixth. The detachment of that regiment must in fact have lost one-third if not one-half of its strength; and, considering that the French in their strong position numbered four hundred against the British three hundred, the action, however

---

to Vaughan, 27th April and 23rd June; Vaughan to Dundas, 6th June 1795.

1795. small in scale, was extremely honourable to the Forty-sixth.[1]

This success seems to have elated Governor Seton unduly, for he now allowed posts to be multiplied all along the windward coast, too numerous to be strong, and yet too remote from each other to give mutual support. The temptation was certainly great, whether it was a civilian or a soldier who was responsible for the blunder, for it was of the utmost importance to occupy Owia, a strong position at the north-east corner of the island, which commanded the little haven that lies nearest to St. Lucia. Owia is twenty-five miles distant from Kingston, and the road on the coast was flanked along its whole length on the western side by wooded mountains impenetrable to Europeans, but containing paths well known to the Caribs and negroes. It was therefore necessary to maintain posts of communication at Dorsetshire Hill, at Calliaqua, at Vigie, three or four miles to east of it, at Baiabu, higher up the eastern coast, and at an intermediate station between Baiabu and Mount Young, where Leighton lay with the main body of the troops. The white soldiers were by this time reduced to four hundred fit for duty, with their clothes in rags and no shoes to their feet. For a month after the action at Chateau Belair the French appear to have given little trouble; but suddenly in the first
Sept. week of September they fell upon the post of Owia by surprise, cut to pieces a part of the garrison of negroes that occupied it, and sent the rest flying in panic along the road to Kingston. Thereupon Colonel Myers at once repaired by order of Vaughan's successor to take the command at St. Vincent, and to make all preparations for evacuating the posts both to windward and leeward; for the enemy were daily receiving small reinforcements at Owia from St. Lucia. Myers delayed the retirement to the last possible moment, fearing lest the negroes on the eastern coast should, by the withdrawal of protection, be driven into the arms of

[1] Seton to Irving, 9th July and 7th August 1795.

the insurgents. At length, on the 18th of September, 1795. the news that the enemy was advancing from Owia in Sept. 18. force, decided him to call in all outlying garrisons to Vigie and Dorsetshire Hill, lest they should be cut off, and the town of Kingston should be taken before they could retreat.

The troops were safely brought in by the 22nd; but Sept. 22. this measure, though inevitable, seems to have plunged the whole Colony into a state of despondency. The Colonial authorities would make no exertion for their own defence; the black rangers were so much shaken by the disaster at Owia that they could not be trusted without regular troops to take them into and out of action; and the regular troops were naked, overworked, and exhausted. On the 23rd the enemy appeared in Sept. 23. force on high ground within two miles of Vigie, and early on the following morning they occupied a ridge Sept. 24. which commanded the road from that post to Kingston. The troops at Vigie numbered two hundred, half British regulars, half negroes; but they were nearly destitute of provisions, the inhabitants having refused to supply Myers on the previous day with the transport necessary for the victualling of the post. In abject terror of the enemy's advance the planters now produced mules in abundance; and Myers, having collected fourteen days' supplies for two hundred men, handed over two hundred regulars and as many negroes — the best part of his force — to Lieutenant-colonel Ritchie of the Sixtieth, to escort the convoy to Vigie. Ritchie marched accordingly by Calliaqua, beyond which he began the ascent of a spur which led him straight upon the post. Here for the first time his advance was opposed, and he ordered some of his troops forward to clear a ridge for the passage of the convoy. The enemy, however, resisted stoutly, and, the advanced parties falling back in disorder upon their supports, the entire body was seized with panic and took to its heels. Ritchie, though wounded, was able with the help of his officers to rally a few men and to check any hostile pursuit, so that the casualties

1795. were few. But the whole of the convoy was lost; and it was only by great skill that the officer at Vigie contrived in the night to lead his men safely into Kingston.[1]

Here, therefore, were the same unpleasant symptoms which had already appeared in St. Lucia and Grenada, displaying themselves at St. Vincent. Soldiers, who, a few months earlier had shown the greatest gallantry, now refused to face the enemy; the scanty remnant of those that survived being debilitated both in body and spirit by excessive strain under a tropical sun. Just at this time, however, as has been seen, four battalions from England arrived at Martinique, of which three were at once despatched under command of Major-general Irving to St. Vincent. These three battalions, the Fortieth, Fifty-fourth, and Fifty-ninth, had served in Flanders during the latter part of the campaign of 1794, including the disastrous retreat to the Ems, had only returned from Germany in May 1795, and had been hastily brought up to strength by large drafts of recruits when ordered to embark for the West Indies. With such slight training and a long voyage superadded to it, they can hardly have been in a very good condition for service. Nevertheless Irving found Kingston so much straitened by the hostile occupation of Vigie that, immediately upon their landing, he marched them Oct. 2. off at three o'clock on the morning of the 2nd of October, and at daybreak attacked the post from two sides. Heavy rain made the ground practically inaccessible, and after a severe struggle Irving called off his troops and retired; but the enemy had been so roughly handled that they abandoned the position during the night, leaving their guns and ammunition undestroyed behind them. Thus Vigie was recovered, though at a cost of one hundred and fifty officers and men killed and wounded, more than half of whom belonged to the Fifty-ninth.

[1] Seton to Vaughan, 5th September; Myers to Seton, 8th and 10th September; to Irving, 14th, 18th, 28th September 1795.

Since the enemy continued still to receive rein- 1795.
forcements from St. Lucia, Irving resolved at first to
stand on the defensive rather than risk the peril
of an advance along a dangerous line of communication upon Owia. Later on, however, he appears, Nov.
notwithstanding the warning given by the results
of Seton's offensive policy, to have reoccupied and
increased the posts for some distance up the eastern
coast, substituting a new station called Mount William,
a little to north of Colonarie Point, for that formerly
occupied on Mount Young. This post was so strong
that he had some right to consider it safe in the hands
of British troops; but the atmosphere of the West
Indies, at this period, seems to have been charged with
the worst spirit of dejection and despondency. "A
degree of apathy and indifference," wrote Myers to
General Grey in November, "seems to have overtaken
not only the troops but all the people in the island.
They complain loudly of neglect, and even the news of
a force coming out from England seems not to cheer
them. The energy which pervaded all ranks when you
and Sir John Jervis were here has been annihilated.
There is talk of capitulation in many of the islands,
the people being tired of the war and of lending their
negroes for defence."[1] One can hardly imagine an
environment better calculated to discourage soldiers
already enervated by the climate of the tropics and disheartened by a service which, always unpopular, had, since
Dundas had deprived the troops of their prize-money,
become positively loathed by all ranks of the Army.[2]

The result of this bad spirit in regiments, which
through no fault of their own were imperfectly disciplined, presently became lamentably apparent. At 1796.
three o'clock on the morning of the 8th of January Jan. 8.
the French made a sudden attack on a battery upon
Mount William, the site of which had been judged
inaccessible. Brigadier Stewart, the officer in command,

[1] Myers to Grey, 2nd November 1795. *Grey MSS.*
[2] Irving to Leigh, 3rd and 6th October 1795.

1796.
Jan. 8.
had taken every precaution against surprise, keeping one-third of the men under arms all night, sending constant patrols to visit the sentries, and taking especial care that the sentinels about that particular battery should be sufficient and properly placed. Whether the guard at this actual point was negligent of its duty or worse is uncertain, for few of the men that composed it were seen after the action; but certain it is that they allowed themselves to be surprised. The troops, however, fell in with perfect order, notwithstanding the confusion which is inevitable upon a dark night, and for a time stood firm; but, before the captured battery could be retaken, the enemy developed their attack along the whole length of the position, and the British, having suffered severely, suddenly gave way at every point. With some difficulty Stewart collected his men, formed a rear-guard, and retreated with inconsiderable further loss to Baiabu, from which at nightfall he retired unmolested to Kingston, picking up the other posts on the way as he went. The troops engaged were the Fifty-fourth, eight companies of the Fortieth, and the flank-companies of the Fifty-ninth, making perhaps six hundred white soldiers in all, besides a detachment of negroes. Their loss was fifty-four killed, one hundred and nine, including eighteen officers, wounded, and two hundred missing; nearly all of the killed and wounded being white soldiers, and three-fourths of the missing black. It was none the less a most dishonourable incident, and the troops were much shaken. Immediately upon the news of this disaster, Major-general Hunter was sent from Martinique to take the command; and all outlying troops were at once called in and concentrated about Kingston, the majority being stationed on Miller's ridge, on the same chain of mountains with Dorsetshire Hill and Sion Hill, to the east of the town. The enemy took

Jan. 20. post opposite to the ridge, and on the 20th Lieutenant-colonel Prevost led two hundred men to attack one of their picquets, which was dangerously isolated; but so strongly were the troops infected with panic that but 1796. eight men would follow him. The French thereupon attacked in turn, and after a severe engagement, which lasted from daylight till dark, were finally repulsed with heavy loss. The beginning of the year 1796 therefore found the British in St. Vincent, as in Grenada, after severe fighting and heavy loss, masters only of a corner of the island about the capital town.[1]

Dominica, though within fifty miles of Point-à-Pitre, 1795. escaped raid and insurrection for longer than her neighbours to south; and it was not until June that a party of revolutionists landed at Pagoua Bay, at the north-east corner of the island. The British garrison, as in all the islands, was weak and sickly, consisting of from four to five hundred men, chiefly of the Fifteenth and Twenty-first, of whom two in every five were on the sick list. A detachment of this force and a few of the local militia accordingly set out from Prince Rupert's Bay, and marching across the whole breadth of the island reached Pagoua Bay on the 8th of June, where, June 8. after a few skirmishes, they surrounded the invaders and captured two hundred and fifty of them on the 17th. About one hundred and fifty more of the enemy June 17. fled to the bush, but were taken by the local negroes in the course of the next few days; and by the 27th June 27. the authorities were able to report not only that the French force had been made prisoners to a man, but that all trace of insurrection had been stamped out. The casualties of the British were trifling; but the march across the island was described by one who took part in it as the most fatiguing that ever was made; and indeed, looking to the extreme steepness, ruggedness and difficulty of the country, it is astonishing that it was even attempted. Two more French expeditions, which had followed immediately upon this one, returned to Guadeloupe when they saw preparations matured to

[1] Stewart to Hunter, 13th January; Irving to Leigh, 19th January; Hunter to Leigh, 24th January; Leigh to Dundas, 21st January 1796.

1795. receive them, and Dominica was troubled no more. The truth is that, unless they could raise the negroes in insurrection, the French were powerless; and Dominica owed its salvation simply to the loyalty of the slaves.[1]

Let us now look at Martinique, the headquarters of the Commander-in-chief to windward during this miserable year. It was the hard lot of Vaughan to be condemned to sit still and see his men engaged in a hopeless struggle against a dangerous enemy and a deadly climate, without the least power to help them. Dundas had promised him reinforcements in the winter, but only three battalions had arrived in December 1794, and with them had come a prohibition against raising black regiments. In April 1795, as has been seen, five more battalions had arrived, a number less than half of what Dundas had led the General to expect, and so poor in quality that they should never have been embarked. Vaughan dealt generously in his distribution of them, keeping the two worst for himself, and sending the others to his colleagues; but he did not fail to give Dundas a warning in plain terms. "It is only filling the hospitals and deceiving yourselves," he wrote, "to send out raw or newly trained levies." It is hardly possible that this warning should not have been repeated a score of times to Dundas by officers of experience in England; but that Minister possessed an infinite capacity for self-deception. While, therefore, St. Lucia, St. Vincent, and Grenada still cried out for troops—and a very few more would have sufficed to save the first and to extinguish the rebellion in the two last—Vaughan was unable to assist them. In May he received ominous hints that one of his officials—a French royalist who had been among the first to invite British protection—was in correspondence with Hugues; and his anxiety was increased by the knowledge that he had, as he said, literally no troops but only boys and sick men. At last in

April.

---

[1] Lieut.-col. Madden to Vaughan, 22nd and 27th June; Capt. George King to Madden, 17th June 1795.

June he received from Dundas a belated and grudging 1795. permission to raise two West India regiments, upon conditions calculated to soothe the tender feelings of the West India Committee. By a curious coincidence Dundas's letter was written apparently on the very day when Vaughan, embittered by the Minister's first rejection of his plan, had sat down to repeat his unanswerable arguments in its favour. But fate was kind to the General, for in the first week of July, July. before he could carry his favourite measure into effect, he died, and, it is to be hoped, was delivered from British War-Ministers for ever.[1]

Upon his death Major-general Irving succeeded to the command at a most terrible time. Between the 7th and the 23rd of July the numbers of the rank and file in the Windward Islands were diminished by over four hundred and fifty deaths; in fact the army was literally decimated by yellow fever in those sixteen days. At Martinique itself the deaths within the same period were one hundred and seventy-seven, and on the 23rd of July the effective men numbered thirteen hundred, the sick seven hundred and sixty-four. "If you want full possession of these islands, and order restored in St. Vincent and Grenada," wrote Irving to Dundas on that day, "twenty thousand men will be necessary. By the end of the campaign there will not be above ten thousand left." Meanwhile, hearing that certain regiments had arrived at Barbados on their way to St. Domingo, Irving begged Major-general Forbes, who was in command, to spare him a part of them; but Forbes very reasonably judged himself unable to consent except in compliance with a positive order. Irving thereupon turned eagerly to the raising of the black regiments, though with many misgivings, for the planters not unnaturally were unwilling to part with their faithful negroes. Further inquiry showed that this unwillingness was an

[1] Vaughan to Dundas, 25th April, 12th May, 16th June; Dundas to Vaughan, 17th April; Irving to Dundas, 8th July 1795.

1795. almost insuperable difficulty. The planters had suffered so much that the whole of the Colonies combined in a declaration that they could not supply negroes even for sale. "Earlier in the course of the disturbance, I am persuaded that there would have been little difficulty," wrote Irving to Dundas, probably unaware how keen a reproach to the Minister lay hidden in his words. It seems indeed to be beyond dispute that if Dundas's sanction for the formation of black regiments had arrived in April instead of at the end of June, the planters would willingly and even joyfully have made over a sufficient quantity of negroes. Thereby the duty thrown upon the white troops would have been lightened, the mortality among them in some degree lessened, many lives and much property would have been saved, and the solution of the whole military problem of the West Indies would have been enormously facilitated. But the arrogance of British Cabinets in military affairs has too often forbidden them to believe that their wisdom could not prevail over time and space ; and hence Downing Street is paved with lost opportunities.[1]

Sept. 24. On the 24th of September, as has been already narrated, there arrived at Martinique the Fortieth, Fifty-fourth, Fifty-ninth, and Seventy-ninth regiments under Major-general Hunter. The Government, upon receiving Vaughan's letters of the month of April, had decided at the end of June to despatch immediately to the Windward Islands four thousand troops, of which four battalions, or more than half, were to set out in that same week and the remainder to follow within ten days. The four accordingly embarked on the 10th of July, but the rest appear to have remained wind-bound in Cawsand Bay until the first week in August, and finally never sailed to the Windward Islands at all. Thus the reinforcements proved to be, as usual, a driblet, not large enough to fill the gaps made by fighting and disease, and therefore insufficient

[1] Irving to Dundas, 8th and 23rd July, 6th September 1795.

CH. XVI   HISTORY OF THE ARMY   453

for any decisive operation; while the Commander-in-chief was, once more as usual, deluded into the belief that his resources would be nearly twice as great as in actual fact they ultimately proved to be.[1]

1795.

Simultaneously with the arrival of the four regiments Major-general Leigh assumed the command at Martinique, having arrived there indeed on the 5th of July, only to find himself unable under his letter of service to displace Irving without further instructions. His fate was even harder than that of his predecessors, for he was doomed to witness the steady deterioration of the British troops in all the islands, and to encounter continued difficulties in the raising of the black regiments. In St. Vincent the tact and energy of Colonel Myers were successful in obtaining from the planters some of the negroes who were already employed as rangers, upon condition that they should not be removed from the island, and that they should be returned to their owners when their services were no longer required. Thus came into being the Second West India Regiment, which fought its first action under that title at Mount William on the 8th of January 1796 and, being still entirely undisciplined, came off with no very great credit. The rest of the islands would not furnish a man; and the embodiment of Malcolm's Rangers, which had done such good service in Grenada, into the First West India Regiment was delayed by a landing of brigands from St. Lucia at Vauclin, on the

[1] Portland to Vaughan, 29th June 1795. Leigh's letter announces the arrival of the 40th, 54th and 59th only, making no mention of the 79th. The Historical Records of the 79th state that they arrived at Martinique on the 20th of September; and the 79th was certainly ordered to embark with the other three regiments (*S.C.L.B.*, 8th July 1795). On the other hand Leigh gives the date of the arrival of the reinforcement at Martinique as the 24th, and not the 20th of September; and he calls the 40th, 54th, and 59th, the *whole* reinforcement (Leigh to Dundas, 2nd October 1795). Nor can I find any mention of the 79th until December, when the flank-companies are described as on their way to Barbados. The matter may appear to be a small one, but in a war of posts a few companies more or less may turn the scale of a campaign.

1795. south-eastern corner of Martinique, in the first week
Dec. of December. A detachment of the Second Queen's under Major Lord Dalhousie, together with a few militia, attacked this party in a strongly entrenched position, and was beaten off with some loss. But on the arrival of the black rangers, originally raised by General Grey, the whole of the invaders were cut off and captured ; and their friends who were starting to join them from St. Lucia and Guadeloupe returned with precipitation to their own place.[1]

So ends the dreary narrative of the campaign in the Windward Islands in 1795. In its later phases it is perhaps the most discreditable that is to be found in the records of the British Army ; and it is quite possible that blame may be cast upon the writer who has ventured to tell the story in its naked truth, and to narrate events which certain regiments, proud of an otherwise honourable career, would gladly have believed to be forgotten. But a military history, if it is to be of the slightest value to soldiers or civilians, must be something more than a transcript of gazettes or a calendar of successes. It is possible that we have still campaigns to fight in the West Indies ; and the aggregation of several thousand white soldiers in any one island may, despite the resources of modern science, again suffice to wake the sleeping demon of yellow fever to his old fury and his old power. Then, if our Governors are wise, they will look back to the year 1795 and observe the effect of the plague upon the troops. It would be unjust severely to criticise regiments which were hastily gathered up from one destructive campaign, stuffed with raw recruits and plunged forthwith into a still more destructive campaign among the graves of thousands of their dead comrades. Even when yellow fever spared them, they were worked to death. The duty thrown upon them would have been hard even in

[1] Leigh to Dundas, 20th September, 2nd and 8th October (with enclosures from Myers), 5th and 10th December 1795 ; 3rd January 1796.

England; in the West Indies where, without proper clothing or comfort of any kind, they were exposed at the best to tropical sun, tropical rain, mosquitos, sand-flies, chigoes, and the myriad torments of the torrid zone, it was insufferable. For a few months they endured it, in conflict continually with a human enemy as dangerous and as cunning as a Red Indian; but the best of them—the men that spared themselves least—soon fell dead, and the exhausted remnant refused to fight. The like was seen in Italy in 1796, where even the victorious remnant of Bonaparte's army declined to follow him, when, standard in hand, he tried to lead them over the bridge of Arcola; and the same story was repeated by the veterans of that same army in Egypt in 1801. There is a limit to human endurance, and what is pardoned to Bonaparte's French in Italy must not be too harshly judged in the British soldier, who was subjected to a far harder trial, in the West Indies.

Nor should we be less careful in criticism of the Generals. At first sight it seems blameworthy in them that they should not have sacrificed one or more of the islands for the greater security of the rest. But this would have signified either the removal of the whole population that remained loyal to the British, or the abandonment of them to massacre by the brigands. The former alternative would have been impossible for want of shipping; the latter would have alienated every planter and loyal negro in the West Indies. Moreover, the despatches of the Secretary of State for War led the commanders constantly to expect large reinforcements from home, which encouraged them always to hope that another week of tenacity might be rewarded by the arrival of the promised succours. Again, the local legislatures of the various islands retained their powers in time of war; and the civil Governors, under their commissions as Commanders-in-chief, interfered whenever they possibly could with the conduct of operations. The legislature of Grenada even at the end of July, 1795, refused to permit martial law to be proclaimed, until

1795. Irving compelled them by the threat that he would withdraw the troops.[1] Moreover, the petty Assemblies and Councils not only worried the Commander-in-chief with incessant outcry, each for the protection of their own particular island, but instructed their agents at home to present memorials with the same request to Dundas, who, instead of declining to receive them, forwarded them to the overworked staff at Martinique. "I have made the best dispositions that I can for the *whole* Government," answered Leigh curtly; and indeed this was all that the Commander-in-chief could do. At first the greatest measure of help had been given to Grenada, as the most valuable of the islands; but, when the yellow fever annihilated the troops, the Generals concentrated their chief strength in St. Vincent, which had escaped the epidemic. More than this they could not do; and the person to blame for the catastrophes in the field was the Minister who sent his scanty battalions not to the British possessions, where his own military policy had created most need for them, but on childish excursions to a Dutch colony in South America and to a barren island in the Atlantic.

[1] Irving to Nicolls, 27th July, enclosed in Irving to Dundas, 6th August 1795.

CHAPTER XVII

WHILE the negro insurrection was going forward in 1794. the Windward Islands, events not less important were passing to leeward in St. Domingo and Jamaica. At the end of 1794, it will be remembered, the British had suffered a heavy disaster in St. Domingo through the loss of Tiburon; though they retained with a handful of men a precarious hold upon Mole St. Nicholas on the Northern peninsula, Jérémie and Irois on the Southern peninsula, and Léogane, Fort Bizothon, and Port-au-Prince, together with a considerable district to the north of the capital, about the Bight of Léogane. The troops on the 1st of January 1795 1795. numbered fewer than eleven hundred of all ranks fit for duty; and Sir Adam Williamson had already set about the formation of large corps of negroes, offering to all recruits emancipation at the close of their service, in order to outbid the French, who had proclaimed liberty to all. "The security of the Colony will depend upon them," he wrote to Dundas, "and the brigands will never be reduced but by negro corps."[1]

The new year opened badly with the loss of Saltrou, a port a little to westward of the Spanish boundary on the southern coast, which was taken in January by the insurgents from the local levies that defended it. Intrinsically the place was of small importance, but it would have been of great value for the reduction of Jacmel, the favourite refuge of the privateers which

[1] Williamson to Dundas, 14th February 1795.

1795. preyed upon the commerce of Jamaica. In February
Feb. there followed a still greater misfortune in the death of
Thomas Brisbane, who was shot dead while making a
reconnaissance on the river Artibonite. Almost from
the first he had been the soul of the defence of St.
Marc, the rich district to north of Port-au-Prince;
and deep and genuine was the lamentation alike of
French and English, of black and white, over the loss
of such a man.   Meanwhile the country generally
March. remained unquiet. In February and March there were
outbreaks about Jérémie, the Mole and Port-au-Prince,
all of which needed to be put down with a strong hand.
Immediately afterwards there occurred another mishap.
The enemy having erected a battery not far from Fort
Bizothon, four British flank-companies were sent to
capture it, which they duly did, destroying one gun,
spiking the rest and inflicting enormous loss on their
opponents; but the casualties of the victors were forty-
five killed and wounded, and among the slain was
Colonel Markham of the Twentieth, the best officer,
after Brisbane, in the whole force. About the same time,
however, arrived letters from Dundas, announcing that
two battalions had actually sailed for St. Domingo, that
three more were embarking, and that, of three thousand
drafts, half would be ready to sail on the 1st of February,
and the rest on the 1st of March. This was encouraging;
and, in the hope of being able at last to undertake
serious operations, Williamson left Jamaica for St.
Domingo at the end of April, to take command in
person.[1]

May 12. On the 12th of May he reached Mole St. Nicholas
and there found the Eighty-first, a new and most
promising regiment, which had lately arrived from
England, but had brought with it only three subalterns
June 17. instead of twenty-nine. After five weeks spent at the
Mole he sailed to St. Marc to inspect five companies

[1] Williamson to Portland, 18th January; to Dundas, 5th and
25th March, 24th April; Lieutenant-colonel Grant (Mole St.
Nicholas) to Dundas, 17th March and 4th April 1795.

CH. XVII   HISTORY OF THE ARMY   459

of Murray's regiment, which had come at the same time as the Eighty-first. On the 11th of April Major Bradshaw, who had succeeded Brisbane in that station, had attacked and captured, with his black troops, two batteries erected by Toussaint l'Ouverture against the town of St. Marc ; and upon the arrival of the redcoats shortly afterwards, the brigands had evacuated all their camps in the valley of the Artibonite and retired to the mountains. When Williamson arrived, however, the whole of the five companies, the dead excepted, were in hospital ; and on perusing the returns of Murray's regiment he discovered that for its ten companies it had brought with it but one captain and four subalterns. Proceeding next to Port-au-Prince, he found the situation most critical. Not only was the sea covered with French privateers, but it was impossible for a man to move a hundred yards outside the British lines without danger of being shot. Worse than this, the duty was so severe that the men had not even one night in bed regularly in the week ; and both they and their officers, being overworked, were succumbing rapidly to the climate. Lastly, in spite of requests constantly repeated both before and since the outbreak of the war, not a single item of ordnance-stores had arrived from England. Williamson's only comforts were the sight of the black troops, now five or six thousand strong and duly clothed in scarlet or green, and the receipt of a further letter from Dundas, reporting the embarkation of two more battalions and of ten troops of Light Dragoons. They were likely to be wanted, for on the 1st of June the returns showed that, of three thousand British soldiers in St. Domingo, seventeen hundred were on the sick list and but thirteen hundred fit for duty.[1]

But meanwhile unexpected events in Jamaica had greatly complicated the situation to leeward. In a

1795.

[1] Williamson to Dundas, 13th May and 6th July 1795. The returns of the five companies at St. Marc on 1st June show 37 fit for duty and 195 sick.

1795. former chapter[1] the reader's attention was specially called to the existence in Jamaica of the Maroons, a wild tribe descended from slaves who had fled from their Spanish masters to the mountains, upon the British conquest of the island in 1655. For two full generations from that time the Maroons had been the scourge of the country, coming down from their fastnesses periodically for the massacre and plunder of the planters; and the annals of Jamaica record a succession of abortive efforts on the part of the white settlers to reduce them to subjection. By natural increase and by the attraction of more runaway slaves to themselves they became at last very formidable; and about the year 1730 a leader sprang up among them who by sheer force of character welded the whole into a single united band. Their strongholds were a chain of deep glens which run from east to west through the mountains at the western end of the island, and are intersected by similar glens running across it in parallel lines from north to south. The sides of these glens, or cockpits as they were called, were of almost perpendicular rock, and the only entrance to them lay through long and deep defiles too narrow to admit two men abreast. The largest of them contained seven acres of fertile land and a spring of water; it was accessible only through a defile half a mile long, being protected by lofty precipices on both flanks; and it further possessed a line of retreat into a succession of similar cockpits. Here the chief of the Maroons made his headquarters, his followers luxuriating in indolent savagery while their provisions lasted, and then descending upon the plantations to live by brigandage. They were excellent marksmen; they were as still in ambush and as stealthy in attack as beasts of prey; they had gradually evolved a code of signals with the horn, whereby they could communicate with each other unseen, and lastly they and they alone knew the secrets of the country around their fastness. After several years of warfare they ended by forcing

[1] Vol. ii. p. 40.

the Government of Jamaica to come to terms; and in 1795. 1738 a treaty was concluded with the chiefs of the Maroons, whereby they obtained amnesty for past offences, a grant of fifteen hundred acres of land, and absolute freedom, independence and self-government. On their part they undertook to surrender all runaway slaves, to admit two white residents to live with them, to accept jurisdiction of these two in all disputes with white men, and finally to assist the King against all enemies from within and from without.

From that time forward until 1795 the Maroons gave little trouble. They were dispersed into five settlements, of which the most important lay at Trelawney, the district of the cockpits; and there they lived in a half-savage, half-civilised state, cultivating their provision-grounds regularly, breeding horses, cattle and poultry, and hunting wild swine and runaway slaves. Physically they were a splendid race, and as free men held the slaves for some years in the greatest contempt; but with the lapse of two generations the authority of their chiefs, who had ruled them with a rod of iron, dwindled gradually to nothing. Discipline among them became relaxed, and the Maroons wandered all over the island, making love to the negro-women, becoming fathers of children by them, and gradually breaking down the barrier which had formerly divided them from their fellow black men. Nevertheless at the beginning of 1795 they were still under some control, thanks to the ascendency of one of their white residents, a man of such physical strength, activity and courage that he could outdo the best of them at their most difficult feats. It so happened, however, that this gentleman succeeded to an estate which detained him for some weeks from his duty; and the Maroons, having no one to keep order among them and to compose their innumerable quarrels, became discontented. The Government thereupon appointed a new resident; but the Maroons, roused to violent rage by the loss of the man whom they adored, turned upon the newcomer

1795. and drove him from their camp. Then they called in all their people, sent their women into the mountains,
July 18. and despatched to the magistrates an insolent message of menace and defiance.

Upon the appointment of Sir Adam Williamson to the Government of St. Domingo, Major-general Lord Balcarres had succeeded him in Jamaica. The Lindsays were a fighting family, and Balcarres came early to the conclusion that he must employ strong measures. Nor can he be blamed for this, seeing that the negroes in the Windward Islands had already risen in insurrection, that Jamaica itself was full of Emigrants, of extremely doubtful character, from St. Domingo, and that there was good reason to believe that French agents had been tampering with the Maroons. By an accident, which he described as providential, the further
July 18. reinforcements destined for St. Domingo arrived at Jamaica on the very day when the difficulty with the Maroons first became serious. These were detachments, numbering together about four hundred men, of the Thirteenth, Fourteenth, Seventeenth, and Eighteenth Light Dragoons, besides the Eighty-third Foot, and a new regiment of infantry raised by Colonel George Pigot[1] in 1794. Owing to one of the Government's usual blunders these troops had been embarked in loaded merchant-ships, which by their charter-party were not bound to take them beyond Jamaica; and, during the fortnight of inevitable delay, while Balcarres was taking up fresh shipping to convey them to St. Domingo, the attitude of the Maroons determined him to detain most of these reinforcements until the rebellion should be repressed. He was not without fair excuse for doing so, since his two regiments of the line, the Sixteenth and Sixty-second, could muster but three hundred men, and the Twentieth Light Dragoons hardly as many; while the Assembly firmly refused to sanction the creation of negro-regiments. Hence it was that, at a moment when troops were most

[1] Then numbered 130th.

sorely needed in St. Domingo, the bulk of the 1795.
second instalment sent out by Dundas was kept in
Jamaica.

Since the Maroons still maintained a defiant attitude,
Balcarres resolved to draw a cordon round them, over
what he described as forty miles of the most difficult
and mountainous country in the universe; whereupon
one entire tribe of Maroons, numbering some two
hundred warriors, retired to the mountains, deter- Aug. 9.
mined to fight the matter out. A few days later they
began hostilities by attacking one of the posts in the
cordon, and killing and wounding a few men; and on
the same day Balcarres essayed a general attack, with
no further result than the entrapping of the Eighteenth
Light Dragoons in an ambuscade, and the loss to the
British of five officers and nearly thirty men killed,
besides about half as many wounded. Mortified by his
failure Balcarres strengthened his cordon with militia,
and began the destruction of the Maroons' provision-
grounds, in the hope of cooping them up and starving
them out; but the cunning savages took advantage of
these dispositions to shoot the soldiers down constantly
by twos and threes, and passed disdainfully between the
posts to plunder, burn, and destroy just as they thought
best. At the end of August the rainy season set in,
and the transport of supplies to the scene of action
became a matter of extreme difficulty. The militia
quickly wearied of the discomfort and dangers of the
campaign and returned to their homes, leaving the regular
troops, as usual, to do all the unpleasant work. The
severity of the duty soon sent many men to hospital;
and the climax of misfortune was reached when on the
12th of September Colonel Fitch, who was supreme Sept. 12.
director of the operations, fell into an ambuscade and
with two more officers was killed. After a month of warfare Balcarres's force had lost more than seventy killed,
including two field officers, besides several wounded
and several more prostrated by sickness; whereas there
was no assurance that a single one of the Maroons

1795. had been even touched. In fact, the idea of destroying the Maroons by means of a cordon was found to be both futile and absurd.

Happily Colonel Walpole of the Thirteenth Light Dragoons, who succeeded Fitch in command, had very different ideas from Balcarres as to the true method of dealing with this troublesome foe. Already the troops were sickly and dispirited, while their enemy was heartened by success, and strengthened by the addition of scores of runaway slaves. Walpole determined at once to take the offensive, and selecting the two troops of the Seventeenth Light Dragoons, who perhaps retained some recollection of their work with Tarleton in America, trained them to fight the Maroons dismounted, on their own ground and with their own weapons. The principal secret of this training was that the men should work together in pairs, so that one should always be at hand to hold the weapons of both, while the other scrambled from ledge to ledge of the rocky sides of the cockpits. It would be unprofitable to follow the innumerable little actions of the three succeeding months. It must suffice that with the help of a howitzer, which Walpole contrived to drag into position so as to drop shells into certain of the cockpits, these men of the Seventeenth, not above one hundred in all, made their way where white men had never penetrated before, and, Dec. 18. notwithstanding heavy losses, drove the Maroons with extraordinary courage from stronghold to stronghold until they fairly cowed them into surrender.

The final scene of the war was a very remarkable one. A party of the Seventeenth and of the Maroons encountered each other on opposite sides of a narrow ravine, at the foot of which was a spring of water. Both sides opened a heavy fire, and, after about a dozen of the Maroons had fallen, the rest began to blow horns as if for a parley. Still not a man of either side dared to move from cover, for all alike were deadly marksmen, until at length a volunteer, Mr. Oswald Werge, sprang up from among the Seventeenth, a target for every weapon of the enemy, and called upon the Maroons to surrender. After some parley it was agreed that both sides should retain their positions until Colonel Walpole could be summoned. Neither party trusted its opponent, and British and Maroons watched each other from their shelter through the whole night, suffering agonies of thirst but not venturing to move. At last the Maroons, unable to endure the torment longer, begged to be allowed to drink ; after which it was arranged that both sides should drink in succession, and return to their posts until Walpole should come. Never was there a finer instance of the triumph of discipline.

1795.

The sequel to the submission of the Maroons was very melancholy. Walpole had pledged himself that they should not be sent out of the island ; but the agreement was violated by Balcarres and the Assembly of Jamaica ; and the unfortunate savages were transported to Nova Scotia. Thereupon Walpole not only refused a sword of honour from the Assembly but resigned his commission. Small though was the scale of the operations, the spirit with which he inspired his troops to a service of extreme danger and exceptional hardship mark him as something more than an ordinary officer ; and it cannot be doubted that he was a loss to the Army.[1]

[1] Accounts of the Maroon War are to be found in Bryan Edward's *History of the West Indies*, Dallas's *History of the Maroons*, Bridges's *Annals of Jamaica*, and *Lives of the Lindsays*, iii. 1-146. In this last the bulk of Balcarres's official correspondence, with its enclosures, is printed, together with a connecting thread of narrative. The original letters are in the Record Office (*Col. Corres. Jamaica*, 37). It must, I fear, be added that the printed correspondence in the *Lives of the Lindsays* is not as complete as it ought to be. Balcarres and Walpole had a serious difference of opinion as to the treatment of the Maroons at the close of the war, arising (so far as I can judge) chiefly from the fact that Balcarres wished to take to himself all the credit for the ultimate success of the operations, which undoubtedly belonged to Walpole, though by him it was generously attributed to the Seventeenth Light Dragoons only. I have no wish to revive a controversy which, apparently, was still

1795. Throughout this period Williamson remained in a state of continued anxiety and suspense, not knowing when the reinforcements detained by Balcarres would reach him. By the 1st of July the seven regiments which had been the first to land in St. Domingo could not muster above five hundred men, and Williamson was obliged to pass an ordinance compelling proprietors to furnish one negro out of every fifteen for service in the field. At the end of the month Major-general Forbes arrived at the Mole with such portions of his force as Balcarres had allowed to go forward from Jamaica. It will be remembered that from Martinique also application had been made to him to spare a part of his troops, so urgent was the need for them at every point; and indeed it was perhaps a pity that he did not comply, for the handful of men which he landed at St. Domingo was too weak even to fill the gaps made by yellow fever. Between the 1st of June and the 1st of August the strength of the force, despite the arrival of Forbes's detachment, fell from three thousand to two thousand living men, of whom half were on the sick list.

July. Towards the end of July the people at Mirebalais and Grand Bois, to north and north-east of Port-au-Prince, rose and drove out the Spanish garrisons which so far had controlled them; and Toussaint L'Ouverture at once marched down from the mountains, hoping to head a general movement which should sweep the British from their posts around the Bight of Léogane.

Aug. 9. On the 9th of August, however, arrived the Eighty-second Regiment from Gibraltar; and, strengthened by this reinforcement, Williamson in September directed

---

bitter when the correspondence was published in 1849; but it is a historian's duty to call attention to the merits or demerits of printed collections of documents; and I must, therefore, point out that, at the stage where Balcarres and Walpole begin to differ, there are omitted in the *Lives of the Lindsays* important passages of Balcarres's letters and several entire letters from Walpole—omissions which are better calculated to flatter the family of Lindsay than to serve the purposes of truth. I have told the story of the Maroon War in my *History of the Seventeenth Lancers*.

his local levies to make a combined advance eastward 1795. in three columns from St. Marc, Arcahais, and Croix des Bouquets. The operations were not successful at every point, but Mirebalais and Grand Bois were gained; whereby Toussaint's designs were checked, the produce of two rich districts was secured, and the communication by land between the brigands in the north and south of the island was cut off. It was, however, impossible to press the advantage further from lack of troops. During the months of August and September over nine hundred British soldiers died, Sept. and by the 1st of October the numbers of the force had sunk again to thirteen hundred soldiers fit for duty and one thousand sick.[1]

The fatal reaction of the Maroon War upon the operations in St. Domingo becomes now more apparent, and Balcarres's responsibility for the initial mismanagement of that troublesome contest is shown to be more serious. Yet it may be doubted whether the driblets of reinforcements sent by Dundas, even if they had arrived at Domingo as he intended, would materially have affected the issue. With the exception of the detachments of light dragoons, the men were raw and untrained. The artillerymen had never seen a gun; the infantry had not even learned their firing-exercise, much less fired a musket. All, being young, were the likelier to fall victims to yellow fever; and it may be questioned whether the operations would have been greatly affected had these troops remained alive in Jamaica instead of coming over to be buried in St. Domingo. In October Balcarres did at length spare a few more men from Jamaica, but the first days of that month were among the deadliest of the sickly season; and though at its close the number of the sick had sunk to eight hundred while that of the well had risen to fifteen hundred, yet the deaths had reached the figure of

[1] Williamson to Dundas, 12th July, 5th, 12th, 31st August, 10th, 16th, 28th September; Forbes to Dundas, 31st July 1795.

1795. nearly five hundred and fifty, and the strength of the force remained practically unchanged.¹

Nov. At the end of November, however, affairs suddenly began to take a more favourable turn. News had arrived of the treaty whereby Spain had ceded St. Domingo to France; and the Spanish planters, who hated the French, seemed disposed to make common cause with the British Government. Letters came in also from Dundas, from which it was apparent that the Ministry had resolved to abandon the policy of reinforcing by small detachments, and to take the offensive in really sufficient strength both to windward and to leeward. In St. Domingo Forbes was to have command, Williamson being allowed to return to England; and he was bidden to expect, by the 1st of December at latest, the arrival of nearly sixteen thousand troops at Mole St. Nicholas. Of these more than one-half were to be British infantry, including seven battalions from England and two from Gibraltar, which, together with three battalions of foreign light infantry, made a total of nearly eleven thousand foot. The rest of the force was to consist of seven regiments of British and two of foreign light cavalry, and of two hundred and fifty artillery.²

Forbes was instructed also to cancel, if he could, the foolish treaty made with Charmilli in 1793, and to gain over the mulattos by promising them the same political privileges as the whites — this last being a point which Williamson had been urging for two years.

¹ Williamson to Dundas, 17th October; Forbes to Dundas, 10th November 1795.

² *British Infantry*: 17th, 32nd, 39th, 56th, 67th (93rd), and (99th), from England—6500 men; 66th and 89th from Gibraltar—2000 men. *British Cavalry*: 13th, 14th, 17th, 18th, 21st, 26th, 29th Light Dragoons—2500 men. *Foreign Infantry*: Salm, Ramsey, Hardy—3000 men. *Foreign Cavalry*: Hompesch, Irving—1400 men. *Artillery*: one company from England, one from Gibraltar, and drafts—257 men. The foreign troops were the remains of those that had served with the Duke of York in Flanders. The 93rd and 99th were not the regiments that now bear those numbers, but two ephemeral corps, which were soon disbanded.

On the other hand, though empowered to raise black 1795. corps, he was forbidden in the most positive terms to promise emancipation after five years' service to negro recruits, which Williamson had represented as absolutely imperative. He was, however, authorised to enter into negotiations with the chiefs of the mulattos and revolted negroes, and to spend £15,000 if necessary in gaining them over. Finally, the operations suggested, though not prescribed, to him were the capture of Cap François and Port de Paix, and the conquest of the Northern Province; while the seizure of the island of Tortuga, which lies a little to the north of the northern peninsula, was likewise put forward for consideration, as providing a base preferable to Mole St. Nicholas for the intended campaign.[1]

These letters reached Forbes on the 20th of No- Nov. 20. vember, and at once stimulated him to activity. As regards the terms to be offered to negro recruits, he absolutely declined to obey Dundas's orders, repeating Williamson's argument that, since the French Convention had decreed emancipation to every slave, it was hopeless to expect to keep negro soldiers from deserting unless the British promised them freedom likewise. The matter, indeed, was one to be decided by the Commander upon the spot, who could see things as they were; not by an ignorant Minister, surrounded by greedy merchants and rapacious, self-seeking Emigrants, four thousand miles away. Forbes began every preparation, however, for the coming operations, and in concert with Williamson at once made overtures to the chiefs of the revolted negroes. The negotiations went forward with unexpected success; and at the beginning of February 1796 Williamson wrote that, though his force at Port-au-Prince was reduced to two hundred men fit for duty, he had never felt so thoroughly at his ease as at that moment. But Forbes, who since the beginning of December had been cruising to windward off the northern coast, was

[1] Dundas to Forbes, 30th September 1795 (four letters).

1796. less sanguine; for during the whole of that month not a ship of the expected convoy had appeared. At last in
Jan. the first week of January 1796 the Sixty-sixth and Sixty-ninth from Gibraltar arrived under General Bowyer's command at the Mole; and by that time, besides other successful negotiations, a definite treaty had been concluded with Titus and Gagnet, the chiefs of a powerful band of negroes, that they should join the British in arms as soon as the reinforcements should land at Cap François.
Feb. 15. On the 15th of February Bowyer with sixteen hundred of his men arrived at Port-au-Prince, and all were in
Feb. 22. high hopes of speedy action. But on the 22nd came further letters from Dundas,[1] announcing that the great armament of sixteen thousand men, which was to have arrived on the 1st of December, had been driven back by a storm, and was consequently to be reduced to three thousand foreign troops and fifteen hundred Light Dragoons, whose time of sailing was uncertain. Deeply chagrined, Forbes saw that offensive operations in the Northern Province were out of the question, and sailed for Port-au-Prince, not without misgiving as to the results of this disappointing news.[2]

His apprehensions proved to be but too well justified. The tidings of a large force coming from England had set all the brigands fighting among themselves in mortal enmity; and there had been a general inclination on the part not only of negroes and mulattos but also of the Spaniards in St. Domingo to come to terms with the British General. When, however, but a handful of soldiers appeared, all was changed. Rigaud, the irreconcilable mulatto, persuaded several of the negro chiefs to break off negotiations with Williamson. The Spaniards

[1] These letters appear by Forbes's acknowledgment to have been dated the 13th and 24th of November 1795; the former I have been unable to discover; the latter is evidently a copy of that addressed by Dundas to Balcarres in *Col. Corres. Jamaica*.

[2] Forbes to Dundas, 9th December 1795, 6th January, 9th and 28th February 1796; Williamson to Dundas, 1st, 2nd, 27th January, 2nd, 4th, 11th, 12th, 16th, 28th February 1796.

caused Titus to be murdered, bribed Gagnet to forsake 1796. the British and to come over to themselves, entered into communications with Toussaint L'Ouverture, and refused permission to the British commissaries to purchase supplies from their territory. In the hope of stemming the current Forbes resolved to strike a blow at Rigaud by an attack on Léogane. By the 1st of March 1. March more troops had been released from Jamaica, and another West India regiment had been raised, which made up the total force in St. Domingo to thirty-five hundred men fit for duty. Moreover, upon his arrival at Port-au-Prince on the 6th of March, Forbes found that Williamson, then on the eve of departure, had already formed a plan for operations against Léogane. Accordingly, on the 18th the troops were embarked, and on the 21st two columns were landed March 21. to east and west of the town, while the fleet cannonaded the fort, which was the principal defence of the place. It was found, however, impossible to make any impression upon the fort without heavy batteries; the British troops soon began to fall down rapidly from sickness; and on the 23rd the enterprise was aban- March 23. doned with the loss of two guns and a few men, and with two ships considerably damaged.[1]

A few weeks of inaction followed; and then in the May. first week of May arrived a part of the long-expected reinforcements from England, both British troops and foreign, raising the force in St. Domingo to some seven thousand five hundred men, of whom over five thousand were fit for duty.[2] But already yellow fever had appeared again at Port-au-Prince; besides which, during the first fortnight of May, reinforcements for the enemy of two line-of-battleships and two thousand troops arrived from France at Cap François. With the

[1] Forbes to Dundas, 2nd and 4th March, 10th April 1796.
[2] *British troops*—17th, 32nd, 56th, 67th, detachments of the 39th, and the regiments (shortly afterwards disbanded) which were then numbered 93rd and 99th. *Foreign troops*—Lewes's Foot, York Hussars, Rohan's Hussars.

1796. support of these troops a French Directory now attempted to assume the government of the whole island; and Forbes, therefore, decided to keep his men together, endeavouring rather to secure the ground already held than to attempt fresh conquests. In truth, the soldiers sent to him were of poor quality, the British infantry thoroughly bad, the foreign cavalry untrustworthy and

June. ready to desert. Early in June yet more troops arrived, namely, seven regiments, more or less complete, of British Light Dragoons, some Dutch artillery, Hompesch's Hussars, and Montalembert's Legion of all three arms, the whole under command of Major-general Whyte. The foreign cavalry, however, were for the present useless, for they had no horses, and it was contrary to their conditions of service to fight on foot. It seems extraordinary that troops calling themselves light cavalry should have been engaged upon such terms; though it is more than probable that the foreigners insisted upon the letter of their contract as a protest against the dreaded and detested service in the West Indies. But yellow fever soon began to reduce Forbes's force to its old proportions. On the 1st of July, despite the reinforcements received in June, the men fit for duty had shrunk to little more than six thousand, while the sick numbered twenty-five hundred. In the months of May and June close upon thirteen hundred men died outright.[1]

In such gloomy circumstances Forbes made his second
June 8. essay in the field by an attack upon Bombarde, for the greater security of Mole St. Nicholas. He captured

[1] Forbes to Dundas, 20th and 23rd May, 1st and 20th June 1795. The force at St. Domingo on the 1st of July included the 13th, 14th, 17th, 18th, 21st, 26th, and 29th Light Dragoons; the 1st, 17th, 32nd, 56th, 66th, 67th, 69th, 81st, 82nd Foot; also detachments of the 39th, 83rd, 93rd, 99th. On that day they numbered 3155 fit for duty, 2099 sick. The foreign troops numbered 3188 fit for duty, 466 sick. The 13th and 17th Light Dragoons had apparently but four troops each in St. Domingo.

the place with little loss; the garrison of three hundred whites laying down their arms on condition that they should be allowed to withdraw to the nearest republican territory. But the conquest proved to be of little value. Within a month it was surrounded and cut off by a large force of brigands; and Whyte, who was in command at the Mole, finding it impossible to keep open communications with the fort by land or (owing to the multitude of French privateers) by sea, contrived by skilful manœuvring to bring the whole of the garrison into the Mole, and abandoned Bombarde for ever. Meanwhile sickness raged with increasing fury among the troops. The garrison stationed by Forbes at the Mole numbered eighteen hundred, of whom in a single month thirty officers and five hundred men died. In the fleet the mortality was even greater than in the army. French gunboats and small craft attacked British traders in the most daring fashion, unchecked; and, at a time when the British line-of-battleships were actually anchored at the Mole, two French frigates captured an ordnance-ship and five transports with four hundred troops on board, at a very short distance from the port. In short, the fleet, like the army, was literally paralysed by yellow fever.

1796.

July.

General Whyte now applied to Balcarres in Jamaica for reinforcements; but there too the yellow fever had fastened savagely upon the raw levies sent from England. Two miserable battalions, known as the Irish Brigade, had recently arrived at Port Royal; and of these Balcarres in August sent one, numbering fewer than four hundred men, to find graves in St. Domingo instead of in Jamaica. What the losses of the troops during the remainder of the sickly season of 1796 may have been it is impossible to state, for the returns are unfortunately undiscoverable; and it is a significant fact that not they only, but several letters written from St. Domingo at this period are missing from the records. All that is certain is that between the 1st of September 1796 and the middle of February

1796. 1797 the mortality among the European troops in St. Domingo was appalling.[1]

Nevertheless, strangely enough, the general position of the British in the island was considered more favourable during the autumn of 1796 than at any previous period. The divisions fostered among the enemy by Williamson and Forbes at the beginning of the year had never subsided; and the landing of white troops from France, together with the establishment of a Directory by the authorities at Paris, had roused bitter animosity among the brigands against the newcomers and their supporters, or, as they were called, the Republican party.

Aug. 8-12. In August determined attacks were made by Rigaud's followers upon Irois and other British posts about Jérémie; all of which were beaten off with heavy loss by the British under General Bowyer.[2] But Rigaud's enmity towards the British was as nothing to that which he nourished against the Republicans. All sections of the population, indeed, seem to have combined against this party—negroes, mulattos, British, and Spaniards; and some of the negroes even went the length of offering their services to General Whyte at Mole St. Nicholas. There are indeed many signs that all the enemies of the Republicans would gladly have placed themselves under the rule of the British,

[1] Forbes to Dundas, 19th July; Whyte to Huskisson, 25th July 1796; Balcarres to Portland, 25th August and 8th September; Simcoe to Dundas, 24th February 1797.

[2] Bowyer's letter to Forbes of 3rd September 1796, describing the actions, was published with some omissions in the *Gazette* of 20th December 1796. It mentions the 17th Light Dragoons as taking part in the operations; and I, therefore, in my *History of the Seventeenth Lancers* quoted the action as one in which the regiment had a share. Having since discovered Bowyer's original despatch (which at the time I was unable to do), I find that the regiment really engaged was the 17th Foot, the letters "L.D." having been inserted after the number 17th by the wanton carelessness of some clerk who prepared the despatch for publication. For this and for several other reasons I must warn students of military history at this period never to accept the despatches printed in the *Gazette* without first collating them with the original.

if there had been a sufficient British force for their 1796. protection. Even the Spaniards, though Spain was at war, or on the verge of war, with Britain, were ready to accept her sovereignty. The mulattos were the most doubtful element; but Rigaud himself seems to have entered into negotiations with Forbes at the beginning of 1797. Confidence was beginning to return. The rich lands at the head of the Bight of Léogane were once more in full cultivation; some of the planters were attempting to import fresh negroes as labourers; and the British garrisons had been pushed far up the river Artibonite even to Banica, beyond the former Spanish frontier. But there was no means of taking advantage of these fair appearances. "Now would be the time to strike a blow," wrote Forbes at the end of October. "Had I eight to ten thousand troops the different parts of the island would fall if attacked. . . . The north of the island will belong to the party that first sends powerful reinforcements." "There is every prospect," wrote Whyte in February 1797, "of the south being added to the British flag; but if Aux Cayes, Tiburon, Jacmel, and Léogane were to be added to us, how could we occupy them?"

The eternal difficulty lay, in fact, in the want of troops. The war with Spain had compelled Dundas to strengthen the garrisons of the Bahamas and Barbados, the former by a regiment of infantry, the latter by a regiment of light dragoons; and these could not be furnished except from the garrison of St. Domingo. The Thirty-second Foot was, therefore, made up by other regiments to a strength of five hundred men and sent to the Bahamas; and the remains of the Light Dragoons, which were then numbered Twenty-sixth and Twenty-ninth, were sent to Barbados. Thus it was that the troops, British and foreign, in St. Domingo, which in July 1796 had numbered nine thousand, had in February 1797 dwindled to a mere fourteen hundred sickly, debilitated men. Not a troop nor a company had arrived during the healthy season of 1796 to reap the harvest which, after such painful and costly labour, seemed at last ripe for the gathering. Let the scene, therefore, be shifted once more to windward, in order to explain the mystery of the neglect of St. Domingo.[1]

[1] Forbes to Dundas, 9th and 25th October, 2nd and 9th December; Whyte to Dundas, 1st November 1796, 4th February 1797.

CHAPTER XVIII

COMPARATIVELY early in the year 1795 the British 1795. Cabinet realised that the condition of affairs in the Windward Islands, consequent upon the negro insurrection, was so serious that nothing less than an expedition of overwhelming strength could amend it. The first sign of the preparations for such an undertaking appears in an order of the 30th of May for the augmentation of sixteen battalions which had recently returned from service in Flanders, a measure which was apparently effected by the drafting of several newly raised regiments into them.[1] The officer selected for the command of the expedition was Sir Ralph Abercromby, who on the 9th of October received his instructions, namely, to sail with his force to Barbados, deal first with Guadeloupe and St. Lucia, which were to be his principal object, and then consider the feasibility of an attack upon the Dutch settlements of Surinam, Berbice, and Demerara.[2]

[1] *S.C.L.B.* 30th May, 17th June, 15th and 20th August, 4th September 1795.

[2] By a return of November 1795 the force under Abercromby's immediate command was as follows:—

26th Light Dragoons, Royal Irish Artillery.
1st Brigade—14th, 27th, 28th, 57th.
2nd Brigade—3rd, 19th, 31st, 33rd.
3rd Brigade—8th, 37th, 44th, 55th.
4th Brigade—38th, 48th, 53rd, 63rd.
5th Brigade—2nd, 10th, 25th, 29th, 88th.
6th Brigade—2 composite batts. of Grenadiers, 42nd.
Hospital Corps.

Total—641 officers, 17,792 non-commissioned officers and men. The force that was designed to start for St. Domingo at the same time is given in the preceding chapter, p. 468, *note* 2.

1795. At the same time he was informed that a part of his force was designed for St. Domingo, but that the officer in command there would correspond with him and receive his orders. How the correspondence from St. Domingo was to make its way to Abercromby over a distance of a thousand miles in the teeth of the trade-wind was a detail that was left unexplained. However, Dundas really seems to have flattered himself that the expedition would be ready to sail at the end of September, so as to arrive in the West Indies at the very beginning of the healthy season. But the wind was contrary until the first days of November; and when the weathered changed it was discovered that the force was not ready to proceed. In what respect the preparations were defective does not, unfortunately, appear, though sundry indications point to the Ordnance Office as the guilty party. In any case the causes of delay were stigmatised by Lord Buckingham, a zealous supporter of Government, as grossly scandalous and criminal; and the delay itself had the worst effect upon the troops. "Among a thousand horrid consequences," wrote Buckingham, "it is not the least important that the officers and men have had leisure to frame to themselves every mischievous apprehension that can arrive from disaffection to this service."[1] Better evidence could hardly be afforded of the utter distrust which Ministers had inspired into all ranks of the military profession; yet it seems never to have occurred to the magnates of Downing Street that they themselves and not the Army were answerable for this. A service which calls men to certain and ignoble destruction without offering a chance of honour, or even the comforting sense that their death may be of benefit to their country, is not a service that is calculated to conciliate affection. Military discipline is great and powerful; but it cannot convince men that they are martyrs to patriotism when they know themselves to be only the victims of imbecility.

[1] *Dropmore Papers*, iii. 142.

Dundas was, very justly and rightly, frantic with rage. 1795. "I shall be glad to know," he wrote to Abercromby, "where the blame lies, for the public will hold me responsible if the wind is lost. Should you not sail with what is ready and let the rest follow? If we are to wait for every transport or boat that may receive a hurt, or for every article that a Department may be negligent in sending, I see no reason to hope that you will be more ready to sail a month hence than you are now. I really feel it a disgrace to the executive Government of this country and to every branch acting under it, that an expedition determined on six months ago should not be in a state to sail seven weeks after the appointed time." This last sentence was no more than just. No doubt the unreadiness of the expedition was a disgrace to the executive Government and to every branch acting under it; but the executive Government had borne such disgraces with remarkable indifference for a full century, and was destined to bear them with like equanimity for the best part of a century more. There had been precisely the same unreadiness in every armament which Dundas had despatched since the beginning of the war; the deficiencies in the expedition under review had actually been brought to his notice by Huskisson; and he had made no effort to furnish a remedy. On the contrary, we shall see the same evils repeated continually up to the end of his administration. Meantime it is not easy to divine what object could be gained by hurrying the troops to sea while still imperfectly equipped. It is true that many expeditions had started not only late but incomplete, sometimes shamefully incomplete, in such trifling details as arms, ammunition, clothing, money, and medical stores; but the result had not been encouraging. Grey, for instance, had arrived at Barbados with a sick-list of twelve hundred men from want of a hospital-ship; and every commander-in-chief, from the Duke of York in Flanders to Sir Alured Clarke at the Cape, had found good reason to

1795. make like complaints. As his letter shows, Dundas desired this expedition also to start incomplete; and Huskisson likewise warned Abercromby that the loss of twelve hours' fair wind might mean a delay of two months. But though the General must have been quite aware of this fact, he was firm in refusing to sail until the defects, whatever they were, had been made good; and it would be contrary to all that we know of his zeal and ability to suppose that he was wrong. Thus the fair wind was lost, with results that were far-reaching beyond all calculation.[1]

On the 16th of November the transports sailed from Portsmouth under convoy of a squadron commanded by Admiral Christian. On the 18th they were off Weymouth, standing down channel with a light breeze and every stitch of canvas set, a sight so beautiful that thousands stood watching it from the shore. On the same afternoon the wind changed to the south-west, freshening continually until at night it attained to the force of a hurricane. The men-of-war took shelter at Portland and many other vessels at Weymouth; but many more, overladen or ill-handled, were driven ashore by the storm, and several were lost with all hands. For a week the coast from Portland to Abbotsbury was strewn with corpses, of which very many were those of soldiers; and the convoy put back to Portsmouth, having suffered much damage.

Nov. 18.

Meanwhile fresh news arrived from the West Indies, which necessitated a change in Abercromby's instructions. The foreign troops, of which the greater part of the force for St. Domingo was to have been composed, had not arrived, and, moreover, the Government now judged it expedient to raise Abercromby's army to a strength which would enable him to attack Guadeloupe and St. Lucia simultaneously. General Whyte was therefore ordered to send forward only

---

[1] Dundas to Abercromby, 9th October (instructions), 3rd November; Huskisson to Abercromby, 21st October and 9th November 1795.

CH. XVIII   HISTORY OF THE ARMY   481

his seven regiments of Light Dragoons to St. Domingo, 1795. and to remain with his infantry at Barbados to await Abercromby's orders. Then, since twelve thousand men were still in a condition to start almost immediately, Dundas gave Abercromby positive instructions to sail with them by the first fair wind after the 28th of November. The fleet accordingly put to sea on the 3rd of December,[1] but was caught once again Dec. 3. by a gale in the Channel and dispersed in all directions. The flag-ship *Glory*, upon which Abercromby had embarked with Admiral Christian, battled with the weather for seven whole weeks in the vain endeavour to get clear of the Channel, but was driven back to Portsmouth. About thirty transports also returned to England; and on the 26th of Dec. 26. December one hundred of them were reported missing, whether in the West Indies or at the bottom of the sea, no one could tell. One vessel, containing a part of the Eighty-eighth, was actually blown through the Straits of Gibraltar, was frapped together at Carthagena and thence navigated once more to Gibraltar, where the men had hardly been landed from her before she fell to pieces.[2] A few ships were captured by the French both in the Atlantic and in the Caribbean Sea. It was owing to this dispersion that the reinforcements arrived, as we have seen, by single vessels at Barbados, enabling the British in St. Vincent and Grenada to hold their own but no more.[3]

On the 10th of January 1796, though Abercromby had not then returned, it was found necessary to draw up for the General a third set of instructions. A wide discretion was allowed to him, but he was informed that the Government now considered St. Domingo the principal object, and was prepared to give him at once six thousand foreign troops and two additional British

[1] Dundas says that it sailed on the 9th.
[2] Cannon's Records of the 88th Foot.
[3] Dundas to Abercromby, 23rd November 1795; to Maj.-gen. Leigh, 9th January 1796.

VOL. IV   2 I

1796. battalions, besides four thousand men more, which were
Feb. to be despatched to join him in April. Finally, when the General and Admiral did return, a fourth set of instructions, drawn up early in February in accordance with later news from the West Indies, made the expulsion of the enemy from Grenada and St. Vincent the first object, the capture of St. Lucia and Demerara the second, and relegated St. Domingo to the background. Eleven thousand of the troops, in all, had returned to England, so it was assumed that six thousand would have arrived at Barbados; but of those that actually reached the island but one regiment was complete, the remainder including fragments of no fewer than twenty corps, varying in strength from six men to four hundred. It was clear therefore that the work of reorganising the force would be severe. Nor was the ill luck of adverse weather confined to England only, for the ships conveying the troops for St. Domingo, which started from Cork on the 10th of February, were also scattered by a storm, and such vessels as returned were not able to start again until the 24th. Never did any expedition pay more dearly for its unreadiness than this to the West Indies in 1795.[1]

The main body of the expedition seems finally to have sailed at the end of February from Portsmouth, where the confusion in getting it to sea was incredible. So miserable was the want of order and method in the naval as well as the military departments that no rendezvous was given to the masters of transports in case the convoy should be dispersed. Abercromby, however, having already sailed independently in a
March 17. frigate, arrived at Barbados on the 17th of March. There he found about five thousand troops on the spot; some eighteen hundred more having been detached to the help of Martinique, Grenada, and St. Vincent, while nearly two hundred of the Eighth and Fifty-

---

[1] Dundas to Abercromby, 10th January, 3rd February, 3rd March 1796; Pitt to Grenville, 3rd January 1796. *Dropmore Papers*, iii. 166.

seventh were serving on board the King's ships *Pique* 1796. and *Charon*. His first care was to reinforce Brigadier Nicolls at Grenada, who was preparing to drive the brigands from their position at Grenville. Six hundred men of the Tenth, Twenty-fifth, Twenty-ninth, and Eighty-eighth had already been sent to that island at the beginning of the month, and to these were now added detachments of the Buffs, Eighth and Sixty-third, which arrived at their destination on the 24th of March. March 24.

The brigands were strongly posted on a ridge overlooking what is now called St. Andrew's Bay, and was then known as Marquis Bay or Port Royal. Their front was towards the south, their left rested on the sea, and their right was protected by ground so difficult as to be impracticable; the ascent to the ridge was steep, and the summit crowned by a fort which was armed with four field-guns and several swivels, and covered by a strong abatis. Landing his troops a thousand yards to south of this ridge, Nicolls spent the night of the 24th in throwing up a battery, and on the following morning opened a cannonade from March 25. two field-guns and a howitzer. Under cover of this fire he sent a party of the Eighty-eighth, supported by a strong detachment of black troops, to carry the right of the enemy's position, hoping thus to cut off their retreat from the interior and to drive them into the sea. This attack was, however, repelled with heavy loss, the enemy closely pursuing the defeated British; and at this critical moment two large French schooners sailed into Marquis Bay with reinforcements from Guadeloupe, threatening to land their troops against Nicolls's flank. Nicolls turned one of his field-guns upon them without effect, and then, seeing that no time was to be lost, ordered a general attack upon the whole front of the enemy's position. The Buffs led the assault, but, though four of their officers and a few of their men broke through the abatis, every one of these was killed and wounded, and the rest gave way.

1796.
March 25.
The Sixty-third and Twenty-ninth, however, came up rapidly in support ; and the whole then advanced with great spirit, carried the summit of the hill, and climbing in at the embrasures swept the enemy out of the fort. In panic terror the brigands fled towards the sea, from which the two French schooners opened fire to check the British pursuit. But Nicolls had kept two troops of the Seventeenth Light Dragoons and a small body of local cavalry under cover on this side ; and these now charged, heedless of a cross-fire from the French ships, and cut down the fugitives without mercy. Only six prisoners were taken, for the enemy were chiefly ruffians of the worst description from Guadeloupe, whose shameful treatment of the prisoners taken at Berville was well known to the troops. The losses of the British in this affair were six officers and one hundred and five men killed and wounded, half of whom belonged to the Buffs. The loss of the enemy was five or six times as great. Such as survived the sabres of the cavalry fled to the woods, allowing Nicolls to reoccupy the ports and to prevent the arrival of further reinforcements from Guadeloupe. In fact the action went so far towards crushing the insurrection in Grenada that Abercromby felt no hesitation in postponing further operations there to a more convenient season.[1]

In all other respects, however, Abercromby's position was extremely difficult and trying. The Quartermaster-general, Knox, had been indefatigable in making all possible preparations in his department, and had collected two thousand four hundred negroes to act as pioneers. But, on the other hand, the West India Regiments, of which Dundas had by this time sanctioned the creation of six, were making no progress, nor were likely to do so until the British Government, as the Generals had

[1] Nicolls to Abercromby, 28th March 1795. *Historical Record of the Buffs*, pp. 210-212. *Autobiography of Sir J. M'Grigor*, pp. 59-64. This last gives an extremely unflattering account of the behaviour of the Buffs, with what justice I am unable to say.

repeatedly recommended, should purchase recruits for 1796. itself. Money, meanwhile, was so scarce that it was scarcely to be obtained even at a cost of ten per cent upon every bill drawn upon England. The season was far advanced, yet half of Abercromby's troops had not arrived; nor did he dare to send more of those which were at his disposal to St. Vincent and Grenada, lest the trade-wind should unduly delay their return to Barbados for the attack on St. Lucia. Moreover, the behaviour of the new levies recently engaged in St. Vincent had been neither creditable nor encouraging. As to St. Domingo, it was ridiculous to suppose that the operations there could be controlled from the Windward Islands, owing to the impossibility of his receiving reports; and the General therefore begged that it might be removed from his command. But the trouble which annoyed him above all others was that the naval Commander-in-chief, Admiral Cornwallis, had not sailed to the West Indies, like himself, in a single frigate, and so was not on the spot to concert operations; though, as the General rightly said, everything depended upon the navy. Abercromby was naturally a man of the gentlest temper and firmest resolution, but after the seven terrible weeks on board ship in continuous gales he began to feel the weight of his sixty-two years, and was probably never so much out of heart with his work as in this West Indian campaign.

At last on the 1st of April a first instalment of April. troops arrived. They were the reinforcements bound from Cork for St. Domingo under General Whyte; and the inspection of them did not reassure the Commander-in-chief. "They are in all respects a very inefficient force," he wrote; "no reliance can be placed on them. I doubt if five hundred of them will be alive on the 1st of November." Three days later arrived April 4. Admiral Laforey, but with only a part of his squadron, the rest having been dispersed in all directions for the blockade of Guadeloupe and other services. However, he was able to spare four frigates to escort Whyte with

1796. the Thirty-ninth and two more regiments to Demerara and Berbice, which had offered to place themselves under British protection; and Whyte, accordingly sail-
April 15. ing for these Colonies on the 15th, was in possession of both of them before the end of the month. A part of the Thirty-ninth was left to hold these new conquests; and the reinforcements for St. Domingo were thus not only weakened but were delayed for several weeks. However, a large quantity of produce was preserved to fill the pockets of British merchants who had invested their capital in the Dutch Colonies; and this was an advantage which, in Dundas's judgment, far outweighed such trivial matters as the general conduct of operations and the lives of a few hundred British soldiers.

April 14-15. Meanwhile on the 14th and 15th of April two divisions of Cornwallis's convoy arrived, though still without the Admiral; and Abercromby, having now a sufficiency of ships and nearly eight thousand men fit for duty, determined no longer to delay his attack upon St. Lucia. It is worth while to mention the names of three remarkable men who were thrown together at Barbados in those days of April. The first was the old Marquis of Bouillé, the hero of the mutiny at Nanci and the projector of the flight to Varennes; the second was Brigadier John Moore, who had recently been sent home from Corsica in consequence of a quarrel with Sir Gilbert Elliot; and the third was Colonel Thomas Maitland, of whose good service we shall soon see more, but who became later still more famous as "King Tom of the Ionian Islands" and lives immortalised in the history of *Mr. Midshipman Easy*.[1]

April 21. On the 21st of April the convoy weighed anchor, and, apparently by Admiral Laforey's wish, made for St. Anne's Bay, just within the southern extremity of Martinique, where it anchored on the evening of the
April 23. 23rd. On the following day Admiral Christian, who had arrived in a frigate, took over the naval command,

[1] Abercromby to Dundas, 9th April (official and private), 2nd May 1796. *Diary of Sir John Moore*, i. 195.

and after three days spent in concerting plans which, 1796. but for his absence, could have been matured long before, the expedition sailed on the night of the 25th April 25. for St. Lucia. Abercromby's design was to effect a landing at three different points under cover of three divisions of the fleet; namely in Anse du Cap, the bay between Pigeon Island and Pointe du Cap, at the northwestern extremity of the island; at Anse du Choc, a few miles to south of it; and at Anse la Raye, from five to six miles south of Port Castries. By daylight of the 26th the fleet was off Anse du Cap, where the Fourteenth April 26. Foot and Forty-second Highlanders were landed under command of Moore, who at once made dispositions to cover a further disembarkation. His skirmishers were engaged all day with small parties of the enemy; and, though an order arrived from Abercromby to delay the landing because the Admiral was not ready, Moore prevailed that the force at this point should be made complete by the debarkation of the Forty-eighth and a battalion of Grenadiers. At three o'clock on the following morning he marched southward along the April 27. shore; and the enemy, finding the batteries which covered Anse du Choc taken in rear, at once abandoned them. A second division of troops, together with Abercromby and the Admiral, thereupon disembarked in Anse du Choc; and on the same evening the General gave orders for a further advance upon Morne Chabot, a commanding post near Morne Fortuné, the possession of which was essential to the investment of that fortress from the north.

The attack was to be made in two columns, the first, April 28. under Moore, consisting of nine hundred men of the Fifty-third, Fifty-seventh, Löwenstein's regiment of foreign riflemen, and two hundred of the Second West India Regiment; the second comprising the remainder of the Fifty-seventh, two small parties of Löwenstein's and the rest of the Second West India Regiment, under Brigadier John Hope. The two columns were to move by different roads; and, since

1796.
April 28.
communication in so rugged a country was practically impossible, Moore arranged with Hope that he himself should open the onset immediately before dawn, upon which signal Hope should attack simultaneously from a different point. Basing their calculations upon the information of their guides, Moore started at midnight and Hope half an hour later, with the not uncommon result that Moore's column struck upon the enemy's advanced picquet an hour and a half before the appointed time. His men being drawn out in single file along a steep and narrow path, Moore had no alternative but to begin the assault forthwith; wherefore he at once led them up the hill, while the enemy hastily formed on the summit. The ground presently permitting him to widen his front to six or eight men abreast, he called upon the advanced companies not to fire but to charge with the bayonet. The men, however, were raw recruits; their officers were as raw as they; and though they faced the enemy bravely enough, they would not charge but insisted upon firing, though they moved forward very slowly as they did so. The enemy replied with effect, for the distance between the two parties was small; and, to make matters worse, the rear-companies of Moore's column also opened fire, thus placing their unfortunate comrades in advance between two fires. Happily by the exertions of Moore and his staff the men at last carried the summit of the hill, where shortly after daybreak he was joined by Hope. The light being now strong, Moore's quick eye at once perceived the importance of the commanding peak of Morne Duchazeau, which dominates Morne Fortuné from the east and forms part of the same ridge with it. Leaving therefore the Fifty-third at Morne Chabot, he, after a weary march over abominable roads, established the rest of his corps in this position, and pushed his outposts forward to within twelve hundred yards of Morne Fortuné. The casualties of the British in this affair were seventy killed and wounded, including three officers, the whole of the loss falling upon the flank-

companies of the Fifty-third. That of the enemy was about the same. Had the British been of the quality which Grey led to the attack of Martinique two years earlier, they would not have lost a dozen men.

The events of the day were not wholly fortunate, for if the two columns had attacked simultaneously few of the enemy would have escaped. However, the occupation of Morne Duchazeau was a great gain, since it ensured a point of communication between the troops already landed and landing to the north of Castries, and the third division which was to disembark at Anse la Raye. This last, which was under the command of Major-general Morshead, effected its debarkation without loss on the 28th. On the 1st of May there was a sharp skirmish between the outposts on the side of Castries, which cost the British some fifty killed and wounded; and on the next day Abercromby directed Morshead's force to advance northward, cross the Cul de Sac River and carry the batteries on the southern slopes of Morne Fortuné, so as to open Cul de Sac Bay to the fleet. Morshead being seized with the gout, the command of his force devolved upon Brigadier Perryn, an officer whom even the charitable Abercromby described as a madman. Unfortunately his mania did not take the form of excessive boldness. He advanced in two columns, of which the left, under Colonel Riddle, duly reached its appointed place and took a battery. Hope, also, who had been detached from the side of Morne Fortuné to help the movement, captured and held a second battery; but Perryn's column, which should have supported and connected these two attacks, did not cross the Cul de Sac River at all. The two isolated detachments of Hope and Riddle were therefore necessarily withdrawn, not without difficulty owing to the skirmishers that harassed them from the jungle on every side; and the operation resulted in total failure with a loss of ten officers and ninety men killed, wounded and missing. Among the killed was Colonel Malcolm, the excellent officer who

1796. may be called the father of our African regiments. Arriving as a Captain with Grey, he had raised his irregular corps of negroes after the capture of Martinique, had lived through two fearful epidemics of yellow fever, and had been engaged in more actions and probably more frequently under fire than any other officer in the West Indies. His name is just remembered as the founder of the First West India Regiment, but he deserves record rather as one of those officers, fortunately not uncommon though too easily forgotten among us, whose skill, courage and magic of leadership can turn the rawest of material into the most devoted and efficient of soldiers.[1]

Much annoyed at this mishap, Abercromby sent General Graham to take command of Morshead's division, and ordered Perryn to prepare to start for St. Domingo. Batteries for ten pieces were thrown up on the ridge of Morne Duchazeau; and the arrival, May 9. on the 9th of May, of the Twenty-seventh and Fifty-seventh Regiments enabled Abercromby to connect the divisions of Moore and Graham and to make the investment of the Morne more or less complete. Several of the enemy were killed in attempting to break through the cordon; but nevertheless the operations dragged on slowly and unsatisfactorily. The labour of making roads over a country so steep and rugged was very great; and the distribution of supplies to an investing line ten miles long and divided by such a mountain as Morne Fortuné, was a work of great difficulty. Moreover, hardly a man in the army took kindly to his work. The soldiers were ill-trained and ill-disciplined, and the officers not only ignorant and inexperienced but poor in quality and the reverse of zealous. Hence neither were to be trusted upon any service, not even to be vigilant when on duty with outposts and picquets. The Major-generals were also

[1] The regiments engaged were the whole or parts of the 14th, 27th, 28th, 42nd, 44th, under Perryn; the 42nd, a light company of the 57th, and the 2nd W.I.R. under Hope.

unfit for their position; while the engineers though unskilful were dogmatic and exacting, and caused much delay by requiring many more guns to be brought up than were necessary. In fact the work of all officers excepting the Commander-in-chief was done by the three brigadiers, Hope, Knox, and Moore, who in consequence could find no rest by day or night. 1796.

At length on the 16th fire was opened from eighteen pieces of ordnance upon Morne Fortuné; but the range was so great and the guns so ill-aimed that little damage was done. On the night of the 17th, by Abercromby's direction, an attack was delivered upon Vigie, on the north side of Port Castries, by the Thirty-first Regiment, which was beaten back with the loss of nearly two hundred officers and men killed, wounded and taken. The result was due to the ignorance of the commanding officer, his neglect of the General's orders, and the bad discipline of the men, in fact to the utter unfitness of one and all for active service. The men instead of moving forward in order silently and swiftly with the bayonet, made a slow and straggling advance, firing as they went. This naturally brought upon them a heavy discharge of grape under which great numbers of them fell, and the rest ran back. Abercromby, though greatly disgusted, took no public notice of the matter. "The censure of their brother-soldiers is sufficient," he said; but in truth this force of Abercromby's did not consist of soldiers at all. It was composed simply of groups of men in the dress and appointments of famous regiments; and it represented only too truly the state to which the Army had been reduced by the insane military policy of Pitt and Dundas. May 16. May 17.

Meanwhile the construction of a second line of advanced batteries had been begun upon the ridge of Morne Duchazeau; and, at the request of Moore, Brigadier Knox was appointed to take command of them and to push forward the operations in that quarter with greater energy. At daylight on May 19.

1796. the 24th these new batteries opened fire; and three
May 24. hours later Moore, at the head of the Twenty-seventh Regiment, stormed a flèche, which formed the principal outwork of Morne Fortuné towards the east, beat off two determined attempts of the enemy to recapture it, and before night had made the post thoroughly secure. The Twenty-seventh in this affair lost eight officers and over eighty men killed and wounded, displaying a steadfastness and gallantry worthy of its best days. On the same evening the enemy sent out a flag of
May 25. truce, and on the following day a capitulation was signed; whereupon the garrison of Morne Fortuné, about two thousand strong but composed chiefly of negroes and coloured men, marched out with the honours of war and laid down their arms.

Thus St. Lucia was recovered, so far as surrender could restore it, having cost the British thirty-nine officers and five hundred and twenty men killed, wounded and missing. It was, as Abercromby confessed, a barren conquest. The island except as a military post had ceased to be of any value; and there was every reason to suppose that the brigands still hiding in the jungle would give much trouble. Moore therefore was left in command with about four thousand men [1] as the officer best qualified for so difficult a charge. "Everything," wrote Abercromby, "is to be expected from his spirit and good sense." Of Hope and Knox he spoke as highly as of Moore; but, now that he had accomplished the first part of his task, he wrote a frank opinion of his officers and his troops. In particular he warned the Government against foreign regiments, many men having deserted from those sent out with him, and but one corps, Löwenstein's, having proved of any value. Then, after repeating his request to be allowed to retire from the service, for which his advanced age unfitted him,
June 3. he embarked on the 3rd of June, having parted his

[1] 31st, 44th, 48th, 55th, York Rangers (Foreign), and black troops.

army into two divisions for the recovery of St. Vincent 1796. and Grenada.¹

Sailing first to the island of Carriacou with the Grenada division, Abercromby arranged with the Admiral the course of operations in that island, and on the 7th returned to St. Vincent, where the appointed troops were already waiting at Kingston. On the 8th they were disembarked and on the following day the entire force marched in one column from Kingston to the insurgents' position on the Vigie, where it halted for the night with each division posted opposite to its selected point of attack. On the following morning a detachment under Brigadier Knox passed round the enemy's seaward flank, so as to cut him off from the northern part of the island; another detachment under Lieutenant-colonel Dickens of the Thirty-fourth was ordered to make a diversion on the opposite flank; and the main body with much difficulty brought forward four field-guns and two howitzers to within six hundred yards of the French redoubts. From seven o'clock until two in the afternoon the cannonade continued, during which time two companies of the Forty-second and some of Löwenstein's Corps, taking advantage of dead ground, crept up close to the works. At two o'clock the assault was delivered by these troops, strengthened by the Buffs, two more companies of the Forty-second, and the foreign corps known as the York Rangers; and the brigands, being swept out of three redoubts, took refuge in their principal post, known as the New Vigie. Here, however, finding retreat cut off by Dickens, they capitulated to the number of six hundred, though not before the Caribs and nearly two hundred of the insurgents had fled to the forest. A detachment was at once pushed northward to Black Ridge or Mount Young to intercept the fugitives, while a second detachment embarked for Owia, where, however, it was unable

June 7.

June 9.

¹ Abercromby to Dundas, 2nd, 4th, 22nd, 30th, 31st May, 1st June 1795. *Diary of Sir John Moore*, i. 195-220.

1796. to land owing to the surf. Seventeen pieces of ordnance and a quantity of ammunition were captured, and the strength of the insurrection in St. Vincent was decisively broken. The loss of the British in this affair was seventeen officers and one hundred and sixty-eight men killed and wounded.[1]

Not less successful were the operations carried on simultaneously at Grenada. There Nicolls landed the
June. troops granted to him by Abercromby at Palmiste, near Goyave, on the western coast, where was the enemy's principal camp; while at the same time a column under Brigadier Campbell advanced from the eastern coast of the island to take it in rear. The French commander and a portion of his force thereupon surrendered; but Fédon with about three hundred followers fled to his own stronghold in the mountains above, where they were at once invested. Abercromby himself visited the besieging force before this position;
June 18. and a few days after his departure Nicolls, under cover of night, pushed some of his troops up to the very summit of Fédon's natural citadel, where the brigands no sooner saw them than they ran down in panic to the woods. They were hotly pursued and over one hundred of them were killed; but Fédon himself escaped. Savage to the last he murdered from twenty to thirty white prisoners before he finally fled, thus ending his career, as he had begun it, by massacre. The losses of the British in these operations were slight, not exceeding seventy officers and men killed and wounded. This was a fatal blow to the insurrection in Grenada. The renegade whites, who had joined themselves to Fédon, surrendered; and the civil courts promptly hanged fourteen out of eighty of them, and would have hanged forty but for the Governor's intervention. Fédon's few remaining followers were quickly hunted

---

[1] The regiments engaged were the whole or portions of the Buffs, 34th, 40th, 42nd, 46th, 59th, 2nd W.I.R., Löwenstein's, York Rangers, and two local black Corps. Abercromby to Dundas, 21st June 1795.

down, and in July he himself was surprised in a hut 1796. on the brink of a precipice, over which he disappeared and, whether dead or alive, was heard of no more.[1]

This final success at Grenada closed the campaign, though affairs were far from settled either in St. Vincent or St. Lucia; but an attack upon Guadeloupe and the eradication of the centre of disturbance was beyond the power of Abercromby's force. After arranging for the distribution of the troops in the various islands he sailed home in August, much broken Aug. in health, leaving General Graham to command in his place. In St. Vincent, however, the work of restoring order proceeded apace, and by November not only Nov. all the negro insurgents but all the Caribs had come in, the latter to be deported in the following March to the island of Rattan in the Gulf of Honduras. In St. Lucia, Moore's task was less easy, partly from the number of brigands still at large, partly from the incapacity of his officers, but chiefly from the frightful mortality among his troops. In St. Lucia and Grenada the yellow fever raged as furiously as in St. Domingo during the hurricane-season of 1796; and in the British islands to windward, including those officially termed Leeward Islands, nearly two thousand five hundred British soldiers died between the 1st of April and the 1st of October. In that same month of October the garrison of St. Lucia buried six hundred and thirty-three men, and there was hardly a regiment in the other islands which did not bury from one to two hundred. By November, Moore's force, which on the first of June had been four thousand strong, was reduced to a thousand fit for duty and fifteen hundred sick, the remaining fifteen hundred having died. At this time the white troops in the islands to windward, including a detachment at Demerara, counted rather more than eleven thousand fit for duty and nearly five thousand sick. The full returns being

[1] Abercromby to Dundas (with enclosures from Nicolls), 22nd and 23rd June 1796.

1797. undiscoverable, it is impossible to state the number of the dead, still less of those who, though surviving, were unfitted by debility for further service. It must suffice that this force of Abercromby's, like that of Grey before it, was practically diminished by one-half through yellow fever.[1]

So ended the third campaign in the West Indies; and it was now plain to every thinking man—it was beginning even to dawn upon Ministers—that so costly a warfare could not be prolonged. The number of men buried annually by the Army and Fleet in the West Indies during the three years 1794, 1795, and 1796 cannot be reckoned at a lower figure than from ten to twelve thousand, or say thirty-five thousand men in all, of which twenty-five thousand may be reckoned as belonging to the Army. Official returns give the number of soldiers killed or dead in the service in all quarters during the year 1794 at eighteen thousand six hundred; and of soldiers discharged as unfit for further service from wounds or other infirmities during 1795 and 1796 at forty thousand six hundred. Adding to these figures eighteen thousand dead during the years 1795 and 1796, and say three thousand dead and discharged during 1793, both of which computations are extremely moderate, we reach the total of eighty thousand soldiers lost to the service, including forty thousand actually dead, the latter number exceeding the total losses of Wellington's army from death, discharges, desertion and all causes from the beginning to the end of the Peninsular War. Yet with all this miserable waste and squandering of life France, as must now be shown, was little the worse, and England even less the better.

[1] Graham to Dundas, 9th September, 16th October, 15th November 1796.

CHAPTER XIX

OUR last glimpse of Europe was at the conclusion of 1795. the Treaty of Bâle, in April 1795, the act which proclaimed in public the final dissolution of the first European Coalition. From that moment it may be said that military operations were practically suspended in Europe until the autumn. The combatants one and all were greatly exhausted. England had chosen to waste her strength in the West Indies. Austria was reserving the best of her armed force to assure to herself the share of Poland that had fallen to her under the Treaty of Partition; and she was determined, unless Russia should guarantee to her possession of this new territory, to make peace with France. In June Russia gave the required guarantee, but still the Imperial troops remained inactive on the eastern bank of the Rhine; for Thugut was resolved that not an Austrian soldier should move against the French until Prussia also should accept the Partition Treaty; and it was not until the 19th of October that, after long hesitation and reluctance, Frederick William finally acquiesced in the new distribution of Poland. The campaign on the Rhine, however, had been opened some weeks earlier by Jourdan and Pichegru, who early in September passed the river, Sept. 7. and for a time met with considerable success. But in October the tide began to turn. On the 29th of the Oct. 29. month Clerfaye gained a brilliant victory over the French before Mainz; and during the following weeks the French were borne steadily back both by him and by his colleague Wurmser. By the end of the year

1795. Mannheim, Mainz, Frankfort, and the greater part of the Palatinate had been recovered by the Austrians, while the French were not only beaten but demoralised. On the other hand, by the victory of Loano on the
Nov. 23. 23rd of November Massena had gained for France the Genoese Riviera and the command of the passes into Piedmont. This success on the side of Italy might fairly be taken to counterbalance the failures of Pichegru and Jourdan on the Rhine.

The victories of Clerfaye and Wurmser had been, however, more than ordinarily timely. On the 18th of February 1795 England had concluded a defensive treaty with Russia, and on the 20th of May a further treaty of alliance with Austria, which agreements were
Sept. 28. consolidated on the 28th of September into a Triple Alliance of Austria, Russia, and England, under which Russia bound herself to furnish a contingent, and Austria to put forth her full strength, in the war against France. The behaviour of Austria in respect of Belgium had not been calculated to inspire England with confidence; and though Fox alone, as leader of the Opposition in the House of Commons, had given voice to the nation's disgust at Austria's faithlessness, yet there can be little doubt that, at heart, every member of the Cabinet was in sympathy with him. Nevertheless, rather than abandon the struggle while there was a chance of adjusting a satisfactory balance of power in Europe, Pitt resolved to bear even with the duplicities and trickeries of Thugut. It was not for England to complain of Austria's subordination of the common interest to her own designs of acquisition. "Our mouths are unfortunately stopped," wrote Windham with his usual candour to Grenville, "by our own proceedings in the East and West Indies."[1] Nevertheless, when the whole summer passed away without the slightest movement of the Austrians on the Rhine,
Sept. Pitt lost patience, and despatched a special emissary to

[1] Windham to Grenville, 13th February 1795. *Dropmore Papers*, iii. 19.

CH. XIX   HISTORY OF THE ARMY   499

Vienna to ascertain, if possible, what the true intentions 1795. of Austria might be. Thugut, however, would say nothing except that, since Prussia had withdrawn from the contest, it was the Emperor's intention to divert the main strength of his force to Italy. This, though Sir Morton Eden knew it not, was the outcome of Thugut's treaty with Russia of the 3rd of January 1795, under which he hoped to gain Venetia for Austria as the prize of a war against Turkey. As to Germany, of which the Emperor Francis was the nominal head and protector, Thugut would not move a finger to save it, unless his master should receive subsidies from England, and troops from the German States, as well as the provinces of Bavaria, Alsace and possibly Lorraine for indemnities. The prospect, therefore, seemed hopeless, for Pitt was rightly determined not to squander more millions upon a power which was always demanding money for the common cause and spending it for her private advantage.[1]

Thugut, however, was unwilling to come to a final decision without consulting Russia and assuring himself of her support. Thereupon Catherine pointed out that peace with France under its existing government was out of the question ; and though, being herself intent upon her Turkish designs, she showed little readiness to take part in the struggle against the French, she none the less urged upon Austria by no means to abandon operations on the Rhine. At this moment Grenville, reassured by the successes of Clerfaye and Wurmser, offered to Russia an annual subsidy of a million sterling in return for a force of fifty thousand men, and to Austria the guarantee of a loan of three millions if she would abandon extensive operations in Italy, assume the offensive vigorously on the Rhine, and agree to a declaration by the Powers of the terms of peace that they would grant to France. It so happened that the Austrian Generals on the Rhine had at the end of December granted, without the Emperor's sanction, a

[1] Sybel, iv. 135-138.

1795. suspension of arms to the defeated French; and this action was quite sufficient to revive the English Cabinet's suspicions as to Austria's good faith. Thugut, however, by this time in desperate straits for money, seized the opportunity to reopen negotiations with England by apologising for the proceedings of his generals; and he now offered, in return for the guarantee of the loan, to raise the army on the Rhine to its former strength and, if Russia would lend assistance, to keep fifty thousand men in Italy also. He likewise gave his assent to the terms which Pitt was prepared to offer to France, though, with a secret reservation of Austria's claim to indemnities; and Grenville thereupon consented to guarantee the loan, as he had proposed, and to
1796. advance £150,000 a month on account of it. Thus
Jan the Triple Alliance assumed at last something of an active form, though, owing to conflicting interests and selfish designs, it was still very far from becoming a potent instrument whether for war or for peace.[1]

1795. Considerably more important were the changes that had come over France in the last six months of 1795. Mention has already been made of the reaction against Jacobinism which drove Carnot, as a former member of the Committee of Public Safety, from the War Office. In August his place was taken, actually though not nominally, for a few weeks by Napoleon Bonaparte, who during his brief tenure of the post poured forth
Oct. plan after plan for the conquest of Italy. In October sterner work was required of him. The Convention had framed a new Constitution, whereby legislative power was entrusted to a Lower Chamber of five hundred members, and an Upper House, called the Council of Ancients, of half that number; while the executive duties were confided to five Directors chosen by the Ancients from a list submitted by the Five Hundred. The Convention, however, had also decreed that two-thirds of its members should form part of the new legislature; and against this Paris rose up in revolt.

[1] Sybel, iv. 138-143.

Bonaparte was placed in command of the troops to quell 1795.
the movement, and very effectually fulfilled the duty. Oct. 4.
This was the insurrection known as that of the 13th of
Vendémiaire ; and one result of its suppression by
military force was to revive new hopes among those
who cherished the old revolutionary and Jacobin ideas.
The will of the majority, comprising the most sensible
and moderate men in France, had been overborne by
bayonets and cannon ; and Bonaparte, as General of the
Interior, gave no chance to any popular movement and
ruled Paris with a rod of iron. On the 26th of October
the Convention came to an end, and on the 4th of
November the Directors, Barras, Rewbell, Lepeaux,
Latourneur, and Carnot, assumed the government of Nov. 4.
France.

It cannot be said that the framers of the new Constitution had done their work very intelligently. They had duly arranged that there should be Ministers, but they had made no provision for Ministerial responsibility. The Ministers were in fact intended only to execute the orders given by the Directors in Council assembled ; and it is therefore not surprising that the Directors, perceiving the hopelessness of attempting to work such clumsy machinery, at once adopted the old procedure of the Committee of Public Safety. The result of this was that Carnot returned to his former place at the War Office. Generally speaking, however, the Directors distributed their duties not according to departments but according to districts ; and since in the selection of functionaries a large majority of royalists and moderate men had been chosen, their first care was to dismiss these and to appoint more fitting instruments, illegally, in their place. The most notable characteristic of the French Revolution is that the men who talked loudest of the rights of the sovereign people were always most violent in preventing the sovereign people from exercising such rights.

The supremacy of the extreme party in the new Legislature was of evil augury for the peace of Europe,

1795. and was rendered doubly formidable by the exhaustion of the French treasury. By the end of 1795 the final bankruptcy, for which Pitt had looked since 1793, seemed to have come at last. Assignats for one hundred francs had fallen to the value of one quarter of a franc in specie; and the French armies of the Rhine, driven back by Clerfaye's victory, were obliged to live on their native soil, as they had lived in foreign lands, by requisitions and plunder. The Directory was forced to make such terms as it could with capitalists for an advance of ready money, thereby placing itself under the control and at the mercy of these financial tyrants. The waste and corruption were appalling. The Directors, Carnot excepted, lived in shameless luxury amid the general distress; and violent denunciations in the press availed little to recall them to decency. They could have given peace to France, if they had wished, with scanty trouble. In Italy the Sardinian Government, following the example of the Austrians, had agreed to a suspension of arms after Loano, and proposed to open negotiations for a final settlement.

1796. Pitt also at the beginning of 1796 insisted, contrary to Thugut's opinion, in proclaiming the terms upon which the Allies would make peace, and even approached the Directory, through the French ambassador in Switzerland, with still more tempting overtures. The old King, George the Third, was vehemently opposed to this last proceeding, and wrote of it openly to Pitt and Grenville with a contempt which to this day retains its sting. Pitt, however, probably with some hope of disarming the criticism of the Opposition, persisted in making the trial, and

March 26. was answered on the 26th of March with an insolence which justified the King's opinion. The Directory was, in fact, puffed up by Hoche's recent successes in La Vendée, where the great rebellion was on the verge of extinction. Stofflet had been taken and shot on the 24th of February, Charette was taken and shot on the very day when the Directory sent its answer to Pitt;

and Hoche, at that moment the most prominent of 1796. the Republican Generals, was eager for a descent upon England. In fact the Directory wanted war for every reason—war to enable the French armies to live at the expense of the stranger, war to fill the empty treasury with the plunder of foreign lands, war as a pretext for establishing a military dictatorship.[1]

Further hostilities were therefore inevitable; and it remained to be seen how the Triple Alliance could resist the shock. England's part consisted only in the providing of money, for such troops as she had were hopelessly entangled in the West Indies. Austria, however, and still more Russia, if she would, could do much. But Austria had not the same inducements as France to put her armed forces upon foreign ground. Vienna was weary of the war; money was wanting for the necessary preparations; and, finally, Wurmser and Clerfaye had quarrelled so bitterly that the Emperor had been compelled to appoint the Archduke Charles Feb. 6. to the chief command on the Rhine. The Archduke, however, received no orders to leave Vienna for the front until the 3rd of April; and, before he could denounce the truce arranged by Clerfaye, Thugut received intelligence that the Empress Catherine, who had refused to send troops to the Rhine on the pretext that they were needed to watch Prussia, had directed an army to march by the Caucasus upon Persia. Thugut's insane jealousy of Prussia at once revived in full strength; and the opening of the campaign on the Rhine was delayed for a month until the news arrived that the insatiable Empress had countermanded the Persian expedition. Nor was this the only quarter where Thugut's suspicions of Prussia wrought untold mischief. Sundry circumstances had conspired to attract his attention towards Italy, and not least the overtures made by Sardinia to the Directory. A demonstration by a formidable Austrian force would have overawed the Court of Turin, and heartened it

[1] Sybel, iv. 153. *Dropmore Papers*, iii. 143, 149-150, 186.

1796. for further effort; and Thugut possessed such a force in the eighty thousand men which he still kept in Moravia, Bohemia, and Galicia as a corps of observation to watch the Prussians. But nothing could induce him to employ these troops for any other purpose. There was, as a matter of fact, no longer anything to fear from Prussia, and both England and Russia strove their utmost to persuade him of the fact; but in vain. The man's prejudices were insuperable. His hatred of the Bourbons forbade him to employ the royalist army under the Prince of Condé, which was paid by England, either in Italy or the Rhine. His intense distrust of Sardinia caused him to reject her overtures, after she had failed to come to terms with France, and to decline to concert with her any operations for the coming campaign. His bitter hatred of Prussia prompted him not only to delay the opening of the campaign on the Rhine, but to wreck the campaign in Italy. Once again Poland was destined to be the salvation of France.[1]

Meanwhile the memoranda drawn up by Bonaparte for operations in Italy had come to the notice of Carnot, who, disgusted by the lugubrious reports of General Schérer from that quarter, determined in spite of the opposition of Barras and Rewbell to supersede him. "If I were there," said Bonaparte, "the Austrians would soon be overthrown." "You shall go there," answered March 26. Carnot shortly; and on the 26th of March the young General reached his headquarters at Nice. There he found the troops in a state of starvation, nakedness, and mutiny; and began at once the difficult task of reviving in them the spirit of energy and order. "Soldiers, you are ill fed and ill clothed," he said, in a general order of the 27th of March. "The Government owes you much, but can give you nothing. . . . I shall lead you into the most fertile provinces of the world. Rich provinces and great cities will fall into your hands. There you shall find honour and glory and riches." "The first principle that should guide us in

[1] Sybel, iv. 145-150.

the direction of our armies," he had written in the 1796.
previous July, "is that they must support themselves
by war at the cost of the enemy's territory." "Behind
the door lies abundance," wrote Carnot in the same
strain, "it is for you to break it open"; and with
such precepts ringing in its ears the ragged army
advanced to the pillage of Italy.[1]

Those who have grasped the false principles which
governed the Austrian operations in the Low Countries
will understand that the like manœuvres executed by
the like senile commanders with inferior troops made
the Imperial armies an easy prey to Bonaparte. In the
second week of April the French General opened his April 10-12.
campaign; and by the 28th he had compelled Sardinia
to abandon the Coalition, to yield up her principal fortresses, and to deliver herself helplessly into the hands
of the Republic. On the 10th of May he forced the May 10.
passage of the Adda at Lodi; on the 16th he entered
Milan; and on the 21st, after some controversy with the
powers at Paris, he finally subjected the Directory to his
will, and reigned thenceforth practically independent and
autocratic in Italy. Then, resuming his march, he on
the 30th of May successfully passed the Mincio, and May 30.
halted at last before the fortress of Mantua.

It now remained for him to gather in the plunder
from such of the distracted states of the Italian peninsula as had not already been despoiled. The countries
that he had traversed had already been shamefully
pillaged alike for the benefit of bankrupt France and
of the penniless officers of her army. On the 15th of May 15.
May Sardinia had concluded a final treaty with the
Directory, whereby she yielded up Nice and Savoy,
and confirmed the military control of France over
Piedmont; and on the 17th Parma and Modena had May 17.
purchased a truce by payment of very large sums. On
the 1st of June arrived an emissary from the craven June 1.
King of Naples, who on the 5th agreed to withdraw
all Neapolitan troops from the Austrian armies, and all

[1] *Corres. de Napoléon*, i. 75. *Vie de Carnot*, ii. 26, 50.

1796. Neapolitan ships from the British fleets; to suspend all hostile movements, and to send an ambassador to Paris to treat for a definite peace. Lombardy, which had already been mercilessly plundered, was reserved for conversion into a republic. Enormous contributions were levied upon the Papal States at the bayonet's point; and, finally, an irruption into Tuscany and a forced march into Leghorn brought the French troops within sight, though not, as Bonaparte had hoped, within reach, of the detested ships of Britain. Leghorn was mulcted in a heavy fine, and the General returned
July. to press the siege of Mantua. But he had made up his mind that Italy should belong to France, and he knew that this was impossible until the British fleet had been driven from the Mediterranean.

Apart from the West Indies the Directory had, with the help of Holland, found another channel into which to divert the energies of England. Early in February the British Cabinet had received intelligence of the preparation of two expeditions at Rochefort and the Texel, whose destinations were suspected to be the Indian Seas and the Cape of Good Hope. Ministers therefore resolved at once not only to reinforce the troops in India but to strengthen the fleet on the Cape station, at the same time taking measures to intercept the hostile armaments at sea. Despite the British cruisers, however, the Dutch fleet succeeded in leaving the Texel on the 23rd of February, while three large French frigates with several smaller vessels also slipped out of Rochefort on the 4th of March. These were
March 6. followed two days later by the first reinforcements, naval and military, from England.

At the Cape itself all was comparatively quiet. The population was indeed inertly hostile, and the Boers at Graaf Reinet were in open but innocuous rebellion against any government except their own; but, in the absence of any help from without, these malcontents were perfectly harmless and their enmity was productive of little inconvenience. Dundas's warnings, however, which reached Craig on the 23rd of April, were 1796. sufficient to disquiet that officer greatly, for his force was April 23. none too strong ; nor dared he take such precautions as he wished, lest the population should guess at the reason and cease to supply him with victuals. Fortunately Commodore Elphinstone at Madras had also received news of the enemy's designs, whereupon with excellent judgment he at once sailed with his fleet and a reinforcement of troops to the Cape. On the way the French frigates from Rochefort, bound to Mauritius, crossed his convoy of transports, which was four days' voyage behind him, and went perilously near to capture it ; but ultimately the entire expedition reached the Cape safely on the 23rd and 27th of May. On the follow- May 23-27. ing day arrived the first reinforcements from England, May 28. and by the end of July six thousand troops were actually concentrated at the Cape, while three thousand more were shortly expected. Elated by the possession of so large a force, Craig and Elphinstone for a moment contemplated an attack upon Mauritius with five thousand men, a design which, though abandoned almost as soon as projected, brought upon Craig a just and welldeserved rebuke from Dundas. "It is scarcely possible," wrote the Minister, "that a case can arise where the upsetting of the Government's arrangements, especially for dependencies at a distance, can be unattended with inconvenience if not danger."[1]

On the 3rd of August, the very day upon which Aug. 3. Craig had renounced the expedition to Mauritius, he received a report from his posts at Saldanha Bay that nine men-of-war had appeared off that part of the coast. Being convinced that, through the capture of a British brig, this fleet must have been apprised of the strength of the British force and of the hopelessness of any attempt at landing, Elphinstone at once prepared for

[1] Dundas to Craig, 16th January, 14th February, 15th April ; Elphinstone to Dundas, 18th and 25th June ; Craig to Dundas, 14th February, 8th March, 12th, 14th, 21st, 28th, 30th April, 5th, 6th, 8th, 10th, 16th, 29th, 30th July, 3rd August 1796.

1796. sea, but owing to stormy weather was unable to leave
Aug. 6. Simon's Bay until the 6th. In the prevailing northeasterly winds, he was likely to find some difficulty in doubling the Cape of Good Hope, while the enemy would almost certainly stand far to westward before doubling it, in order to avoid him. On the morning of the 6th, however, the strange fleet anchored in Saldanha Bay, showing pretty clearly that the commander counted upon a rising of the Dutch on shore. Craig, therefore, at once sent ships in quest of the Commodore, and, leaving nearly four thousand men in Cape Town, lest the enemy should descend upon it in
Aug. 7. his absence, set out on the morning of the 7th with about twenty-five hundred men[1] for Saldanha Bay.

This was the first real march ever made by British troops in South Africa, a dreary tramp of ninety miles through so barren a country that but five houses were seen in the whole of it. The burghers with surprising readiness helped Craig to impress waggons and cattle, as well as horses and saddles for the cavalry; but, even so, the subsistence of the force was with difficulty provided for. The men suffered every privation except that of meat, and the column took nine days to reach
Aug. 16. Saldanha Bay. On descending from the heights to the shore, however, Craig was met by the welcome sight of Elphinstone's fleet, still at a distance, but with all sail crowded before a fair wind. The Commodore, misled by false intelligence, had steered south and south-west, and after six days of tempestuous weather had returned on the 12th to Simon's Bay, where he learned the true position of the Dutch fleet. He at once made signal to sail; but a gale sprang up which blew two of his ships into imminent danger, and notwithstanding every effort the fleet could not put

---

[1] These troops consisted of a composite battalion of Grenadiers, the 78th, the 80th, and detachments of the 25th and 28th Light Dragoons. The other regiments in Cape Colony at the time were the 33rd, 84th, two regiments, afterwards disbanded but then numbered (95th) and (98th), and part of the 19th.

to sea until the 15th. As Craig's force marched down 1796. to the beach a Dutch frigate of light draught opened fire on it, but was quickly silenced by a few shots from a howitzer; and, as the fleet was close at hand, Craig refrained from doing her further damage. At sunset Elphinstone entered the harbour, and, anchoring for the night, on the following morning summoned the Aug. 17. Dutch Admiral to surrender. Having but three line-of-battle ships against seven, and five frigates and smaller craft against six, that unfortunate officer had no option but to yield, and the entire squadron passed into Elphinstone's hands.[1]

This, so far as it went, was a solid success, but it did not in the slightest degree affect the main operations of France, nor the general circumstances in the Mediterranean. Nearly two years earlier Bonaparte had pressed for the deliverance of his native Corsica; and immediately upon his entry into Milan he had sent agents to Genoa to rouse insurrection in the island. Now, while engaged with the siege of Mantua, July. he found time to organise a body of Corsican refugees at Leghorn. That port throughout the summer had been watched by Nelson's squadron, while the main Mediterranean fleet under Sir John Jervis blockaded Toulon, and seven ships of the line under Admiral Mann observed a French squadron which had taken refuge in Cadiz. But the subjection of Genoa and Tuscany to French influence raised serious difficulties as to the victualling of the British ships. Sir Gilbert Elliot, the Viceroy of Corsica, being profoundly impressed by the importance of British operations in the Mediterranean, had more than once in 1794 and 1795 suggested that Corsica should be turned into a base of offensive operations. The squandering of British troops in the West Indies had, however, made this, like all other effective military measures, absolutely impracticable; and in July the symptoms

[1] Craig to Dundas, Elphinstone to Admiralty, 19th August 1796.

1796. of discontent in Corsica became so threatening that
July. Elliot ordered Nelson to seize Elba, as a station more easily to be held than the larger island. Nelson accordingly received the surrender of Porto Ferrajo
July 10. on the 10th of July, and thus the new base in the Mediterranean was assured.[1]

But in the following weeks misfortunes crowded thick and fast upon the Coalition. In the first place, Spain, which so far had observed neutrality since making peace with France, now became hostile. The fact was that Godoy, whose power rested solely upon the intimacy that bound him to the Queen, had become nervous lest the Courts of Naples, Parma, and Lisbon should put pressure on her to dismiss him, as the adviser who had brought Spain to terms with the regicide democracy of France. He therefore looked for solid support in France itself, desiring, however, only a defensive alliance in case of an attack by England. The Directory on the other hand was strongly for an offensive alliance, offering, in return for the cession of Louisiana, to assist Spain in the reconquest of Gibraltar and the conquest of Portugal. Formal negotiations were opened in April 1796, and the victories of Bonaparte quickened Godoy's zeal for a speedy alliance even upon the French terms. Finally,
Aug. 19. on the 19th of August a treaty was signed which engaged Spain to declare war against England within a month. Meanwhile, the first attempt of the Austrians under Marshal Wurmser to relieve Mantua was, owing to their incurably vicious military methods, foiled by
July 29- Bonaparte through the series of operations that are
Aug. 14. bound up with the names of Lonato and Castiglione. The campaign on the Rhine, tardily opened on the 1st of June, had also been marked so far by nothing but failure. The Archduke Charles had retired hastily before the two armies of Jourdan and Moreau ; and the French had plundered Swabia, Franconia, and

---

[1] *Memoir of Lord Collingwood*, i. 40. Sir G. Elliot to Dundas, 16th October 1794 and 23rd February 1795.

Bavaria with the same rapacity, both as an army and 1796. as individuals, that had disgraced their irruption into Italy. The German potentates too had shown themselves no less contemptible than the Italian, by the haste wherewith they placed their precious persons in safety and bought indulgence from the invaders. Lastly, as a climax, Prussia on the 5th of August signed Aug. 5. a treaty with France in order to secure to herself favourable treatment upon the conclusion of a general peace.[1]

In these circumstances the British Government on the 31st of August despatched orders to Jervis to evacuate Aug. 31. Corsica, Elba, and the Mediterranean at large; but the letter did not reach him until the 25th of September, and meanwhile the situation had changed. In Italy, indeed, a second attempt of Marshal Wurmser to relieve Mantua, having been even more fatuously conducted than the first, had ended still more disastrously in the rout of a part of his force at Bassano, Sept. 7. and the shutting of the main body under Wurmser's own command within the walls of Mantua. But Oct. 1. in Germany the tide had completely turned. There Moreau and Jourdan, under the inspiration of the Directory, had imitated Austrian methods, and, pressing on in two independent columns, had laid themselves open to a brilliant counter-attack by the concentrated forces of the Archduke. On the 3rd of September Sept. 3. the Archduke delivered his stroke upon Jourdan at Würzburg, inflicting on him a defeat which forced his army back in demoralisation to the Rhine, and, with a little more energy, might have brought about its utter destruction. Then turning southward upon the communications of Moreau the prince compelled him also to make a hasty retreat from Augsburg to the western Oct. 25. bank of the same river. Thereby the designs of the Directory for a junction of the Armies of Germany and Italy, and for an advance of both upon Vienna, were utterly overthrown.

This success revived the hopes alike of Austria and

[1] Sybel, iv. 233-246.

1796.
Oct.
of England; and on the 21st of October the British Government countermanded its orders to Jervis for the evacuation of Corsica, if they should not have been already executed; directing that in any case Elba was still to be held. It was, however, too late to save Corsica, for the last of the troops had been safely em-
Oct. 19. barked under the guns of Nelson's ships on the 19th of October. Sir John Jervis, nevertheless, remained in the
Nov. 2. bay of San Fiorenzo till the 2nd of November, waiting for Admiral Mann's squadron, which he had ordered to rejoin him from Gibraltar. Unfortunately Mann, from some incomprehensible motive, took his ships home, thus dangerously weakening the Mediterranean fleet at the very moment when it might be required to encounter the united armaments of France and Spain. Being short of provisions Jervis was obliged to return to Gibraltar, receiving on the way his new instructions to defer the evacuation. Elba, as it happened, was still held by a British garrison, for, whatever the Government's intentions, it had sent no orders to General de Burgh, who commanded the troops, to withdraw from that island; and he did not think himself justified in evacuating it upon Jervis's commands alone. After some delay De Burgh did receive in April 1797 his instructions to leave Elba; and, though they were then accompanied by censure for his refusal to quit it earlier, yet, as he justly said, the only orders with which the Government had honoured him were that he should hold the island. The fault in fact lay not with the General but with the Ministers, who had entangled themselves in such a multitude of enterprises that they knew neither what they were doing nor what they wanted to do. Nevertheless, to the great relief of Bonaparte, the British fleet was withdrawn from the Mediterranean; and this was something more than a mere military movement; it was a confession of military impotence and almost of despair.[1]

[1] Mahan. *Sea-power in the French Revolution*, i. 212-218. De Burgh to Dundas, 6th April 1797.

In truth, the sudden renewal of the hopes and resources of France by Bonaparte's successes in Italy had profoundly affected Pitt. In June he had anticipated that before the end of the year England would be left to fight single-handed against the rest of Europe, and had written, with the courage that rarely failed him, that with proper exertion she could hold her own against them all.[1] But in his heart he longed for peace; and, quite apart from such men as Grey and Fox who were always urging peace in season and out of season, there was beyond all doubt a strong party in the country which yearned for the end of the war. In the first place the expenditure, between the cost of England's own military enterprises and the subsidies paid to foreign powers, had been enormous; and the taxation was consequently very heavy. Trade had suffered greatly from the depredations of the French cruisers, and the financial situation was rapidly becoming very serious. Then there were the Radical Associations, which talked of reform and played with revolution, ever powerful for mischief even if anxious for good. Repressive statutes had been passed and many prosecutions instituted; but a series of triumphant acquittals due to the eloquence of Erskine, in the course of 1794, had enlisted public sympathy less with the accusers than the accused. Bad harvests both in 1794 and 1795 aggravated the general discontent; and in 1795 there were riots in various parts of the country, the most serious of them in Sussex, where four hundred men of the Oxford Militia broke out of barracks with loaded arms and plundered the butchers' and bakers' shops. On the 29th of October 1795 the King was attacked on his way to and from the opening of Parliament, the windows of his coach were smashed, and a bullet fired from an air-gun passed close to him. "My Lords, I have been shot at," was the only remark of the intrepid monarch when he reached Westminster; and, as if to show his contempt of such demonstrations, he went to

1796.

---

[1] Pitt to Grenville, 23rd June 1796. *Dropmore Papers*, iii. 214.

the theatre on the following night. But the King's courage was not sufficient of itself to dispel the anxiety of Ministers over such an occurrence.

There was a cruel irony in the fate which exposed Pitt, who had done so much to restore the stability of British finance and had hoped himself to institute the reform of Parliament, to such a storm of discontent. "If I were to resign to-day," he said in November 1796, "my head would be gone in six weeks." Yet in truth, setting the misfortune of bad harvests aside, he himself was chiefly to blame, owing to his deplorable misconduct of the war. Here was the root of the mischief. The Opposition in Parliament must always criticise a Government's actions, for that is its proper function; and in time of war there is no task more delicate and difficult than so to tone that criticism that it shall be profitable to the country and unprofitable to the enemy. For Governments are as unscrupulous as Oppositions, and always claim, in the name of patriotism, that the nakedness of their incapacity shall not be uncovered. There were many utterances of the Opposition which were deliberately mischievous and therefore unpatriotic; there were many more, vindicating the purity and innocence of the Revolutionary Government of France, which were simply childish; but their condemnation of the Government's manner of conducting war was just and unanswerable. Had it been otherwise, Pitt could well have afforded to ignore it; as matters stood he could not do so, and he knew that he could not. If by sheer incompetence Ministers waste the country's resources and reduce it to perilous impotence, then—unless ministerial responsibility be no more than a name—they are guilty of a capital crime. Newcastle had incurred this guilt and escaped; North and Sackville had incurred it and escaped; now Pitt and Dundas had incurred it, and their hearts misgave them lest they should not escape.

Then there was the eternal danger of Ireland, now more than ever acute and threatening. There, in greater measure than in other countries, the French

Revolution had stirred inert minds to activity, and 1791-3. active minds to precipitation. The Presbyterians of the north, already almost Republicans since the American Revolution, followed the vagaries and insurrections of Paris with rapture, and quickly set on foot an agitation, upon the French model, for Parliamentary reform. The Irish Catholics, being burdened with grievous and humiliating disabilities, were roused in the name of the Rights of Man to demand complete and immediate relief. The Presbyterians sympathised with them, designing to make Catholic emancipation a stalking-horse for their own coveted reforms; and in 1791 the two parties were actually combined for political union in the Society of United Irishmen, founded by Theobald Wolfe Tone. Such an alliance was something new in Ireland, though at first it came to little. The leaders of the United Irishmen were to a man Protestants, Presbyterians or freethinkers; and it was Belfast, now the stronghold of loyalty, which was then the chief centre of political disaffection. The Volunteers of 1782 were not extinct, and they were supplemented in Belfast itself, in Dublin, and in one or two more cities by new organised bodies called by the French title of National Guards. So dangerous was this movement in the north that it was found necessary to suppress these National Guards; and in Dublin this was not effected without calling out the troops. At the same time conciliation was not neglected, and in 1792 and 1793 two Acts were passed which removed so many of the Catholic disabilities that it seemed ridiculous not to abolish the rest. Thus, the electoral franchise was granted to Catholics, but not the right to sit in Parliament. A Catholic might enter the Army and command a regiment, but might not rise to be a General. Many wise men urged that it would be better to end all grievances while their removal could still be conceded as a favour; but to this the ruling cabal at Dublin Castle was obstinately opposed, and most unfortunately their stubbornness prevailed.

1793-4. The concessions of 1792 and 1793 were, however, not without some good effect for the time, though the outbreak of war between England and France roused the Presbyterians of the north to the bitterest indignation. But meanwhile an old source of disturbance had arisen in the revival, under a new form, of the body known as Defenders. Originally the Defenders had represented simply a Catholic faction, intended to withstand the aggressive Presbyterians, who, under the name of Peep-of-Day-Boys, had organised themselves in the county of Armagh; and in 1791 and 1792 there were contests between the rival sects which turned some counties almost into a seat of civil war. But in 1793 the Defenders became a secret society of the kind usual in Ireland, designed for the avenging of wrongs and the venting of discontent by outrage, violence and crime. The objects of the society seem to have been twofold: political among the better educated, purely agrarian among the poor and ignorant; but it served as the main channel through which the Roman Catholics of Ireland passed into the ranks of disaffection. Gradually a vague idea began to spread among the Defenders that a French invasion would be the cure for all evils, and that it would be their duty to abet such an invasion if attempted. Quite independently of them, the United Irishmen had entered into communication with the French Government, themselves making the first overture unsuccessfully in 1792, but receiving a second, which was immediately discovered by the British Government, in 1794. None the less the year 1794 passed away quietly on the whole in Ireland, while the Irish Parliament supported the war from the beginning with the greatest heartiness and loyalty.

Early in 1795, however, a new excitement threw the country once more into confusion. The junction of the Whigs under the Duke of Portland with Pitt had raised high hopes of final Catholic emancipation in Ireland; and those hopes were immoderately flattered by the appointment of Lord Fitzwilliam, who was known to be Portland's nominee, to the Lord-Lieutenancy at 1795. the close of 1794. Arriving in Ireland on the 4th Jan. 4. of January 1795, Fitzwilliam found the agitation for emancipation in full vigour, and gave it as his opinion that relief to the Catholics should be granted at once, and should be immediately followed by the establishment of a body of Yeomanry Cavalry to enforce law, order and tranquillity. It enters not into the province of this history to describe the quarrel which thereupon arose between him and the British Government, chiefly, as it appears, because Ministers did not know their own minds, and because Fitzwilliam had consequently misconceived his own powers. He was recalled, and left Dublin on the 25th of March amid signs of March 25. general mourning; and the disappointment in Ireland found vent in the growth of a savage hatred towards England.

Lord Camden shortly afterwards succeeded as Lord-Lieutenant ; and, since the British Government had definitely determined not to yield emancipation to the Catholics, his instructions practically bade him to rouse a feeling against them, or in other words to ally himself with the Protestants for a renewal of the old religious warfare. The Society of United Irishmen, whose meetings had been suppressed in 1794, revived under the stimulus of the general discontent and unrest, and became definitely republican and treasonable. The Defenders likewise increased rapidly, with a fervour of animosity against the Protestants which not only overthrew all the schemes of the United Irishmen for an alliance between the Irish of all creeds, but called into existence the powerful rival called the Orange Society. A furious fight in the county of Armagh Sept. 21. between Defenders and Peep-of-Day-Boys, wherein the Catholics were the aggressors, was the immediate cause of the formation of this new Protestant League ; which at once girded itself for new reprisals, and by continuous outrages drove a number of the poorer Catholics homeless from the land. Lawlessness and crime reduced the

1796. country to such a state of anarchy that in the spring of 1796 a severe Insurrection Act was passed to enable the Government to cope with it; but an Act is useless without the means to enforce it, and the army at Camden's disposal was small. The demand for men in the West Indies had drained every old soldier and very nearly every regular regiment from Ireland; and the troops in the island consisted chiefly of Fencible Infantry, with a few old regiments of Cavalry, all of them in bad order, and a few recently created corps of Dragoons, both Regular and Fencible. The whole of these did not number fifteen thousand effective men, who were dispersed in small parties all over the country for the protection of isolated buildings and individuals. This in itself was sufficient to ruin all discipline; and the evil was not mitigated by the absence of great numbers of officers from their posts. In addition to these troops there was the Militia, some sixteen thousand strong, but ill-officered, ill-disciplined, and known not only to have been tampered with by Defenders, but actually to include many members of the Society in its ranks.

June. To an Ireland thus seething with excitement, violence and discontent, came the news in June 1796 that a French invasion of the country was imminent. Divided and even antagonistic as were the Defenders and the United Irishmen, the prospect of a common rallying point drew the two parties steadily together. Many of the Defenders took the oath of union; an increased number of malcontents was passed into the Catholic regiments of the Militia; and the United Irishmen began to devise for the Society a military organisation, which was fully elaborated by the close of the year. Camden, not ill apprised of all that was going forward, wrote urgently for reinforcements. His troops, as he said, were so much dispersed on police-duty that few were left free to act against an invasion; and he therefore urged the creation of a Yeomanry, the very measure which, when proposed by Fitzwilliam, had been scouted as impossible. The British Government thereupon sent 1796. over four regiments, two of regular Cavalry and two of Fencibles. Camden took exception to three of these upon the ground that they were entirely composed of Irishmen ; and finally at the end of August Portland August. yielded permission for the formation of Yeomanry, both cavalry and infantry, provided that care were taken in the selection of officers and men. The patriotism of the Irish gentry had already prompted them to raise a few corps of Fencible Cavalry; and within six weeks over one hundred troops and companies of Yeomanry were formed to relieve the regulars of police-duty in the event of a landing of the French. "Of course I shall be construed as arming the Protestants against the Papists by arming property," wrote Camden pathetically, " but no time is to be lost." A few Catholics were indeed enrolled ; but the leaders both of the disaffected Catholics and of the United Irishmen discountenanced the movement ; and, since the Yeomanry at first was formed chiefly in the north, where disloyalty was most systematic and most dangerous, the force necessarily consisted chiefly of Orangemen.[1]

In such circumstances it is not surprising that Pitt should have grown more and more anxious to end the war ; and accordingly in September he made up his Sept. mind to send an ambassador to Paris, informing the Court of Vienna at the same time that he had no intention of making a separate peace. Thugut answered angrily that such overtures would destroy all the effect of the Archduke Charles's victories, and that the withdrawal of the British fleet would be the ruin of Italy ; but nevertheless Pitt was firm, and on the 16th of October Lord Malmesbury, his selected Oct. 16. envoy, left England for Paris. Meanwhile the Ministers racked their brains for some expedient to avert, if possible, the threatened invasion ; but the awful

[1] *S.P. Ireland.* Camden to Portland, 6th, 18th, 24th August, 1st September; Portland to Camden, 29th August ; *Dublin Gazette*, 13th and 18th October 1796.

1796. millstone of the West Indies was still round their necks, and they could not yet shake it off. Already in September they had it in contemplation to concentrate all the British troops in St. Domingo about Mole St. Nicholas, to administer and protect the rest of the island by means of local levies, to send no further reinforcements and to incur no further expense. But meanwhile Dundas was in frequent conference with Abercromby about the next campaign to windward, recommending attacks upon the Spanish West Indies, and yet assuring the general that he could not possibly spare a reinforcement of more than fifteen hundred men. It was evident that Ministers were beginning to sicken of St. Domingo ; but not even the prospect of invasion could keep Dundas from wasting troops upon the capture of additional pestilent islands in the Caribbean Sea.[1]

There were, however, by chance two battalions which for the moment were occupied by no special duty ; and Dundas promptly seized the opportunity to send them on an useless errand. One of the British agents in Holland had in April transmitted to Grenville a scheme for a counter-revolution in the provinces of Friesland, Overyssel, Groningen and Drenthe, aided by British expeditions to the Texel and to the islands that lie north and east of it. In September some person unknown had supplemented this by a project for throwing a small force by surprise into the northern extremity of North Holland, so as to take the batteries of the Helder and of Texel Island in rear, and to enable the British fleet to destroy the Dutch fleet at its anchorage in the Texel. Possession of the Helder, observed this sage observer, and of a position upon the Maas would give England the keys of Dutch commerce without the expense of a blockading squadron ; and to this counsel is perhaps in part to be ascribed the despatch of a second expedition to the Helder in 1799. Undoubtedly at the moment the destruction of the

[1] Dundas to Abercromby, September and October 1796.

Dutch fleet at the Texel was well worth the risk of two 1796. battalions, if there were really any prospect of accomplishing it; and the Tenth and Eighty-seventh Foot were accordingly placed under the orders of Colonel John Doyle of the latter regiment, to do the necessary work ashore. His instructions set forth the immediate object of the expedition, and added that, if victorious, he would no doubt be able to maintain himself until the fleet had accomplished its task, and indeed for some time longer. Since surprise was essential to the success of his attack, the Government gave out that the two battalions were designed for the defence of Portugal, a pretext which was too flimsy to deceive any man, and made Doyle very uneasy. "I see no paragraphs in the Ministerial papers sending us round to accompany Lord Macartney to the Cape," he wrote. "By God, I cannot defend Portugal much longer." Doyle need not have fretted himself. After some days of adverse weather he on the 20th of October fell in with Admiral Oct. 20. Duncan's blockading squadron, when he found that the object of the expedition had, as usual, for some time been the talk of the whole fleet. Moreover, the Dutch Admiral, evidently possessing full information of everything that was going forward, had withdrawn his ships to a safer anchorage. Finally, Admiral Duncan gave Doyle to understand, with the full assent of his captains, that the project, though in itself feasible, was absolutely out of the question at that season of the year, and ordered him straight back to Spithead. The reader may think it strange that this fact should not have been ascertained before the troops were sent to sea. I can only remind him that he must consider no sins of omission or commission strange in the military enterprises of Henry Dundas.[1]

Meanwhile a new Parliament, elected during the summer, had been opened by the King on the 6th of

[1] The few papers relating to this expedition will be found in *W.O. Orig. Corres.*, 61, at the beginning of the volume. See also *Dropmore Papers*, iii. 189-191.

1796. October; and on the 18th Pitt brought forward his measures for meeting the threatened invasion. The first was an Act for levying fifteen thousand men from parish to parish to recruit the Navy and the troops of the Line; the maritime counties being assigned to the Fleet and the inland counties to the Army. For the formation of this levy the parochial authorities were empowered to pay a stated bounty to the so-called volunteers who should come forward as recruits; a method which, though frequently employed before to obtain men for the Navy, had not for many years been used for the Army. But the fact was that the Government had exhausted the supply of voluntary recruits. Eighty thousand had been enlisted in 1794 and 1795, most of whom had been buried or broken down for life in the West Indies, and there was no great eagerness either in England or Ireland to share their fate. This was one among many signs that the day of retribution for the follies, ignorances, and negligences of the Government was close at hand.

The second measure was an Act for the gradual levy by ballot of a Supplementary Militia of sixty thousand men, according to a fixed quota for each county. Substitutes were allowed, and encouragement was given for volunteers to come forward and save their district from the ballot; and it was intended that this levy should be called out in fractions of one-sixth, until the whole had passed, in succession, through twenty days' training. To this there was added a further force called the Provisional Cavalry. Owners of horses kept for riding or carriages were required to provide one trooper and horse for every ten of such horses, while those that possessed fewer than ten were lumped together to provide their horsemen jointly. This Provisional Cavalry was entitled to pay if embodied, and was reckoned to comprise fifteen thousand men. It is somewhat singular that in spite of the peril of the country the new companies of volunteers formed during 1796 were extremely few. The whole of these measures were of course passed, though not 1796. always with the best grace. Fox sneered at the idea of invasion. "But," he added, "were I compelled to take my choice between that evil and a continuance of the present war for two years, I should, as the friend of the real interests of the country, prefer invasion as the lesser calamity." It was such utterances as these that kept Pitt and Dundas in office to mismanage the war with impunity for as long as they would.

The various Acts had hardly been passed before there came news of further misfortune in Italy. The third force sent to relieve Mantua under General Alvintzy, after defeating Bonaparte at Caldiero on the 12th of November, had been beaten by him at Arcola on the 16th and 17th and finally driven back a Nov. 16-17. few days later. The victory of the French had not been decisive; indeed the Directory regarded it as so doubtful that on the 25th they sent an emissary, Nov. 25. General Clarke, to Bonaparte to obtain from him passports, so as to open negotiations for peace at Vienna. Meanwhile Lord Malmesbury's overtures at Paris had been checked by a question from the French Directors whether he were empowered to act on behalf of the Court of Vienna as well as that of St. James's. Malmesbury was obliged to refer to Grenville for the answer, and on the 7th of November Grenville wrote Nov. 7. to Sir Morton Eden insisting that Austria should take part in the negotiations in Paris, and threatening, in case of her refusal, that England would make a separate peace. This announcement roused Thugut to the highest pitch of anger and suspicion, and he resolved to break with England and to throw himself wholly upon Russia. The man, to do him justice, possessed courage, and was determined to fight on until he had attained his desires; wherefore he dismissed Clarke without listening to his proposals, and strained every nerve to reinforce Alvintzy for a fourth attempt to relieve Mantua. But Thugut was not destined so easily to free Austria from the golden chains that bound

1796. her to England. In this same fateful month of
Nov. 16. November, at the very moment when Catherine
seemed inclined at last to take an active part against
France, the great Empress died; and her successor,
hastily recalling all her expeditions, gave England
and Austria to understand that they must make
peace for themselves, for that Russia was in no condition to go to war. Once again, therefore, Thugut
found himself driven back for his only ally upon
England, the mistrusting and mistrusted.

Grenville's threat of a separate peace was, however,
Dec. 18. more idle than he knew, for on the 18th of December
Malmesbury with marked rudeness and discourtesy was
ordered to withdraw from Paris. The explanation of
Dec. 15. this curious proceeding soon appeared. On the 15th
the French expedition for Ireland, having been designed to start first in the early autumn and then in
November, at last sailed out of Brest. It consisted
of seventeen ships of the line, nineteen frigates and
corvettes, and seven transports only, the troops to the
number of some eighteen thousand being crowded on
board the men-of-war after a fashion which must inevitably have ensured disaster in case of a meeting with
a British fleet. But, to the shame of the Admiralty,
there was no British fleet to interfere with them; and
the greater part of the armament, beset by no difficulties nor alarms except those arising from inferior
Dec. 20. seamanship, arrived safely on the 20th at the mouth of
Bantry Bay. A few ships only had gone astray, so few
as little to weaken the actual force of the expedition,
had not one of the missing vessels carried not only the
naval Commander-in-chief, but also the General who
was the soul of the enterprise, Lazare Hoche.
Dec. 22. On the 22nd General Dalrymple, who held command
at Cork, first learned of the danger that was impending,
and admirably supported by Mr. Richard White, the
chief resident proprietor near Bantry, and by his tenantry,
made such dispositions as he could to meet it. He at
once occupied Bandon, to check any advance on Cork;

but he reckoned that he could not concentrate even two thousand men there for some days at least, while to assemble as many as nine thousand about Cork before the 1st of January would have been impossible. The country, with the exception of Belfast and some parts of the north, showed the best possible spirit, and the strength of the Yeomanry rose rapidly to over twenty thousand men. But the fact remains that, if the French had been able to land even two-thirds of their force by Christmas Day, they would almost infallibly have captured Cork, with an enormous quantity of naval supplies and stores. Bad weather and bad seamanship, however, wrecked the whole enterprise. Foul winds prevented the French ships from working to the head of Bantry Bay; a heavy gale on the 25th drove the greater part of them to sea, and the remainder, judging themselves too weak for any profitable operations, joined their companions. On the 29th the flagship with General Hoche on board, which had been first chased away and afterwards blown away from Bantry Bay, met what remained of the fleet at sea; and the whole sailed back gloomily to Brest.

Five of the ships had been lost or destroyed by their officers to avoid capture, and six more had been taken by a few British frigates that were lying at Cork. As to the British fleets, that of Admiral Colpoys off Brest did not even discover that the French had sailed until they had been for two days outside Bantry Bay, when it ran first to Falmouth and from thence to Spithead, which it entered on the 31st of December. Lord Bridport with the Channel fleet was lying at Spithead when the news, that the Brest fleet had sailed, reached him on the 21st or 22nd of December. He was not ready to get under way until the 25th, and owing to a sudden change of wind was unable to take his whole fleet to sea until the 3rd of January. Yet the Ministers maintained that neither they nor he could have done more; and probably they believed it, though Sir John Jervis would have been of a different opinion.

1797. A very few weeks only were to elapse before the seamen themselves were to pronounce damning judgment both upon the Ministers and the Admiral.[1]

This fearful danger, therefore, by great good fortune passed away; but Camden's nerve had not unnaturally been shaken by the safe coming and going of Hoche's expedition, and he renewed his entreaties for reinforcements especially of regular troops. "You know our nakedness in the matter of regular troops," answered Portland plaintively; "we could not have spared you above a thousand regular infantry unless we sent the Guards." Shortly afterwards arrived more bad news from Italy. Alvintzy had made a fourth attempt to relieve Mantua, always upon the old false principles, Jan. 14. had been beaten at Rivoli on the 14th of January, and had retired with an army in miserable plight and utterly demoralised to Friuli and Innsbrück.[2] Mantua capitulated on the 2nd of February; and at Vienna all except Thugut were in blank despair. He was now more than ever embittered against England, for in December 1796 there had been delay, owing to financial difficulties in London, in payment of the loan promised to the Emperor. Those difficulties culminated in the third week in February, when the Bank of England was compelled to suspend cash-payments; but confidence Feb. 27. was restored by an agreement of the principal bankers and merchants to accept bank-notes; and the restriction on cash-payments was shortly afterwards authorised by Act of Parliament.

In the midst of the crisis came the extraordinary

[1] For the Irish expedition see the evidence collected by Mr. Lecky from the Irish State Paper Office and other sources, *History of Ireland in the Eighteenth Century*, chapter viii. ad fin; Mahan's *Influence of Sea Power in the French Revolution*, i. chapter xi.; James's *Naval History*, ii. 1-19; S.P. Ireland, Camden to Portland, 25th and 26th December 1796.

[2] Colonel Thomas Graham summarised the story as follows—"With half our army we had beaten Bonaparte and must have destroyed him with the other half, but for the damnable stupidity of our Generals and the disgraceful and unaccountable terror that seized our men." *Life of Lord Lynedoch*, p. 152.

intelligence that a body of twelve hundred French had 1797. landed at Fishguard, on the north coast of Pembrokeshire, on the 23rd of February, but that being overawed Feb. 23. by detachments of the Cardigan Militia and of other local levies, and by the red cloaks of the Welsh women who crowned the surrounding hills to witness so interesting a spectacle, these heroes had at once laid down their arms. They proved to be a gang of galley-slaves and ruffians of every description, dressed in uniform and commanded by one Colonel Tate, who carried instructions signed by Hoche to burn Bristol, raise insurrections and make mischief generally. On their way to the Welsh coast the frigates escorting this force had stopped at Ilfracombe, then a remote and tiny village on the coast of North Devon, scuttled a few merchantmen and attempted to destroy the shipping in the haven; but they sailed away before the North Devon Volunteers, who were at once assembled by Colonel Paul Orchard of Hartland Abbey, could march thither to attack them. The whole enterprise was inspired by such motives as prompt a burglar to befoul the doorstep of a house which he has failed to enter, and would never have been sanctioned but by a government of blackguards such as the Directory. However, little harm was done. The promptitude with which the local levies responded to the call for their services was reassuring; and the Welsh Militia and North Devon Volunteers had the satisfaction of reading the history of their exploits in the *Gazette*.[1]

Moreover, this petty raid, added to financial difficulties, was the means of saving England from yet another military failure. It will hardly be credited that, at a moment when the Army was hopelessly overburdened by the many enterprises already undertaken by the Cabinet, Dundas actually gave orders for a force of eighteen hundred men to be detached from the Cape of Good Hope for an expedition to Spanish South

[1] *London Gazette*, 25th-27th February 1796; Adolphus, vi. 526-528.

1797. America. Such a project had been put forward originally in 1780 and had been then approved by Lord North's Cabinet. James Craig had revived it at the time of the dispute over Nootka Sound; and the British Ministers in January 1797 proposed to send a thousand men to replace the troops that should be drawn from the Cape for this adventure, and to set him in command. The point of attack first suggested was Rio de la Plata, but this was presently changed, with almost ludicrous vagueness, to the south-west coast of America; and it was ordained that the petty police-corps at New South Wales should contribute a certain number of men to the force. The idea, no doubt, was to rouse the whole of the Spanish Colonies to a struggle against their mother-country; but it is difficult to see what help eighteen hundred men could have afforded to such a movement. The number was too small to give any countenance to an insurrection, though large enough to raise false hopes such as the Ministry had already kindled and permitted to be extinguished, in La Vendée. Huskisson, Dundas's Under-Secretary, appears to have been the soul of the enterprise; and when, by the mercy of Providence, circumstances forced him at the end of February to abandon it, he declared that he had never put pen to paper with such reluctance as when he cancelled the orders for a plan of operations which presented to England such "fair prospects of glory and permanent advantage." It is, therefore, tolerably plain that the Ministers aimed not merely at deliverance of South America from the Spanish yoke, but at actual annexation of territory. In other words, they recklessly proposed further to exhaust the military strength of England by adding yet more to her innumerable foreign garrisons. The whole plan presents such a picture of the Cabinet's misconception of the meaning of war as almost to forbid sober criticism. It is difficult to know whether to describe it as frivolity or madness.[1]

[1] *W.O. Orig. Corres.*, 61. Memo. of proposed expedition, 17th

Fortunately on the 5th of March came news which 1797. showed that England possessed a man who dared to strike at Spain where she might really feel the blow. On the 14th of February Sir John Jervis with fifteen sail Feb. 14. of the line engaged the Spanish fleet of twenty-seven sail off Cape St. Vincent, and completely defeated it, capturing four ships. The story of the action and of Nelson's part in it is too well known to need repetition; but it must not be forgotten that the soldiers of the Sixty-ninth Foot in the *Captain* were the foremost among the boarders of the *San Nicolas*, and that a private of that regiment took the lead even of Nelson himself. "A victory," Jervis had said on the morning of the action, "is very essential to England at this moment"; and he had won it against odds of nearly two to one. The Spanish fleet, long dreaded as a menace to Ireland, now became a mere subject for contempt; and the people, as the naval historian well says, thanked God and took courage.[1]

Nevertheless the moment of greatest peril was still to come. On the 15th of April Lord Bridport made April 15. signal to the Channel fleet, which was lying at Spithead when it ought to have been cruising off Brest, to weigh anchor and proceed to sea; whereupon the whole crew of the flagship, instead of manning the capstan, ran up the shrouds and gave three cheers. The remaining ships responded by the like action; and England was face to face with a great and general mutiny of the fleet. Isolated risings had given warning of some such event. In Admiral Hotham's fleet the men of the *Windsor Castle* had mutinied in November 1794, and the Admiral had been obliged to remove the Captain and First Lieutenant from the ship. At Spithead the discontent was provoked by real and substantial grievances, not against individuals, but against the country at large.

January 1797. Huskisson to Craig, 21st January; to Lord Spencer, 2nd March; Dundas to Admiralty, 22nd January; to Duke of Portland, 21st February; to Cornwallis, 22nd February 1797.

[1] *Nelson's Despatches*, ii. 345; Mahan, *Influence of Sea Power*.

1797. The men in fact asked only for fair wages, decent and sufficient food, better care for the sick, protection from embezzlement, and a short leave of absence on returning from sea; and they declined to do their duty until their demands were granted and secured to them by Act of Parliament, unless (for this exception was always inserted) the enemy's fleet should put to sea. Within April 22. a week the whole of the men's demands had been granted, and Bridport rehoisted his flag; but a fortnight later the mutiny was renewed, apparently owing to the ineradicable suspicion of the men that the Government would not keep faith. Lord Howe after some trouble set this matter right by bringing an Act of May 17. Parliament in his hand, and on the 17th of May Bridport sailed to his station before Brest.

Hardly was this mutiny at Spithead brought to an end when another mutiny broke out among the ships at the Nore, and infected nearly the whole of Admiral Duncan's squadron in the North Sea. This was less a mutiny than a political riot organised by seditious leaders, and was for the moment the more dangerous on that account; for it was feared that it might spread to the troops. As a matter of fact there were isolated cases of disaffection among the artillery at Woolwich, which were publicly disavowed by the mass of the men;[1] and there were also unpleasant symptoms, which were probably much exaggerated, in one of the battalions of the Guards in London. But the Government soon found that it could depend upon the whole country, civil and military, and resolved to put down the disloyalty at the Nore with a strong hand. Measures were taken to cut off from the mutineers all supplies of food and water, and, if necessary, to throw shells upon their ships; and meanwhile the people at large, rising to the occasion, hastened to join the ranks of the civil army, insomuch that thirty-one corps of Yeomanry and nearly two hundred and fifty of Volunteers were either created or augmented in the course of the year. Very

[1] Duncan's *History of the Royal Artillery*, ii. p. 72.

soon the mutineers began to quarrel among themselves; 1797.
by the 22nd the mutiny was at an end; and on the June 22.
25th the ringleader, Richard Parker, was hanged at the
yard-arm of the *Sandwich*. It is worthy of note that
Sir Charles Grey was called in to take command at
Portsmouth during the outbreak, owing to his immense
popularity with the seamen. It is still more noteworthy that on the 25th of May the Government May 25.
suddenly granted to the Army the solid increase of
pay for which the military authorities had entreated
in vain from 1784 to 1792.

Little though it has been noticed by historians, this
fact furnishes in itself a damning commentary upon
Pitt's administration. It is absolutely incontestable
that he refused to make the slightest concession to the
just claims of the Navy and the Army until overawed
by a mutiny, and that thereby he exposed England to
the greatest peril that had threatened her since the days
of the Spanish Armada. It is one of the chief functions
of a statesman to forestall revolutions by the wise and
timely initiation of political and administrative reform;
and, compared with such a task, the maintenance of due
subordination in the military forces of the Crown, by
the exercise of common sense and common justice, is
simple indeed. Yet this latter elementary duty was
completely overlooked by Pitt. It is true that both in
the Navy and in the Army there were hard and brutal
martinets whose tyranny would have driven even angels
to rebellion; and it is true that the most terrible of the
many mutinies of the Navy—that in the *Hermione*—
was provoked by the excesses of a commander of this
type. But the mutiny at Spithead, without which that
at the Nore could never have attained to so formidable
dimensions, was no revolt against individual oppression,
for the men spoke with warm affection both of Howe
and of Bridport; no insolent challenge to the Government to yield or perish, for they protested their willingness to do their duty upon any terms if the French
fleet should put to sea. It was an appeal to the nation

1797. for relief from long neglect and long injustice, and if it were accompanied by threats, the reason was that without threats it could have compelled no attention.

Whether the Government had received such warnings from the naval commanders as it had received from the military, I cannot say; that point is for the naval historian to make clear. But it is at any rate certain that no man, reading the despatches of Hood and Hotham from the Mediterranean in 1794 and 1795, and observing the pitiful shifts to which the country was driven for manning the fleet, could fail to see that the state of the Navy from the very beginning of the war had been in the highest degree dangerous. Yet the Ministers moved not a finger to set the evil right. On the contrary, when two such officers as Grey and Jervis, through the ascendency which they had gained over their men by true care and consideration for them, evoked from both sailors and soldiers the astonishing efforts which conquered the French West Indies, the Government instantly picked a quarrel with them over the prize-money, which was their sole reward. Finally, when the patience of the men was worn out, the Government hurriedly acknowledged that it was in the wrong, and hastened, under the compulsion of fear, to redress the grievances not only of the Navy but of the Army. It is idle to talk of statesmanship in connection with such proceedings, futile to put forward Pitt's ambitious schemes for the settlement of Europe in support of his claim to such a talent. A man is not a good manager who lays out a pleasing landscape before his windows, when his house is tumbling about his ears and may bury him at any moment in its ruins. The reparation wrung from the Government by the mutiny at Spithead was an abject and humiliating confession of crime; and if any deserved to be hanged for that crime it was not the mutineers.

Throughout these miserable months the news from the Continent had grown steadily worse. Even before the capitulation of Mantua had been signed,

Bonaparte had repaired to Bologna with ten thousand 1797.
men to open the campaign against the Papal States. Feb. 1.
The resistance offered was contemptible. On the 18th
of February messengers arrived from the Pope to sue
for peace; and, on the following day, a treaty was Feb. 19.
signed whereby the Pontiff confirmed to France all
that she had taken, and undertook to pay a large contribution, pending discharge of which several provinces
were to remain in French occupation. Then rejoining
his headquarters at Bassano on the 9th of March, March 9.
Bonaparte on the following day began his advance
into Austria; having meanwhile arranged for a revolutionary outburst in Venice, which should give him an
excuse for seizing Venetia and using it for his own
purpose in the negotiations which he anticipated with
the Court of Vienna.

There was little opposition to his forward movement
by the demoralised Austrian army. The Archduke
Charles had been recalled from the Rhine to take the
command against Bonaparte; but he judged it wisest, with
sound reason, not to fight until he had drawn the French
far into the heart of Germany. Bonaparte followed
the Austrians rapidly until, on reaching Klagenfurth, March 20.
the capital of Carinthia, he grew nervous at hearing no
news of the army of the Rhine, which he had expected
to co-operate with him. Suddenly halting, he wrote a
letter to the Archduke proposing a negotiation for peace.
The suggestion was welcomed at Vienna, where even
Thugut, finding himself estranged alike from Prussia,
Russia, and England, was prepared to come to terms;
and, on the 18th of April, Bonaparte concluded, with- April 18.
out reference to the Directory, the preliminary Treaty
of Leoben.[1] Hereby Belgium was openly made over
to France, while by secret articles the Emperor

---

[1] Count Starhemberg, the Austrian Ambassador in England, who did not hesitate to express to Grenville his own disgust at the conduct of his chiefs in Vienna (*mes* . . . *supérieurs*), declared that the conclusion of peace was due to *ce vilain Archiduc*. *Dropmore Papers*, iii. 325, 331.

1797. renounced all his Italian possessions west of the Oglio, receiving in return the territory of Venice east of that river. Venice was also to cede to France her territory west of the Oglio, and to gain in compensation Romagna, Ferrara, and Bologna. The main point for England, however, was that Austria had made a separate peace, and had left her isolated in the contest with France.

The preliminaries of Leoben signed, Bonaparte returned at once to the subjugation of Venice. For this the disturbances which he had himself excited May 24. furnished a sufficient pretext. On the 24th of May he entered upon a new negotiation with Austria for the remodelling of the preliminaries; and, since the cession of Zante and Corfu to France formed a part of the proposed arrangements, a French expedition on the 28th of May seized Corfu. Meanwhile, once again by his own machinations, a factitious revolution had broken June 6. out in Genoa, wherein he intervened to impose upon Genoa also a new Constitution after the French model. At the same time his mind became filled with designs for the extension of French rule in the Mediterranean. While reporting the strength of the fleet taken from Venice, he expressed his fears that the British might prevent the transport of it to Toulon. When announcing the expedition to Corfu, he pointed out to the Directory that Malta would be of priceless value to France. Nor did he leave out of sight the chance of an expedition against England herself.[1]

Amid such an accumulation of misfortunes, it is not surprising that Pitt, on hearing on the 5th of May of the Treaty of Leoben, decided immediately to renew his overtures of peace to France. Grenville was strongly opposed to this step, being, in truth, a more resolute man than Pitt, while the King, as always, had nothing but contempt to spare for the project;[2] but Pitt prevailed, and Lord Malmesbury at the beginning of July

---

[1] *Corres. de Napoléon*, iii. 66, 86, 100, 26th May and 7th June 1797.
[2] *Dropmore Papers*, iii. 327-330.

met the French plenipotentiaries at Lille. In France 1797. itself recent events had been adverse to the gang of unscrupulous rogues who held the preponderance of power in the Directory. Elections held in March for the renewal of one-third of the Legislature resulted in the return of an overwhelming majority of moderate men, who were of one mind with Carnot, the only honest man in the Directory, in favour of order and peace. In May the two Councils met, and proceeded not only to repeal several oppressive laws against royalists, but to vote the recall of Santhonax and his fellow ruffians from St. Domingo and to censure the Directory's treatment of Venice. As a matter of fact, Bonaparte was solely responsible for this last affair, and was violently irritated by their criticism. The Directory therefore found him in a willing mood when they appealed to him for help, since they had already June 24. decided, as usual, to overthrow the opposition of the moderate party by violence.

Plans had earlier been approved for a second attempt to invade Ireland; and twelve thousand men were on march from the Sambre to Brest, in order to take part in the expedition. A pretext was easily found for diverting these to Paris; and meanwhile Bonaparte kept stirring up his own troops to march to the rescue of the Directory, and exhorting the Directors to be firm. Finally, in July, he sent General Augereau from his army to Paris, where that officer was at once installed as the Governor of the capital. Nevertheless, the Directory hesitated to strike the final blow, until at length fear of a counterstroke by their opponents forced them to act. On the night of the 3rd of September Sept. 3. the leaders of the Moderates were arrested, and on the next day the Legislature was intimidated into the repeal of its conciliatory measures. Carnot, having evaded seizure, fled to Geneva; the remainder of the arrested leaders were deported to Cayenne; and, by this triumph of the Directors, France was subjected once more to the rule of a tyrannical minority.

1797. This was the revolution known as that of the 18th of Fructidor, and its first result was the rupture of the negotiations at Lille. The event was a great disappointment to Pitt. He had been led to expect that the Directory would cede Ceylon and the Cape of Good Hope to England in return for a bribe of £450,000, and had already devised the means for depleting the Treasury of this sum without disclosure of the transaction to Parliament. There can be no question of the venality of some of the Directors, and in particular of their recently appointed Foreign Minister, Talleyrand; nor can Pitt be blamed if, in genuine zeal for his country's welfare, he were inclined to close with so tempting an offer. Yet Grenville could not, and would not, approve of it. "If this country could but be brought to think so," he wrote to Pitt, "it would be ten thousand times safer (and cheaper too, which they seem to consider above all other things) to face the storm than to shrink from it. And above all I dread the loss of consideration which must, I fear, infallibly result from any mode of *purchasing* our safety; and such this is and will be felt to be, let us say or do what we will." These words breathe a higher statesmanship, as well as a nobler spirit, than Pitt's. "Let us trust to nothing but God and ourselves," Colonel Calvert had written from Flanders at the close of 1794, "for I repeat it again and again, there is nothing else left on which we can rely with safety." This was the lesson which Ministers were at last beginning to learn; and it was well that, when the course of events left England isolated in the great struggle with France, there was one of them who preferred to face the storm rather than shrink from it. It was not for nothing that this proud, shy scholar shared the blood of Richard Grenville of the *Revenge*.[1]

[1] *Dropmore Papers*, iii. 328, 369, 378.

CHAPTER XX

Long before the disasters of 1797 had begun to burst
upon England, Abercromby had again sailed for the
West Indies. The rapid course of untoward events
had caused frequent changes in his instructions in
October and November 1796; and, before he finally
embarked on the 15th of the latter month, Dundas had
given him to understand that Ministers could furnish
him with few troops and few ships for the coming
campaign. As regards operations against the French,
therefore, the Cabinet looked for no more than the
retention of the conquests already made, and were
prepared even for the evacuation of the whole of St.
Domingo, excepting Mole St. Nicholas. But the declaration of war by Spain had introduced a new element into
the struggle in the West Indies. The planters of Grenada
and Tobago had represented strongly the danger that
threatened them from the vicinity of the Spaniards
at Trinidad; and the reduction of that island was
therefore the object first recommended to Abercromby.
" Even if you cannot hold it," wrote Dundas, " you
will remove a source of danger to our own islands";
forgetting that the only possible source of danger to
the British Islands from Spain lay not in Spanish
harbours but in Spanish ships. However, a month's
consideration decided Dundas to favour rather an
attempt on Porto Rico, for which purpose Abercromby
was to employ most of the troops at St. Domingo.
Having taken Porto Rico, the General was then to
transport thither the people who claimed King George's

1796.

Nov. 15.

1796. protection in St. Domingo itself. The Minister's last word, in fact, was that, though he left the General a free hand, he would recommend Porto Rico as the prior object. The only obstacles to the plan were, firstly, that the troops at St. Domingo were little more than a name; secondly, that neither the Government nor Abercromby possessed the slightest trustworthy information as to the strength of the Spaniards at Porto Rico; and thirdly, that, even if Porto Rico were taken, it might be a little difficult to transport some tens of thousands of people with their goods and property for some five hundred miles in the teeth of the trade-wind. Such a voyage would take some time; the vessels would all require to be escorted by men-of-war; and it was not very easy to say how they were to be victualled for so long a passage. Moreover, since the people at St. Domingo had not been consulted as to this plan, it was by no means certain that they would be willing to migrate. These practical matters, however, naturally escaped the notice of Dundas.

At the last moment, however, Abercromby was delivered of all responsibility for St. Domingo; and his command, to his great relief, was restricted to the windward sphere of operations. The Duke of Portland was anxious to entrust to General Simcoe the winding up of affairs in St. Domingo; and, since his Grace was not backward to assert his rights as the head of the Colonial administration, the business, though essentially a military question, was left to him. The conflict of jurisdiction, indeed, between the Military and the Colonial departments throughout these West Indian campaigns, was such that the Generals were evidently often puzzled whether to address themselves to Portland or to Dundas.[1] Nor was the confusion limited to these two departments only. Dundas, after endless foolish intrigues with the Emigrant French

[1] There was friction as to the limits of Portland's and Dundas's spheres of administration even later than this. *Dropmore Papers*, iv. 79.

nobility, had in January 1796 grown weary of the 1796. labour of fitting out expeditions to the French coast, and tried very unceremoniously to shift that burden on to the Foreign Office; only, however, to be checked by Grenville with most disconcerting decision.[1] But, even though released from all anxiety as to St. Domingo, Abercromby could not but doubt gravely his power to accomplish everything prescribed to him. The garrisons judged necessary for the security of the islands to windward were reckoned at twelve thousand white soldiers; the force at present in occupation of them did not exceed nine thousand effective men; and the only troops that he could hope to receive in the course of the winter were twelve hundred Germans of extremely inferior quality. However, he was an officer of sufficient experience not to expect too much from Ministers. On his arrival at Portsmouth he found that, as usual, the clothing and camp equipment for the troops were, owing to the neglect of the Regimental Agents, not ready for shipment; and with a final expression of his opinion that Trinidad should be his first object, he sailed on the 17th of November for Martinique.[2]

Early in January 1797 he arrived at that island 1797. and found the troops to windward reduced beyond all calculation by the ravages of disease, in spite of every care in the hospitals. He waited, however, only for the arrival of some of the foreign regiments that he was expecting from England, and then, embarking a force of about four thousand men of all ranks,[3] assembled the fleet and transports at the island of Carriacou, from whence on the 15th of February he sailed to Trinidad. Feb. 15. On passing through the Dragon's Mouth, the British

[1] Grenville to Pitt, 25th January 1796. *Dropmore Papers*, iii. 167.
[2] Dundas to Abercromby, 28th October (four letters) and 13th November (two letters); Abercromby to Dundas, 31st October, 4th, 15th, 17th November 1796.
[3] The troops engaged in this expedition were the 2nd Queen's, 14th and 53rd, the flank-companies of the 3rd, detachments of the 38th and 60th, Hompesch's and Löwenstein's foreign corps.

1797. squadron discovered four Spanish ships of the line and
Feb. 16. a frigate lying under cover of a fortified islet, and came to anchor almost within gun-shot of them, while the transports worked up towards Port of Spain and took up their station within five miles of the town. All preparations were made for a landing and for a general attack by sea and land at daybreak on the following
Feb. 17. morning; but at two o'clock the Spanish squadron was seen to be on fire. The troops were immediately disembarked; the town was captured after trifling resistance, and on the following morning the island capitulated, having cost the British no further loss than a single officer killed. The garrison numbered about six hundred of all ranks, the marines and seamen of the squadron sixteen hundred; and these with nearly one hundred guns and a single line-of-battle ship, which was saved from the conflagration, fell into the hands of the captors.[1]

Notwithstanding Dundas's hint that Trinidad need not be occupied, Abercromby decided to leave there one thousand men under command of Lieutenant-colonel Picton, with instructions to obtain all possible information as to the neighbouring Colonies on the mainland. The feebleness of the Spanish resistance had struck him as characteristic of a decaying race; and, being a liberal in politics, he had seen visions of an America liberated by British help from the Spanish yoke, free and self-governed, with nine-tenths of its commerce in British hands and such a wealth of tropical produce as would enable Britain to dispense with troublesome and costly sugar-islands. All this, however, lay in the future. The immediate object was now Porto Rico, and, before Abercromby could make any attempt upon it, it was necessary for him to return to Martinique to await the reinforcements and stores that were on their way from England. With the troops that had already reached him he was extremely ill-satisfied.

[1] Abercromby to Dundas, 16th and 26th January, 20th February 1797.

These were exclusively foreigners, partly Germans, 1797. " which at best could only be compared to the condottieri of the sixteenth and seventeenth centuries," and partly nondescripts of the Irish Brigade, a corps which had been taken over with great ceremony from the service of France in 1794, and had since tried in vain to maintain its existence by recruiting in its native island. However, in the military destitution of England at this time better things were hardly to be expected; and Abercromby could only hope that the other reinforcements, when they arrived, would prove no worse.[1]

By the 8th of April the preparations were complete. April 8. About four thousand troops were embarked,[2] and the armament, after some days' delay at St. Kitts, anchored on the 17th of April in extremely bad ground off April 17. Congrejos Point, some eight miles to east of the town of San Juan, Porto Rico. Then the difficulties of the enterprise were first seen. The town itself lay at the point of a small island, covered by powerful fortifications both to seaward and landward, with two redoubts to guard the principal access to it across the narrow channel that parted it from the mainland, and a swarm of gunboats to hinder the passage at any other point. Further, the whole of the coast was barred by a reef, through which there was but one narrow and difficult channel to permit even small craft to approach the shore. None the less Abercromby landed his troops; but after endeavouring in vain, owing to the enormous superiority of the enemy's fire, to force a passage opposite to the two redoubts, he fell back on an attempt to bombard the town from a distance. Then, finding that his fire at extreme range was wholly ineffective, he re-embarked his force on the 30th of April, and returned to April 30. Martinique. His losses amounted to just over one

---

[1] Abercromby to Dundas, 20th February and 13th March 1797.
[2] Detachments of 26th Light Dragoons, Artillery and Engineers, 14th, 42nd, 53rd, 3/60th, 87th Foot; 150 of the Tobago Negro Corps; total 3706. Return of 2nd May 1797.

1797. hundred killed and wounded and one hundred and twenty missing, of which last the majority, being from the foreign corps, were probably deserters; and he was obliged also to destroy and abandon thirteen pieces of ordnance. The whole enterprise had, as Abercromby said, been undertaken too lightly; the Spanish garrison, which had been reported weak, actually outmatching the attacking force both in numbers and in weight of artillery. It was only fortunate that the attempt should have ended without serious failure or serious success; for success would only have locked up another garrison of one thousand men in the West Indies, or in other words have killed another five hundred men every year for no object worth the cost.[1]

Herewith ended the campaign to windward, without need for Dundas to order, as in June for good reasons he did order, that the General should stand strictly on the defensive, save every penny that could be saved, and above all look to the good management of the hospitals. There remained, therefore, nothing for Abercromby to do but to superintend the raising of negro regiments, which the Government had decided to increase to the number of eight. The method prescribed was to obtain a quota of negroes in each island by contract, at a price not exceeding £70 a head. The Assemblies in the most important islands, however, at once exerted themselves to the utmost to thwart the measure, and with complete success. In the first place, the islands being now more or less secure, the planters were unwilling that the negroes should be distracted from the task of making money for their owners to so trivial an employment as defence of the country. In the second place, as Abercromby said, they delighted in opposition and made speeches from the *London Magazine*. In the third place, they were furious at the behaviour of the British officers, who trained the black recruit to self-respect, and taught him as his first lesson that he was better than other black men. Aber-

[1] Abercromby to Dundas, 2nd May 1797 (two letters).

cromby returned to England in August, before the 1797.
difficulty had been solved; and it fell to his successors,
Generals Cuyler and Bowyer, to execute Dundas's
final instructions, which were to buy negroes direct
from Africa, taking every precaution to conceal the fact
that the Government was the purchaser. Cuyler fulfilled his task discreetly and warily; and by July 1798
the Eighth of the West India Regiments had been
formed in Dominica, where it took over the duty at
Prince Rupert's Bay. The withdrawal of British troops
from this single pestilent station saved the lives of
hundreds of British soldiers.

But such considerations carried little weight with the
planters, whose hatred for the black troops now found
a new vent. Under the servile code of the islands any
one magistrate might order a black soldier, being a
slave, to be publicly whipped, and two magistrates
could order him to be hanged; and since the magis-
tracy consisted to all intent exclusively of planters, such
a chance of asserting their rights to the annoyance
of officers was not overlooked. The officers naturally
objected to such summary treatment of their men; but
Dundas settled the dispute with commendable good
sense, by simply ordering the General to use his legal
right to enfranchise his recruits, and so to render them
amenable either to civil or to military law. Thus by
a curious sequence of causes the creation of West India
Regiments directly favoured the work of Clarkson and
Wilberforce. A final attempt was made by the Legislature of Antigua to prevent the quartering of black
troops in that island, by passing a series of violent and
extremely foolish resolutions. General Bowyer reported
the matter, as in duty bound, to Dundas, who very
loyally stood by him with all his authority. "It is
your duty," he wrote, "to countenance and support
the black corps against the unwarrantable jealousies and
prejudices of the planters, and to impress upon them
that, owing to the difficulty of providing recruits, their
defence cannot be provided for in any other way."

1797. Five years of bitter experience had at last taught Dundas the lesson which Grey and Williamson in 1794 had urged upon him in vain; and, to do him justice, he had learned it thoroughly.¹

1798. From the end of 1797 and the beginning of 1798 the islands to windward may be said to have returned to peace. The brigands had been thoroughly subdued or destroyed. The Black Caribs to the number of nearly five thousand men were deported to Rattan, where pestilence, which they had brought with them from St. Vincent, destroyed nearly half of them in five months. One transport with three hundred of them on board was captured by the Spaniards and 1797. carried into Truxillo; whereupon the frigate *Experiment* April 27. promptly sailed thither after them, attacked the fort at midnight with fifty convalescent soldiers of the Irish brigade, Forty-second and Fifty-third, spiked eight guns, and carried off the missing transport in triumph.² With this incident the Black Caribs vanish from history, none too soon for the peace of St. Vincent. For the rest it will be convenient in this place to anticipate matters a little, so as to release the reader finally from these wearisome Antilles. The West India Regiments were increased to twelve by the middle of 1799, and the West Indies were practically guarded by them and by the Sixtieth Regiment. To this last a Fifth battalion was added by the incorporation of some of Hompesch's infantry in January 1798 and of Löwenstein's far more efficient Chasseurs a few months later. A Sixth battalion, raised in 1799, was also ordered to the West Indies in November of that year. It may be added that Surinam was bloodlessly made

¹ Dundas to Abercromby, 28th October 1796; to Cuyler, 17th January and 14th November 1798; to Trigge (Bowyer's successor), 23rd March 1799; Abercromby to Dundas, 26th January, 19th and 20th March, November 1797; Cuyler to Dundas, 23rd and 29th March, 3rd April 1798; Bowyer to Dundas, 13th July and 8th September 1798; 19th January 1799; to Colonel Brownrigg, 6th September 1798.

² Major John Wilson to Dundas, 9th July 1797.

over by its Dutch commander to a paltry expedition in 1797. 1799, in consideration of the sum of £100,000, and that Curaçoa invoked and received British protection in September 1800. Thus the whole of the Dutch West Indies passed into British hands ; and the Windward Islands may be practically dismissed from the sphere of active military operations.[1]

It is now needful to return to St. Domingo, where, as will be remembered, though the general situation had improved, the British force was too weak to take advantage of the improvement. By this time, the Government, appalled at the cost of the island in blood and treasure, had resolved to alter its former system entirely, and had appointed General Simcoe to carry out the change of policy. The instructions, given first to Abercromby and from him passed on to Simcoe, prescribed the following as the principal objects to be pursued. First, all possible provision was to be made for securing the interests and property of those who had placed themselves under British protection, and for the preservation of the most valuable parts of the Colony. But, secondly, this was to be effected by turning to the best account the personal exertions of the various classes of the people ; for the Government was resolved to send no further reinforcement of British troops, and was positively pledged to reduce the expenditure hitherto defrayed by the British Treasury. The British regiments were therefore to be gradually withdrawn to Mole St. Nicholas, and the rest of the country was to be committed to the charge of the Colonial troops under such French or Colonial officers as the General might appoint, subject always to his supreme control. If the islands of Tortuga or Cap François were of immediate importance to the safety of the Mole, one or other of them might also be occupied by British troops. Finally, the annual expense to the British nation on account of the island was not to

[1] Cuyler to Dundas, 1st January 1798 ; Trigge to Dundas, 4th June 1799 ; Dundas to Trigge, 6th and 7th November 1799.

1797. exceed £300,000; and this was in reality the cardinal point upon which the whole of the new system was to turn. So far the cost of St. Domingo had risen steadily from £300,000 in 1794 to close upon £800,000 in 1795, to more than two millions in 1796, and to £700,000 for the month of January 1797 alone. There could be no question but that this expenditure had been shamefully extravagant and profligate; but whether the preservation of St. Domingo were compatible with its immediate reduction was an extremely difficult question.[1]

Simcoe's own idea before setting out for the island was to occupy Tortuga, which was rich in pasture, horses, cattle, and timber, and to use it as the base for a flotilla of armed vessels, which could not only follow the enemy's privateers into every refuge and sweep them off the sea, but also land a force at any point on the coast for the reduction of a fortress or for the dispersion of any large body of brigands. The project had been conceived by him first during the American War, from his knowledge of the use made of Tortuga by the buccaneers in the seventeenth century; and only accident had prevented him from proving himself as able a partisan-leader by sea as by land. He now returned to his design in the assurance that the possession of the island, together with that of the Mole, would give the British a defensive position, with powers of offence so formidable as practically to control the greater part of French St. Domingo, particularly if the flotilla and the force attached to it were placed under the orders of Colonel Thomas Maitland. On his
Feb. 20. arrival, however, at the Mole on the 20th of February he found himself at once crippled by the lamentable weakness of the British regiments, and by the debility even of the few men that were returned as effective. The recruits, which had been promised to him to raise

[1] Dundas to Abercromby, September; to Simcoe, 25th November 1796. *Parl. Hist.* Commons Debate of 18th May 1797.

their strength, had not arrived; the foreign regiments, 1797. which had been sent out as reinforcements, were ruffians and marauders of the worst description; and he was fain to remain inactive until Balcarres could send him some troops from Jamaica.

But, meanwhile, events began to move rapidly. In the hope of rallying the Spaniards, who in their hatred of the French were strongly inclined to join the British, a detachment of troops under Sir William Cockburn had been pushed out to Banica, nearly a hundred miles east of St. Marc, into the territory which, until its recent cession to France, had always been Spanish. In the first days of March the posts adjacent to this were March. attacked and carried by the Republicans; and it was necessary to send orders to Cockburn to abandon Banica and retire. Before he could do so, however, the outposts of Mirebalais were also carried by Toussaint l'Ouverture's levies; a reinforcement sent to the relief of Mirebalais itself under Montalembert was defeated; and finally both that post and those at Grand Bois were suddenly evacuated, greatly endangering the retreat of Cockburn and enabling the enemy to close in all round Port-au-Prince.[1]

These mishaps were untoward in themselves; but Simcoe soon discovered that behind them lay facts still more serious. News of Malmesbury's mission to Paris had reached the island; it had been noised abroad, not untruly, that the British Government only retained possession of St. Domingo as a useful card in the game of negotiation; and Simcoe's arrival had been interpreted to signify the immediate evacuation of Port-au-Prince. Moreover, Simcoe had already been active in detecting and suppressing abuses, and was rapidly feeling his way to an immediate reduction of nearly £200,000 of expense. Montalembert and the Viscount de Bruges, the two officers responsible for the evacuation of Mirebalais and Grand Bois, were both of them

[1] Simcoe to Dundas, 13th, 14th, 16th November 1796; 24th February, 7th and 9th March 1797.

1797. Emigrants who had long been fattening on the gold of England and on indiscriminate plunder; and it soon became evident that their abandonment of their fortified posts had been deliberately contrived. Montalembert presently retired from the island; and the Emigrants and others who had enriched themselves, even as he had, by peculation and misconduct of all kinds, began to resign their commissions and to hurry away with their spoil to America. In fact it was becoming plain that, if the British Government ceased to waste money, the men who as proprietors of St. Domingo had invoked England's protection had no intention of moving a finger to help her.[1]

April 11. On the 11th of April six hundred men of the Fortieth, of the Irish brigade, and of other small detachments, arrived at Port-au-Prince, together with Thomas Maitland, who had hoped for the command of the flotilla at Tortuga. Disappointed of this owing to the lack of men, he devoted all his energy to supporting Simcoe in the suppression of abuses, a task which his abomination of all Emigrants made peculiarly congenial to him. He also drew up for the benefit of Dundas a summary of the whole situation, in exceedingly trenchant terms; with a recommendation that Port-au-Prince and the entire district of St. Marc should be evacuated immediately. Simcoe, however, no sooner received the troops from Jamaica than by a series of skilful

April 13-17. movements he drove back Toussaint from his positions round Port-au-Prince. He was pursuing his operations with great success, when he was interrupted by news

April 18. that Rigaud had attacked Irois on the night of the 18th of April and, though repulsed, was evidently preparing to capture the post by a regular siege. Simcoe was therefore obliged to break off his own movements, and to send some of his troops in hot haste under Maitland to Jérémie. They would, however, have arrived too late had not Captain Ricketts of the frigate

[1] Simcoe to Dundas, 12th and (two letters) 13th April; Maitland to Dundas, 13th April 1797.

Magicienne happened by chance to call at Irois; when 1797. perceiving Rigaud's store-ships lying at anchor, he de- April 23. stroyed the whole of them and compelled the mulatto to retreat. Thus by pure accident Irois was saved, and with Irois, Jérémie, and Grand Anse, the loss of which, as Maitland said, would have meant the loss of the whole Colony. Nevertheless, even if it had been saved by design, through the arrival of Maitland's reinforcement, this end could have been attained only at the sacrifice of important operations about Port-au-Prince. While such things were possible, it was vain to expect the people to feel confidence in British protection; and while the General was liable to such calls for sudden and immediate efforts, necessarily involving unexpected expense under the pressure of the moment, it was futile to lay any plans for present retrenchment or future security. In brief, the continued tenure of St. Domingo was incompatible with sudden economy of British troops and British gold.[1]

Having placed Maitland in charge of Jérémie, and taken his predecessor, Brigadier Churchill, under his own command, Simcoe, as soon as he could reassemble his troops, entered upon operations for the recovery of Mirebalais, and for clearing the enemy once more from May 30- the south of the Artibonite. But Churchill had no such June 2. ability as Maitland; and, though Mirebalais and Grand Bois were indeed recaptured with slight loss, little real injury was inflicted upon Toussaint's forces. Moreover, a second expedition, designed to drive the enemy from their post at Verrettes, was a failure, owing to the June 16-20. incapacity of Churchill and the misconduct of his troops. Simcoe's disappointment was great. "Had Toussaint been dealt with as I had a right to expect," he wrote, "the affairs of the island would have been most prosperous." The Spaniards were universally desirous of submitting to the British Government; Rigaud was seriously at variance with the negro leaders, and was possibly also to be gained by the British; another large

[1] Simcoe to Dundas and Maitland to Dundas, 8th May 1797.

1797. body of negroes in the north had made friendly overtures; yet for want of troops nothing could be done. "Not a day has passed since my arrival," Simcoe wrote, "in which a reinforcement of two thousand troops or six thousand new troops would not have ensured the conquest of French St. Domingo"; and it seems possible, looking to the exhaustion and weariness of the country, that this may have been true. Finally, in the middle of June, the General wrote a long report in reply to the voluminous instructions of Dundas, and gave it as his opinion that the diminution of expenditure was irreconcilable with the continuance of British protection. The commanders of the various foreign and native corps were unwilling to forego the enormous advantages which they had gained by peculation and corruption. Nor was it only the foreign officers who were thus tainted. British officers also had become farmers of sequestrated estates, and one of them had refused to resign that office, alleging Simcoe's orders thereupon to be illegal. Simcoe had placed the Colonial regiments upon the most economical footing, but, "owing to the universal depravity of the military profession," would not answer for the consequences. He had done the like for the foreign corps, but doubted the result owing to the insubordinate character of the commanding officers. As to concentrating the British force at the Mole, it would lead to the immediate loss of all the valuable parts of the island, and very speedily of the Mole itself. It was its position, not its strength, which had given it the name of Gibraltar, for it was indefensible against attack by land, and could only be fortified at enormous expense. In short, it was impossible to preserve the island with the sum assigned for the purpose.[1]

July. In the middle of July both Simcoe and Maitland returned to England, as had been originally arranged, and Major-general Whyte was left in command. Evils increased rapidly as the reforms of Simcoe began

[1] Simcoe to Dundas, 15th, 16th, 25th, 26th June 1797.

to make themselves felt. Two of the foreign corps, at the instigation of their officers, insisted on being shipped back to England; and the men of many others, being the recruits that had been enlisted by Charmilli, began to desert in numbers. Two of them were caught and executed, but suffered death, according to Whyte's account, with all imaginable composure. Toussaint's forces were again descending from the mountains upon the plain of Cul de Sac, and during August and September the weary war of posts was renewed once more. The situation became most dangerous; and Whyte found but sorry encouragement in a letter which Dundas had written to Simcoe in June, adjuring him to withdraw to the Mole and reduce expenditure to £25,000 a month, at whatever sacrifice. "Parliament has been assured," the Minister wrote, "that the service of St. Domingo shall not exceed £300,000 a year. The difficulties to you in executing your instructions are nothing to the embarrassments which must occur here through your neglecting them"; and he added as a final argument that circumstances forbade the despatch of any reinforcements. A Minister might be excused for yielding to a somewhat hysterical tone during the height of the naval mutiny; but Whyte, who now heard of the new policy for St. Domingo apparently for the first time, was anything but sympathetic. "I must tell you," he answered, "that if evacuation takes place, desolation will ensue, and the faith of the country, pledged by every general in command here, will be broken. If such a thing should be in agitation, what are a handful of worn-out British soldiers to do against six thousand disciplined blacks, backed by the French, who have no gratitude, and only think of what use we can be to them?" There was not one of the follies of Pitt and Dundas that did not recoil upon their heads during that miserable year, 1797.[1]

Meanwhile Maitland and Simcoe had arrived in

[1] Dundas to Simcoe, 7th June; Whyte to Dundas, 24th July, 28th August, 29th September 1797.

1797.
Oct.

London to give counsel in person; and the result was seen in a new set of instructions drawn up in October, after the failure of Lord Malmesbury's negotiations at Lille. These were to the effect that a proposal had been made to the Directory that St. Domingo and Jamaica should remain neutral during the rest of the war, and that meanwhile the British troops must be withdrawn without delay to the Mole and Jérémie. If the people at Port-au-Prince were inclined to defend themselves, then provisions, stores and money to the amount of £60,000 were to be furnished to them; but if not, arrangements must be made, if possible, for their escape, and Ministers were prepared to give a bounty of from two months' to six months' pay to all officers, civil and military. It was, however, significant that these instructions expressed a doubt whether, owing to the naval superiority of Britain, the possession of St. Domingo was quite so important as had been thought at the opening of the war.

The officer finally selected to carry out these measures was General Nesbitt, with Maitland for his assistant; and it seems that Maitland left England almost immediately after the instructions had been communicated to his chief, on the 1st of January 1798. Before Nesbitt could sail, however, the irrepressible Charmilli and others of the self-styled proprietors of St. Domingo came forward with an offer to contribute a revenue of half a million sterling annually. Thereupon, incredible as it may seem, the Government actually modified its instructions. It now empowered the General to delay the evacuation of Port-au-Prince for two months, in order to consider the feasibility of collecting this contribution, and even to maintain the existing order of things in St. Domingo if the money should be forthcoming. Nesbitt surpassed this folly by recommending the despatch of six priests and thirty or forty Emigrant nobles to St. Domingo, pointing out that the Ministers would thereby rid themselves of a number of troublesome suitors, and provide

1798.

officers for the black regiments in the island. How 1798.
Nesbitt, and still more the Ministers, after their long
experience of these adventurers, could have listened to
their representations for one moment is a matter that
passes human understanding.[1]

Meanwhile the situation at St. Domingo had remained
unchanged through the beginning of the winter, the
enemy making only a few desultory attempts upon the
posts on the side of Port-au-Prince, which were easily
repulsed. At the end of January, however, the brigands Jan.-Feb.
began a general movement against every station occupied by the British. At the Mole Colonel William
Stewart of the Sixty-seventh met the attack by a spirited
counter-movement, which checked the enemy so completely that he was able to spare one hundred men of
his garrison for the assistance of St. Marc. But elsewhere the onset of the foe was irresistible. On the
side of Port-au-Prince Toussaint bore down with sudden
swiftness and overwhelming strength upon Mirebalais,
Grand Bois and other posts to the north and east; while
simultaneously another coloured leader, La Plume,
attacked the posts on the side of Léogane, and Rigaud
once again advanced against Irois. In some cases the
Colonial troops made a gallant resistance; in others,
they not only gave way, but actually deserted to the
enemy. By the beginning of March Mirebalais and March.
Grand Bois had fallen into Toussaint's hands, together
with several minor posts. St. Marc was seriously
threatened. The cordon defending the plain of Arcahais had, through the treachery of an officer of the
Irish Brigade, been utterly broken, and the enemy had
again closed round Port-au-Prince. Lastly, Rigaud
was pressing Irois with a science and an energy beyond
any that he had hitherto displayed. The most alarming
feature of this offensive movement was that Toussaint,
La Plume, and Rigaud, though known to have been
divided by bitter differences of colour and opinion,

[1] Dundas to General Hunter, October 1797; to Nesbitt, 1st
January 1798; Nesbitt to Dundas, 18th, 20th, 28th January 1798.

1798. seemed to be agreed, at any rate, upon the expediency of driving the British from the island.

Such was the state of affairs when, on the 12th of March, Maitland arrived at Mole St. Nicholas—worse, as he said, than with all his pessimism he could possibly have imagined. On the 20th he reached Port-au-Prince, whereupon Whyte very excusably at once withdrew to Mole St. Nicholas. The footing upon which Maitland stood was, in fact, extraordinary and very unfair to his superiors. Though he was no more than a Lieutenant-colonel, he enjoyed the Government's confidence in far greater measure than any General in the West Indies, and held a kind of roving commission to report upon all military matters and military persons in the Archipelago. Having touched at Barbados and Martinique on his outward voyage, he had written to Dundas the dry opinion that the service would not essentially suffer if ill-health or some other cause compelled General Cuyler to return to England. Before leaving London he had urged that the evacuation of Port-au-Prince should be deferred until General Whyte had relinquished his command. "Behaviour different from Whyte's is required," he had said, "and *hauteur* should be studiously avoided"; which was a delicate way of conveying the indubitable fact that Whyte, though a good soldier, was not conspicuous for tact or conciliatory manners. The Ministers no doubt expected that Nesbitt would arrive on the spot as soon as Maitland, and would at once relieve Whyte, who had many months before asked permission to resign. It so happened, however, that Nesbitt was detained by very severe illness at Madeira, and, being unable to send news of himself to the West Indies, was given up as lost at sea. Whyte, who could not be ignorant of Maitland's direct correspondence with Ministers, asked him, immediately after his arrival, if he was aware of the Government's intentions; to which Maitland replied that he was, but did not feel at liberty to disclose them. Whyte then pressed him to say whether he thought himself to be sufficiently master 1798. of the Government's plans to feel authorised to take over the command; and on Maitland's replying in the affirmative, though with a careful disclaimer of proposing such a thing, Whyte tacitly abdicated in his favour.

Maitland thereupon ordered the offensive to be resumed in the plain of the Arcahais, with the result that the enemy was defeated in two successive actions, with the loss of seven hundred killed. But this measure was taken only with the view of evacuating Port-au-Prince and the adjacent country with the greater ease, for the safety of Irois and Jérémie demanded every man that could be spared. Rigaud's energy in his attack had been remarkable. Formerly the chief security of Jérémie and its outworks had lain in the difficulty of the country, which prohibited the transport of cannon and stores except by sea; but the mulatto chief, with astonishing industry and labour, had constructed military roads on every side, so that the natural defences of the place had been in great measure broken down. With good communication by land thus opened, Rigaud had established himself in force over against Irois, which was the key of Jérémie, and refused to be moved. Maitland blamed Brent Spencer, who commanded the station, very greatly for allowing Rigaud thus to ensconce himself. "Spencer's failure," he said, "is due to the received and practised mode of carrying on the war in this island—that of stuffing all his men into posts without leaving any moving force, so that when one of his posts was attacked, he could not hope to relieve it." But whether Spencer had fallen into Austrian methods or not, it was certain that his troops, which were almost exclusively Colonial, were little to be trusted for any offensive movement.

Still the maintenance of Jérémie was so important that, on the 1st of April, Maitland sent Spencer one April 1. thousand men, and waited three weeks longer in the hope of Nesbitt's arrival. On the 20th, however, news April 20.

1798. from several quarters roused the British commander to decided action. Toussaint was preparing a great force to renew his attack on Arcahais; Stewart reported certain information of an intended assault upon the Mole, and begged for reinforcements; and finally, Whyte formally resigned to Maitland the command. Without delay, Maitland sent three hundred men to Stewart, and, having thus stripped Port-au-Prince so bare that there were not troops enough to relieve the guards, he began the embarkation of his heavy stores. At the same time he despatched an officer to Toussaint l'Ouverture to negotiate for the peaceable evacuation of Port-au-Prince, St. Marc, Arcahais, and their dependencies. Toussaint met him in a very friendly spirit, agreeing to respect the lives and properties of the inhabitants; and on the 10th of May a suspension of arms was agreed to for five weeks. By the 18th of May the British had left Port-au-Prince for ever.[1]

May 10.
May 18.

Maitland's action in thus conciliating Toussaint was a political stroke which practically decided the ultimate fate of St. Domingo. In the summer of 1797 the moderate party in the French Legislature, revolted by the brutality of Santhonax, had insisted upon his removal; and, as a consequence, General Hédouville had arrived in the island on the 10th of April 1798, with full powers from the Directory. All real authority had hitherto been divided pretty equally between the three coloured leaders, Toussaint l'Ouverture in the north, La Plume and Rigaud in the south; but the treaty of evacuation gave a decided preponderance to Toussaint, and Maitland, alive to the negro's ambitious disposition, felt confident that he would not readily yield up his supremacy to Hédouville. Having thus laid a sure foundation for a policy that would meet any later emergency, Maitland repaired, after a short stay at the Mole, to Jérémie, taking with him some four thousand Colonial

April 10.

May 23.

[1] Maitland to Dundas, 5th April (enclosing correspondence with Whyte), 8th April, and 10th May; to Huskisson, 5th April; Whyte to Dundas, 8th April 1798.

levies. Despite the large reinforcement sent to him on 1798. the 1st of April, Spencer had effected remarkably little in that quarter. He had lost over four hundred men killed and wounded in constant petty engagements ; and it was evident that if Rigaud remained in position opposite to him for much longer the British force would be completely worn out. The advent of the British squadron from Port-au-Prince caused the mulatto to withdraw from several of his posts to eastward of Jérémie, but, until he had been thoroughly beaten, Maitland knew that there was no security for the district of Grande Anse and no possibility of reducing expenses within the limits prescribed by the British Government. He therefore decided to attack Rigaud as soon as possible from the south side of the peninsula, and to drive him back by the capture of Tiburon.

Heavy rains delayed the operation for nearly three weeks, but on the 11th of June Maitland sailed from Jérémie with eight hundred British and twenty-three hundred Colonial troops. Anchoring below Irois, he landed seventeen hundred of the latter, with orders to march south over the mountains to Baie des Anglais, where he himself intended to disembark the remainder of the force, so as to sever communication between Tiburon and Aux Cayes. The march across the mountains was a complete success ; for the enemy, being taken by surprise at Baie des Anglais, fled pre- June 16. cipitately, abandoning a battery of five guns. But from June 15. the moment of Maitland's arrival the wind blew fresh, raising so heavy a surf that it was impossible to land any number of men. For three days Maitland waited, hoping that the sea would abate, and even losing a few men by drowning in attempts to land ; but the weather showed no signs of improvement, and, the provisions of the detachment ashore being exhausted, he was obliged to order it to retire and to abandon the June 18, whole enterprise.[1]

June 11.

Meanwhile there was still no news of Nesbitt ; but

[1] Maitland to Dundas, 23rd May, 3rd June, 19th June 1798.

1798. instead of the Commander-in-chief there had arrived Charmilli with five and sixty Emigrant officers, all with intimate friends in the British Cabinet, and all expecting salaries and appointments. Charmilli further informed Maitland that the King's orders were for Port-au-Prince and its dependencies to be held at all costs, alleging, as was indeed the case, that the intentions of the Cabinet had been altered since Maitland's departure from England. The disgust of the British commander was unspeakable. He could not believe that the Government would employ such a man as the bearer of its orders, and yet he was evidently more disquieted by Charmilli's assertions than he cared to own. Finally, Charmilli produced the paper, signed by the so-called proprietors of St. Domingo, which had induced the Ministers to modify their first instructions; and then Maitland's wrath knew no bounds. "Who these proprietors are," he wrote to Dundas, "and what they have to give, I know not; but this I do know, that we have not been able to make them pay taxes; much less can we do so now with no military force. But really the farce is too great. Who are your friends, for whom you have paid so much? I have recently seen Frenchmen of the highest rank in the Colony tearing off their ribbons and crosses of St. Louis, waiting impatiently to pay their court to the brigands, and actually intriguing with the remaining negroes of their own estates—and this driven not by force nor by being sacrificed, but while acknowledging at the same moment the fairness and generosity of His Majesty's Government. This is the fact as to most of the proprietors here. Not an estate remains in Cul-de-Sac, not a coffee plantation in Arcahais; half the sugar plantations there are deserted, and the managers in treaty with the enemy. If the Government had meant the old system to go on (which I do not believe), the only result would have been abundance of promises against the next crop, and when the next crop was ready, they would themselves have managed

an invasion of the enemy to satisfy your claims and 1798.
their promises. But I have no patience with this
absurdity, when I know that if every shilling's worth of
produce made and shipped in the island were placed to
the credit of Government, it would not pay the cost of
three months of British defence."[1]

Considering that the Government had been guilty
of precisely the folly that Maitland professed to think
incredible, Dundas must have read this letter with
uncomfortable feelings. But the arrival of Charmilli
was but a very small factor in a very grave situation. Whatever the differences between Toussaint,
La Plume, and Rigaud, it was certain that all three
were still bent upon the expulsion of the British,
Toussaint chiefly from ambition, and Rigaud to
reconcile himself with the Directory at Paris, by which
he had been outlawed. Maitland had made over Port-au-Prince to Toussaint in order that the strongest of the
three chiefs might be the most remote from Jérémie.
But Toussaint had lately moved a strong force to
the vicinity of Mole St. Nicholas; and the Mole was
not a place that could resist a really serious attack.
Jérémie also, since Rigaud's recent work, had lost all
its old security. As to troops, there were six[2] battalions
of British, with an effective strength of about eight
hundred men, which, added to detachments of the
Sixtieth, the Irish Brigade, the Twenty-first Light
Dragoons, and the York Hussars, made up a total of
about twenty-three hundred Europeans. Most of
these men, though fairly seasoned, had been weakened
by the climate; but the Sixtieth, being newcomers,
were suffering severely from sickness, and a great
many of them, originally deserters from the Dutch
service, were deserting once more to the enemy. Of
Colonial troops Maitland had six thousand, half of whom
were much worn down by the recent severe struggle
with Rigaud, and the other half, brought from Port-

[1] Maitland to Dundas, 23rd May 1798.
[2] 17th, 40th, 56th, 66th, 67th, 69th.

1798. au-Prince, were by no means to be trusted. But, apart from this, it was absolutely out of the question to maintain troops enough for the security of the Mole and Jérémie for less than £500,000, or nearly double the sum named by the British Government as its maximum; and it was exceedingly doubtful whether the advantages to be gained were worth either the money or the lives of British soldiers. In fact, by
July. the beginning of July, Maitland had made up his mind that the wishes of the Government could only be met by the total evacuation of St. Domingo.

The responsibility of such a decision, however, was greater than he would at first take upon himself, knowing the outcry that would probably be raised by the planters in Jamaica over the triumph of the negroes, by the Navy over the loss of Mole St. Nicholas, by the West India Committee in London, and even by certain members of the Cabinet. Maitland consulted Balcarres at Jamaica as to his views on the matter, but Balcarres, while frankly admitting that Jérémie could not be held and that the Mole was not worth keeping without it, would not be answerable for withdrawal from the whole island. On
July 31. the 31st of July, however, there came to Maitland from Dundas a copy of Nesbitt's instructions, upon which he decided to evacuate St. Domingo entirely and without delay. Negotiations were again begun with Toussaint and with Rigaud, and conventions were agreed to with both for the peaceable departure of the British. With Toussaint also there were concluded secret articles, stipulating that the English and Toussaint should not attack each other nor interfere in each other's political business in Jamaica and St. Domingo, so long as the war lasted, and that the British should send provisions to Toussaint at certain ports of St. Domingo, to be paid for by the produce of that island. Admiral Hyde Parker and Balcarres both of them protested strongly against the evacuation; but Maitland would not be deterred from his purpose. The ultimate supremacy in St. Domingo must fall, as he knew, either

to Toussaint, the negro, or to Rigaud, the mulatto; 1798. and it lay in great part with himself to decide between the two. Circumstances so far had led him to favour Toussaint; and it was tolerably certain that the Agents of the French Directory, having no power of their own, would ally themselves with Rigaud for the negro's overthrow. Rigaud, as has been seen, possessed no common energy and ability, but he had proved himself also to be faithless, and he was vindictive, as none but a cross-bred man can be, against the whites. No one who has had to do with mulattos, or indeed with coloured men of every shade, can have failed to notice their extraordinary faculty for sulking. They are intelligent, they are affable, they seem to be perfectly easy and even pleasant to manage; when, all of a sudden, one discovers that, for no apparent reason, they have taken offence, and are consumed by a silent, jealous hatred which seems incapable of total extinction. On the other hand, Maitland had been struck by the intense fidelity and affection of the emancipated negro-slaves towards their former owners. Toussaint himself had begged, as the greatest favour that could be granted to him, for the liberation of his old master, who was a prisoner in the hands of the British, and had restored him at once to his former position and estate. Toussaint also had most loyally and scrupulously observed the Convention of Port-au-Prince; and there was therefore good prospect that if, as was his ambition, he established the independence of St. Domingo, he would keep faith with the British. Maitland, for his part, was careful to warn him of Hédouville's designs, and to throw as much power as possible into his hands.[1]

It is extraordinary that a transaction of such transcendent importance as this Convention between Maitland and Toussaint should have been so utterly forgotten. Maitland's audacity alone, apart from his sagacious political wisdom, should have sufficed to redeem

[1] Maitland to Dundas, 13th July, 26th August, 26th December 1798.

1798. it from oblivion. He justified his action by reference to the instructions to Nesbitt, but I can find nothing whatever in them to sanction, much less to suggest, an agreement with any of the coloured leaders. Indeed, after the Convention had been signed, but before the news of it had reached England, the Government had issued fresh instructions to Nesbitt's successor to hold at any rate Jérémie and the Mole, granting him sixteen hundred troops, with authority to expend £500,000 annually instead of £300,000 for that purpose. But, apart from all instructions, the bare notion of an agreement with a negro, much more with a chief of insurgent negroes, was an abhorrence to every white man in the West Indies. The proceeding, therefore, was bound to gain Maitland the enmity of every planter in the British tropical possessions, of every West Indian proprietor or agent in England or elsewhere, of every naval and military commander, of every Emigrant and every royalist. Lastly, it was more than likely that he would give grievous offence to every member of the Cabinet, for his action was neither more nor less than an absolute reversal of the Government's cherished policy. Yet, with full knowledge of all the consequences, this Lieutenant-colonel deliberately took upon himself so great a responsibility with a steadfastness, a courage and a constancy which, to me at least, seem worthy of no ordinary admiration and honour. And, be it remarked, his action was no mere temporary makeshift for the shelving of a troublesome question; it laid the foundation of a sound and solid policy in the future, namely, the turning of the demon of destruction, which France had conjured up in the West Indies, against herself. Maitland's agreement extended no further than to the conclusion of the war; after which he recommended that England should abstain from all interference in St. Domingo, so as to encourage France to the re-establishment of the old Colonial system, and, as he grimly wrote, to let her waste her men and money in the attempt. His insight had pierced deep into the true

meaning of the negro revolt in St. Domingo. The 1798.
black man in that island had discovered his own
strength and the white man's weakness; he was like
an elephant who has turned upon his mahout, beyond
control from henceforth for ever. Recognising this
fact, Maitland laid in St. Domingo a snare for the
ruling powers at Paris, and into that snare fell the First
Consul, Napoleon Bonaparte.

It was the 3rd of October before St. Domingo was Oct. 3.
finally evacuated, and during that time and for months
afterwards Maitland's troubles were incessant. Balcarres
turned against him, partly because he had presumed to
make terms for Jamaica without consulting his superior
officer. The Admiral, Sir Hyde Parker, turned against
him also, from personal pique as well as on general
grounds. The Assembly of Jamaica was almost beside
itself with fury, and vented its rage and its spite in
disgraceful persecution of the French planters and their
slaves, whom Maitland had been obliged, for want of
a better refuge, to transport for a time to that island.
Nothing would serve these selfish oligarchs but that
every French negro must be shipped off from
the shores of Jamaica, in spite of all protests and
entreaties. Balcarres himself testified that the attach-
ment between the French slaves and their masters was
such that death seemed to them better than separation:
but, none the less, special laws were passed to chase
them from Jamaica. Then too late the planters awoke
to the fact that these negroes could teach them the
cultivation of coffee, and that some of the handicrafts-
men among them were valuable beyond all estimation in money. It is refreshing to know that the
blind vindictiveness of the Assembly brought its own
punishment.

Maitland, meanwhile, went home, and was at once
sent out to America to negotiate for the sharing of
the trade of St. Domingo exclusively between England
and the United States, a necessary as well as a gracious
concession, since Toussaint depended for all his food-

1799. stuffs upon America. It was a difficult and trying business, but was at length successfully accomplished June 13. in June 1799. In ordinary circumstances it would not have been easy to conclude an agreement whereby a neutral country might furnish provisions to the enemy of a belligerent, for Toussaint was now reckoned by France as an open enemy; but fortunately the principal obstacle had been overthrown by the insane folly of the Directory itself, which had picked a quarrel with the United States by insisting on its right to confiscate British merchandise carried in American ships. While Maitland was absent from Jamaica, Balcarres upheld his policy with a loyalty that did him honour. It was long, indeed, before he could overcome his suspicions of Toussaint; nor was he wholly without justification. Rigaud was very anxious for an attack on Jamaica, and there seemed to be signs that Toussaint might join with him in the enterprise. Negro agents despatched by Rigaud were actually arrested at Port Royal at the end of 1799, distributing hat-bands emblazoned with a death's head and the misspelt motto *Vincre ou mourir*. Nevertheless, Toussaint kept honourable faith with the British, refusing to take part in the expedition against Jamaica, and thereby hastening the open rupture between himself and Rigaud. The Agents of the Directory threw in their lot with the mulatto; but Toussaint, by finally subduing him, in the course of 1800 established his own supremacy in St. Domingo. Events, therefore, turned out exactly as Maitland had foreseen and predicted; and by the end of 1800 it was recognised alike in Downing Street and Port Royal that England's interests to leeward were safe so long as Toussaint l'Ouverture was her friend.[1]

[1] Balcarres to Portland, 16th September, 29th October, 2nd December 1798; 5th February, 19th May, 28th October, 7th December 1799; 1st and 2nd January, 23rd March, 14th September 1800; Portland to Balcarres, 19th March 1801; Maitland to Huskisson, 10th January; to Dundas, 3rd and 20th April, 23rd May, 3rd and 17th June 1799; Dundas to Maitland, 26th May 1799.

CH. XX   HISTORY OF THE ARMY   565

Thus, by the supreme strength and courage of a 1799. single subordinate officer, England was plucked from the awful morass of confusion, extravagance, death and disaster into which she had been plunged by the thoughtless incapacity of Pitt and Dundas. The amount of blood and treasure drained from England by that miserable island of St. Domingo will never, I think, be truly known. The expenditure acknowledged to the House of Commons was over four millions sterling, a far greater sum in those days than in these, and the mortality up to September 1796 was set forth in a return at seven thousand five hundred men. The returns preserved in the Record Office are so imperfect that I am unable to substitute for this latter figure another which shall be absolutely correct; but I have no hesitation whatever in saying that the number given above is positively misleading, and should at the very least be doubled. Moreover, these figures take no account of the deaths of seamen, nor of troops serving on board ship; nor is any mention made of the men who returned home only to die, or, at best, to be disabled for life from further service. After long and careful thought and study I have come to the conclusion that the West Indian campaigns, both to windward and to leeward, which were the essence of Pitt's military policy, cost England in Army and Navy little fewer than one hundred thousand men, about one-half of them dead, the remainder permanently unfitted for service. And in return for this frightful cost of life, there could be shown only the British islands of Grenada and St. Vincent utterly devastated and ruined, and the French islands of Tobago, intact but of small value, of Martinique, much damaged and with difficulty held, and of St. Lucia, so wasted as to be no more than a naval station. For this England's soldiers had been sacrificed, her treasure squandered, her influence in Europe weakened, her arm for six fateful years fettered, numbed and paralysed.

Now, however, thanks to Thomas Maitland, the

1799. hateful incubus was shaken off, and England was free —free to move, and free to strike. We have no more part in St. Domingo until the time comes to tell how Napoleon, falling into the pit that Maitland had digged for him, emulated and outdid the folly of Pitt and Dundas.

CHAPTER XXI

In September 1797, as will be remembered, the revolution of the 18th Fructidor re-established the party of violence and war in France, and abruptly ended Lord Malmesbury's negotiations for peace. In October the preliminaries of Leoben received more permanent form in the Treaty of Campo Formio between Austria and France. Hereby Austria ceded to the French Republic the Belgic provinces, and recognised the independence of the newly formed Cisalpine State, which included Milan, Modena, Bologna, and, roughly speaking, the Venetian territory west of the Adige. The partition of the Venetian State was completed by the cession of the Ionian Islands also to France, while Austria took Venice itself and the rest of the Venetian possessions on both shores of the Adriatic. Further details of the agreement between France and the Empire were to be adjusted at a congress to be held at Rastadt, Austria engaging herself secretly to secure for France the left bank of the Rhine, while France promised to gain for Austria compensating advantages on the side of Bavaria. Thugut was very ill-satisfied at the treaty, and well he might be, for, in the words of a German historian, France acquired by it twice as much territory as she yielded to Germany in 1871; but he flattered himself with the thought that the peace thus purchased was but a truce, and that the Emperor Paul might hereafter become an ally for the renewal of the war.[1]

Meanwhile England was left to battle with France

[1] Sybel, v. 135-137.

1796. alone, at a moment when her most vulnerable point
Dec. 29. seemed positively to invite attack. Since the departure of the French expedition from Bantry Bay, the situation in Ireland had grown steadily worse. In the north the Government had lost practically all authority and con-
1797. trol; and in March 1797 Lord Camden again begged earnestly for reinforcements. The British Government responded at once by sending two regiments of Fencible Cavalry, one of which, Sir Watkin Wynn's Ancient British Fencibles, was to leave no enviable reputation behind it; but no regular soldiers could accompany them, for there was not a regiment that was not composed of Irish recruits, and the disloyal party had been unwearied in its efforts to corrupt the troops. General Lake was ordered to disarm the most disturbed districts of the north; and just at this moment occurred the new com-
April-June. plication of the mutinies at Spithead and at the Nore, in which there was some reason to believe that the United Irishmen had been concerned. Scores if not hundreds of Irish insurgents had been illegally deported to serve on board the fleet by the Commander-in-chief, Lord Carhampton; and it was supposed that Richard Lee, the ringleader of the mutinous marines, being the brother of one of the original United Irishmen, had enlisted in the Navy for the express purpose of sowing disaffection. A Dutch fleet at the Texel, to be followed later by a French fleet from France, was actually preparing for the invasion of the British Isles at the time, and could have sailed to Ireland almost without hindrance; for the mutiny had reduced Admiral Duncan's squadron of observation to but two ships. Whether, however, their preparations were incomplete, or whether they were deceived by the cunning device of Duncan, who continued to make signals as if his main fleet were still in the offing, the Dutch made no attempt to take advantage of their opportunity; and the worst of the peril passed harmlessly away.[1]

[1] Camden to Portland, 9th March, 15th April, 28th April to 1st July; Cooke to Grenville, 4th July; Dundas to Camden, 22nd

But order had hardly been restored in the Navy 1797. before the Dutch expedition was ready for sea; and on the 8th of July Wolfe Tone, the leading spirit in the July 8. Irish conspiracy against England, arrived at the Texel to sail with it. The armament was far from contemptible, the fleet consisting of fifteen ships of the line besides ten smaller vessels, and the troops of nearly fourteen thousand men. Moreover, both the Admiral, De Winter, and the General, Daendels, were thoroughly capable officers. At sea Duncan was thought by the Dutch to have but thirteen ships of the line. In Ireland, though four more regiments of Fencible Infantry and two of Fencible Cavalry had arrived from England in the course of May and June, it may be doubted whether fourteen thousand men could have been concentrated at any one point within less than a fortnight. Even if assembled, the quality of the troops would have been very far from good, and their commander, Lord Carhampton, was by no means of the first order. Moreover, the intelligence of the British Government was so defective that no warning was sent to Camden of the impending invasion until the beginning of August. The elements, however, which had fought so hard against the British in their West Indian expeditions, now interposed in their defence. The Texel was an anchorage which could not be cleared without a favourable concurrence of wind and tide; and for six consecutive weeks the wind blew foul from the southwest. Meanwhile the best of the campaigning season slipped away. The Dutch fleet exhausted its provisions. The north of Ireland subsided under the vigorous measures of Lake; and Duncan's fleet was reinforced to superior strength. In the middle of August Wolfe Aug. Tone learned to his infinite mortification that the expedition to Ireland, upon any considerable scale, had

---

April 1797. Mr. Lecky, in his account of the mutiny, doubts if Duncan's fleet was reduced so low as to two ships. Portland, however, wrote to Camden on 1st June that the only ships in that fleet untainted with mutiny were the *Venerable* and *Adamant*.

1797.
Sept. 18.
Oct. 11.

been abandoned. Shortly afterwards, a heavy blow fell upon all projects of invasion through the death of Hoche; and nearly a month later the Dutch fleet, sallying forth alone, was met by Duncan with ships of equal number but superior strength, and completely defeated with the loss of nine vessels of the line, off the dunes of Camperdown.[1]

None the less, Lord Camden's uneasiness as to the condition of Ireland increased steadily during 1797; and with good reason. The Fencibles and Militia, which constituted practically the whole of his garrison, were at best none too well disciplined; and the officers, particularly those of the Militia, were for the most part both ignorant and neglectful of their duty. Moreover, these troops had been scattered broadcast over Ireland in small parties for the protection of isolated houses and petty towns, under very imperfect supervision or control. Now flattered and feasted by the country-gentlemen, now cursed and pelted by the poorer classes, now courted and bribed by the agents of the disloyal, they were misled and encouraged to excesses by the example of their officers and their betters, and seldom called to account for indiscipline or oppression. It was a trial which would have corrupted the Ironsides under Oliver in person; and many corps had disgraced themselves by shameful cruelty and license. Camden, though no soldier, had been roused to some perception of the danger by the difficulty of assembling a force when the French sailed into Bantry Bay; and, being still apprehensive of an invasion, he had for some time past been trying to obtain a really strong Commander-in-chief, who would relieve him of some responsibility. In the autumn of 1796 he had asked for Sir Charles Grey, who, however, had declined on the score of age. Camden had then been fain to accept Lord Carhampton in the hope that David Dundas would join his staff; but Dundas was needed in England and

[1] Camden to Portland, 10th July; Portland to Camden, 2nd August 1797.

unwilling to leave it. A few months' trial satisfied 1797. Camden that Carhampton, notwithstanding many merits, was not of a calibre to deal with the situation, and in May 1797 he asked for Cornwallis. Once again he met with a refusal, for Cornwallis by no means approved the policy of the Government in Ireland. A far abler soldier, Lord Moira, was excluded even from the offer, owing to his much stronger antagonism to the Ministry on Irish questions. Finally, on the return of Abercromby from the West Indies, Camden begged that the post might be offered to him ; and the veteran very reluctantly, but from a strong sense of duty, accepted the command.[1]

His arrival in Ireland chanced nearly to coincide in Nov. time with the delivery of a speech by Lord Moira in the House of Lords, severely and justly criticising the misconduct and indiscipline of the troops in Ulster. Abercromby knew little of Moira, and, though holding liberal opinions in politics, was careful, as became a soldier, to keep them to himself. Upon his arrival in Dublin his first discovery was that, whether through the carelessness of Lord Carhampton or, as is more likely, the encroachment of the Lord-Lieutenant's officials, it had become the practice for Generals to address their letters to Dublin Castle direct instead of to the Commander-in-chief. Here was a first point of discipline to be set right ; and Abercromby without delay insisted that he must have absolute command of the troops, saying with perfect truth that good military administration was impossible, if authority were divided between himself and the Lord-Lieutenant. Camden, who was as grossly ignorant as any of his colleagues of the meaning of military discipline, thought Abercromby somewhat exacting ; but while alleging the impossibility of delegating to him entire command, he

[1] Portland to Camden, 7th and 8th September, 1st October 1796 ; May and 5th October 1797. Camden to Portland, 17th and 22nd September 1796 ; 30th January and 28th April 1797. *Cornwallis Correspondence*, ii. 327.

1797. agreed to give him full powers in substance. A little further knowledge of the demoralisation and indiscipline of the army, and of the encouragement given thereto by the dispersion of the forces in small detachments, satisfied Abercromby that the existing state of things must be ended at once. But the root of the evil lay somewhat outside the strict range of the Commander-in-chief's powers. It was the country-gentlemen who, through their timidity in calling upon the troops at all times to protect them, were chiefly responsible for the ruin of military efficiency; and over them, of course, the Commander-in-chief had no control. Three things were essential before discipline could be restored. The first was that the country-gentlemen should awake to a sense of their duties and their powers, and employ only the Yeomanry for duties of police, thus releasing the troops; the second, that all detachments should be gathered in and the army concentrated as far as possible so as to be ready in case of invasion; the third, that the military, when inevitably employed in aid of the civil power, should observe the bounds of legality. No one of these measures could suffice to meet the case without the other two. One and all required to be carried out simultaneously and without delay, otherwise the troops would simply become ruthless persecutors when employed as policemen, and a disorderly mob in the presence of an enemy. But, though in one aspect purely military, not one of these matters could be touched by the Commander-in-chief without real or apparent encroachment upon the authority of the Lord-Lieutenant.

As the person responsible for the defence of the kingdom and, to that end, for the efficiency of the
Nov. military forces, Abercromby pressed urgently for these reforms; and Camden was in principle at one with him. But the General's policy was not likely to commend itself to the hundreds of gentlemen who were crying out for military protection, or to the officials at the Castle who had tacitly connived at the burning of houses and

the other illegal acts of violence which Abercromby 1798. so emphatically condemned. From the first moment of his arrival the Commander-in-chief issued several injunctions, both general and particular, for restraining disorder and reviving subordination among the troops, but with little or no effect; and accordingly he issued on the 26th of February 1798 a General Order which has become famous. "The very disgraceful frequency of courts-martial and the many complaints of irregularities in the conduct of the troops in this kingdom have too unfortunately proved the army to be in a state of licentiousness which must render it formidable to every one but the enemy." With this preamble Abercromby required all commanders to exact the strictest discipline from their officers and men, and recalled to their notice the standing orders under which troops were forbidden, unless attacked, to act in aid of the civil power without the presence and authority of a magistrate.

This Order burst upon the three kingdoms like a thunderclap, and upon Dublin Castle with the greater violence, since a proclamation by the Lord-Lieutenant, of the 18th May 1797, had authorised the military to act without waiting for civil direction. The Duke of Portland wrote frantically from England to ask if the document were not a forgery, being unable to conceive how it could have other than a political purpose. "Our friends here," he said, "cannot suppress the regret which they feel at the apparent triumph of Moira and the disaffected. The Irish whom I have seen conceive that they are to be abandoned and forced to join the insurgents." No better example could be found of the failings which are bred in public men by our Parliamentary system. Lord Moira, who was, it is true, a strong political opponent of the Ministry, had described the army in Ireland as undisciplined and demoralised; and the accuracy of his description had been avouched by the testimony not only of Abercromby but of Chief Secretary Pelham. Ministers had

1798. answered Moira, according to the received practice, by belittling and evading his assertions; which would have signified little, had they realised the seriousness of the situation and striven at once to amend it. But it was not so. These deplorable men imagined that by blinking facts they had disposed of them; and, when the state of the army in Ireland was forced upon their notice by Abercromby's General Order, their first thought was not of the frightful peril of committing Ireland, then on the verge of revolt and under threat of invasion, to the protection of such a force, but of the apparent triumph of Moira in a political controversy.

It need hardly be said that Abercromby was far too straightforward, as well as too able a man, to dream of political trickery. He conceived himself to have been sent to Ireland to set right what he knew to be wrong in the Army, and he needed no Moira to point out its glaring defects. He has left his own account of the true purpose of his order, which was to force the country-gentlemen to use the Yeomanry for their protection, so that the Fencibles and Militia might be ready and able to oppose a foreign enemy.[1] Whether such action were legitimate or not is an extremely difficult question. The struggle was to decide, as he said, whether he was to have command of the Army really or nominally; whereby he meant not whether he was to wrest the supremacy from the Lord-Lieutenant, but whether

[1] "Now for the order—The abuses of all kinds I found here can scarcely be believed or enumerated. I tried various means with little success; it was necessary to speak out; the order is strong, but be assured it was necessary. The way in which the troops have been employed would ruin the best in Europe. Here are 3500 Yeomanry, raised for the express purpose of protecting the country. To them I have urged the necessity of applying for assistance, but in vain. I therefore restricted the troops to the standing orders of the Kingdom, that their discipline might be pursued if possible, and that the gentlemen might be obliged to trust to the Yeomanry, on whom they must ultimately depend, in case the troops should be called away to oppose a foreign enemy" (Abercromby to his son). Dunfermline's *Life of Abercromby*, p. 114.

he was to recover the military authority which had been usurped from his office by the Lord-Lieutenant's advisers. By the connivance of those advisers the troops had become a gang of insubordinate ruffians, committing every kind of enormity and openly defying their officers. Was it the duty of a man, who had accepted the command-in-chief, against his own inclination and from purely patriotic motives, to shut his eyes to these things; or to shrug his shoulders and disclaim all responsibility; or to resign forthwith; or to go even to extremity in endeavouring to right what was wrong? It has been said that the time was past for Abercromby's remedies, that they were excellent but that they came too late; and it seems certain that he did not realise how far Ireland was advanced on the road to rebellion and how near was the danger. Even so, however, matters could not have been improved by the confirmation of disorder in the Army; and it is a hard saying to be accepted by a General, who has just been made answerable for the defence of a country, that he may not restore discipline in the armed forces wherewith he is to defend it.

The truth of course is that Abercromby's situation was impossible. When military considerations are paramount in a country, as was then the case in Ireland, it is absolutely necessary that all authority, both civil and military, shall be invested in a single military head. But of such measure the Government was extremely shy. In Corsica, which was essentially a military station and liable to attack at almost any moment, a very able soldier and administrator, Charles Stuart, had in 1794 been displaced to make way for Sir Gilbert Elliot, a civilian who, though doubtless possessed of talent, was a child in military matters. The result had been an immediate quarrel between Elliot and Colonel John Moore, who was not only one of the most capable officers in the service, but the only man on the island who could have defended it in case of attack. In such cases it is idle to attempt to apportion the blame between the two parties. The true fault lies with the Government for placing a civilian in command where circumstances demand a soldier. This was even more true of Ireland in 1797 than of Corsica in 1794, with, however, this difference, that no soldier with the slightest claim to thoughtfulness, ability, and self-respect would condescend to execute the policy of the Ministers. Grey pleaded age as an excuse for declining. Cornwallis declined unequivocally. Moira was disqualified even from receiving the chance of refusal. David Dundas, who knew Ireland intimately, evaded re-employment there even as Chief of Carhampton's Staff. Charles Stuart, as shall presently be related, was in Portugal; but it may be asserted with positive certainty that he of all men would have been least likely to touch so dirty a task. Abercromby, who had accepted the military command, had found himself to be in opposition to the Government from the first moment of his arrival in Dublin. Stronger ground would be difficult to find for the condemnation of the Ministry.

Nevertheless, so highly did Camden value Abercromby that both he and Pelham strove earnestly to explain away, and even to justify, the General Order, in the hope of retaining him as Commander-in-chief. It so happened that Abercromby had set out on a tour of inspection in the north immediately after issuing it, so that the Lord-Lieutenant could not immediately call upon him for an explanation of his action. The clique of reactionary officials took advantage of his absence to organise a cabal so as to ensure his removal. They had their correspondents in London, Lord Auckland the chief of them; and through him and others they speedily gained the ear of Ministers, and frightened the Duke of Portland into writing the foolish letter of which two sentences have already been quoted. It is one of the gravest reproaches against Pitt as an administrator that he was not steadily loyal to the subordinates of his own appointment, but too often preferred the underhand advice of external and irresponsible counsellors. Thus he had 1798. listened to the West India merchants rather than to Jervis, Grey, and the Generals in the West Indies; he had given heed to Charmilli and other adventurers despite the warnings of Simcoe and Maitland; he would not even consult Cornwallis, the only military member of his Cabinet, upon the most important military matters, but sought the advice, behind his back, of other and junior officers;[1] and now, without waiting to hear Camden and Pelham, he lent a willing ear to the insinuations of Abercromby's enemies at Dublin.[2] So unscrupulous were these last that, at a moment when Camden was still striving fruitlessly to propitiate Abercromby, the Speaker, taking advantage of the speech usually made on the presentation of a money bill, expressed the confidence of the Irish House of Commons in the "order, alacrity, vigour, and discipline" of the Army. It would not be easy, even in the records of Dublin Castle, to find a match for such an example of mischievous effrontery.

Fortunately Abercromby had already withdrawn himself from all further dealing with these men. Immediately upon being taken to task for his General Order he sent in his resignation, and, notwithstanding all Camden's arguments and even entreaties, refused to withdraw it. The British Cabinet, on learning Camden's sentiments, also made conciliatory overtures to him, but in vain.[3] From sheer pity for the weak and helpless Lord-Lieutenant Abercromby consented, upon Camden's positive order, to go in person to quell disturbances in Tipperary, and he even bowed to his instructions that the military should act without awaiting the sanction of the civil magistrates. But he announced to his sub-

[1] *Cornwallis Correspondence*, ii. 336.
[2] "Your Grace thought fit, in declaring the sentiments of the British Cabinet, to give countenance to the cabal here . . . to condemn without hearing not only Sir Ralph Abercromby but Lord Camden." Pelham to Portland, April 1799.
[3] Portland to Camden, 19th March; Henry Dundas to Abercromby, 20th March 1798.

1798. ordinate Generals that he expected to be relieved in his command immediately, and he told Camden that he considered himself ruined and disgraced. Camden confessed that the Army must suffer from the contemplation "of the victory which they would consider themselves to have gained over the Commander-in-chief"; and yet both he and the British Cabinet professed themselves greatly injured when Abercromby still refused to recall his resignation. But the General declined, as he said, to be a cipher, or still worse a tool, in the hands of the party that governed the country. After several times pressing for the speedy appointment of his successor, and urgently recommending Lord Camden to apply for a reinforcement of disciplined troops, Abercromby at the end of April quitted Ireland.

The outcry in the Cabinet against him was loud. Portland described his conduct as most distressful and unjustifiable, and Cornwallis wrote that he had been exceedingly wrong-headed. But King George, taking him aside at the levée, told him that he had been extremely ill-treated, but that he would now go Commander-in-chief to Scotland, where people would know how to respect him.[1] To Scotland accordingly he went; but it is significant that the old soldier, though the gentlest of men, never wholly forgave Pitt for his disloyalty to him in Ireland.[2] The Cabinet, meanwhile, was at its wit's end to find a new

[1] Portland to Camden, 31st March 1798; *Cornwallis Correspondence*, ii. 335. Dunfermline's *Life of Abercromby*, p. 125.

[2] In 1800, on hearing that his son had met Pitt at dinner, Abercromby wrote. "In Mr. Pitt you gained an agreeable companion at table and very nearly a great man in the Cabinet. If his mind were equal to his abilities and talents he would deserve the name of a first-rate statesman." Dunfermline's *Abercromby*, p. 217. The expression is a little obscure, but its meaning after study reveals itself to be that Pitt's magnanimity was not equal to his talent. A high-minded man would have heard Camden, Pelham, and Abercromby before listening to a clique at Dublin, and would have supported them against it. The reproach was just.

CH. XXI HISTORY OF THE ARMY 579

Commander-in-chief. Much pressure was put upon 1798. Cornwallis to accept the office in combination with the Lord-Lieutenancy, but he declined it. The defence of Ireland, as he rightly held, could not be dissociated from political measures; and to the Government's Irish policy he was strongly opposed. He shared, in fact, the views which had been embodied in Abercromby's General Order, though he had not the courage to defend it; and this fact betrays the limitations both of his character and of his intelligence. Despite his professions he was so far biassed by the representations of the cabal at Dublin that he joined the rest of the Cabinet in condemning Abercromby, who was certainly his equal and probably his superior both in administrative and military ability, and at all events far surpassed him in knowledge of Ireland. In despair the Government left the command for the present to the senior officer, General Lake, who, though a brave soldier, was above all other officers identified with the military abuses which Abercromby had striven to check. Lest Lake also should by chance endeavour to restore discipline, Camden ordained that no General Order should in future be issued until first submitted to himself. Thus the reign of violence and the ruin of the soldiery were erected into a sacred principle; and a rebellion in Ireland was finally assured. No better measures could have been taken by the ablest and subtlest French agent for the success of a French invasion.[1]

Such an invasion seemed at the moment in the highest degree to be apprehended. On the 5th of December 1797 Napoleon Bonaparte had arrived at Paris, and had been received with wild enthusiasm. His busy brain was seething with projects for seizing the government of France, for further spoliation of Holland and Italy, for the plunder of Switzerland,

[1] The whole story of Abercromby's command is written so fully in Lecky's *History of Ireland in the Eighteenth Century*, chapter ix., and in Dunfermline's *Life of Abercromby*, chapter iv., that it is unnecessary to give further references than to these two works.

1798. for an invasion of Egypt, and ultimately for an attack upon England. He had already stripped Venice bare before delivering it to Austria, and ordered a French squadron under Admiral Brueys to proceed to Corfu, there to take over twelve vessels of the Venetian fleet. On the 14th of December he gave Brueys further directions to sail with this armament to Brest, taking care to avoid Jervis's blockading squadron before Cadiz. At the same time he hastened the despatch of a few ships at Toulon to the same destination, urging also that Spain should make ready every possible vessel of war, and fifteen thousand troops together with transports to convey them. On the 9th of January 1798 he began to organise his army for the invasion of England, and a month later he left Paris for Dunkirk to supervise the preparations for himself. The result
Feb. 23. was not, apparently, to his satisfaction, for on returning to Paris he wrote that the expedition to the British Isles could not take place until the following year, even if then, and that the true moment for it had been lost, perhaps for ever. "Make what efforts we will," such were his opening words, "we shall not for many years gain control of the sea. To make a descent upon England without mastery of the sea is the boldest and most difficult operation ever attempted." Despairing, therefore, of the feasibility of throwing fifty thousand infantry and four thousand cavalry upon the coast of Kent or Sussex, he proposed an expedition to the Levant to threaten British trade with the East Indies.[1]

Meanwhile the French government had embarked upon a huge scheme of aggression, directed partly against British commerce, but designed chiefly for the purpose of obtaining money and material for future military enterprises. On the 8th of January 1798 a law was passed declaring all vessels with English goods on board to be lawful prize, and forbidding all ships that had touched at an English port to enter any French

[1] *Corres. de Napoléon*, iii. 328, 418, 431, 462, 486-493.

harbour. The execution of this decree, of course, 1798. demanded a naval force, to provide which Bonaparte resorted to Holland. But the Dutch, who had not yet succeeded in providing themselves with a constitution which was to their mind, were so much exhausted and depressed by the loss of their Colonies, by the heavy demands of France and by the defeat of Camperdown, that they refused to make any effort. The French agents thereupon contrived by the usual means to overthrow the existing administration and to place their own instruments in power; after which Bonaparte enforced a requisition for two hundred and fifty gunboats without further trouble. Simultaneously the Directory showed equal activity in Italy. On the 11th of January 1798 a force was ordered to march Jan. 11. into the new Roman Republic to punish a riot, which had been kindled by French intrigues. The provocation from Rome came rather too early to suit Bonaparte's plans, but the troops were set in motion under command of Berthier, who wrote cheerfully that his chief had made him treasurer of the army of England, and that he would do his best to fill the chest. He thereupon levied a large contribution on the Pope; while the soldiers of all ranks under his command threw themselves upon the spoil of Rome, both public and private, with the most shameless rapacity. Very soon afterwards came the turn of Switzerland. The country was invaded on the flimsiest of pretexts by General Brune, who, by a long series of treacherous and faithless acts, took possession of Berne on the 6th of March. Once again officers and men March 6. fell upon the unfortunate people like hungry wolves, pillaging, stealing, and extorting. One million sterling found its way to the treasury at Paris; more than half a million remained unaccounted for, having stuck to the fingers of Brune and his colleagues. Finally, the newly constituted Cisalpine Republic having, under a mistaken idea that it was free, presumed to raise difficulties about paying for a garrison of twenty-five

1798. thousand French troops, the obnoxious members of the government were, as in Holland, expelled by force, and more complaisant instruments appointed in their stead. Such were the gentle methods of France, under the guidance of Bonaparte, for replenishing her empty coffers in the spring of 1798.[1]

Meanwhile the preparations for Bonaparte's expedition were pushed steadily forward, always ostensibly for the object of invading England. It was indeed significant that the destination of the French ships at Corfu was changed from Brest to Toulon, and that it was not in the Atlantic ports but at Toulon itself, Genoa, and Civita Vecchia, that the signs of a coming embarkation were most evident. But at all of these centres of activity the troops were designated to the various commandants as the Army of England; and the Courts of Europe exhausted themselves in conjectures as to the true destination of the armament. The Emperor Paul suspected it to be designed against the Balkan Peninsula, and began to set his army and navy in motion; for, though he did not share Catherine's greed after Turkey, he had no idea of suffering any influence to rival that of Russia in that country. At Vienna it was feared that Bonaparte's heart was set upon Sicily, and Thugut began to seek closer relations with the Court of Naples. In London the Cabinet was equally puzzled, and full of apprehension. Bonaparte's thoughts, however, were intent
March 5. upon Egypt and the East Indies, and on the 5th of March he drew out the details of the force necessary for an Egyptian expedition, together with the orders for the several embarkations. Five weeks later the
April 12. Directory committed itself definitely to the enterprise; and Bonaparte was authorised to seize Malta and Egypt, to drive the British from all their possessions in the East, and particularly from the Red Sea, and to cut a canal through the isthmus of Suez. As a further means to that end, the French ships at Mauritius were

[1] Sybel, v. 166-214.

ordered to make their way forthwith to Suez itself. 1798. A library of Oriental literature, a map of Bengal, and a French agent who had resided at the Court of Tippoo Sahib, formed part of Bonaparte's equipment for his operations in the East.[1] Curiously enough one of Grenville's agents in Paris supplied the Foreign Office with exact information upon all these details on the day before the order was signed by the Directory.[2] There can be no doubt that this intelligencer had obtained a sight of the document.

It is difficult to understand exactly what object Bonaparte proposed to himself in this extremely hazardous enterprise, or by what means he thought to compass it. It is certain that he had intended to sail not later than the end of April; for, since the British fleet had for more than a year been withdrawn from the Mediterranean, he might reasonably hope that it would not appear there again until he had at least reached his destination in safety. Indeed there is ground for supposing that he counted upon the conquest of Malta and Egypt within three or four months at most, and upon a safe return to France at the end of that time. But, even if these hopes were realised, it was certain that, from the moment when the British fleet entered the Mediterranean, the communication between France and Egypt would be severed, and the garrison, which he was bound to leave in the valley of the Nile, cut off. It was apparently his idea either to invite Austria and Russia to the partition of Turkey, or to obtain an alliance with the Porte in exchange for the restoration of Egypt; but it was extravagant to look for such expectations to fulfil themselves before the British Navy should intervene. Moreover, to call up the French squadron in eastern waters to Suez was the surest means of calling the British fleet in those seas to follow in its wake, with the practical certainty that the French vessels would be captured or destroyed, and that

---

[1] *Corres. de Napoléon*, iv. 1-9, 27, 40, 50-63, 68, 71, 96.
[2] *Dropmore Papers*, iv. 193.

1798. all egress for the French force to the southward would thereby be effectually barred.

In fact, as it seems to me, this expedition to Egypt was not a military operation at all but a mere gambling adventure, utterly unworthy the hazard of fifteen ships of the line and a force of thirty thousand men. To affirm that an unwieldy raid of this kind upon British commerce in the East was at that moment the most effective means of injuring England is, looking to the state of Ireland, ridiculous. Moreover, Bonaparte knew it. "The Cisalpine Republic gives us perhaps the best military frontier in Europe"; he had written in October 1797, "we have Mainz and the Rhine, we have Corfu, extremely well fortified, in the Levant, and the other Ionian Islands. What more do we want? Are we to scatter our forces so that England may continue to take the Colonies of France, Spain, and Holland, and delay still longer the restoration of our trade and navy? . . . Let us rather concentrate all our activity upon the navy and destroy England. That done Europe is at our feet." For one moment he reverted to this idea, and on the 13th of April sketched a plan for the invasion of England in December,[1] as though the destruction of British commerce in the East would by that time have been complete; but the matter ended with the dictation of the document. A really patriotic Frenchman would never for a moment have lifted his eye from Ireland, where even five thousand men, landed at the right moment, would have been more dangerous to England than thirty thousand in Egypt. If a diversion and the destruction of British commerce were so desirable, Bonaparte's true and obvious course would have been to anticipate Maitland in making Toussaint supreme in St. Domingo, and to give the negro chief a roving commission to root the British out of the West Indies. It was idle to say that the opportunity for effective attack on England was gone for ever. The naval mutiny was indeed

[1] *Corres. de Napoléon,* iv. 56.

over, but a great opportunity still remained. Had 1798. Bonaparte seized it he might later have fulfilled his dream of Oriental empire.

With enormous difficulty, owing to lack of naval stores and sailors, the expedition was made as ready as could be expected by the appointed time; and, though the ships were but half-manned with seamen, the troops were embarked. Then came an unexpected impediment. True to the old policy of the Jacobin Convention, Bernadotte, the French ambassador at Vienna, had been foolish enough to turn his embassy into a general rendezvous for Polish revolutionary conspirators; and on the 13th of April the building April 13. was assailed by the mob and the tricolour torn down. Rejecting all the Austrian apologies Bernadotte at once demanded his passports, and the Archduke Charles thereupon set the army in motion, so as to be ready for the possibility of war. Orders were therefore issued on the 23rd of April for the troops at Toulon April 23. to disembark; and, though the quarrel was speedily adjusted and the troops re-embarked five days later, yet it was the 3rd of May before Bonaparte could venture May 3. to leave Paris for Toulon. He had hoped to sail on the 8th, but was delayed by contrary winds; and it was not until the 19th, from three to four weeks late, May 19. that the armament finally put to sea.

Meanwhile the British Government had come to a momentous decision. For some time past the Austrians had been urging in vain that the British fleet should re-enter the Mediterranean; and the Tsar, alarmed at the proceedings at Vienna, now joined in these representations, finally offering to England a part of his Baltic fleet to blockade the coast of Holland. But the Ministry was moved also by other considerations. All reports agreed that there were few French ships in Brest, and that the French armament at Toulon was designed against Ireland. Since the beginning of the year the fleet on the north coast of Ireland had, by Camden's request, been con-

1798. siderably strengthened; but it was obvious that, if the Government's intelligence were correct, the right place for the British squadron was the mouth of Toulon harbour. Moreover, a British fleet in the Mediterranean was the best possible diversion to parry a threatened attack on the British Islands, and offered the best chance for the rescue of Italy and the conclusion of a durable peace.

Such were the motives which prompted the Government at the end of April to order twelve line-of-battle ships, nine of which were from the coast of Ireland, to join Lord St. Vincent off Cadiz, so as to enable him to detach a squadron of that strength under Nelson to Toulon. The deepest secrecy was rightly observed over the despatch of this reinforcement. The Admiralty's letter of advice to St. Vincent concerning it is dated the 2nd of May; but not a word was said to the foreign ambassadors upon the subject until at least three weeks later, nor was it until the 21st that the Duke of Portland ventured, still under seal of the strictest secrecy, to write the news to Lord Camden in Ireland.[1] Meanwhile,

May 24. the twelve ships sped on their way, and on the 24th joined St. Vincent's fleet off Cadiz, but out of sight of the port. Nine of the newly arrived vessels were then painted to resemble as many of the inshore blockading squadron, so as to lull all suspicion on the part of the Spaniards at Cadiz; and, with five more ships added to these last, Nelson sailed to search for Bonaparte's expedition. There for the present let us leave him, merely remarking that for England this transaction marked the turn of the tide in her favour in Europe, and, taken in conjunction with Maitland's convention with Toussaint a few months later, not in Europe only but all over the world. The Ministry so far had done little but go on from blunder to blunder; but this wise and courageous decision to resume the offensive in the Mediterranean deserves nothing but the highest praise.

[1] Portland to Camden, 21st May 1798.

CH. XXI   HISTORY OF THE ARMY   587

Meanwhile, Dundas had embarked simultaneously 1798. upon an enterprise of a very different kind, undertaken on the advice of that ever restless sailor, Home Popham. There had recently been completed, at a cost of five millions sterling, a canal from Bruges to Ostend, fourteen miles long, one hundred yards broad, and thirteen feet deep, extremely convenient for the transport of men, stores, and even gunboats to Ostend, for a descent upon the British Isles. It occurred to Popham that, if the lock of this canal at Saas, a mile from Ostend, were blown up, much damage would be done to the port itself, while the principal internal communication between Holland and West Flanders would be destroyed, and the hostile coast of the Low Countries at any rate alarmed. General Sir Charles Grey, who was also an advocate for offensive measures, was much attracted by the plan, as likewise was Huskisson at the War Office; and, accordingly, it was approved by the Government. Preparations, therefore, went busily forward all through April; but the Admiralty, either from distrust of Popham or for other and still sounder reasons, did not favour the adventure. It is only certain that the department threw every obstacle in the way of the expedition, and succeeded in delaying its departure until the 14th of May. The troops em- May 14. barked consisted of four light companies of the First Guards, as many of the Coldstream and Third Guards, the light and grenadier-companies of the Twenty-third and Forty-ninth Regiments, the Eleventh Foot, about one hundred of the Royal Artillery, and nine men of the Seventeenth Light Dragoons, in all about fourteen hundred men of all ranks, under the command of Major-general Eyre Coote. It is not without significance that, in the general dearth of trained men, it was necessary to call upon the Guards for this paltry enterprise.

The expedition sailed from Margate, escorted by a flotilla of frigates and smaller vessels under the command of Popham himself, but, owing to bad weather,

1798.
May 19. did not anchor off Ostend until one o'clock on the morning of the 19th. Very shortly afterwards the wind shifted to westward with such threatening appearance of a gale that Popham was disposed to go to sea and await a more favourable opportunity. It had, however, been ascertained that transports for the invasion of England were to move immediately by way of the new canal from Flushing to Dunkirk and Ostend, as also that the garrisons at Nieuport, Ostend, and Bruges were very weak; and Coote, therefore, begged that the troops might be landed, no matter how great the risk to his retreat. Accordingly, the men were thrown ashore forthwith without respect to the prearranged order of disembarkation; nor were they discovered until past four o'clock, when the enemy's seaward batteries opened fire upon the shipping, and were answered, not only by broadsides but by shells, directed by two bomb vessels upon the town and harbour. By five o'clock the troops had all been landed, excepting the four companies of the First Guards, which had strayed from the rest of the convoy on the voyage; and Coote pushed forward six companies under Major-general Burrard to seize the approaches to the lock. After some brisk skirmishing with the enemy's sharpshooters, these were gained; and, the remainder of the soldiers having been so disposed as to cover the operations from interruption, the dock-gates were successfully blown up. By eleven o'clock the force had returned to the beach with its work fully done, and only a single casualty; but by that time the wind and surf had increased to a height that forbade re-embarkation. Coote, therefore, entrenched himself as well as he could among the sandhills, and bivouacked for the night.

May 20. The first light of dawn showed two strong columns of French advancing in front, which were soon followed by others upon each flank. The action presently began, and for two hours Coote held his own gallantly enough, until severely wounded while rallying some broken men; when Burrard, unwilling to sacrifice lives in useless resistance to overwhelming numbers, surrendered at discretion. The losses of the force were one hundred and sixty-three of all ranks killed and wounded, and rather over eleven hundred taken prisoners; and, though in official circles the tone was to treat the expedition as successful, yet the general opinion pronounced the object attained to be not worth the cost. Indeed, later events proved that the internal navigation between France and Holland had suffered little injury. Huskisson, in writing to Sir Charles Grey, laid the whole blame of the mishap upon the Admiralty, since its dilatoriness had caused the loss of a week of fine weather; but in truth so petty a service should have been left to some skilful and daring captain of a frigate to accomplish with his own ship's company. There is evidence that Huskisson favoured this tiny attempt at the offensive in the hope of putting heart into some of the Cabinet. "Too many men in high office are fond of croaking," he wrote; but it must be confessed that for such an evil, however deplorable, the destruction of the Bruges Canal was an inadequate remedy.[1]

Three days after the capture of Coote's little force, and within a month of Abercromby's departure, the rebellion which had for so long been smouldering in Ireland broke out at last into flame. Into the details of the miserable story I think it no part of my duty to enter, for but a very small fraction of the Regular Army was concerned in it. To all intent the rebellion was a savage fight between two factions of half-disciplined and wholly undisciplined Irish; and the only troops, other than Irish, that entered with true native spirit into the struggle were the Welsh Fencibles, known as the Ancient Britons. The arrangements of the rebel leaders were disconcerted by the arrest of Lord Edward Fitzgerald, who was the military chief of the conspiracy; for which reason the rising was but partial,

1798.

May 23.

---

[1] Besides the official account of this expedition in the Record Office there are interesting letters in the *Grey MSS*. Huskisson to Grey, 13th April, 14th and 22nd May 1798.

1798. and only in Wexford assumed a really formidable aspect. The officers both of the Regular Army and of the Militia and Fencibles undertook the business of suppression at first with a light heart and with the greatest contempt of their opponents; and it was thought that the perambulation of a number of small columns, after the practice of Hoche in La Vendée, would suffice to restore order. They were undeceived by the furious battle of New Ross, where the insurgents, partly, it is true, under the influence of liquor, showed desperate and most splendid bravery. A great defeat of the troops was only averted by the superhuman exertions of a few officers of the Regular Army; and Robert Craufurd, who was one of them, declared that such courage and enthusiasm could only be safely encountered by large and concentrated bodies of men.[1]

The danger would have been less serious had the regiments at the disposal of the authorities possessed any military value; but in this respect Abercromby's criticisms were proved, by overwhelming evidence, to be just and true. There were, indeed, battalions of British Fencibles which conducted themselves honourably as became disciplined men; but the rest, and in particular the Irish Militia, could not have behaved worse. Craufurd described this Militia as quite ungovernable. John Moore used still harder words. "The officers of every description are so bad that it is quite discouraging. Except that they are clothed with more uniformity, they are as ignorant and as much a rabble as those that have hitherto opposed them. . . . The composition of the officers is so bad that I see it will be impossible ever to make soldiers of them."[2] "The Irish Militia," wrote Cornwallis in his turn, "are totally without discipline, contemptible before the enemy when any serious resistance is made to them, but ferocious and cruel in the extreme when any poor wretches with or without arms come within their

[1] Craufurd to Lake, 7th June 1798.
[2] *Diary of Sir John Moore*, i. 303, 307, and *see generally* ch. xxi.

power."[1] To keep such men within bounds was 1798. impossible; and though the majority of the British Generals, particularly the finer officers such as Moore, exerted themselves from the first to restrain them, yet there were a few who thought that they were serving their country well by turning loose their unmanageable levies to burn, torture, and destroy. Happily, on the 20th of June, Cornwallis arrived in Dublin as Lord-Lieutenant and Commander-in-chief, and instituted with great firmness a policy of mercy and conciliation.

By that time the insurrection was at an end as a serious movement; but the justification of Abercromby was not yet fully accomplished. Yielding to the repeated importunities of Wolfe Tone, the French Directory at the end of July gave orders that a number July. of small expeditions should make simultaneous descents upon the Irish coast. Of these the first and, as it proved, the only effective one, was a small armament of three frigates, with just over one thousand regular troops under General Humbert, which sailed from the Isle of Aix on the 6th of August. These had intended to Aug. 6. enter Donegal Bay, but, being prevented by contrary winds, anchored at Killala Bay in the county of Mayo on the 22nd of August, and landed on the same Aug. 22. evening. A small party of about fifty Yeomen and Fencibles, which attempted to oppose them, was quickly overpowered; and the French at once occupied the buildings in the bay. Their troops were composed of veterans from the armies of Italy and the Rhine, who conducted themselves with a moderation and good discipline which was beyond praise; but they found little enthusiasm for the French Revolution in Mayo; and it was only by the distribution of gaudy uniforms that they contrived to attract a few hundreds of simple peasants to the ranks. Connaught had taken no part in the rebellion, and was wholly unmoved by the evangel of the Rights of Man.

The officer in command of the province of Con-

[1] Cornwallis to Portland, 8th July 1798.

1798. naught was Major-general Hutchinson, whom we shall presently know better as Abercromby's successor in Egypt. On receiving intelligence of the enemy's landing he at once collected two regiments of Irish Militia, a detachment of Fencible Infantry, a few Fencible Cavalry and four guns, and moved with them
Aug. 25. towards Castlebar. Arriving there on the 25th he found the country perfectly quiet; but, hearing exaggerated statements of the numbers of Irish which had joined Humbert, he thought it prudent to ask for reinforcements before venturing to attack. Meanwhile, Cornwallis had sent Lake, as an officer of greater experience, to take command in Connaught; and, after directing large bodies of troops to occupy the passages of the Shannon at Athlone and Carrick, he started himself with the Ninety-second Highlanders, two composite battalions of light infantry and four flank-companies of Militia by forced marches for Athlone. On the
Aug. 27. 27th he reached Kilbeggan, having traversed sixty miles in two days; and here on the following morning there reached him the astonishing news that Lake had been completely defeated.
Aug. 26. Lake had arrived at Castlebar on the 26th, where Hutchinson had already assembled about four thousand men, chiefly Militia and Fencibles. About twelve hundred more, chiefly Yeomanry, under General Taylor, lay some thirteen miles to northward, at the village of Foxford, guarding what was thought to be the only passage possible for an army across the river Moy. Humbert, meanwhile, had begun his advance southward from Killala on the same day, when, leaving Ballina at three o'clock in the afternoon, he evaded Taylor by following a rough rocky track, and at six
Aug. 27. o'clock on the following morning had reached the heights before Castlebar. There he found Lake, who had been advised of his approach, duly awaiting him in a strong position with some seventeen hundred men and eleven guns, his flanks being covered by a lake and a bog. After a heavy cannonade, during which

the French suffered much loss and their Irish allies instantly took to their heels, Humbert ordered his veterans to attack with the bayonet; and thereupon almost the whole of Lake's men fled away in panic. The Artillery, a little band of one hundred men of the Sixth Foot, and a small body of Lord Roden's Fencible Dragoons, alone stood firm and showed gallantry enough; but the remainder, namely, the Longford and Kilkenny Militia, a detachment of Fraser's Fencibles, some Galway Volunteers and the Sixth Dragoon Guards, behaved infamously. There seems to be little doubt that many of the Militiamen were disaffected, and it is certain that several of them deserted to Humbert after the action. Too much again could not be expected of half-disciplined Fencibles; but that a regiment of regular Cavalry should behave itself worse than the worst was a disgrace indeed. Nor was it only in action that these troops misconducted themselves; for their depredations on the march had exceeded all description. Yet it is not upon the regiments nor even upon their officers that the hardest censure should fall, but upon the Governments of Ireland and of Britain, which had encouraged indiscipline and refused to support the General who would have restored obedience.

1798.

Humbert entrenched himself at Castlebar, but very soon found that all hopes of real help from the Irish were groundless. Reinforcements came over from England, and Cornwallis, having gathered a considerable force at Athlone, began his advance westward on the 30th. Arriving on the 4th of September at Hollymount, about fifteen miles south-east of Castlebar, he heard that Humbert, having called in all detachments of his French troops, had doubled back northward to Foxford. The object of this movement could only be conjectured; wherefore Cornwallis ordered Lake to follow up the French and to harass their march without risking an action, while he himself turned back northeastward before Carrick. Ascertaining, however, early

Aug. 30.
Sept. 4.

Sept. 6.

1798. on the 6th, that the French were certainly making for Sligo, he sent three regular battalions under John Moore to reinforce Lake, and ordered the garrison of Sligo not to await attack but to retire on Ballyshannon or Enniskillen. Meanwhile Humbert, moving by forced marches, had turned east from Foxford for about ten miles and then northward upon Coloony, where early on
Sept. 5. the morning of the 5th he was boldly engaged, under a misapprehension of his strength, by three hundred of the Limerick Militia under Colonel Vereker. So stoutly did this little party fight, that Humbert took a full hour to clear them out of his way; after which judging them, apparently, to be the advanced guard of
Sept. 6. an army, he turned short to the east upon Drummahair, thence north-eastward to Manor Hamilton, and thence abruptly southward as if heading for Carrick. Corn-
Sept. 7. wallis accordingly at once hastened his troops to that town, while Humbert, with Lake close at his heels, passed the Shannon at Ballintra as if making for Granard. Cornwallis thereupon moved eastward from Carrick to intercept him; and, after a short action
Sept. 8. on the 8th at Ballinamuck, Humbert and the eight hundred men who survived of his force surrendered. If ever commander did himself honour by the exemplary behaviour of his troops, by moderation towards the inhabitants of an invaded country, and by indomitable courage in a desperate situation, it was this rough, illiterate Humbert. It was not mere vainglorious boasting when he wrote after his landing to the Directory that, if he were reinforced by two thousand men, Ireland would be free.

This most shameful episode did not end the disgrace of the troops in Ireland. The rebellion which had been kindled in Connaught by Humbert's landing needed now to be suppressed; and, notwithstanding a succession of severe orders issued by Cornwallis to restrain the prevailing military disorder, the unhappy peasants were pursued with a ferocity which even to the present day has never been forgiven. Yet they had been guilty of no grave crimes ; and a conciliatory 1798. proclamation would probably have brought nearly every man to willing submission. Such were the ultimate results of Camden's weakness, and of the ignoble truckling of the Ministry to the cabal that ruled Ireland under shelter of his name. Nor were the immediate consequences less serious. At the end of August an officer of the Guards wrote that if his men were kept in the country for another six months he would not answer for their subordination, so freely was whisky bestowed upon the soldiery by the faction that abetted the outrages against the rebels, and so demoralising generally was the contact of the Irish with the army. The same alarms were entertained for the English Militia which had crossed St. George's Channel, and assuredly not without reason,[1] for some of the regular regiments around them set the worst possible example. At length insubordination outstepped all bounds. The officers of the Perthshire Fencibles declined to convict some of their brethren of proved misconduct, and at the recommendation of Cornwallis the regiment was very rightly disbanded.

A still more melancholy case followed soon after. A conspiracy was discovered in the Fifth Dragoons to attack and destroy, in concert with a party of rebels, a small detachment of Dragoons and Militia, which was employed in the work of stamping out the last dying embers of insurrection. The whole of the men concerned were recruits who, apparently, had enlisted for the express purpose of doing this mischief; but the affair was judged too grave to be passed over. It was true that the Government had drafted countless insurgents into the Navy and the Sixtieth, and had pardoned many others on their engaging for military service in the West Indies. It was true also that the Fifth had behaved very well throughout the rebellion, and notably at New Ross ; but it was evident that the regiment was rotten to the core. On the 1st of 1799.

[1] *Castlereagh Papers*, i. 341-343.

1799. January 1799 Cornwallis made formal complaint of the want of discipline and inattention of the officers, and of the dangerous and disloyal conduct of the non-commissioned officers and men. There had been much desertion, and there were soldiers in the ranks who were known to have taken the oath of the United Irishmen. The commanding officer, Lieutenant-colonel Charles Stewart, had used his utmost endeavours to restore subordination, but in vain, being unsupported by his inferiors. Altogether Cornwallis pronounced the men to be so radically bad and depraved that he despaired of rendering the corps in the smallest degree serviceable; and he therefore recommended that it should be removed from Ireland and drafted out. But the King Jan. 12. took a far stronger view; and on the 12th of January the sentence was pronounced that the regiment should be dissolved. The officers petitioned for a Board of April 12. Enquiry, but this was refused; and on the 12th of April a General Order was issued for the Fifth Dragoons to be disbanded and for the officers to be placed on half-pay, though with the reservation that the deserving men among them, notably Charles Stewart, would not be forgotten. We shall see more of Stewart, who was Lord Castlereagh's brother, and was destined to play some part in the Peninsula; but the majority of the officers neither received nor deserved consideration. The example, indeed, was intended chiefly for the officers, and was very grievously needed.

Thus the Fifth Royal Irish Dragoons were swept from the Army-list, their place being for years left blank as a standing reproach. The regiment's career had been most distinguished. It had taken three kettledrums at Blenheim, and received them as a trophy from Marlborough himself. In company with the Greys, according to tradition, it had captured at Ramillies two battalions of Regiment Picardie, and had cut a third to pieces; and with the Greys it had won the distinction of wearing the Grenadiers' cap. It had fought forty years later under the Duke of Cumberland at

Fontenoy; after which it had remained in Ireland, 1799. dispersed, according to the fashion of that kingdom, in troops and fractions of troops for fifty years. Warning had been given to the Government of the state of the Cavalry in Ireland in 1784 and 1786, but had remained unheeded; and the misconduct of the Fifth and of the Carbineers was the natural consequence. In July the Carbineers were drafted out; and the four regiments of "Irish Horse," that is to say the Fourth, Fifth, Sixth and Seventh Dragoon Guards, were removed to England to relearn the discipline which, through small fault of their own, they had forgotten.[1]

July.

Yet one more aspect of the Irish rebellion requires notice before the subject is finally dismissed, namely, the inefficacy of the measures taken by the Government for the internal defence of the British Isles. In June 1798, when Camden was crying loudly for troops, there were sent to him from England, with much reluctance, four weak regiments of Fencible Cavalry, as many weak battalions of Fencible Infantry, three, or at most four, weak battalions of the Line, one weak brigade of Guards, and one regiment of foreign riflemen, the whole hardly amounting to ten thousand men. It was therefore necessary to call upon the English Militia to volunteer for duty in Ireland, and to pass an Act to enable them to perform that service. The Bucks and the Warwickshire, numbering together nearly three thousand men, were the first to cross the water in June, to be followed in September by twelve regiments more; and great pressure was put on some of these corps to remain there even in December 1798, when the rebellion was wholly extinguished. Thus, in spite of all the levying of Fencibles to release the regular Army for foreign service, it was actually found impossible to make an end of one thousand French troops without throw-

[1] Cornwallis to Portland, 1st January and 18th July; Portland to Cornwallis, 12th January 1799.

1798. ing Ireland on the mercy of the British Militia, and denuding England of the territorial garrison which strictly and legally belonged to it. In plain language, the whole of the Government's measures for home-defence stood utterly and completely condemned, and that at the one moment when invasion was seriously threatened.

Fortunately the remaining expeditions prepared by the Directory came to little. In October 1798 a line-of-battle ship and eight frigates with three thousand troops reached the neighbourhood of Lough Swilly; but half of the squadron was captured, and the remainder dispersed by a British fleet of superior force. A fortnight later four more ships of war, with two thousand troops, anchored in Killala Bay, but returned with all speed to France on learning of the fate of their predecessors. For the rest, Bonaparte was in Egypt, and had lost the greatest opportunity of his life.

Oct. 12.
Oct. 27.

END OF PART I

Printed by R. & R. CLARK, LIMITED, *Edinburgh.*

FORTESCUE'S
A History of the British Army

The Naval and Military Press have reprinted this valuable and timeless work in its entirety, faithful to the originals in all respects.
The contents of the individual volumes are as follows:

Volume I – From the Battle of Hastings to the end of the Seven Years' War (1713). Includes such battles as Bannockburn, Crecy, Agincourt, Flodden, the battles of the English Civil War, Dunkirk Dunes, Tangiers and the battles during Marlborough's campaigns. The volume also traces the development of European armies, infantry, cavalry and artillery, and the specific changes in Britain during the period.

Volume II – Covers from 1713 to 1763 and includes the Jacobite Rebellion of 1715, the scandals of the reign of King George I, the war with Spain and the dispute over the Austrian Succession, and the Battles of Fontenoy and Culloden. It also covers the situation in India and the contest for mastery with the French. The expansion into North America is described and the differences that arose between the French and the British, together with Wolfe's campaigns in North America. The volume includes much material on the development of the British Army, and the problems that arose regarding recruitment and conditions of service at that time.

Volume III – Continues the story from 1763 to 1792. The continuing problems in North America are joined by the growing pains of Empire. The loss of the Americas is covered in detail, as is the state of the British Army, especially in the light of Cornwallis' disastrous contributions to the American failure. Developments in India follow, and again Cornwallis contributes to failure.

Volume IV Part I – Deals with the French Revolution from 1789 to the Treaty of Amiens in 1798. It includes British operations in the Netherlands, the West Indies, South Africa and Ireland. The whole European area is described with the French and Allied nations included. Naval matters are also included, and the campaigns in Egypt and the Mediterranean are treated in detail. At the same time a close eye is kept on developments within the British Army.

Volume IV Part 2 – Continues the theme of the previous part and goes up to 1801. The examination of the British Army is also expanded, and an important appendix gives exact details of British Army pay.

Volume V – The period 1803 to 1807. Detailed treatment of the situation and operations in the East Indies and Ceylon, the West Indies, Europe and the Mediterranean. There are important chapters on conditions at home, and the air of war-weariness that was appearing. Finally, there is a description of operations in South America.

Volume VI – 1807-1809. The Napoleonic War continued, with further details of operations in Egypt and in the Mediterranean. The Swedish situation is covered, the British expedition to Copenhagen and operations in Portugal. The Spanish theatre is also examined in fine detail.

Volume VII – 1809-1810. This volume is concerned mainly with these two years in the Peninsula, but also covers the expedition to the Scheldt and operations in the East Indies, Mauritius and Java.

Volume VIII – 1811-1812. This volume covers two more years of the campaign in the Peninsula, together with the War with the United States. There are details of many battles, including Barosa, Badajoz, Fuentes de Onoro, Albuera, Ciudad Rodrigo, Salamanca and others of fame during the Peninsula War.

Volume IX – 1813-1814. The French invasion of Russia is followed by descriptions of the situation in the Peninsula, and in North America. Throughout, developments in Europe are covered so that the picture of the war for the reader in these years is complete, and second to none in detail.

Volume X – 1814-1815. The whole of Europe was aflame in these two years, and Fortescue writes most effectively of the military activity and the political background. Italy, the Peninsula, the Low Countries and the American War are all interwoven from the British point of view in a tour de force of military history. He then includes a really valuable summary of events in Europe from 1803 to 1814 before setting out to describe the culminating battle at Waterloo. From the Duchess of Richmond's Ball to the exhaustion on the night after the battle, Fortescue maintains a pace and directness which is fascinating to read.

Volume XI – 1815-1838. Fortescue looks at the British Army in 1815, and particularly the recruit in England. Every detail of his life is included, and the picture is an important one for all who are interested in this period of military and social history. The War with Nepal, the Pindari War, the War in Ceylon and the War with Burma all occupy the subsequent pages, followed by the Ashanti campaign and the Kaffir War of 1834-35. This volume also includes details of Home Affairs and Foreign Policy.

Volume XII – 1839-52. This volume is mainly concerned with India and covers operations in Afghanistan and on the Khyber Pass, together with internal security operations in India itself. There is also a section dealing with the revolt in Australia and operations in New Zealand. Finally, there is a description of the Kaffir War and the Boer revolt.

Volume XIII – 1852-1870. This volume includes the Crimean War, the War in Persia and the Indian Mutiny and the campaign in China. It then goes on to look at the Ambela and Abyssinian campaigns, and the Wars in New Zealand. Finally, Fortescue looks at affairs in Great Britain and the position of the East India Company. He then turns his attention to the new army from 1870 to 1914 and includes the territorial system, the new social engineering going on for men's welfare in the army. The series ends, however, with an important look at the end of the era of purchase, and what the army was going to do next.

Map Compendium
An amalgamation of all six separate map volumes in a single binding containing the complete set of large maps which accompanied *Fortescue's History of the British Army*.

www.ingramcontent.com/pod-product-compliance
Lightning Source LLC
Chambersburg PA
CBHW050522300426
44113CB00012B/1923